Diversity in Advertising

Broadening the Scope of
Research Directions

Advertising and Consumer Psychology
A Series sponsored by the Society for Consumer Psychology

Aaker/Biel: *Brand Equity and Advertising: Advertising's Role in Building Strong Brands* (1993)

Clark/Brock/Stewart: *Attention, Attitude, and Affect in Response Advertising* (1994)

Englis: *Global and Multi-National Advertising* (1994)

Goldberg/Fishbein/Middlestadt: *Social Marketing: Theoretical and Practical Perspectives* (1997)

Kahle/Chiagouris: *Values, Lifestyles, and Psychographics* (1997)

Kahle/Riley: *Sports Marketing and the Psychology of Marketing Communications* (2004)

Mitchell: *Advertising Exposure, Memory, and Choice* (1993)

Schumann/Thorson: *Advertising and the World Wide Web* (1999)

Scott/Batra: *Persuasive Imagery: A Consumer Response Perspective* (2003)

Shrum: *The Psychology of Entertainment Media: Blurring the Lines Between Entertainment and Persuasion* (2004)

Thorson/Moore: *Integrated Communication: Synergy of Persuasive Voices* (1996)

Wells: *Measuring Advertising Effectiveness* (1997)

Williams/Lee/Haugtvedt: *Diversity in Advertising: Broadening the Scope of Research Directions* (2004)

Diversity in Advertising

Broadening the Scope of Research Directions

Edited by

JEROME D. WILLIAMS
The University of Texas at Austin

WEI-NA LEE
The University of Texas at Austin

CURTIS P. HAUGTVEDT
Ohio State University

Psychology Press
Taylor & Francis Group

New York   London

First Published by Lawrence Erlbaum Associates, Inc., Publishers
10 Industrial Avenue
Mahwah, New Jersey 07430

Published 2008 by Psychology Press
711 Third Avenue, New York, NY 10017
27 Church Road, Hove, East Sussex, BN3 2FA

First issued in paperback 2014

Psychology Press is an imprint of the Taylor & Francis Group, an informa business

Cover design by Sean Trane Sciarrone

Library of Congress Cataloging-in-Publication Data

Williams, Jerome D., 1947–
    Diversity in advertising : broadening the scope of research directions /
  by Jerome D. Williams, Wei-Na Lee, Curtis P. Haugtvedt.
      p. cm.—(Advertising and consumer psychology)
    ISBN 0-8058-4794-4 (casebound)
    1. Advertising—Psychological aspects.   2. Communication
in marketing.   3.Consumers—Attitudes.   I. Lee, Wei-Na, 1957-II. Haugtvedt,
Curtis P., 1958-III. Title. IV. Series.
    HF5822.W495   2004
    659.1′08—dc22
                                                        2003022327

ISBN 13: 978-0-8058-4794-9 (hbk)
ISBN 13: 978-1-138-01282-0 (pbk)

Jerome D. Williams, Curtis P. Haugtvedt, and Wei-Na Lee

Contents

Contributors

Swee Hoon Ang
National University of Singapore

Osei Appiah
Ohio State University

Ludy T. Benjamin, Jr.
Texas A & M University

Sjaak (J.) G. Bloem
*Janssen-Cilag b.v., Unit Business
Intelligence*

Anne M. Brumbaugh
Wake Forest University

Caryl A. Cooper
University of Alabama

Johan de Heer
Telematica Instituut

Devon DelVecchio
University of Kentucky

David Fair eld
University of Houston-Downtown

Geraldine Fennell
Consultant

Ronald C. Goodstein
Georgetown University

Timothy B. Greenlee
Miami University

Sonya A. Grier
Stanford University

Geraldine R. Henderson
*Howard University/University of
Virginia*

Madeline Johnson
University of Houston-Downtown

Charles M. Judd
University of Colorado

Carrie La Ferle
Michigan State University

Jinkook Lee
Ohio State University

Robert W. Livingston
University of Wisconsin-Madison

David Luna
Baruch College, CUNY

Gillian K. Oakenfull
Miami University

So e E. W. M. Paijmans
Valkenbosch Consultancy

Bernadette Park
University of Colorado

Robert Pennington
National Chung Hsing University

Laura A. Peracchio
University of Wisconsin-Milwaukee

Joel Saegert
The University of Texas at San Antonio

Michael J. Sargent
Bates College

Joan Scattone Spira
Consultant

David W. Schumann
University of Tennessee

Denise Sekaquaptewa
University of Michigan

Patricia A. Stout
The University of Texas at Austin

Marye Tharp
Emerson College

Patrick T. Vargas
University of Illinois

Jorge Villegas
University of Florida

William von Hippel
University of New South Wales

Kittichai Watchravesringkan
University of Arizona

Tommy E. Whittler
DePaul University

Bernd Wittenbrink
University of Chicago

Christopher Wolsko
University of Alaska Fairbanks

Preface

This volume grew out of the 18th annual Advertising and Consumer Psychology Conference held in 1999 in San Antonio, Texas, sponsored by the Society for Consumer Psychology (SCP), Division 23 of the American Psychological Association. The theme of the conference was Diversity in Advertising. Over 70 academicians and practitioners attended the conference, and over 30 papers were presented. As Co-Chairs of that Conference, we also took on the task of organizing and editing this volume. We selected 19 papers from that conference and asked the authors to revise and update their papers from the presentations made at the conference. In addition, we invited other authors to prepare 5 papers that we felt would signi - cantly add to the value of this work, thus resulting in the 24 chapters comprising this book.

Although the need for such a volume may seem obvious to many academics and practitioners as a result of the rapidly changing demographic landscape, it may be helpful for us to provide some additional background as to why we felt it was important to undertake this effort. These demographic changes are challenging the effectiveness of traditional advertising techniques and marketing strategies. More and more advertisers are nding that they must appeal to narrower segments of consumers, who express distinctive ethnic, age-cohort, or lifestyles values by what and how they buy. Marketers hoping to attract these diverse groups of consumers must build relationships with them by mirroring the values and multiple identities with which they identify. More sophisticated advertising and marketing insights and tools based on contemporary, cutting-edge research and methodologies are needed.

In addition, we feel that diversity in advertising is more than effectiveness in the marketplace; it is also a recognition and welcoming sign for immigrants and other individuals who, over the years, have been considered as "minorities." We hope this book on diversity in advertising will contribute to the understanding of the diversity of people, the changing landscape of the United States, and, what is more important, the need for a more inclusive society.

This book provides a vast array of information for those academics and practitioners seeking to better understand how individual characteristics affect the sending, receiving, and processing of communication efforts. The book highlights (a) past and current knowledge on diversity in advertising, (b) important questions that have not been addressed satisfactorily in this area, and (c) how current theories can be used to construct better communication plans and message content. The chapters in the book represent a collection of research from academics from the elds of social psychology, advertising, and marketing, all focusing on discussing existing and needed research to face the challenges of diversity in the next millennium.

This book is unique in that it is research driven. The various chapters draw on existing literature from the elds of psychology, marketing, and related disciplines to amplify our understanding and insight into developing effective advertising approaches to reach diverse audiences. What is even more important is that the contributors to this volume are researchers who have pushed the envelope in understanding diversity in advertising, rather than merely relying on theoretical frameworks developed decades ago when the demographics of the population were much different. As diversity increases in the marketplace, it becomes questionable whether theories developed and tested within the dominant White Anglo consumer group can be appropriately applied to the many contemporary diverse consumer groups, who likely differ in terms of household composition, values, lifestyles, self-perceptions, and aspirations. As far as we know, there are no other books that focus on marketing and consumer psychology theory and research as the drivers of advertising decisions in a contemporary diverse environment.

ORGANIZATION OF THE CHAPTERS

The twenty-four chapters of this book are divided into six parts. Here we provide a brief glimpse of the parts and their respective chapters.

Part I. Historical Perspectives on Diversity and Advertising: Where We've Been and Where We're Going

There are two chapters in this rst part. In the introductory chapter (chap. 1), Wei-Na Lee, Carrie La Ferle, and Jerome D. Williams provide a historical perspective on the role of advertising as it relates to diversity. They stress the need for advertisers to broaden the de nition of diversity if we are to understand the changing face of the United States and to really grasp the meaning of diversity in the 21st century. In addition to summarizing the literature, they also raise a number of questions that still must be addressed, thereby establishing a foundation for a diversity research agenda. Next, Ludy T. Benjamin, Jr. (chap. 2) looks back on American psychology and debunks the historical myth that during the early days psychologists rarely strayed from their laboratories into the real world to advance the science in applied settings. By discussing the legacy of some of the early pioneers, Benjamin demonstrates that applied psychology has always been a part of American psychology and shows how advertising and scienti c psychology became linked in a common time of transformation.

Part II. The Dark Side of Diversity in Advertising: Discrimination, Prejudice, and Bias

The six chapters in this part explore what we refer to as the "dark" side of diversity in advertising, namely topics dealing with discrimination, prejudice, and bias exhibited by both consumers and marketers or advertisers. In the rst chapter, Michael J. Sargent (chap. 3) reviews relevant studies on the use of implicit measures of prejudice to predict behavior under speci c conditions, with an emphasis on one popular measure, the Implicit Association Test. Sargent links this to advertising by suggesting that, like other media portrayals, the use of stigmatized sources in advertising may in uence implicit attitudes toward those categories. He further concludes that although consumers' implicit racial attitudes may in uence their responses to advertisements that feature members of stigmatized groups, those same implicit racial attitudes may be in uenced by the advertisements themselves. Robert W. Livingston (chap. 4) follows with a discussion of thoughts or behaviors that show evidence of occurring outside of conscious awareness, intent, or control, and he links this research with issues of nonconscious bias in the media and advertising. He suggests that biased advertising may sometimes re ect the deliberate economic or political goals of its creator, because race and gender do in uence the effectiveness of advertising. Livingston concludes that it seems plausible to assume that more positive portrayals of minorities in the media could go a long way toward reducing bias in society, even at the automatic level.

Next, Christopher Wolsko, Bernadette Park, Charles M. Judd, and Bernd Wittenbrink (chap. 5) focus primarily on the ethical consideration of addressing ethnic diversity in advertising. They present theoretical and empirical arguments on the consequences of messages that focus on ethnic similarities versus ethnic differences, and, in the process, they examine whether focusing on ethnic-group differences necessarily leads to greater prejudice, or if there is a way in which people may positively value ethnic diversity. Then Patrick T. Vargas, Denise Sekaquaptewa, and William von Hippel (chap. 6) examine a divergent view of prejudice by starting with the premise that *what* people think about a particular group may often differ from *how* they think about it. Their research suggests that there is an important information-processing component to prejudice. The analysis they provide offers some evidence that implicit measures of prejudice that tap biased information processing can be quite useful in predicting cognitive and behavioral responses to stigmatized others.

David W. Schumann's chapter (chap. 7) is based on his 1999 Society for Consumer Psychology Presidential Address and provides a historical overview of the study of prejudice, highlighting what are thought to be the four causal processes underlying the existence of prejudice. Most relevant for this volume, he describes two forms of marketing communication that can serve as reinforcement transmitters, namely the ongoing way in which certain groups of people are presented to consumers by means of advertising, and market segmentation and its resulting communication strategies. In the concluding chapter of this part, Caryl A. Cooper (chap. 8) examines diversity issues in the context of media. Cooper provides evidence to substantiate the frequently stated claims that Black-oriented radio stations do not receive advertising revenues that re ect their strength in the market, hence raising accusations of foul play and questions about the agenda of those responsible for placing advertising dollars. Cooper stresses that such discrimination in today's diverse marketplace is not acceptable, as it not only threatens the government's overriding philosophy of broadcasting in the public interest but also hits the nation's Black community where it hurts.

Part III. The Influencing Role of Language in Diversity in Advertising

Three chapters address issues related to language and its role in in uencing diversity in advertising. First, David Luna and Laura A. Peracchio (chap. 9) review research examining the issue of language in advertising that targets bilinguals, and they provide a cognitive framework for the study of how bilingual consumers process advertisements. Their ndings suggest that factors such as picture–copy congruity and processing motivation, both previously studied in monolingual consumer research, may have different effects depending on the language in which the ad is written. Next, Wei-Na Lee, Carrie La Ferle, and Marye Tharp (chap. 10) study the communication patterns of four ethnic groups. Their ndings indicate Chinese and Hispanic Americans appear to have both English and ethnic in-language media competing for their time and attention, and African Americans use the most word-of-mouth communication whereas Chinese Americans talk the least about advertising and products. Finally, Robert Pennington (chap. 11) demonstrates how to apply a psycholinguistic methodology to discover what public affective meanings that brands have for consumers. This application can discover consumers' perceived distinctions among publicly consumed brands according to brand personality, and it can allow consumers to de ne brand personality through their own words rather than through a previously developed list.

Part IV. The Influencing Role of Social and Information Contexts in Diversity in Advertising

The two chapters in this part focus on the role of context as an in uencing factor in diversity in advertising; the rst chapter deals with social context based on distinctiveness theory and the second deals with information context. Sonya A. Grier and Anne M. Brumbaugh (chap. 12) discuss the signi cance of distinctiveness theory for understanding advertising persuasion in multicultural marketplaces. Their assessment suggests that distinctiveness theory presents a powerful basis for understanding advertising effects in a multicultural market. They conclude that additional theoretical and practical progress related to multicultural advertising can be made by further exploration of advertising cues, consumer contexts, intervening variables, and mechanisms that contribute to the influence of distinctiveness on advertising response. Johan de Heer, Sjaak (J.) G. Bloem, and Sofie E. W. M. Paijmans (chap. 13) examine diversity in advertising from a theoretical perspective, namely the influence of contextual information on attitude toward the ad. Over products, brands, consumer segments, and time, advertising messages are characterized by a high degree of variability, and, based on the ad's nature, spatial layout, visual aesthetics, goal, content, target group, or medium, there can be virtually an unlimited number of unique and distinct messages. Given this ad diversity, de Heer, Bloem, and Paijmans examine whether contextual information influences attitudes toward the ads.

Part V. The Influencing Role of Source Effects in Diversity in Advertising

In this part, each chapter looks at source effects and their influencing role, particularly spokesperson and celebrities sources. In the first chapter, Joan Scattone Spira and Tommy E. Whittler (chap. 14) discuss some of the research that has examined individuals' responses to race or ethnicity in persuasive messages. They discuss what effect a spokesperson's race has on persuasion, and then they consider individual difference, environmental, and contextual variables that may influence who is likely to be influenced by the spokesperson's race and when such influence is likely to occur. They also discuss how these race effects are manifested by considering the psychological processes underlying them. The next two chapters both deal with celebrities. Devon DelVecchio and Ronald C. Goodstein (chap. 15) investigate the role of ethnic identity and other-group orientation on the effectiveness of African American and White celebrity endorsers. They find that matching viewers and endorsers' ethnicity and other-group orientation adds significantly to the explained variance in ratings of endorsers. These results highlight the need to consider the perceived ethnic identity of both endorsers and audiences in future research. Geraldine R. Henderson and Jerome D. Williams (chap. 16) discuss other-race contact and link it to celebrity endorser recognition. Their assessment suggests that advertisers can draw on the literature on celebrity endorsers and the phenomenon of other-race effect to develop more effective strategies for advertising executions using celebrity endorsers to appeal to diverse market segments.

Part VI. Broadening the Concept of Diversity: Going Beyond Black and White

The concluding part broadens the concept of diversity by examining it from many perspectives beyond the traditional "Black and White" focus, including a broader definition of diversity, adolescents, Asian Americans, sexual orientation, gender, religion, and international perspectives. The rst chapter challenges the traditional de nition of diversity, as Geraldine Fennell and Joel Saegert (chap. 17) highlight the theme that diversity itself is a diverse construct. They emphasize the distinction between market diversity and population diversity. Adopting a marketing perspective on advertising in the context of diversity, Fennell and Saegert discuss how management uses marketing analysis to describe and strategically respond to market diversity and then consider the extent to which taking cognizance of population diversity may add to a marketing analysis. Osei Appiah (chap. 18) looks at a younger segment by examining differences in adolescents' responses to ads that vary in the extent to which they contain race-related cultural cues. His results indicate that both White and Black adolescents respond more favorably to Black-character ads than they do to White-character ads. Appiah ties his research to theories of distinctiveness and identi cation and also considers the implications of "cultural voyeurism." Asian Americans are the focus of the next chapter, as David W. Schumann, Jinkook Lee, and Kittichai Watchravesringkan (chap. 19) explore the contention that differential marketing efforts may be warranted for the "Asian" category as a whole, given the within-group differences. Their results reinforce the contention the Asian American ethnic groups should be considered as separate entities when marketers consider their targeting strategies and that categorizing the various Asian groups under one umbrella label has signi cant potential to create ineffective marketing strategies.

The next topic area contains two chapters that highlight issues related to sexual orientation. Timothy B. Greenlee (chap. 20) focuses on the communications strategies available to mainstream marketers targeting the gay and lesbian community by means of gay- and lesbian-oriented print media. He also provides a research agenda designed to provide insight for mainstream marketers as they attempt to secure a portion of the gay and lesbian consumer dollar. Gillian K. Oakenfull (chap. 21) examines the advertising strategies that are available to advertisers in pursuit of the gay market, and she re ects on the issues that advertisers must consider to carefully balance gay goodwill with the potential stigma attached to courting the gay market. She develops a framework based on sexual orientation, gay identity, and attitude toward homosexuality and offers advertising strategies that may allow marketers to target gay and "gay-friendly" consumers without risk of alienating heterosexual consumers who may disapprove of such a strategy.

Gender is the focus of the next chapter, as Patricia A. Stout and Jorge Villegas (chap. 22) examine issues in women's health. They investigate how gender differences might in uence message design for delivery by using interactive technology. Stout and Villegas also tie their work to theory by assessing structural features of interactive technology, using the selectivity hypothesis as an explanatory framework for how gender differences might affect information processing of Web-based health-promotion messages. Next, David Fair eld and Madeline Johnson (chap. 23) extend the concept of diversity to religion and the international arena by analyzing the presence of religious symbols and values in advertising in southern India. In showing that values most frequently portrayed in the ads were not consistent with Hinduism but instead re ected more Western values, Fair eld and Johnson provide evidence to support the theory that advertising content can be a distorted mirror of culture. Finally, Swee Hoon Ang and Jerome D. Williams (chap. 24) also extend diversity to the international arena by comparing youths from East Asian countries with youths from Western countries in terms of their beliefs on business ethics and social responsibility, Machiavellianism, and a variety of social values. Their ndings provide implications on the use of such advertising appeals as psychological, symbolic association, lecture, celebrity endorsement, and comparative advertising in these respective cultures.

ACKNOWLEDGMENTS

An eclectic group of businesses, agencies, and academic units helped sponsor the conference. Bromley Aguilar + Associates provided signi cant nancial support for the conference and a fun- lled Friday evening reception at the agency's new building in downtown San Antonio, complete with a Mariachi band and a continuous supply of margaritas. Three of the largest Black-oriented agencies in the country, Burrell Communications Group, UniWorld Group, and Chisholm-Mingo Group, also contributed nancially to the conference. BankOne sponsored all three coffee breaks and was represented at the conference. In addition, The University of Texas at Austin, College of Communication and its Of ce of Survey Research and the Department of Advertising provided nancial as well as technology support.

We acknowledge the support of the SCP executive board for having the faith in us to tackle this important topic and Division 8 (Society for Personality and Social Psychology) for helping cosponsor the conference. Special thanks are given to Marian Friestadt and Karen Machleit, who worked closely with us as Secretary and Treasurer of the SCP during the time of the conference. We thank Anne Duffy at Lawrence Erlbaum Associates for her patience and guidance and Lawrence Erlbaum Associates themselves for their continued support of the Advertising & Consumer Psychology series.

We thank all the authors for making the conference a success and for sticking with us as we moved this book project toward publication. We especially thank the authors who came on board after the conference and contributed invited chapters (Michael J. Sargent, Robert W. Livingston, Sonya A. Grier, Anne M. Brumbaugh, and Geraldine R. Henderson). We cannot thank all of you enough for your patience and always positive attitude throughout the process. The editing of this book has coincided with a dif cult period in our lives, as each of us suffered the loss of a parent. This has made our work all the more demanding and important.

Jerome acknowledges all the helpful support he received from the administrative staff at the several institutions where he was on the faculty or visited over the past few years while working on this book, including the University of Michigan

Business School, Wharton School of Business, Penn State University Smeal College of Business, Howard University School of Business, Georgia State University Robinson College of Business and the University of Texas at Austin. Jerome is especially thankful for the loving support of his wife, Lillian, who was a beacon of light and encouragement and provided the moral, emotional, and spiritual compass in his life to keep him focused, especially during times when he needed to be uplifted. He also thanks all of his children, Denean, Derek, Daniel, Dante, and Dachia, for always willingly accepting the family sacri ces that sometimes had to be made to accommodate his working on this book. Finally, Jerome dedicates this book in memory of three people who were instrumental in touching and shaping his life: his parents, Jerome J. and Gloria E. Williams, and his father-in-law, Charles R. Harrison.

Wei-Na thanks several of her former and current students—Carrie La Ferle, Gigi Taylor, Wenling Amber Chen, Jorge Villegas, and Ji-Young Hong. Their diligence and upbeat outlook helped make the experience an enjoyable one. Wei-Na especially thanks her colleague and friend, Marye Tharp, for her willingness to share her vast knowledge in the topic area and for her enthusiastic celebration of diverse cultures. Wei-Na also thanks Carrie La Ferle for coming on board to help write the introductory chapter. It was fun and exciting to meet the challenge. In addition, Wei-Na thanks her husband, Hao, who is always honest in giving his opinions. Finally, Wei-Na dedicates this book to the memory of her father, Ying-Hsiang Lee, who was an ambivalent immigrant to the United States at the age of 65.

Curt dedicates this book to the memory of his father, Roy Haugtvedt, a farm laborer, expert jack-of-all trades, and an open, caring individual who was very interested in everyone he met. Roy taught his children and grandchildren to explore the world with courage and patience.

—Jerome D. Williams, Wei-Na Lee, and Curtis P. Haugtvedt

EDITORS

Jerome D. Williams is the F. J. Heyne Centennial Professor in Communication, Department of Advertising, at The University of Texas at Austin, with a joint appointment in the Center for African and African American Studies. He received his PhD from the University of Colorado. His current research interests cover ethnic minority consumer behavior and advertising strategies, consumer racial pro ling, social marketing, target marketing of food and beverage products, Internet privacy, and marketing and religion. He is a Co-Chair of the Committee on Ethnic Minority Affairs of the Society for Consumer Psychology.

Wei-Na Lee is an Associate Professor of Advertising at the University of Texas at Austin. She received her PhD from the University of Illinois at Urbana-Champaign. Her research interests include cross-cultural consumer behavior, multicultural marketing communication, and consumer acculturation in a technology-mediated environment. She is a Co-Chair of the Committee on Ethnic Minority Affairs of the Society for Consumer Psychology and is currently its representative to the American Psychological Associations's Committee on Women in Psychology Network.

Curtis P. Haugtvedt is an Associate Professor of Marketing and Logistics at Ohio State University. He recevied his PhD in Social Psychology from the University of Missouri—Columbia. His basic and applied research interests include attitude change and persuasion, the use of personality variables in consumer and social psychological research, health psychology, and environmental psychology. He is a former President of the Society for Consumer Psychology and a former Associate Editor of the *Journal of Consumer Psychology*. He currently serves as the Chair of the Society for Consumer Psychology Strategic Planning Committee.

Diversity in Advertising

Broadening the Scope of
Research Directions

I. HISTORICAL PERSPECTIVES ON DIVERSITY AND ADVERTISING: WHERE WE'VE BEEN AND WHERE WE'RE GOING

CHAPTER ONE

Diversity in Advertising:
A Summary and Research Agenda

Wei-Na Lee
Jerome D. Williams
The University of Texas at Austin

Carrie La Ferle
Michigan State University

Advertising is a major tool of the capitalist system in the United States and has contributed to one of the highest standards of living in the world. In 2003, the U.S. advertising industry was reported to generate $245 billion dollars in annual spending (McCarthy & Howard, 2003). Quite frequently, advertising expenditures account for approximately 3% of a developed country's gross national product and the U.S. often leads this rate with $534.8 spent per capita in 2002 (Frith & Mueller, 2003). Numbers like these are evidence that advertising is a powerful economic force and an important institution in the United States (Carey, 1989).

Similarly, advertising is also a powerful social and cultural force in American society (Jhally, 1995; Pollay, 1986). Advertising has been attributed as being both a mirror of societal values and a molder of our beliefs and norms (Holbrook, 1987; Lantos, 1987; Pollay, 1986). In fact, many would argue that, with the current level of media and technology available, advertising and the mass media have become more powerful than other institutions such as education, religion, and even the family (Pollay, 1986). With advertising's ability to yield both economic and cultural power, it is important for advertisers and consumer researchers to understand how it is both influenced by and influences individuals in society. This point is particularly true in light of the major demographic shifts occurring in the United States. For example, people over 50 years of age will soon make up the largest age group in the United States, and ethnic minorities are predicted to account for close to 50% of the population by 2050 (U.S. Census, 2000). Information on how individual characteristics affect the sending, receiving, and processing of communication is crucial for marketers to communicate and serve tomorrow's consumers in an increasingly diverse marketplace.

Increasing levels of consumerism over the years have led many researchers to question and examine the social effects of advertising (Mittal, 1994). Since the 1960s, several studies have been undertaken to assess attitudes toward advertising as an institution (Bauer & Greyser, 1968; Mittal, 1994; Zanot, 1984). Time and time again, we find that the economic effects of advertising are praised, whereas the social effects are considered negative (Bauer & Greyser, 1968; Pollay & Mittal, 1993). In a pivotal piece written in 1986, Pollay outlined a number of the unintended consequences of advertising. Advertising has also been attributed with creating higher levels of materialism and consumption in society, as well as with encouraging people to seek happiness from products as opposed to family and friends. It has also been charged with perpetuating stereotypes, particularly for minority groups. As Pollay (1986) argued, "while it may be true that advertising reflects cultural values, it does so on a very selective basis, echoing and reinforcing certain attitudes, behaviors, and values far more frequently than others" (p. 33). Over its history, advertising has been especially criticized for presenting an Anglo American male viewpoint of the world; this viewpoint is one that has both underrepresented and misrepresented other groups in society, particularly women and ethnic minorities (Wilson & Guitierrez, 1995).

The successful advertiser of the 21st century must understand the importance of diversity in American society (Gardyn & Fetto, 2003; Raymond, 2001; Tharp, 2001). Within the United States, advertisers need to recognize the distribution of consumers across a number of characteristics, including gender, age, ethnicity, sexual orientations, and so on, if they hope to build relationships and maintain market share in today's ever-growing diverse society. Diversity of people, products, and images is crucial in the 21st century for an advertiser's bottom line; it also helps to contribute to a more representative and inclusive society.

U.S. POPULATION TRENDS

One need only to look at the breakdown of the American population by different indicators to see that today's American society is diverse. Of the 281 million citizens reported in the U.S. Census 2000, almost one fourth of Americans identified themselves as something other than White alone (Raymond, 2001). In 2003, Hispanics became the nation's largest minority group, with an estimated 37 million people. This number just surpassed African Americans, who make up roughly 36.2 million Americans (Clemetson, 2003). The growth is said to stem from higher birth rates among the Hispanic population compared with other groups as well as from high levels of immigration. Asian Americans are also rapidly expanding in size in the United States and now account for 4.2% of the population (Raymond, 2001). According to Raymond (2001), the multicultural nature of the United States demands a new business approach, particularly if marketers want to effectively reach the billions of dollars in annual spending that ethnic minority groups have been reported to control.

Reports from the Selig Center for Economic Growth at the University of Georgia indicate that African Americans accounted for $646 billion in buying power in 2002, followed by Hispanic Americans at $581 billion and Asian Americans at $296 billion (Gardyn & Fetto, 2003). These numbers have more than doubled in size from those reported across the three groups in 1990 (Raymond, 2001). Furthermore, although the buying power of White Americans accounts for $6.3 trillion in annual spending, the size of the White non-Hispanic population is decreasing and is expected to drop from approximately 70% of the population today to close to 50% by 2050 (Gardyn & Fetto, 2003; U.S. Census, 2000). In contrast, the Hispanic population is estimated to grow and account for 20% of the population by 2020 (U.S. Census, 2000). Asian Americans are also predicted to continue growing and to account for just over 5% of the U.S. population by 2010 (U.S. Census, 2000).

However, other groups and trends must also be noted if we are to understand the changing face of the United States and to really come to understand what diversity means in the 21st century. The projected estimates in 2003 of those people aged 55 and over include almost 63 million Americans (U.S. Census, 2000). One of every four Americans will be over 55 years of age by 2010 (Tharp, 2001). This group is particularly attractive for providers of health-care services, travel, and luxury products, with predictions that "by 2007, the number of households headed by people ages 55 to 74 is expected to grow about 15 percent, while the number of those with an annual income of $100,000 or more is expected to rise a whopping 63 percent" (Francese, 2002, p. 41). By the same token, the gay, lesbian, bisexual, and transgender (GLBT) community has been estimated at between 4% and 8% of the population, with approximately $340 billion in discretionary spending (Gardyn, 2001). With the U.S. population growing ever more complex and diverse, it is important to examine issues of diversity in advertising and especially to define what diversity means in today's American culture.

THE ROLE OF ADVERTISING

If we look back over the history of advertising, we can see that advertising has always had a role to play in society, but the focus of criticism toward advertising has shifted as societal assumptions have changed and as technology has advanced (Carey, 1989). Pope (1991) discussed how early complaints about advertising were really targeted more toward the demand for safe products. Then the focus shifted to a desire and demand for honest and truthful advertising messages. Later, in the

1960s, these concerns turned to the mass distribution of advertising by means of television. According to Pope (1991), television was very different than any media before it, because it came directly into your living room with vivid images and sounds.

At this time, several researchers started to talk about the power of advertising to act like a magic bullet. It was suggested that people would see ads and be manipulated by them to go and buy the products advertised (Pope, 1991). Several popular books such as Vance Packard's 1957 *The Hidden Persuaders* came out at the same time and talked of subliminal advertising, or hitting consumers with messages below the conscious level of thought. During this time, people started to become very worried about motivational research. They also started to worry that advertisers were now not simply presenting information about their products in ads, but they were brainwashing consumers and designing special messages for different segments of the population such as children (Pope, 1991). Here we see the psychology of advertising coming into play and many theories from the discipline of psychology being borrowed to better help advertising researchers understand how consumers receive, process, and react to persuasive messages.

The 1960s were also greatly influenced by the civil rights movement, which further contributed to a widening of criticism toward the advertising industry and the lack of diversity in advertisements. Criticism increased over the images of various minority groups, in particular women, African and Hispanic Americans, and later Asian Americans (Wilson & Guitierrez, 1995). The portrayals were considered stereotypical, limited, and in many cases derogatory. As an example, Belkaoui and Belkaoui (1976) were able to show portrayals from the 1950s up through the 1970s depicting women as domestic, decorative, and dependent on men. Other studies on the portrayals of women have focused on differences in products advertised between men and women (Bresnahan, Inoue, Liu, & Nishida, 2001), the number of voice-overs and the frequency of central figure roles for women (Furnham & Mak, 1999), images of dependence and unintelligence as well as the types of professional roles presented (Milner & Collins, 2000), and, especially, women as sex objects (Lin, 1998). Although women have come a long way in the images portrayed in advertising, many representations of them still are limited and reminiscent of the findings from previous research (Furnham & Mak, 1999).

For ethnic minorities, the 1960s saw the beginning of a consistent stream of research assessing African American images in advertising (Barban, 1969; Barban & Cundiff, 1964; Bristor, Lee, & Hunt, 1995; Dominick & Greenberg, 1970; Kassarjian, 1969). These studies were followed in the 1980s by research examining Hispanic American representations (O'Guinn & Meyer, 1984; Wilkes & Valencia, 1986, 1989) and then in the 1990s by studies focusing on the representation of Asian Americans (Taylor & Lee, 1994; Taylor, Lee, & Stern, 1995; Taylor & Stern, 1997). Now we are starting to see representation studies expanding to include the representation of other growing, yet often underrepresented, groups such as Asian-Indian Americans (Khairullah & Khairullah, 1999), the elderly population (Benet, Pitts, & LaTour,

1993; Peterson & Ross, 1997), the gay community (Gardyn, 2001; Kates, 1999; Penaloza, 1996), and the mobility disabled (Burnett & Paul, 1996).

Beyond the goals of academic researchers who want better and more accurate representation of different groups in American society, there are serious financial reasons for marketers to better understand and represent today's diverse consumer groups. Because advertising is a form of social communication, only by presenting what is familiar can advertisers hope to connect with consumers through their messages (Bush, Smith, & Martin, 1999). As noted by Duff (1993), growing numbers of non-White consumers may find it increasingly difficult to relate to advertising that continues to rely on the traditional White-only models. Therefore, it is crucial for advertisers to understand individual characteristics and cultural values of consumers in different groups if they hope to communicate their messages effectively and build strong relationships with these consumers (de Mooij, 1998; McCracken, 1986). Groups once ignored because of their size and low disposable incomes have grown and become very attractive, and they can now be reached more efficiently through technological advances. Therefore, success in the 21st century will come only to marketers who understand the diversity that exists within the American culture.

DEFINING DIVERSITY

The United States has been called a melting pot, referring to people of different races, cultures, and religions that have come to blend and assimilate into one nation, often by shedding their traditional cultural identities (Orndoff, 2003; Tharp, 2001). However, the melting pot has been criticized for stifling diversity (Carr-Ruffino, 1996) and for having several negative implications for people who have tried to assimilate and either were not accepted or who ended up being ashamed of their heritage (Simons, Vasquez, & Harris, 1993). Today, some people have begun to expand existing definitions, whereas others have created new definitions to describe the changing face of the United States (Glazer, 2000; Suro, 1999).

Frey (2002), for example, said that the melting pot now extends to include multiple languages, with approximately one in five Americans (17.9%) over the age of 5 speaking a foreign language at home in the year 2000. In fact, the U.S. Census (2000) reported that although 28 million Americans speak Spanish at home, Chinese (including both Mandarin and Cantonese) is now the second most common foreign language spoken at home, followed by French (1.6 million) and German (1.4 million; Fetto, 2003). In contrast, a new term describing the United States as a "salad bowl," where people maintain their cultural heritage but within a U.S. lifestyle, has emerged (Tharp, 2001).

In light of the changing trends in the United States as well as a culture that is more accepting of differences, it is important to have a broad definition of diversity. In a special issue of the *Journal of Advertising* on gender and multicultural issues in advertising, Stern (1999) defined multiculturalism as "applying to the study of nonmajority populations within, between, and across cultures.... [T]he term is used in its popular sense as a descriptor of the study of populations other than white, European, heterosexual, educated men..." (p. 1). Although the definition is quite broad, it is not adequate for the future of American society and the trends that are now taking place. Any definition of diversity must be one that incorporates all citizens, White, Black, old, young, Christian, Muslim, gay, heterosexual, and so on. Advertisers as well as other major institutions in society must recognize that diversity includes everyone. According to Cavanaugh (2001), old terms of diversity that focus on race and gender are ineffective in today's world. He suggests that the term "inclusiveness" is on the road to becoming a market leader and that this term can go as far because it encompasses variables such as personal style as well as age, culture, and ethnic origin. The mind-sets of younger generations such as Generation Y are already at this place, where multiculturalism is their reality and race is not necessarily the defining variable (Irwin, 2003).

Across a wide range of fields, evidence exists for the expanding definitions of diversity that Cavanaugh (2001) has suggested. Books such as *Managing Diversity: People Skills for a Multicultural Workplace* are supporting broad definitions of diversity such as those that include women, men, racial and ethnic minorities, gay persons, persons with disabilities, obese people, and older people (Carr-Ruffino, 1996). In his article on teaching about diversity in family nursing, the characteristics Friedman (1997) considered important include variables such as immigration experience, generational differences, language, class and poverty, residence or regional differences, and family forms as well as the traditional variables of race, ethnicity, and religion. Wellner (2002) suggested that diversity training is expanding to move beyond the "primary dimensions" of diversity such as age, ethnicity, gender, physical ability, race, and sexual orientation to also include "secondary dimensions of diversity" such as educational background, marital status, parental status, work experience, and so on.

Although diversity was defined in *Webster's Dictionary* (1977) simply as "the condition of being different; an instance or a point of difference...," commonality can actually be attained in recognizing and appreciating differences. With these more inclusive definitions, we become much closer to recognizing that everyone is included in diversity; from this vantage point, advertisers can consider segmenting on more than simply belonging to one group. According to Chideya, author of *The Color of Our Future*, "America is a constantly reinvented country and a constantly reinvented concept.... [W]e're in a transitional phase right now where [foreign influences] are going to be seen as 'Latin American,' 'Asian American,' and so on...but eventually, they'll be identified as simply 'American'" (as cited in Fetto, 2001a). Therefore, in defining diversity in the 21st century, we might follow Tharp's (2001) suggestion of a salad bowl as a model for multiculturalism in which "individuals can express the part of themselves that is African American or gay or teenage or Texan or working class and still belong (or aspire to belong) to mainstream America" (p. 23). In other words, multiculturalism is about "the simultaneous influence of multiple value systems" (Tharp, 2001, p. 21).

This broader and more inclusive view of diversity might help many marketers who have already fallen prey to defining their target segments too narrowly, based on one primary dimension of diversity. Several failed campaigns have shown that simply because some people have labeled themselves as Hispanic does not mean that effective marketing will occur by simply targeting "Hispanics" as a homogeneous group. According to Herbig and Yelkur (1998), there are over 20 different Spanish-speaking nationalities that make up the U.S. Hispanic population, and each has its own national holidays, foods, values, and cultural characteristics. The authors go on to provide examples of companies that have tried a "one slogan fits all," such as Tang, that ended up with a Puerto Rican idiom for orange juice that was not relevant for other Hispanics.

A variety of other studies have shown differences in levels of ethnic identification that can greatly influence attitudes and behavior (Green, 1999; Lee, 1993; Webster, 1994; Whittler, Calantone, & Young, 1991; Williams & Qualls, 1989), not to mention the many other variables such as age, lifestyle, region of the country, or even work schedules. In an article on increasing flexible opportunities in the workplace, Fetto (2001b) discussed how more companies are offering their employees options such as telecommuting, job sharing, compressed workweeks, and flextime. Certainly these expanding opportunities have implications for consumer behavior and may create new segments with which marketers can consider targeting consumers.

As changes continue to occur in the United States, from shifting sizes of various demographic groups to increases in purchasing power, it becomes important for advertisers and researchers to understand the differences and similarities in attitudes and behaviors both between and within groups. Culture is said to influence the cognitions, attitudes, and behavior of people, including why, when, and how people shop as well as people's preferences for and responses to advertising messages (de Mooij, 1998; Gudykunst, 1997; Han & Shavitt, 1994; Markus & Kitayama, 1991; Tharp, 2001; Triandis, 1989). However, culture consists of a variety of demographic and psychographic elements, and, in some cases, variables such as income or beliefs about shopping may transcend the cultural boundaries of one's ethnicity, gender, or age. In other cases, however, ethnic identification or lifestyle preferences may be the best predictors of behavior for certain products; therefore these variables would be the most appropriate segmentation variables for efficient and effective marketing communications.

Tharp's book, *Marketing and Consumer Identity in Multicultural America* (2001), provides an up-to-date synthesis of past research that has examined the diversity of people and the influence of different cultural and individual characteristics on buyer behavior and message effectiveness. Based on extensive analysis, Tharp's book also suggests a multitude of issues to consider in order to market effectively to consumers in the America of the 21st century. We are now at a juncture where additional and updated research is needed in order to address these issues and advance the field.

FUTURE RESEARCH ON DIVERSITY ISSUES

Culture, simply put, is a way of life shared by a group of people (Swidler, 1980). When cultural contact takes place, adaptations follow. Depending on the nature of contact, the subsequent cultural adaptations may be long or short in duration, attitudinal or behavioral, and unidirectional or bilateral. Scholars in anthropology, sociology, psychology, and marketing have all studied issues related to those adaptations. Collectively, they provide the broad context for research on diversity in advertising and highlight key avenues for future research.

Recognize Within-Group Variations

Generations of immigrants have helped make the United States a great land of opportunities and a society with a mosaic makeup. It has long been suggested that differences in cultural origin imply that people are open to different parts of the American experience, interpret it in different ways, and use these interpretations for different ends (Glazer & Moynihan, 1963). Kumanyika and Odoms (2001) further noted how immigrant status, in addition to origin, may be considered as a within-group segmentation variable.

Whereas earlier immigrants were largely characterized as laborers with little education and skills, recent newcomers appear to be bimodal in terms of characteristics. Although some still concentrate on blue collar work, others have been credited for being better educated, highly skilled, and willing to work for lower wages in the United States (Boyd, 1979; Gold, 1989; U.S. Census, 2000). To keep our research current, we need to examine the special characteristics of these "new" immigrants and how they differ from the "old" or even the second- or third-generation immigrants as consumers in the marketplace.

African Americans are a good case in point. Over the past three decades, the United States has seen an increasing number of immigrants of African descent. In 1980, approximately 3% of African Americans were foreign born. By 1998, that percentage had almost doubled (Pollard & O'Hare, 1999). Although individuals of African descent share a common origin, differences in immigration patterns have resulted in variations in a number of things such as dietary practices and preferences for music. Likewise, *Asian American* is simply a blanket term that includes various Asian heritages such as the Chinese, Filipinos, Koreans, Japanese, and so on. For this group, interestingly, Generation X makes up a larger percentage than among any other ethnic minority groups (Wellner, 2002). One would think that their presence would surely produce a different demand for consumer goods and services. The Hispanic population, while heavily populated by recent immigrants, is further segmented by country of origin, with Mexicans, Puerto Ricans, and Cubans as the largest subgroups (Wellner, 2002). Their use of language and preference for media outlets speak loudly to how these immigrants are all unique in their own right. Rather than each of these groups being treated as one homogeneous, monolithic group, it behooves researchers to pay close attention to how these within-group cultural differences manifest themselves in issues such as self-labeling, the use of media and interpersonal sources, and attitude and decision-making processes.

Consider Multicultural Individuals

The Census Bureau, for the first time in Census 2000, allowed people to identify with more than one race. The idea of the "marginal man" (Park, 1931) and the concept of "double consciousness" (DuBois, 1907) remind us of the double role of being an American and being an X-American and the perpetual struggle between them (Williams, 1992).

Researchers have suggested that individuals can be "multicultural" and exhibit behavior and attitudes from extensive life experiences in two or more cultures (Williams & Qualls, 1989). For example, multicultural African Americans who measure as strong bicultural identifiers (Airhihenbuwa, Kumanyika, TenHave, & Morssink, 2000) might exhibit diet and exercise behavior representative of "typical" Black cultural values in one setting and exhibit diet and exercise behavior representative of Anglo mainstream cultural values in other situations. In the latter case, the switch in behavior may be due to being a minority in a majority setting where there is more normative pressure to conform to mainstream values, or it may be that the individual is genuinely comfortable with the mainstream values, that is, multicultural, and prefers that behavior for that particular setting.

Williams and Qualls (1989) further suggest that African American consumers who have moved up the socioeconomic ladder may have similar responses to their Anglo counterparts, but they should not necessarily be viewed as having lost strong ethnic identity. In other words, accepting one set of values does not necessarily mean rejecting another set. A multicultural individual is able to feel comfortable with both mainstream and his or her group identity and values. Take banda music, for example. It is neither American nor Mexican. Instead, it is a mixture of rock, country western, salsa, and traditional folk music of northern Mexico. Together, these types provide a unique combination of the music from two cultures (Suro, 1999). Future research should recognize that individuals can simultaneously belong to more than one group and reflect the complexity of their psychological dispositions and behaviors.

Conduct Research That Is Inclusive

Almost right from the start, American society was characterized by the ideal of *e pluribus unum*. Over the years, there has been an ongoing struggle between nativism and cosmopolitan liberalism. Spencer (1994), in his discussion of the politics of identity, correctly pointed out that the movement of multiculturalism is an effort by previously excluded groups to overcome historical and social exclusion in order to construct new identities for the country.

Identity-based production, distribution, and consumption are all characteristics and functions of modern consumer culture (Chasin, 2000). Capitalism in the United States has made possible the path from identity politics to identity-based niche markets. For example, when women earned the constitutional right to vote in 1920, they became a viable market and were aggressively targeted. After the Civil Rights Act and the Voting Rights Act, African Americans drew advertisers and marketers' attention as a noteworthy consumer segment (Chasin, 2000). D'Emilio (1983) suggested that the modern gay identity took shape only after gay individuals obtained economic independence from heterosexual families. The formation of the gay identity and, consequently, the gay market then became a reality in the United States.

Given this view of American identity politics and the evolution of niche markets, future research on diversity should (a) not only study people with different ethnic origins but also expand to include those with different value systems originating from whatever groups significantly contribute to forming their identities; (b) conduct historical and sociological analyses to provide a better understanding of how various groups emerge as target markets and the subsequent ramifications; and (c) broaden traditional theories that were developed on the basis of limited populations.

Expand Acculturation Research

For years, research on diversity issues has used acculturation as the theoretical framework. Acculturation was first used in 1880 by P. W. Powell to describe the process of culture borrowing. Lesser (1933, p. 9) provided an even broader perspective by referring to acculturation as "the process by which aspects of elements of two cultures mingle and merge." The notion of "what gets changed in what situation and how" forms the basic premise for subsequent acculturation studies in disciplines such as anthropology, sociology, psychology, communication, and marketing. To be thorough in the scope of our investigation and for future acculturation research to be relevant, we must expand that research beyond simply studying immigrant groups.

The traditional notions of a culture's powerful force and the dominant paradigm of assimilation may have to be reconsidered. Factors such as country of origin, generations, life stages, and even sexual orientations will all have an impact on how the process of acculturation takes place and evolves. Because acculturation is said to be an ongoing process, the earlier theoretical propositions made by Triandis and his associates (1986) on the circular stages of accommodation–overshooting–affirmation or the so-called ping-pong effects seem worthy of our consideration in explaining differences in behavior. Furthermore, some research evidence has suggested that acculturation could be temporal and may lead to behavior that is situation dependent (Stayman & Deshpande, 1989; Williams & Qualls, 1989). Because consumption-related activities may be different in terms of the context they take place in and the amount of time they require, the issue of situational identity has to be addressed.

Another important factor to consider in future acculturation research is that of motivation for change. Culture is generally regarded as a potentially powerful force, rewarding those who conform and punishing those who deviate. Therefore, the motivation to conform could simply be that of pressure. For first-generation immigrants, this motivation is usually considered high. This is because immigrants take the initiative to come to America either to avoid difficulties in their home countries or in search of a better life and opportunities. However, for everybody else, the opposite may be true. For an African American who traces his or her ancestry to Africa, for a second- or third-generation Japanese American, for a gay person or for an elderly person, the desire to integrate is probably less important than the desire to claim ownership of the American culture and preserve his or her unique identity. The image of a minority culture wholeheartedly embracing the majority culture's way of life may have to be updated. Therefore, it is necessary to refocus our research on understanding the motivation and functional need for acculturation (Helweg, 1987; Taylor, 1969).

Examine Policy Implications

While exploring the opportunities offered by their environment, individuals must also submit themselves to the limitations imposed by the environment. A society, to a certain extent, may accommodate minority cultures and help preserve them. Many other countries may be ahead of the United States in this regard. In Canada, for example, the Constitution defines itself as a multicultural society having the following guidelines with regard to ethnic groups in that (a) they maintain and develop themselves; (b) they be accepted by other members of the society; (c) they share and interact with other groups; and (d) they learn the official languages. Though many challenges have been raised against the true functions of such guidelines, they are found to be useful in easing acculturation stress and problems. Sweden has also established three criteria, that is, equality of living, retaining and developing one's ethnic identity, and working with other groups, to develop a multicultural society. Future research has to examine diversity issues within the context of sociopolitical environments in order to fully assess the impact of public policies on citizens who belong to different groups in the United States.

The many ethnic "towns" or locales within most major U.S. metropolitan areas (e.g., Japanese villages, Italian streets, East Indian neighborhoods, Jewish communities, little Taipei, and China towns) stand witness to the need for one to affirm his or her cultural heritage. The same is true for sexual orientation, such

as the gay-oriented city pockets found in San Francisco or the elderly populations found in regions of California or Florida. Recently, the Internet has also
emerged as an important virtual community for various groups such as Gay.com or
CommercialCloset.org for gay and lesbian Americans, aan.net and asianamerican.
net for Asian Americans, and aarp.org for elderly persons. These communities help
preserve an individual's group identity by selling ethnic products, holding special
social events, establishing schools or support groups, and developing their own media outlets, programming, and online groups in which news specific to the group
shares equal footing with news of the mainstream culture. Eventually the communities and networks help to form political groups that aid in advancing group
interests. The presence of these communities offers minorities the confidence to
identify socially with their group culture. An important issue to consider, then, is
the significance that individuals attach to these communities and the impact of
group dynamics and networks on intergroup relations.

Although the 1960s civil rights movement has helped show the necessity to
accommodate people of different cultures, views, and opinions, tensions often
emerge from beliefs about the inequities that exist (e.g., education opportunities
and career advancement) between groups in the society. Recent discussions ranging from affirmative action (e.g., University of Michigan's admissions policies),
political correctness, and White male bashing to racial profiling, gay bashing, and
a woman's right to be in the military are all reminders of the changing social
and political climates and potential implications of such changes. Tensions and
confrontations between groups have also demonstrated their ability to stimulate
a minority group's cohesiveness and self-identity. Consequently, it is necessary
to situate future research within the context of group community influences and
public policies.

Study Diversity Practice in Advertising

Because "people shop on the basis of their identities, or on the basis of their inclusion in an identifiable social group" (Chasin, 2000, p. 32), advertising becomes an
important tool for legitimizing and publicizing the existence of their target groups.
Advertising influences identity formation and identity enhancement in two important ways. First, advertising acknowledges individuals by rendering them identifiable and intelligible in the mass media. Second, advertising recognizes consumers
as members of a discernible social group, with which they identify. Therefore, advertising may function to bring the marginalized population groups into public
being. Whether this practice is desirable or beneficial requires further investigation
(Lee & Callcott, 1994).

Through the use of content analysis, an extensive stream of studies has been
focused on examining diversity representation in advertising. The underlying assumption is twofold. First, representative or inclusive advertising is likely to produce
positive attitudes among minority populations and therefore is more effective. The

ingroup bias theory (Brewer, 1979; Wilder & Shapiro, 1991) suggests that a member of any group should have a more favorable response to another member of the same group in an advertisement. In other words, Whites should respond more favorably to ads with other Whites, gays or lesbians should respond more favorably to ads with other gays or lesbians, and elderly persons should do likewise. Second, representative or inclusive advertising is thought to help promote positive self-esteem among minority populations and is therefore socially desirable.

Past research has studied the impact of specific types of inclusive advertising such as the use of models, images, and visual cues (Kerin, 1979; Qualls & Moore, 1990; Schlinger & Plummer, 1972; Tolley & Goett, 1971; Whittler, 1991; Williams & Qualls, 1989; Williams, Qualls, & Grier, 1995) as well as language (Alsop, 1984; Dillard, 1972; Giles, Taylor, & Bourhis, 1973; Haskins & Butts, 1973; Kochman, 1981; Terrell & Terrell, 1983; Williams, 1997; Williams, Atwater, Nelson, & Toy, 1989; Williams & Dillon Grantham, 1999) on a limited number of minority consumer groups. Although interesting findings have emerged, future research will have to expand this investigation to other population groups in order to gauge the generality of effects.

On the issue of whether inclusive advertising contributes to social good, reaction to gay advertising may serve as the most recent example. For many participants of the gay community, the expanding gay market and increasing gay images in advertising are signs of progress, if not success. This optimistic perspective argues that advertising to the gay community serves to legitimize members of this group as individuals and members of an intelligible subculture in the United States. However, the excitement of being noticed and praised by marketers has grown into a more skeptical and critical attitude as the gay market grows (Burnett, 2000). Many have voiced their concerns about the possible negative consequences of stereotypes of gay men and lesbians in the mass media (see, e.g., CommercialCloset.org). Moreover, they have critiqued the presentation of certain eccentric gay images, such as drag queens and the paucity of lesbians or gay people of color in advertising. Thus gay advertising reflects the ambivalence of legitimacy and vulnerability of assimilation and confrontation. The study of stereotyping and the effects of stereotypical images in advertising may help shed some light on this issue, and, obviously, a lot more has to be done.

Finally, as suggested by Williams (1992), influences from family members, church, professions, and so on may outweigh advertising in an individual's decision-making process. Culture, as we know it, consists of objects, symbols, stories, and rituals that a group of people share (McCracken, 1986). Furthermore, culture manifests itself in actions, behavioral styles, lifestyles, and ways of expressions (Berry, 1980; Kahle, 1983; Padilla, 1980). Both the subjective and objective aspects of a culture provide the parameters for defining who we are (Triandis, 1972). Members of minority groups must continuously define and redefine their identity between the reality of their world and that from the mainstream culture. Exactly what are some of the other important factors that an individual considers in his or her decision-making process? Do these vary from group to group? How do media sources compare with interpersonal sources in terms of usage and importance? How does the struggle between the dominant and minority cultures manifest itself in day-to-day situations? Is consumption behavior different from other types of behavior? Does it matter if the behavior is public or private? Future research on diversity issues will have to respond to all of these questions and more. Given the demographic and psychographic landscape of the United States in the years to come, it would seem prudent to begin answering these questions now.

REFERENCES

Airhihenbuwa, C. O., Kumanyika, S. K., TenHave, T. R., & Morssink, C. B. (2000). Cultural identity and health lifestyles among African Americans: A new direction for health intervention research? *Ethnicity and Disease, 10,* 148–164.

Alsop, R. (1984, October 25). Firms still struggle to devise best approach to Black buyers. *Wall Street Journal,* p. 35.

Barban, A. M. (1969). The dilemma of "integrated" advertising. *Journal of Business, 42,* 477–496.

Barban, A. M., & Cundiff, W. (1964). Negro and white response to advertising stimuli. *Journal of Marketing Research, 1,* 53–56.

Bauer, R. A., & Greyser, S. (1968). *Advertising in America: The consumer view.* Boston, MA: Harvard University Press.

Belkaoui, A., & Belkaoui, J. M. (1976). Comparative analysis of the roles portrayed by women in print advertising: 1958, 1970, 1972. *Journal of Marketing Research, 13,* 168–172.

Benet, S., Pitts, R. E., & LaTour, M. (1993). The appropriateness of fear appeal use for health care marketing to the elderly: Is it ok to scare granny? *Journal of Business Ethics, 12,* 45–55.

Berry, J. W. (1980). Acculturation as varieties of adaptation. In A. Padilla (Ed.), *Acculturation: Theory, models and some new findings* (pp. 9–25). Boulder, CO: Westview.

Boyd, M. (1979). The changing nature of Central and Southeast Asian immigration to the United States: 1961–1972. *International Migration Review, 8,* 507–519.

Bresnahan, M., Inoue, Y., Liu, W. Y., & Nishida, T. (2001). Changing gender roles in prime-time commercials in Malaysia, Japan, Taiwan and the United States. *Sex Roles, 45,* 117–131.

Brewer, M. B. (1979). In-group bias in the minimal intergroup situation: A cognitive-motivational analysis. *Psychological Bulletin, 86,* 307–324.

Bristor, J. M., Lee, R. G., & Hunt, M. R. (1995). Race and ideology: African-American images in television advertising. *Journal of Public Policy and Marketing, 14,* 48–59.

Burnett, J. J. (2000). Gays: Feelings about advertising and media used. *Journal of Advertising Research, 40,* 75–84.

Burnett, J. J., & Paul, P. (1996). Assessing the media habits and needs of the mobility-disabled consumer. *Journal of Advertising, 25,* 47–59.

Bush, A. J., Smith, R., & Martin, C. (1999). The influence of consumer socialization variables on attitude toward advertising: A comparison of African-Americans and Caucasians. *Journal of Advertising, 28,* 13–24.

Calfee, J. E., & Ringold, D. J. (1994). The 70% majority: Enduring consumer beliefs about advertising. *Journal of Public Policy and Marketing, 13,* 228–238.

Carr-Ruffino, N. (1996). *Managing diversity: People skills for a multicultural workplace.* Cincinnati, Ohio: International Thomson Publishing.

Carey, J. W. (1989). Advertising: An institutional approach. In R. Hovland & G. B. Wilcox (Eds.), *Advertising in society* (pp. 11–26). Lincolnwood, IL: NTC Publishing Group.

Cavanaugh, W. (2001). New definition of diversity. *Executive Excellence, 8*(1), 5.

Chasin, A. (2000). *Selling out.* New York: St. Martin's Press.

Clemetson, L. (2003, January 22). Hispanics now largest minority, census shows. *The New York Times* (nytimes.com).

de Mooij, M. (1998). *Global marketing and advertising: Understanding cultural paradoxes.* Thousand Oaks, CA: Sage.

D'Emilio, J. (1983). Capitalism and gay identity. In A. Snitow, C. Stansell, & S. Thompson (Eds.), *Powers of desire: The politics of sexuality* (pp. 100–113). New York: Monthly Review Press.

Dillard, J. L. (1972). *Black English: Its history and usage in the United States.* New York: Random House.

Dominick, J. R., & Greenberg, B. S. (1970). Three seasons of Blacks on television. *Journal of Advertising Research, 26,* 160–173.

DuBois, W. E. B. (1907). Souls of Black folk. Chicago: McLurg.

Duff, C. (1993, March 3). You, too, could be a model for catalogs. *Wall Street Journal,* p. B1.

Fetto, J. (2001a, July). Toplines: An all-American melting pot. *American Demographics, 23,* 8–10.

Fetto, J. (2001b, July). Toplines: Flexing our options. *American Demographics, 23,* 10–11.

Fetto, J. (2003, February). Chinese at home. *American Demographics, 25,* 12.

Francese, P. (2002, November). Older and wealthier. *American Demographics. 24*(10), 40–41.

Frey, W. H. (2002, July/August). Multilingual America. *American Demographics, 24,* 20–23.

Friedman, M. (1997). Teaching about and for diversity in family nursing. *Journal of Family Nursing, 3*(3), 280–294.

Frith, K. T., & Mueller, B. (2003). *Advertising and Societies: Global Issues.* New York: Peter Lang Publishing.

Furnham, A., & Mak, T. (1999). Sex-role stereotyping in television commercials: A review and comparison of fourteen studies done in five continents over 25 years. *Sex Roles, 41,* 413–437.

Gardyn, R., & Fetto, J. (2003, February 25). Race, ethnicity and the way we shop. *American Demographics, 1,* 30–33.

Gardyn, R. (2001, November). A market kept in the closet. *American Demographics, 23,* 36–43.

Giles, H., Taylor, D. M., & Bourhis, R. Y. (1973). Toward a theory of interpersonal accommodation through language: Some Canadian data. *Language in Society, 2,* 177–192.

Glazer, N. (2000). On beyond the melting pot, 35 years after. *International Migration Review, 34,* 270–279.

Glazer, N., & Moynihan, D. P. (1963). *Beyond the melting pot.* Cambridge, MA: MIT Press.

Gold, S. J. (1989). Differential adjustment among new immigrant family members. *Journal of Contemporary Ethnography, 17,* 408–434.

Green, C. L. (1999). Ethnic evaluations of advertising: Interaction effects of strength of ethnic identification, media placement and degree of racial composition. *Journal of Advertising, 28,* 49–64.

Gudykunst, W. B. (1997). Cultural variability in communication. *Communication Research, 24,* 327–348.

Han, S., & Shavitt, S. (1994). Persuasion and culture: Advertising appeals in individualistic and collectivist societies. *Journal of Experimental and Social Psychology, 30,* 326–350.

Haskins, J., & Butts, H. F. (1973). *The psychology of Black language.* New York: Barnes and Noble Books.

Helweg, A. (1987, June). Why leave India for America? A case study approach to understanding migrant behaviour. *International Migration, 25,* 165–177.

Herbig, P., & Yelkur, R. (1998). Marketing to Hispanics. *Services Marketing Quarterly, 16*(2), 171–180.

Holbrook, M. B. (1987). Mirror, mirror, on the wall, what's unfair in the reflections on advertising? *Journal of Marketing, 51,* 95–103.

Irwin, T. (2003). Diversity moves to the forefront. *Adweek, 53*(2), 5.

Jhally, S. (1995). Image-based culture. In G. Dines & J. M. Humez (Eds.), *Gender, race, and class in media: A text-reader* (pp. 77–87). Thousand Oaks, CA: Sage.

Kahle, L. R. (Ed.). (1983). *Social values and social change: Adaptation to life in America.* New York: Praeger.

Kates, S. M. (1999). Making the ad perfectly queer: Marketing "normality" to the gay men's community? *Journal of Advertising, 28*, 25–37.

Kassarjian, H. H. (1969). The Negro and American advertising, 1946–1965. *Journal of Marketing Research, 6*, 29–39.

Kerin, R. (1979). Black model appearance and product evaluation. *Journal of Communication, 29*, 123–128.

Khairullah, D. Z., & Khairullah, Z. Y. (1999). Relationships between acculturation, attitude toward the advertisement, and purchase intention of Asian-Indian immigrants. *International Journal of Commerce & Management, 9*, 46–65.

Kochman, T. (1981). *Black and White styles in conflict.* Chicago: University of Chicago Press.

Kumanyika, S. K., & Odoms, A. (2001). Nutrition issues for African Americans. In R. L. Braithwaite and S. E. Taylor (Eds.), *Health issues in the Black community* (pp. 419–447). San Francisco: Jossey-Bass.

Lee, W. (1993). Acculturation and advertising communication strategies: A cross-cultural comparison of Chinese and Americans. *Psychology & Marketing, 10*, 381–397.

Lee, W., & Callcott, M. F. (1994). Billboard advertising: A comparison of vice products across ethnic groups. *Journal of Business Research, 30*, 85–94.

Lantos, G. P. (1987). Advertising: Looking glass or molder of the masses? *Journal of Public Policy and Marketing, 6*, 104–128.

Lesser, A. (1933). The Pawnee ghost dance hand game. In M. J. Herskovits (Ed.), *Acculturation: The study of culture contact* (pp. 6–9). New York: Augustin.

Lin, C. A. (1998). Uses of sex appeals in prime-time television commercials. *Sex Roles, 38*, 461–475.

Markus, H. R., & Kitayama, S. (1991). Cultures and the self: Implications for cognition, emotion, and motivation. *Psychological Review, 98*, 224–253.

McCracken, G. (1986). Culture and consumption: A theoretical account of the structure and movement of the cultural meaning of consumer goods. *Journal of Consumer Research, 13*, 71–84.

McCarthy, M., & Howard, T. (2003, January 20). Last year's rookies back for more. *USA Today*, p. 3B.

Milner, L. M., & Collins, J. M. (2000). Sex-role portrayals and the gender of nations. *Journal of Advertising, 29*, 69–79.

Mittal, B. (1994). Public assessment of TV advertising: Faint praise and harsh criticism. *Journal of Advertising Research, 34*, 35–53.

O'Guinn, T., & Meyer, T. P. (1984). Segmenting the Hispanic market: The use of Spanish-language radio. *Journal of Advertising Research, 23*, 9–16.

Orndoff, K. (2003). Assessing American diversity. *The Futurist, 37*(1), 22.

Packard, V. O. (1957). *The hidden persuaders.* New York: D. McKay Co.

Padilla, A. M. (1980). *Acculturation: Theory, models and some new findings.* Boulder, CO: Westview Press.

Park, R. E. (1931). Mentality of racial hybrids. *American Journal of Sociology, 36*, 534–551.

Penaloza, L. (1996). We're here, we're queer, and we're going shopping! A critical perspective on the accommodation of gays and lesbians in the U.S. marketplace. In D. L. Wardlow (Ed.), *Gays, lesbians, and consumer behavior* (pp. 9–41). New York: Haworth.

Peterson, R. T., & Ross, D. T. (1997). A content analysis of the portrayal of mature individuals in television commercials. *Journal of Business Ethics, 16*, 425–433.

Pollard, K. M., & O'Hare, W. P. (1999). A history of disadvantage. *Population Bulletin, 54*, 5.

Pollay, R. W. (1986). The distorted mirror: Reflections on the unintended consequences of advertising. *Journal of Marketing, 50*, 18–36.

Pollay, R. W., & Mittal, B. (1993). Here's the beef: Factors, determinants, and segments in consumer criticism of advertising. *Journal of Marketing, 57*, 99–114.

Pope, D. (1991). Advertising as a consumer issue: An historical view. *Journal of Social Issues, 47*, 41–56.

Qualls, W. J., & Moore, D. J. (1990). Stereotyping effects on consumers' evaluation of advertising: Impact of racial differences between actors and viewers. *Psychology & Marketing, 7*, 135–151.

Raymond, J. (2001, November). The multicultural report. *American Demographics, 23*, S3–S6.

Simons, G. F., Vazquez, C., & Harris, P. R. (1993). *Transcultural leadership.* Houston, TX: Gulf.

Schlinger, M. J., & Plummer, J. T. (1972). Advertising in black and white. *Journal of Marketing Research, 9*, 149–153.

Spencer, M. E. (1994). Multiculturalism, "political correctness," and the politics of identity. *Sociological Forum, Special Issue: Multiculturalism and Diversity, 9*, 547–567.

Stayman, D., & Deshpande, R. (1989). Situational ethnicity and consumer behavior. *Journal of Consumer Research, 16*, 361–371.

Stern, B. (1999). Gender and multicultural issues in advertising: stages on the research highway. *Journal of Advertisment, 28*(1), 1–9.

Suro, R. (1999, March). Recasting the melting pot. *American Demographics, 21*, 30–32.

Swidler, A. (1980). Culture in action: Symbols and strategies. *American Sociological Review, 51*, 273–286.

Taylor, C. R., & Lee, J. Y. (1994). Not in vogue: Portrayals of Asian Americans in magazine advertising. *Journal of Public Policy & Marketing, 13*, 239–245.

Taylor, C. R., Lee, J. Y., & Stern, B. B. (1995). Portrayals of African, Hispanic, and Asian Americans in magazine advertising. *American Behavioral Scientist, 38*, 608–621.

Taylor, C. R., & Stern, B. B. (1997). Asian-Americans: Television advertising and the "model minority" stereotype. *Journal of Advertising, 26*, 47–61.

Taylor, R. C. (1969). Migration and motivation: A study of determinants and types. In J. A. Jackson (Ed.), *Migration* (pp. 99–133). Cambridge, England: Cambridge University Press.

Terrell, S., & Terrell, F. (1983). Effects of speaking Black English upon employment opportunities. *American Speech and Hearing Association, 25*, 27–29.

Tharp, M. C. (2001). *Marketing and consumer identity in multicultural America.* Thousand Oaks, CA: Sage.

Tolley, B. S., & Goett, J. J. (1971). Reactions to blacks in newspapers. *Journal of Advertising Research, 11*, 11–17.

Triandis, H. C. (1972). *The analysis of subjective culture.* New York: Wiley.

Triandis, H. C. (1989). The self and social behavior in differing cultural contexts. *Psychological Review, 96*, 506–520.

Triandis, H. C., Kashima, Y., Shimada, E., & Villareal, M. (1986). Acculturation indices as a means of confirming cultural differences. *International Journal of Psychology, 21*, 43–79.

U.S. Bureau of the Census (2002). Retrieved from http://www.census.gov. April 15, 2003 retrieved

Webster, C. (1994). Effects of Hispanic ethnic identification on marital roles in the purchase decision process. *Journal of Consumer Research, 21*, 319–331.

Webster's New Collegiate Dictionary (1977). 5th edition. Massachusetts: G. & C. Merriam Co., 334.

Wellner, A. (2000). How do you spell diversity? *Training, 37*(4), 34–38.

Wellner, A. S. (2002, November). Our true colors. *American Demographics, 24*, S2–S20.

Whittler, T. E. (1991). The effect of actor's race in commercial advertising: Review and extension. *Journal of Advertising, 20*, 54–60.

Whittler, T. E., Calantone, R. J., & Young, M. R. (1991). Strength of ethnic affiliation: Examining black identification with black culture. *The Journal of Social Psychology, 131*, 461–467.

Wilder, D. A., & Shapiro, P. (1991). Facilitation of outgroup stereotypes by enhanced ingroup identity. *Journal of Experimental Social Psychology, 27*, 431–452.

Wilkes, R. E., & Valencia, H. (1986). Shopping-related characteristics of Mexican Americans and Blacks. *Psychology & Marketing, 3*, 247–259.

Wilkes, R. E., & Valencia, H. (1989). Hispanics and Blacks in television commercials. *Journal of Advertising, 18*, 19–25.

Williams, J. D. (1992). Reflections of a Black middle-class consumer: Caught between two worlds or getting the best of both? In J. F. Sherry, Jr. & B. Sternthal (Eds.), *Diversity in consumer behavior: Advances in consumer research* (Vol. 19, pp. 850–856). Provo, UT: Association for Consumer Research.

Williams, J. D. (1997, March 4). Ebonics controversy: Relevance for marketers. *Marketing News*, p. 5.

Williams, J. D., Atwater, D. F., Nelson, J., & Toy, D. R. (1989). Ebonics and advertising to the Black consumer: A need for research to analyze language and communication styles in a linguistic perspective. In J. M. Hawes & J. Thanopoulos (Eds.), *Developments in marketing science, volume XII. Proceedings of the Thirteenth Annual Conference of the Academy of Marketing Science* (pp. 637–642). Orlando, FL: Academy of Marketing Science.

Williams, J. D., & Dillon Grantham, K. (1999). Racial and ethnic identity in the marketplace: An examination of nonverbal and peripheral cues. In E. J. Arnould & L. M. Scott (Eds.), *Advances in consumer research* (Vol. 26, pp. 451–454). Provo, UT: Association for Consumer Research.

Williams, J. D., & Qualls, W. J. (1989). Middle-class Black consumers and intensity of ethnic identification. *Psychology & Marketing, 6,* 263–286.

Williams, J. D., Qualls, W. J., & Grier, S. (1995). Racially exclusive real estate advertising: Public policy implications for fair housing practices. *Journal of Public Policy and Marketing, 14,* 225–244.

Wilson, C. C., & Guitierrez, F. (1995). Advertising: The media's not-so-silent partner. In C. C. Wilson & F. Guitierrez (Eds.), *Race, multiculturalism, and the media: From mass to class communication* (pp. 109–138). Thousand Oaks, CA: Sage.

Zanot, E. J. (1984). Public attitudes towards advertising: The American experience. *International Journal of Advertising, 3,* 3–15.

CHAPTER TWO

Science for Sale: Psychology's Earliest Adventures in American Advertising

Ludy T. Benjamin, Jr.
Texas A&M University

It is estimated that more than half of the world's psychologists today live and work in the United States, and more than half of those are employed outside of the colleges and universities where the science of psychology began. Most of these applied psychologists work in clinical and counseling settings, but approximately one third of them are employed in business and industry. This chapter describes the origins of psychology in service to the world of business through its point of initial entry, the application of the new scientific psychology to the world of advertising, an applied field that began more than 100 years ago.

When the fledgling science of psychology with its new laboratories and shiny brass instruments was beginning to try its wings in the late nineteenth century, there were those psychologists who were eager to put their science to the ultimate test of application to real-world problems. The initial applications were in education, principally studies on teacher training and curriculum design, and, in business, studies on advertising.

That psychology's entry in the field of business was through advertising was no random event. The advertising industry, which began in America in the second half of the 19th century, was undergoing a transformation as the new century dawned. Advertisers, who had long been content to describe their products mostly for local markets, were now looking at expanded markets made available by the growth of the railroad and the telegraph, by the rise of national magazines, and by the capacity for surplus production. Business historians Bryant and Dethloff (1990) described that metamorphosis as follows:

> Advertising became increasingly important after the 1890s as manufacturers reduced price competition and stressed product differentiation. As manufacturing capacity came to exceed demand, firms used advertising to create additional markets. Profit levels provided for ever-expanding advertising budgets and for the hiring of experts in advertising techniques as well as in sales.... In an economy of excess, advertising became the means to dispose of an oversupply. The effect, in the long run, was the development of a consumer society with advertising as one of its major institutions. The advertising industry would come to exert great influence, with few responsibilities, while it stimulated materialism and sanctioned the drives and anxieties it created as national social values. (p. 190)

What was more important was that advertisers were no longer focused on mere product descriptions. Instead, they wanted to create a demand for their products. Advertising was about understanding the mind of the consumer, about capturing the consumer's attention, about persuading the consumer in favor of a particular product, and, of greatest importance, about directing the consumer's behavior so that action was taken—action that resulted in purchase. In short, advertising was about the elements of the mind, and so it was natural that the new scientific experts on the mind would be drawn to this field.

This chapter describes the emergence of the psychology of advertising in the late 19th century and its evolution in American business through the 1920s. It begins with the invention of the science of psychology and the applied psychology myth attendant to that story. Next there is brief coverage of the historical development of advertising in America. Finally, the focus of the chapter is on the contributions of three early pioneers in the psychology of advertising who worked in the field between 1900 and 1930.

THE BEGINNINGS OF APPLIED PSYCHOLOGY

To historians of psychology and most psychologists, the term *scientific psychology* refers to the laboratory-based psychology that originated in Germany with Wilhelm Wundt and his contemporaries. That kind of psychology adopted several names to distinguish itself from psychology that was philosophical discourse, usually labeled *mental* or *moral philosophy*. It called itself the "New Psychology" or "Physiological Psychology" or "Experimental Psychology."

There was, however, another psychology that predated scientific psychology, and it was especially popular in America throughout much of the 19th century. This psychology was an applied psychology, although not the one we think of today, and its practitioners offered such services as helping individuals select careers, helping schools select teachers, helping businesses select employees, helping people choose marital partners, and advising people about a multitude of personal decisions. At times these practitioners called themselves psychologists, but more commonly they were known as phrenologists, physiognomists, characterologists, graphologists, spiritualists, and psychics. These practitioners had decades of experience in applying their pseudosciences by the time the first of the American psychology laboratories appeared (Benjamin & Baker, 2004).

When scientific psychology began in America, it had to fight for its legitimacy against a public image of psychology that assumed the field was about characterology, mental telepathy, clairvoyance, and communicating with the dead (see Benjamin, 1986; Coon, 1992). The confusion of terms was considerable. The British journal, *Psychological Review*, founded in 1878, was a journal about paranormal phenomena and spiritualism. When Wundt began publication of his journal in 1881, he had to name it *Philosophical Studies* because the title *Psychological Studies* was already claimed by a parapsychology journal. The term *psychical* was used to connote events that were mental or psychological as opposed to events that were physical; thus Wundt and his followers talked about consciousness in terms of its composition in psychical elements and psychical compounds.

The early scientific psychologists were very much aware of the public's confusion, and they launched a public-image campaign to educate Americans about the new psychology, a campaign that included a psychology exhibition at the Chicago World's Fair in 1893 and a host of articles in popular magazines and newspapers by such psychological luminaries as G. Stanley Hall, Hugo Münsterberg, Edward Bradford Titchener, and James McKeen Cattell. It was an orchestrated advertising campaign designed to educate the public about what scientific psychology was and was not, and, perhaps of greatest importance, to tell the public about the value of psychology when applied to their lives, schools, and businesses.

One of the historical myths of American psychology—reinforced by the two editions of E. G. Boring's textbook on the history of psychology (Boring, 1929, 1950) and other sources—has been that, in its first 40 years, psychologists stayed in their laboratories and advanced the science of psychology, whereas only a few misfits ventured into the real world to seek fortune and fame by applying an imperfect science. In this version of history, applied psychology emerged after World War I when so many psychologists involved in war work suddenly recognized the relevance of their science. It's a nice story, but it just isn't so, and there is considerable historical scholarship in the past 30 years to debunk that myth (see Fagan, 1992; Napoli, 1981). Even so, most myths die hard. It is a fact that while the paint on the laboratory walls was still drying, American psychologists were busy applying their new science.

Although in the early years, applied psychologists were outnumbered by their pure science colleagues, they were not small in number; nor were they the misfits of the discipline. These psychologists, steeped in American pragmatism and Yankee know-how (and usually in need of money), would not be restrained. The new science of the mind was arguably the most applicable of all sciences, and these pioneering psychologists wasted little time trying to prove it.

America in the late 19th century was undergoing a social metamorphosis brought on by increased industrialization, new waves of immigration, growth of the cities, and reform movements in labor and education, including child labor laws and compulsory school attendance (Fagan, 1992; Napoli, 1981). There were,

TABLE 2.1
Harlow Gale's 1895 Survey of Minnesota Businesses

Question Blank No. 3 in Experimental Psychology. For the Study of Advertising.
Advertisements seem to have two aims, viz: 1. To attract attention. 2. To induce to buy. If you have any corrections to make with this they will be gladly received. We have classified the chief ways of advertising into four groups, viz:
  1. Magazines and periodicals.
  2. Newspapers and handbills or posters.
  3. Show-windows.
  4. Painted signs and placards.
Do you know of other ways of advertising?
What are the best ways you have found in your experience for attracting attention under these four ways of advertising?
  Please name them in the order of their importance from best to poorest.
  Give your reasons why each way of attracting attention does attract attention.
What are the best ways you have found in your experience for inducing people to buy? (e.g., constant reiteration of firm or article, odd figure prices, leaders, testimonials, prizes, use of superlatives, argument, plain statement, etc.)
  Please name them in the order of their importance from best to poorest.
  Give your reasons why each way of inducing people to buy does induce them to buy.

---

of course, numerous problems inherent in such social upheaval. What was needed was an applied science to solve those problems. Psychology may not have had the science to solve those problems, but psychologists were smart enough to recognize the importance of the moment. They stepped forward to offer their services.

By 1892 the child study movement was underway under the leadership of G. Stanley Hall. The principal goal of this movement was to apply psychology to the problems of education, particularly curricular reform and teacher training (see Davidson & Benjamin, 1987). Four years later, in 1896, Lightner Witmer opened what may have been the first psychological clinic in the world, founding the applied specialties of school and clinical psychology (Baker, 1988; McReynolds, 1997).

Psychology in the business world was begun at the same time. In the fall of 1895, Harlow Gale, an instructor in the Psychology Department at the University of Minnesota, began his research on the psychology of advertising. It was, perhaps, the first work by any American psychologist in the field that would become known as business psychology and later as consumer psychology and industrial–organizational psychology.

Gale sent a brief questionnaire to approximately 200 businesses in the twin cities of Minneapolis and St. Paul (see Table 2.1 for the complete text of the questionnaire). His cover letter stated the following:

> At the University of Minnesota we are making a psychological investigation of advertisements. It is an entirely new field for psychological work and one of great and increasing importance. It is our aim to find the mental processes which go on in the

minds of the customers from the time they see the advertisement until they have purchased the article advertised. To get down to the bottom of our subject and make our work successful, we need the aid of experienced advertisers, and to that end we have sent out this circular with the following questions and will be greatly indebted to you if you will send us your answers to them. (Gale, 1900, p. 39)

Although psychologists may have been ready and eager to apply their science to the problems of American business, it is not clear that the business community shared that enthusiasm. Gale reported that approximately 20 of the advertising questionnaires were returned, which is a return rate of only 10%.

Gale was especially interested in attention and investigated several components of magazine advertisements, including location on the page, wording differences, and color. Although Gale was the first psychologist to work on advertising issues, his research did not get much attention from the advertising community. However, psychologists were just a few years away from being sought out by advertising firms. Advertiser David Gibson (1908) echoed the beliefs of many in his field:

Most advertising would be a great deal better investment if there were more psychology in it. . . . Instead of finding out by cut-and-try methods, wouldn't it pay to listen to the college professor's say-so on such subjects as attention, interest, association, desire, and all the other things that bear directly upon the success of advertising copy? (p. 955)

A BRIEF HISTORY OF THE ORIGINS OF ADVERTISING IN AMERICA

Before the work of the early psychologists who pioneered the psychology of advertising is discussed, a brief history of the development of advertising in America is needed to establish some of the context for the psychological work. We could begin a historical analysis by asking this question: How might the present state of advertising be characterized?

The most obvious characteristic is the pervasiveness. Advertising is ubiquitous. It has invaded all fields and every medium. . . . The mails are swollen and the postal deficit increased by torrents of circulars, which scarcely anyone reads but which an indulgent Government transmits cheaply. Newspapers and magazines, . . . unoccupied buildings, fences and open lots, even roofs and walls, are employed to exploit merchandise. . . . Ingenuity has exhausted itself in devising new places from which to win the passing tribute of a glance. (Dwight, 1909, p. 201)

This sentiment about the omnipresence of advertising is often voiced today in response to a landscape from roadsides to computer screens that is obliterated by advertisements; yet the quotation just given was written nearly 100 years ago, in 1909, in the first decades of advertising as an industry. It verifies a long-standing public disaffection for the intrusiveness of advertising. Such public dislike has not been able to stop or even slow the growth of advertising. Thus it joins Benjamin Franklin's short list of certainties: death, taxes, and advertising.

The first individuals specializing in advertising in America began offering their skills to businesses in the years immediately prior to the Civil War. They were located principally in the cities of the northeast, particularly New York, Boston, and Philadelphia. Initially these advertising agents served merely as brokers between businesses wishing to sell their goods and newspapers eager to sell their page space. For their services, the newspapers and magazines paid these agents a fee, eventually standardized at around 15%. In the course of approximately 25 years, the job of the "advertising man" would be transformed from one in which a person sold blank space to one in which a person wrote advertising copy and designed ads (Fox, 1984; Laird, 1998; Norris, 1990).

In writing advertising headlines and copy and in designing advertisements, the successful advertising agents likely qualified as amateur psychologists. That is, they possessed a knowledge of human nature that they used to make their ads more effective. As the advertising industry grew in the last quarter of the 19th century, so too did the belief in the importance of human psychology for effective advertising (see Benton, 1896; Herzberg, 1895, 1897).

Most advertising agents in the 19th century were self-employed, but there were some collectives organized as advertising firms as early as 1869. Soon there were trade journals and magazines that gave the field some additional respectability and visibility. The best known of the 19th-century advertising journals was *Printer's Ink*, which began publication in 1888.

Respectability for the advertising agent was a key issue. The unsavory image of a carnival huckster was often the picture held by many businesses, and in fact these early "ad men" often referred to themselves as hucksters. In 1906, George Rowell, a principal figure in the growth of advertising on a national scale, wrote that advertising is "one of the easiest sorts of business in which a man may cheat and defraud a client without danger of discovery" (as cited in Lears, 1994, p. 90). To businesses, the price of advertising was not clear; that is, the value was almost impossible to ascertain, as a business decision, so that advertising agents were free to ask whatever they thought they could get. It was not a profession for the timid.

Advertising agents sought greater respectability. One avenue to legitimacy was to form alliances that promoted ethical behavior in the field and fostered research on advertising practices. Thus were born the advertising clubs. In New York City the New York Men's Advertising League was founded in 1905, and its counterpart in Philadelphia opened the next year as the Poor Richard Club. These clubs are fascinating social and business institutions whose histories are beyond the scope of this chapter, but consider just briefly a few facts about the Poor Richard Club.

The club opened in 1906 with 75 members. The following year the group bought a clubhouse, actually a very large Victorian home, where they could host monthly dinners and weekly lunches. By 1911 there were 350 members. The bylaws of the club listed a single objective: to promote the scientific study of advertising. The single biggest event for the Poor Richard Club each year was its banquet, which in 1915 was attended by 500 people. The perceived legitimacy of these advertising men's clubs is evident in the banquet speakers of the Poor Richard Club, which included William Howard Taft, Woodrow Wilson, Will Rogers, and Amelia Earhart, among many other dignitaries (Lutz, 1953).

Apparently all of the clubs announced the promotion of the science of advertising as a principal aim, yet there is little evidence that that goal received much attention. Occasionally scientists were invited for luncheon speeches and workshops (see Benjamin, 2000). These clubs, however, were clearly social and political entities. Businesses had always recognized the value of social and political connections; science had yet to prove itself an equal contributor to economic gain.

Still, the business world was willing to give science its chance. Historian Donald Napoli (1981) wrote that with "the formation of large industrial empires came new management problems and a growing problem with efficiency" (p. 28). Psychologists, equipped with a battery of mental tests and other techniques, were poised to answer the questions that American business had about advertising, selling, personnel selection, job analysis, efficiency, and management styles. By the turn of the 20th century, American businesses were beginning to seek the services of psychologists to solve their problems in much the same way that they had sought the services of phrenologists in the previous century. Research on advertising would lead psychologists into the world of business.

There was another reason that advertisers would be led to the world of psychology. At the end of the 19th century, two theories of advertising were being debated. The dominant theory is usually labeled the *rationalist school*. It argued that consumers were rational beings and thus advertisements should appeal to reason. Therefore, advertisements should be kept simple and straightforward, mentioning only the most relevant facts. The alternative view has been called the *impressionist theory*, and it emphasized sensory qualities of advertisements, including wording that suggested sensory images. The belief was that consumers were not always rational; they often were guided in their behaviors by sensory impressions that proved more influential than reason. For the rationalists, then, advertisements should be about the presentation of information, whereas for the impressionists, advertising was a form of persuasion in which the appeal was to influence the subconscious mind (Kuna, 1976). This debate was an open invitation for the new science of psychology.

THREE EARLY PSYCHOLOGICAL PIONEERS

Although this chapter focuses on the advertising theory and work of three psychologists, the reader should be aware that by 1930 there were perhaps 40 to 50 psychologists working in this field, including the following people who wrote

influential books on the subject: Henry Foster Adams, Charles E. Benson, Joseph
V. Breitweiser, Harry L. Hollingworth, Harry D. Kitson, Albert T. Poffenberger,
Walter D. Scott, Carl E. Seashore, Daniel Starch, and Edward K. Strong, Jr. Although Harlow Gale may have been the first psychologist to work on the subject
of advertising, he did not pursue that work or related work as a career. He was not
really a business psychologist or an industrial–organizational psychologist as the
label would be used today. Likely the honor of being the first business psychologist
goes to Walter D. Scott (1869–1955).

Walter Dill Scott

Like Gale and Lightner Witmer, Scott had received training from Wundt at the
University of Leipzig, earning his doctorate there in 1900 and joining the faculty
at Northwestern University later that year. In his first year at Northwestern, at the
encouragement of a magazine advertising executive, Thomas Balmer, Scott agreed
to give a lecture on the new psychology at a meeting of the Agate Club, Chicago's
organization of advertising executives. One of those in attendance was John L.
Mahin, head of a leading Chicago advertising agency. He was intrigued by Scott's
remarks and met with him later to discuss the potential contributions of psychology
to advertising. Mahin offered to start publication of a magazine on advertising if
Scott would write a series of 12 articles on psychology for that publication. Scott
agreed, and the magazine, *Mahin's Magazine*, began monthly publication in 1902
with Mahin's promise to his readers to work toward developing advertising as
an exact science. Scott's initial contribution was a brief discussion of the laws of
association of ideas—habit, recency, vividness—with little direct indication of their
relevance for advertising.

The article on association was followed by others on suggestion, on argumen-
tation, on perception, on illusions, on mental imagery, and on the psychological
value of the return coupon. Perhaps at the encouragement of Mahin or perhaps with
growing self-assurance of his ability to apply psychology to advertising, Scott's articles grew in their direct relevance for Mahin's readers. Only one of those articles—a
study of type face timetables for the Burlington Railroad—was based on any research by Scott. All the others were the result of armchair theorizing that seemed
to appeal to Mahin and his readers.

Those dozen articles were reprinted as Scott's first book, *The Theory of Advertising*, which was published in 1903 and was the first book in the field of industrial
psychology by one of the new psychologists. Presumably Scott had titled the book
"The Psychology of Advertising," but the publisher insisted on substituting the
word "Theory" for the word "Psychology" (Hollingworth, 1938).

Apparently Scott's contributions were quite popular, and Mahin invited him
to continue. He wrote another 21 articles for the magazine through the end of
1904, and these were collected in a second book, *The Psychology of Advertising*
(1908), using the title that Scott had wanted for his first book. At the same time

Scott wrote about advertising for a number of other magazines, including *Atlantic Monthly*, *Business World*, and *Advertising World*. Many of the articles written for one magazine were published in identical form in other magazines, but some of them were new contributions, including a series of seven articles in *The Woman's Herald* (Ferguson, 1962).

By 1905, Scott was engaged full time in applied research, mostly investigating practical problems supplied to him by businesses that were willing to pay for the research to be done. Scott's popularity in the advertising community derived in part from the commonsense nature of his advice, from his motivational prescriptions, and from his knowledge of public speaking (indeed, he published a book on public speaking in 1906).

Despite the commonsense approach of Scott, or perhaps because of it, in the first decade of the 20th century, he was considered the leading scientific expert on advertising by the advertising community. David Kuna, a historian of psychology and an authority on the history of psychology in advertising, wrote that Scott's popularity derived from his support for the impressionist theory, the theory that came to dominate advertising copy after 1910, whether the scientific evidence justified its ascendancy or not. Kuna (1976) wrote that Scott's theory argued that the consumer was "a nonrational, suggestible creature under the hypnotic influence of the advertising writer" (p. 353). Kuna (1976) noted that it was through Scott's writings "that advertising men learned about the psychology of suggestion" (p. 347). Psychologists also learned a great deal about suggestion from Scott, who was the author of the annual review articles on suggestion that were published in the *Psychological Bulletin* from 1910 through 1916.

Scott believed that all humans were suggestible and that suggestion was a compelling force for action. The secret of effective advertising for Scott was to suggest a course of action, that is, buying some product, and to produce the advertisement in such a way that no contrary actions would be considered. In his 1903 book, Scott wrote the following: "Man has been called the reasoning animal but he could with greater truthfulness be called the creature of suggestion. He is reasonable, but he is to a greater extent suggestible" (p. 59).

In applying suggestion to advertising, Scott promoted two techniques in particular: the direct command and the return coupon. The direct command was often the headline of an ad: "Use Peterson's Tooth Powder" or "Get the Promotion You Deserve." According to Scott, such statements were effective because they suggested a particular action without arousing competing actions. He believed that individuals were inherently susceptible to such direct suggestion. Similarly, the return coupon was effective because it suggested a specific action to be taken, namely tearing out the coupon, filling it out, and mailing it in. Both techniques were thought to stimulate compulsive obedience.

Scott also promoted the importance of mental imagery and the way in which such imagery defined suggestion. He noted that advertisements for pianos should describe the instrument so "vividly that the reader can hear it" (1904, p. 34).

Similarly, foods should be advertised so that readers could taste them, and perfume advertisements should cause readers to experience the exotic smells.

Scott believed that individuals differed with regard to their dominant sense. According to him, some people were "eye minded" whereas others were "ear minded." In many cases the nature of the product being advertised would dictate the senses to be aroused; thus some advertisements might be largely visual, whereas others would focus on olfactory images. However, where possible, Scott urged advertisers to appeal simultaneously to as many senses as possible, "for in this way variety is given, and each reader is appealed to in the sort of imagery which is the most pleasing to him, in which he thinks most readily, and by means of which he is most easily influenced" (1904, p. 34).

By 1908, when Scott's second book on the psychology of advertising appeared, there was evidence of growing respect in the advertising community for what psychological science might provide. Scott's dedication page in his new book was meant to acknowledge this change: "The author respectfully dedicates this volume to that increasing number of AMERICAN BUSINESSMEN who successfully apply science where their predecessors were confined to custom."

Suggestion continued to be Scott's hallmark for advertising effectiveness. He did not deny the occasional role of other factors. Indeed, in his 1908 book he acknowledged the important role that emotion or state of mind could play in the reception or rejection of suggestions (Kuna, 1976). Still, he maintained his emphasis on suggestion as the chief force in the success of advertising. The following example, about his purchase of a suit, illustrates Scott's belief in the enormous power of the suggestibility of advertising:

> Some time ago a tailor in Chicago was conducting a vigorous advertising campaign. I did not suppose that his advertising was having any influence upon me. Some months after the advertising had begun I went into the tailor's shop and ordered a suit. While in the shop I happened to fall into conversation with the proprietor and he asked me if a friend had recommended him to me. I replied that such was the case. Thereupon I tried to recall who the friend was and finally came to the conclusion that this shop had never been recommended to me at all. I had seen his advertisements for months and from them had formed an idea of the shop. Later, I forgot where I had received my information and assumed that I had received it from a friend who had patronized the shop. I discovered that all I knew of the shop I had learned from advertisements.... (Scott, 1908, pp. 183–184)

Kuna (1976) wrote that Scott's "influence in the advertising profession was substantial" (p. 353). The validity of Scott's ideas was not really substantiated by research but by testimonials. Articles began to appear in *Mahin's Magazine*, *The Woman's Herald*, and other advertising journals that reported the success of advertising campaigns using Scott's ideas about suggestion. His role in the history of this field cannot be overstated. He gave scientific credibility to psychology's involvement with advertising. Scott's work so affected the nature of advertising that by 1910 "suggestive advertising" was a redundant phrase.

Harry Levi Hollingworth

Scott's popularity and reputation opened the doors for other psychologists to enter the advertising field, most notably Harry Hollingworth (1880–1956), who would lead advertising psychology in a very different direction. Hollingworth received his doctorate with James McKeen Cattell at Columbia University in 1909. Like Scott, Hollingworth's invitation to the world of business came early in his career. He was an instructor at Barnard College in New York City, married, and drawing an annual salary of $1,000. As a way to supplement his salary he taught night courses through the extension division of Columbia, where he encountered people in business who were interested in the applications of psychology to their work. Apparently it was three lectures that he gave on psychology and advertising in an applied psychology course that led to an invitation to give a series of lectures in 1910 on the psychology of advertising to the Advertising Men's League of New York City. At the time, there was nothing in Hollingworth's training or research interests to suggest any expertise in advertising. Indeed, he had none. But he needed money and he believed that the experimental psychology that he had learned gave him the tools that he needed to study the psychology of advertising. His lectures before the New York advertising group were especially well received, and the group inquired about the possibility that Hollingworth would conduct research for them. Several events followed as a result of those lectures.

First, the Advertising League established a graduate fellowship in psychology at Columbia University for a student to do advertising research. The initial recipient of that fellowship was Edward K. Strong, Jr., later the creator of the *Strong Vocational Interest Blank* and author of *The Psychology of Selling and Advertising* (1925). Second, Hollingworth published his lectures in 1913 as a book entitled *Advertising and Selling*, a book whose royalties Hollingworth shared with the Advertising League. Third, Hollingworth began a series of research studies on advertising funded by the League.

The Zeitgeist in psychology was changing from the mentalistic views of consciousness that focused on will, attention, apperception, and decision processes to a behavioristic view emphasizing observable responses. Both Gale and Scott were part of the earlier mentalistic tradition. They viewed advertising as a means for influencing the mind, and they felt that the insights to advertising effectiveness would be found in the mental processes and introspections of consumers. However, at Columbia University, under the guidance of such psychologists as Cattell, E. L. Thorndike, and Robert Woodworth, students were being trained in a more objective psychology that anticipated the ideas of John B. Watson (Kuna, 1979). It is interesting that Watson delivered his call for a behavioral psychology in an address that he gave at Columbia University in February 1913 (Benjamin, 1991).

That behaviorist manifesto was published later that year (Watson, 1913), as was Hollingworth's first book on advertising.

The difference between the two approaches is perhaps best illustrated in the controversy over attention as a predictor of advertising success. Those in the older tradition measured attention because of their belief in the power of attention in controlling action. It was assumed that if an advertisement held a reader's attention, that is, was attention grabbing, then behavior would follow. Gale and Scott studied those elements of the advertisement that they believed captured attention and suggested action, such as color, wording, placement on the page, repetition, and sensory involvement. Yet Hollingworth and his contemporaries, including many workers in the advertising field, focused more on the endpoint of the advertising process—the purchase as response—recognizing that the proof of the advertisement was in its ability to complete the sale, and that advertisements could be attention grabbing without being effective. In his 1913 book, Hollingworth wrote the following:

> After all has been said, the final value of an appeal depends entirely upon the effectiveness with which it leads to the desired specific action. No amount of care in framing a solicitation so as to catch the eye, to hold attention, and to stick in the memory, will be worth the trouble if the reader's reaction does not go beyond the appeal itself [to the final response]. (p. 216)

That quote reveals what Hollingworth believed to be the four tasks of an effective advertisement. The first task was to get attention; the second was to hold it; the third was to fix the impression in memory; and the fourth was to motivate the person to take the desired action. If the fourth did not occur, then the money was wasted on the other three.

Hollingworth began a program of pretesting the effectiveness of advertisements. Such testing programs had been done before by advertising agents, especially through the use of return coupons, which provided an obvious measure of advertisement success. Hollingworth argued that the testing done by advertisers was suspect because of a host of uncontrolled variables such as seasonal sales, multiple media, actions of competitors, and range of circulation. Further, those tests were not able to isolate variables that were part of the advertisement; thus one could never be certain which components were more or less effective in resultant sales. Finally, Hollingworth argued that an additional advantage of the pretesting was that advertisers could then use only the most effective ads, thus preventing considerable waste in advertising budgets.

To demonstrate the effectiveness of laboratory testing of advertisements, Hollingworth tested multiple ads for various products (e.g., lathes, soaps, and electric lights) sent to him by local advertising agents who knew the relative effectiveness of those ads in terms of sales figures for each advertisement but who did not share that information with Hollingworth in advance of his studies. He sent the results of his laboratory tests to the advertisers for comparison with actual sales. The correspondence between the two sets of figures was remarkably high, producing an average correlation of .82 (Hollingworth, 1913; Kuna, 1979).

As a psychologist, Hollingworth was interested in more than just the bottom line of an advertisement's success. He was curious about the stimulus variables that were important in each of the four tasks. He investigated many of the variables that had been looked at by Gale and Scott—wording, images, typefaces, color, and position—and he did so not by relying on introspective accounts but by studying the responses to the variations in the stimuli he was studying. In some studies he looked at a single independent variable, whereas in others he looked at the interactions that might be produced from multiple independent variables.

Hollingworth (1913) recognized that person variables were important as well, so he did research that looked at gender differences and socioeconomic differences. As part of this research, he selected 25 couples in the New York City area and asked them to keep records of their purchases of 80 items. These data are among the earliest systematic attempts to record consumer behavior in terms of such person variables. Again, most of this research was funded through the Advertising League or through New York City businesses.

Hollingworth's second book on advertising (Tipper, Hollingworth, Hotchkiss, & Parsons, 1915) again listed the four principal functions of an advertisement: secure attention; hold attention; establish associations; and influence conduct by making associations dynamic. Making associations dynamic meant understanding the role of human motives and emotions and appealing to those in structuring advertisements. Wants and needs were the motivating factors in purchasing behavior; advertisements that aroused those were most likely to be successful. This conceptual shift may owe its origins to the dynamic psychology of Robert Woodworth and his emphasis on organismic variables and to E. L. Thorndike's views on motives (Kuna, 1979). As noted earlier, Hollingworth had studied with both men.

Hollingworth's laboratory testing that focused on measuring stimulus–response connections and motivation became the dominant paradigm in the work of other advertising psychologists such as Daniel Starch, E. K. Strong, Jr., and A. T. Poffenberger. The demonstrated efficacy of the procedures strengthened the role of consulting psychologists in their work with businesses and further demonstrated to experimental psychologists the applicability of their methods to problems in the world outside of the academy. Eventually this work evolved into marketing research in which the laboratory was replaced by external settings, but the testing methods remained much the same. Further, Hollingworth's objective approach to advertising and the success of his laboratory and market-based studies paved the way for advertising firms to employ psychologists as full-time researchers.

John Broadus Watson

John B. Watson (1878–1958) had not planned to work in the advertising field. Instead, in 1920 he was comfortable rocking America's psychological boat with his theory of behaviorism. He was chair of the Psychology Department at Johns

Hopkins University and editor of one of the field's most prestigious journals, the *Psychological Review*. However, that year an affair with one of his graduate students led to a scandalous divorce and the loss of his academic position. Depressed and jobless, he visited a friend in New York who introduced him to Stanley B. Resor, the president of the J. Walter Thompson advertising agency. Watson (1913) had written that a science of psychology should be able to predict and control behavior. It is easy to understand why such a claim would gain the interest of the advertising world. Resor, a graduate of Yale University and a man acknowledged in his time as the "dean of American advertising" (Fox, 1984; Larson, 1979), was convinced that science could be of considerable aid to advertising effectiveness by measuring consumer behavior and predicting consumer trends (Buckley, 1989). Thus Watson went to work for J. Walter Thompson in 1920.

Resor hired Watson to work in Thompson's Research Department, which he had started in 1915. Yet before Watson was ready for that assignment, Resor required of him what he required of all executive hires, and that was learning about the business from the bottom up. In a brief autobiographical chapter, Watson (1936) described that experience:

> [Resor] sent me on a temporary investigation job, studying the rubber boot market on each side of the Mississippi River from Cairo to New Orleans. I was green and shy, but soon learned to pull doorbells and stop wagons in order to ask what brand of rubber boots were worn by the family.... On January 1, 1921, I ... was sent out immediately to sell Yuban Coffee to retailers and wholesalers in Pittsburgh, Cleveland, and Erie. I carried my pack for over two months. This job was just what I needed to rub off the academic. When I returned to the agency, I went through every department, media, research, and copy. I felt one distinct need. I knew little about the great advertising god, the consumer. Accordingly I made private arrangements to clerk in Macy's Department Store for two months.... (pp. 279–280)

Watson enjoyed early successes, partially because he was such a great self-promoter, and in 1925 he was made a Vice President. He wrote a lot for popular magazines, especially about child training, so he was a very visible figure in the public. Thompson took advantage of that visibility and made much of the fact that this eminent psychologist and former president of the American Psychological Association worked for the company.

Watson had created behaviorism as a psychology of utility. Early in his writings as an academic he had noted the applied value of a behavioral psychology, especially for the business world. From his offices in New York City's business district he set out to prove the validity of his science. Apparently ignoring the work of his predecessors in psychology, or else having examined that work and found it wanting, Watson argued that there was no science of advertising. Advertisers were wasteful, he declared. He wrote in 1921 to Adolf Meyer, his former colleague at Johns Hopkins: "No one knows just what appeals to use.... It is all a matter of instinctive judgment. Whether I can establish certain principles or not remains to be seen" (Buckley, 1989, p. 136).

Watson proposed creating a society of predictable consumers through the use of conditioned emotions. He planned to use the innate emotions of fear, rage, and love to influence consumption. He was not caught up in theories of rationalism or impressionism. It mattered not whether humans were governed by reason or by sensory impressions; for Watson the issue was to identify the variables that impelled action and to learn how to control those actions.

Following World War I, Americans were enjoying considerable economic prosperity. Social historians have touted the decade as a time of euphoria in America. Psychologists enjoyed enormous popularity during that time. For example, the first popular psychology magazines appeared in the 1920s, at least eight of them. One of those was entitled *Industrial Psychology* and was published monthly, primarily for business managers and executives (Benjamin & Bryant, 1997). National marketing began during this time, which called for a more scientific approach to advertising and marketing. Watson could not have chosen a better time for his new profession.

Watson understood the importance of targeting advertising campaigns for particular markets, and that meant knowing the consumers. He organized a number of demographic studies that formed the base for his ad appeals. For example, in an ad campaign for Johnson & Johnson's baby powder, Watson decided to appeal to fear in mothers, emphasizing the dangers of infection in infants and how baby powder would offer protection. He used the testimony of medical experts in ads intended to convince mothers that folk wisdom and family traditions were barriers to modern child training and that the answers for the modern world lay in the hands of science (Buckley, 1989).

Watson is said to have promoted style rather than substance in advertising campaigns. Historian of science and Watson biographer Kerry Buckley has written that, "In the case of automobiles, . . . Watson reasoned that since all models were mechanically similar and served the same function, a constantly changing design and style that appealed to the wish fulfillment of the consumer should be the basis for sales" (1989, p. 139). Thus advertisements should emphasize the obsolescence and unfashionableness of products, thereby generating new sales to replace products that were still serviceable but now out of fashion.

Watson headed a number of successful campaigns for Thompson and is generally credited with bringing back testimonial advertising, an advertising form that had earlier fallen out of favor because of its association with patent medicines. He is believed to have secured the services of celebrities such as Queen Marie of Romania and Mrs. Marshall Field to testify to the benefits of Pond's cold cream, an advertising campaign that was especially effective.

Further, Watson used himself as scientific authority, especially to promote Thompson's clients via radio advertising. Watson's visibility as an expert on all topics psychological, especially child rearing—promoted principally through his frequent contributions to popular magazines such as *Harper's Monthly Magazine, McCall's, Collier's,* and *Cosmopolitan*—gained him frequent invitations to speak on radio programs. Buckley (1989) described how Watson used those opportunities to advertise, although the public may not have recognized it as such:

> . . . a radio broadcast sponsored by Pebeco toothpaste featured Watson in a seemingly scientific discussion of salivary glands and their function in digesting food. Watson, not surprisingly, stressed the importance of brushing teeth to stimulate gland activity. But listeners who responded to an offer of additional information received a circular and samples of the sponsor's product. (p. 140)

Watson also used what he called "indirect testimonials," advertising appeals that used symbols to stimulate one of the three innate emotions. For example, in an advertising campaign for Pebeco toothpaste, Watson's advertisements pictured a seductively dressed young woman smoking a cigarette. It was not fashionable for women to smoke; it was seen as a behavior that represented independence and assertiveness. The ad emphasized that women's smoking was okay but only if they used Pebeco toothpaste to ensure that their breath remained fresh.

> The ad associated cigarettes with sexuality and seduction and raised fears that attractiveness might be diminished by the effects of smoking on the breath and teeth. Toothpaste was promoted not as a contribution to health and hygiene but as a means of heightening the sexual attraction to the user. Consumers were buying not merely toothpaste, they were buying sex appeal. (Buckley, 1982, p. 216)

This method of indirect testimonial has been touted as perhaps Watson's one unique contribution to advertising.

As noted earlier, the 1920s were a time of enormous popularity for psychology in America. Watson was one of several prominent psychologists who served as a popularizer of psychology in that time. In daily newspaper columns and magazine articles by psychologists and nonpsychologists, the public read of the advantages in seeking the services of psychologists. People were encouraged to use them to select careers, to hire employees, to find marital partners, and to raise their children. Advertisers, too, grew in their belief in the power of psychology, fueled by business and industry's adoption of the scientific management system of Frederick Winslow Taylor, the efficiency studies of Frank and Lillian Gilbreth, and the growing impact of industrial psychologists, particularly in the area of personnel selection.

Watson, however, was more than just a popularizer of psychology. That he was an effective advertising executive seems evident; that he changed the course of advertising in the image of his behavioral psychology is less clear (Coon, 1994). What is clear is that Watson's scientific authority and his visibility as the showpiece of Thompson's Research Department did much to enhance the reputation of psychologists working in advertising in the 1920s and the growth of the field in subsequent decades.

SUMMARY AND CONCLUSIONS

Applied psychology has always been a part of American psychology. It existed before the advent of scientific psychology in the late 19th century in the form of characterology and phrenology. It existed in the earliest days of advertising in the sales techniques and copywriting themes of the hucksters who sold advertising space or wrote copy and did so successfully because of their instincts about human nature or what they had learned of the subject on the job.

Advertising and scientific psychology became linked in a common time of transformation. As the status of science grew at the end of the 19th century, advertisers recognized the need for the application of scientific principles to their work. Psychology, a young science, was looking for an opportunity to validate the meaningfulness of the discipline and the utility of its methods for understanding the mind. Advertising was about appeal to the mind. It was a marriage made of mutual need.

The psychology of advertising evolved from the mentalistic approaches of Gale and Scott that emphasized the role of suggestion and the methods of introspection to the more objective approach of Hollingworth and Watson that relied on discovery of stimulus–response relationships and later the inclusion of organismic variables such as motives and emotions. Watson's goal was to create an advertising science that could control consumer behavior. Although Watson's behaviorism never achieved for advertising what he promised, his presence in the field further legitimized the scientific base for advertising. It seems likely that the advertising field was headed in behavioral directions already, but the presence of Watson gave a visibility to the union of psychology and advertising that promoted considerable growth in the following decades.

Some business historians have argued that psychological research in advertising "became widespread only with the Depression" (Pease, 1958, p. 170) or still later in the 1940s (Fox, 1984). That is true in the sense that the number of psychologists working in industry increased substantially during those decades. The cause of that may reflect a change in attitude within the advertising industry, perhaps keyed by the trumpeted successes of J. Walter Thompson with Watson on board as expert psychologist, and it may reflect the need for additional job outlets for psychologists as the academic market shrunk during the Great Depression, followed by increased job opportunities in business in a postwar growth economy. Not only have psychologists increased in numbers in advertising, but the scope of their work has increased as well. Psychologists' presence today in the fields of consumer studies, marketing, and advertising is testimony to the important legacy of the early pioneers discussed in this chapter.

REFERENCES

Baker, D. B. (1988). The psychology of Lightner Witmer. *Professional School Psychology, 3*, 109–121.

Benjamin, L. T., Jr. (1986). Why don't they understand us? A history of psychology's public image. *American Psychologist, 41*, 941–946.

Benjamin, L. T., Jr. (1991). A history of the New York Branch of the American Psychological Association, 1903–1935. *American Psychologist, 46*, 1003–1011.

Benjamin, L. T., Jr. (2000). A platform disaster: Harry Hollingworth and the psychology of public speaking. *Nebraska History, 81*, 67–73.

Benjamin, L. T., Jr., & Baker, D. B. (2004). *From séance to science: A history of the profession of psychology in America*. Belmont, CA: Wadsworth.

Benjamin, L. T., Jr., & Bryant, W. H. M. (1997). A history of popular magazines in America. In W. Bringmann, H. E. Luck, R. Miller, & C. E. Early (Eds.), *A pictorial history of psychology*, (pp. 585–593). Carol Stream, IL: Quintessence.

Benton, J. (1896). Psychology of advertising. *Printers' Ink, 14*(2), 14.

Boring, E. G. (1929). *A history of experimental psychology*. New York: Century.

Boring, E. G. (1950). *A history of experimental psychology* (2nd ed.). New York: Appleton-Century-Crofts.

Bryant, K. L., Jr., & Dethloff, H. C. (1990). *A history of American business* (2nd ed.). Englewood Cliffs, NJ: Prentice-Hall.

Buckley, K. W. (1982). The selling of a psychologist: John Broadus Watson and the application of behavioral techniques to advertising. *Journal of the History of the Behavioral Sciences, 18*, 207–221.

Buckley, K. W. (1989). *Mechanical man: John Broadus Watson and the beginnings of behaviorism*. New York: Guilford.

Coon, D. J. (1992). Testing the limits of sense and science: American experimental psychologists combat spiritualism, 1880–1920. *American Psychologist, 47*, 143–151.

Coon, D. J. (1994). "Not a creature of reason": The alleged impact of Watsonian behaviorism on advertising in the 1920s. In J. T. Todd & E. K. Morris (Eds.), *Modern perspectives on John B. Watson and classical behaviorism* (pp. 37–63). Westport, CT: Greenwood.

Davidson, E. S., & Benjamin, L. T., Jr. (1987). A history of the child study movement. In J. Glover & R. Ronning (Eds.), *Historical foundations of educational psychology* (pp. 41–60). New York: Plenum.

Dwight, F. (1909, August). The significance of advertising. *The Yale Review*, pp. 197–205.

Fagan, T. K. (1992). Compulsory schooling, child study, clinical psychology, and special education: Origins of school psychology. *American Psychologist, 47*, 236–243.

Ferguson, L. (1962). *The heritage of industrial psychology, I. Walter Dill Scott: First industrial psychologist*. Hartford, CT: Finlay Press.

Fox, S. (1984). *The mirror makers: A history of American advertising and its creators*. New York: Morrow.

Gale, H. (1900). On the psychology of advertising. *Psychological Studies, 1*, 39–69.

Gibson, D. (1908). The common sense of psychology. *Profitable Advertising, 17*, 955.

Herzberg, O. (1895). Human nature as a factor in advertising. *Printers' Ink, 13*(14), 1–2.

Herzberg, O. (1897). Hidden forces in advertising. *Printers' Ink, 20*(5), 10.

Hollingworth, H. L. (1913). *Advertising and selling: Principles of appeal and response*. New York: Appleton.

Hollingworth, H. L. (1938). Memories of the early development of the psychology of advertising suggested by Burtt's "Psychology of Advertising." *Psychological Bulletin, 35*, 307–311.

Kuna, D. P. (1976). The concept of suggestion in the early history of advertising psychology. *Journal of the History of the Behavioral Sciences, 12*, 347–353.

Kuna, D. P. (1979). Early advertising applications of the Gale-Cattell order-of-merit method. *Journal of the History of the Behavioral Sciences, 15*, 38–46.

Laird, P. W. (1998). *Advertising progress: American business and the rise of consumer marketing*. Baltimore: Johns Hopkins University Press.

Larson, C. A. (1979). Highlights of Dr. John B. Watson's career in advertising. *The Industrial-Organizational Psychologist, 16*(3), 3–5.

Lears, J. (1994). *Fables of abundance: A cultural history of advertising in America.* New York: Basic Books.

Lutz, J. (1953). *The Poor Richard Club.* Philadelphia: The Poor Richard Club.

McReynolds, P. V. (1997). *Lightner Witmer: His life and works.* Washington, DC: American Psychological Association.

Napoli, D. S. (1981). *Architects of adjustment: The history of the psychological profession in the United States.* Port Washington, NY: Kennikat Press.

Norris, J. D. (1990). *Advertising and the transformation of American society, 1865–1920.* New York: Greenwood.

Pease, O. (1958). *The responsibilities of American advertising: Private control and public influence, 1920–1940.* New Haven, CT: Yale University Press.

Scott, W. D. (1903). *The theory of advertising.* Boston: Small, Maynard.

Scott, W. D. (1904). The psychology of advertising. *Atlantic Monthly, 93*(1), 29–36.

Scott, W. D. (1906). *The psychology of public speaking.* Philadelphia: Pearson Brothers.

Scott, W. D. (1908). *The psychology of advertising.* Boston: Small, Maynard.

Strong, E. K., Jr. (1925). *The psychology of selling and advertising.* New York: McGraw-Hill.

Tipper, H., Hollingworth, H. L., Hotchkiss, G. B., & Parsons, F. A. (1915). *Advertising: Its principles and practice.* New York: Ronald Press.

Watson, J. B. (1913). Psychology as the behaviorist views it. *Psychological Review, 20,* 158–177.

Watson, J. B. (1936). Autobiography. In C. Murchison (Ed.), *A history of psychology in autobiography,* (Vol. 3, pp. 271–281). Worcester, MA: Clark University Press.

II. THE DARK SIDE OF DIVERSITY IN ADVERTISING: DISCRIMINATION, PREJUDICE, AND BIAS

On the Predictive Utility of the Implicit Association Test: Current Research and Future Directions

Michael J. Sargent

Bates College

A great deal of research in marketing and social psychology has investigated the effectiveness of persuasive appeals when the source of the appeal is a member of a stigmatized group. For example, do White message recipients respond more favorably to White spokespersons, Black spokespersons, or does it not matter? When might it matter more or less?

One approach common to several studies of this issue has been to examine the impact of Whites' racial prejudice on their evaluations of advertisements featuring Black or White individuals. The results of these investigations have been mixed. Cagley and Cardozo (1970), for example, exposed White participants to three print ads: one featuring only Black models, one featuring only White models, and one with a racially heterogeneous cast. Cagley and Cardozo also measured participants' racial prejudice by using a self-report measure. They found that low-prejudice individuals responded similarly to all three ads, but high-prejudice individuals responded more favorably to the all-White ad than to either of the others. In contrast, Bush, Hair, and Solomon (1979) found little evidence that high-prejudice Whites evaluated advertisements more favorably if they featured White models than if they featured Blacks. Similarly, Whittler (1989) found little evidence that high-prejudice Whites discriminated in their evaluation of ads featuring Black and White actors. Although on one product, high-prejudice Whites reported greater difficulty identifying with the Black actor, their product evaluations and evaluations of the advertisement were unaffected by the actor's race. Consistent with this result, Whittler and DiMeo (1991) found that high-prejudice Whites evaluated a product equally favorably, regardless of whether a Black or White spokesperson had appeared in its advertisement. In fact, it was *low-prejudice* individuals who rated the products less favorably when a Black actor had appeared rather than a White one.

One factor that may have contributed to the inconsistency of these results is the researchers' reliance on explicit, self-report measures of racial attitudes. These measures, although convenient to use, are characterized by a serious problem. As this chapter notes later, these measures may reveal some individuals' feelings toward African Americans, but other individuals may be motivated and able to distort their responses in ways that reduce the validity of the measures. Thus, variance in the validity of self-report measures of racial attitudes could contribute to variance in the findings obtained with those measures. Of course, this problem of motivated response distortion is one that social psychologists have recognized for decades (Jones & Sigall, 1971; Sigall & Page, 1971; Warner, 1965). Recent years, however, have seen the development and proliferation of implicit racial attitude measures, which promise a new solution to this problem. The present chapter reviews relevant research in this area, with an emphasis on one particular measure—the Implicit Association Test (IAT). The chapter also reports one study in which a collaborator and I have examined the predictive utility of this measure, and it closes with an eye to future research and marketing strategy.

IMPLICIT RACIAL ATTITUDES

Recently, the use of implicit measures of attitudes has spread rapidly. In fact, at least 48 research laboratories have used the IAT in recent studies (Nosek, 2001). This growth is the result of at least two causes—one methodological and one conceptual. First, self-report measures of many attitudes, including racial attitudes, are subject to response distortion. In the case of racial attitudes, respondents who want to appear unprejudiced—either in their own eyes or the eyes of others—can alter their responses in an effort to appear egalitarian. Even self-report measures that are designed to offset this problem still appear to be quite reactive (cf., McConahay, 1986; McConahay, Hardee, & Batts, 1981). For example, Fazio, Jackson, Dunton, and Williams (1995) randomly assigned White participants to complete the Modern Racism Scale (MRS) in the presence of either a Black or White experimenter, who, according to the experimental cover story, would read their responses. Participants who believed a Black experimenter would see their answers gave less prejudiced responses than those who believed a White experimenter would see their responses. Individuals in both groups reported less prejudice than they had in a mass testing session earlier in the semester. However, this shift was more pronounced with the Black experimenter, suggesting that self-presentational concerns were higher in her presence. These data call into question the claim that the MRS is not reactive.

A second reason for the development and popularity of implicit measures is that some researchers endorse a conceptual distinction between implicit and explicit attitudes. Greenwald and Banaji (1995), for instance, propose that implicit attitudes represent a trace of past experience that can mediate evaluative responses to objects, even if the actor is unable to accurately identify the trace. Or, as Greenwald, McGhee, and Schwartz (1998) say, "implicit attitudes are manifest as actions or judgments that are under the control of automatically activated evaluations, without the performer's awareness of that causation" (p. 1464). Because this reasoning proposes that actors may not always be able to identify their implicit attitudes, accurately it implies that valid measurement by means of self-report is unlikely.

Consistent with the assumption that implicit attitudes are conceptually separable from explicit attitudes, Wilson, Lindsey, and Schooler (2000) propose a model of dual attitudes, one that postulates that a single individual can hold two, distinct attitudes toward a single object, one implicit and one explicit. According to Wilson et al., the implicit attitude is defined by (a) unknown origin, (b) automatic activation, and (c) influence on implicit responses, those responses that the actor does not view as influenced by his or her attitude. Importantly, Wilson et al. assume that individuals may override their implicit attitudes through controlled processes. For example, a White might hold a positive explicit attitude toward African Americans but a negative implicit attitude toward members of the same category. According to Wilson et al., such an individual may experience spontaneous negative feelings upon seeing or thinking about Blacks, because the negative implicit attitude will be automatically activated. Nevertheless, this person will be motivated to override the implicit attitude and respond on the basis of the explicit attitude. If this same overriding occurs while individuals complete self-report measures of racial prejudice, then those measures are likely to be poor indicators of implicit racial attitudes.

Implicit Attitude Measures

Because self-report measures are likely to be insensitive to implicit attitudes, a number of indirect measures have been developed as alternatives. For example, Russ Fazio and colleagues have developed an evaluative priming measure of racial attitudes (Fazio et al., 1995). While completing this measure, participants are exposed to positive adjectives (e.g., "wonderful") and negative adjectives (e.g., "disgusting") that appear on a computer monitor, and their task is to indicate, by pressing one of two keys, whether each word is a good word or bad word. Prior to the appearance of each target adjective, a prime is displayed briefly (for 315 ms). Some of the primes are photographs of Blacks and some primes are photos of Whites. Fazio et al. find that participants' response latencies on the good word–bad word judgments are differentially facilitated by the faces. In general, White participants classify positive adjectives as "good" faster after exposure to White faces than Black faces, but the opposite tends to be true with negative adjectives. Importantly, there is considerable variance among participants in their tendency to show this pattern, and participants can be assigned scores that indicate the extent to which they show this pattern of differential facilitation. Moreover, two pieces of evidence suggest that these scores are reliably associated with participants' positivity or negativity toward Blacks. First, Blacks show a very different pattern of responding, one that suggests ingroup bias (i.e., White faces facilitate responding to negative adjectives).[1] Second, Fazio et al. demonstrated that Whites' scores on the racial priming measure were correlated with their behavior toward a Black experimenter. Even though the experimenter was blind to individuals' scores, she rated those Whites whose priming scores indicated more negative attitudes as less friendly and less interested in what she was saying.

The IAT is another popular measures of implicit attitudes. This implicit measure, originally proposed by Greenwald et al. (1998), involves the presentation of stimuli on discrete trials, after each of which the respondent's reaction time is measured. Typically, participants must give one of two keyboard responses (striking either a specified key on the left-hand side of the computer keyboard or one on the right-hand side) to each stimulus that appears. In one version of this task, participants are exposed to stimuli from four categories: African American names (e.g., Aiesha), White names (e.g., Amber), pleasant words (e.g., love), or unpleasant words (e.g., death). As Table 3.1 indicates, the first two blocks of trials are learning trials that acquaint the participant with the procedure. However, the third block of trials is critical. On this block of trials, two of the stimulus categories are assigned to each of the two response keys. So, Black and unpleasant share a response key, as do White and pleasant. Then, on a later block of trials (the fifth), the task is modified so that Black and pleasant share a response key, as do White and unpleasant. Consistently (e.g., Dasgupta, McGhee, Greenwald, & Banaji, 2000; Greenwald et al., 1998), participants are slower to give the same response to Black and pleasant (as well as White and unpleasant) than they are to give the same response to White and pleasant (as well as Black and unpleasant). This "IAT effect" is interpreted as an indication of an implicit preference for Whites over Blacks. In other words, it is assumed that slower responding on the Black + pleasant version of the task indicates more positive implicit attitudes toward Whites than toward Blacks. Importantly, this mean difference is obtained regardless of the order of the critical blocks. Although Fig. 3.1 describes an IAT in which the Black + pleasant block comes second, participants tend to respond more slowly on that block of

TABLE 3.1
Sample Structure of a Black–White IAT

Block	Left Hand	Right Hand
1	White names	Black names
2	Pleasant words	Unpleasant words
3	White names *and* pleasant words	Black names *and* unpleasant words
4	Black names	White names
5	Black names *and* pleasant words	White names *and* unpleasant words

trials, even when it comes before the Black + unpleasant block (Greenwald et al., 1998).

As with order effects, so must other plausible alternative explanations be ruled out if confidence in the validity of the IAT is to be justified. One plausible alternative interpretation is based on stimulus familiarity. It could be that Black names are simply less familiar to most respondents than are White names. Given that familiarity with stimuli can produce liking (Zajonc, 1968), this alternative explanation is, on its face, quite plausible. Nevertheless, recent research has demonstrated that this stimulus familiarity explanation does not fully account for the IAT effect. Most participants are slower to give the same response to Black exemplars and pleasant words than to White exemplars and pleasant words, even when the stimuli used are equally unfamiliar Black and White faces (Dasgupta et al., 2000). Moreover, the IAT effect is still obtained on an IAT using Black and White names (and pleasant and unpleasant words), even after the effects of stimulus familiarity are controlled for. These data undermine the plausibility of the familiarity interpretation, and, as a consequence, bolster the case for the validity of the IAT as a measure of implicit attitudes.

Arguably, however, the utility of the IAT depends on demonstrations of its ability to reliably predict behavior. Just as social psychologists once questioned the utility of the explicit attitude construct because of controversies over its predictive utility (LaPiere, 1934; Wicker, 1969), so might researchers and practitioners question the utility of the implicit attitude construct in the absence of data showing a relationship between it and overt behavior. Indeed, researchers have begun addressing this very question and are also beginning to reap fruit. McConnell and Leibold (2001), for instance, found that the Black–White IAT could predict Whites' tendency to exhibit different nonverbal behavior with a Black experimenter than with a White experimenter. For example, participants whose IAT indicated an implicit preference for Whites over Blacks exhibited more speech errors and hesitations with the Black experimenter than with the White. This demonstration is of practical importance, given that nonverbal behaviors such as these can have important consequences. For instance, Word, Zanna, and Cooper (1974) demonstrated that White participants who were interviewing a confederate showed a more negative pattern of nonverbal behavior with a Black confederate than with a White (including a tendency to commit more speech errors with the Black target). In a second study, Word et al. showed that White participants who were then the *targets* of the same nonverbal behavior that the Blacks had received performed worse in the interview.

These data suggest that the IAT may indeed be a reliable predictor of important behavior. Two purposes of this chapter are (a) to review evidence confirming that the IAT can predict behavior and (b) to suggest some of the conditions under which it is more or less likely to do so. The predictions that my students and I have tested were derived from Fazio's MODE model of attitude–behavior relations as well as from research conducted to test its assumptions.

Fazio's MODE Model

Fazio's MODE model proposes two ways that attitudes can influence behavior—spontaneously and deliberatively (Fazio, 1990; Fazio & Towles-Schwen, 1999). When individuals respond spontaneously, their attitudes, once activated, guide behavior without the actor's necessarily reflecting on them. In contrast, deliberative responding does involve conscious reflection on, at the very least, any relevant attitudes. One possible motivation for this deliberation is a desire to be accurate. For example, a consumer shopping for a new automobile might experience spontaneous positive feelings upon seeing a red Porsche, but because this purchase represents an expensive and prolonged commitment, she may deliberate and consider other alternatives in order to ensure her long-term satisfaction. Of course, there are other potential motivations for deliberation besides accuracy. Importantly, egalitarian motivations could cause actors to be deliberative when responding to stigmatized targets (e.g., African Americans). Individuals who worry that their spontaneous response could be prejudiced may act to override or correct it (Wegener & Petty, 1995).

The "MO" in the MODE model is for motivation and opportunity, the two factors that determine whether a response is likely to be spontaneous or deliberative. Simply put, an actor must have both the motivation to deliberate and the opportunity to deliberate in order for a spontaneous response to be avoided. This is because deliberation is a controlled process that consumes scarce cognitive resources. If either motivation or opportunity is low (or if both are low), one's response is more likely to be spontaneous.

Whites, in their interactions with Blacks, will deliberate on their responses in order to minimize the influence of prejudice, but only if they have the required motivation and opportunity to do so. In that deliberative process, implicit racial attitudes—even if automatically activated—may be overridden. Wilson et al. (2000) also described this process of "motivated overriding," whereby an automatic response (e.g., a negative implicit attitude toward Blacks) is inhibited through a controlled process. In other words, automatically activated racial attitudes serve as the "starting point" for race-related judgments and behaviors, but, with sufficient motivation and opportunity to override them, they are unlikely to govern controllable judgments and behavior (Fazio, 2001).

This logic implies that valid measures of implicit attitudes may not predict controllable responses when individuals are motivated to override their implicit attitudes. However, when individuals are not motivated to override their implicit attitudes, valid implicit measures may indeed predict controllable responses. In fact, Fazio et al. (1995) found that one sort of controllable response (responses on the MRS) could be predicted by their racial priming measure—but only among individuals low in a specific kind of motivation to control prejudice. Fazio et al. prescreened participants on the Motivation to Control Prejudiced Reactions Scale (Dunton & Fazio, 1997). This scale consists of two subscales, one of which describes individual differences in *concern with acting prejudiced*. Among individuals high in this concern, the relationship between the priming measure and the MRS was notsignificant. In fact, these participants actually showed a nonsignificant trend indicating that as their implicit attitudes toward Blacks became more negative, their responses on the MRS became *less* negative toward Blacks. Fazio and colleagues interpret this pattern as indicative of overcompensation for presumed bias.[2] In other words, Whites whose implicit attitudes toward Blacks are negative but who are motivated not to appear prejudiced "bend over backward" so far that they respond even more positively toward Blacks (on the MRS) than do individuals whose implicit attitudes are actually positive. In terms of the MODE, when these participants completed the MRS, they had the opportunity to deliberate (e.g., there was no time pressure) and the motivation to deliberate (i.e., they did not want to give racist responses). As a consequence of their deliberation, they overrode—and overcompensated for—their implicit racial attitudes.

The pattern was quite different among individuals low in concern with acting prejudiced. Here, the relationship between the racial priming measure and the MRS was significant in the direction opposite of that obtained with individuals high in concern. Scores indicating more negative implicit attitudes toward Blacks were associated with more negative responses to Blacks on the MRS. In other words, the implicit attitude measure predicted controllable responses on the MRS, but only when individuals lacked the motivation to override their automatically activated attitudes, a pattern that has since been replicated (Dunton & Fazio, 1997). Thus, it appears the MODE model is correct in its suggestion that motivation (in this case, motivation to respond without prejudice) can moderate the relationship between implicit attitude measures and controllable responses.

Assessing the Predictive Validity of the Black–White IAT

Ongoing research in my laboratory has examined the predictive validity of the IAT. In a straightforward application of the MODE model, we expected that the Black–White IAT could predict Whites' controllable responses to a Black person (or the symbolic equivalent), but we also expected that this relationship would depend on Whites' motivation to control prejudice. Among Whites whose motivation was low, we predicted that the IAT would be a reliable predictor of controllable responses. That is, IAT scores indicating implicit preferences for Whites over Blacks would be associated with relatively positive reactions to Whites and relatively negative reactions to Blacks. However, among Whites whose motivation was high, that relationship was expected to be weaker, null, or possibly even reversed (suggesting overcompensation). The results of one study conducted thus far confirm these predictions.

The goal of this study was to determine if attributional ambiguity would moderate the predictive validity of the Black–White IAT. Prior studies have shown that people often act on socially unacceptable motives (e.g., prejudice) under conditions of attributional ambiguity (Gaertner & Dovidio, 1977; Snyder, Kleck, Strenta, & Mentzer, 1979). In other words, when a socially unacceptable motive is but one of a number of plausible explanations for a particular behavior, people are more likely to act on that motive. For example, Snyder et al. presented individuals with a choice between two seating areas, in either of which they could view a film while seated near another person. In one area, the potential seating partner appeared to have a physical disability (implied by leg braces and Canadian crutches). The person in the other area did not. Snyder et al. found that participants who believed that different movies would be shown in the two seating areas were more likely to choose the nondisabled partner than participants who believed that the same movie would be showing in each area. Snyder et al. assumed that many participants were motivated to avoid sitting near the disabled person, but they deemed this avoidance motive socially unacceptable and only acted on it when their choice could be attributed to a preference for one movie over another. Put differently, the existence of attributional ambiguity (in the different movies condition) may have lowered participants' concern with appearing prejudiced against the disabled. In contrast, low ambiguity (in the same movie condition) maintained or heightened their concerns with appearing prejudiced.

In the present study (Sargent & Theil, 2001), we modified the Snyder et al. (1979) paradigm to present White male participants with a choice between two partners, one of whom was Black and another for whom race was left unspecified.[3] Upon arrival, each participant was convinced that he was the third of four participants to arrive for the session, and that the first two had left their personal belongings in the laboratory while they worked on preparatory tasks elsewhere. The participant was further informed that, after each participant had finished these preparatory tasks, he and one of the first two participants would work together on an intellectual task. Consistent with this cover story, the laboratory was divided into two workspaces, each of which contained a table and two chairs. In one workspace, the participant could clearly see a sweatshirt emblazoned with a photo of a Black family, and the label "Jackson Family Reunion."[4] This sweatshirt was said to belong to "Jamal," one of the participants. In the other workspace, the other participant, "Christopher," had apparently left only a nondescript blue jacket. Each participant was asked to choose his desired workspace and to leave any of his personal belongings there. Whether participants chose to work with Jamal or Christopher was the dependent variable. Participants made this choice under either high or low attributional ambiguity. In the high-ambiguity condition, participants were told that different intellectual tasks were available in the different workspaces. (Of course, counterbalancing ensured that Jamal was paired with each of the two tasks half the time.) In the low-ambiguity condition, participants were told that the same task was available regardless of the chosen workspace. After making his choice, each participant was then escorted to a private room for his preparatory tasks, which, naturally, included completion of the Black–White IAT.

Our central assumptions were that concern with appearing prejudiced motivates individuals to override their implicit racial attitudes, but that high ambiguity lowers concern about appearing prejudiced. Thus, we expected that the IAT would predict participants' likelihood of choosing the Black partner, but only under conditions of high ambiguity. In that condition, participants would be less motivated to override their implicit racial attitudes, and, as a consequence, those attitudes would be more influential of their behavior.

Consistent with our expectations, the interaction between IAT score and attributional ambiguity was significant, as Fig. 3.1 illustrates. Under conditions of high ambiguity (i.e., the different task condition), the IAT was a significant predictor of behavior. As expected, IAT scores indicating an implicit preference for Whites were associated with lower likelihood of choosing the Black partner. In contrast, there was no significant relationship between the IAT and behavior under conditions of low ambiguity (i.e., the same task condition). In fact, there was a nonsignificant trend in the opposite direction (suggesting possible overcompensation). Thus, these data are consistent with the MODE model in that the implicit attitude measure (in this case the IAT) predicted a controllable response (likelihood of choosing the Black partner), but only among individuals in the high attributional ambiguity. Our interpretation is that those individuals' motivation to control their prejudice was temporarily reduced by the presence of a plausible nonracial explanation for their behavior.

It will be important for future research to replicate this effect and to explore its boundary conditions. It may be, for instance, that this effect will only emerge on

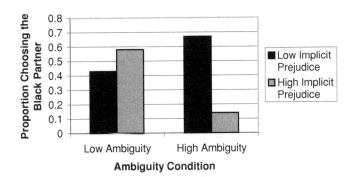

FIG. 3.1. The IAT was scored so that higher numbers represented a tendency for participants to respond more quickly when "Black" and "unpleasant" shared the same response key than when "Black" and "pleasant" shared the same response key. Higher scores are interpreted as indicating an implicit preference for Whites over Blacks. Although the data were analyzed in logistic regression, for illustrative purposes, a median split distinguished "high implicit prejudice" individuals (i.e., above the median) from "low implicit prejudice" individuals. *Source:* From Sargent and Theil (2001).

certain types of dependent measures. In the present study, the dependent measure was a tendency to choose between a Black partner and a presumably White partner. As a consequence, this measure may have been influenced by both reactions to the Black partner and the presumably White partner. In other words, the IAT may have predicted approach toward the White as much as avoidance of the Black. Similarly, McConnell and Leibold (2001) found that the IAT predicted difference scores, each of which represented the tendency to respond more favorably toward a White experimenter than a Black. It is possible that the IAT—which itself involves simultaneous responses to White and Black stimuli—only predicts responses of a comparative nature. In other words, the IAT might not predict individuals' reactions to Blacks in isolation from their reaction to Whites.[5] At any rate, resolving this issue is one of a number of questions for future research, to which I now turn.

FUTURE DIRECTIONS

Research on Stigmatized Sources and Persuasion

Recent research on attitude change has demonstrated that recipients of persuasive messages may be motivated to process information from a source who belongs to a stigmatized group—even under conditions where such processing is not usually expected. For example, White and Harkins (1994) demonstrated that White participants processed a persuasive message from a Black source, even under conditions of low relevance. In other words, even when the message pertained to an issue that would not affect these individuals directly, they still were more persuaded by a Black source whose arguments were strong than a Black source whose arguments were weak. Under the same conditions, exposure to a White source did not lead to message scrutiny (i.e., strong and weak arguments were equally persuasive). White and Harkins concluded that this effect was driven by aversive racism (Gaertner & Dovidio, 1986). According to the aversive racism model, Whites endorse egalitarian values and are motivated to think of themselves as unprejudiced, but they still harbor negative feelings toward Blacks. Whites are more likely to act on their negative feelings when a plausible nonracial explanation exists. Scrutinizing the Black source's message, according to White and Harkins, is one way that White message recipients can seek a nonracial justification for a negative response. According to this interpretation, then, it is negativity toward the Black source that motivates processing the message, and that processing is assumed to be a search for weak arguments that would justify rejecting the message. Thus, it might be that people high in prejudice would be most prone to this tendency to process the Black source's message.

In fact, Petty, Fleming, and White (1999) found the opposite to be true. It was low-prejudice individuals (as indicated by the MRS) who were most likely to process the Black source's message.[6] They also demonstrated that individuals low in prejudice against gays were more likely to process a message from a gay source than a straight source, whereas individuals high in antigay prejudice were not. Petty et al. argued that these data support a "watchdog hypothesis." That is, low-prejudice individuals are vigilant in their efforts to respond fairly to a stigmatized source. They are watchdogs against prejudice and discrimination. Their processing of the stigmatized source's persuasive message, according to Petty et al., is to ensure they give the source due consideration. In other words, low-prejudice Whites are assumed to be high in motivation to control prejudice. As Petty et al. said, "the increased processing of persuasive messages from stigmatized others could be part of low-prejudiced individuals' chronic attempt . . . to be unprejudiced and to prevent themselves from discriminating against stigmatized sources" (p. 30).

I agree with this characterization, but, on the basis of the data reported earlier (Sargent & Theil, 2001), I expect that watchdogs sometimes let down their guard. Even if egalitarian vigilance is what activates scrutiny of a stigmatized source's persuasive message, once the message recipient realizes that the message contains weak arguments, he or she may relax those efforts. Sargent and Theil found that Whites' preference for a Black or White task partner could be predicted by their implicit racial attitudes, but only when there was a plausible nonracial justification. Likewise, once Whites have identified a plausible nonracial justification for rejecting a Black's message (i.e., weak arguments) at that point, their implicit racial attitudes may predict their response to the message.[7] So, even if source negativity is not what motivates the processing of messages from stigmatized sources, it may be relevant in other ways. It may be that implicit measures of negativity (e.g., the Black–White IAT) can predict Whites' responses to persuasive appeals featuring stigmatized individuals, but only when there is a plausible justification that is irrelevant to the stigma.

For example, a Black source who presents only weak arguments in endorsing a product creates attributional ambiguity for rejecting his or her message and the product; it is unclear whether the rejection was because of the specious arguments or the source's race. In that case, a measure such as the IAT might predict Whites' response to the product and to the message. Moreover, a Black source who presents a mixture of strong and weak arguments may also create attributional ambiguity, because any response to the message (positive or negative) can be attributed to the arguments and not to one's attitude toward the source's category. In contrast, a Black source whose position is known but who presents no arguments may create a case of low attributional ambiguity, because there are no arguments to which one can attribute a response (R. Petty, personal communication, February 11, 2001). In future research, my collaborators and I hope to address this question by manipulating attributional ambiguity in a persuasion context and then determining the extent to which implicit racial attitude measures, such as the IAT, can predict Whites' responses to the message.

Practical Implications

The Effects of Ad-Based Diversity on Product Attitudes.   If future studies confirm that there are conditions under which implicit racial attitudes (or implicit intergroup attitudes in general) predict consumers' evaluations of advertisements featuring stigmatized sources, this result could have important implications for advertising effectiveness. For example, this research could reinforce the importance of presenting strong arguments in messages delivered by stigmatized sources. Earlier research on source effects (Petty et al., 1999; White & Harkins, 1994) already demonstrates the importance of utilizing strong arguments with stigmatized sources, because message recipients are likely to process those messages, even under conditions of low personal relevance. As suggested earlier, the presence of weak arguments could constitute one form of attributional ambiguity, and, if so, it might reduce message recipients' concerns with appearing prejudiced. In that case, implicit racial attitudes may predict message recipients' responses to the source, the message, and the product. So, measures such as the IAT could identify which individuals respond most extremely to strong and weak arguments from stigmatized sources. It may be, for instance, that Whites with negative implicit attitudes toward Blacks will be more sensitive to the quality of a Black source's arguments than will Whites with neutral or positive implicit attitudes toward Blacks. If the Black source presents weak arguments, they may respond more negatively than Whites with neutral or positive attitudes, but if all his or her arguments are strong (or if he or she presents no arguments at all), they may respond more positively, as a result of overcompensation.[8] If future data support these predictions, they would suggest that implicit racial attitudes might be useful to marketers in determining when it is most critical to pretest arguments to ensure that all the weak ones are eliminated from persuasive appeals. Specifically, if a Black source is featured in ads that are run in a market where implicit prejudice against Blacks is prevalent, the unintended presence of weak arguments in his or her message could be extremely counterproductive to the campaign, more so than with a White source.

Of course there may be practical difficulties associated with assessing consumers' implicit racial attitudes. Even if future studies confirm that the IAT (and other implicit measures) can predict consumers' responses to persuasive messages, frequent testing may be difficult (although web-based administration of the IAT may make even that possible). One potential long-term goal for future marketing research will be to identify demographic correlates of the IAT so that its predictive power can be readily translated into practical use.

The Effects of Ad-Based Diversity on Implicit Prejudice. Thus far, this chapter has adopted a narrow focus in examining the impact of stigmatized sources on advertising effectiveness, where effectiveness is gauged by message recipients' evaluations of the ad and the product. Nevertheless, there may be other effects worth considering. It seems plausible that—like other media portrayals—the use of stigmatized sources in advertising may influence implicit attitudes toward those categories. In fact, a burgeoning literature on context effects attests to the malleability of implicit attitudes (Maddux & Barden, 2001; Wittenbrink, Judd, & Park, 2001).

Dasgupta and Greenwald (2001) reported data more directly supportive of the notion that exposure to stigmatized sources could affect the implicit intergroup attitudes of message recipients. Their participants completed the Black–White IAT after exposure to (a) images of popular Black males (e.g., Michael Jordan) and unpopular White males (e.g., Jeffrey Dahmer), (b) images of unpopular Black males (e.g., Mike Tyson) and popular White males (e.g., Tom Hanks), or (c) nonracial images, exposure to which represented a control condition. Participants in the control condition were faster on the Black + unpleasant trials than on the Black + pleasant trials, a pattern indicating an implicit preference for Whites. Participants who saw unpopular Blacks and popular Whites showed virtually the same pattern. In contrast, this difference was significantly reduced among participants who had been exposed to popular Blacks and unpopular Whites. Notably, this attenuation was still evident 24 hr later on another IAT. Moreover, explicit racial attitude measures were insensitive to these effects.

Although it will be important for future studies to confirm that this attenuation of implicit racial preferences was at least partially attributable to exposure to the popular Blacks (and not merely the unpopular Whites), this result raises interesting possibilities for advertisers. Although consumers' implicit racial attitudes may influence their responses to advertisements that feature members of stigmatized groups, those same implicit racial attitudes may be influenced by the advertisements themselves. In other words, consumers who are exposed to ads featuring popular minority spokespersons may develop more positive implicit attitudes toward that group as a consequence. So, Nike's use of Michael Jordan's image may not only be good for the company's sales; it may also reduce implicit prejudice among viewers of its ads. This is a question of great practical importance and one that should guide future research.

CONCLUSION

The effects of stigmatized sources in persuasive appeals may be more complex than previous analyses suggested. Whereas explicit, self-report measures of racial attitudes might appear to account for little variance in responses to advertisements featuring Blacks, for example, implicit measures may prove more useful. But even where implicit measures may be useful predictors of consumers' responses to stigmatized sources, it seems plausible—based on the MODE and on the research reviewed here—that their utility will depend on motivational factors. Among individuals whose concern about appearing prejudiced is temporarily reduced, implicit intergroup attitudes may predict how positively or negatively they will respond to ads featuring members of stigmatized categories. In contrast, individuals who are concerned about appearing prejudiced may override any implicit negativity that is activated upon encountering a stigmatized source.

Future studies should address these issues so that a comprehensive understanding of the effects of stigmatized sources can be developed. As future studies test the ways that implicit intergroup attitudes can influence the persuasiveness of ads, effective marketing strategy will be informed. Moreover, as future studies test the ways that implicit intergroup attitudes may themselves be partially determined by exposure to advertising, socially responsible marketing strategy will be informed as well.

ACKNOWLEDGMENT

I am grateful to Marilynn Brewer, Monique Fleming, and Rich Petty for helpful comments on an earlier version of this chapter.

REFERENCES

Bush, R. F., Hair, J. F., Jr., & Solomon, P. J. (1979). Consumers' level of prejudice and response to Black models in advertisements. *Journal of Marketing Research, 16*, 341–345.

Cagley, J. W., & Cardozo, R. N. (1970). White response to integrated advertising. *Journal of Advertising Research, 10*, 35–39.

Dasgupta, N., & Greenwald, A. G. (2001). On the malleability of automatic attitudes: Combating automatic prejudice with images of admired and disliked individuals. *Journal of Personality and Social Psychology, 81*, 800–814.

Dasgupta, N., McGhee, D. E., Greenwald, A. G., & Banaji, M. R. (2000). Automatic preference for White Americans: Eliminating the familiarity explanation. *Journal of Experimental Social Psychology, 36*, 316–328.

Dunton, B. C., & Fazio, R. H. (1997). An individual difference measure of motivation to control prejudiced reactions. *Personality and Social Psychology Bulletin, 23*, 316–326.

Fazio, R. H. (1990). Multiple processes by which attitudes guide behavior: The MODE model as an integrative framework. In M. Zanna (Ed.), *Advances in experimental social psychology* (Vol. 23, pp. 75–109). San Diego, CA: Academic Press.

Fazio, R. H. (2001, February). *Automaticity-activated attitudes as the "starting point" for race-related judgments and behavior.* Paper presented at the Attitudes Preconference to the meeting of the Society for Personality and Social Psychology, San Antonio, TX.

Fazio, R. H., Jackson, J. R., Dunton, B. C., & Williams, C. J. (1995). Variability in automatic activation as an unobtrusive measure of racial attitudes: A bona fide pipeline? *Journal of Personality and Social Psychology, 69*, 1013–1027.

Fazio, R. H., & Towles-Schwen, T. (1999). The MODE model of attitude-behavior processes. In S. Chaiken & Y. Trope (Eds.), *Dual-process theories in social psychology* (pp. 97–116). New York: Guilford.

Gaertner, S. L., & Dovidio, J. F. (1977). The subtlety of white racism, arousal, and helping behavior. *Journal of Personality and Social Psychology, 35*, 691–707.

Gaertner, S. L., & Dovidio, J. F. (1986). The aversive form of racism. In J. Dovidio & S. Gaertner (Eds.), *Prejudice, discrimination, and racism* (pp. 61–89). Orlando, FL: Academic Press.

Greenwald, A., & Banaji, M. (1995). Implicit social cognition: Attitudes, self-esteem, and stereotypes. *Psychological Review, 102*, 4–27.

Greenwald, A. G., McGhee, D. E., & Schwartz, J. L. K. (1998). Measuring individual differences in implicit cognition: The Implicit Association Test. *Journal of Personality and Social Psychology, 74*, 1464–1480.

Jones, E. E., & Sigall, H. (1971). The bogus pipeline: A new paradigm for measuring affect and attitude. *Psychological Bulletin, 76*, 349–364.

LaPiere, R. T. (1934). Attitudes vs. actions. *Social Forces, 13*, 230–237.

Macrae, C. N., Bodenhausen, G. V., Milne, A. B., & Jetten, J. (1994). Out of mind but back in sight: Stereotypes on the rebound. *Journal of Personality and Social Psychology, 67*, 808–817.

Maddux, W. W., & Barden, J. (2001, February). *The contextual nature of implicit racial attitudes*. Poster session presented at the annual meeting of the Society for Personality and Social Psychology, San Antonio, TX.

McConahay, J. B. (1986). Modern racism, ambivalence, and the Modern Racism Scale. In J. Dovidio & S. Gaertner (Eds.), *Prejudice, discrimination, and racism* (pp. 91–125). Orlando, FL: Academic Press.

McConahay, J. B., Hardee, B. B., & Batts, V. (1981). Has racism declined in America? It depends on who is asking and what is asked. *Journal of Conflict Resolution, 25*, 563–579.

McConnell, A. R., & Leibold, J. M. (2001). Relations among the Implicit Association Test, discriminatory behavior, and explicit measures of racial attitudes. *Journal of Experimental Social Psychology, 37*, 435–442.

Nosek, B. (2001). *IAT research worldwide* [Online]. Retrieved from http://buster.cs.yale.edu/implicit/worldwide/index.html on 2/15/01.

Petty, R. E., Fleming, M. A., & White, P. H. (1999). Stigmatized sources and persuasion: Prejudice as a determinant of argument scrutiny. *Journal of Personality and Social Psychology, 76*, 19–34.

Sargent, M. J., & Theil, A. (2001). *When do implicit racial attitudes predict behavior? On the moderating role of motivation*. Unpublished manuscript.

Sargent, M. J., & Theil, A. (2002, February). *Assessing the predictive utility of the "Black-White" Implicit Association Test: Evidence for moderators*. Paper presented at the annual meeting of the Society for Personality and Social Psychology, Savannah, GA.

Sigall, H., & Page, R. (1971). Current stereotypes: A little fading, a little faking. *Journal of Personality and Social Psychology, 18*, 247–255.

Snyder, M. L., Kleck, R. E., Strenta, A., & Mentzer, S. J. (1979). Avoidance of the handicapped: An attributional ambiguity analysis. *Journal of Personality and Social Psychology, 37*, 2297–2306.

Warner, S. L. (1965). Randomized response: A survey technique for eliminating evasive answer bias. *Journal of the American Statistical Association, 60*, 63–69.

Wegener, D. T., & Petty, R. E. (1995). Flexible correction processes in social judgment: The role of naïve theories in corrections for perceived bias. *Journal of Personality and Social Psychology, 68*, 36–51.

White, P. H., & Harkins, S. G. (1994). Race of source effects in the Elaboration Likelihood Model. *Journal of Personality and Social Psychology, 67*, 690–807.

Whittler, T. E. (1989). Viewers' processing of actor's race and message claims in advertising stimuli. *Psychology & Marketing, 6*, 287–309.

Whittler, T. E., & DiMeo, J. (1991). Viewers' reactions to racial cues in advertising stimuli. *Journal of Advertising Research, 31*, 37–46.

Wicker, A. W. (1969). Attitude versus actions: The relationship of verbal and overt behavioral responses to attitude objects. *Journal of Social Issues, 25*(4), 41–78.

Wilson, T. D., Lindsey, S., & Schooler, T. Y. (2000). A model of dual attitudes. *Psychological Review, 107*, 101–126.

Wittenbrink, B., Judd, C. M., & Park, B. (2001). Spontaneous prejudice in context: Variability in automatically activated attitudes. *Journal of Personality and Social Psychology, 81*, 815–827.

Word, C. O., Zanna, M. P., & Cooper, J. (1974). The nonverbal mediation of self-fulfilling prophecies in interracial interaction. *Journal of Experimental Social Psychology, 10*, 109–120.

Zajonc, R. B. (1968). Attitudinal effects of mere exposure. *Journal of Personality and Social Psychology Monographs, 9*(2, Pt. 2).

ENDNOTES

1. These data should, however, be interpreted with caution, as the sample of Black participants was rather small ($n = 8$).
2. What Fazio et al. call "overcompensation" seems similar to what has elsewhere been termed "over-correction" (Wegener & Petty, 1995). Although I will consistently use the former term, I see the two as interchangeable. In either case, an actor is attempting to undo or avoid the effects of a presumed bias, but because of a flawed implicit theory about the magnitude of the bias, the corrective or compensating process is excessive.
3. Given the demographics of the student body from which participants were drawn (overwhelmingly majority White), we suspect that most participants assumed that the alternative to the Black partner was, in fact, a White partner.
4. In pretesting, the majority of participants indicated that they would assume the owner of such a sweatshirt was Black. I thank Joanne Miller for suggesting the use of the sweatshirt to imply the owner's race.
5. In fact, a follow-up study suggested that the IAT did not predict scores on either the MRS or the Attitudes Toward Blacks Scale (Sargent & Theil, 2002), each of which solicits reactions to only Blacks. Importantly, this was true even among individuals low on either subscale of the Motivation to Control Prejudiced Reactions Scale (Dunton & Fazio, 1997). Just as the participants in the high attributional ambiguity condition of the experiment just reported were presumed to be relatively unconcerned about appearing or acting prejudiced because of the presence of a plausible nonracial excuse for their behavior, so were participants low in motivation to control prejudiced reactions assumed to be similarly unconcerned. However even among that group, the IAT did not predict either self-report measure of prejudice. It may be that, even under the most favorable of conditions (e.g., among individuals unmotivated to override their implicit attitudes), the IAT will not predict either reactions to Blacks or Whites separately but will only predict the difference between the two or an explicit choice between a Black and a White.
6. Unlike White and Harkins (1994), Petty et al. (1999) left unspecified whether message recipients would be personally affected by the policy described in the persuasive message, so relevance was uncertain.
7. Incidentally, this proposal implies that primacy effects on recall might be obtained with stigmatized sources. If, for example, a Black source's message begins with weak arguments, then attention to, and consequent recall of, later arguments might be weaker than for early arguments.
8. Of course, one wonders if successful inhibition of negative implicit racial attitudes will be followed by subsequent rebound effects, as have been observed with stereotypes (Macrae, Bodenhausen, Milne, & Jetten, 1994).

CHAPTER FOUR

Demystifying the Nonconscious: Unintentional Discrimination in Society and the Media

Robert W. Livingston
University of Wisconsin-Madison

As early as the 19th century, psychologists proposed that human thought and behavior were largely influenced by nonconscious impulses (Freud, 1896/1963) and could be easily habituated, obviating the need for conscious intervention (James, 1890). Conceptualizations of "automaticity" were theoretically refined and empirically substantiated in the latter half of the 20th century as researchers continued to examine the impact of nonconscious processes on social perception and behavior (see Bargh, 1994; Wegner & Bargh, 1998 for review). Automatic processes are generally defined by at least one of four components: awareness, intent, control, or efficiency (Bargh, 1994). To be sure, there is no strict dichotomy between exclusively conscious and automatic processes; most thoughts and behaviors fall somewhere on a continuum between these two extremes (Bargh, 1994). However, for purposes of this chapter, any thought or behavior that shows evidence of occurring outside of conscious awareness, intent, or control will be considered automatic.[1] I begin the chapter with a discussion of the role of automaticity in everyday thought and behavior, followed by an overview of the research on automatic bias in intergroup perception and behavior. In the final section, I explore the issue of nonconscious bias in the media and advertising.

AUTOMATICITY IN EVERYDAY PERCEPTION AND BEHAVIOR

Contrary to the intuitive assumption that individuals know why they do what they do, early automaticity research showed that people possess surprisingly little insight into the psychological underpinnings of their thoughts and behaviors (Nisbett & Wilson, 1977). In their seminal paper, aptly subtitled "Telling More Than We Can Know," Nisbett and Wilson report the results of several studies demonstrating that cognitions are primarily determined by nonconscious mechanisms and environmental cues, even though individuals *believe* that they are aware of the reasons underlying their choices. In one study, participants from introductory psychology courses were asked to memorize a list of word pairs. Among some of these lists were paired items that the researchers believed would "prime" Tide brand laundry detergent. It was hypothesized that students who memorized word pairs such as "ocean–moon" would be more likely to reply "Tide" when asked to name a detergent compared with participants who had not previously been exposed to semantically relevant word pairs. (This study was conducted prior to the existence of Surf brand laundry detergent.) The study yielded highly significant results ($p < .001$), revealing that participants were twice as likely to name Tide compared with some other brand of detergent when they had memorized word pairs such as ocean–moon (Nisbett & Wilson, 1977).

The novelty of this study, however, was not the demonstration of a priming effect. Indeed, other research had confirmed the passive effect of stimulus exposure on subsequent cognitive processing (Higgins, Rholes, & Jones, 1977; Meyer & Schvaneveldt, 1971; Neely, 1977; Segal & Cofer, 1960; Storms, 1958; Zajonc, 1968). The interesting (and ironic) finding emerged when participants were asked to explain why they had chosen Tide over another brand. Instead of replying "Gee, it might have had something to do with those semantically related words that you had me memorize" or "I have no clue" (either of which would have been a correct response), participants gave rather elaborate (and erroneous) explanations for their consumer preferences, citing the high quality or popularity of the product, or the fact that their family used the product, or even the extent to which they liked the box.

In a similar experiment, Nisbett and Wilson (1977) invited shoppers at a commercial establishment to participate in a "consumer survey" in which they evaluated the quality of several articles of clothing. Shoppers evaluated four identical pairs of nylon stockings and provided reasons for their choices. Given the pervasive "right-hand bias" (among right-handed individuals), the researchers reasoned that all else being equal participants as a whole would prefer stockings located on the right to identical stockings positioned on the left. Indeed, participants preferred stockings on the right to those on the left by a ratio of nearly 4:1! However, not one of the participants mentioned the right-hand location of the stockings as a factor in their evaluation of the product. In fact, when the researcher suggestively questioned the participants as to whether the location of the stockings might have influenced their evaluation, "virtually all subjects denied it, usually with a worried glance at the interviewer suggesting that they felt either that they had misunderstood the question or were dealing with a madman." (Nisbett & Wilson, 1977; p. 244). In short, these experiments effectively demonstrate that although individuals are unaware of the true source of their preferences, they nonetheless believe that they hold such insight.

Inspired by these earlier findings, more recent researchers have further challenged the role of conscious will in governing everyday cognition and behavior. Harvard psychologist Daniel Wegner has argued emphatically that people have little or no control over their thoughts and actions. According to Wegner (2002), the *experience* of consciously willing an action and the *causation* of an action by will are quite distinct. He contends that people often experience the illusion of conscious will, even though most human thought or behavior is the product of nonconscious reponses to environmental cues (see Wegner, 2002). Similarly, researchers such as Yale psychologist John Bargh have shown that environmental stimuli can have direct, unmediated effects on behavior, independent of the intent or awareness of the perceiver. This phenomenon has been labeled by Bargh and colleagues as the "perception–behavior link" (see Bargh, Chen, & Burrows, 1996; Chartrand & Bargh, 1999). According to this model, inspired by William James' principle of ideomotor action, cognitive representations of actions activate the propensity to perform actions encapsulated within those representations. Because cognitive representations, such as those of "the elderly," for example, contain information about traits associated with the group (e.g., forgetfulness) as well as information about behaviors associated with the group (e.g., walking slowly), schema activation can cause individuals to behave in a manner consistent with those representations.

Consistent with this notion, Bargh et al. (1996) empirically demonstrated that the activation of a group representation is sufficient to induce group-consistent behaviors. In one study, participants were randomly assigned to unscramble words related to the elderly stereotype (e.g., "old," "Florida," or "retired") or words that were unrelated to the elderly stereotype. After this priming phase, the experimenter "concluded" the session, dismissed the participant, and directed him or her to proceed toward the elevator located at the end of a long corridor. Using a hidden stopwatch, a confederate of the experimenter surreptitiously recorded the amount of time it took the participant to walk to the end of the hallway. Results from two separate studies confirmed that participants in the elderly prime condition took significantly longer to walk down the hallway compared with those in the control condition.

In a conceptual replication using African American stimuli, participants were subliminally primed with the face of either a Black male or a White male in what they were told was a monotonous computerized visual task. After several dozen presentations of these faces, the computer ostensibly crashed, at which point the experimenter informed the participant that she or he would have to start the task over from the beginning. Meanwhile, hidden cameras recorded participants' facial reactions to the news that they would have to redo the tedious experiment because of the computer crash. The experimenter also rated the hostility of participants' expressions upon receiving the unfortunate news. Results indicated that participants subliminally primed with Black faces exhibited significantly more hostility than participants primed with White faces, both when hostility was judged by the experimenter and when it was judged by blind coders of the videotape.

On the basis of these results, the researchers concluded that exposure to environmental stimuli can have a direct influence on behavior through the activation of stereotypic representations. Because participants in the first experiment did not report any suspicion of links between the elderly word primes and their sluggish behavior, the researchers concluded that these behavioral effects are automatic in nature. Supportive of this conclusion, participants in the second study were unaware of the (subliminal) African American primes altogether, so their behavior could not have been consciously induced.[2] These effects have been replicated by researchers in Europe as well (Dijksterhuis & van Knippenberg, 1998).

In addition to static cues and concepts, the perception of dynamic actions can also produce behavior-consistent responses. Consistent with the folk belief that yawning is contagious (which may not be apocryphal; see Provine, 1986), research by Chartrand and Bargh (1999) has found that individuals nonconsciously imitate the behavior of others. In one study, a confederate of the experimenter was trained to rub his or her face while describing photographs to a participant. Hidden cameras recorded the extent to which the participant rubbed his or her face as a function of whether the confederate engaged in the same behavior. Judgments by coders blind to the experimental hypotheses indicated that participants rubbed their face more when the confederate also rubbed her or his face. Similar results were found with foot-wiggling behavior (Chartrand & Bargh, 1999).

Importantly, in a funneled debriefing session after the experiment, none of the participants reported noticing any unusual face rubbing or foot wiggling from the confederate, let alone that they had responded in kind. Consequently the authors concluded that the mimicry was a nonconscious response to the behavior of the confederate. Follow-up studies have found that mimicry effects are stronger when participants report liking the confederate or when they scored high on an individual measure of empathy, indicating that nonconscious mimicry may serve an evolutionary function by strengthening social bonds (Chartrand & Bargh, 1999; Chartrand, Maddux, & Lakin, in press). However, other studies have shown that people may also mimic facial expressions and movements that they see on television, suggesting that the fortification of social relationships is not the only motive for nonconscious mimicry (Hsee, Hatfield, Carlson, & Chemtob, 1990).

Although the present compendium is by no means an exhaustive account of the evidence for automaticity (see Wegner & Bargh, 1998 for review), I have reported evidence indicating that many everyday behaviors occur nonconsciously as a function of cues in the environment. These automatic effects may also have downstream consequences for real-world intergroup interactions. For example, Chen and Bargh (1997) found that exposure to subliminal African American primes caused White participants to behave in a hostile fashion, which caused their African American interaction partners to respond in kind, resulting in a "self-fulfilling prophecy"

(Merton, 1957; Rosenthal & Jacobson, 1968). These effects may also have implications for performance. As I discuss later in the chapter, automatically activated stereotypes can hinder athletic or academic performance, depending on the content and relevance of the stereotype (Davies, Spencer, Quinn, & Gerhardstein, 2002; Shih, Pittinsky, & Ambady, 1999; Steele & Aronson, 1995; Stone, Lynch, Sjomeling, & Darley, 1999). In the next section, I provide a brief overview of the measurement of nonconscious bias and discuss societal contexts in which such biases can lead to negative outcomes.

CONCEPTUALIZATION, MEASUREMENT, AND CONSEQUENCES OF NONCONSCIOUS BIAS

In the mid-1980s, Sam Gaertner and Jack Dovidio proposed their highly influential theory of Aversive Racism, which posits that unlike old-fashioned forms of racism, contemporary prejudice is characterized by the paradoxical combination of egalitarian values and anti-Black affect (Gaertner & Dovidio, 1986). To cope with threats to the nonprejudiced self-concept posed by this inherent contradiction, aversive racists push their negative Black feelings into the subconscious, and they only discriminate when their behaviors can be readily attributed to some factor other than race. In subsequent years, researchers developed a number of measures to gauge nonconscious or automatic prejudice by using reaction time procedures.

Although a detailed discussion of the construct validity of automatic racial attitudes is beyond the scope of this chapter (see Devine, 1989; Dovidio, Kawakami, Johnson, Johnson, & Howard, 1997; Fazio, Jackson, Dunton, & Williams, 1995; Fazio & Olson, 2003; Greenwald & Banaji, 1995; Lepore & Brown, 1997; Livingston & Brewer, 2002; Wilson, Lindsey, & Schooler, 2000 for theoretical debate), I briefly describe two of the most common methods of measuring automatic attitudes. One measure, Fazio et al.'s (1995) "bona-fide pipeline" task, is a sequential priming task that measures reaction time to judge target words as "good" or "bad" as a function of whether they are preceded by the brief presentation of a Black or White facial prime. The underlying assumption, based on spreading activation theory, is that the presentation of an attitude object (e.g., an African American) will automatically activate associated evaluations from memory, which in turn facilitate (speed up) responses to evaluatively congruent words and inhibit (slow down) response times to evaluatively incongruent words following the prime. Thus, for someone high in prejudice, the brief presentation of a Black facial prime on a computer screen should speed up responses to negative words following the facial prime while slowing down response times to positive words following the prime. The presentation of a White face, in contrast, should facilitate response times to positive target words and inhibit response times to negative target words. These differences (measured in milliseconds) in response times to positive versus negative words as a function of whether the prime preceding it is a Black or White face are used to compute an index of automatic prejudice (see Fazio et al., 1995).

Another popular measure of automatic racial attitudes is the Implicit Association Test, or IAT (Greenwald, McGhee, & Schwartz, 1998). The IAT is a response competition task that involves the classification of race concepts (i.e., Black or White faces or proper names such as Tyrone vs. Adam) and evaluative attributes (i.e., pleasant or unpleasant words such as flower or garbage) by use of two computer keys. Participants first practice this task by classifying only race concepts by pressing keys labeled as "Black" or "White," and then only evaluative words by pressing keys labeled as "pleasant" or "unpleasant." In the critical trials, the two judgment tasks are combined such that one of the concept categories (e.g., "Black") is paired with one of the attribute categories (e.g., "unpleasant") by using the same key, while the other race concept and attribute category are paired on the other key. The underlying assumption is that White participants should be faster to complete blocks involving "compatible" pairings (i.e., Black–unpleasant, White–pleasant) compared with blocks involving "incompatible" pairings (i.e., Black–pleasant, White–unpleasant). Participants' average overall reaction time to classify words and names in the compatible block is subtracted from their reaction time to classify words in the incompatible block. This score serves as the index of implicit ingroup bias (visit the IAT Web site at implicit.harvard.edu for a test demonstration).

It may be informative to know that such measures do not produce large absolute differences in reaction time. In most priming tasks, differences in response times to negative words preceded by Black versus White faces are under 100 ms, or a fraction of an eyeblink (most people can blink ~5 times in 1 s/1000 ms, giving the average eyeblink a duration of 200 ms). Nevertheless, these seemingly miniscule differences provide enough meaningful variability to accurately differentiate individuals by their level of prejudice (Wittenbrink, Judd, & Park, 1997). Dozens of studies have found that individual differences in automatic prejudice are related to nonverbal discrimination (Fazio et al., 1995; McConnell & Leibold, 2001), as well as other behavioral outcomes (see Fazio & Olson, 2003 for review). Livingston (2001) also found that the IAT predicted racial bias in criminal sentencing. In this study, White participants were randomly assigned to read about a physical assault perpetrated by either a Latino or White defendant. After reading about the crime, participants made decisions regarding the severity of punishment the defendant should receive. Because aversive racism theory maintains that individuals will discriminate only in ambiguous situations in which discriminatory behavior can be rationalized on some basis other than race, sentencing responses were chosen such that there was no one "correct" sentence, but rather a range of seemingly appropriate sentences that could be assigned to the defendant without appearing prejudiced.

Results of this study showed that participants assigned significantly harsher sentences to the minority defendant compared with the White defendant. This differential sentencing was further moderated by scores on a Hispanic version of the

IAT, such that higher levels of implicit prejudice correlated with harsher sentencing of the minority defendant, even when individual differences in motivation to avoid discrimination were controlled for. As a way to verify that discrimination was unintentional and was not due to a lack of motivation to avoid discrimination, participants in a follow-up study were made aware of the possibility of bias, were told *not* to respond in a biased fashion, and were informed that their responses might be reviewed by a circuit court judge (Livingston, 2001). Despite these inducements to be fair, participants still discriminated against the minority defendant, suggesting that participants were unable rather than unwilling to avoid bias. The results of several follow-up studies reveal similar results and suggest that unintentional sentencing bias is most likely to emerge when (a) there is stereotypic fit between the crime and defendants' ethnicity, (b) there is high response ambiguity, and (c) participants are high in automatic prejudice.

Discrimination at earlier stages in the criminal justice system may also be the result of unintentional bias. In February 1999, four White, plain-clothed New York City police officers searching for a rape suspect shot and killed a 22-year-old West African immigrant, Amadou Diallo, despite the fact that Diallo was both innocent and unarmed. A series of studies by Payne (2001) sought to test the idea that nonconscious racial biases may play a role in the propensity to shoot minority targets. In this study, participants were primed with the face of either a White or Black male followed by a picture of a tool (e.g., power drill or screwdriver) or a gun. The participants' task was to identify the objects following the faces as quickly and as accurately as possible by pressing a key labeled "tool" or "gun." Dependent variables consisted of both reaction time to identify objects as well as errors in identification. Results from the first study showed that participants were faster to identify guns when primed with Black rather than White faces, showing evidence of strong cognitive associations between African Americans and crime. Even more compelling was a second study that showed that participants were more likely to *misidentify* a tool as a gun when primed with a Black rather than a White face. Using a process-dissociation procedure (Jaccoby, 1991), Payne (2001) found that, in both studies, these effects were accounted for by automatic rather than controlled processes. In sum, these findings indicate that individuals are more likely to mistake everyday objects for guns when their cognitive representations of African Americans are activated, and that these effects are driven by automatic rather than conscious processes.[3]

Research by Correll, Park, Judd, and Wittenbrink (2002) took this finding a step further by investigating actual shooter bias in a more realistic context. In this experiment, participants played a videogame in which White or Black targets appeared in a variety of settings such as in parking lots or shopping malls, holding an object such as a camera or cell phone or holding a gun. The object of the game was to shoot targets who posed an imminent danger (i.e., those holding a gun) and to refrain from shooting innocent bystanders (e.g., those holding a cell phone) as quickly as possible by pressing buttons labeled "shoot" or "don't shoot." Results showed that participants mistakenly shot an unarmed target more often when he was Black than when he was White, and erroneously decided *not* to shoot an armed target more often when he was White than when he was Black. Participants were also significantly quicker to shoot a Black target compared with an White target, regardless of whether he was armed or unarmed.

In brief, these studies suggest that police officers may be predisposed to shoot Black targets more quickly and erroneously than White targets and that this tendency may be the unintentional result of automatic prejudice (Payne, 2001) or awareness of Black stereotypes (Correll et al., 2002). Thus, both shooter bias and sentencing bias may represent cases of what Wilson and Brekke (1994) refer to "mental contamination," or the process by which cognitive biases exert unwanted and detrimental influences on judgment and behavior outcomes. As the authors explain, "when teachers assign a C to a student's paper, they probably believe that they have given it a fair and unbiased evaluation, even if they were biased by how much they like the student" (Wilson & Brekke, 1994, p. 121). Similarly, a juror or judge might unfairly convict or sentence an African American defendant, adhering to the fallacious belief that his or her decision was not influenced by the race of the defendant. The next section extends this discussion to unintentional bias in the media and advertising, focusing on the manner in which minorities are stereotypically portrayed in the media as well as the unintended consequences that exposure to these stereotypic representations may produce.

INSTANCES AND CONSEQUENCES OF BIAS IN ADVERTISING AND THE MEDIA

Numerous studies have found that women and minorities are systematically portrayed in a biased fashion by advertisers and the media (see Ruscher, 2001 for review). For instance, African Americans are overrepresented in media portrayals of poverty or crime, and underrepresented in portrayals of hardworking Americans. In a study examining hundreds of photographic representations of the poor in major print media outlets, Gilens (1996) found that African Americans are overrepresented in images of the poor, relative to their actual proportion of the poor population. Specifically, over 60% of the pictoral representations of the poor depicted African Americans despite the fact that, according to recent Census estimates, approximately 30% of individuals at or below the poverty line in the United States are African American. In contrast, Blacks are underrepresented in visual images of the working poor, relative to the actual proportion of poor African Americans who are employed. Less than 15% of the pictoral representations of poor African Americans were portrayed as working individuals, although nearly 45% of the African American poor in America are employed (Gilens, 1996).

Similarly, the news media may misrepresent Black criminality (Entman, 1994). On one hand, arrested Blacks are more likely than Whites arrested for similar crimes to be shown being physically restrained. On the other hand, arrests of Whites are more likely to contain soundbites in which the defendant utters statements in his or her defense, whereas arrests of Blacks typically do not contain such statements. It is not clear whether these media biases are the product of automatic or deliberate processes. Nevertheless, the cumulative effect of exposure to these biased media representations could be the continual activation and reinforcement of distorted African American stereotypes, resulting in an increased likelihood of unwanted discriminatory outcomes such as shooter bias (Correll et al., 2002; Payne, 2001) or sentencing bias (Livingston, 2001).

Research has also documented systematic bias in the way in which minorities are *spatially* depicted in movies, television, and magazines. Miron Zuckerman and others have found that women and Blacks are portrayed on screen and in photographs with lower levels of facial prominence, or "face-ism," compared with men and Whites (Archer, Iritani, Kimes, & Barrios, 1983; Zuckerman & Kieffer, 1994). Face-ism is assessed by computing the ratio between the distance from the top of the head to the lower point of the chin, over the distance between the top of the head and the lowest part of the body that is depicted in the frame or photograph (Goffman, 1976). The more the frame is occupied by the face, the higher the level of face-ism. Zuckerman found across several hundred magazine advertisements that men were likely to have higher face-ism scores than women (Zuckerman, 1986). Likewise, Whites are likely to have higher face-ism scores than members of ethnic minority groups, and members of high status occupations are likely to have higher face-ism scores than members of low status occupations (Zuckerman & Kieffer, 1994).

Interestingly, however, differences in face-ism between men and women were attenuated in more "feminist" outlets such as *Ms.* and *Working Women*, compared with more traditional periodic publications such as *Time* and *Newsweek*. Likewise, differences in face-ism between Blacks and Whites dissipated in Black-controlled media outlets (Zuckerman & Kieffer, 1994). On the basis of these findings, Zuckerman and colleagues reasoned that differences in face-ism are determined to some extent by individual differences in creators' attitudes toward the targets that are being depicted. However, such differences in face-ism are probably the result of nonconscious rather than conscious bias. Specifically, they argue that although "sex differences in face-ism were smaller for publications considered as more feminist ... and race differences in face-ism disappeared for portraits painted or designed by Black artists ... this is not to say that the photographers of the painters are aware of the impact of face-ism, much less that they intend to deliver a message through a particular level of face-ism. In all likelihood, the values one holds can affect the level of face-ism in the picture one produces without awareness or intention" (Zuckerman & Kieffer, 1994; p. 91). In short, individual differences in stereotyping or prejudice toward women or Blacks may affect face-ism; however, it does not seem to be the case that photographers or camera people consciously produce these facial prominence effects.

Notwithstanding, differences in face-ism can have an insidious effect on social perception; faces high or low in face-ism actually *cause* members of the social groups to be perceived more or less stereotypically. Specifically, high face-ism reinforces judgments of power and dominance. To demonstrate the effect of face-ism empirically, Zuckerman and colleagues manipulated the face-ism level of photographs of male, female, Black, and White targets, prepared from a single negative, such that one photograph of the target appeared high in face-ism while the second photograph was identical except that it reflected lower face-ism. These low and high face-ism photographs were mixed to form two "impression formation" booklets, identical in all respects apart from the level of face-ism for a given target. Results reveal that photographs higher in face-ism were perceived as being more dominant or powerful than identical photographs depicting lower face-ism (Zuckerman & Kiefer, 1994), indicating that how individuals are portrayed in the media has a significant impact on how those individuals are perceived.

Research evidence also indicates that exposure to bias in advertising can lead to increased stereotyping and discrimination. For example, Rudman and Borgida (1995) found that exposing men to sexist advertising caused them to perceive female job candidates more stereotypically (Rudman & Borgida, 1995). In one experiment, male participants were randomly assigned to either an experimental or control condition in which they watched 20 videotaped advertisements. The videotape in the experimental condition contained 16 sexist ads and 4 neutral ads, whereas the control condition contained 20 neutral ads. Participants were told that they were rating the ads on general appeal for a marketing research study. Following an intervening computer task, participants were then asked to interview a female candidate (actually a confederate to the experimenter) as a favor to the experimenter. The dependent variables in this study consisted of interpersonal ratings of the interviewee as a function of exposure to sexist versus nonsexist commercials. Results show that participants who viewed the sexist ads rated the female candidate as being less competent than did participants who viewed the nonsexist ads. However, participants in the sexist ad condition rated the female candidate as being more *likeable* than those in the nonsexist condition. These results are consistent with Glick and Fiske's (1996) model of benevolent sexism, which posits that sexist attitudes may be characterized by positive affect toward women mixed with negative beliefs concerning the competence of women. In other words, sexist men *like* women (usually more than they like men), but they do not necessarily *respect* women.

In addition to sexist perceptions, Rudman and Borgida (1995) showed that exposure to sexist ads actually increased the incidence of sexist *behavior* toward women. Men in the primed sexist ad condition asked more sexist questions (i.e., questions that dealt with appearance or interpersonal factors as opposed to questions related to the job per se) than did those in the nonsexist ad condition. Furthermore, men exposed to sexist ads sat closer to the female candidate than did men in the control condition, presumably as a means of conveying sexual interest. Additionally, the candidate herself as well as independent female observers (who were all blind to the male participants' experimental condition) indicated in several postexperimental questions that, compared with males in the nonsexist condition, males exposed to sexist ads showed greater dominance and sexualized behavior toward the confederate. These researchers summarized their findings by stating that "the pernicious effects of culturally normative material such as sexist advertising may be that it (1) encourages men to mentally cast women into subjugative, sexualized roles and (2) facilitates access to norms advocating use of a sexist subtype. The cognitive effects may in turn leak *unintentionally* [italics added]... into even relatively nonsexist men's behavior" (Rudman & Borgida, 1995, p. 514).

Finally, exposure to sexist advertising can impair women's academic performance. Research by Davies et al. (2002) found that exposure to sexist television commercials made women more susceptible to "stereotype threat" (Steele & Aronson, 1995). Stereotype threat effects occur when activation of negative stereotypes about one's group disrupts performance on tasks that are behaviorally relevant to the stereotype (see Steele, 1997 and Steele & Aronson, 1995 for discussion). The particular stereotype examined in this study was the belief that women are not good at math. Consistent with stereotype threat, Davies et al. reasoned that exposure to sexist stereotypes would hinder women's performance on a math exam. Across three studies, these researchers found that, compared with women exposed to counterstereotypic ads, women exposed to sexist ads did worse in math. These women also showed less interest in careers involving math compared with women shown stereotypic ads.

It is worth mentioning that none of the sexist or counterstereotypic ads depicted math-relevant content. Rather, one of the sexist ads showed a woman jumping on a bed after trying a new acne product, whereas one of the counterstereotypic ads showed a woman impressing a man with her knowledge of auto mechanics. Thus, the effect is not contingent on the existence of a direct link between the specific (math) stereotype and stereotype-consistent performance. Rather, the activation of *any* negative stereotype can disrupt performance. To be sure, it is unlikely that advertisers consciously design acne commercials to sabotage women's math performance, or that women consciously attribute their underperformance in math to sexist commercials on television. Although advertisers and consumers alike may be unaware of the deleterious effects of biased advertising, exposure to these stereotypic representations in the media can and do have unintended effects on stereotypic perception, discriminatory behavior, and academic performance.

SUMMARY

I have presented a number of findings confirming the notion that human thought and behavior can be influenced by exposure to environmental cues and the activation of preexisting cognitive representations, independent of will or intent.

Although automatic processes play a role in intergroup stereotyping and discrimination, these behaviors may also result from more conscious or "rational" motives. Indeed, research has shown that discrimination can arise from competition over scarce resources (Campbell, 1965; Sherif, Harvey, White, Hood, & Sherif, 1961) or from the desire to establish or maintain group-based social hierarchy (Sidanius & Pratto, 1999). Moreover, because race and gender stereotypes enhance the effectiveness of advertising, media bias may sometimes reflect economic or political motives. Research has shown the following: (a) people evaluate same-race characters or spokespeople more favorably than other-race spokespeople; (b) race affects memory for products, particularly among high-prejudiced or high-identified individuals; and (c) race affects likelihood to purchase or learn more about the product (Ruscher, 2001). Race may also affect the degree to which individuals scrutinize advertisements (Petty, Fleming, & White, 1999). Consequently, advertisers may deliberately cast minorities in stereotypic roles because it generates profit. Moreover, stereotypic portrayals of women shopping for peanut butter or musical, happy-go-lucky African Americans enjoying chicken wings may serve the added psychological function of providing comfort and security to "traditional" audiences by affirming their cultural worldviews as opposed to challenging them (Solomon, Greenberg, & Pyszczynski, 1991).

Whatever the underlying cause of media bias, research confirms that its existence creates negative social consequences. Thus, socially conscious advertisers who take care to *avoid* bias in advertising will diminish the risk of increasing discrimination; those who take the extra step of providing *positive* or counterstereotypic portrayals of minorities in the media may actually *decrease* societal prejudice. For instance, Dasgupta and Greenwald (2001) found that exposing participants to positive African American exemplars reduced automatic prejudice on the IAT, and Rudman, Ashmore, and Gary (2001) showed that educating students about the positive contributions of African Americans led to a significant decrease in automatic prejudice. Given these findings, it is plausible that more positive portrayals of minorities in the media could go a long way toward reducing bias in society, even at the automatic level. Furthermore, the diminution in stereotypes and prejudice produced by these changes in media images would, in turn, increase the economic viability of fair and unbiased portrayals of women and minorities in the media.

REFERENCES

Archer, D., Iritani, B., Kimes, D. D., & Barrios, M. (1983). Face-ism: Five studies of sex differences in facial prominence. *Journal of Personality and Social Psychology, 45,* 725–735.

Bargh (1994). The fours horsemen of automaticity: Awareness, intention, efficiency and control in social cognition. In R. S. Wyer & T. K. Srull (Eds.), *Handbook of social cognition* (pp. 1–40). Hillsdale, NJ: Lawrence Erlbaum Associates.

Bargh, J. A., Chen, M., & Burrows, L. (1996). Automaticity of social behavior: Direct effects of trait construct and stereotype activation on action. *Journal of Personality and Social Psychology, 71*, 230–244.

Campbell, D. T. (1965). Ethnocentric and other altruistic motives. In D. Levine (Ed.), *Nebraska symposium on motivation.* (pp. 283–311) Lincoln, NE: University of Nebraska Press.

Chartrand, T. L., & Bargh, J. A. (1999). The chameleon effect: The perception-behavior link and social interaction. *Journal of Personality and Social Psychology, 76*, 893–910.

Chartrand, T. L., Maddux, W. W., & Lakin, J. L. (in press). Beyond the perception-behavior link: The ubiquitous utility and motivational moderators of nonconscious mimicry. In R. Hassin, J. Uleman, & J. A. Bargh (Eds.), *Unintended Thought 2: The New Unconscious.* New York: Oxford University Press.

Chen, M., & Bargh, J. A. (1997). Nonconscious behavioral confirmation processes: The self-fullfiling consequences of automatic stereotype activation. *Journal of Experimental Social Psychology, 33*, 541–560.

Correll, J., Park, B., Judd, C. M., & Wittenbrink, B. (2002). The police officer's dilemma: Using ethnicity to disambiguate potentially threatening individuals. *Journal of Personality and Social Psychology, 83*, 1314–1329.

Davies, P. G., Spencer, S. J., Quinn, D. M., & Gerhardstein, R. (2002). Consuming images: How television commercials that elicit stereotype threat can restrain women academically and professionally. *Personality and Social Psychology Bulletin, 28*, 1615–1628.

Dasgupta, N., & Greenwald, A. G. (2001). On the malleability of automatic attitudes: Combating automatic prejudice with images of admired and disliked individuals. *Journal of Personality and Social Psychology, 81*, 800–814.

Devine, P. G. (1989). Stereotypes and prejudice: Their automatic and controlled components. *Journal of Personality and Social Psychology, 56*, 5–18.

Dijksterhuis, A., & van Knippenberg, A. (1998). The relationship between perception and behavior, or how to win a game of Trivial Pursuit. *Journal of Personality and Social Psychology, 74*, 865–877.

Dovidio, J. F., Kawakami, K., Johnson, C., Johnson, B., & Howard, A. (1997). On the nature of prejudice: Automatic and controlled processes. *Journal of Experimental Social Psychology, 33*, 510–540.

Entman, R. M. (1994). Representation and reality in the portrayal of blacks on network television news. *Journalism Quarterly, 71*, 509–520.

Fazio, R. H., Jackson, J. R., Dunton, B. C., & Williams, C. J. (1995). Variability in automatic activation as an unobtrusive measure of racial attitudes: A bona fide pipeline? *Journal of Personality and Social Psychology, 69*, 1013–1027.

Fazio, R. H., & Olson, M. (2003). Implicit measures in social cognition research: Their meaning and use. *Annual Review of Psychology, 54*, 297–327.

Freud, S. (1963). Further remarks on the defense neuropsychoses. In P. Rieff (Ed.), *Freud: Early psychoanalytic writings* (pp. 151–174). New York: Collier. (Original work published 1896)

Gaertner, S. L., & Dovidio, J. F. (1986). An aversive form of racism. In J. F. Dovidio & S. L. Gaertner (Eds.), *Prejudice, discrimination, and racism* (pp. 61–89). New York: Academic Press.

Gilens, M. (1996). Race and poverty in America: Public misperceptions and the American news media. *Public Opinion Quarterly, 60*, 515–541.

Glick, P., & Fiske, S. T. (1996). The ambivalent sexism inventory: Differentiating hostile and benevolent sexism. *Journal of Personality and Social Psychology, 70*, 491–512.

Goffman, E. (1976). *Gender advertisements.* New York: Harper & Row.

Greenwald, A. G., & Banaji, M. R. (1995). Implicit social cognition: Attitudes, self-esteem, and stereotypes. *Psychological Review, 102*, 4–27.

Greenwald, A. G., McGhee, D. E., & Schwartz, J. L. K. (1998). Measuring individual differences in implicit cognition: The Implicit Association Test. *Journal of Personality and Social Psychology, 74*, 1464–1480.

Greenwald, A. G., Spangenberg, E. R., Pratkanis, A. R., & Eskenazi, J. (1991). Double-bling tests of subliminal self-help audiotapes. *Psychological Science, 2,* 119–122.

Higgins, E. T., Rholes, W. S., & Jones, C. R. (1977). Category accessibility and impression formation. *Journal of Experimental Social Psychology, 13,* 141–154.

Hsee, C. K., Hatfield, E., Carlson, J. G., & Chemtob, C. (1990). The effect of power on susceptibility to emotional contagion, *Cognition and Emotion, 4,* 327–340.

Jaccoby, L. L. (1991). A process dissociation framework: Separating automatic from intentional uses of memory. *Journal of Memory and Language, 30,* 513–541.

James, W. (1890). *Principles of psychology.* New York: Holt.

Lepore, L., & Brown, R. (1997). Category and stereotype activation: Is prejudice inevitable? *Journal of Personality and Social Psychology, 72,* 275–287.

Livingston, R. W. (2001). *Bias in the absence of malice: The phenomenon of unintentional discrimination.* Unpublished doctoral dissertation, Ohio State University, Columbus.

Livingston, R. W., & Brewer, M. B. (2002). What are we really priming?: Cue-based versus category based processing of facial stimuli. *Journal of Personality and Social Psychology, 82,* 5–18.

McConnell, A. R., & Leibold, J. M. (2001). Relations among the Implicit Association Test, discriminatory behavior, and explicit measures of racial attitudes. *Journal of Experimental Social Psychology, 37,* 435–442.

Merton, R. K. (1957). *Social theory and social structure.* New York: The Free Press.

Meyer, D. E., & Schvaneveldt, R. W. (1971). Facilitation in recognizing pairs of words: Evidence of dependence between retrieval operations. *Journal of Experimental Psychology, 90,* 227–234.

Neely, J. H. (1977). Semantic priming and retrieval from lexical memory: Roles of inhibitionless spreading activation and limited-capacity attention. *Journal of Experimental Psychology: General, 106,* 226–254.

Nisbett, R. E., & Wilson, T. D. (1977). Telling more than we can know: Verbal reports on mental processes. *Psychological Review, 84,* 231–259.

Payne, B. K. (2001). Prejudice and perception: The role of automatic and controlled processes in misperceiving a weapon. *Journal of Personality and Social Psychology, 81,* 181–192.

Petty, R. E., Fleming, M. A., & White, P. H. (1999). Stigmatized sources and persuasion: Prejudice as a determinant of argument scrutiny. *Journal of Personality and Social Psychology, 76,* 19–34.

Provine, R. R. (1986). Yawning as a stereotyped action pattern and releasing stimulus. *Ethology, 72,* 109–122.

Rosenthal, R., & Jacobson, L. (1968). *Pygmalion in the classroom: Teacher expectations and student intellectual development.* New York: Holt, Rinehart & Winston.

Rudman, L. A., & Borgida, E. (1995). The afterglow of construct accessibility: The behavioral consequences of priming men to view women as sexual objects. *Journal of Experimental Social Psychology, 31,* 493–517.

Rudman, L. A., Ashmore, R. D., & Gary, M. L. (2001). "Unlearning" automatic biases: The malleability of implicit prejudice and stereotypes. *Journal of Personality and Social Psychology, 81,* 856–868.

Ruscher, J. B. (2001). *Prejudiced communication: A social psychological perspective.* New York: Guilford.

Segal, S. J., & Cofer, C. N. (1960). The effect of recency and recall on word association. *American Psychologist, 15,* 451.

Sherif, M., Harvey, O. J., White, B. J., Hood, W. R., & Sherif, C. W. (1961). *Intergroup conflict and cooperation: The Robber's Cave experiment.* Norman, OK: University of Oklahoma, Institute of Group Relations.

Shih, M., Pittinsky, T. L., & Ambady, N. (1999). Stereotype susceptibility: Identity salience and shifts in quantitative performance. *Psychological Science, 10,* 80–83.

Sidanius, J., & Pratto, F. (1999). *Social dominance.* New York: Cambridge University Press.

Solomon, S., Greenberg, J., & Pyszczynski, T. (1991). A terror management theory or social behavior: The psychological function of self-esteem and cultural worldviews. In M. Zanna (Ed.), *Advances in experimental social psychology* (Vol. 24, pp. 93–159). San Diego, CA: Academic Press.

Steele, C. M. (1997). A threat in the air: How stereotypes shape intellectual identity and performance. *American Psychologist, 52,* 613–629.

Steele, C. M., & Aronson, J. (1995). Stereotype threat and the intellectual test performance of African Americans. *Journal of Personality and Social Psychology, 69,* 797–811.

Stone, J., Lynch, C. I., Sjomeling, M., & Darley, J. M. (1999). Stereotype threat effects and Black and White athletic performance. *Journal of Personality and Social Psychology, 77,* 1213–1227.

Storms, L. H. (1958). Apparent backward association: A situational effect. *Journal of Experimental Psychology, 55,* 390–395.

Strahan, E. J., Spencer, S. J., & Zanna, M. P. (2002). Subliminal priming and persuasion: Striking while the iron is hot. *Journal of Experimental Social Psychology, 38,* 556–568.

Wegner, D. M. (2002). *The illusion of conscious will.* Cambridge, MA: MIT Press.

Wegner, D. M., & Bargh, J. A. (1998). Control and automaticity in social life. In D. T. Gilbert, S. T. Fiske, & G. Lindzey (Eds.), *The handbook of social psychology* (4th ed., Vol. 1, pp. 446–496). New York: McGraw-Hill.

Wilson, T. D., & Brekke, N. (1994). Mental contamination and mental correction: Unwanted influences on judgments and evaluations. *Psychological Bulletin, 116,* 117–142.

Wilson, T. D., Lindsey, S., & Schooler, T. Y. (2000). A model of dual attitudes. *Psychological Review, 107,* 101–126.

Wittenbrink, B., Judd, C. M., & Park, B. (1997). Evidence for racial prejudice at the implicit level and its relationship with questionnaire measures. *Journal of Personality and Social Psychology, 72,* 262–274.

Zajonc, R. B. (1968). Attitudinal effects of mere exposure. *Journal of Personality and Social Psychology, 9* (Suppl. 2, Pt. 2).

Zuckerman, M. (1986). On the meaning and implications of facial prominence. *Journal of Nonverbal Behavior, 10,* 215–229.

Zuckerman, M., & Kieffer, S. C. (1994). Race differences in face-ism: Does facial prominence imply dominance? *Journal of Personality and Social Psychology, 66,* 86–92.

ENDNOTES

1. Many terms in the literature have been used to describe the same general processes. The terms *automatic, nonconscious, implicit,* and *unintentional* are used interchangeably throughout the chapter.

2. Although there is evidence that subliminal priming can affect perception and behavior (cf. Bargh et al., 1996; Strahan, Spencer, & Zanna, 2002), the popular notion that exposure to subliminal messages embedded in tape recordings or advertisements can drastically alter behavior tends to be grossly exaggerated (Greenwald, Spangenberg, Pratkanis, & Eskenazi, 1991).

3. Many cases of police brutality, such as the beating of Rodney King or the torture of Abner Louima, are not as amenable to explanation by automatic processes. These events were not the result of reflexive, split-second decisions but rather involved more deliberative actions.

CHAPTER FIVE

Interethnic Ideology in Advertising: A Social Psychological Perspective

Christopher Wolsko
University of Alaska Fairbanks

Bernadette Park
Charles M. Judd
University of Colorado

Bernd Wittenbrink
University of Chicago

Concerns about ethnic diversity and the problems of interethnic conflict have always been a part of our social heritage. However, in recent decades, dramatic technological advances and population growth have placed humans into greater contact with one another and, in some sense, have made our fates more interdependent. Cultural groups are becoming less and less isolated from one another, and the intersection of very different customs and belief systems is now commonplace. In the United States, we are currently experiencing a heightened awareness of the increasing level of contact between diverse ethnic groups. Some estimate that by the middle of the 21st century, the majority of Americans will trace their origins to "Africa, Asia, the Hispanic world, the Pacific Islands, Arabia—almost anywhere but white Europe" (Henry, 1990, p. 31). When combined with opinions and ideals that vary substantially between cultures, these changing demographics have the potential for creating tremendous chaos and conflict. Thus we must consider, for ourselves, for the way we navigate our social interactions, and for the manner in which we conduct business, how to best address the demands of a complex world composed of people from many different ethnic backgrounds.

Addressing ethnic diversity is perhaps a particularly thorny issue for those individuals and organizations involved in the construction of social interventions—as are those who participate in the enterprise of advertising. We view it as a difficult issue for advertisers for two primary reasons. First of all, one must engage in the complicated task of determining the extent to which the effectiveness of a given advertisement is contingent upon how much the characteristics of the ad (e.g., the type of product, the name of the product, the ethnicity of the actors, and the activities engaged in by the actors) match the cultural characteristics shared by members of the target audience. For example, if a company is interested in expanding into an African American market, is it sufficient (or even necessary) to change the ethnicity of the people who promote their products? Or are there certain additional cultural characteristics of African Americans that have to be taken into consideration? The complexities of the relationships between effective marketing strategies and the consumer behavior of different ethnic groups are no doubt extensive.

This concern over whether or not to utilize culturally specific messages relates to a second difficult issue that many advertisers must inevitably confront—one that may have serious ethical implications. Namely, to what extent does focusing on cultural differences in advertisements perpetuate stereotypes and prejudice between ethnic groups? Advertisers are often criticized for depicting ethnic group members in certain ways (e.g., Hispanics as family oriented, Blacks as athletic, Whites as wealthy and intelligent, or women as weak and submissive). The argument is that such ads reinforce common stereotypes, setting a poor precedent for a society that should be based on treating one another as unique individuals instead of as interchangeable group members. Such criticism may place the socially sensitive advertiser in a difficult predicament—one in which she or he believes it is important to address the needs of a diverse audience (by having actors of various ethnicities act in ways "consistent with their cultural background") but fears that too much emphasis on ethnic differences may ultimately serve to perpetuate or even exacerbate ethnic conflict.

In this chapter, we focus primarily on this ethical consideration of addressing ethnic diversity in advertising. Mass media serves as a tremendously powerful socializing agent in today's world, and so those with the power to direct the content of the messages running through popular culture are in a position to influence the ways in which people from different ethnic groups relate to one another. The purpose of this chapter is to present theoretical and empirical arguments that address the consequences of messages that focus on ethnic *similarities* versus ethnic *differences* and, in the process, to help advertisers consider the types of media efforts that may appeal to a more diverse audience and that may be capable of facilitating interethnic harmony.

We approach these issues by considering the implications of interethnic ideology—the different ideals that people have for the optimal path toward interethnic harmony. In recent years, within the United States there has been a passionate ideological debate over how to best approach the "problem" of diversity. As we frame it, the basic dichotomy in this debate is between a *colorblind* perspective, which values dissolving ethnic boundaries and promotes judging others on the basis of their individual merits, and a *multicultural* perspective, which values maintaining ethnic boundaries and having respect and appreciation for different cultural characteristics. In part on the basis of on our own research findings, which we present later in this chapter, we believe that whether or not one adopts a colorblind versus a multicultural perspective can have profound consequences for attitudes toward and beliefs about different ethnic groups. More specifically, we examine whether focusing on ethnic group differences *necessarily* leads to greater prejudice, or if there is a way in which people may positively value ethnic diversity.

Before describing our theoretical and empirical approach, which is grounded in the social psychological tradition, we find it important to first provide the reader with a sense of the broader context in which this ideological dispute over ethnic diversity is taking place. Therefore, we begin our discussion in the field of education, where the pros and cons of colorblind and multicultural perspectives have been heavily debated.

EDUCATIONAL REFORM

The debate between supporters of colorblind versus multicultural perspectives is quite apparent in the contrasting strategies adopted in recent work toward educational reform in the United States. In support of a colorblind perspective, many scholars argue that because our society is becoming more diverse, we must strive harder than ever to live up to our creed of *e pluribus unum*. It is suggested that this unity can be achieved by teaching a common core curriculum in our schools—one that is founded primarily in European intellectual traditions (e.g., Bennet, 1987; Bloom, 1987; Finn, 1991; Hirsch, 1996; Schlesinger, 1992). Invoking an economic metaphor, Hirsch (1996) referred to this common knowledge base as consisting of intellectual capital, the raw materials with which individual citizens may pursue their own version of the American dream. In general, those who adopt this perspective argue that we must work toward a colorblind ideal by assimilating diverse ethnic groups into the American "melting pot"—a cohesive nation of individuals who are united by a common intellectual heritage.

This perspective objects to the development of bilingual and multicultural educational initiatives. The argument is that allowing ethnic groups to have their own specific curricula will lead to a practice of separatism and the eventual loss of common democratic values. Perhaps one of the most outspoken critics of cultural relativism is Allan Bloom (1987):

> ... cultural relativism succeeds in destroying the West's universal or intellectually imperialistic claims, leaving it to be just another culture. So there is equality in the republic of cultures. Unfortunately the West is defined by its need for discovery of nature, by its need for philosophy and science. This is its cultural imperative. Deprived of that it will collapse. The United States is one of the highest and most extreme achievements of the rational quest for the good life according to nature. (p. 39)

The colorblind educational agenda is therefore defined by a desire to dissolve ethnic boundaries and to unite a nation of individuals under a common set of Western intellectual, economic, and political principles. In this conception, then, preserving the cultural characteristics of diverse ethnic groups is undesirable, because of the general chaos and conflict it would presumably create, and because it would undermine the sanctity of Western accomplishments.

In opposition to this relatively conservative agenda, others argue that the traditional notion of the great American melting pot is in some sense an outdated and unattainable ideal (e.g., Takaki, 1993; Yinger, 1994). Scholars who adopt more of a multicultural perspective acknowledge that some degree of social consensus among diverse groups is necessary for the smooth functioning of society, but they suggest that this consensus should not be achieved by dissolving ethnic group differences into a colorblind melting pot. The argument is that the traditionally colorblind alternative fails to provide all students with an accurate depiction of their cultural background because it advocates unity only under European cultural principles; furthermore, the colorblind approach does not do an adequate job of preparing students to function in a truly democratic society, where sensitive interactions between fellow citizens can only take place with knowledge of cultural differences (Nieto, 1996; Sleeter & McLaren, 1995). As an alternative, proponents of a multicultural perspective suggest that a cooperative society should be based on an ethic that recognizes and appreciates ethnic diversity. Therefore, multicultural reformers advocate an educational curriculum that better incorporates the historical experiences of diverse ethnic groups (Cummins, 1989; Skutnabb-Kangas & Cummins, 1988; Weis, 1988).

This multicultural educational agenda is therefore defined by a desire to recognize and appreciate ethnic group differences and to facilitate a harmonious society by achieving consensus among the experiences of diverse groups. In this conception, then, ignoring cultural differences is devastating, because it invalidates the lives of minorities and less powerful groups, forcing them to either assimilate to the ways of dominant culture or to suffer the consequences of discrimination based on their physical or cultural divergence.

SOCIAL PSYCHOLOGICAL APPROACHES TOWARD AMELIORATING PREJUDICE

This brief discussion of educational approaches to dealing with ethnic diversity should illustrate the potential significance of the colorblind and multicultural perspectives for shaping the nature of interethnic relations in the larger society. In social psychology, researchers have addressed the issue of prejudice reduction from these same two basic perspectives: one that stresses the importance of judging one another as individuals and downplaying the importance of one's ethnic group membership, and another that emphasizes the importance of recognizing and appreciating group differences. In contrast to the educational approaches, however, social psychological efforts are much less politically motivated and do not generally contain explicit assumptions about such things as the general superiority of one cultural worldview over another (as the colorblind educational agenda described herein tends to do). In our discipline, the colorblind and multicultural perspectives have evolved more from a basic scientific understanding about the fundamental ways in which humans interact with their social world, than from idealized notions about the way society "should be."

Theoretical and empirical research in social psychology has traditionally tackled the issue of prejudice reduction with a colorblind ideal in mind. In this approach, the major task for researchers has been to define conditions that help people respond to one another as unique individuals rather than as interchangeable members of social categories (e.g., male or female, and Black or White). The goal is to cultivate an environment in which people are encouraged to consider their common "humanness," instead of their "blackness," "whiteness," or other specific group memberships.

This approach toward prejudice reduction is grounded in the argument that prejudice may result directly from the process of categorizing people into different groups (see Tajfel, 1969, 1970). This argument is supported by a wealth of experimental research demonstrating that simply assigning people to different groups can lead to significant intergroup biases, even when group membership is based on very trivial criteria. For example, in one classic experiment, Billig and Tajfel (1973) randomly assigned different code numbers to research participants (half received numbers in the 40s and half received numbers in the 70s). When later prompted to divide rewards among the other people in the experiment, participants discriminated in favor of their ingroup (those who shared their code number) at the expense of their outgroup (those who were assigned a different code number). This basic pattern of findings has been replicated extensively by researchers using variants of this minimal group paradigm (for reviews see Brewer, 1979; Diehl, 1990; Wilder, 1986).

Why should simple ingroup–outgroup categorization lead to significant intergroup bias? Underlying the basic motivation that we have to identify positively with our ingroup(s) relative to our outgroup(s) is the fundamental need to see ourselves positively rather than negatively—the well-documented motivation to establish and maintain positive self-esteem (see Baumeister, 1996; Rosenberg, 1979). Because much of our self-image is defined in terms of our group memberships, we have preferences to see our ingroups in a positive light in relation to those groups to which we do not belong. Such are the tenets of social identity theory (Tajfel, 1978, 1982; Tajfel & Turner, 1979). Interpreting prejudice and ingroup biases through the lens of this theory of esteem-based group identity suggests that the development and maintenance of a satisfactory identity requires that individuals search out various forms of positive distinctiveness for their ingroup; if these cannot be found, then they must search out a new ingroup. From this it follows that threats to people's social identities should be responded to by increased attempts to differ-entiate the ingroup positively from outgroups. Research findings examining these predictions of social identity theory are generally consistent with Triandis' (1994) notion that all people are ethnocentric—that all people positively identify to some degree with their own groups' customary ways of interacting with the world, and that people will go to great lengths to defend and preserve them.

In accordance with a colorblind approach, then, the focus for social psychologists working on prejudice reduction has essentially been to find ways to undermine the foundation of ethnocentrism—namely, the ingroup–outgroup categorization process. Researchers have typically pursued this issue by creating conditions under which people are encouraged to judge one another on the basis of their individual attributes and *not* on the basis of their particular group memberships. The specific methods used have taken one of two forms.

In one approach, researchers have focused on downplaying the significance of social categories (i.e., rejecting ethnic stereotypes as a valid basis for judgment). The work of Brewer and Miller (1984, 1988) has been exemplary in its focus on promoting interpersonal rather than category-based interactions. In examining the effectiveness of intergroup contact interventions (involving artificial groups in the laboratory and ethnic groups in school classrooms), these and other researchers have found that cooperative interactions between group members result in more positive intergroup attitudes when participants are encouraged to relate to others as individuals, rather than as members of social categories (Bettencourt, Brewer, Rogers-Croak, & Miller, 1992; Cook, 1984; Miller, Brewer, & Edwards, 1985).

With the similar goal of undermining the basis for intergroup bias, a second approach has been to alter the ways in which social categories are applied (i.e., rejecting the labels of "Black" and "White" and substituting a more inclusive category of "American"). Gaertner, Dovidio, and their colleagues have suggested that a valuable path toward reducing prejudice involves establishing a common ingroup identity ("we") rather than dividing the social world into a potentially antagonistic "us" versus "them" (Gaertner, Mann, Murrell, & Dovidio, 1989; Gaertner, Dovidio, Anastasio, Bachman, & Rust, 1993). Research adopting this approach has found more positive intergroup attitudes when intergroup contact involves cooperative interaction and is defined as one in which the participants comprise one single group, as opposed to individuals or different groups (see also Sherif, 1966; Sherif, Harvey, White, Hood, & Sherif, 1961).

In summary, the majority of research on prejudice reduction in social psychology has assumed that the process of dividing people into different groups is sufficient to create prejudice and, therefore, that bias can be reduced by either avoiding or altering this categorization process. This approach embodies a colorblind ideal because it is clearly focused on deemphasizing the relevance of group differences and instead advocates treating one another as unique individuals.

In contrast to the colorblind approach, some researchers have adopted more of multicultural perspective. The foundation of this perspective begins with the notion that groups of people differ in their subjective culture—their historically acquired patterns of interpreting and behaving in their respective social environments. In a diverse society, people from different backgrounds bring different ideas about appropriate behavior to their interactions with one another, creating the potential for significant conflict. In this approach to prejudice reduction, then, the goal is to reduce this potential for conflict by promoting greater awareness and understanding of these different group experiences, or subjective cultures.

In a synthesis of work from anthropology and social psychology, researchers have attempted to foster greater appreciation of group differences by developing a variety of cross-cultural training programs (Bennett, 1986; Brislin & Pedersen, 1976; Cushner & Brislin, 1995; Fielder, Mitchell, & Triandis, 1971; Triandis, 1975; Weeks, Pedersen, & Brislin, 1982). The goal of these programs is to help cross-cultural interactions run more smoothly by encouraging participants to accurately comprehend the perspective of members from the other culture. This approach has been successful in reducing misunderstandings in business negotiations (e.g., Lee & Duenas, 1995; Triandis, 1995), and, in situations where there is less motivation to form cooperative relationships (i.e., everyday interactions between members of different ethnic groups), a few studies have obtained positive results, such as reduced anxiety, increased liking of outgroup members, and more ease of interaction (see, e.g., Randolph, Landis, & Tzeng, 1977, and Triandis, 1976, on Black–White relations; Stephan & Stephan, 1984, on Chicano–White relations).

Thus, rather than treating social categories as an invalid basis for judgment, as the colorblind approach tends to, this multicultural perspective actually encourages the recognition and appreciation of group differences. Although the consequences of focusing on group differences have received relatively little empirical attention from mainstream social psychologists, many do believe that such focusing is a critical task for future research (see Berry, 1984; Hewstone & Brown, 1986; Schofield, 1986; Stephan & Stephan, 1984; Tajfel, 1981; Turner, 1981; Van Knippenberg, 1984).

Both of these research approaches hold promise for reducing prejudice. Appreciating cultural differences and treating others as individual members of a common humanity seem equally important. However, one argument against the multicultural perspective is that, because it divides people on the basis of their group memberships, it will only serve to perpetuate stereotypes and lead to greater prejudice. As discussed in the introduction to this chapter, this type of argument may similarly be voiced against advertisers who portray members of ethnic groups in certain stereotypic roles, or who generally highlight ethnic group differences. Indeed, the research we described herein as motivating the colorblind approach demonstrates that simply dividing people into different groups is in some cases sufficient to motivate prejudiced reactions. Thus it appears that there is a valid concern about the consequences of promoting a multicultural ideology: that preserving ethnic group differences simply ends up preserving the basis for ethnic group conflict.

Does highlighting ethnic group differences inevitably lead to greater prejudice and conflict? If so, then could advertisements and other social interventions that emphasize group differences or that highlight the cultural characteristics of a given ethnic group actually promote prejudice? In a series of experiments, we have begun to address such questions.

EFFECTS OF COLORBLIND VERSUS MULTICULTURAL MESSAGES

In recent research, (Wolsko, Park, Judd, & Wittenbrink, 2000), we compared the consequences of being persuaded to adopt either a colorblind or a multicultural perspective, with two basic purposes in mind. First, we were interested in examining whether accentuating ethnic group boundaries necessarily leads to greater prejudice. In other words, can people simultaneously look more positively at members of an ethnic outgroup and still recognize substantial group differences? Answering this question seems very important for advertisers who are concerned with addressing the needs of a diverse audience but who also wonder about the potential harm they may be causing by highlighting cultural differences. A second purpose of our research was to simply examine how perceptions of different groups would be altered as a function of one ideological message versus the other. The social guidelines prescribed by both colorblind and multicultural perspectives are highly salient in popular American culture today (and increasingly so in various advertising campaigns), and we believe that our findings may serve as a fair approximation of how people's beliefs and attitudes are influenced by the receiving of these messages.

In a series of experiments, we first primed White American college students to think in terms of either a colorblind or a multicultural perspective and then examined their subsequent expressions of attitudes toward and beliefs about different ethnic groups (Wolsko et al., 2000). In each of these experiments, the ideological prime, so to speak, consisted of a half-page essay, said to be motivated by the consensual opinions held by social scientists regarding issues relevant to ethnic relations in the United States. In the colorblind condition, experimental participants read the following essay:

> Issues surrounding relations between people of different ethnicities are a #1 concern for the United States. At the present time we are experiencing a great deal of conflict among various ethnic groups. Social scientists note that it is extremely important to heed our creed in the Declaration of Independence that "all men (and women) are created equal." That is, in order to overcome interethnic conflict and fighting, we must remember that we are all first and foremost human beings, and second, we are all citizens of the United States. In order to make the U.S. as strong and successful as possible, we must think of ourselves not as a collection of independent factions, but instead as parts of a larger whole. We must look beyond skin color and seek to

understand the person within, to see each person as an individual who is part of the larger group, "Americans." Currently, we are spending a great many resources on conflict between ethnic groups. If we can recognize our "sameness" we will be able to rechannel those resources to work on difficult and important other problems within our society such as education, caring for the elderly, and medical reform. Thus, social scientists encourage us to look beyond skin color and learn to treat others as unique individuals, and also to see the larger picture—recognizing that at our core we really are all the same.

In the multicultural condition, participants read the following essay:

Issues surrounding relations between people of different ethnicities are a #1 concern for the United States. We are in the unique position of having many different cultural groups living within our borders. This could potentially be a great asset because different cultural groups bring different perspectives to life, providing a richness in styles of interaction, problem solving strategies, food, dress, music, and art. Each ethnic group within the United States can contribute in its own unique way. Recognizing this diversity would help to build a sense of harmony and complementarity among the various ethnic groups. Each group has its own talents, as well as its own problems, and by acknowledging both these strengths and weaknesses, we validate the identity of each group and we recognize its existence and its importance to the social fabric. We can allow each group to utilize its assests, to be aware of its own particular problems or difficulties, and overall to live up to its potential. Thus, social scientists argue that understanding both the similarities and differences among ethnic groups is an essential component of long-term social harmony in the United States, and that the ability to recognize the unique social characteristics of each cultural or ethnic group will lead to smoother interactions between people.

To strengthen these messages, participants read through a list of 20 reasons that other participants had given for why the particular ideological perspective was valuable, and then they circled the ones they agreed with. In addition, in some of this research, participants were assigned to a control condition. They received relatively minimal instructions—informing them that we were simply interested in their perceptions of a variety of social groups.

We examined the effects of this manipulation of the ideological context on a variety of group perceptions. Our research participants to date have been White American college students, making judgments about Whites, Blacks, and Hispanics. We basically examined two types of group perceptions: *ethnocentrism* and *category differentiation*.

Ethnocentrism

First, we assessed differences in ethnocentrism (Tajfel, 1969; Tajfel & Turner, 1979), the degree to which one has more positive feelings toward and beliefs about the ingroup (Whites, in this case) than the outgroup. In this research, feelings were measured on a thermometer scale, in which participants rated how warmly they felt toward a variety of groups (on a 100-point scale on which 0 meant they felt very cool toward the group and 100 meant they felt very warm). Additionally, beliefs about these groups were measured on a percent estimate task in which participants estimated the percentage of members of a particular group who possess various positive versus negative characteristics (e.g., intelligence, athleticism, uptightness, or laziness).

Results from the analysis of these measures indicated that, relative to a control condition, participants who received either the multicultural or the colorblind message expressed less ethnocentrism—or in other words, an increase in positive feelings toward and beliefs about Blacks relative to Whites. It is important to note that participants responding from either perspective displayed this tendency equivalently (i.e., levels of ethnocentrism did not differ between the colorblind and multicultural conditions). This suggests that motivating people to think about the importance of improving interethnic relations (through either a colorblind or a multicultural message) can have the effect of producing, at least on a temporary basis, less prejudiced interethnic attitudes.

Category Differentiation

However, a major question posed by this research is whether this decrease in ethnocentrism can co-occur with perceptions of greater differences between groups. In other words, does presenting a multicultural ideological message enable people to value diversity positively? To address this question, we also collected in the same studies a number of measures designed to assess what we refer to as category differentiation. These are measures that determine the extent to which participants' beliefs make distinctions between the characteristics associated with different groups. In these measures, participants made judgments about the prevalence of both positive and negative characteristics among different groups, and so the degree of category differentiation reflected in the judgments of a given participant was unrelated to the valence of the characteristics being judged. In other words, category differentiation is a measure of the extent to which groups are perceived as "different" and *not* a measure of the extent to which one group is viewed as positive and the other as negative.

Although both of the two ideological perspectives encourage intergroup harmony, they differ in that the colorblind perspective suggests that this harmony can be best achieved by judging one another as individuals and not on the basis of skin color; the multicultural perspective underscores the importance of recognizing group differences. Therefore, on these measures of category differentiation, we expected that the multicultural message would cause participants to make more distinctions between groups than would the colorblind message. This was in fact the case for a variety of measures.

For example, on one measure of beliefs, we had participants estimate the percentage of Black and White Americans who possess certain traits, such as intelligence, uptightness, athleticism, and laziness. In this task, participants were presented with a list of 56 attributes and were asked to estimate the percentage of White (Black) Americans that possessed each attribute. Half the attributes were typically associated with Blacks (and less so with Whites, e.g., athleticism and laziness), and half were typically associated with Whites (and less so with Blacks, e.g., intelligence and uptightness). In addition, half of each of these were positive and half were negative. In this measure, category differentiation is defined as assigning particular patterns of traits to Blacks relative to Whites, orthogonal to the valence of the traits. So, in differentiating between these groups, one would say that Whites are relatively intelligent and uptight, and not very athletic or lazy—whereas Blacks are relatively athletic and lazy, and not very intelligent or uptight.

We found that participants receiving the multicultural message engaged in greater category differentiation than did participants receiving either the colorblind message or the control instructions. It is important to note that this tendency did not depend on the valence of the attributes being judged. Thus, accentuating category boundaries did not focus attention solely on negative characteristics of Blacks—it also increased the recognition of positive traits. This multicultural tendency to recognize between-group differences in *both* positive and negative characteristics equivalently was found on all of the measures of category differentiation discussed in the paragraphs that follow.

On a measure of belief accuracy, we again asked participants to estimate the prevalence of certain characteristics among Black and White Americans, and we were able to compare these estimates to their actual prevalence. For this, we used 16 items asking about things such as unemployment rates, attendance at church, white-collar crimes, and median income—attributes for which we were able to find objective criteria. As in the measure of beliefs just described, half the attributes were associated with Blacks (and less so with Whites, e.g., being unemployed and being religious) and half were associated with Whites (and less so with Blacks, e.g., being wealthy and being a white-collar criminal). Half of each of these were positive and half were negative. We found that participants receiving the multicultural message engaged in a more accurate level of category differentiation than did participants receiving the colorblind message. In other words, they more accurately estimated the different attributes of Black versus White Americans—at least in a small number of domains.

This multicultural tendency to differentiate more between the social characteristics of different groups was also revealed on a task in which participants indicated the values, or life-guiding principles, that they thought were important in the lives of Black and White Americans in general (e.g., a comfortable life, true friendship, and family security). In this task, participants completed the Rokeach (1973) value sort according to how they thought White Americans in general would respond and according to how they thought Black Americans in general would respond. This task required participants to rank order two separate sets of values, one consisting of 18 instrumental values and the other consisting of 18 terminal values.

Instrumental values essentially reflect different preferred ways of interacting with one's world (e.g., being ambitious, broad minded, or courageous), and terminal values reflect desired end states of existence (e.g., having an exciting life, a world at peace, or social equality). For each group, participants were required to rank order the two sets of values and to record their order of importance.

For both value types, results indicated that the values that participants deemed important in the lives of Black versus White Americans differed to a greater extent under a framework supporting multiculturalism than under one supporting colorblindness. This suggests that influencing people to think in terms of ethnic diversity, as opposed to ethnic similarity, creates the perception that different ethnic groups may have different agendas underlying their social actions.

We also examined how these ideological messages influence the extent to which people use ethnicity as a cue for judging the behavior of specific individuals. After a manipulation of the ideological message, participants read through descriptions about the past behaviors of 12 White and 12 Hispanic target individuals. The participants were then asked to predict the future behavior of these individuals in situations that would require a response that was either consistent or inconsistent with how members of the group are generally viewed. For example, in one of the situations, targets could adhere to the wishes of their family (consistent with how Hispanics are generally viewed but inconsistent with Whites) or they could engage in more individualistic behavior (consistent with how Whites are generally viewed but inconsistent with Hispanics). In this example, the pattern of past behaviors performed by the various targets differed on the dimension of being family-motivated versus personally motivated (i.e., some targets had performed all family-motivated behaviors in the past, some all personally motivated ones, and others had performed a mixture). There were 12 patterns of past behavior in all, and each combination was paired once with a White target and once with a Hispanic target. This design enabled us to determine the extent to which participants used category information (ethnicity) and individuating information (specific pattern of past behavior) in making their predictions about the behavior of targets.

Our findings indicated that participants who received a multicultural message weighted the ethnicity of the target individuals more in their judgments than did those who received a colorblind message. That is, on average, multicultural participants predicted that the target individuals would behave in a manner consistent with their ethnic background (i.e., Hispanics would be more likely to adhere to the wishes of their family than Whites would), whereas colorblind participants did not predict any differences in behavior as a function of ethnicity.

One argument against a multicultural approach is that, in its emphasis on cultural differences, it may cause perceivers to ignore important information about the individual—information that might receive greater attention under a colorblind approach. However, in their judgments of White and Hispanic individuals, participants presented with a multicultural message attended to individuating information as much as participants presented with a colorblind message. In sum, results on our measures of category differentiation indicate that being presented with a multicultural perspective causes one to highlight ethnic group differences, and that being presented with a colorblind perspective leads one to basically ignore ethnicity and instead judge others as individuals.

POSITIVELY VALUING DIVERSITY

By integrating the results from our measures of ethnocentrism and category differentiation, we were able to determine that presenting the multicultural message caused our research participants to positively value group differences. Relative to the colorblind message, presenting participants with a multicultural message led to more category differentiation, more accurate differentiation, and more use of category information in judgments of individuals. In conjunction, this increased category differentiation occurred equivalently for both positive and negative attributes and was paired in some cases with greater overall positivity toward the outgroup.

Given these findings, we must question the assumption made by a strictly colorblind approach to prejudice reduction: that the relevance of ethnicity must be deemphasized. The findings we present here demonstrate that increased differentiation of the outgroup from the ingroup and reduced ethnocentrism can coexist. In other words, messages that highlight group differences do not necessarily perpetuate prejudice, and they may even improve interethnic relations—provided that these differences are framed in terms of a multicultural ideology that positively values diversity. In making this argument, however, our intention is not to criticize efforts at prejudice reduction coming from a colorblind approach. As we mentioned previously, both perspectives seem to have considerable merit. We simply believe that a multicultural approach has received limited attention in the field of social psychology, and we hope to raise awareness here about its potential benefits.

INTERETHNIC IDEOLOGY IN ADVERTISING

There are various levels at which we might apply this discussion of interethnic ideology to the enterprise of advertising. To begin with, it is very important to recognize that our research findings relevant to the multicultural perspective *do not* give the advertiser the license to engage in the reckless stereotyping of different ethnic groups, particularly on negative traits. There is a very extensive social psychological literature that testifies to the fact that such a practice is quite capable of promoting negative and rigid evaluations of ethnic group members. Instead, we advocate media efforts that foster a general sense of multicultural appreciation. A message of this type might involve presenting people from different ethnicities engaging in *different* but *positive* activities. Alternatively, an advertisement might promote a product as valuable precisely because it fits the needs of an ethnically diverse audience, with their different experiences and lifestyles.

Thus, we support media that sensitively encourages the appreciation of group differences and that displays diversity in a positive light. If the advertiser does wish to portray ethnic group members in stereotypic roles (i.e., Hispanics as family oriented), we suggest that it would be important to first conduct market research using participants from the stereotyped group. In the process of determining a campaign's potential effectiveness, gauging the group members' general evaluation of a stereotypic versus nonstereotypic advertisement would help to address ethical considerations (i.e., whether the group accepts or rejects the stereotype about their group).

It may also be useful to consider that there are cultural differences in the adherence to different interethnic ideologies, and that advertisements will no doubt be more effective when the particular ideological perspective present in the message matches that of the target population. For example, an appeal directed at rural Whites of the Western states may be most effective if framed in terms of something approximating a colorblind ideology, which focuses on the importance of individual freedom. In contrast, an appeal directed at urban Blacks may be most effective if framed in terms of something approximating a multicultural ideology, which focuses on the importance of one's particular ethnic or cultural experience. In this sense, then, being sensitive to the interethnic ideology of the target audience may produce more effective advertisements.

Apart from these specific suggestions, we believe that the future challenge for those concerned with prejudice reduction, and for those concerned about the ethical implications of mass media for interethnic relations, will be to develop more creative interventions that are not entirely specific to a given segment of the population, that are not strictly colorblind or multicultural in focus, and, therefore, that seek to legitimize diversity and freedom at both the individual and cultural levels. The colorblind notion of accepting the common humanness and individuality of people from diverse backgrounds is critical in today's world more than ever. To provide balance with this colorblind ideal, we suggest that it would be beneficial to incorporate an ethic of respect and appreciation of ethnic diversity. Although our own empirical research does not indicate that such an ethic is necessary for improved intergroup relations, it does suggest that preserving or even emphasizing ethnic group boundaries is not inconsistent with improved intergroup relations. Thus we are currently left with a judgment call, simply based on how much we value the maintenance of ethnic diversity. With this in mind, consider the following argument from Wilson (1995) for the preservation of biological diversity:

> The ethical imperative should therefore be, first of all, prudence. We should judge every scrap of biodiversity as priceless while we learn to use it and come to understand what it means to humanity. We should not knowingly allow any species or race to go extinct. And let us go beyond mere salvage to begin the restoration of natural

environments, in order to enlarge wild populations and stanch the hemorrhaging of biological wealth. There can be no purpose more enspiriting than to begin the age of restoration, reweaving the wondrous diversity of life that still surrounds us. (p. 351)

Applying this argument from evolutionary biology to the cultural realm, we suggest that the maintenance of ethnic and cultural identity is important for people's psychological health and for the future adaptability and creativity of the human species in a rapidly changing social and physical environment. Integrating these ideas with those of a colorblind perspective results in a sort of hybrid vision of improving interethnic relations. In this vision, it is unproductive to argue that a multicultural approach is more valid or beneficial than a colorblind approach. Both perspectives are important and should be thought of as complementary rather than as contradictory. In this sense then, we share the opinions of researchers who recognize that reducing prejudice will require learning to relate to one another as unique individuals *and* as members of cultural subgroups *and* as constituents of a common humanity (e.g., Brewer, 1996; Dovidio, Gaertner, & Validzic, 1998; Gaertner, Rust, Dovidio, Bachman, & Anastasio, 1994, 1996; Marcus-Newhall, Miller, Holtz, & Brewer, 1993).

It may be difficult to visualize the form that such an integrative, flexible approach might take. Yet if we are going to apply it in our social world, then we do in fact need a vision. Advertising succeeds on the basis of projecting a suitable image, and perhaps the ultimate image, or metaphor for such an integrative approach, for creating unity from diversity is one of music. So we close with a passage on jazz from Cornell West, found in his book, *Race Matters* (1993):

> I use the term "jazz" here not so much as a term for a musical art form, as for a mode of being in the world, an improvisational mode of fluid and flexible dispositions toward reality suspicious of "either/or" viewpoints, dogmatic pronouncements, or supremacist ideologies. ... The interplay of individuality and unity is not one of uniformity and unanimity imposed from above, but rather one of conflict among diverse groupings that reach a dynamic consensus subject to questioning and criticism. As with a soloist in a jazz quartet, quintet or band, individuality is promoted in order to sustain the creative tension with the group—a tension that yields higher levels of performance to achieve the aim of the collective project. This kind of critical and democratic sensibility flies in the face of any policing of the borders and boundaries of "blackness," "maleness," "femaleness," or "whiteness." (p. 105)

In the present context, this, is to say that, in a diverse society, we cannot afford to embrace a dogmatic colorblindness—which fails to appreciate the extent to which human life is shaped by the cultural environment—nor can we afford to embrace a dogmatic multiculturalism—which blindly engages in stereotyping and exaggerates the extent to which groups differ. Instead, we must adopt an ideology of flexibility, which is characterized by a recognition that everyone is a unique individual, that an important part of this uniqueness is one's particular experience as an ethnic group member, and that we are members of a common humanity, ultimately more similar to one another than we are different. Those working in the field of advertising may find that the sort of dynamic open-mindedness that such a perspective engenders is tremendously appealing to consumers, especially those in younger generations.

REFERENCES

Baumeister, R. F. (1996). Self-regulation and ego-threat: Motivated cognition, self-deception, and de-structive goal-setting. In P. M. Gollwitzer and J. A. Bargh (Eds.), *The psychology of action* (pp. 27–47). New York: Guilford.

Bennett, M. J. (1986). A developmental approach to training for intercultural sensitivity. *International Journal of Intercultural Relations, 10*, 179–196.

Bennett, W. (1987). *James Madison High School: A curriculum for American students.* Washington, DC: U.S. Department of Education.

Berry, J. W. (1984). Cultural relations in plural societies: Alternatives to segregation and their sociopsy-chological consequences. In N. Miller & M. B. Brewer (Eds.), *Groups in contact: The psychology of desegregation* (pp. 11–28). Orlando, FL: Academic Press.

Bettencourt, B. A., Brewer, M. B., Rogers-Croak, M., & Miller, N. (1992). Cooperation and the reduction of the intergroup bias: The role of reward structure and social orientation. *Journal of Experimental Social Psychology, 28*, 301–319.

Billig, M., & Tajfel, H. (1973). Social categorization and similarity in intergroup behaviour. *European Journal of Social Psychology, 3*, 27–52.

Bloom, A. (1987). *The closing of the American mind.* New York: Simon & Schuster.

Brewer, M. B. (1979). Ingroup bias in the minimal intergroup situation: A cognitive-motivational analysis. *Psychological Bulletin, 86*, 307–334.

Brewer, M. B. (1996). When contact is not enough: Social identity and intergroup cooperation. *International Journal of Intercultural Relations, 20*, 291–303.

Brewer, M. B., & Miller, N. (1984). Beyond the contact hypothesis: Theoretical perspectives on deseg-regation. In N. Miller & M. B. Brewer (Eds.), *Groups in contact: The psychology of desegregation* (pp. 281–302). Orlando, FL: Academic Press.

Brewer, M. B., & Miller, N. (1988). Contact and cooperation: When do they work? In P. A. Katz & D. A. Taylor (Eds.), *Eliminating racism: Profiles in controversy* (pp. 315–328). New York: Plenum.

Brislin, R. W., & Pedersen, P. (1976). *Cross-cultural orientation programs.* New York: Gardner.

Cook, S. W. (1984). Cooperative interaction in multiethnic contexts. In N. Miller & M. B. Brewer (Eds.), *Groups in contact: The psychology of desegregation* (pp. 156–186). Orlando, FL: Academic Press.

Cummins, J. (1989). *Empowering minority students.* Sacramento, CA: California Association for Bilin-gual Education.

Cushner, K., & Brislin, R. W. (1995). *Intercultural interactions: A practical guide.* Thousand Oaks, CA: Sage.

Diehl, M. (1990). The minimal group paradigm: Theoretical explanations and empirical findings. In W. Stroebe & M. Hewstone (Eds.), *European review of social psychology* (pp. 263–292). Chichester, England: Wiley.

Dovidio, J. F., Gaertner, S. L., & Validzic, A. (1998). Intergroup bias: Status, differentiation, and a common in-group identity. *Journal of Personality and Social Psychology, 75*, 109–120.

Fielder, F., Mitchell, T., & Triandis, H. C. (1971). The culture assimilator: An approach to cross-cultural training. *Journal of Applied Psychology, 55*, 95–102.

Finn, C. A. (1991). *We must take charge: Our schools and our future.* New York: The Free Press.

Gaertner, S. L., Dovidio, J. F., Anastasio, P. A., Bachman, B. A., & Rust, M. C. (1993). The common ingroup identity model: Recategorization and the reduction of intergroup bias. In W. Stroebe & M. Hewstone (Eds.), *European review of social psychology* (pp. 1–26). Chichester, England: Wiley.

Gaertner, S. L., Mann, J., Murrell, A., & Dovidio, J. F. (1989). Reducing intergroup bias: The benefits of recategorization. *Journal of Personality and Social Psychology, 57,* 239–249.

Gaertner, S. L., Rust, M. C., Dovidio, J. F., Bachman, B. A., & Anastasio, P. A. (1994). The contact hypothesis: The role of a common ingroup identity on reducing intergroup bias. *Small Group Research, 25,* 224–249.

Gaertner, S. L., Rust, M. C., Dovidio, J. F., Bachman, B. A., & Anastasio, P. A. (1996). The contact hypothesis: The role of a common ingroup identity on reducing intergroup bias among majority and minority group members. In J. L. Nye & A. M. Brower (Eds.), *What's social about social cognition? Research on socially shared cognition in small groups* (pp. 230–260). Thousand Oaks, CA: Sage.

Henry, W. A. (1990, April 19). Beyond the melting pot. *Time, 135,* 28–31.

Hewstone, M., & Brown, R. J. (1986). Contact is not enough: An intergroup perspective on the "contact hypothesis." In M. Hewstone & R. J. Brown (Eds.), *Contact and conflict in intergroup encounters* (pp. 1–44). Oxford, England: Blackwell.

Hirsch, E. D. (1996). *The schools we need: And why we don't have them.* Garden City, NY: Doubleday.

Lee, Y.-T., & Duenas, G. (1995). Stereotype accuracy in multicultural business. In Y.-T. Lee, L. J. Jussim, & C. R. McCauley (Eds.), *Stereotype accuracy: Toward appreciating group differences* (pp. 157–188). Washington, DC: American Psychological Association.

Marcus-Newhall, A., Miller, N., Holtz, R., & Brewer, M. B. (1993). Cross-cutting category membership with role assignment: A means of reducing intergroup bias. *British Journal of Social Psychology, 32,* 124–146.

Miller, N., Brewer, M. B., & Edwards, K. (1985). Cooperative interaction in desegregated settings: A laboratory analogue. *Journal of Social Issues, 41,* 63–81.

Nieto, S. (1996). *Affirming diversity: The sociopolitical context of multicultural education.* White Plains, NY: Longman.

Randolph, G., Landis, D., & Tzeng, O. C. S. (1977). The effects of time and practice on cultural assimilator training. *International Journal of Intercultural Relations, 1,* 105–119.

Rokeach, M. (1973). *The nature of human values.* New York: The Free Press.

Rosenberg, M. (1979). *Conceiving the self.* New York: Basic Books.

Schlesinger, A. M. (1992). *The disuniting of America: Reflections on a multicultural society.* New York: Norton.

Schofield, J. W. (1986). Causes and consequences of the colorblind perspective. In J. F. Dovidio & S. L. Gaertner (Eds.), *Prejudice, discrimination, and racism* (pp. 231–254). New York: Academic Press.

Sherif, M. (1966). *Group conflict and cooperation.* London: Routledge & Kegan Paul.

Sherif, M., Harvey, O. J., White, B. J., Hood, W. R., & Sherif, C. W. (1961). *Intergroup conflict and cooperation: The Robbers' Cave experiment.* Norman, OK: University of Oklahoma Press.

Skutnabb-Kangas, T., & Cummins, J. (Eds.). (1988). *Minority education: From shame to struggle.* Clevedon, England: Multilingual Matters.

Sleeter, C. E., & McLaren, P. L. (Eds.). (1995). *Multicultural education, critical pedagogy, and the politics of difference.* Albany, NY: State University of New York Press.

Stephan, W. G., & Stephan, C. W. (1984). The role of ignorance in intergroup relations. In N. Miller & M. B. Brewer (Eds.), *Groups in contact: The psychology of desegregation* (pp. 229–257). Orlando, FL: Academic Press.

Tajfel, H. (1969). Cognitive aspects of prejudice. *Journal of Social Issues, 25,* 79–98.

Tajfel, H. (1970). Experiments in intergroup discrimination. *Scientific American, 223,* 96–102.

Tajfel, H. (Ed.). (1978). *Differentiation between social groups: Studies in the social psychology of intergroup relations.* London: Academic Press.

Tajfel, H. (1981). Social stereotypes and social groups. In J. C. Turner & H. Giles (Eds.), *Intergroup behaviour* (pp. 144–167). Oxford, England: Blackwell.

92

WOLSKO ET AL.

Tajfel, H. (1982). *Social identity and intergroup relations.* Cambridge, England: Cambridge University Press.

Tajfel, H., & Turner, J. C. (1979). An integrative theory of group conflict. In W. G. Austin & S. Worchel (Eds.), *The social psychology of intergroup relations* (pp. 33–47). Monterey, CA: Brooks/Cole.

Takaki, R. (1993). *A different mirror: A history of multicultural America.* Boston: Little, Brown.

Triandis, H. C. (1975). Culture training, cognitive complexity, and interpersonal attitudes. In R. W. Brislin, S. Bochner, & W. J. Lonner (Eds.), *Crosscultural perspectives on learning* (pp. 39–78). Beverly Hills, CA: Sage.

Triandis, H. C. (Ed.). (1976). *Variations in Black and White perceptions of the social environment.* Urbana, IL: University of Illinois Press.

Triandis, H. C. (1988). The future of pluralism revisited. In P. A. Katz & D. A. Taylor (Eds.), *Eliminating racism: Profiles in controversy* (pp. 31–52). New York: Plenum.

Triandis, H. C. (1994). *Culture and social behavior.* New York: McGraw-Hill.

Triandis, H. C. (1995). *Individualism and collectivism.* Boulder, CO: Westview Press.

Turner, J. C. (1981). The experimental social psychology of intergroup behavior. In J. C. Turner & H. Giles (Eds.), *Intergroup behaviour* (pp. 144–167). Oxford, England: Blackwell.

Van Knippenberg, A. (1984). Intergroup differences in group perceptions. In H. Tajfel (Ed.), *The social dimension: European developments in social psychology* (pp. 560–578). Cambridge, England: Cambridge University Press.

Weeks, W. H., Pedersen, P., & Brislin, R. W. (1982). *A manual of structured experiences for cross-cultural learning.* Chicago: Intercultural Press.

Weis, L. (Ed.). (1988). *Class, race, and gender in American education.* Albany, NY: State University of New York Press.

West, C. (1993). *Race matters.* Boston: Beacon.

Wilder, D. A. (1986). Social categorization: Implications for creation and reduction of intergroup bias. In L. Berkowitz (Ed.), *Advances in experimental social psychology.* Orlando, FL: Academic Press.

Wilson, E. O. (1995). *The diversity of life.* Cambridge, MA: Harvard University Press.

Wolsko, C., Park, B., Judd, C. M., & Wittenbrink, B. (2000). Framing interethnic ideology: Effects of multicultural and colorblind perspectives on judgments of groups and individuals. *Journal of Personality and Social Psychology, 78,* 635–654.

Yinger, J. M. (1994). *Ethnicity: Source of strength? Source of conflict?* Albany, NY: State University of New York Press.

CHAPTER SIX

It's Not Just What You Think, It's Also How You Think: Prejudice as Biased Information Processing

Patrick T. Vargas
University of Illinois

Denise Sekaquaptewa
University of Michigan

William von Hippel
University of New South Wales

Prejudice has traditionally been conceptualized as negative attitudes toward members of an outgroup that are based on stereotypes and beliefs concerning that outgroup. Traditional measures of prejudice tend to reflect this conceptualization in that they assess individuals' explicit attitudes toward outgroup members, or issues pertaining to outgroup members. That is, prejudice has largely been measured in terms of *what* people think about an outgroup. We have proposed that *what* people think about a particular group may often differ from *how* they think about it (von Hippel, Sekaquaptewa, & Vargas, 1995, 1997). For example, a person may be unwilling to entertain prejudiced explicit attitudes toward a particular group, yet those attitudes may nevertheless influence information processing about individual group members (e.g., White & Harkins, 1995). Thus, measures of *how* people think about outgroup members might fruitfully assess the stereotypic biases that people show when they process information about these groups. Furthermore, these biases in information processing have the potential to influence both cognitive and behavioral responses to outgroup members.

Before further discussing the current perspective on prejudice assessment, we believe it may be useful for us to briefly review more traditional work in this domain.

Following our discussion of prejudice measurement, we delve more deeply into the perspective of prejudice as biased information processing, and we introduce some measures that we have developed by relying on this perspective. Next, we discuss a series of studies using our biased processing measures. Finally, we discuss some implications of this perspective for researchers in psychology and advertising.

A BRIEF HISTORY OF PREJUDICE MEASUREMENT

Old-Fashioned Prejudice and Direct Measures

The earliest work attempting to measure prejudice was more an assessment of stereotypes about outgroup members than an assessment of the extent to which individuals held negative opinions about outgroup members. Researchers were more concerned with assessing group-level beliefs about stigmatized others than with measuring individual differences in prejudice. However, because most, if not all, stereotypes have some negative components (Wittenbrink, Judd, & Park, 1997), it seems reasonable to assume that measuring stereotype endorsement is closely related to measuring prejudice (Kawakami, Dion, & Dovidio, 1998).[1] Katz and Braly (1933) presented 100 members of the (then all-male) Princeton student body with a list of 84 adjectives, and they asked respondents to indicate those adjectives that described a particular target group (e.g., African Americans). Additionally, respondents were asked to indicate 5 adjectives that seemed most typical of the target group. Those adjectives that were most frequently used to describe a particular group were identified as the group's stereotype. This initial focus on the content of stereotypes faded and was replaced by a focus on individual-level analyses, that is, personality.

The authoritarian personality type (Adorno, Frenkel-Brunswick, Levinson, & Sanford, 1950) was the subject of a great deal of focus in the 1940s and 1950s. This marked a return to the study of individual differences in prejudice, but the focus was not strictly on prejudice. The study of the authoritarian personality focused on a Freudian interpretation of children's repressed impulses. According to the theory, these squelched impulses manifested themselves later in life as an intense dislike of individuals and groups who were not a part of middle-class America (e.g., Jews or African Americans). Research on the authoritarian personality fell out of favor[2] as serious methodological and conceptual questions arose (Brown, 1965), and overt expressions of prejudice began to slowly creep underground.

Unobtrusive Measures of Prejudice

Although there seemed to be a steady decrease in prejudice in America according to survey data (Schuman, Steeh, & Bobo, 1985), there was no shortage of prejudice uncovered in unobtrusive field and laboratory studies (Crosby, Bromley, & Saxe,

1980). Although overt expressions of prejudice were becoming less and less prevalent, a number of subtle studies demonstrated that prejudice was very much still present. For example, Caucasian subjects reliably delivered more punishment to African American confederates than to Caucasian confederates (e.g., Donnerstein & Donnerstein, 1975); Caucasian subjects also reliably offered less help to African American than to Caucasian confederates, particularly in remote situations (e.g., Benson, Karabenick, & Lerner, 1976). To explain the apparent discrepancy between survey and experimental data, researchers theorized that more subtle forms of prejudice had become normative.

Three influential theories guided the measurement of prejudice during the 1970s and the 1980s. Symbolic racism (Sears & Kinder, 1971; Sears & McConahay, 1973), aversive racism (Gaertner & Dovidio, 1986), and racial ambivalence (Katz & Hass, 1988) differed in their conceptualization of prejudice, but they all relied on a common theme in their attempts to measure prejudice. Symbolic racism suggested that Caucasian Americans were uncomfortable overtly expressing prejudice but were willing to express prejudice under the guise of preference for the status quo (e.g., unfavorable attitudes toward school bussing). Following this conceptualization of prejudice, McConahay and Hough (1976) developed the Modern Racism Scale (MRS). The MRS measured prejudice indirectly, presenting respondents with questions about political issues that favored African Americans rather than questions about the likeability of African Americans.

Aversive racism posited that prejudice against African Americans was thought to arise as a result of simultaneously held, conflicting ideals of egalitarianism and the Protestant work ethic (PWE). Egalitarian ideals suggest that individuals are equal and that all individuals, regardless of race or creed, should be given equal opportunity to resources, jobs, and the like. The PWE, in contrast, suggests that people get what they deserve and that all individuals are responsible for "pulling themselves up by their own bootstraps." According to the theory of aversive racism, Whites may be prejudiced, but they are unwilling to admit their prejudices to others and perhaps even to themselves. Because of this, direct measures of prejudice are unlikely to be useful. Instead, aversive racism suggests that prejudice might best be assessed indirectly, through respondents' egalitarian and PWE ideals. Endorsement of egalitarian beliefs tends to be related to the liking of African Americans, whereas endorsement of PWE ideals tends to be related to antipathy toward African Americans. Not unlike aversive racism theory, racial ambivalence suggested that prejudice might best be conceptualized as arising from simultaneously held, conflicting pro- and anti-African American attitudes. Prejudice, conceptualized as racial ambivalence, was assessed with pro- and anti-Black scales.

To tap into these apparently more subtle forms of prejudice, researchers developed more indirect measures of prejudice (e.g., the symbolic racism scale, or SRS, Kinder & Sears, 1981; the MRS, McConahay, Hardee, & Batts, 1981; and egalitarianism and PWE measures, Gaertner & Dovidio, 1986). Indirect measures of prejudice are essentially disguised self-report measures, wherein respondents provide information that is ostensibly unrelated to the attitude object under consideration and researchers infer respondents' attitudes based on this information. In the case of the MRS, prejudiced attitudes were tapped under the guise of political concerns. Prejudiced attitudes were inferred on the basis of respondents' desire to maintain the status quo regarding racially sensitive political issues (e.g., bussing, affirmative action).

More recently, however, indirect measures of prejudice such as the MRS have come under attack for at least two reasons. First, it is unclear whether these measures really tap prejudiced attitudes or whether they tap attitudes toward the issues disguising the measures. For example, the MRS is disguised as a measure of political attitudes; thus it is possible that the MRS is tapping political conservatism rather than prejudice per se (Sinderman, Piazza, Tetlock, & Kendrick, 1991; Sniderman & Tetlock, 1986). Indeed, some of the items on the MRS could conceivably be endorsed by individuals who are nonprejudiced but are against government intervention (e.g., "over the past few years, African Americans have gotten more economically than they deserve").

Second, disguised self-report measures of prejudice have become relatively transparent. That is, respondents are generally able to deduce that the MRS is, in fact, tapping attitudes toward African Americans. For example, people respond to the MRS differently depending on whether the experimenter administering the measure is African American or Caucasian; mean scores on the MRS were lower when the experimenter was African American (Fazio, Jackson, Dunton, & Williams, 1995). Presumably, respondents were motivated to appear nonprejudiced when they believed that an African American experimenter was going to see their responses. Additionally, measures of prejudice such as the MRS obtain floor effects at some universities (e.g., Etling, 1993; LeCount, Maruyama, Petersen, Petersen-Lane, & Thomsen, 1992). In response to these problems, researchers turned to still more subtle measures of prejudice.

Implicit Prejudice

Current perspectives suggest that prejudice exists at two different levels (Devine, 1989; Divine & Monteith, 1993; Divine, Monteith, Zuwerink, & Elliot, 1991; Monteith, 1993; Greenwald & Banaji, 1995; but see also Gilbert & Hixon, 1991). Stereotypes about African Americans are thought to be so overlearned as to be automatically activated by the suggestion or presence of an African American person. That is, the mere sight of an African American individual may evoke stereotype-congruent or stereotype-relevant cognitions (e.g., hostile). One difference between prejudiced and nonprejudiced individuals, however, is in the controlled response to stereotype activation (Devine, Plant, Amodio, Harmon-Jones, & Vance, 2002; see also Lambert et al., 2003). Nonprejudiced individuals are careful to effortfully suppress these stereotypic thoughts, whereas prejudiced individuals are not and thus allow negative stereotypes to influence judgment. This notion that prejudice has automatic and controlled components has been very influential in the development of new measures of prejudice. To the extent that stereotype activation (and subsequent stereotype use) is automatic, a measure that taps automatic processing would seem to lend itself well to the study of prejudice.

Implicit measures are intended to assess attitudes outside of respondents' conscious awareness. That is, implicit measures do not require respondents to consciously consider their attitudes toward the object under consideration—the measures tap automatic evaluations associated with the object. A number of implicit prejudice measures have been developed. Fazio, et al. (1995) developed an implicit priming measure that relies on the automatic activation of evaluative information from memory. Primed words should facilitate the categorization of evaluatively consistent target words, and they should interfere with the categorization of evaluatively inconsistent words. If presented with the negatively valenced prime "cockroach," for example, respondents should be faster to identify "vomit" as bad than to identify "paradise" as good. Conversely, a positive prime such as "flower" should facilitate identification of "paradise" as good and interfere with identification of "vomit" as bad.

The implicit prejudice measure used by Fazio et al. (1995) relied on individual differences in facilitation and interference for identification of positive or negative words when participants were primed by African American or Caucasian faces. Greater prejudice was indicated by the magnitude of each respondent's prime by adjective valence interaction, that is, facilitation for African American-negative, Caucasian-positive pairings and interference for African American-positive, Caucasian-negative pairings. Similar priming-type paradigms were also used to measure prejudice by Dovidio, Kawakami, Johnson, Johnson, and Howard (1997) and by Wittenbrink et al. (1997). A second, qualitatively different measure of implicit prejudiced attitudes was developed by Greenwald, McGhee, and Schwartz (1998).

The Implicit Association Test (IAT; Greenwald et al., 1998) also relies on the automatic activation of attitudes. Rather than relying on a priming technique, however, the IAT requires participants to sort target words into categories. Initially, participants simply have to identify words as belonging to one of two categories. For example, participants must decide, as quickly as possible, whether the word "vomit" is positive or negative; later, participants must decide whether the word "viper" belongs to the snake category or the bird category. During critical trials of the IAT, all four categories are divided into two pairs, e.g., positive or bird versus negative or snake. Participants are again presented with a series of target words, and they must decide to which of the category pairs the word belongs. Completion of the categorization task is facilitated when the category pairs are evaluatively consistent (e.g., positive–bird vs. negative–snake), compared to when the category pairs are inconsistent (e.g., positive–snake vs. negative–bird).

A number of studies now exist demonstrating that reliable individual differences emerge when participants are asked complete the IAT with positive, negative,

African American and Caucasian categories. Initial testing with the IAT provided evidence for implicit prejudice against African Americans by Caucasians, against Koreans by Japanese, and against Japanese by Koreans (Greenwald et al., 1998). Other research has revealed evidence for negative implicit attitudes against both Aboriginals and Asians by Caucasian Australians (Vargas, Forgas, & Williams, 1999), as well as implicit sexism (i.e., facilitation of female-home compared with female-work; Greenwald et al., 2002). More negative implicit attitudes against outgroup members have even emerged following minimal group manipulations (e.g., random assignment to groups ostensibly based on some judgment task; Ashburn-Nardo, Voils, & Monteith, 2001; Greenwald, Pickrell, & Farnham, 2002).

Such measures can be considered valid indicators of prejudice to the extent that they predict a prejudicial outcome, such as a negative judgment or behavior directed at an outgroup member, or are related to self-report prejudice measures. Interestingly, although the methods used to measure implicit prejudice are conceptually similar to one another, their relationships to these validating factors are quite different. Some methods show a significant positive correlation with self-report prejudice measures (e.g., Cunningham, Preacher, & Banaji, 2001; Hense, Penner, & Nelson, 1995; Kawakami et al., 1998; McConnell & Liebold, 2001; Schnake & Ruscher, 1998; Wittenbrink et al., 1997; see also Lepore & Brown, 1997), whereas others do not (e.g., Brauer, Wasel, & Niedenthal, 2000; Dovidio, Kawakami, & Gaertner, 2002; Fazio et al., 1995; Greenwald et al., 1998). Even within methods there are discrepancies (e.g., Dovidio et al., 1997, report both a significant correlation with explicit measures in one experiment and no correlation in another). Furthermore, the utility of implicit measures to predict actual prejudicial behavior seems to be limited to spontaneous (outside of conscious control) behaviors (e.g., Dovidio et al., 1997, 2002; Fazio et al., 1995; McConnell & Liebold, 2001; Wilson, Lindsey, & Schooler, 2000). In the current research we examine these issues with a conceptually distinct measure of implicit prejudice, reflecting the extent to which individuals tend to think in stereotype-congruent terms.

The approach of the current research is not based on a response-time inhibition–facilitation paradigm; indeed, the response required is much more thoughtful and elaborative. The technique is based on the possibility that prejudicial responding involves chronic stereotyping as well as negative affect. Although prejudice and stereotyping are traditionally separated as "feelings" and "beliefs," respectively, evidence indicates that chronic stereotyping and stereotype-affirming processing should lead to discrimination (Dovidio, Brigham, Johnson, & Gaertner, 1996). Fiske (1998) offered a distinction between "hot" discrimination as the result of affect-laden prejudices and "cold" discrimination based on "calm, cool, collective stereotypes" (p. 26). In a similar vein, Brewer and Miller (1996) argued that intergroup bias can result even in groups without a history of "hot" prejudice against one another, as a result of categorization and ingroup favoritism. Thus, it seems that people who chronically engage in stereotypic processing are likely to discriminate against others whether or not they harbor "hot" prejudice against them. Furthermore, although a person may be aware that he or she is engaging in stereotypic processing, this will not necessarily result in discrimination. Even nonconscious stereotypic processing can influence people's reactions to members of other social groups (see Chen & Bargh, 1997). Indeed, it may be that this latter case is when controlling prejudiced reactions is less likely to occur.

PREJUDICE AS PROCESS

In the remainder of this chapter, we discuss work with a few implicit measures of prejudice that are based on biased information processing; more specifically, our measures tap the encoding and interpretation of stereotype-relevant information that is biased toward confirming the stereotype.

Prejudice as Biased Processing

The notion that psychological factors such as mood, expectancies, and attitudes influence information processing is one of the oldest and most pervasive ideas in social psychology (e.g., Allport, 1935; Bruner, 1957; James, 1890; Lewin, 1935). Campbell (1963, p. 97), for example, noted that attitudes contain "residues of experience of such a nature as to *guide, bias, or otherwise influence later behavior*" [italics added], and presumably later information processing as well. Allport (1935, p. 810) suggested that "an attitude is a mental and neural state of readiness, organized through experience, *exerting a directive or dynamic influence* upon the individual's response to all objects and situations with which it is related" [italics added]. Krech and Crutchfield (1948) defined attitude as "an enduring organization of motivational, emotional, perceptual, and cognitive processes with respect to some aspect of the individual's world" (p. 152). Prejudice, as an attitude toward some outgroup, ought to be reflected, at least to some extent, in biased information processing about that group.

How might prejudice be manifested as biased information processing? Among many examples of stereotypic biases available in the literature, we chose to examine two: the linguistic intergroup bias (LIB) and the stereotypic explanatory bias (SEB). The LIB is the tendency to describe others' stereotype-congruent behaviors at a higher level of abstraction than stereotype-incongruent behaviors (Maass, Milesi, Zabbini, & Stahlberg, 1995; Maass, Salvi, Arcuri, & Semin, 1989). For example, if one expects members of the Hell's Angels motorcycle club to be aggressive, seeing a member of the club punch out a police officer would likely elicit an abstract dispositional attribution: "Gee, that Hell's Angels fellow sure is aggressive." In contrast, seeing a member of the club help a little old lady across the street would likely elicit a much more concrete description of the event, such as "Gee, that Hell's Angels fellow is walking a little old lady across the street," rather than a more abstract description, such as "Gee, that Hell's Angels fellow sure is helpful."

Maass et al. (1989, 1995) have suggested that the LIB may be associated with prejudice toward other groups. Additionally, the LIB seems to mediate expectancy maintenance (Karpinski & von Hippel, 1996). Thus, the LIB may be an important cause and consequence of prejudice; and the extent to which one demonstrates the LIB should indicate the degree of prejudice one has (see Schnake & Ruscher, 1998).

The SEB is the tendency for people to be more likely to provide explanations for behaviors that are inconsistent with their expectancies than for behaviors that are consistent with their expectancies (Hastie, 1984). If one expects "Don" to be intelligent, learning that "Don received a D on the test" may instigate attributional processing in an attempt to make sense of the incongruity ("... because he was ill that day"). Learning that "Don received the highest grade in the class," in contrast, is unlikely to instigate attributional processing. Importantly, however, explaining away incongruency renders that information ineffective in changing the perceiver's impression (see Lord, Ross, & Lepper, 1979, Munro & Ditto, 1997). Thus, explanatory biases are both likely to emerge and likely to maintain expectancies in the face of disconfirming evidence. In the same fashion, explanatory biases can help maintain stereotypes in the face of inconsistency. If a person tends to explain stereotype inconsistency but not stereotype consistency, then stereotype inconsistency will have less of an effect on impressions and judgments.

These measures do not, like traditional prejudice measures, require respondents to indicate what they think about the outgroup; rather, these measures operationalize prejudice in terms of encoding processes, or "the proclivity of an individual to think in stereotype-congruent ways," (von Hippel et al., 1995, p. 225). Thus, to the extent that stereotype use results in discrimination (Fiske, 1998), an assessment of stereotype-biased information processing such as the LIB and the SEB may be used as a predictor of prejudicial judgments and behaviors (Sekaquaptewa, Espinoza, Thompson, Vargas, & von Hippel, 2003; von Hippel et al., 1997). We have conducted a number of studies, using two measures of biased information processing, to predict both cognitive and behavioral responses to stereotyped groups. We first review a number of studies that have been conducted by using this approach to prejudice, and then we consider how this approach might be of interest to psychologists, advertisers, and researchers in attitudes and persuasion.

Prejudice and LIB

The first challenge in using the LIB as an individual difference measure of prejudice was in developing an individual difference measure.[3] We developed a series of ersatz newspaper articles featuring African American and Caucasian targets engaging in stereotypically congruent or incongruent behaviors. For example, one article, designed to be stereotype congruent for African Americans, described the winner of a slam-dunk contest as being naturally athletic, a resident in a housing project in the inner city, having a criminal past, and being somewhat ostentatious. Following each article, respondents were presented with four sentences, varying in their level of abstraction, that described the article. Respondents had to indicate the extent to which each sentence did a good job of describing the main point of the article. The last sentence was always a trait-level description of the main character, such as "Johnson is athletic." Greater prejudice was indicated by a respondent's willingness to endorse the most abstract sentences for the stereotype-congruent articles.

In an initial test of the efficacy of the LIB as a measure of prejudice, we sought to compare our new measure with a more traditional, explicit measure of prejudice (the MRS) in predicting evaluations of African American or Caucasian targets (von Hippel et al., 1997). Participants watched a videotaped interaction featuring either an African American or a Caucasian man ask another man for some money. Figure 6.1(a) shows that participants who were low in prejudice according to the

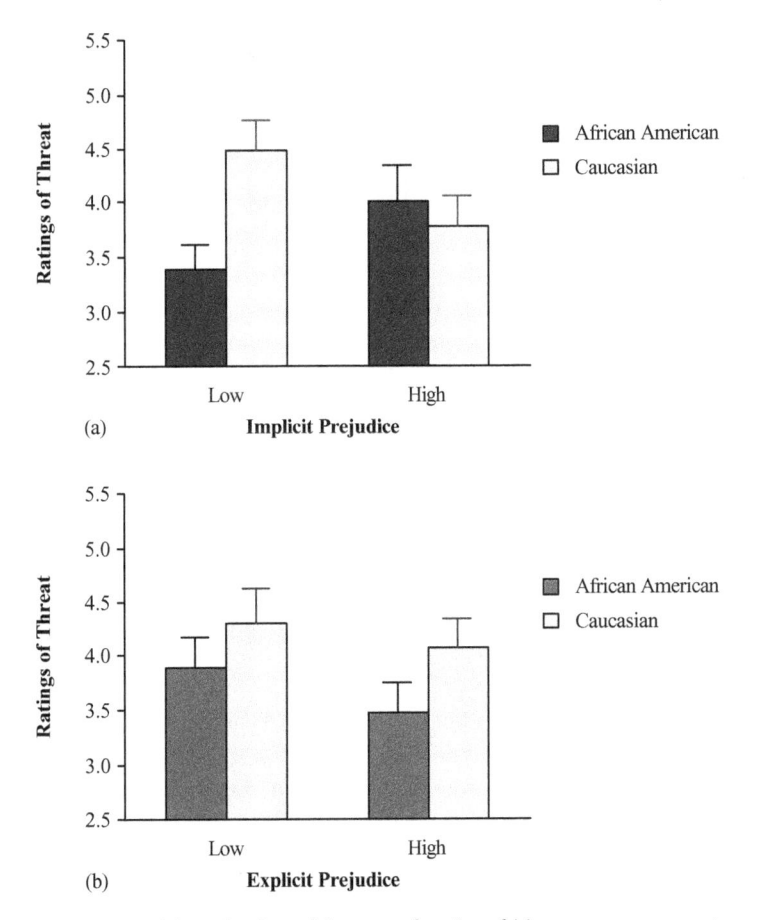

FIG. 6.1. Participants' ratings of threat as a function of (a) stereotype-congruent implicit prejudice and race of the requester and (b) explicit prejudice and race of the requester.

LIB measure rated the White target as more threatening than the African American target. Those high in prejudice showed the opposite pattern: the African American target was (nonsignificantly) more threatening than the White target. Figure 6.1(b) shows no such interaction: high- and low-prejudice MRS respondents both rated the White target as more threatening than the Black target. The LIB measure and the MRS were uncorrelated ($r = -.05$; ns).

One surprising aspect of this first study was that individuals who were identified as high in prejudice, according to the LIB measure, showed very little difference in their ratings of the African American and Caucasian targets. We thought that this might have occurred because of the explicitness of our dependent measure. That is, social desirability concerns may have prevented even highly prejudiced people from describing an African American target as threatening. In a second study using the LIB prejudice measure, we sought to attenuate social desirability concerns by asking more subtle questions about the target. Instead of asking people to indicate how threatening the target was, we asked about their memory for a potentially threatening event, and we also asked for an indirect rating of threat.

Thus, our second study used the same stimuli but different dependent measures. Our first dependent measure asked respondents to recall whether the man asking for money touched the man who was asked for money. We reasoned that a touch on the arm by a stranger asking for money could be an aggressive or threatening act, so recalling a touch on the arm could be a marker indicating the belief that the target is threatening. As can be seen in Fig. 6.2(a), the LIB prejudice measure predicted differential recall for the requester touching the arm of the requestee. Participants who were high in LIB prejudice were more likely to recall a touch when the target was African American, than when he was Caucasian. Recall for participants low in LIB prejudice were unaffected by the race of the target. Note, also, in Fig. 6.2(b), that the MRS showed the opposite pattern: individuals low in prejudice apparently demonstrated more prejudice than did individuals high in prejudice. Additionally, the LIB and MRS measures were, again, uncorrelated with one another ($r = -.05$; ns).

In this same study, we also asked participants about the meekness of the person who was asked for money. The logic behind this request may be best explained by way of example. Imagine someone holding a gun and asking for money. Giving money to an armed, apparently dangerous person would certainly not be considered very meek. However, giving money to an unarmed individual who simply asks for money could certainly seem meek. Similarly, giving money to an African American man would seem not at all meek, if the perceiver believed that African Americans were hostile, dangerous, or threatening. As can be seen in Fig. 6.3(a), individuals high on the LIB prejudice measure thought the man giving money was more meek when he gave money to the Caucasian requester, compared to when he gave money to the African American requester. This implies that high-prejudice individuals perceived the African American requester as more threatening. Individuals low in LIB prejudice showed the opposite pattern: giving money to the African American was perceived as being meek, implying that the African

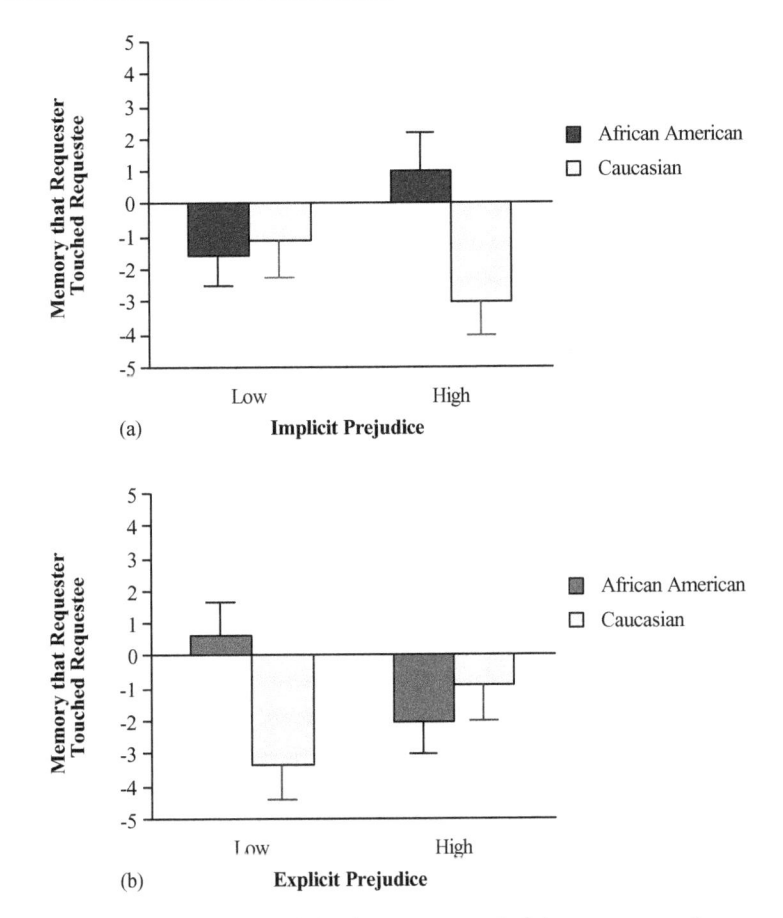

FIG. 6.2. Participants' recall that the requester touched the requestee as a function of (a) stereotype-congruent implicit prejudice and race of the requester and (b) explicit prejudice and race of the requester.

American requester is not very threatening. Once again, the same analysis using the MRS suggested greater prejudice among the low-prejudice respondents; see Fig. 6.3(b). The MRS and LIB measures were uncorrelated with one another ($r = -.03$; *ns*).

Our work using the LIB as an indicator of racial prejudice showed that those who engaged in the LIB were more likely to judge an African American panhandler as more threatening than those who did not engage in the LIB (von Hippel et al., 1997, Experiments 1 and 2). In addition, scores on the LIB measure were unrelated to scores on an traditional prejudice measure, the MRS.

Although many implicit prejudice measures assess racial prejudice, most have been, or theoretically can be, adapted to assess gender prejudice as well (e.g.,

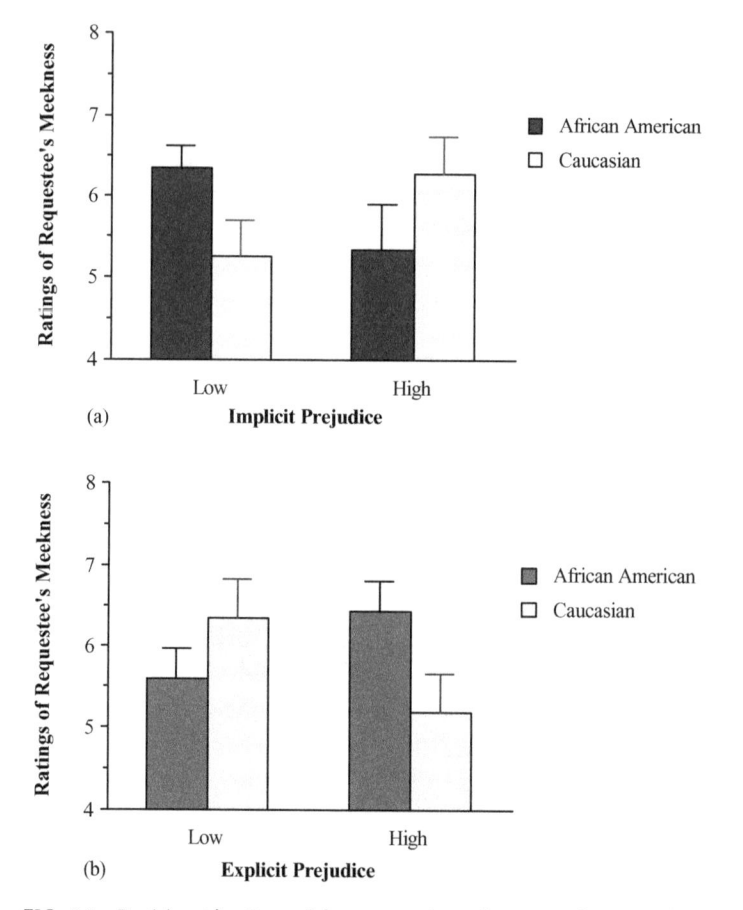

FIG. 6.3. Participants' ratings of the requestee's meekness as a function of (a) stereotype-congruent implicit prejudice and race of the requester and (b) explicit prejudice and race of the requester.

Greenwald et al., 1998; von Hippel et al., 1997). In a third study we sought to expand our repertoire of measures. We did this in two ways: first, we developed an LIB measure of prejudice against women; second, we developed an additional measure of prejudice that also relied on biased information processing—the SEB. For our LIB measure, we again relied on ersatz newspaper articles, written to be consistent with stereotypes for women. For example, one article described a person who was exceptionally dependent on her spouse. After her spouse left her, she had been unable to manage anything around her house (e.g., she was living in the dark because she could not change a blown fuse). Like the race LIB prejudice measure, prejudice was operationalized as the respondents' proclivity to think in stereotype-congruent terms; that is, it was operationalized as the extent to which they endorsed the abstract, stereotype-congruent descriptions of the articles.

The SEB measure consisted of a series of 22 sentence beginnings. Of these sentence beginnings, 10 described gender-neutral behaviors (e.g., Alina brushed her teeth), 6 described stereotypically female behaviors (e.g., Wendy baby-sat the neighbors' kids), and 6 described stereotypically male behaviors (e.g., Steve studied the engineering manual). Half of the behaviors were paired with a male name, and half were paired with a female name, and the specific pairings of a behavior with a name were counterbalanced between subjects. Subjects were instructed to read the sentence beginnings and continue them in any fashion that created a grammatically correct sentence (see Hastie, 1984). Prejudice was operationalized as respondents' proclivity to explain stereotype-incongruent behaviors. For example, the sentence beginning "Tina drove the pickup truck" could be either explained, "because her boyfriend broke his leg," or continued, "with her friends in the back." Note that we did not code for the stereotypicality of the responses (i.e., explicit stereotyping), only whether there was evidence of attributional processing.

Relationships Among Measures of Biased Processing

The goal of this study was simply to examine the relationships among our two measures of biased processing, and an explicit measure of prejudice toward women, the Attitudes Towards Women Scale (ATWS; Spence, Helmreich, & Stapp, 1973). The LIB and SEB measures were correlated with each other ($r = .21$; $p < .01$), whereas neither was correlated with the ATWS ($r < .10$; $p > .25$). This study provided further evidence that prejudice may be conceptualized and operationalized as biased information processing. Two very different types of biased information processing were reliably correlated with one another—people who tended to describe stereotype-congruent events abstractly also tended to explain stereotype-incongruent events.

In a related study (Sekaquaptewa , Vargas, & von Hippel, 1997), we sought to test whether the SEB measure would be correlated with yet another type of biased information processing: recall for stereotype-consistent information. Memory for stereotype-relevant information has received a great deal of empirical attention (for reviews, see Fyock & Stangor, 1994; Rojahn & Pettigrew, 1992; Srull & Wyer, 1989; Stangor & McMillan, 1992). An early and surprising finding from this literature was that expectancy-inconsistent items were often better recalled than expectancy-consistent items (Hastie & Kumar, 1979; Srull, 1981). A meta-analysis of this literature revealed that weak stereotypes or expectancies result in memory-incongruency effects; strong stereotypes or expectancies lead to better recall of consistent information (see Stangor & McMillan, 1992). Thus, it seems that memory for stereotype-relevant information is biased toward stereotype maintenance. To the degree that these attributional and memorial biases reflect a general pattern of stereotype-maintaining cognitive processes, they should be intercorrelated and thus likely to emerge in the same individuals. Just as our previous research showed that people who evince the SEB are also likely to display stereotypic linguistic biases (von Hippel et al., 1997), we hypothesized that people who show the SEB are likely to have biased memorial processing, resulting in better recall for stereotype-confirming information. Furthermore, this bias should be particularly likely if the stereotype-congruent and stereotype-incongruent information is designed to be unambiguous and therefore not amenable to the process of explaining it away. In our next experiment, we explored these ideas.

Male participants came to the lab and were informed that they would be watching some videos and completing some unrelated questionnaires (the SEB sexism measure and the ATWS). They read five different, one-paragraph descriptions of five different video segments, and they were asked to rank-order the videos from those they were most interested in watching to least interested. The experimental manipulation involved two of the video summaries. We manipulated the content of the summaries so that the videos appeared to be either stereotype congruent or incongruent. One summary described a video on race car driving, explaining that men (or women) were biologically better suited to be champion drivers because they tended to be better able to predict the movements of other drivers, diagnose engine trouble by sound, and so on. The other summary described a video about a hunting competition, in which the top winners, who happened to be male (or female), would offer advice on guns and ammo. Each participant read one stereotype-congruent summary and one stereotype-incongruent summary.

Participants' SEB scores were reliably correlated with recall for the stereotype-congruent race car driver video ($r = .26$, $p < .03$). Individuals who were more likely to explain stereotype-incongruent information on the SEB were also more likely to recall stereotype-congruent information about the race car driver summary. There was no relationship between SEB scores and recall for the stereotype-incongruent race car driver summary (i.e., that women were genetically superior drivers) ($r = -.08$, $p = .51$). Thus, SEB scores predicted enhanced recall for stereotype-congruent information but not diminished recall for stereotype-incongruent information. Participants' ATWS scores were unrelated to recall for either stereotype-congruent ($r = .06$, $p = .60$) or stereotype-incongruent ($r = .07$, $p = .58$) information.

Participants' SEB scores were not correlated with either the stereotype-congruent or stereotype-incongruent hunting video summaries ($r = -.02$, $p = .85$, and $r = -.03$, $p = .81$, respectively). Likewise, ATWS scores were not correlated with either the stereotype-congruent or stereotype-incongruent hunting video summaries ($r = .10$, $p = .43$, and $r = .02$, $p = .89$, respectively).

Why might individuals who tend to explain stereotype-incongruent behaviors (i.e., individuals high in SEB sexism) remember more stereotype-congruent information? At first glance, this seems contrary to what one might expect—greater attributional processing of stereotype-incongruent material should lead to better recall (Hastie, 1984; Srull & Wyer, 1989). However, the SEB items and the racing story differ quite strongly in the extent to which they are incongruent. The SEB items are only mildly stereotype incongruent (e.g., Jane read the engineering manual), whereas the racing summary was very stereotype incongruent (e.g., women are naturally gifted at racing). Following the meta-analytic review of memory for unexpected events (Stangor & McMillan, 1992), mildly incongruent events ought to instigate attributional processing (as in the SEB measure) and strongly congruent events ought to be better remembered (as in the video-summary recall).

Also interesting is the fact that SEB predicted enhanced recall for stereotype-congruent information but not diminished recall for stereotype-incongruent information. That is, SEB sexism may be manifested as ingroup favoritism rather than outgroup derogation. This type of prejudice was noted previously—Brewer and Miller (1996) suggested that prejudice may be expressed as "preferential treatment of those who share a common category membership [that] produces biases that benefit the ingroup ... even without any negative prejudice against outgroups" (p. 48). Although this perspective on prejudice helps explain the results from the racing summary, it does not explain the lack of findings from the hunting summary.

The failure to replicate differences by SEB level across both racing and hunting summaries may simply be due to an idiosyncrasy in the study, or it may be due to some systematic difference in the materials. In the female version of the race car summary, evidence is provided suggesting that women are genetically superior to men on many of the characteristics that are most important to race car drivers. These gender differences are provided as a general truth about the categories men and women, and were thus designed to be difficult to explain away. In contrast, the female version of the hunter summary describes a specific counterstereotypic event—a group of women have won in a stereotypically masculine event. Because such an event could be considered atypical, respondents may have simply discounted the summary as an example of masculine women, or an amusing episode of "News of the Weird." In any event, the results of this study do provide at least preliminary evidence that the measure may be used to predict cognitive responding to conuterstereotypical events.

What remains to be seen is whether a scale assessing SEB can itself predict independent variance in judgments and behavior and thus be considered a useful measure of implicit prejudice. The goal of our next set of studies (Sekaquaptewa et al., 1997) was to test this possibility.

Prejudice and SEB

To test whether the SEB sexism measure would predict sexist behaviors, we modeled a study after Rudman and Borgida (1995). More specifically, male participants came to a lab and were informed that they were to help train a (male or female) research assistant (RA) for a role the RA would be playing in an upcoming experiment. In this study we employed two female confederates—one who dressed as a traditional female (flowery dress, makeup, long hair), and one who dressed as a nontraditional female (men's clothing, no makeup, very short hair, and a T-shirt with the slogan, "This is what a feminist looks like.") in order to see whether differences emerged for stereotype-congruent and stereotype-incongruent targets. As a part of this training, participants would be interviewing the RA for a position as restaurant supervisor. Participants were presented with a clipboard listing questions that they could ask the RA. The questions on the clipboard were arranged in pairs; each pair asked essentially the same thing, but one of the questions always had a sexist tone to it. For example, participants could ask either "Do you have any physical restrictions that we should know about?" (nonsexist) or "Will you need one of the maintenance men to help you unload boxes from the delivery truck?" (sexist). In this study, the primary dependent measure was the number of sexist questions that participants selected. In addition, immediately following the interview, the RAs rated the participants on liking and friendliness. These ratings were collapsed into a single impression score.

As can be seen in Fig. 6.4(a) individuals who were high in SEB sexism tended to ask more sexist questions of the traditional female RA than individuals who were

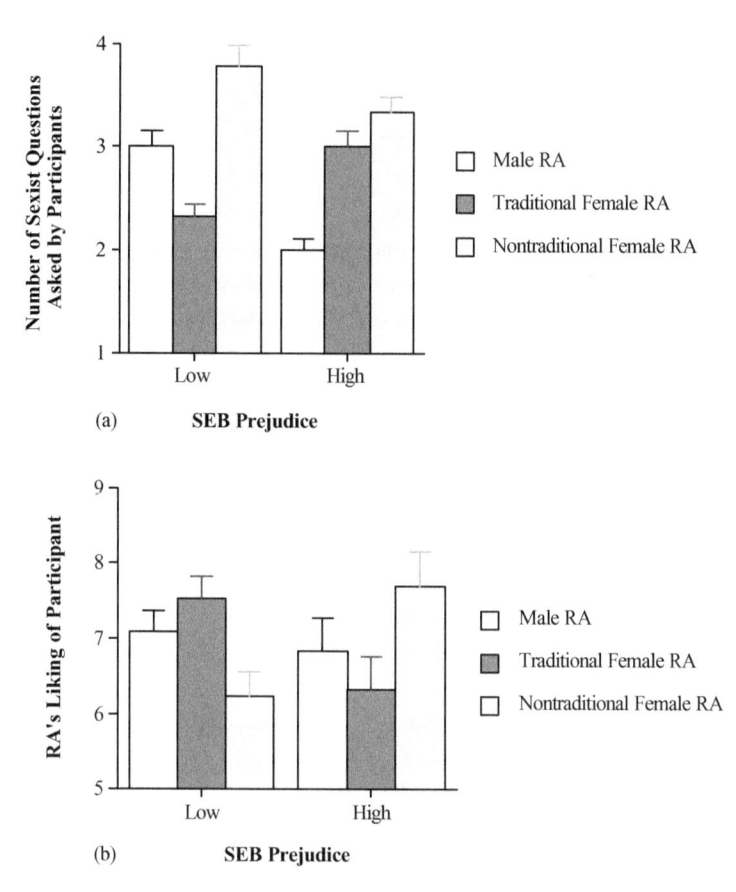

FIG. 6.4.   (a) Number of sexist questions asked by participants as a function of SEB prejudice and RA type (b) RAs' liking of participants as a function of participants' SEB prejudice and RA type.

low in SEB sexism. There were no differences by SEB sexism in the sexist questions asked of the nontraditional female. Individuals high in SEB sexism also asked fewer sexist questions of the male RA compared with individuals low in SEB sexism. No significant effects emerged when the ATWS was used.

As predicted, men who were more likely to explain mildly stereotype-incongruent behaviors were more likely to behave in a sexist manner toward a traditional woman. The lack of a difference for high and low SEB participants in number of sexist questions asked of the nontraditional woman may be due to the participants' awareness of the inappropriateness of asking sexist questions to a woman wearing a T-shirt with a feminist slogan; or it may be due to a tendency to discriminate only against stereotype-congruent targets. Stereotype-incongruent targets may not elicit stereotyping or prejudiced behavior (e.g., Banaji, Hardin, & Rothman, 1993). Somewhat surprisingly, individuals high on the SEB measure were less likely to ask sexist questions of other men, compared with individuals low on the SEB measure. This difference may have emerged because high SEB partici-pants were attending to the sexist quality of some of the questions and felt that they were inappropriate for other men—somehow threatening to their masculinity or otherwise insulting. Nonsexist participants may not have been so concerned with sex roles and therefore would not have avoided the sexist questions when inter-viewing a male RA.

As can be seen in Figure 6.4(b), there was a significant interaction for the RAs' impressions of the participant by SEB sexism and RA gender. The male RA's ratings did not differ depending on the participant's SEB level, but both female RAs differed in their evaluations of the high and low SEB participants. The traditional female RA liked low SEB men more than she liked high SEB men. The nontraditional female RA, in contrast, liked the high SEB men more than she liked the low SEB men. No significant effects emerged when the ATWS was used.

As predicted, a male confederate showed no difference in his impressions of high and low SEB participants, and a traditional female confederate liked individ-uals who were low in sexism over those who were high in sexism. But why did the nontraditional female confederate like the high sexist participants better than the low sexist participants? One possibility is that sexist men tend to treat traditional-looking women in a sexist manner, but they do not treat nontraditional-looking women the same way. The nontraditional confederate may have liked the sexist men more because they did not treat her in a stereotypical fashion. Consistent with this hypothesis, recall that high and low SEB participants did not differ in the num-ber of sexist questions asked of the nontraditional woman. However, number of sexist questions was not correlated with the RAs' impression scores ($r = -.16$; ns), suggesting that impressions were not entirely driven by question choice. Alterna-tively, this interaction may have emerged as a result of high SEB men's treating the traditional woman as a potential dating partner, and low SEB men's treating the nontraditional woman as a potential dating partner. Negative impressions could have emerged to the extent that high and low SEB male participants were leering at the traditional and nontraditional female RAs, respectively.

We have presented a number of studies demonstrating that our implicit prejudice–sexism measures reliably predict cognitive and behavioral responses to outgroup members, whereas more explicit measures (MRS and ATWS) do not. Given that our implicit measures are qualitatively different from response-time-based implicit prejudice measures, next we decided to compare our measure with a response-time-based implicit measure of prejudice—the Implicit Association Test (IAT; Greenwald et al., 1998).

We used a paradigm similar to that used in the previous study, although this time we returned to a focus on prejudice against African Americans. We adapted the SEB sexism measure to feature stereotypically African American and Caucasian names and behaviors (e.g., "Marcellus easily made the team" and "Adam got a job at Microsoft" are both stereotype congruent; they would be stereotype incongruent if the names were reversed). Participants were randomly assigned to play a game with either an African American or Caucasian confederate. The primary dependent measures were the confederates' ratings of the participants' behaviors (made eye contact, initiated conversation, crossed his or her arms) and the confederates' impressions of the participants themselves (friendly, selfish, etc.). These were both coded such that higher numbers reflected greater positivity; hereafter they are referred to as behavior and feeling scores, respectively.

Both implicit prejudice measures, as well as the MRS, were entered in four, separate simultaneous multiple regression analyses to predict behavior and feeling scores for both African American and Caucasian confederates (see Table 6.1). First, both implicit measures predicted unique variance in the African American confederates' feeling scores, but the explicit measure did not. African American confederates reported less positivity toward individuals who showed greater levels of the SEB and toward individuals who showed more implicit prejudice on the

TABLE 6.1
Positive Feelings and Behavior Scores of Black and White Confederates

	Black			White		
	Test	β	p	Test	β	p
Feelings						
	SEB	−.628	.01	SEB	−.227	.23
	IAT	−.506	.02	IAT	−.045	.81
	MRS	.243	.27	MRS	.210	.27
Behaviors						
	SEB	−.495	.05	SEB	−.195	.31
	IAT	−.492	.05	IAT	−.235	.22
	MRS	.373	.12	MRS	.004	.98

IAT. Second, none of the measures predicted the Caucasian confederates' feeling scores. Third, both implicit measures predicted unique variance in the African American confederates' behavior scores, but the explicit measure did not. African American confederates reported seeing fewer positive behaviors from individuals who showed greater levels of the SEB, and from individuals who showed more implicit prejudice on the IAT. Fourth, none of the measures predicted the Caucasian confederates' behavior scores. Thus, both the SEB and the IAT predicted unique variance, above and beyond one another, in how African American confederates felt about participants, and in the number of positive behaviors reported by the African American confederates. The two implicit measures were uncorrelated ($r = -.13$), and the SEB was uncorrelated with the explicit measure ($r < .01$), but the IAT was correlated with the explicit measure ($r = .30$).

This study offers further support that implicit measures of prejudice that rely on biased information processing (SEB) can aid in the prediction of prejudiced behavior. Importantly, the measure of biased processing predicted unique variance, beyond that predicted by a response-time-based implicit measure, in both feelings and behaviors.

GENERAL DISCUSSION

The results of these experiments provide evidence that implicit measures of prejudice based on biased information processing can predict both cognitive and behavioral reactions to members of stereotyped groups. The research by Maass et al. (1989, 1995) suggests that the LIB may be associated with prejudice toward other groups. In our first pair of studies, our adaptation of the LIB reliably predicted judgments about a videotaped interaction featuring either an African American or a Caucasian panhandler who requested money from a Caucasian. A traditional, more explicit measure of prejudice, the MRS McConahey et al., 1981), obtained inconsistent patterns that were often contrary to the LIB measure: high-prejudice participants perceived the Caucasian to be more threatening than the African American, and vice versa for low-prejudice participants.

In attempting to expand the utility and validity of the bias approach to measuring prejudice, a second set of studies (Sekaquaptewa et al., 1997) was designed to predict prejudice toward women, or sexism. This set of studies relied on a different measure of biased processing, which we had previously found to be correlated with the LIB (von Hippel et al., 1995), that is, the SEB. Individuals who showed the SEB had better memory for stereotype-consistent stories, and people who didn't show the SEB had a nonsignificant reversal of this effect. A further study used the SEB to predict sexist behavior during a mock interview for a restaurant job. Participants in both studies also completed a traditional, explicit questionnaire assessing sexism, that is, the ATWS (Spence et al., 1973); however, participants' ATWS scores were unrelated to the dependent variables in both studies. Finally, the SEB measure was adapted to assess prejudice against African Americans and reliably predicted unique variance (beyond that predicted by a response-time-based measure of prejudice, that is, the IAT) in African American confederates' liking of participants, as well as the frequency of positive behaviors when interacting with an African American confederate.

Together these studies suggest that there is an important information processing component to prejudice. Whereas most paper-and-pencil measures of prejudice require respondents to indicate their attitudes toward stereotyped outgroup members, or issues ostensibly unrelated to prejudice, the present measures rely on individuals' information processing biases. These ideas form the basis of the information processing perspective on prejudice (von Hippel et al., 1995), which indicates that prejudice involves not only the content of negative attitudes but also the way that people process information about outgroup members.

There are a number of notable implications of this approach to prejudice that may be of interest to psychologists, advertisers, and persuasion researchers, in general. First, attempts to measure prejudice would benefit from adding a measure of biased information processing. These measures have an advantage over more traditional measures of prejudice (e.g., the MRS and ATWS) in that they are relatively implicit, relying on biases in information processing rather than on explicit evaluations concerning members of stereotyped groups. Even if people are aware that these measures are somehow tapping information about socially undesirable attitudes, respondents may not know how to alter their responses to appear nonprejudiced. Biases in information processing should be more difficult to control than explicit evaluations. Furthermore, these measures of prejudice have an advantage over other implicit attitude measures (e.g., the IAT) in that they are comparatively easy to administer and score. It also appears that implicit measures tapping biased processing may be unrelated to implicit measures based on response-time paradigms; therefore, bias measures may provide information beyond that provided by response-time-based measures. We would not, of course, advocate the elimination of more traditional disguised self-report measures of prejudice, but rather we suggest that both types of measures can be useful in predicting responses to stereotyped outgroups (e.g., Fazio et al., 1995).

Second, because measures of biased information processing have been demonstrated to predict cognitive and behavioral responses to information about stereotyped group members, we might expect that such measures would be particularly useful for researchers looking to understand responses to persuasive communications. That is, the tendency toward biased information processing may be an important factor in the relationship between argument quality and attitude change, particularly for information presented by members of stereotyped groups (e.g., Petty, Fleming, & White, 1998, Vargas, 2003; White & Harkins, 1995). In addition, the biased processing approach to prejudice might suggest that individuals who tend to process information in stereotype-congruent ways would be less likely to recall information presented by stereotyped group members, particularly when that information is incongruent with their stereotypes. Thus, attempts to reduce prejudice by portraying outgroup members in stereotype-incongruent ways would be met with indifference by a prejudiced audience, as such people would tend to explain away mild incongruency and dismiss extreme incongruency.

Third, measures of biased processing may also be used to assess other socially undesirable attitudes and to predict socially undesirable behaviors (e.g., dishonesty; Vargas, von Hippel, & Petty, in press). In advertising or consumer behavior, for example, bias measures may tap nationalistic biases against Japanese products, where other, more direct measures would not.

Fourth, this biased processing approach to measuring prejudice suggests that prejudice is unlikely to be significantly reduced by simply presenting new, individuating, or counterstereotypical information about stereotyped group members. Efforts to reduce prejudice would also benefit by addressing changes in processing style (Devine et al., 1991; Monteith, 1993; Monteith, Sherman, & Devine, 1998). Divine, Monteith, and colleagues have referred to prejudice as "a bad habit" that can be broken: people seem to have knowledge in place that both supports and rejects stereotypes—people know the stereotypes, but they also know that the stereotypes are frowned upon and may be false. Because content-based and biased processing measures tend to be independent of one another, simply teaching people new content may not successfully replace stereotype-congruent ways of thinking. By teaching people new, stereotype-incongruent ways of processing information about African Americans (Hispanics, women, etc.), one may be able to reduce prejudice. It will also be important to learn whether newly learned processing strategies to stereotyped outgroup members will be more resistant to decay than content-based persuasive appeals.

Fifth, the biased information processing approach to the measurement of prejudiced attitudes has also proven to be useful in the study of attitudes more generally. A series of studies by Vargas et al. (in press) have relied on a slightly different measure of biased information processing to predict both self-reported and actual behavior, regardless of social desirability concerns.

In these studies, we developed an implicit attitude measure that relied on the tendency for people's attitudes to color the way they perceive events. This is a very intuitively appealing idea that may be best exemplified by the way in which two people can observe the exact same event yet "see" very different things. Consider two fans of opposing baseball teams watching a close play at home plate—the runner and the ball are speeding toward the plate at the same time, the runner crashes into the catcher at the same time the ball reaches the catcher's glove, there is a cloud of dust, and . . . the umpire shouts "Safe!" Both fans were privy to the exact same objective event, but their differential perceptions of the event cause one fan to jump up for joy and the other to groan woefully about how runner was "out by a mile."

Our implicit measures may not have been quite so dramatic, but they were effective predictors of behavior, beyond what was predicted by traditional, explicit attitude measures. We relied on a well-known attitudinal bias, contrast effects (Sherif & Hovland, 1963), as an implicit measure of attitudes. The measures consisted of a series of brief vignettes, each of which described a different individual engaging in ambiguous or inconsistent behaviors. For example, one of the vignettes used to assess attitudes toward religion read as follows:

> Mary didn't go to church once the whole time she was in college, but she claimed that she was still a very religious person. She said that she prayed occasionally, and that she believed in Christian ideals. Sometimes she watched religious programs on TV like the 700 Club, or the Billy Graham Crusade.

Following each of these vignettes, participants were asked to indicate the extent to which the target was religious. According to the logic behind this measure, these behaviors should fall in latitudes of rejection for both religious and atheistic people alike. In this way, the targets should be perceived as relatively atheistic by religious people, and as relatively religious by atheistic people. Indeed, this was the case. Perceived religiosity reliably predicted self-reported behavior.

In four studies, using three different attitude objects, we were able to use implicit attitude measures tapping biased information processing to predict unique variance in both self-reported and actual behavior, whether social desirability was a concern (e.g., attitudes toward dishonesty) or not (e.g., attitudes toward religion; political conservatism). Furthermore, the implicit measures were consistently unrelated to explicit attitude measures. Perhaps most importantly, with the use of simultaneous multiple regression equations, the implicit measures predicted unique variance in self-reported and actual behavior, above and beyond what was predicted by the explicit attitude measures. In all cases the implicit attitude measures significantly increased the amount of explained variance.

CONCLUSIONS

The research reviewed in this chapter offers some evidence that implicit measures of prejudice that tap biased information processing can be quite useful in predicting cognitive and behavioral responses to stigmatized others. The primary benefit of these measures, over more traditional prejudice measures such as the MRS, is self-evident: namely, the bias measures may be implicit—they do not seem to be susceptible to social desirability concerns. An additional reason that the implicit measures described herein may be particularly attractive is their relative ease of use. Implicit prejudice measures relying on automatic evaluations of, say, African Americans require quite sophisticated computing facilities (Dovidio et al., 1997; Fazio et al., 1995), whereas the SEB and LIB measures require nothing more than paper and pencil. Furthermore, both the SEB and LIB measures hint at processes that help individuals maintain stereotypes and prejudice. Thus, they suggest that encountering stereotype-incongruent individuals will have little lasting effect on prejudice, and that simply teaching people that stereotypes are untrue or otherwise harmful will have little effect on prejudice. A more effective way of reducing prejudice would involve actually changing not just *what* we, as a society, think about stigmatized others, but also changing *how* we think about them.

More broadly, this biased processing approach to measuring attitudes seems to be beneficial regardless of social desirability concerns. Implicit attitude measures have generally been reserved for use when social desirability concerns have been expected to limit the efficacy of direct measures. However, recent research has suggested that implicit measures tapping biased processing may be of use even when social desirability is not a concern. The notion that behavior is guided not only by *what* we think but also by *how* we think suggests that attitudes have an important processing component. To the extent that we can measure this biasing component of attitudes, we will have taken an important step in reaching toward some of social psychology's most important goals: expanding our understanding of the attitude construct and enhancing our ability to predict behavior.

REFERENCES

Adorno, T. W., Frenkel-Brunswick, E., Levinson, D. J., & Sanford, R. N. (1950). *The authoritarian personality.* New York: Harper.

Allport, G. W. (1935). Attitudes. In C. Murchison (Ed.), *Handbook of social psychology* (pp. 133–175). Worcester, MA: Clark University Press.

Ashburn-Nardo, L., Voils, C. I., & Monteith, M. J. (2001). Implicit associations as the seeds of intergroup bias: How easily do they take root? *Journal of Personality and Social Psychology, 81,* 789–799.

Banaji, M. R., Hardin, C., & Rothman, A. J. (1993). Implicit stereotyping in person judgment. *Journal of Personality and Social Psychology, 68,* 181–198.

Benson, P. L., Karabenick, S. A., & Lerner, R. M. (1976). Pretty pleases: The effects of physical attractiveness, race, and sex on receiving help. *Journal of Experimental Social Psychology, 12,* 409–415.

Brauer, M., Wasel, W., & Niedenthal, P. (2000). Implicit and explicit components of prejudice. *Review of General Psychology, 4,* 79–101.

Brewer, M. B., & Miller, N. (1996). *Intergroup relations.* Pacific Grove, CA: Brooks/Cole.

Brown, R. (1965). *Social psychology.* New York: The Free Press.

Bruner, J. S. (1957). On perceptual readiness. *Psychological Review, 89,* 369–406.

Campbell, D. T. (1963). Social attitudes and other acquired behavioral dispositions. In S. Koch (Ed.), *Psychology: A study of a science* (Vol. 6, pp. 94–172). New York: McGraw-Hill.

Chen, M., & Bargh, J. (1997). Nonconscious behavioral confirmation processes: The self-fulfilling consequences of automatic stereotype activation. *Journal of Experimental Social Psychology, 33,* 541–560.

Cunningham, W. A., Preacher, K. J., & Banaji, M. R. (2001). Implicit attitude measures: Consistency, stability, and convergent validity. *Psychological Science, 121,* 163–170.

Crosby, F., Bromley, S., & Saxe, L. (1980). Recent unobtrusive studies of black and white discrimination and prejudice: A literature review. *Psychological Bulletin, 87,* 546–563.

Devine, P. G. (1989). Stereotype and prejudice: Their automatic and controlled components. *Journal of Personality and Social Psychology, 56,* 5–18.

Devine, P. G., & Monteith, M. J. (1993). The role of discrepancy-associated affect in prejudice reduction. In D. E. Mackie & D. L. Hamilton (Eds.), *Affect, cognition, and stereotyping: Interactive processes in group perception* (pp. 317–344). San Diego, CA: Academic Press.

Devine, P. G., Monteith, M. J., Zuwerink, J. R., & Elliot, A. J. (1991). Prejudice with and without compunction. *Journal of Personality and Social Psychology, 60,* 817–830.

Devine, P. G., Plant, E. A., Amodio, D. M., Harmon-Jones, E., & Vance, S. L. (2002). The regulation of explicit and implicit race bias: The role of motivations to respond without prejudice. *Journal of Personality and Social Psychology, 82,* 835–848.

Donnerstein, E., & Donnerstein, M. (1975). White rewarding behavior as a function of potential for black retaliation. *Journal of Personality and Social Psychology, 24,* 327–333.

Dovidio, J. F., Brigham, J. C., Johnson, B. T., & Gaertner, S. L. (1996). Stereotyping, prejudice, and discrimination: Another look. In N. Macrae, C. Stangor, & M. Hewstone (Eds.), *Stereotypes and stereotyping* (pp. 276–319). New York: Guilford.

Dovidio, J., Kawakami, K., & Gaertner, S. (2002). Implicit and explicit prejudice and interracial interaction. *Journal of Personality and Social Psychology, 82,* 62–68.

Dovidio, J., Kawakami, K., Johnson, C., Johnson, B., & Howard, A. (1997). On the nature of prejudice: Automatic and controlled processes. *Journal of Experimental Social Psychology, 33,* 510–540.

Etling, K. (1993). *Stereotyping of African-American businesspeople: The effects of cognitive load, target race, performance level, and racism level.* Unpublished master's thesis, University of Virginia, Charlottesville, VA.

Fazio, R. H., Jackson, J. R., Dunton, B. C., & Williams, C. J. (1995). Variability in automatic activation as an unobtrusive measure of racial attitudes: A bona fide pipeline? *Journal of Personality and Social Psychology, 69,* 1013–1027.

Fiske, S. T. (1998). Stereotypes, prejudice, and discrimination. In D. T. Gilbert, S. T. Fiske, & G. Lindzey (Eds.), *The handbook of social psychology* (4th ed.). New York: McGraw-Hill.

Fyock, J., & Stangor, C. (1994). The role of memory biases in stereotype maintenance. *British Journal of Social Psychology, 33,* 331–343.

Gaertner, S. L., & Dovidio, J. F. (1986). The aversive form of racism. In J. F. Dovidio and S. L. Gaertner (Eds.), *Prejudice, discrimination, and racism* (pp. 61–89). San Diego, CA: Academic Press.

Gilbert, D. T., & Hixon, J. G. (1991). The trouble of thinking: Activation and application of stereotypic beliefs. *Journal of Personality and Social Psychology, 60,* 509–517.

Greenwald, A. G., & Banaji, M. R. (1995). Implicit social cognition: Attitudes, stereotypes, and self-concept. *Psychological Review, 102,* 4–27.

Greenwald, A. G., Banaji, M. R., Rudman, L. A., Farnham, S. D., Nosek, B. A., & Mellott, D. S. (2002). A unified theory of implicit attitudes, stereotypes, self-esteem, and self-concept. *Psychological Review, 109,* 3–25.

Greenwald, A. G., Pickrell, J. E., & Farnham, S. D. (2002). Implicit partisanship: Taking sides for no reason. *Journal of Personality and Social Psychology, 83,* 367–379.

Greenwald, A. G., McGhee, D. E., & Schwartz, J. L. K. (1998). Measuring individual differences in implicit cognition: The Implicit Association Test. *Journal of Personality and Social Psychology, 74,* 1464–1480.

Hastie, R. (1984). Causes and effects of causal attribution. *Journal of Personality and Social Psychology, 46,* 44–56.

Hastie, R., & Kumar, P. A. (1979). Person memory: Personality traits as organizing principles in memory for behaviors. *Journal of Personality and Social Psychology, 37,* 25–38.

Hense, R., Penner, L., & Nelson, D. (1995). Implicit memory for age stereotypes. *Social Cognition, 13,* 399–415.

James, W. (1890). *The principles of psychology.* New York: Dover.

Katz, D., & Braly, K. W. (1933). Racial stereotypes of 100 college students. *Journal of Abnormal and Social Psychology, 28,* 280–290.

Katz, I., & Hass, R. G. (1988). Racial ambivalence and value conflict: Correlational and priming studies of dual cognitive structures. *Journal of Personality and Social Psychology, 55,* 893–905.

Karpinski, A., & von Hippel, W. (1996). The role of the linguistic intergroup bias in expectancy maintenance. *Social Cognition, 14,* 141–163.

Kawakami, K., Dion, K., & Dovidio, J. F. (1998). Racial prejudice and stereotype activation. *Personality and Social Psychology Bulletin, 24*, 407–416.

Kinder, D. R., & Sears, D. O. (1981). Prejudice and politics: Symbolic racism versus racial threats to the good life. *Journal of Personality and Social Psychology, 40*, 414–431.

Krech, D., & Crutchfield, R. (1948). *Theory and problems of social psychology.* New York: McGraw-Hill.

Lambert, A. J., Payne, B. K., Jacoby, L. L., Shaffer, L. M., Chasteen, A. L., & Khan, S. R. (2003). Stereotypes as dominant responses: On the "social facilitation" of prejudice in anticipated public contexts. *Journal of Personality and Social Psychology, 84*, 277–295.

LeCount, J., Maruyama, G., Petersen, R. S., Petersen-Lane, R. P., & Thomsen, C. J. (1992). *How reactive are measures of modern racism?* Paper presented at the 100th annual meeting of the American Psychological Association, Washington, DC.

Lepore, L., & Brown, R. (1997). Category and stereotype activation: Is prejudice inevitable? *Journal of Personality and Social Psychology, 72*, 275–287.

Lewin, K. (1935). *A dynamic theory of personality.* New York: McGraw-Hill.

Lord, C. G., Ross, L., & Lepper, M. (1979). Biased assimilation and attitude polarization: The effects of prior theories on subsequently considered evidence. *Journal of Personality and Social Psychology, 37*, 2098–2109.

Maass, A., Milesi, A., Zabbini, S., & Stahlberg, D. (1995). Linguistic intergroup bias: Differential expectancies or in-group protection? *Journal of Personality and Social Psychology, 68*, 116–126.

Maass, A., Salvi, D., Arcuri, L., & Semin, G. (1989). Language use in intergroup contexts: The linguistic intergroup bias. *Journal of Personality and Social Psychology, 57*, 981–993.

McConahay, J. B., Hardee, B. B., & Batts, V. (1981). Has racism declined? It depends on who's asking and what is asked. *Journal of Conflict Resolution, 25*, 563–579.

McConahay, J. B., & Hough, J. C., Jr. (1976). Symbolic racism. *Journal of Social Issues, 32*, 23–45.

McConnell, A. R., & Liebold, J. M. (2001). Relations among the Implicit Association Test, discriminatory behavior, and explicit measures of racial attitudes. *Journal of Experimental Social Psychology, 37*, 435–442.

Monteith, M. J. (1993). Self-regulation of prejudiced responses: Implications for progress in prejudice-reduction efforts. *Journal of Personality and Social Psychology, 65*, 469–485.

Monteith, M. J., Sherman, J. W., & Devine, P. G. (1998). Suppression as a stereotype control strategy. *Personality and Social Psychology Review, 2*, 63–82.

Munro, G. D., & Ditto, P. H. (1997). Biased assimilation, attitude polarization, and affect in reactions to stereotype-relevant scientific information. *Personality and Social Psychology Bulletin, 23*, 636–653.

Petty, R. E., Fleming, M. A., & White, P. H. (1999). Stigmatized sources and persuasion: Prejudice as a determinant of argument scrutiny. *Journal of Personality and Social Psychology, 76*, 19–34.

Pratto, F., Sidanius, J., Stallworth, L. M., & Malle, B. F. (1994). Social dominance orientation: A personality variable predicting social and political attitudes. *Journal of Personality and Social Psychology, 67*, 741–763.

Rojahn, K., & Pettigrew, T. F. (1992). Memory for schema-relevant information: A meta-analytic resolution. *British Journal of Social Psychology, 31*, 81–109.

Rudman, L., & Borgida, E. N. (1995). The afterglow of construct accessibility: The behavioral consequence of priming men to view women as sexual objects. *Journal of Experimental Social Psychology, 6*, 493–517.

Schnake, S. B., & Ruscher, J. B. (1998). Modern racism as a predictor of the linguistic intergroup bias. *Journal of Language and Social Psychology, 17*, 484–491.

Schuman, H., Steeh, C., & Bobo, L. (1985). *Racial attitudes in America: Trends and interpretation.* Cambridge, MA: Harvard University Press.

Sears, D. O, & Kinder D. R. (1971). Racial tensions and voting in Los Angeles. In W. Z. Hirsch (Ed.), *Los Angeles: Viability and prospects for metropolitan leadership.* New York: Praeger.

Sears, D. O., & McConahay J. B. (1973). *The politics of violence: The new urban blacks and the Watts Riot.* Boston: Houghton Mifflin.

Sekaquaptewa, D., Espinoza, P., Thompson, M., Vargas, P. T., & von Hippel, W. (2003). Stereotypic explanatory bias: Implicit stereotyping as a predictor of discrimination. *Journal of Experimental Social Psychology, 39,* 75–82.

Sekaquaptewa, D., Vargas, P., & von Hippel, W. (1997). *Explanatory bias as an implicit indicator of prejudice.* Symposium presentation at the New England Social Psychological Association Conference, Williamstown, MA.

Sherif, M., & Hovland, C. I. (1963). *Social judgment: Assimilation and contrast effects in communication and attitude change.* New Haven, CT: Yale University Press.

Sidanius, J., Pratto, F., & Bobo, L. (1996). Racism, conservatism, affirmative action, and intellectual sophistication: A matter of principled conservatism or group dominance? *Journal of Personality and Social Psychology, 70,* 476–490.

Sniderman, P. M., Piazza, T., Tetlock, P. E., & Kendrick, A. (1991). The new racism. *American Journal of Political Science, 35,* 423–447.

Sniderman, P. M., & Tetlock, P. E. (1986). Symbolic racism: Problems of political motive attribution. *Journal of Social Issues, 42,* 129–150.

Spence, J., Helmreich, R., & Stapp, J. (1973). A short version of the Attitudes Toward Women Scale. *Bulletin of the Psychonomic Society, 2,* 219–220.

Srull, T. K. (1981). Person memory: Some tests of associative storage and retrieval models. *Journal of Experimental Psychology: Human Learning and Memory, 7,* 440–463.

Srull, T. K., & Wyer, R. S. (1989). Person memory and judgment. *Psychological Review, 96,* 58–83.

Stangor, C., & McMillan, D. (1992). Memory for expectancy-congruent and expectancy-incongruent information: A review of the social and social developmental literatures. *Psychological Bulletin, 1,* 42–61.

Strobe, W., & Insko, C. A. (1989). Stereotypes, prejudice, and discrimination: Changing conceptions in theory and research. In D. Bar-Tal, C. F. Grauman, A. W. Kruglanski, & W. Strobe (Eds.), *Stereotypes and prejudice: Changing conceptions* (pp. 3–34). New York: Springer.

Vargas, P. T. (2003). *Saving it for when it counts: Stereotypic matching of source and message increases message scrutiny.* Unpublished manuscript, University of Illinois at Urbana-Champaign.

Vargas, P. T., Forgas, J. P., & Williams, K. (1999). *Implicit attitudes towards outgroups, old and new.* Unpublished manuscript, University of Illinois, Urbana-Champaign.

Vargas, P. T., von Hippel, W., & Petty, R. E. (in press). Using partially structured attitude measures to enhance the attitude-behavior relationship. *Personality and Social Psychology Bulletin.*

von Hippel, W., Sekaquaptewa, D., & Vargas, P. (1995). On the role of encoding processes in stereotype maintenance. In M. P. Zanna (Ed.), *Advances in experimental social psychology* (Vol. 27, pp. 177–254). San Diego, CA: Academic Press.

von Hippel, W., Sekaquaptewa, D., & Vargas, P. (1997). The Linguistic Intergroup Bias as an implicit indicator of prejudice. *Journal of Experimental Social Psychology, 33,* 490–509.

White, P. H., & Harkins, S. G. (1995). Race of source effects in the Elaboration Likelihood Model. *Journal of Personality and Social Psychology, 67,* 790–807.

Wilson, T. D., Lindsey, S., & Schooler, T. Y. (2000). A model of dual attitudes. *Psychological Review, 107,* 101–126.

Wittenbrink, B., Judd, C. M., & Park, B. (1997). Evidence for racial prejudice at the implicit level and its relationship with questionnaire measures. *Journal of Personality and Social Psychology, 72,* 262–274.

ENDNOTES

1. Although prejudice and stereotyping are obviously not isomorphic concepts, stereotypes (consensual beliefs about outgroup members) and prejudice (negative attitudes toward outgroup members) are related to one another. Stereotypes may be considered the cognitive component of prejudice

(Strobe & Insko, 1989). Indeed, this approach foreshadows our own and others' (Wittenbrink et al., 1997), very recent developments in prejudice assessment, wherein implicit or nonconscious stereotype endorsement serves as a measure of prejudice.

2. Personality variables have not fallen by the wayside, altogether. There has been a recent surge in interest in social dominance orientation as a personality variable that is correlated with prejudice (e.g., Pratto, Sidanius, Stallworth, & Malle, 1994; Sidanius, Pratto, & Bobo, 1996).

3. Here we shall only review the essence of the measures used; for a complete description of the materials and methods, see von Hippel, Sekaquaptewa, & Vargas (1997).

CHAPTER SEVEN

The Transmission of Prejudice: What Do Our Marketing Strategies Really Reinforce?

David W. Schumann
University of Tennessee

Richard Suinn, the incoming President of the American Psychological Association, selected two topics for psychology to focus on during his presidency. One is the psychology of cancer; the other is the topic of diversity. In this spirit, I have selected a related topic to the latter focus that I believe is in keeping with Dr. Suinn's agenda.

I begin by providing a historical overview of the study of prejudice. From that overview, I present what are thought to be the four causal processes underlying the existence of prejudice. One of these processes involves the transmission of certain forms of communication that serve to reinforce prejudicial attitudes within our society. I then proceed to describe, in turn, two forms of marketing communication that, I believe, serve as reinforcement transmitters. Within each description, I briefly review the past and present state of social scientific investigation. I then conclude by offering my thoughts regarding future research.

Many types of social stratification appear to influence the distribution of power and resources in our society: racism, ethnocentrism, sexism, classism, heterosexism, ageism, ableism, and others. Each of these stratifications has its own history, dynamics, and conditions of existence. Each has produced its own social movement in the 20th century.

In his 1992 *American Psychologist* piece entitled "Psychology and Prejudice: A Historical Analysis and Integrated Framework," and in his 1992 book entitled *The Social Psychology of Prejudice*, John Duckitt, from the University of the

---

This chapter was presented as a Presidential address to the membership of the Society for Consumer Psychology on February 19, 1999.

Witwatersrand, in Johannesburg, South Africa, suggested several distinct periods that separate the way in which psychologists have understood and examined prejudice. I briefly summarize each period and also attempt to fill certain gaps.

Prejudice emerged as a social scientific construct in the early part of this century. It surfaced primarily as it relates to differences between races. Sadly, during the 19th century, race inferiority in both America and Europe was accepted by social scientists. The idea of superiority of one race over another was well established. Evolutionary backwardness, limited intellectual capacity, and even excess sexual drive were three popular hypotheses of the day explaining inferiority. In 1925, an influential paper by Thomas Garth appeared in *Psychological Bulletin*, reviewing 73 studies on the issue of race and intelligence. Garth concluded that these "studies taken together seem to indicate the mental superiority of the white race." Please note that the recent publication and publicity surrounding the book entitled *The Bell Curve* (Herrnstein & Murray, 1996) suggests that this question still persists in the minds of some today.

However, during the latter part of the 1920s, the superiority of one race over another began to be challenged. Prejudice was viewed as irrational and unjustified, conceptualized as a social problem. Two social movements of the day seemed to challenge the legitimacy of racial superiority: the Black Civil Rights Movement, and the question of European colonial rule and White domination of colonized populations. One secondary influence for psychology was the emergence of several key Jewish psychologists into the profession, including Freud and Adler. It is believed that Floyd Allport, in 1924, was the first social psychologist to specifically pose the question that, if inferiority did not exist, then how could deficiencies and stigmatizations by Whites about Blacks exist? Thus scientists shifted their focus to trying to understand racial attitudes.

The 1930s and 1940s shifted to the identification of universal processes underlying prejudice. Psychodynamic theory ruled the day and offered an explanation for prejudice. Universal processes, such as defense mechanisms located in the unconscious, resulted from channeling tensions that arose either internally from personality or externally from an environment filled with approach–avoid contexts. Projection, frustration, and the displacement of hostility reflected a variety of psychodynamic processes.

Dollard and his colleagues (Dollard, Doob, Miller, Mowrer, & Sears, 1939) believed these processes could be integrated into a coherent explanation of prejudice in terms of aggression—originating from chronic social dysfunctions. The rise of Nazism and blatant anti-Semitism fueled this reasoning. Although overall studies testing psychodynamic theory and prejudice were inconclusive, the theoretical approaches are still alive and well today. In Elizabeth Young-Bruehl's (1998) new book entitled *The Anatomy of Prejudices*, published by Harvard Press, she suggests that social psychologists have long erred in their treatment of prejudice as a single phenomenon. She claims there are three distinct types of prejudice, each guided by a different need structure. She labels them *obsessional, hysterical,* and *narcissistic.*

She considers ethnocentrism, such as anti-Semitism, to be an obsessional prejudice characterized by a person with rigid superego-dominated traits. Racism is viewed as a hysterical prejudice in which a person unconsciously appoints a group to act out in the world of forbidden sexual and sexually aggressive desires. Finally, sexists are individuals who cannot tolerate the idea that other individuals exist who are not like them—specifically anatomically. This prejudice has a strong narcissistic foundation.

Returning to our history, the 1950s saw a shift in focus yet was still psychodynamically based. World War II and Nazism provided a context in which anti-Semitism could not be ignored. A theory of a personality type emerged, labeled the *authoritarian* individual. The Berkeley group, put together by Ned Sanford, posited multiple factors and attempted to measure the trait. Although the specific wording by Adorno, Frenkel-Brunswik, Levinson, and Sanford (1951/1964) of items posited to measure authoritarianism was appropriately challenged, their work gained significant exposure through their book entitled the *Authoritarian Personality*. The ideas of others followed quickly, including Rokeach's (1960) dogmatism, Smith and Rosen's (1958) worldmindedness, and Martin and Westie's (1959) tolerant personality. This work moved from a psychodynamic orientation to more one of an individual difference focus.

The 1960s and 1970s appeared to evolve to a sociocultural perspective. There was a marked decline in studies of individual prejudice during that time. A realization that the southern region of the United States held different social norms provided a catalyst for comparative study. The question thus focused on understanding group differences toward prejudice. By examining this normative approach, social scientists were optimistic about overcoming prejudice by ending social conformity to actions such as segregation. However, with the urban revolts in the late 1960s and resistance to the civil rights movement, this optimism faded. Sociologists sought to explain intergroup conflict and the conditions of social structure that could contribute to racism and discrimination. Although Sherif and Sherif (1953) had earlier provided research directly examining conflict theory, this was a time when psychology appeared to lose interest in the study of prejudice. Some attribute this loss of interest to the question posed by Alan Wicker in 1969 regarding the predictability of behavior from attitudes. In fact, surveys at the time reflected a decline in racial prejudice but not racial discrimination.

The 1980s found a reemergence of focus on the individual. Several programs of research seemed to reflect that prejudice may not be on the decrease at all but exist as a more subtle, complex phenomenon. Tajfel and his colleagues (1970) found evidence for prejudice in their well-known minimal intergroup studies. Although individuals were divided into groups on a random basis with no contact or interaction with other groups, they still showed bias and discrimination in favor of ingroups and against outgroups. Intergroup bias and discrimination were thus viewed as inevitable, part of the cognitive process that facilitates survival within a social environment. Prejudice and stereotyping were viewed as consequences of the cognitive processes involved in categorization. People's memberships in fundamental categories such as age, gender, and race seem to be attended to automatically. Associated stereotypes are activated upon perception of the category and, in turn, may influence judgments and behaviors.

Interestingly, the notion that negative stereotypes are automatically activated upon perception of a category member dates back to Gordon Allport's 1954 book, The Nature of Prejudice. However, the bulk of the work on automatic response has occurred within the past two decades. More recent research by Devine (1989), Lepore and Brown (1997), and others has begun to tease out similarities and differences between people who are high and low in ratings of prejudice, as well as the motivational determinants behind those who, when primed, appear to respond without expressing prejudice.

Duckett provided an integrative framework for conceptualizing the causation of prejudice. In his historical analysis, he presented four causal processes identified to date (Duckett, 1992a): (a) universal psychological processes that build in human potentiality or propensity for prejudice; (b) social and intergroup dynamics describing the conditions and circumstances of contact and interaction between groups that elaborate this propensity or potentiality into normative and socially shared patterns of prejudice characteristic of entire social groups; (c) mechanisms of transmission explaining how these intergroup dynamics and shared patterns of prejudice are socially transmitted to individual members of these groups; and (d) individual difference dimensions that determine individuals' susceptibility to prejudice that appear to modulate the impact of these social transmission mechanisms on individuals.

ADVERTISING THAT REINFORCES PREJUDICE

Duckitt's (1992a) third causal process directly involves the reinforcement of prejudice through mechanisms of transmission or communication. The remainder of this chapter describes and discusses two mechanisms of transmission within marketing strategy that communicate intergroup dynamics and shared patterns of prejudice. The first mechanism involves the media in the form of advertising. Advertising that reinforces prejudice, as perceived and responded to by the consumer, has been and continues to be a hot topic for academics in psychology, communication, advertising, and marketing.

Douglas Kellner (1995), Professor of Philosophy at the University of Texas at Austin, summed up the media's role in this form of transmission:

> Radio, television, film and the other products of media culture provide materials out of which we forge our very identities, our sense of selfhood; our notion of what it means to be male or female; our sense of class, of ethnicity and race, of nationality, of sexuality, of "us" and "them." Media images help shape our view of the world and

our deepest values: what we consider good or bad, positive or negative, moral or evil. Media stories provide the symbols, myths and resources through which we constitute a common culture and through the appropriation of which we insert ourselves into this culture. Media spectacles demonstrate who has power and who is powerless, who is allowed to exercise force and violence and who is not. They dramatize and legitimate the power of the forces that be, and show the powerless that they must stay in their places or be destroyed. (p. 5)

As I just mentioned, one such media product that has been found to transmit material deemed to be prejudicial is advertising. Historically, the most common example, the most sensitive, and the most publicized has been the role of African Americans in advertising.

Marilyn Kern-Foxworth (1994), the first African American awarded a PhD in Advertising, provides a provocative look back at the history of "Blacks in Advertising, Yesterday, Today, and Tomorrow" in her book entitled *Aunt Jemima, Uncle Ben, and Rastus*. This book, with a forward by Alex Haley, is a fascinating and scholarly treatise on the use and role of African Americans in advertising dating back to the early newspaper promotions for the sale of slaves and bringing us forward into the 1990s. In this book she reviews numerous studies and case histories denoting usage rates, stereotyping, and consumer perceptions. Although she reported an increased usage of African Americans in advertising over time, with more sensitivity to stereotyping, by no means has prejudice disappeared from advertising. She cites numerous examples of underrepresentation and continued stereotyping.

Kern-Foxworth concludes her book by stating that "the advertising industry has been reluctant to 'colorize' its advertisements, it commercials, and its boardrooms because it may alienate white consumers. In other words, the people who visit our homes day in and day out, trying to get us to buy this or that, are still not reflective of the society in which we live" (p. 167).

Last summer I was involved in a mentoring program for minority undergraduates interested in graduate studies. I worked with a young woman, from Wittenburg University in Ohio. Together we collected and analyzed academic research from the previous 25 years that we felt reflected the possible transmission of prejudice through advertising. From this review, we found that four major types of stratification have been researched in the advertising literature: gender, ethnicity, age, and attractiveness. Within each type, we found several dimensions that provided possible transmission of prejudice. These included (a) the roles in which people were presented; (b) the presence or absence in advertising (usage); (c) the types of behaviors and habits shown to be representative; (d) the perceptions that are represented, including beliefs and attitudes; (e) the types of product associations projected; and (f) the environmental settings presented.

These studies, taken as a whole, reflect the continuing existence of prejudice and stereotyping in advertising and its effect on the consumer. Although it appears that advertisers have become more sensitive by including minorities in more ads, recent content analyses suggest stereotyping is still present. For example, Charles

Taylor's recent research (Taylor & Lee, 1994; Taylor, Lee, & Stern, 1995; Taylor & Stern, 1997) consistently found that Asians are overrepresented in advertising and are stereotyped as possessing an intense work ethic. They are also most likely to appear in advertising for technical products. Furthermore, Asians are more likely to appear in the background than other minority groups. Although Asians are very family oriented, they rarely appear in ads with children. Taylor also found that Hispanics are significantly underrepresented in advertising. I would also ask, how often you see someone disabled in consumer advertising? How often do you see someone obese in nonhumorous advertising? Although there are exceptions, they are very rare occurrences.

By the way, another related form of transmission of prejudice, stereotyping, and discrimination to consumers is through the exchange relationship. Although I have yet to begin to investigate this literature, it is well known that some sales people will make decisions on the basis of race, age, weight, disability, or even how wealthy a person looks. These decisions include which potential customer to address, how long to stay with a customer, and what types of products and services should be shown to customers.

PREJUDICE RESULTING FROM MARKET SEGMENTATION

Let's move to the second type of transmission. This type of transmission occurs primarily through a more systematic marketing strategy. It is very directed and today is ever present in our society. In part, the modes of transmission through advertising and the exchange relationship that I just mentioned are pieces of this larger marketing phenomenon. The name of this phenomenon is *market segmentation*. So now you're thinking, "Schumann's going to take on market segmentation? This smacks of tilting at windmills." Perhaps, but perhaps not.

Let's go back to Kern-Foxworth's (1994) second statement in her quote: "In other words, the people who visit our homes day in and day out, trying to get us to buy this or that, are still not reflective of the society in which we live" (p. 167). Who are these people who come into our homes day in and day out, trying to get us to buy this or that? Why do we receive direct mail for certain types of products and not others? Who is responsible for the specific print ads and commercials that we are exposed to that are included in the media we select? What determines what types of catalogs we receive unsolicited? The answer to these questions is target marketing. What drives target marketing? A long-standing strategy by marketers to segment the marketplace.

Joseph Turow (1997), from the Annenberg School for Communication at the University of Pennsylvania, has written several books on media. One of his books, entitled *Breaking Up America: Advertisers and the New Media World*, takes a hard look at market segmentation and it impact on advertising and society. From the past 20 years of studying the media, Turow noted that "I noticed that media were increasingly encouraging people to separate themselves into more and more specialized groups and to develop distinctive viewing, reading, and listening habits that stressed differences between their groups and others" (p. ix).

Turow's book was based on research incorporating three methods of study that all focus on relationships with the media industry: in-depth reading of advertising and media trade magazines, attendance at industry conferences, and interviews with executives from a variety of industries. He interviewed nearly 100 media practitioners in preparation for this book.

With budgets that add up to hundreds of billions of dollars, the media industry, including advertising, is arguably better than the church or schools in its ability to promote images about our place in society—where we belong, why, and how we should act toward others. The increase in cable stations, radio, and speciality magazines, catalogs, and direct mail is no accident. It is the result of advertisers seeking to segment their markets.

As Turow suggested, "these activities have centered on entering individuals' private spaces—their homes, their cars, their offices—with lifestyle-specific news, information, entertainment, and especially, commercial messages. They also have involved tailoring public spaces—concerts, (automobile) races, and other open-to-the-public events—so that they attract customers who fit narrow profiles demanded by particular sponsors."

As authors like Turow, Peppers and Rogers (1993), and others have suggested, marketers know exactly who we are, where we live, what we do, who we socialize with, what we read, what we watch, and how we work. Simply put, they can predict us with uncanny accuracy. So what do they do with this information? I believe they formulate communication strategies that feed what they believe to be our basic narcissistic tendencies. They may very well be accurate in their belief. This past Christmas one of the most popular new toys on the market was not in the stores. It was the $200 mail-order doll. You take a picture of your child and send it to the company. The Twin Doll is made in the likeness of your son or daughter and is returned to you through the mail.

In his book, Turow tries to demonstrate how "marketers look for splits in the social fabric and then reinforce and extend the splits for their own ends." How do they do this? By giving consumers an incentive to use media specially designed for them and discouraging the use of media designed for others.

Historical Roots of Market Segmentation

So is market segmentation a new phenomenon? No. The roots of target marketing go back at least as far as the first quarter of this century. In 1911, the great copywriter Elmo Calkins noted in his book, *The Business of Advertising*, the differences in how periodicals could target different audiences. Nonetheless, in the early part of the century up until the 1980s, mass marketing dominated marketing strategy. Newspapers were aimed at large and diverse urban populations that manufacturers and department stores targeted daily. The modern ad agency developed in sync with mass marketing. Indeed, perhaps the richest man ever in the advertising business, Albert Lasker, told his staff, "We are making a homogenous people out of a nation of immigrants."

However, target marketing was still hanging around. The 1960s and 1970s, with their emphasis on freedom of expression and differences of opinion, led to an emphasis on grouping individuals with common attitudes and beliefs. Many groups were labeled *disadvantaged minorities* and included certain ethnic groups, women, and disabled individuals. With this emphasis on new forms of expression and overcoming hardship came strong pressure from advertising to begin differentiating television audiences. The advent of cable television and commercial satellite feed soon followed. Pressure was brought to bear on market researchers, including some of the pioneer consumer psychologists that started Society for Consumer Psychology, to provide greater specificity regarding audiences. New market research tools that attempted to group Americans emerged. Examples include VALS, PRIZM, and the Yankelovich Monitor.

By the 1980s and into the early 1990s, market segmentation was being used to signal the consumer. Media and marketers routinely split their customers into different categories so as to reach them differently. By the mid-1990s, we seem to have moved from signaling to "incentivizing." We incentivize everything and this activity depends on target marketing. I recently signed up for a credit card from an alliance between Delta Airlines and American Express. I get a mile added to my frequent flyer mileage for every dollar I charge. What is interesting is that, subsequent to my signing up, a major telecommunications company has phoned or mailed me at least once a week, with a similar deal. So now we are in the age of incentive target marketing with alliances between major brands.

The Consequences of Market Segmentation

Let's think for a moment: What are the consequences of market segmentation? To a marketer, there are numerous positive consequences, including (a) the ability to match products and services to certain value drivers that define a segment, thus creating the potential for more loyal customers; (b) the ability to accurately target consumers most likely to be customers; (c) the ability to collect more accurate and timely market data; (d) the ability to purchase more cost-effective media; (e) the ability to create an effective sales proposition that is unique to a segment; (f) the ability to design cost-efficient distribution systems; and (g) the ability to keep "undesired" segments away from a product. To society, it also has positive benefits, including the greater likelihood of receiving a product designed to meet the customer's needs and lower prices that are due to cost efficiencies in promoting and delivering the product.

These benefits are important to both the marketer and consumer but, in my view, they may not be without cost to society. The strategy of segmenting markets, whether intentional or not, minimizes exposure and knowledge of other groups in our society. It presents a "me" as owning certain products, doing certain activities, and socializing with certain people, and a "they" as being different in their choice of products, activities, friends, and so on. Is it possible that market segmentation reinforces a type of market segregation? The degree to which market segmentation is harmful to society and perhaps counter to basic positive societal values is an empirical question—one that I believe deserves further investigation.

FUTURE RESEARCH QUESTIONS

What are the questions that we as researchers should be asking? How should we be examining these questions? In considering the first form of transmission, although there is a significant amount of existing research that has attempted to document prejudice and stereotyping within product presentation, it would be helpful to take our research a step further, just as social psychology has. Borrowing (marketers call it applying) the social psychology agenda, we might want to address the following questions:

1. Can advertising stimuli, believed to transmit direct or indirect prejudicial messages, influence the audiences' automatic prejudicial responses?
2. If so, what types of specific advertising stimuli are particularly influential?
3. What, if any, emotion is involved in transmission that might serve to establish or reinforce an automatic prejudicial response?
4. Are there certain motivational and/or personality factors that might moderate this influence?
5. Is it possible to desensitize the automatic prejudice response by providing more, not less, mixed group advertising and promotion?

I would also recommend that we move beyond examining simple consumer response, such as recall, advertising and brand attitude, and purchase intention, as dependent measures and begin to look more long term at how this transmission of prejudice influences individual values, and people's attitudes and treatment of others not in their defined ingroup.

In considering the second form of transmission, market segmentation, we can address several questions:

1. Does market segmentation result in significantly less exposure to other groups in our society?
2. Does market segmentation serve to enhance insecurity or fear toward outgroups?
3. What impact does market segmentation have on the formation or reinforcement of prejudicial attitudes toward outgroups?

4. Do market segmentation strategies alter cognitive categorization?

5. What are the long-term costs of market segmentation on society?

It is possible that the study of the potential negative impact of segmentation will require more creative methodologies. One strategy to consider might be a derivative of Tajfel's minimal intergroup studies (1970). It might be possible to create some form of simulation that can provide the experience of a targeted audience.

CONCLUSIONS

In this chapter, I have attempted to make a case for our need as consumer psychologists to consider the negative impact that certain transmissions of prejudice have on society. I have outlined two forms of transmission through marketing communication strategies. The first form considers the ongoing way in which certain groups of people are presented to consumers by means of advertising. The second form, market segmentation and its resulting communication strategies, is a broader phenomenon.

I want to leave you with a fact. In 1994, over one third of all new housing construction in Southern California was in the form of gated communities. It appears that many of us take significant measures to wall ourselves in from the outside. Who do we perceive threatens us? I feel confident in saying that the perceived threat is not likely to come from people like me, the people I am exposed to the most and know the most about. The perceived threat is more likely to come from those whom I know the least about. Furthermore, I am constrained by a lack of time and easily available information as well as a lack of exposure to many other groups that *do* exist in the society in which I live.

REFERENCES

Adorno, T. W., Frenkel-Brunswik, E., Levinson, D. J., & Sanford, R. N. (1951). *The authoritarian personality*. New York: Wiley. (Original work published 1964)

Allport, F. H., & Hartmann, D. A. (1925). Measurement and motivation of atypical opinion in a certain group. *American Political Science Review, 19*, 735–760.

Allport, G. W. (1954). *The nature of prejudice*. Reading, MA: Addison-Wesley.

Calkins, E. E. (1911). *The business of advertising*. New York, London: D. Appleton & Company.

Devine, P. G. (1989). Stereotypes and prejudice: Their automatic and controlled components. *Journal of Personality and Social Psychology, 56*, 5–18.

Dollard, J., Doob, L., Miller, N. E., Mowrer, O., & Sears, R. (1939). *Frustration and aggression*. New Haven, CT: Yale University Press.

Duckitt, J. (1992a). Psychology and prejudice: A historical analysis and integrative framework. *American Psychologist, 47*, 1182–1193.

Duckitt, J. (1992b). *The social psychology of prejudice*. New York: Praeger.

Garth, T. R. (1925). A review of racial psychology. *Psychological Bulletin, 22*, 343–364.

Herrnstein, R. J., & Murray, C. (1996). *The bell curve: Intelligence and class structure in American life.* New York: The Free Press, Simon & Schuster.

Kellner, D. (1995). Cultural studies, multiculturalism and media culture. In G. Dines & J. M. Humez (Eds.), *Gender, race and class in media* (pp. 5–17). Thousand Oaks, CA: Sage.

Kern-Foxworth, M. (1994). *Aunt Jemima, Uncle Ben, and Rastus: Blacks in advertising, yesterday, today, and tomorrow.* Westport, CT: Greenwood.

Lepore, L., & Brown, R. (1997). Category and stereotype activation: Is prejudice inevitable? *Journal of Personality and Social Psychology, 72,* 275–287.

Martin, J. G., & Westie, F. R. (1959). The tolerant personality. *American Sociological Review, 24,* 521–528.

Peppers, D., & Rogers, M. (1993). *The one-to-one future: Building relationship one customer at a time.* New York: Doubleday.

Rokeach, M., Smith, P., & Evans, R. (1960). Two kinds of prejudice or one? In M. Rokeach (Ed.), *The open and the closed mind* (pp. 132–168). New York: Basic Books.

Smith, H. P., & Rosen, E. W. (1958). Some psychological correlates of worldmindness ad authoritarianism. *Journal of Personality, 26,* 170–183.

Sherif, M., & Sherif, C. W. (1953). *Groups in harmony and tension.* New York: Harper.

Tajfel, H. (1970). Experiments in intergroup discrimination. *Scientific American, 223,* 96–102.

Taylor, C. R., & Lee, J. Y. (1994). Not in Vogue: Portrayals of Asian Americans in magazine advertising. *Journal of public policy & marketing, 13,* 239–245.

Taylor, C. R., Lee, J. Y., & Stern, B. (1995). Portrayals of African, Hispanic, and Asian Americans in magazine advertising. *American behavior scientist, 38,* 608–621.

Taylor, C. R., & Stern, B. B. (1997). Asian-Americans: Television advertising and the "model majority" stereotype. *Journal of advertising, 26,* 49–60.

Turow, J. (1997). *Breaking up America: Advertisers and the new media world.* Chicago: Chicago University Press.

Wicker, A. (1969). Attitudes vs actions: The relationship of verbal and overt behavioral responses to attitude objects. *Journal of Social Issues, 25,* 41–78.

Young-Bruehl, E. (1998). *The anatomy of prejudices.* Boston: Harvard University Press.

CHAPTER EIGHT

When Perceptions Affect Broadcasting in the Public Interest: Advertising Media Buyers as an Economic Hurdle for Black-Oriented Radio Stations

Caryl A. Cooper
University of Alabama

If there is one prevailing assumption that permeates the radio advertising industry, it's this: higher rated radio stations earn greater advertising revenues than their lower rated competitors in the same market. Radio stations that fail to earn revenue shares commensurate with their ratings are not uncommon. Certainly, other elements are involved: the format, the availability of advertisers placing ad dollars in the market, an advertiser's or ad agency's assessment of the buying power, spending patterns and responsiveness of the radio station's audience, and economies derived from common ownership all play a part in a station's ability to attract advertisers (Ofori, 1999). However, patterns in rating-to-revenue share discrepancies not only raise eyebrows; they also raise accusations of foul play and questions about the agenda of those responsible for placing advertising dollars. Moreover, because advertising plays a pivotal role in a station's ability to broadcast in the public interest, patterns of revenue discrepancy raise the consternation of the Federal Communications Commission (FCC).

For more than 20 years, owners and salespeople of Black-oriented radio stations have maintained that their stations do not receive advertising revenues that reflect their strength in the market. There is evidence to support this perception. A special report released in January 1999 by the Civil Rights Forum (CRF) of the Federal Communications Commission shows that a disparity between general-formatted radio stations and their minority-formatted contemporaries exists. General-formatted stations earn revenue shares that are greater than their audience share, with a power ratio of 1.16. (A power ratio is the measure comparing a radio station's audience share with its revenue share. A power ration of 1.00 is considered average, one above 1.00 is considered good, and one below 1.00 is considered poor.) Minority-formatted (including Black-oriented and Hispanic) radio stations, however, do not earn revenue shares equal to or greater than their audience shares, with a power ratio of .91 (Ofori, 1999).

Minority owners and salespeople are not reserved about offering reasons for this disparity. Many contend that some advertisers encourage economic discrimination by issuing "no urban–Spanish" dictates that exclude these stations from consideration, severely limiting a media buyer's ability to consider including ethnic stations on a buy.

Minority owners and salespeople also claim that advertisers and their agencies fail to appreciate the virtues of advertising to African Americans (Ofori, 1999a; "Black Buying Power," 1998):

1. Household earning are estimated to be $367 billion.
2. Researchers estimate that the buying power of African Americans will reach $533 billion in 1999.
3. Blacks outspend the average non-black consumer in several categories, including telephone services, utilities, major appliances, and new cars and trucks.
4. In 1999, African American consumers will account for 8.2% of the nation's total buying power, compared with 7.4% in 1990.
5. The African American population will increase in importance as the population increases in the year 2000. Alfred Schreiber, a managing partner of TN Media, the media-planning division and multicultural marketing arm of True North Communications, agrees. He says that media-planning departments are "ignorant of the strength of minority groups' buying power" ("Different Strokes," 1999, p. 16).

Despite the increased trend in target marketing ("Niche Market," 1998), Judith Ellis, Senior Vice President of Emmis Broadcast, believes that "the Black consumer is less valued than the White consumer and therefore they're [advertisers] going to pay less for Black consumers" (Ofori, 1999, p. 13). For example, advertisers and media buyers who pay $1 per listener for general-market radio stations pay 78 ¢ for minority-owned and minority-formatted stations (Tienowitz, 1999). This type of economic discrimination forces owners to undersell their radio stations in order to get media schedules. These steep discounts create a disproportionate gap in spending between general and minority media ("Niche Market," 1998).

In addition to "no urban–Spanish" dictates and the advertiser's ignorance of the Black consumer market, the government report mentions other reasons for the disparity in radio station incomes. The report indicates that advertisers and their agencies share a general belief that minorities can be reached through general-market media and share racial or ethnic stereotypes that may influence media-related decisions. The report also singles out media buyers as persons who are unfamiliar with ethnic consumer behavior. The report concludes that further research is needed to assess the impact of these elements, as well as the race and gender of ad agency personnel, on discriminatory advertising buying practices.

Unlike the FCC study, which presented anecdotal data gathered by the surveying of owners and managers of minority-formatted radio stations, this study focuses on advertising agency personnel: media buyers. This study, conducted in 1993, is an exploratory examination of media buyers and their perceptions regarding a specific type of minority-formatted radio station and its audience: urban contemporary. This study attempts to answer the following research question: In comparison with their attitudes about other formats, do media buyers have a negative attitude about urban contemporary radio stations? It is hypothesized that media buyers do have negative attitudes and perceptions about the urban contemporary format, which, in part, lead to lower power ratios and hurt the growth of urban contemporary stations, contrary to Congressional and FCC guidelines, and to the detriment of serving the Black audience.

Media buyers were selected for this study for several reasons. First, the FCC highlights media buyers as persons who are particularly ignorant of Black consumer behavior. Second, media buyers are usually responsible for analyzing demographic and rating information and placing advertising buys, which ultimately led to the disparities in ad revenues for minority-formatted stations reported by the FCC. Third, the relationship between radio stations and media buyers is a primary concern for most radio managers because of the large amount of advertising dollars they place.

Because the study focused on a specific radio format, the media buyers selected for this survey were those who were buying spot radio for agencies billing the most in spot radio ("Agency income by top ten broadcast," 1990).

The urban contemporary format was selected for the following reasons. First, advertisers have singled out the urban format for exclusion through their "no urban–Spanish" dictates. Second, the urban format has a unique audience composition that should be attractive to most advertisers. Using data collected by MediaMark Research Inc., a 1991 study prepared by Interep Radio Store suggested that the urban format, and its core of Black listeners, would be the growth market for advertisers (Bunzel, 1991).

The study revealed the following information.

1. Sixty-nine percent of urban contemporary's cumulative audience is Black; 27.3% is White; and 4% is described as other.
2. Urban contemporary stations are top ranked in most major markets.
3. Forty-five percent of listeners earn household incomes in excess of $30,000 per year.

4. Over 33% are employed in white-collar jobs; 26% are employed in clerical, sales, or technical positions; and 10.6% are employed in professional, executive, or managerial positions.

5. Urban contemporary listeners spent $33.3 million on CDs, tapes, and records; $1 billion annually on home improvements; $2.6 million on foreign air trips and $10.4 million on domestic air trips; $600 million weekly on groceries; and $1.4 billion on men's clothing and $1.4 billion on women's clothing.

AFRICAN AMERICANS IN ADVERTISING

Studies about African Americans in advertising have branched into two primary areas: Images in advertising and the historical and cultural context of Blacks in advertisements. In her essay, "Advertising," in *Split Images: African Americans in the Mass Media,* Janette Dates (1993) described the evolution of stereotypical images since the early 1800s. Kern-Foxworth (1994) expanded this line of inquiry by examining the symbolic significance of Black images from 18th-century slavery advertisements to the Black-nationalist images of the 1980s. Image studies have not been the sole line of inquiry about diversity issues in advertising. Since the 1960s, in addition to exploring Black role modeling in advertising (Humphrey & Schuman, 1984), researchers have also explored White consumer reactions to Blacks in advertisements (Cagley & Cordozo, 1970; Bush, Solomon, & Hair, 1977).

BLACK-ORIENTED RADIO STATIONS AND THE GOVERNMENT

Three studies serve as the foundation for analyzing Black-oriented radio stations. Bachman (1977) and Edmonston (1954) focused on the historic and economic development of Black radio, including Black-owned-and-operated (O & O) radio stations and Black-oriented radio stations. These studies provide an important foundation, as the history of the urban contemporary format is rooted in the history of Black radio. Included in each study is a brief discussion of the relationship between Black O & O radio stations and the economic forces influencing their growth—the ratings services and advertising agencies. Although the Bachman study elicited comments from the heads of advertising agencies, it contained few direct references to the role media buyers play in the advertising placement process.

Stuart Surlin (1972) surveyed the management of 74 Black-oriented radio stations to identify the methods used to meet the needs of the Black communities they served. The study was prompted by public criticism of White-owned Black-oriented radio stations' inability to serve the Black community. The study revealed that most stations were not prepared to meet the needs of their audiences.

As a result of the criticism, Blacks began to form lobbying groups to challenge the licenses of White-owned Black-oriented stations in their communities. They had several goals in mind: to stop negative stereotyping by gaining access to the medium, to upgrade the quality of programming, and to increase radio station ownership by Blacks (Hicks, 1978). Black ownership of radio stations increased slowly during the 1950s and 1960s. In 1970, 12 stations in the United States were reported as being owned by Blacks. By 1976, that number had grown to 56 (Bachman, 1977).

Accompanying the rise in Black ownership of radio stations came complaints of unfair practices at advertising agencies. These complaints were first formally voiced to the FCC and advertising agencies in a congressional hearing in 1977 ("Minorities Charge Discrimination," 1977). Almost 10 years later, the charge of discriminatory buying practices was voiced again in another congressional hearing in 1986. With evidence gathered by his station's rep firm, James Hutchinson, Vice President and General Partner of Inter Urban Broadcasting of New Orleans, submitted an availability request that directed the rep firm not to submit Black–ethnic stations. "It is this practice," Hutchinson said, "that is at the heart of the problem. It is patently discriminatory to preclude a station out of hand, because it has a black or Urban format" (Hearing before the Subcommittee of Telecommunications, Consumer Protection and Finance, HR. 5373, Serial No. 99–173).

In response to those charges, Daniel Jaffe (Senior Vice president of the Association of National Advertisers), after surveying some of the organization's members, stated that because media buys are based on "reach, efficiency and effectiveness, the solution to any perceived problems could only come from the marketplace. Neither the Congress nor the FCC could resolve these issues" (Minority-Owned Broadcast Stations, 1986). In light of the FCC's recent report, it seems obvious that the marketplace has provided no solutions.

Mr. Jaffe's position in 1986 does not mirror the advertising industry's response in 1998. Prior to the release of the new report, industry critics took advertisers and media specialists to task ("No Double Standards," 1998):

> Top managements at advertisers and agencies have a duty to scrutinize media buying for any hint that bigotry is affecting buying decisions, and promptly take any corrective actions necessary. This question cannot be allowed to fester.... Advertisers have no specific obligation to use their media budgets to support government policy to encourage minority ownership of media.... But advertisers—and agencies—do have an obligation to fairly and accurately value minority audiences; to see that racially inspired stereotypes play no part in that valuation; and to insure that all media—regardless of ownership—are honestly compensated for value received, without consideration of race. There's no room for a double standard. Period. (p. 34)

Since the Civil Rights Forum on Communications Policy issued its report, advertising agency representatives have met behind closed doors with the FCC and minority-formatted radio stations owners to seek solutions to this decades-old problem (Tienowitz, 1999).

ADVERTISING AGENCY PERSONNEL

To date, few scholarly articles have been published about media specialists. In their review of media-planning literature, Pasadeos, Barban, Yi, and Kim (1997) identified a scant 20 articles spanning 30 years. Turk and Katz (1992) focused on important developments affecting the media planning and buying process from 1985 through 1991. By analyzing scholarly and trade journal articles, the researchers reviewed media departments from an organizational perspective. They found that media specialists are becoming increasingly important as the analysis of media alternatives becomes more critical to the marketing process. However, neither the study by Pasadeos et al. nor that by Turk and Katz looks at media buyers in particular.

One recent study, however, focused on media buyers and their perceptions about specific media. The study by King, Reid, and Morrison (1997) of media specialists' opinions of newspaper advertising for national accounts begins to fill the void in scholarly literature. The study thus described agency media specialists:

> [They are] major gatekeepers of national advertising expenditures.... Our study therefore was designed and executed on the assumption that the opinions of those gatekeepers must be assessed and understood if the newspaper industry is to cope effectively and strategically with the problem of declining advertising revenues from national accounts." (p. 2)

This study adds to the scant body of literature about media buyers' perceptions by focusing on minority-formatted radio because, as King et al. (1997) stated, perceptions of media buyers must be assessed if change is to take place. The results of this study should give direction to minority-formatted radio station owners and salespeople as they develop strategies to correct discriminatory agency practices.

METHODOLOGY

Sample

A self-administered survey was mailed to a purposive sample of media buyers. The media buyers selected for this survey were those who were buying spot radio for agencies handling the nation's top 25 spot radio advertisers (*Advertising Age*, 1990). Although spot radio buyers were targeted, it should be noted that buyers are often responsible for buying a variety of media.

Names of survey participants were collected through telephone calls to the agencies. The telephone call was either fielded by the agency receptionist or forwarded to the media supervisor. Media buyers named by receptionists were sent a cover letter describing the project, a questionnaire, and a prepaid business reply envelope. In addition, the questionnaire, a cover letter, and a prepaid business reply envelope were sent to media supervisors who felt there would be a higher response if they dispersed the materials. There were 381 buyers who were identified for participation in the study.

Questionnaire Pretest

Two questionnaires were created and pretested. Five media buyers from agencies based in St. Louis participated in the pretest. All buyers were encouraged to share their feelings about the questionnaire and the purpose of the survey. The first survey was a four-page questionnaire composed of seven identical statements about eight different radio program formats, followed by a Likert-type response scale ranging from "strongly agree" to "strongly disagree." This version was rejected because the buyers coded most of statements as "disagree" or "strongly disagree," leaving an inadequate range for measurement.

The second questionnaire consisted of different buying scenarios that asked the buyer to select the best formats for each product or service. The media buyers preferred this survey because it simulated a buying situation. Consequently, the second questionnaire was used for this study.

The Instrument

The questionnaire (available from the author by request) consisted of seven different buying scenarios. Each scenario contained information that buyers consider of primary importance when selecting radio stations to be included on a buy: the product, cost per point, and the target demographic. Products for the scenarios were selected through interviews with urban contemporary radio station salespeople and by analyzing the Black Consumer Spending Index (Campenelli, 1991). The scenarios attempted to get a mixture of products and services for which urban contemporary stations typically received orders, and products and services for which they do not receive orders. Telephone interviews with three urban contemporary station salespeople in St. Louis, Chicago, and Norfolk, Virginia said their respective radio stations still had a problem attracting advertising schedules for banks, automobile dealerships (especially foreign automobiles), airline travel, and real estate. The products urban contemporary stations generally have success in attracting are soft drinks, clothing, and some health and beauty aids.

In addition, the scenarios did not contain any specific market locations, such as Chicago or Houston. The buyers were instructed to apply "general market conditions." This clause was included in the questionnaire in an attempt to get the buyers to consider formats in general terms rather than for specific markets.

In an attempt to ensure that the remaining variables were constant, the efficiency information for each scenario remained the same: There were seven differently formatted radio stations in the market from which to choose, all stations met the required cost per point, and all stations had comparable ratings. The scenarios did not contain any information regarding the market's ethnicity.

The buyer was instructed to choose four of the seven formats for the buy and to rank them in order of desirability, with 1 being the best and 4 being the worst.

Each selection was given an index for desirability. Desirability was determined by the number of times a format was selected (frequency). All of the formats selected as the first choice were given a score of 4 points; the second selection was given a score of 3 points; the third selection was given a score of 2 points; and the fourth selection was given a score of 1 point. The total amount of points given each format was tabulated and then divided by the number of respondents. This figure was considered to be the "desirability index." The four formats with the highest index were considered the most desirable for reaching the specified target demographic assigned to each scenario.

The questionnaires were mailed during the last week of March in 1992. The survey deadline was set for April 25, 1992, giving respondents approximately 4 weeks to respond. The questionnaires were coded by color into five regions. This method was used to provide easy identification of areas where survey response was low.

Follow-up phone calls and postcards were mailed during the first week of May. These techniques were used to increase the response rate.

RESULTS

Responses

The mailing of 381 questionnaires yielded a sample of 67 ($N = 67$) responses (17.5%).

Demographics

According to the demographic data provided by the respondents, the average media buyer is a 31-year-old White female who has graduated from college, bought media for an average of 7 years, and has worked at her present company for almost 5 years. The respondents listed adult contemporary and rock–classic rock as the formats they listened to most.

Product: Banking Services

Scenario 1 asked media buyers to identify the four most desirable formats for reaching adults aged 25–54 years who were purchasers of bank certificates of deposit. This product was chosen because, according to Daryl Green, sales manager for WGCI-FM in Chicago (D. Green, personal communication, February 13, 1992), urban contemporary radio stations traditionally have not been able to attract a large amount of bank advertising (see Table 8.1).

TABLE 8.1
Scenario 1

Format	Desirability Index
Adult contemporary	2.95
News–talk	2.49
Rock–classic rock	1.79
Country	1.05
Easy listening	0.60
Hot-hit	0.35
Urban contemporary	0.22
Classical	0.06
Oldies	0.06
Jazz	0.04

TABLE 8.2
Scenario 2

Format	Desirability Index
Hot-hit	3.76
Rock–classic rock	2.61
Urban contemporary	2.03
Adult contemporary	0.97
Country	0.52
Easy listening	0.03
News–talk	0.01

Media buyers did not consider the urban contemporary format a practicable contender for placement of bank buys with a target demographic of adults aged 25–54. Even though urban stations average more that 33% of their audience in the 25- to 54-year age bracket, for the product and demographic, urban stations probably would not receive an order.

Product: Soft Drinks

Scenario 2 asked media buyers to rank the four best formats for a product called "Drink Me Cola" (see Table 8.2). The target demographic was Teens and adults aged 18–34 years. The campaign was designed to increase product awareness.

Media buyers considered the urban format a practicable contender for a soft drinks with a target demographic of adults aged 18–34. According to the Black Consumer Spending Index (BCSI), African Americans are 4% more likely to purchase nonalcoholic beverages (Campenelli, 1991).

TABLE 8.3
Scenario 3

Format	Desirability Index
Adult contemporary	3.01
News–talk	2.22
Rock–classic rock	1.44
Easy listening	1.29
Country	1.29
Oldies	0.16
Urban contemporary	0.10
Classical	0.10

TABLE 8.4
Scenario 4

Format	Desirability Index
Adult contemporary	3.00
Hot-hit	2.88
Urban contemporary	1.40
Rock–classic rock	1.06
Country	0.80
Easy listening	0.46
News–talk	0.09
Other	0.09
Oldies	0.04

Product: Airline–Vacation Travel

Scenario 3 asked buyers to identify the four most desirable formats for reaching the airline traveler. The target demographic was 25- to 54-year-old men and women with incomes of $30,000 or more. The campaign was designed for vacation travel (see Table 8.3).

Media buyers did not consider the urban contemporary format a practicable contender for placement on airline buys with an adults aged 25–54 target demographic. Data indicate that the urban format should be highly considered. In the 1991 Interep Radio Store Report (Bunzel, 1991), Urban listeners spent $2.6 million on foreign air trips and $10.4 million on domestic air trips. Despite this evidence, the urban format probably would not be placed on an airline buy.

Product: Women's Clothing

Scenario 4 asked the media buyer to identify the four most desirable formats for reaching young, working women. The target demographic was 18- to 34-year-old women. The product was a moderately priced women's clothing store that was advertising a sale (Table 8.4).

TABLE 8.5
Scenario 5

Format	Desirability Index
Adult contemporary	3.12
News–talk	2.24
Rock–classic rock	1.61
Country	1.72
East listening	0.76
Urban contemporary	0.27
Hot-hit	0.13
Classical	0.03
Oldies	0.04
Jazz	0.01

Media buyers considered the urban format a desirable format for reaching buyers of women's clothing. According to the BCSI, African Americans are 22% more likely to purchase apparel (Campenelli, 1991).

Product: Foreign and Domestic Cars

In Scenario 5, the media buyer was asked to identify the four most desirable formats for reaching 25- to 54-year-old adults with an income of $30,000 or more. In this scenario, the product was an automobile dealership that sells domestic and Japanese cars (Table 8.5).

Media buyers did not consider the urban format desirable for this product. Research suggests that the format should have gotten stronger support. According to the *Profile of the Urban Contemporary Listener* (1991), 58.1% of urban listeners are aged 25–54 years, and 45.5% have yearly household incomes of $30,000–60,000.

Product: Real Estate

Scenario 6 asked media buyers to identify the four most desirable formats for reaching 25- to 54-year-old men. The product for this scenario was real estate, specifically targeting new home and condominium buyers earning yearly incomes in excess of $40,000 (Table 8.6). This product and demographic was chosen because urban contemporary stations have found it extremely difficult to attract real estate advertisers.

Media buyers considered the urban format the least suitable for new home sales even though the format delivers the audience, the age, and the income level desired by the advertiser. The BSCI is low for this category. African Americans are 27% less likely to own their own home. In part, this is due to the fact that many Black households are located in large cities where renting is more common: 55% live in cities, 26% live in suburban areas, and 19% live in rural areas (Campenelli, 1991).

TABLE 8.6
Scenario 6

Format	Desirability Index
News–talk	2.45
Rock–classic rock	2.25
Country	1.70
Adult contemporary	1.65
Easy listening	0.67
Oldies	0.28
Classical	0.16
Hot-hit	0.10
Urban contemporary	0.07

TABLE 8.7
Scenario 7

Format	Desirability Index
Adult contemporary	3.38
Country	2.04
Urban contemporary	1.32
Rock–classic rock	1.17
Easy listening	0.65
Hot-hit	0.62
News–talk	0.56
Oldies	0.19

Product: Grocery Stores

Scenario 7 asked media buyers to identify the four most desirable formats for reaching 25- to 54-year-old adults with children and modest incomes of $20,000 or more. The product was a local grocery store chain. This product and demographic was chosen because of the universality of the product. Groceries are a necessity for all people, regardless of ethnicity and income (Table 8.7).

Media buyers considered the urban format suitable for grocery chain accounts. According to the BCSI, African Americans are 62% more likely to purchase meats, poultry, fish, and eggs; 20% more likely to purchase fruits and vegetables; and 12% more likely to purchase cereals and bakery products (Campenelli, 1991).

DISCUSSION

The results of this survey support the hypothesis for the study: Media buyers have negative perceptions about the urban contemporary radio format. For overall desirability, media buyers ranked the urban format sixth. They consider the format suitable for a narrow range of products and services that are targeted to younger adults with moderate incomes (grocery stores, soft drinks, and clothing). These are also products and services for which urban stations have had no problems attracting in the past. Media buyers did not consider the urban format suitable for banks, new home sales, domestic or foreign cars, or airline travel. These are products and services that urban stations have had a difficult time attracting.

In addition, it is interesting to note the relationship between the formats that buyers listened to most and the formats overwhelmingly chosen as the best for each product. The adult contemporary and rock–classic rock formats were consistently chosen as formats most suitable for the products and services included in the survey. Similarly, media buyers listed these same formats as their personal favorites. None of the respondents listed the urban format as a personal favorite. Because there appears to be a positive relationship between favorite format and desirability index, this may indicate that media selection is not a totally objective process. Most importantly, the audience delivered by urban contemporary stations meets the criteria for inclusion in the media buy for banks, cars, and airline travel, and yet this format was not selected. The most obvious explanation is bias against this format and its listeners.

LIMITATIONS

Clearly, a higher response rate would have helped the validity of this study. A 20% to 40% response rate is common for most mail surveys (Wimmer & Dominick, 1991). The response rate for this study was 17.5%. As a result, these findings are not generalizable to the entire population of media buyers.

There also seemed to be little consistency in the choices made by the media buyers for each category. For example, when asked to choose a format for reaching 25- to 54-year-old adults with children and modest incomes of $24,000 or more, media buyers chose eight different formats in the first choice category. Even though a large percentage of the selections clustered around two formats (adult contemporary = 63%; rock–classic rock = 18%), the variety of format selections could mean several things:

1. There was not enough information in each scenario to enable the respondents to make a narrower selection. However, ethnic information was deliberately omitted in an attempt to get the media buyers to think in general terms. It would seem that media buyers may not be comfortable with making buying decisions based on general information.

2. The proliferation of format selections could also mean that the responses forced media buyers to tread the gray area between objectivity and opinion. As one buyer who responded to the survey put it, "What I wrote are my personal opinions. These have no influence on my buying. Stations bought depend on client

suggestions, and more importantly, on individual market research. The opinions expressed don't influence a normal buy" (unidentified response from a survey respondent). The evidence from this study, combined with the FCC's report, however, suggests that opinions do influence media buying decisions.

CONCLUSION

Perhaps the best that could be said is that, under certain buying conditions, some media buyers will choose some radio formats some of the time. However, in general, media buyers do not consider the urban contemporary format as objectively as other formats in the media mix, even for products that Blacks might be expected to buy. For example, in one scenario, media buyers were asked to choose the four most desired formats for reaching 18- to 34-year-old women who were purchasers of clothing. Even though the urban contemporary format received the third highest desirability index in the scenario, it appears that the buyers did not consider relevant research. Research shows that Black women are 27% more likely than non-Black women to purchase women's and girl's apparel (Campenelli, 1991). In addition, the Black consumer, in this case women, is not as effectively reached on radio stations with other formats. Taken together, these facts suggests that the urban contemporary format is worthy of a higher index.

When the data for this survey were collected, 6 years had passed since the congressional hearing at which the topic of discriminatory buying practices and its effects on Black-oriented radio stations was discussed. This researcher had hoped that the perceptions of discrimination in media buying had diminished over time. It seems, however, that the charges of discrimination have strengthened, and, because of the efforts of the Civil Rights Forum of the FCC, they are now substantiated in a government report.

The advertising industry seems to be saying and doing the right things. Advertising officials have met in closed meetings with the FCC, the Civil Rights Forum, and representatives from minority-owned media and marketers to find solutions to the problem, which include discussions about the government's proposed code of ethical buying behavior (Tienowitz, 1999). However, there is still much to be done. During the round-table discussion, Sam Chisholm, president-CEO of Chisholm/Mingo, an advertising agency specializing in advertising to African Americans, claimed that a representative from Walt Disney Co. told him that she did not see the value in targeted marketing (Tienowitz, 1999). Such assertions from a company the size and influence of Disney is, to say the least, difficult to understand and illustrates the depth of the problem faced by minority broadcasters and the government.

The FCC awards radio licenses for two main reasons: to ensure diversity of opinion and to ensure that these stations serve the country's diverse population. However, when an individual or company is awarded a license, there are expenses and, often, debt because the company must invest in equipment, personnel, programming, and research. These elements are necessary tools for a station to be attractive to advertisers as well as to serve the community. Debt can often amount to millions of dollars. For Black-oriented and Black O&O radio stations, making the bottom line is a matter of survival. Revenue lost as a result of media buyers' prejudices hinders a radio station's ability to service the debt that might have been incurred by owners upon purchasing a station. If owners cannot service their debt, a station faces bankruptcy.

Most importantly, media buyer discrimination hinders Black-oriented and Black O & O radio stations from servicing the communities in which they operate—the purpose for which these stations have been licensed. These stations not only provide valuable information for the Black community but also act as a forum for the discussion of issues pertaining to the Black community. Historically, general market media outlets have not immersed themselves in the issues relevant to the Black community; nor is there a trend for these outlets to do so. If a Black-oriented or Black O & O station goes out of business, the Black community loses a vital source of information and an important means of communication.

Media buyers claim to be objective and fair when placing a buy because the buying decision is based on market information and cost efficiencies. This study, however, reinforces the government's study and clearly demonstrates that the media-buying community is less than objective when considering the urban contemporary format. This study reveals that media buyers have negative perceptions about urban contemporary radio stations. Perhaps urban contemporary salespeople could show the results of this study to media buyers to help them recognize their prejudices and correct the error in their thinking. However, the researcher also realizes that prejudices are deeply ingrained in the psyche, are painful to recognize, and, frequently, difficult to change. Change, however, must happen.

This study indicates that Black-oriented and Black O & O radio stations will have to continue to work harder than their general market competitors to receive orders from advertising agencies. They will have to continue to invest in research and take the extra time to combat discrimination by educating media buyers and their clients about the value of reaching the Black consumer.

In defense of charges of discriminatory media-buying practices that surfaced during the Subcommittee on Telecommunications hearing in 1986, one unnamed editorial writer claimed the following ("Media Buying is Discriminatory," 1986):

Media buying has to be discriminatory. With a set amount of dollars to spend, advertisers try to get the widest exposure for the lowest cost. . . . Who is to determine that an advertiser with a broadly based media plan is discriminating against a certain segment of our society? . . . If an advertiser wrongly believes black readers, listeners and viewers are never good prospects for their products and services, that's his problem—and one that should in and of itself hit the company where it hurts. (p. 17)

No, as the new millennium approaches, we can see that such discrimination threatens the government's overriding philosophy of broadcasting in the public interest and hits the nation's Black community where it hurts.

REFERENCES

Bachman, R. D. (1977). *Dynamics of Black radio: A research report.* City: Creative Universal Products.

Bunzel, R. L. (1991, August). Interep study pushed value of urban format. *Broadcasting,* 29.

Bush, R., Solomon, P., & Hair, J. (1977). There are more blacks in TV commercials. *Journal of Advertising Research, 17,* 21–25.

Cagley, J., & Cardozo, R. (1970). White response to integrated advertising. *Journal of Advertising Research, 10,* 35–40.

Campenelli, M. (1991, May). The African-American market: Community, growth, and change. *Sales & Marketing Management,* 75–81.

Dates, J. L., & Bardow, W. (1993). *Split Image: African Americans in the mass media.* Howard University Press.

Minority-Owned Broadcast Stations (1986). *Hearing before the subcommittee on telecommunications, consumer protection, and finance of the committee on energy and commerce* (Serial No. 99–173). Washington, DC: U.S. Government Printing Office.

Edmonston, E. (1954). *The American negro in United States professional radio, 1922–1953.* Unpublished master's thesis, University of California, Los Angeles.

Hicks, R. G. (1978). *Black-owned radio stations 1949–1978.* Unpublished master's thesis, University of Missouri-Columbia, Columbia.

Humphrey, R., & Schuman, H. (1984). The portrayal of blacks in magazine advertisements: 1950–1982. *Public Opinion Quarterly, 48,* 551–563.

Kern-Foxworth, M. (1994). *Aunt Jemima, Uncle Ben, and Rastus: Blacks in advertising, yesterday, today, and tomorrow.* New York: Praeger.

King, K. W., Reid, L. N., & Morrison, M. (1997). Large-agency media specialists' opinions on newspaper advertising for national accounts. *The Journal of Advertising, 26,* 2.

Pasadeos, Y., Barban, A., Yi, H., & Kim, B. (1997). A 30-year assessment of the media planning literature. *Journal of Current Issues and Research in Advertising, 19,* 1.

Surlin, S. (1972, Summer). Black oriented radio: Programming to a perceived audience. *Journal of Broadcasting, 16,* 289–298.

Tienowitz, Ira. (1999, January). Minority media: Next step debated. *Advertising Age, 70,* 10.

Tienowitz, I., & Cordona, M. (1999, January). Sharpton sets timetable for minority ad changes. *Advertising Age, 70,* 18.

Turk, P., & Katz, H. (1992). Making headlines: An overview of key happenings in media planning, buying and research from 1985–1991. *Journal of Current Issues and Research in Advertising, 14,* 2.

Wimmer, R., & Dominick, J. (1991). *Mass media research. An introduction* (3rd ed., p. 123).

Agency income by top 10 broadcast (1990, March). *Advertising Age, 61,* S56.

Black buying power is rising; to reach $533 billion by 1999, new survey projects (1998, August). *Jet, 94,* 22–23.

Different strokes. (1999, May). *American Demographics, 21*(16), 18.

Media buying is discriminatory. (1986, October). *Advertising Age, 57,* 17.

Minorities charge discrimination in broadcast ratings, agency practices. (1977, December). *Broadcasting, 57,* 35–36.

Minority-Owned Broadcast Stations. (1986). *Hearing before the subcommittee on telecommunications, consumer protection, and finance of the committee on energy and commerce* (Serial No. 99–173). Washington, DC: U.S. Government Printing Office.

Niche market. (1998, November). *Advertising Age, 69,* 16.

No double standards. (1998, September). *Advertising Age, 69,* 34.

Power of ethnic radio seen. (1989, April). *Television/Radio Age, 36,* A10, A19.

Profile of the urban contemporary listener. (1991, June).

Ofori, K. A. (Principal Investigator). (1999). *When being no. 1 is not enough: The impact of advertising practices on minority-owned & minority-formatted broadcast stations.* (Report prepared by the civil rights forum on communications policy; access at http://www.civilrightsforum. org/fccadvertising.html).

III. THE INFLUENCING ROLE OF LANGUAGE IN DIVERSITY IN ADVERTISING

CHAPTER NINE

Language in Multicultural Advertising: Words and Cognitive Structure

David Luna
Baruch College, CUNY

Laura A. Peracchio
University of Wisconsin-Milwaukee

LANGUAGE AND CROSS-CULTURAL ADVERTISING

Advertisers are operating in an increasingly multicultural marketplace. As U.S. consumers become more diverse, they represent a growing variety of ethnic and cultural backgrounds and many are likely to speak other languages in addition to English. As a result, advertisers who target ethnic bilingual segments of the population must often address these questions: Should we translate our ads into our consumers' first language even though they understand English? If so, what types of ads should be translated?

Language, a manifestation of culture (Hofstede, 1997), influences consumers' reactions to marketing communications. Recently, a number of consumer research studies examined the relationship between the language of a stimulus (e.g., ads or brand names) and individuals' cognitive and affective responses to that stimulus. Most of those studies followed a psycholinguistics approach in that they adapted methods from cognitive psychology to examine how people who speak different languages process information. Research exploring language effects on consumer behavior can be classified in two groups: (a) studies that compare how monolingual speakers of different languages process information and (b) studies that examine how bilingual individuals may process a stimulus differently depending on its language. The study of bilingual individuals is particularly relevant to advertisers operating in a diverse cultural marketplace in which consumers speak the culture's dominant language but also speak their subculture's language. For instance, in the United States, many members of ethnic subcultures who speak non-English languages and take an active role in the marketplace are relatively fluent in English as well. For example, 72% of U.S. Hispanics speak both English and Spanish (Levey, 1999). Thus, it is important for marketers to understand how bilingual consumers process language.

We now briefly review a number of studies examining language-related topics in an advertising context to both monolingual and bilingual consumers. This review primarily focuses on how bilingual individuals process messages differently in their first and second languages because of the relevance of this issue for advertisers in a culturally diverse society. It will be evident from the existing studies on bilingual consumers that there is a need for theory-based research extending psycholinguistics theories to advertising to bilinguals.

Language Differences in Monolinguals

Recent studies compared monolingual processing across languages. For example, Schmitt, Pan, and Tavassoli (1994) and Tavassoli (1999) compared speakers of Chinese and English and the implications that structural differences in languages have for consumers' information processing and mental representations. They examined whether visually or auditorily presented information is remembered better by speakers of each of the languages. Their findings showed that, for example, unaided brand recall is differentially affected in Chinese and English when it is spoken compared with when it is written. Also using a cognitive approach, Pan and Schmitt (1996) found that a logograph-based writing system (i.e., Chinese writing) promotes visual processing whereas alphabetic systems promote aural processing. This effect of writing system on cognitive processing also has an impact on attitudes toward a brand, so Chinese brand attitudes are primarily affected by the match between script associations and brand associations, but brand attitudes of English names are primarily affected by the match between sound associations and brand associations. Going one step further, Schmitt and Zhang (1998) suggested that language shapes the representation of categories in consumers' minds. Thus, language differences may result in different cognitive structures, which in turn may lead to differences in consumers' inferences, attitudes, and, ultimately, choices.

Altogether, these studies suggest that the structure of a language indeed influences the cognition of individuals. This is consistent with recent conceptualizations of the Whorfian hypothesis (Carroll, 1956; Hunt & Agnoli, 1991) that describe how linguistic forms may affect the concepts and categories that denote objects and relations in the world. This is an important proposition for advertisers targeting consumers across cultures: It implies that a message, even after it is accurately translated and all other cultural factors have been taken into account, may not offer the same results in foreign countries. Consumers' processing and interpretation of the ad claims may differ just because they process language differently.

Language Differences in Bilinguals

Very few consumer behavior studies have examined how bilingual individuals process information in their respective languages. One of these studies, by Dolinsky and Feinberg (1986), examined language and how consumers from bilingual subcultures process information in their first versus their second language. They found that second-language processing leads to information overload and suboptimal decisions more easily than first-language processing. Following a sociolinguistics approach, Koslow, Shamdasani, and Touchstone (1994) applied a sociolinguistic approach in their study of advertising that targeted U.S. Hispanics. The authors used a sociolinguistics theory, accommodation theory, to explain their results and argue that Hispanic consumers' perception of the advertiser's sensitivity to their culture mediates the effectiveness of ads. Positive responses to ads are evoked if they include at least some portions in Spanish language. Other researchers have taken an anthropological, interpretive approach in the study of the relationship between symbols and cognition. For example, Sherry and Camargo (1987) examined the effect of language on consumers' cognition. Their study suggested that mixed-language (Japanese–English) ads communicate certain values that single-language ads could not express.

Two main issues emerge from the existing literature on advertising to bilinguals. First, second-language conceptual processing seems to be more effortful than first-language processing. Second, meaning structures seem to be different across languages, even within an individual. Thus, the same word may mean different things in different languages for the same person. Although these issues can be inferred from existing research, there is a need to explain why we should expect these differences in language processing. An understanding of the processes underlying these two phenomena will help advertisers design more effective materials to target bilingual consumers. The rest of this chapter presents two complementary psycholinguistics models that explain (a) why there is a difference in cognitive effort regarding the processing of first versus second language, and (b) why different languages may elicit different world views. The models help explain how bilingual individuals process information. In addition, a series of empirical studies that extend the models to advertising are described.

PROCESSING DIFFICULTY OF FIRST VERSUS SECOND LANGUAGE

In this section, a psycholinguistics model, the Revised Hierarchical Model (RHM; Kroll, 1993), is presented to show that second-language conceptual processing is more effortful than first-language conceptual processing. Two types of moderators of this effect are identified: individual-level variables (i.e., processing motivation) and stimulus characteristics (i.e., ad pictures). First, the RHM is presented. Then, the process through which the two types of moderators influence language effects is described and empirical evidence is provided in the form of the results of several experimental studies.

The Revised Hierarchical Model

The topic of conceptual representation in a bilingual individual's memory has been extensively discussed in the psycholinguistics literature. Specifically, a question subject to frequent enquiry is whether, in a bilingual's mind, each language she or he knows possesses its own memory store. Some studies have reported evidence for the independence between a bilingual's two language representations (e.g., Kolers, 1963). Other theorists suggest that all languages known by an individual share a single representational system (e.g., Schwanenflugel & Rey, 1986). A recent and widely accepted model that synthesizes both views is the RHM (Dufour & Kroll, 1995; Kroll & de Groot, 1997). This model builds on previous findings (Durgunoglu & Roediger, 1987; Snodgrass, 1984) that suggest that there exist two levels of representation: the lexical (word) level and the conceptual (meaning) level. At the lexical level, each language seems to be stored separately. However, at the conceptual level, there is a unitary system in which words in each language access a common semantic representation or meaning. Thus, according to Dufour and Kroll (1995), bilingual individuals possess a "hierarchical arrangement of words and concepts, with a separation at the lexical level but with connections to a semantic system that is shared across languages" (p. 166).

The connections between words in different languages made at the lexical level are referred to as word associations or *lexical links*, whereas the connections in memory between lexical representations in either language and the meanings they represent are referred to as *conceptual links*.

Figure 9.1 depicts the RHM in graphical form. The model specifies a stronger lexical link from the individual's second language (L2) to his or her first language (L1) than from the individual's L1 to his or her L2.[1] This is a residual effect from the L2 acquisition process, in which it is assumed that individuals begin learning words in their L2 by relating them to words in their L1. Hence, words in the bilingual individual's L2 are closely associated with L1 words, and this initial association is based on lexical links.

The same residual effect accounts for the stronger conceptual links between lexical representations in an individual's L1 and the semantic representations in memory (concepts). Conceptual links to the individual's L2 are weaker because it is only after individuals have achieved a high level of proficiency in their L2 that they rely less on their L1 to gain access to meaning. Thus, the strengths of both lexical and conceptual links are a function of the L2 proficiency of the individual in

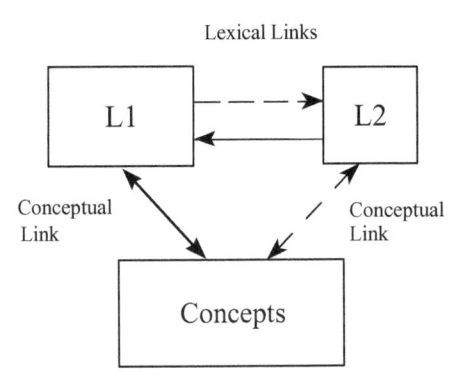

FIG. 9.1. The Revised Hierarchical Model.

question. However, even after the individual has become relatively fluent in both languages, there is a residual asymmetry in both lexical and conceptual links as represented in Fig. 9.1. The model also specifies that the L2 lexical store is smaller than the L1 store, which indicates a pervasive lexical (vocabulary) superiority of the L1 over the L2.

The RHM has been tested in psycholinguistics mainly by use of translation tasks. For example, Kroll and Stewart (1994) theorized that translation from L1 to L2 (forward translation) is more likely to involve conceptual mediation than translation from L2 to L1 (backward translation) because L1 can activate concepts more readily than L2 can. In contrast, the stronger lexical links from L2 to L1 should facilitate fast lexical-level backward translation without access to meaning. In general, lexical-level translation is faster than translations that involve conceptual access (Sholl, Sankaranarayanan, & Kroll, 1995). Accordingly, in an empirical study, Kroll and Stewart (1994) hypothesized and confirmed that backward translation is faster than forward translation and also less sensitive to the effects of semantic factors such as whether the word to be translated is inserted in a categorized list or in a randomly mixed list.

Pictures as Moderators of Language Effects

The studies presented in the previous section lend support to the relationships hypothesized by the RHM. The processing of L1 stimuli is more likely to involve conceptual mediation than the processing of equivalent L2 stimuli. In other words, L1 stimuli have more direct access to concepts than L2 stimuli. This is due to the asymmetry in the strength of L1 and L2 lexical and conceptual links as depicted in Fig. 9.1. At the same time, research in psycholinguistics testing the RHM has found that the accessibility to concepts of an L2 text may be facilitated by manipulation of other elements of the stimulus, such as whether it is accompanied by a congruent picture. La Heij, Hooglander, Kerling, and Van Der Velden (1996) exposed bilingual subjects to words that had to be translated into a different language. Subjects were native speakers of Dutch (their dominant language) and were relatively proficient in English. In Experiment 1, the words were accompanied by either congruent or incongruent pictures, such as the word *shark* in combination with the picture of a shark or the picture of a bottle. In Experiment 2, the words were accompanied by either semantically related or semantically unrelated pictures, such as the word *shark* in combination with the picture of a whale or the picture of a bottle.

La Heij et al. (1996) found that translation of the written stimuli was facilitated in the form of shorter latencies by both congruent (Experiment 1) and semantically related (Experiment 2) pictures, whereas incongruent and unrelated pictures resulted in higher latencies. Thus, pictures seem to aid or hamper language processing, depending on their level of relatedness to the textual stimulus. Consistent with the RHM, La Heij et al. (1996) concluded that relatively fluent bilinguals are able to access concepts from their L2 but do so with more difficulty than from their L1 (latencies were higher for backward translation than for forward translation even in the picture-congruent conditions). Hence, the asymmetry in conceptual link strength hypothesized by the RHM is supported. Most importantly, the findings by La Heij et al. (1996) imply that L2 conceptual links can be "strengthened" by a pictorial cue that facilitates activation of the concept represented by the L2 word. Next, we briefly review consumer research on the effect of pictures on advertising effectiveness. This research will help us consider picture effects in a bilingual advertising context.

Picture Effects in Advertising.   Advertising researchers have examined the role of pictures in ad processing by monolinguals (Alesandrini, 1983; Holbrook & Moore, 1981; Houston, Childers, & Heckler, 1987; Lutz & Lutz, 1977; Schmitt, Tavassoli, & Millard, 1993; Unnava & Burnkrant, 1991). Previous studies have theorized that pictures that are congruent with the brand name of the product featured in an ad (interactive pictures) facilitate processing of the message by providing a frame to process the ad claims. Interactive pictures serve as an advance organizer that creates an expectation of the claims that follow. At the same time, the ad claims may or may not be congruent with the picture. If they are congruent (consistent), processing of the claims is facilitated. If the ad claims are incongruent (inconsistent), processing is more difficult because the consumer needs to resolve the incongruity between the new information presented by the ad claims and the prior knowledge established by the picture (Houston et al., 1987).

Other studies (Schmitt et al., 1993) have used the spreading activation paradigm (Anderson, 1983) to explain picture effects on ad processing. They suggest that the picture activates a conceptual node, which then may become closely associated with the concept(s) described by the subsequent text if there is a high level of picture–text congruity. The strong linkages between these sets of nodes then facilitate further relational processing, in turn making the conceptual links stronger. As a result, the probability of retrieving a concept is higher when picture and text are congruent than when they are not. Paivio's (1971) dual-code theory validates this reasoning. Activation can spread from the imagery to the verbal system and vice versa, creating linkages between the two structures. Because, in memory, pictures are more easily accessed than verbal information, the probability that a concept will be retrieved is higher if it is closely associated with a picture than if it is not (Schmitt et al., 1993; Unnava & Burnkrant, 1991).

On the basis of this research, we suggest that if the ad copy expresses the same (or a similar) concept as the picture, strong linkages will be formed in memory that will facilitate relational processing of the ad claims. This will make retrieval of the information easier during recall. The findings by La Heij et al. (1996) with single-word stimuli lend support to this reasoning and establish a theoretical link with the psycholinguistics literature on bilingual language processing and the RHM.

Empirical Support

An empirical study was conducted to test the moderating effect of an ad's picture on memory for L1 versus L2 ads (see Luna & Peracchio, 2001). The study conceptualized the degree of picture–text congruity and its effect on ad memory by adapting a method used by Houston et al. (1987). Two ad factors were manipulated to produce different levels of picture–text congruity: interactivity of the product's brand name (whether the brand name is congruent or incongruent with the picture) and consistency of the copy (whether the product attribute described in the copy is congruent or incongruent with the picture). As already described, the level of picture–text congruity determines the degree to which the picture will help process the ad claims semantically.

Greater congruity suggests that stronger linkages are created in memory between pictorial and verbal concepts, facilitating relational processing and increasing the likelihood that the ad claims will be correctly recalled. For example, if the brand name is interactive with the picture, the concept activated by the picture is similar to the one activated by the brand name. As a result, the ad will be easier to process than if the brand name is noninteractive (i.e., the brand name and picture activate dissimilar concepts). This effect will be noted not only on brand recall but also on memory for other textual elements of the ad (Houston et al., 1987), presumably because the expectation communicated by the picture is confirmed by the brand name. For the same reason, if the product attribute described in the text (i.e., ad claims) is consistent with the picture, processing of the ad will be similarly aided relative to ads describing an inconsistent product attribute.

Three levels of picture–text congruity result from the manipulation of brand name and product attribute congruity with the picture: (a) high-congruity ads in which picture, brand name, and product attribute are all congruent; (b) moderate-congruity ads in which either the brand name or the product attribute is not congruent with the picture; and (c) low-congruity ads in which neither the brand name nor the product attribute are congruent with the picture.

For ads in the low-congruity condition, strong linkages between the concepts represented by the picture and the text will not be formed and relational processing of the ad claims will not occur. Thus, pictures are not expected to facilitate processing and subsequent recall of the ad claims in either language. L1 and L2 ads will not benefit from the pictorial information in the ad, so subjects in both the L1 and L2 conditions will generally fail to remember the correct ad claims.

As the congruity of the ads is increased in the moderate-congruity condition, memory for the L1 ad claims should increase significantly. Subjects in the L1 condition will be able to easily establish a connection between the picture and at least one element of the ad text, so relational processing will be facilitated. However, as postulated by the RHM, L2 ads are intrinsically difficult to process at the conceptual level because of the weaker L2 conceptual links, so subjects in this condition will continue to have difficulty making the connections between the pictorial and verbal concepts. In this moderate-congruity condition, there is only partial congruity between picture and text, so subjects exposed to L2 ads cannot establish strong linkages across presentation modalities. As a result, memory for L2 ad claims will be significantly lower than memory for L1 claims in this condition.

Finally, ads in the high-congruity condition represent total overlap between the pictorial and verbal information. In this condition, both brand name and product attribute are congruent with the picture, so the entire text of the ad communicates the same concept as the picture. This condition parallels La Heij et al.'s (1996) congruity condition: the picture serves as a means to access concepts directly, thus facilitating processing of the ad claims. Hence, memory for L2 ad claims should experience a significant improvement over the low- and moderate-congruity conditions. This increase should bring L2 memory to approximately the same level as L1 memory. This is the condition most interesting for advertisers targeting bilingual markets with limited capabilities to produce customized campaigns, because both L2 and L1 ads should produce similar high memory.

In our empirical study, we manipulated three factors between subjects: language, consistency of the product attribute described in the ad, and interactivity of the brand name of the product featured in the ad. Three ads, all in the same condition, were presented in either English or Spanish to the subjects. For the purposes of analysis, the ad's language was coded as L1 or L2, depending on the language in which the subjects were most fluent. Thus, if the language in which a subject was most proficient (e.g., Spanish) was the same as the language in which the ad was presented to the subject, then she or he was in the L1 condition; otherwise, the subject was in the L2 condition. Consistency of the product attribute and interactivity of the brand name were two-level factors: Ads were designed to have either an interactive or a noninteractive brand name and to describe either a consistent or an inconsistent product attribute as defined by Houston et al. (1987).

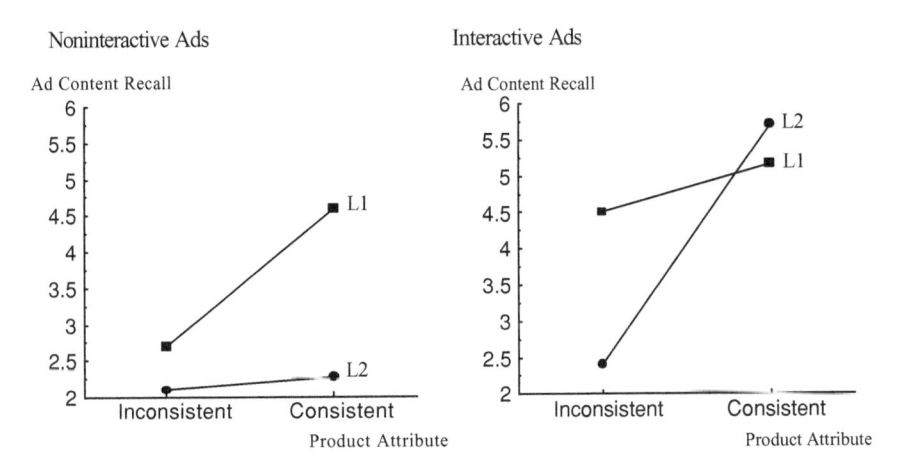

FIG. 9.2.   Three-Way Interaction on ad Content Recall.

The results of the study confirmed our expectations. Figure 9.2 depicts the findings. In the noninteractive–inconsistent condition (low-congruity ads), there was no significant difference between the L1 and the L2 conditions. In addition, memory for both L1 and L2 ads is relatively low, as can be seen in Fig. 9.2. In the noninteractive–consistent condition (moderate-congruity ads), L1 messages were recalled better than L2 messages. Similarly, in the interactive–inconsistent condition (also moderate-congruity ads), there was a parallel superiority of L1 ads over L2 ads. Finally, in the interactive–consistent condition (high-congruity ads), L2 ads were recalled equally as well as L1 ads. As can be observed in Fig. 9.2, the increase between interactive–inconsistent and interactive -consistent ads in the L2 condition was highly significant. Recognition memory results followed the same pattern.

The next section describes how an individual-level variable, processing motivation, can also moderate language effects on cognitive measures of ad effectiveness. Two empirical studies are described to confirm our reasoning.

Processing Motivation as a Moderator of Language Effects.   Individuals who are highly motivated to process an ad tend to engage in elaborative processing of the ad claims (Unnava et al., 1991), which may in turn result in higher recall of the ad content. At the same time, according to dual-process models of persuasion such as the Elaboration Likelihood Model (Petty & Cacioppo, 1986), subjects must have the ability to process the ad claims in order to benefit from a high level of motivation. The RHM suggests that L2 messages are more difficult to process than L1 messages, so consumers exposed to L1 ads have a higher ability to process messages than consumers exposed to L2 ads. Consequently, only memory for L1 ads should benefit from a higher level of motivation. As a result, we can predict that, under high-motivation conditions, there will be a memory superiority of L1 ads in conditions of moderate picture–text congruity, whereas under low-motivation conditions, both L1 and L2 ads should experience similar levels of low memory. This reasoning is consistent with previous research (Unnava et al., 1991) that examined the role of pictures under high-motivation conditions.

To test our reasoning, we conducted a second empirical study (see Luna & Peracchio, 2001). The procedure and materials used in this study were similar to the picture study described in the previous section. Subjects were exposed to the ad booklet and then completed a questionnaire containing the dependent measures. The experimental ads included manipulations for brand name and product attribute congruity with the ads' pictures. The present study differed from the previous one in two ways: (a) only ads in the moderate-congruity conditions were used, because ads in the high- and low-congruity conditions had shown similar memory results for L1 and L2; and (b) subjects' processing motivation was manipulated following a procedure used in previous research (Peracchio & Meyers-Levy, 1997). Individuals in the low-processing-motivation condition were told that they were part of a large group of people in the country who were participating in the study and that their opinion about the ads might be used after it was aggregated with that of other individuals. In contrast, individuals in the high-processing-motivation condition were told that they were part of a small group of people in the city who were participating in the study and that, because their opinion was very valuable to the companies represented in the ads, they would be offered special discounts on any advertised product or service that they wished to purchase.

The results revealed a significant two-way interaction of processing motivation and ad language for moderate-congruity ads. Examination of this interaction revealed the anticipated outcomes. In the high-motivation condition, there was a memory superiority of L1 messages over L2 messages. In the low-motivation condition, L1 and L2 messages resulted in similar, low recall of the ad content. As Fig. 9.3

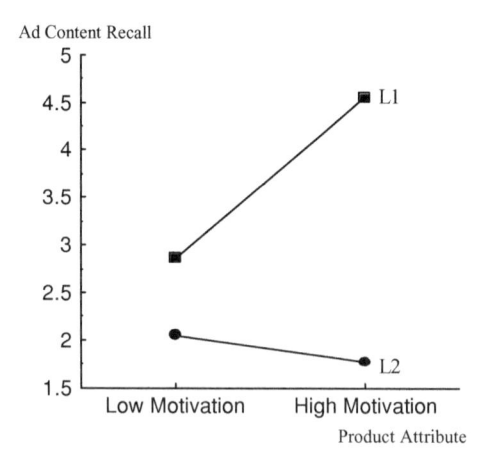

FIG. 9.3.   Motivation and ad Content Recall.

suggests, it seems that L1 ads benefited from processing motivation whereas L2 ads did not. Therefore, processing motivation increased memory for L1 ads but not for L2 ads. Because L2 ads are inherently difficult to process at the conceptual level, individuals exposed to L2 ads could not elaborate on the ad content as effectively as individuals exposed to L1 ads. Luna and Peracchio (2002a) conducted follow-up research showing that need for cognition, a measure of intrinsic motivation, interacts with extrinsic motivation (i.e., resulting from an experimental manipulation). When both forms of motivation are high, L2 processing can be facilitated.

In sum, the results of these experiments suggest that (a) congruent pictures facilitate memory for L2 ads, and (b) motivation facilitates memory for L1 ads but not L2 ads, unless individuals also have a high need for cognition. The studies used to achieve these results were based on the RHM (Kroll, 1993), which suggests that L2 processing is less likely to involve conceptual mediation than L1 processing. In the next section, we present the Conceptual Feature Model (CFM; de Groot, 1992a). The model complements and is consistent with the RHM (Kroll & de Groot, 1997) and can be used to substantiate the second topic that emerged from our review of the literature on advertising to bilinguals: A bilingual individual may possess different cognitive structures for each of the languages that the individual knows.

DIFFERENT LANGUAGES, DIFFERENT WORLD VIEWS

The Conceptual Feature Model

De Groot (1992a) developed a model of bilingual lexicosemantic organization, the CFM, in which words in each language known by a bilingual individual activate a series of conceptual features. These features, or concepts, are language independent and are distributed so that one word is connected to a number of concepts that ultimately define the subjective meaning of the word for each individual. The features activated by a word, say, *friend*, are not necessarily the same features activated by its Spanish-language translation equivalent, *amigo*. For example, *friend* may be associated with the concepts [McDonalds] and [honesty], whereas *amigo* may be associated with the concepts [honesty] and [male]. The difference in the conceptual features linked to each translation-equivalent word could be due to the different contexts in which the words are learned and normally used. Figure 9.4 shows the hypothetical links between two translation-equivalent words and the concepts with which they are connected. As shown, the conceptual nodes connected to *friend* may not be the same as the ones connected to *amigo*.

The example in Fig. 9.4 can be interpreted as depicting two language-specific knowledge schemas: the English *friend* schema and the Spanish *amigo* schema. Tests of the CFM have found that concrete words (e.g., *window*) share more conceptual features across languages than abstract words (e.g., *love*). This difference is apparent in that abstract words often do not seem to have an exact translation. De Groot (1992a) theorized that the reason for this difference may be that the function and appearance of concrete entities (e.g., apple or chair) tend to be the same across

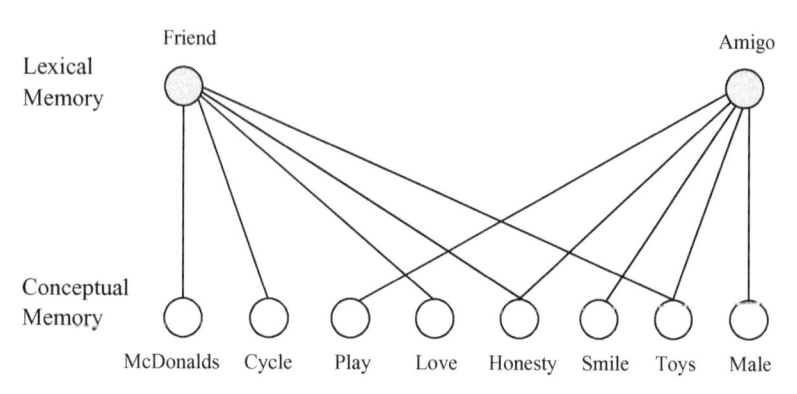

FIG. 9.4. The Conceptual Feature Model (adapted from de Groot, 1992a).

different language communities. Thus, the language learner creates a representation for a new concrete word that varies relatively little across languages. Abstract words do not have external referents that can be inspected during the learning process, so there is no guarantee that the content of the developing representations across languages will be similar. An individual has to acquire the meanings of abstract words from an objective source (e.g., a dictionary) or, more importantly, by deducing them from the contexts in which they are used. Because contexts are likely to differ between languages or cultures, the meanings of these words are also likely to be different. The difference between concrete and abstract words also appears in monolingual settings. For example, in an experiment with monolingual subjects, de Groot (1989) found that concrete words have more and stronger links with the concepts they represent than abstract words.

Another variable that has an impact on lexicosemantic organization is the cognate status of words. A word is a cognate when its translation equivalent sounds and looks like it. For example, *addiction* and *adicción* are cognates, whereas *book* and *libro* are noncognates. According to the CFM, cognates share a great deal more conceptual features across translation equivalents than do noncognates. Cognate effects on lexicosemantic organization may be due to two factors. First, cognate translation-equivalent words generally derive from the same root in a common parent language (e.g., Latin or Greek), so they have probably preserved the meaning of this root over time. Consequently, cognates may have similar meanings. Another reason for the cognate effect may be that L2 learners, noticing the form similarity between a cognate word and its translation, assume that the two also have a meaning similarity conveniently linking the new L2 word with the concept representation of the L1 word (de Groot, 1992a).

Theoretical Support for the CFM

The duality specified in the CFM finds support in a number of theories that help explain the underlying processes resulting in language-specific schemas. The repeated coupling of certain concepts with an L1 word, for example, the concept [play] and the Spanish word *amigo* (friend) during L1 learning and the life of the individual provides consistent and strong mappings from those concepts to the L1 word (Kroll & de Groot, 1997; MacWhinney, 1997). These consistent mappings result in strong links between the L1 word and the concepts. Different associations are likely to happen during L2 learning. Other concepts are likely to be consistently present when the individual learns L2 words, for example, the concept [McDonalds] and the English word *friend*, so alternate L2-specific links will be created between these nodes. This reasoning is consistent with the theory of spreading activation (Anderson, 1983; Collins & Loftus, 1975), which predicts that links that are "practiced" or observed many times become stronger. Therefore, if we assume that the *amigo*–[play] link was practiced more than the *friend*–[play] link, the former will be stronger than the latter.

Barsalou's (1982) research also helps explain the notion of language-specific schemas. Properties, or concepts associated with a stimulus, become automatically activated with that stimulus after being frequently associated with it during processing. Frequent pairings of a stimulus and a concept cause an automatized relation between them to be established in memory. Barsalou indicated that there are two types of concepts likely to be frequently active during the processing of a stimulus: concepts having high diagnosticity ([gills] for *fish*), and concepts relevant to how people typically interact with instances of the respective stimulus ([edible] for *apples*). Hence, an individual's experience may be a source of differences in cognitive structure. Because culture shapes human experience, cultural differences may give origin to different patterns of activation or cognitive structures in individuals.

Finally, according to spreading activation principles, encoding context plays a large role in the memory for an item. Anderson (1983) asserted that

> The encoding context determines the sense of the word chosen [i.e., one of its meanings] and that a trace is formed involving that sense and, perhaps, the encoding context. When the subject is tested, context will again determine the sense chosen and activation will spread from the chosen sense. Probability of recognition will be greater when the same sense is chosen because activation will be spreading from a sense node directly attached to the trace. (p. 283)

The language of a message can be considered a contextual cue that helps a particular word activate a series of nodes that would not be activated in another language, thus priming the language-specific schemas implied by the CFM. Note that this effect is similar to encoding specificity (Tulving & Thompson, 1971).

What are the implications of the CFM for advertisers? Consider the following ad (see Fig. 9.5) for AFLAC insurance that recently appeared in *Hispanic* magazine: "Twenty million hijas are covered by AFLAC. Is yours?"

In Spanish, the word *hija* means daughter. *Hispanic* is a publication that targets Latinos who are fluent in English, so the majority of its articles are in English. However, many of the ads are either in English and Spanish or entirely in Spanish. AFLAC hopes that the word *hija* may have associations in the minds of bilingual consumers that the English-equivalent word does not have. For example, the concepts [love] or [responsibility] may be activated by *hija*, but not by *daughter*. When these language-specific associations are activated by the use of the Spanish word, then the Spanish schema will shape consumers' subsequent information processing, thus affecting their response to the ad. Hence, it is important that advertisers know which associations are elicited by their bilingual ad. The next section discusses the topic of language-specific schemas and argues that bilingual individuals seem to possess different cognitive structures for each of the languages they know. We label this phenomenon *cognitive duality*.

Cognitive Duality

Cognitive duality may occur when an individual possesses different cognitive schemas linked to the same word. In the case of bilingual individuals, activation of either schema depends on the language in which the individual encounters the word. In a sense, then, an individual's perception of reality could depend on the language the individual uses, and either cognitive structure may be readily activated by a simple cue like language of presentation.

Cognitive duality, or the existence of language-specific schemas, is implicit in the CFM (see Fig. 9.4) but has not been explicitly addressed by the psycholinguistics studies that test the model. Language-specific schemas may originate because certain contexts are normally present when one of the languages is used but not when the other language is used. For example, for a bilingual Hispanic child of Spanish-speaking parents who is growing up in an Anglo community, the English word *telephone* may be associated with technical or electronic concepts, because most of the time when the word is presented to the child, it is in a technical context. In contrast, the Spanish-equivalent translation, *teléfono*, may be more strongly associated with family or friendship-related concepts because the child normally uses and hears the Spanish word in the context of communication with friends and family.

The existence of such language-specific structures would have important implications for advertisers. It would mean that language in bilingual ads could be manipulated to communicate certain connotations not activated by ads in only one language (Sherry & Camargo, 1987). Acknowledging the relevance of this issue, we describe in this section an empirical study that investigated two possible manifestations of cognitive duality (see Luna & Peracchio, 2002b, 2003). First, some words may be associated with specific categories of concepts, depending on the language in which they are presented. For bilingual Hispanics, for example, Spanish words could more easily access concepts that are emotionally charged or Hispanic in

FIG. 9.5. Ad containing words in two languages.

nature. Latinos in the United States normally associate the Spanish language with family and home-related topics (Guernica, 1982). Consequently, they tend to express emotions in Spanish. At the same time, language can be considered a cultural cue: use of a language is associated with behaviors and objects typical of a particular culture (Grossjean, 1982; Gudykunst & Schmidt, 1988; Scotton & Ury, 1977). Therefore, concepts relating to the Hispanic culture should be more readily available when a Spanish word is presented.

Bilingual Hispanics who live in a predominantly Anglo society will likely approach certain topics in English, particularly topics that relate to the Anglo culture and imply an interaction with it. For example, concepts related to financial and technical matters (i.e., technology or technical terms) may be more easily associated with words in English than with words in Spanish. This phenomenon can be observed when individuals from a minority culture switch to the standard or majority language when they treat business or technical topics (Grossjean, 1982; Scotton & Ury, 1977).

The second manifestation of cognitive duality examined in this study is the implication that some specific concepts may be associated with a word in one language (e.g., English) but not in the other (e.g., Spanish). For example, as already indicated, the words *telephone* and *teléfono* may activate different, language-specific schemas. Because, by definition, any analysis designed to test this implication is based on a posteriori inspection of the data, this proposition was tested by use of a qualitative method.

Empirical Study

Eight words, all nouns, were selected for the study based on their cognate status and concreteness level. The words were chosen from an initial list of 120 nouns that appeared in advertisements. The selection process consisted of filtering the initial list through two pretests, one for the cognate status of the words (de Groot, 1992b) and another for their concreteness (de Groot & Hoeks, 1995; Paivio, Yuille, & Madigan, 1968). Thus, in the final list of eight words there were two words in each of the 2 (concrete; abstract) × 2 (cognate; noncognate) conditions. The final eight words were matched for word frequency by using Francis and Kucera's (1982) standards, in which a corpus of English-language words is rated for frequency of use.

Subjects participated in three sessions in which they had to perform a continuous word association task for each of the eight experimental words. The sessions were held approximately 1 month apart. Subjects were told that they had 1 minute to write down all the words that came to their mind when they read the experimental word on top of each page. They were asked not to repeat words and to try not to think of the other words they had written before when they gave each answer. Subjects were told that there were no right or wrong answers and that they should write down whatever came to their mind. After subjects read the written instructions, the experimenter reiterated them verbally. Each experimental word was written on top of a page in boldface, capital letters. The same word was repeated numerous times down the page, forming a column, with a space to the right of each repetition where subjects were asked to write their associations. The eight words were randomly ordered, and the order was varied. Across the three sessions, half the subjects performed the task in Spanish–English–Spanish, and the other half in English–Spanish–English. Within each session, only one language was used. All instructions, stimuli, responses, and "small talk" were carried out in the language corresponding to the session.

The first manifestation of cognitive duality described herein stated that certain categories of concepts are more likely to be associated with words in one language than to their translation equivalents in the other language. For this proposition to be tested, subjects' lists of associates were pooled across the eight keywords, resulting in two lists of associative responses for each subject: one in English and another in Spanish. These lists were searched for associates belonging to each of the four categories of interest. Emotion words were any associates that carried positively or negatively valenced affect, such as the words *love* or *family*. Hispanic words were associates that made reference to concepts specific to any Hispanic culture, such as the words *taco* or *Puerto Rican*. Technical words were those related to technology or to formal definitions of a term, such as the words *Internet* or *data*. Financial words were those related to business or money matters, such as the words *money* or *cost*. After the lists of associates were coded according to the four categories relevant to the hypotheses tests, it was observed that certain associates of a neutral nature were frequently written by subjects in response to the keywords in both languages. These neutral associates represent concepts that have very strong links to the keywords but were irrelevant for our study, because they do not relate to any hypotheses. Examples include *dress* as a response to *bride* or *big* in response to *size*. These associates were elicited very frequently both in Spanish and in English. Thus, the 10 most frequent neutral associates for each of the keywords account for an average of 24% and 22% of the total number of associates in English and Spanish, respectively.

Two analyses were performed to test our hypotheses. First, responses for the whole sample were analyzed. Then, a subsample of culturally homogenous subjects of Puerto Rican origin was selected to validate the results with respect to the whole sample. For each of the two analyses, the dependent measure was the ratio of each subject's associative responses in each of the four relevant categories over the total number of associates produced by that subject. The ratios were submitted to an arcsine transformation. A within-subjects, repeated measures, multivariate analysis of variance with one within-subjects factor (language: Spanish or English) and four measures (category: emotion, Hispanic, technical, or financial) was performed.

The results for the total sample show that subjects produced a higher proportion of emotion associates in Spanish than in English. There were also more Hispanic associates in Spanish than in English. Similarly, there were more technical associates in English than in Spanish. However, English words did not elicit significantly more financial concepts than Spanish words. A similar analysis was performed with a subsample of 25 subjects of Puerto Rican origin. Subjects of only one national background were selected to minimize the cultural heterogeneity of the sample and test the validity of the whole-sample results. All subjects in this subsample had learned Spanish at home before learning English, and, at the time of the experiment, they still communicated with their parents mostly in Spanish. The results for the subsample parallel those for the whole sample. Subjects produced more emotion associates in Spanish than in English. There were more Hispanic associates in Spanish than in English, and there were more technical associates in English than in Spanish. As with the whole sample, English words did not elicit significantly more financial concepts than Spanish words.

The second manifestation of cognitive duality stated that some specific concepts are activated by words in one language but not in the other. The data from the Puerto Rican subsample were exclusively used to test this proposition. The smaller and more homogenous sample was used in this instance exclusively, because this group of subjects had less variation that was due to cultural differences. A qualitative analysis examines this proposition. The responses to the word-association task were pooled across all subjects, so 16 lists, or 8 (words) × 2 (English or Spanish) lists, were developed that included the responses from all 25 subjects. The lists were searched for concepts frequently associated with a word in one language but not in the other. Thus, if an association was to be considered English (Spanish) specific, it had to meet two rules: First, it had to be mentioned by at least 4 more subjects in English (Spanish) than in Spanish (English). Second, it had to be listed at least three times as often in English (Spanish) as in Spanish (English) by subjects. For example, suppose that the Spanish associate *familia* was listed by 5 subjects in response to the keyword *restaurante* and the English associate *family* was mentioned by only 1 subject in response to *restaurant*. *Familia* would be considered a Spanish-specific association, because it was mentioned by at least 4 more subjects than *family* and was also mentioned by at least three times as many subjects as *family*. A number of language-specific associates were found for each language and are included in Table 9.1. Language-specific associates were consistent with the findings with respect to the categories of associates found herein (e.g., Spanish-specific associates included emotion concepts, and English-specific associates included technical concepts).

Therefore, the notion of cognitive duality is supported by the results of this study. Furthermore, cognitive duality seems to be robust across subcultures, because our expectations were supported for the whole sample in addition to the smaller, more homogeneous, subsample. Language, not subculture, seems to drive cognitive duality.

These results are consistent with the categories found in our analysis of the first manifestation of cognitive duality. For example, the words *kitchen* and *telephone* tended to elicit the concept [microwave] and [dial], respectively, in English but

TABLE 9.1
Language-Specific Associates

Word	English Associates	Spanish Associates
Kitchen	Microwave (5–1) Cabinet (5–1)	
Culture		Dance (2–6)
Bride	Bridesmaid (7–0) Flowers (7–2) Husband (5–0) Marriage (7–2)	Beautiful (1–7)
Telephone	Dial (7–1) Ring (6–2)	
Size	Car (8–2) Medium (10–3) Petite (4–0)	Sew (2–9)
Restaurant	Chinese (4–1) People (6–2)	Flavor (0–4) Napkin (0–4) Family (1–4)
Rate	Cost (6–0) Expensive (5–0) Increase (4–0) Judge (4–0) Price (4–0) Speed (9–0) High (6–2)	Book (0–4) Sports (0–6) Work (1–5)
Information	Letter (5–0) Mail (4–0)	School (1–7) Important (2–6) Books (3–9)

Note. Frequencies in English–Spanish are in parentheses.

not in Spanish. This may be because English-language words are more strongly associated with technical concepts than are Spanish-language words. In contrast, the Spanish word for *culture* tended to elicit the concept [baile] (dance), and the Spanish version of *restaurant* tended to elicit [family], an emotionally charged concept, and *sabor* (a culturally charged term for the word *flavor*) and *servilleta* (napkin), both of which can be considered more culturally Hispanic than Anglo. At the same time, when the Spanish word for *size* was presented, it elicited the associate *sewing* frequently, but it did not when the word was presented in English. Indeed, sewing-related concepts such as needle and thread were mentioned 24 times (by a total of 11 subjects) in Spanish whereas they were only mentioned 3 times (by a total of 2 subjects) in English. Language was revealed to be a significant factor in a test of the likelihood that subjects would mention sewing-related concepts in English versus Spanish. It is possible that sewing is seen as an activity typically performed by Hispanic women, so it may be more easily activated by the Spanish word for *size* (a clothing-related word) than by its English-equivalent translation.

CONCLUSIONS

In this chapter, we reviewed research examining the issue of language in advertising that targets bilingual individuals. Language is an important component of any marketing communication, so the lack of theory-based research in this area is surprising. From our review of the literature, two issues that required further attention were identified: (a) the differential processing demands that L1 messages and L2 messages seemed to exert on individuals, and (b) the effect of language on semantic structures. These two issues were addressed in this chapter through the extension of two psycholinguistics models, the RHM and the CFM. The two models are complementary and together offer a framework to study how bilingual individuals process and store language (Kroll & de Groot, 1997). The chapter outlines the results of several experimental studies that test and extend these models in an advertising context. The results are promising in that they confirm our reasoning that cognitive processing is different in different languages, and they open a new avenue for advertising research.

Our research extending the RHM contributes to both psycholinguistics and consumer behavior research. Previous studies seeking to test the RHM had only considered single-word stimuli and either translation or priming tasks. In this research, we applied the RHM to more complex stimuli: advertisements. We tested the implications of the RHM for memory and found that the model predictions apply to this task as well. More importantly, the moderating effect of nonlanguage variables on the RHM is highlighted in this research.

Future research studies that seek to apply the RHM must examine whether learning context (c.g., classroom or immersion learning), situation (e.g., home or work), medium (e.g., print or TV), or subject matter (e.g., home life issues or shopping) moderate the relationships described by the model. For example, it is possible that, for some Hispanics, L2 (e.g., English) conceptual links are stronger when the topic of conversation revolves around shopping matters. Conversely, the same individuals' L1 (e.g., Spanish) conceptual links could be stronger when the subject matter is home life issues. Peñaloza's (1994) research seems to imply that Mexican immigrants in the United States may be experiencing this phenomenon because they frequently learn consumer-related concepts in English (their second language) for which there are no Spanish equivalents. Our studies used an operationalization of L1 and L2 in which general language proficiency was measured and then used to assign subjects to the L1 or L2 conditions. This general proficiency measure included items that asked how well subjects could perform day-to-day tasks such as reading newspaper headlines or writing notes to friends. Future research must examine language proficiency in specific contexts such as shopping to determine whether the predictions of the RHM are indeed context specific.

Consumer researchers will benefit from this chapter in that it provides a cognitive framework for the study of how bilingual consumers process advertisements. Our findings suggest that factors such as picture–copy congruity and processing motivation, both previously studied in monolingual consumer research, may have different effects depending on the language in which the ad is written. If similar conclusions can be applied to other constructs examined in consumer behavior, a number of theories may have to be revisited. For example, the conclusion of Unnava and Burnkrant (1991) that motivation enhances memory is qualified by our findings—only memory for L1 messages is enhanced. Reviewing existing theory to account for bilingualism is no trivial matter if we consider that much of the world's population speaks more than one language.

This chapter also explores the extension of the CFM to advertising. In particular, we investigate whether there are language-specific cognitive structures, or schemas, unique to a word when it is presented in English, but not in Spanish, and vice versa. The existence of language-specific schemas would support our notion of the cognitive duality of the bilingual mind. Previous research in psycholinguistics has not explicitly addressed this question. This research reveals that indeed some concepts tend to be associated with a word in one language but not in the other. From these findings, it can be inferred that those unique associates are part of language-specific schemas. Additionally, our findings suggest that words or messages in Spanish may elicit more emotional concepts and thoughts that assert the consumer's "Hispanicness." English words or messages, in contrast, seem to be more strongly associated with technical terms.

Complementing existing sociolinguistic theory (Gudykunst, 1988), these results suggest that language is used by bilingual individuals as a cultural or emotional cue. The schemas corresponding to culturally stereotypical norms may be activated by a word in Spanish (English), but not by the same word in English (Spanish). The results support the notion of the cognitive duality of bilingual individuals. This has important implications for advertisers, who could use bilingual ads or statements to elicit the most desirable associations to their product. For example, marketers such as AFLAC insurance could use the Spanish word *hija* instead of the English word *daughter* in order to elicit feelings of love, tenderness, and family that the English translation may not be associated with. Another application of the CFM to advertising would consist of manipulating the congruity between the concepts described in the ad and the consumers' expectations as determined by their language-specific schemas. Future research must now examine the notion of cognitive duality in more depth, test its robustness across different contexts, and apply it more directly to ad copy testing.

The studies described in this chapter focused on print advertisements. Previous research, however, suggests that ethnic consumers in general and Hispanics in particular are heavy consumers of other media, such as TV or radio (O'Guinn &

Meyer, 1983). Future research must now examine whether messages presented in different media are subject to the same phenomena as found in this study.

REFERENCES

Alesandrini, K. L. (1983). Information processing research in advertising. In R. J. Harris (Ed.), *Information processing research in advertising* (pp. 65–82). Hillsdale, NJ: Lawrence Erlbaum Associates.

Anderson, J. (1983). A spreading activation theory of memory. *Journal of Verbal Learning and Verbal Behavior, 22,* 261–295.

Barsalou, L. (1982). Context-independent and context-dependent information in concepts. *Memory and Cognition, 10,* 82–93.

Carroll, J. B. (Ed.). (1956). *Language, thought and reality: Selected writings of Benjamin Lee Whorf.* Cambridge, MA: MIT Press.

Collins, A., & Loftus E. (1975). A spreading-activation theory of semantic processing. *Psychological Review, 82,* 407–428.

Dolinsky, C., & Feinberg, R. A. (1986). Linguistic barriers to consumer information processing: Information overload in the hispanic population. *Psychology and Marketing, 3,* 261–271.

Dufour, R., & Kroll, J. (1995). Matching words to concepts in two languages: A test of the concept mediation model of bilingual representation. *Memory & Cognition, 23,* 166–180.

Durgunoglu, A., & Roediger, H. (1987). Test differences in accessing bilingual memory. *Journal of Memory and Language, 26,* 377–391.

Francis, W. N., & Kucera, H. (1982), *Frequency analysis of english usage.* Boston: Houghton Mifflin.

Groot, A. de (1989). Representational aspects of word imageability and word frequency as assessed through word association. *Journal of Experimental Psychology: Learning, Memory and Cognition, 15,* 824–845.

Groot, A. de (1992a). Bilingual lexical representation: A closer look at conceptual representations. In R. Frost & L. Katz (Eds.), *Orthography, phonology, morphology, and meaning* (pp. 389–412). Amsterdam: Elsevier.

Groot, A. de (1992b). Determinants of word translation. *Journal of Experimental Psychology: Learning, Memory, and Cognition, 18,* 1001–1018.

Groot, A. de, & Hoeks, J. (1995). The development of bilingual memory: Evidence from word translation by trilinguals. *Language Learning, 45,* 683–724.

Grossjean, F. (1982). *Life with two languages: An introduction to bilingualism.* Cambridge, MA: Harvard University Press.

Gudykunst, W. (1988). *Language and ethnic identity.* Philadelphia: Multilingual Matters.

Gudykunst, W., & Schmidt, K. (1988). Language and ethnic identity: An overview and prologue. In W. Gudykunst (Ed.), *Language and ethnic identity* (pp. 1–14). Philadelphia: Multilingual Matters.

Guernica, A. (1982). *Reaching the Hispanic market effectively: The media, the market, the methods.* New York: McGraw-Hill.

Hofstede, G. (1997). *Cultures and organizations: Software of the mind.* New York: McGraw-Hill.

Holbrook, M., & Moore, W. (1981, June). Feature interactions in consumer judgments of verbal versus pictorial Presentations. *Journal of Consumer Research, 8,* 103–113.

Houston, M., Childers, T., & Heckler, S. (1987, November). Picture-word consistency and the elaborative processing of advertisements. *Journal of Marketing Research, 24,* 359–69.

Hunt, E., & Agnoli, F (1991, July). The Whorfian hypothesis: A cognitive psychology perspective. *Psychological Review, 98,* 377–389.

Kolers, P. (1963). Interlingual word associations. *Journal of Verbal Learning and Verbal Behavior, 2,* 291–300.

Koslow, S., Shamdasani, P., & Touchstone, E. (1994, March). Exploring language effects in ethnic advertising: A sociolinguistic perspective. *Journal of Consumer Research, 20,* 575–585.

Kroll, J. F. (1993). Accessing conceptual representations for words in a second language. In R. Schreuder & B. Weltens (Eds.), *The bilingual lexicon* (pp. 53–81). Philadelphia: Benjamins.

Kroll, J. F., & de Groot, A. (1997). Lexical and conceptual memory in the bilingual: Mapping form to meaning in two languages. In A. de Groot & J. F. Kroll (Eds.), *Tutorials in bilingualism: Psycholinguistic perspectives* (pp. 169–200). Mahwah, NJ: Lawrence Erlbaum & Associates.

Kroll, J. F., & Stewart, E. (1994). Category interference in translation and picture naming: Evidence for asymmetric connections between bilingual memory representations. *Journal of Memory and Language, 33,* 149–174.

La Heij, W., Hooglander, A., Kerling, R., & Van Der Velden, E. (1996). Nonverbal context effects in forward and backward word translation: Evidence for concept mediation. *Journal of Memory and Language, 35,* 648–665.

Levey, R. H. (1999, May). Give them some credit. *American Demographics, 21,* 41–43.

Luna, D., & Peracchio, L. A. (2001, September). Moderators of language effects in advertising to bilinguals: A psycholinguistic approach. *Journal of Consumer Research, 28,* 284–295.

Luna, D., & Peracchio, L. A. (2002a). "Where There Is A Will . . .": Motivation as a moderator of language processing by bilingual consumers. *Psychology and Marketing, 19,* 573–594.

Luna, D., & Peracchio, L. A. (2002b). Uncovering the cognitive duality of bilinguals through word association. *Psychology and Marketing, 19,* 457–476.

Luna, D., & Peracchio, L. A. (2003). Bilinguals and frame-switching: An empirical investigation. Manuscript in preparation.

Lutz, K., & Lutz, R. (1977). Effects of interactive Imagery on learning: application to advertising. *Journal of Applied Psychology, 62,* 493–498.

MacWhinney, B. (1997). Second language acquisition and the competition model. In A. de Groot & J. Kroll (Eds.), *Tutorials in bilingualism: Psycholinguistic perspectives* (pp. 113–144). Mahwah, NJ: Lawrence Erlbaum Associates.

O'Guinn, T., & Meyer, T. (1983). Segmenting the Hispanic market: The use of Spanish-language radio. *Journal of Advertising Research, 23,* 9–16.

Paivio, A. (1971). *Imagery and verbal processes.* New York: Holt, Rinehart & Winston.

Paivio, A., Yuille, J., & Madigan, S. (1968). Concreteness, imagery, and meaningfulness values for 925 nouns. *Journal of Experimental Psychology Monograph Supplement, 76* (1, Pt. 2), 1–25.

Pan, Y., & Schmitt, B. (1996). Language and brand attitudes: Impact of script and sound matching in Chinese and English. *Journal of Consumer Psychology, 5,* 263–277.

Peñaloza, L. (1994, June). Atravesando fronteras/border crossings: A critical ethnographic exploration of the consumer acculturation of Mexican immigrants. *Journal of Consumer Research, 21,* 32–54.

Peracchio, L. A., & Meyers-Levy, J. (1997, September). Evaluating persuasion-enhancing techniques from a resource-matching perspective. *Journal of Consumer Research, 24,* 178–191.

Petty, R., & Cacioppo, J. (1986). The elaboration likelihood model of persuasion. In L. Berkowitz (Ed.), *Advances in experimental social psychology* (Vol. 19, pp. 123–205). Orlando, FL: Academic Press.

Schmitt, B., Pan, Y., & Tavassoli, N. (1994, December). Language and consumer memory: The impact of linguistic differences between Chinese and English. *Journal of Consumer Research, 21,* 419–431.

Schmitt, B., Tavassoli, N., & Millard, R. (1993). Memory for print ads: Understanding relations among brand name, copy, and picture. *Journal of Consumer Psychology, 2,* 55–81.

Schmitt, B., & Zhang, S. (1998, September). Language structure and categorization: A study of classifiers in consumer cognition, judgment, and choice. *Journal of Consumer Research, 25,* 108–122.

Schwanenflugel, P., & Rey, M. (1986). Intralingual semantic facilitation: Evidence for a common representational system in the bilingual. *Journal of Memory and Language, 25,* 605–618.

Scotton, C. M., & Ury, W. (1977). Bilingual strategies: The social functions of code-switching. *Linguistics, 193,* 5–20.

Sherry, J. F., Jr., & Camargo, E. G. (1987, September). "May your life be marvelous": English language labeling and the semiotics of Japanese promotion. *Journal of Consumer Research, 14,* 174–188.

Sholl, A., Sankaranarayanan, A., & Kroll, J. (1995). Transfer between picture naming and translation: A test of the asymmetries in bilingual memory. *Psychological Science, 6,* 45–49.

Snodgrass, J. (1984). Concepts and their surface representations. *Journal of Verbal Learning and Verbal Behavior, 23,* 3–22.

Tavassoli, N. (1999). Temporal and associative memory in Chinese and English. *Journal of Consumer Research, 26,* 170–182.

Tulving, E., & Thompson, D. M. (1971). Retrieval processes in recognition memory: Effects of associative context. *Journal of Experimental Psychology, 87,* 116–124.

Unnava, H. R., & Burnkrant, R. (1991, May). An imagery-processing view of the role of pictures in print advertisements. *Journal of Marketing Research, 28,* 226–231.

ENDNOTES

1. It is worth noting that, in this study, language proficiency or fluency is the construct used to conceptualize L1 and L2. Thus, the chronological order in which each language was learned is not used in the analyses. This is because it is possible that a person could have learned Spanish (English) first and yet be more proficient in the other language at the time of the test. In such a case, the RHM would predict that the language learned chronologically first would suffer from weaker conceptual links and a smaller lexicon and would be best described as L2, whereas the language learned chronologically second would be the "dominant" language and would be best described as L1. Thus, in the rest of this paper, L1 denotes the language in which a bilingual is most fluent and L2 denotes the language in which a bilingual is less fluent.

CHAPTER TEN

Ethnic Influences on Communication Patterns: Word of Mouth and Traditional and Nontraditional Media Usage

Wei-Na Lee
The University of Texas at Austin

Carrie La Ferle
Michigan State University

Marye Tharp
Emerson College

As the American population becomes more diverse, marketers seek to better understand the impact of consumer characteristics such as ethnicity on activities ranging from communication patterns to purchasing decisions. Communication appeals to specific ethnic groups and other "targeted" marketing efforts have vastly expanded their share of all U.S. marketing activities in the past decade (Jandt, 1995). According to Solomon (1996), "almost half of all Fortune 500 companies now have an ethnic marketing program" (p. 465). Advertising targeted to U.S. Hispanics in Spanish-language media alone, for example, exceeded $1 billion in 1996 (Goldsmith, 1996). Although U.S. Hispanics' buying power is valued at over $225 billion, the African American market is estimated to be worth in excess of $270 billion (Phillips, 1993). The Asian American market as a whole is small by comparison, but Asian American household incomes can average 23% more than those of comparable Anglo Americans (O'Hare, Frey, & Fost, 1994). The new and exciting possibilities brought on by the integrated marketing communication perspective are also helping marketers to direct their efforts synergistically. Buying power, media availability, and holistic marketing strategies are combining to make ethnic groups attractive markets.

As a result, advertisers are demanding expertise in ethnic-oriented communication; advertising agencies that specifically offer aptitude in designing and placing ads for minority audiences, such as Burrell Advertising, Caroline Jones Advertising Inc., Conill Advertising, and Muse, Cordero, and Chen, are on the rise. These types of agencies are not only representing impressive clients from McDonald's, Kmart, and Polaroid to Nike, Coors, Chrysler, and AT&T, but they are also seeing results. Companies taking the time to get to know their minority audiences are reaping the rewards with increases in market share and brand loyalty.

Similarly, a growing number of research articles in the academic arena are focusing on minority consumers, attempting to find differences in the various aspects of consumer behavior of particular ethnic groups (Delener & Neelankavil, 1990; Deshpande, Hoyer, Donthu, 1986; Faber, O'Guinn, & McCarty, 1987; Hirschman, 1985; Lee, 1993; Lee & Tse, 1994; Mehta & Belk, 1991; O'Guinn & Faber, 1985, 1986; Penaloza, 1994; Penaloza & Gilly, 1986; Saegert, Hoover, & Hilger, 1985; Stayman & Deshpande, 1989; Wallendorf & Reilly, 1983; Webster, 1992, 1994). However, a critical examination of the literature to date leads to the conclusion that the majority of studies are lacking in rendering a clear picture of media-consumption patterns among ethnic groups. In any one study, the comparison of three or more ethnic groups is rare. The studies also define key constructs such as culture, ethnicity, and acculturation in different ways under various contexts. Often, differing methodologies in data collection are used. Thus, cross-comparisons between studies are difficult. As a consequence, the extent to which the findings from these studies contribute to our substantive understanding of ethnic consumer behavior, particularly media usage, is somewhat questionable.

Because communication pattern is a key component in the overall consumer decision-making process, a study focusing on this topic is a necessary beginning toward expanding our knowledge regarding ethnic consumers. Research focusing on U.S. ethnic markets is not only useful and necessary in the American market but also can provide fruitful insight for other countries facing populations with multiple ethnic groups. By simultaneously incorporating four ethnic groups from one geographic location into one study, the research reported here attempts to establish an initial descriptive "portrayal" of ethnic media behavior and interpersonal communication.

Specifically, the research questions raised are these:

1. How do ethnic consumers use English mass media?
2. How are ethnic in-language media used?
3. To what extent do ethnic consumers engage in interpersonal communication in the form of advertising or product talk?
4. How do ethnic consumers respond to nontraditional media efforts?

DEFINING ETHNICITY

There has been much debate over the classification of race and ethnicity on the U.S. Census. For researchers as well, the distinction among ethnicity, race, and ethnic group is quite ambiguous. Each term has been defined and operationalized in many ways in mass media and cross-cultural studies (Deshpande et al., 1986; Deshpande & Stayman, 1994; Saegert et al., 1985; Stayman & Deshpande, 1989; Subervi-Vélez, 1986; Wallendorf & Reilly, 1983; Whittler, Calantone, & Young, 1991; Williams & Qualls, 1989). However, Deshpande et al. (1986) have found that adequate measures for differentiating between two ethnic groups can be obtained either by asking respondents to self-designate their ethnic group membership or by asking respondents to provide their strength of ethnic identification. Therefore, in this study, with the focus on between-group as opposed to within-group differences, ethnicity was defined in terms of self-designated ethnic group membership. Defined in this manner, ethnic group membership allowed for individuals to take into consideration race, culture, and region in their response; these are the three main criteria suggested by the Harvard Encyclopedia of American Ethnic Groups (1980) for defining ethnicity.

ETHNICITY AS AN INFLUENCE ON COMMUNICATION PATTERNS

Culture influences many aspects of society. At the individual level, it affects how people view the world by influencing their cognitions, motivations, and behavior. It is generally agreed that the culture of an individual constitutes that person's norms and values (Rokeach, 1968). From a societal perspective, Hofstede (1991) has been able to illustrate how culture can orient people along various dimensions. Communication style has also been said to vary by culture, affecting people's preferences for high- or low-context communication, direct or indirect modes of communication, and verbal or nonverbal communication (de Mooij, 1998). Therefore, cultural orientation should have a profound effect on media usage and other related communication patterns.

Several studies have been able to discern ethnic patterns in communication style and information search even while recognizing the diversity within each group. For example, Webster (1992) found radio and billboard advertising, coupons and displays, and family and coworkers to be preferred sources of product information among Spanish-dominant Hispanics. English-dominant Hispanics, in contrast, used magazine ads, brochures, the Yellow Pages, *Consumer Reports*, window shopping, and product labels more frequently. Both groups relied on television and newspaper ads and friends and salespeople for product information (Webster, 1992). In a study of Asian versus Hispanic consumers, Delener and Neelankavil.

(1990) concluded that television and radio were the best media to reach Hispanics, whereas English and ethnic in-language print media, especially newspapers, were preferred by Asian buyers. Other findings have suggested that Asian Americans like electronic programming and advertising when it is in their own language (Wiesen-danger, 1993). Dates (1993) reported that African Americans are best reached by means of Black-oriented media, and Delener and Neelankavil (1990) found that they have high overall usage of electronic media. Although such studies contribute to our appreciation of ethnic differences, they usually only focus on one or two eth-nic groups at a time and they do not survey preferences and use of traditional and nontraditional media; nor do they contrast word-of-mouth activity with media us-age patterns. Thus we are left with a fragmented view of the overall communication pattern.

Ethnic in-language media are generally considered as those media vehicles using a specific ethnic group's native language in their transmission of messages. The relative impact of English versus ethnic in-language media on consumer decision making has not been directly studied. Several researchers have noted that Spanish-language media validate the Hispanic consumer's cultural heritage and thus are attributed with higher source credibility (Koslow, Shamdasani, & Touchstone, 1994; O'Guinn & Meyer, 1984). Likewise, an individual's preference for media in the language of origin, even when the person has spent significant time in a new country, has been noted by other researchers (Delener & Neelankavil, 1990; Lee & Tse, 1994; Penaloza, 1994; Webster, 1992). In general, aside from situational factors and specific product categories, we would expect ethnic preference for information from one's native ethnic in-language media (Deshpande & Stayman, 1994). Therefore, one objective of this study was to examine the use of English and ethnic in-language media among the different ethnic groups.

WORD-OF-MOUTH COMMUNICATION

Word of mouth and advertising were initially viewed as competing sources of influence in consumer purchasing decisions, with word of mouth dominating in terms of its potential for persuasion (Arndt, 1967; Bearden & Etzel, 1982; Cohen & Golden, 1972; Dichter, 1966; Ford & Ellis, 1980; Sheth, 1976; Stafford, 1966; Witt & Bruce, 1972). Recent research suggests that word of mouth appears to be stronger in certain situations (e.g., adoption of new products), at particular stages in the purchase decision (e.g., immediately before purchase choice), among certain individuals (e.g., consumers with stronger social networks or higher susceptibility to interpersonal influence), and for certain types of products (e.g., visible, consumer goods and services; see Bearden, Netemeyer, & Teel, 1989; Bone, 1995; Brown & Reingen, 1987; Frenzen & Nakamoto, 1993; Hayseed, 1989; Herr, Kardes, & Kim, 1991; Higie, Feick, & Price, 1987; Reingen, Foster, Brown, & Seidman, 1984; Reingen & Kernan, 1986; Singh, 1990; Swan & Oliver, 1989). Even while recognizing that individuals vary in both the giving and receiving of interpersonal influence (Stern, 1994), research indicates that consumers do tend to approximate group norms (Bearden et al., 1989; Burnkrant & Cousineau, 1975).

Several studies have been conducted to explore the issue of unique patterns of interpersonal influence for different ethnic groups. Herr et al. (1991) found that both media and word-of-mouth information were used as inputs for product choices when the information was accessible and perceived to be relevant. Endorsement of a brand by means of word of mouth from members of the same ethnic group may help consumers assign that brand to one cognitive category, making that information more accessible. Chinese American consumers have been found to use more reference group information in general, whereas Hispanic Americans utilize more family sources (Delener & Neelankavil, 1990; Deshpande et al., 1986; Hecht, Collier, & Ribeau, 1993; Lee, 1993; Lee & Tse, 1994; Penaloza, 1994; Webster, 1992). Further, Hecht et al. (1993) have described the communication style of African Americans as one that emphasizes the spoken word, use of code switching between regular and Black English, and call-response participation of speaker and audience. Feick and Price (1987) also discovered that African Americans tended to be "market mavens." However, both Asian and Latino Americans are thought to rely more heavily than other cultural groups in the United States on social networks within their ethnic communities (Penaloza, 1994; Webster, 1992). In regard to consumption, earlier studies of ethnic groups suggested that African Americans and U.S. Latinos were less likely to complain about products with which they were dissatisfied (Hilger & English, 1978). These findings may indicate that some groups will engage in word of mouth less than others, given their unlikeliness to complain.

The shared values of members of an ethnic group may provide a basis for interpersonal communication and influence (Moschis, 1976). Some products have been found to be more culturally sensitive than others (Webster, 1994). Thus, word of mouth by consumers may vary by product category. Likewise, some advertisements generate more consumer "talk" than others, depending on both form and content of the ad itself, as well as on situational and general characteristics of the receivers (Bearden et al., 1989; Brown & Reingen, 1987; Childers & Rao, 1992; Hayseed, 1989; Herr et al., 1991; Mick & Buhl, 1992; Richins, 1991; Webster, 1991). Before we can gain a better understanding of how ethnicity relates to word-of-mouth communication, we need to find out the extent of such usage. Therefore, a second objective of the present study was to examine if consumers in different ethnic groups differ in their extent of advertising talk and product talk.

NONTRADITIONAL MEDIA COMMUNICATION

In recent years, marketers have expanded their use of so-called nontraditional media in an attempt to more precisely match media audiences with product users and to try to circumnavigate the increased level of noise in traditional media

(Schultz, Tannenbaum, & Lauterborn, 1994). Integrated marketing communications planning emphasizes the use of public relations, event marketing, direct mail, telemarketing, direct marketing by means of television, targeted promotions, and electronic marketing as complements to a firm's advertising program. Thus, many consumers find their traditional sources of product or service information, mass media and word of mouth, to be only two options in today's information society. Unfortunately, the literature on ethnic usage of nontraditional media, such as coupon use, is scarce and often controversial (Awhigham-Desir, 1997; Bejou & Tat, 1994; Green, 1995). For example, Bejou and Tat (1994) reported that Blacks were more favorable than Whites toward coupon use, whereas Green (1995) found opposite results. It is expected in this study that consumers in different ethnic groups differ in their response to nontraditional media. For the relationship between ethnicity and communication pattern to be explained adequately, all the available communication variables—mainstream English media, ethnic in-language, word of mouth, and nontraditional media such as telemarketing, direct marketing, promotions, and event marketing—must be taken into consideration.

THE STUDY

A cross-cultural survey with individuals from four ethnic groups (Anglo, African, Chinese, and Hispanic Americans) was carried out in Houston, Texas. Houston, Texas is an ethnically diverse city supporting a population that is 52.7% White, 28.1% Black, 27.6% Hispanic, 4.1% Asian and Pacific Islander, 0.18% American Indian–Eskimo–Aleut, and 14.9% people who classify themselves as Other (Bureau of the Census, 1990). Because to its geographic proximity, a majority of the people of Hispanic origin in Houston are from Mexico. Many of these people retain their Mexican culture and values, and often they can be found celebrating significant Mexican holidays. Likewise, a majority of Asian and Pacific Islanders are Chinese persons from Taiwan and, more recently, China. A fair amount of effort is also made by these people to maintain their Chinese way of life.

The study was designed with the main goal of providing an initial portrayal of English and ethnic in-language media usage among the four ethnic groups. In addition, although literature directly relating to this area is scarce, the following three research hypotheses were suggested as guidelines to the investigation:

1. Hypothesis 1 (H_1): Consumers in different ethnic groups differ in their extent of advertising talk.
2. Hypothesis 2 (H_2): Consumers in different ethnic groups differ in their extent of product talk.
3. Hypothesis 3 (H_3): Consumers in different ethnic groups differ in their response toward nontraditional media.

Measurement of Communication Behavioral Indicators

There were several communication behavioral indicators used in the study, namely, mass media use (both English and ethnic in-language), interpersonal communication in the form of advertising and product talk, and nontraditional media behavior. Mass media use was defined as weekday time spent with English-language media such as television, radio, newspapers, and magazines. Respondents of the Chinese and Hispanic American groups were also asked to estimate their ethnic in-language media usage. Ethnic in-language media use was operationalized as the amount of time spent with the native-language media (either Chinese or Spanish) available in Houston. In Spanish, this included television, radio, newspapers, and magazines; in Chinese, only television, newspapers, and magazines were available. It should be noted that Anglo and African Americans were assumed to have English as their native language.

Likert-type statements for interpersonal advertising, product talk, and nontraditional media statements were developed from in-depth personal interviews as well as from related literature. Nontraditional media were identified as sales promotion, catalogs, direct marketing, telemarketing, public relations, and event-marketing-related activities (Schultz et al., 1994). Appendix A contains a list of items used in the survey questionnaire. Finally, respondents were asked to report demographic information such as ethnic group, age, income, employment status, education, marital status, and gender. With respect to ethnic group membership, respondents were asked to self-categorize according to who they considered themselves to be ethnically. For statistical purposes, once respondents had made their selection, their self-categorizations were then treated as groups at the nominal level, providing the definition of ethnic group in this study.

Extensive pretests were conducted to make sure that the questionnaire contained relevant and ethnically accurate questions and response items. The questionnaire was also translated into Chinese and Spanish by using the back-translation technique. Chinese and Hispanic American respondents were asked to choose either English or Chinese–Spanish versions of the questionnaire.

Sampling and Data Collection Procedure

Census track information and *The Sourcebook of Zip Code Demographics* were used in the selection of zip codes for data collection sites in Houston. Specific ethnic shopping malls or areas were then located within selected zip code regions. Quotas were assigned to each data collection site. The field workers were instructed to randomly approach prospective respondents. Once consent was obtained, the field worker handed over the questionnaire for the respondents to fill out in a self-administered format. Each respondent was offered $1 as an incentive or token of appreciation for participation upon turning in a completed questionnaire.

APPENDIX A
Questionnaire Items

Advertising Talk Statements ("almost always" to "almost never")
  We talk at home about advertising we have seen that we like.
  We talk at home about advertising we have seen that we don't like.
  My friends and I talk about advertising we have seen that we like.
  My friends and I talk about advertising we have seen that we don't like.

Product Talk Statements ("almost always" to "almost never")
  We talk at home about products or brands we have been satisfied with.
  We talk at home about products or brands we have been dissatisfied with.
  My friends and I talk about products or brands we have been satisfied with.
  My friends and I talk about products or brands we have been dissatisfied with.

Nontraditional Media Statements ("almost always" to "almost never")
  I like to order product I see in catalogs.
  I like to order products I learn about from telephone salespeople.
  I try new products when I have a coupon for one.
  I like to enter contests or sweepstakes whenever I can.
  I prefer to buy brands that offer a rebate.
  I prefer to buy brands from companies I've heard good things about.
  I like to receive catalogs or direct mail from companies offering something to buy.
  I like to receive phone calls from companies offering something to buy.
  I use coupons whenever I can.
  I like to buy from companies that sponsor my ethnic festivals or sports events.

Field workers were carefully chosen (they were bilingual in either Spanish–English or Chinese–English) and trained. Two field supervisors were on site to help troubleshoot incidental problems. Each of the four groups had at least one interviewer matching the dominant ethnicity of the neighborhood. The overall refusal rate was low, at approximately 9%. Of those who were approached, 97% of the African Americans, 96.5% of Hispanic Americans, 80% of Anglo Americans, and 90% of Chinese Americans participated in the study.

RESULTS AND DISCUSSION

Sample Check

The total sample size was 1,142, with 271 Chinese Americans, 289 African Americans, 288 Hispanic Americans, and 294 Anglo Americans. Statistics (Bureau of the Census, 1990) on the population of Houston were compared with those obtained from the sample groups (Table 10.1).

The majority of demographic variables across the four ethnic groups were similar to those in the population. Exceptions occurred with the percentage of people in the population under 17 years of age, as they were not sampled. In addition, in

TABLE 10.1

Demographic Statistics for the Four Sample Groups and Population

Demographics	Anglo American		African American		Chinese American		Hispanic American	
	Sample	Pop.	Sample	Pop.	Sample	Pop.	Sample	Pop.
Gender								
Male	112(38.1)	429,112(50)	125(43.3)	215,484(47.1)	152(56.1)	34,669(51.7)	120(41.7)	236,391(52.5)
Female	176(59.9)	429,957(50)	145(50.2)	242,506(53.0)	118(43.5)	32,444(48.3)	160(55.6)	214,092(47.5)
Education level								
High School/Below	79(26.9)	263,585(42.2)	109(37.7)	179,640(61.8)	27(10.0)	15,759(36.3)	148(51.4)	189,127(79.0)
Technical & Comm.	91(31.0)	167,557(26.8)	96(33.2)	76,284(26.2)	33(12.2)	10,086(22.2)	67(23.3)	34,498(14.4)
Bechelor Degree	74(25.2)	128,327(20.5)	44(15.2)	23,970(8.2)	73(26.9)	10,497(24.2)	33(11.5)	10,408(4.3)
Master's & phD	36(12.2)	65,767(10.5)	12(4.2)	11,007(3.8)	134(49.4)	7,081(16.3)	7(2.4)	5,611(2.3)
Age distribution (years)								
17–34	93(31.6)	273,119(40.3)	162(56.1)	151,631(46.9)	117(43.2)	23,339(47.8)	159(55.2)	172,457(61.1)
35–54	118(40.1)	235,291(34.8)	100(34.6)	108,434(33.6)	118(43.5)	19,994(41.0)	96(35.3)	86,243(30.6)
55+	76(26.5)	168,787(24.9)	8(3.0)	62,937(19.5)	23(8.9)	5,448(11.2)	17(6.3)	31,203(11.1)
Marital status								
Married	160(54.4)	357,044(50.8)	86(29.8)	117,071(34.6)	178(65.7)	29,460(57.0)	151(52.4)	161,942(52.0)
Income ($)								
25,000 or less	65(22.1)	141,442(38.1)	153(52.9)	101,929(63.4)	60(22.1)	9,584(45.5)	167(58.0)	72,212(60.8)
25,001–45,000	80(27.2)	101,992(27.5)	100(34.6)	37,184(23.1)	72(26.6)	5,232(24.8)	73(25.3)	30,075(25.3)
45,001–65,000	59(20.1)	54,768(14.8)	24(8.3)	13,434(8.4)	55(20.3)	2,921(13.9)	26(9.0)	9,847(8.3)
65,001+	70(23.8)	72,824(19.6)	8(2.8)	8,319(5.2)	71(26.2)	3,347(15.9)	5(1.7)	6,667(5.6)

Note. The number of respondents is as follows: Anglo American, 294; African American, 289; Chinese American, 271; Hispanic American, 288. Raw numbers are listed in the table; percentages are given in parentheses. "Missing" data account for percentages that are short of totaling to 100.

the categories of education and income, the sample underrepresented the Houston population of people with less than a junior high school education and persons making $15,000 or less per year. Therefore, the sample's education and income were skewed toward higher brackets. This was true for all ethnic groups, except Hispanic Americans in the sample, whose incomes matched Houston population statistics.

English and Ethnic In-Language Media Usage

Respondents' use of English media was measured by asking the following question: "How much time (in minutes and hours) in a typical weekday do you spend with each of the following media?" All groups were asked the question with regard to the following four media categories: watching English TV, listening to English radio, reading English newspapers, and reading English magazines. In addition, both the Chinese and Hispanic American groups were asked extra questions about watching Chinese–Spanish TV, listening to Spanish radio (there was no Chinese language radio programming in Houston), reading Chinese–Spanish newspapers, and reading Chinese–Spanish magazines. A continuous response scale was used, ranging from less than 30 min of use to 4 hr or more for all of the questions.

English and ethnic in-language media usage by ethnic groups is reported in Fig. 10.1. All groups used more electronic media than print in mainstream English-language media. This was also true for Hispanic Americans in ethnic in-language media. Chinese Americans did not appear to use any one of the media very much over another. Except for watching English TV, Chinese Americans uniformly reported very little media use compared with the other groups. In contrast, African Americans indicated a preference for TV and radio. Finally, Hispanics appeared to enjoy a wide range of media, with the highest usage in Spanish-language radio followed by English-language radio.

Both Chinese and Hispanic Americans consume English and ethnic in-language media. As Lee and Tse (1994) suggested, this could be due to their "need to be informed" in a new cultural environment. Lower media usage for Chinese Americans across the board suggests that these "newcomers" may have more than they can handle in terms of available English and available ethnic in-language media. The end result of "too little time, too many choices" is that some ethnic consumers may simply tune into each medium to gather essential information, such as using electronic media for a quick update of world, national, and local news. Consequently, the balance between using English and ethnic in-language media has to be researched further.

Advertising and Product Talk

The next objective of the study (H_1 and H_2) was to see if there would be any significant differences across ethnic groups concerning the extent of talking about

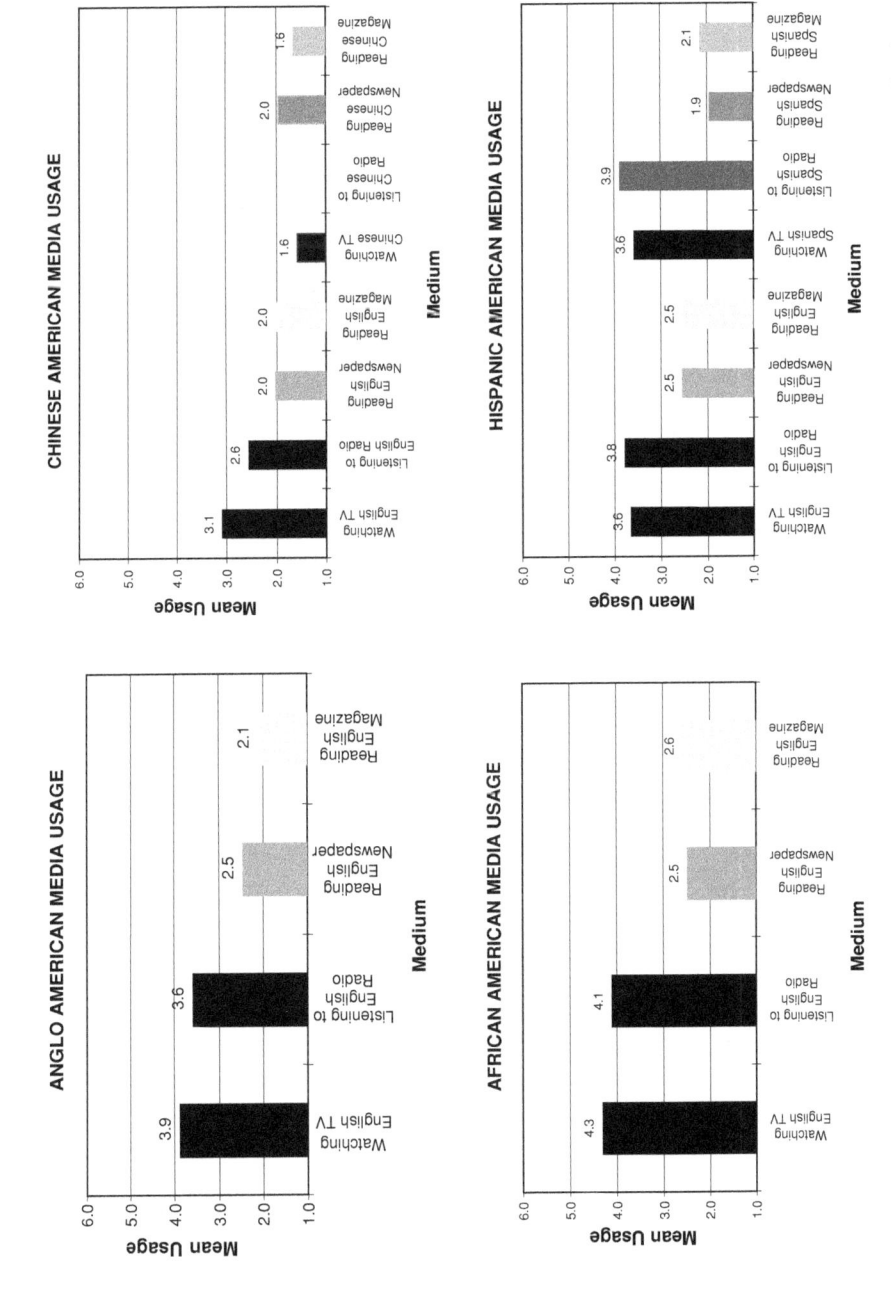

FIG. 10.1. Media usage by ethnic group. Scale: 1 = < 30 min; 2 = 30–59 min; 3 = 1 hr–1hr, 59 min; 4 = 2hr–2hr, 59 min; 5 = 3 hr–3hr, 59 min; 6 = 4 hr or more.

187

TABLE 10.2
ANCOVA Summary of Advertising Talk and Product Talk Indices

Dependent Variable	Adjusted Group Means				F Value	Bonferroni (p <.0083)
	Anglo American	African American	Chinese American	Hispanic American		
Advertising talk	2.90₃	2.37₁	3.16₄	2.66₂	11.30**	ab, bc, bd, cd
Product talk	2.51₄	2.19₁	2.33₂	2.46₃	2.93*	—

Note. The mean scores represent 1 = almost always to 5 = almost never. The numbers next to adjusted means indicate lowest to highest mean values. Five sociodemographic variables are held constant. Lettering is as follows: a = Anglo, b = African c = Chinese, and d = Hispanic Americans.
*Significant at .05;   **Significant at .01.

advertising and products. There were four different statements relating to each of the two concepts (Appendix A). As the four statements for both advertising talk and product talk held together in reliability tests with alpha values greater than .8, they were collapsed into two indices—Advertising talk and product talk. A series of chi-square analyses were run examining relations between ethnic group and each of the sociodemographic variables of gender, education, marital status, household income, and age. Each chi-square was found to be significant. Therefore, to see if a significant difference existed between ethnic group membership and advertising and product talk, sociodemographic variables were held constant by use of analyses of covariance (ANCOVAs). Table 10.2 reports the ANCOVA results and adjusted means, indicating that significant differences between ethnic group and extent of both advertising talk ($F = 11.30$; $p < .00001$) and product talk ($F = 2.93$; $p < .033$) were found. Therefore, both H_1 and H_2 were supported. Consumers in different ethnic groups differ significantly in their extent of advertising talk and product talk.

In order to detect which ethnic groups differed significantly on the extent of advertising and product talk, a series of pairwise comparisons were then conducted. In each analysis, the Bonferroni adjustment was used to maintain the Type I error rate (Hair, Anderson, Tatham, & Black, 1995). African Americans were found to talk the most about advertising compared with the other ethnic groups. Chinese Americans were shown to talk significantly less about advertising than both African Americans ($t = 3.50$; $p < .00049$) and Hispanic Americans ($t = 5.74$; $p < .00001$). Anglo Americans were also found to talk less about advertising than African Americans ($t = 4.00$; $p < .00007$). As the Bonferroni test is quite conservative (Hays, 1988), it should be noted that Chinese Americans also talked less about advertising than Anglo Americans ($t = 2.11$; $p < .0354$), although not at the Bonferroni level of adjustment of .0083. With respect to extent of product talk, although African Americans were again found to talk the most as compared with the other ethnic groups, no significant differences resulted between the groups by use of the Bonferonni test.

The two constructs of advertising and product talk were then broken down into their respective statement variables, and each variable was tested across the four different ethnic groups by use of ANCOVAs. Of interest was whether or not any differences would be found between talking with friends and talking with families across the four ethnic groups. Table 10.3 reports the ANCOVA results and adjusted means, indicating that significant differences between the groups were found for every statement regarding degree of advertising talk. For two of the four variables dealing with talking about products, significant differences were found only on those items that included talking with friends about products that the participant was satisfied and dissatisfied with.

Advertising Talk at Home and With Friends. To detect which ethnic groups differed significantly on the dependent variables, a series of pairwise comparisons were then conducted. On all advertising talk variables, the same pattern was found. African Americans talked the most, followed by Hispanic Americans, then Anglo Americans, and finally Chinese Americans, who talked the least. Specific to talking *at home* (i.e., "we talk at home about advertising we have seen that we like"), African Americans were found to talk significantly more about advertising than both Chinese ($t = 4.64$; $p < .00001$) and Anglos ($t = 3.66$; $p < .00027$). There was also a significant difference found between Chinese and Hispanic groups ($t = 3.11$; $p < .00196$), with Chinese talking less at home about advertising liked than Hispanics. The t test for "we talk at home about advertising that we have seen that we don't like" showed that Chinese Americans talk significantly less than all other ethnic groups—Anglo Americans ($t = 4.03$; $p < .00006$), African Americans ($t = 5.39$; $p < .00001$), and Hispanic Americans ($t = 4.42$; $p < .00001$).

African Americans were found to talk significantly more *with friends* about advertising they liked than Anglos ($t = 3.03$; $p < .00255$), Chinese ($t = 3.04$; $p < .00241$), and Hispanics ($t = 3.08$; $p < .00214$). Finally, African Americans were again found to talk significantly more with friends about advertising *disliked* than both Anglos ($t = 3.13$; $p < .00182$) and Chinese ($t = 3.95$; $p < .00008$).

Product Talk at Home and With Friends. On the questions regarding product talk, African Americans were found to talk the most across all four variables. However, on the topic of talking about products *at home*, whether the participant was satisfied or dissatisfied, no significant differences were found between the ethnic groups. However, product talk *with friends* showed a different pattern. On the question "my friends and I talk about products or brands we have been satisfied with," Anglos were found to talk significantly less than both African Americans ($t = 2.74$; $p < .00626$) and Chinese ($t = 3.02$; $p < .00259$). Hispanics also talked with friends less about products they were satisfied with than African Americans ($t = 2.18$; $p < .02988$), but not at the Bonferroni level of adjustment. Finally, on the question of "my friends and I talk about products or brands we have been

TABLE 10.3
ANCOVA Summary of Advertising Talk and Product Talk Variables

Dependent Variable	Adjusted Group Means				F Value	Bonferroni ($p < .0083$)
	Anglo American	African American	Chinese American	Hispanic American		
Advertising talk						
Talk at home about advertising liked.	3.10_3	2.52_1	3.29_4	2.75_2	7.98**	ab, bc, cd
Talk at home about advertising disliked.	2.77_3	2.50_1	3.39_4	2.62_2	10.85**	ac, bc, cd
Talk friends about advertising liked.	2.84_3	2.38_1	2.87_4	2.83_2	4.77**	ab, bc, bd
Talk friends about advertising disliked.	2.84_3	2.35_1	2.99_4	2.70_2	5.72**	ab, bc
Product talk						
Talk at home about products satisfied with.	2.51_4	2.29_1	2.39_3	2.32_2	.89(ns)	
Talk at home about products dissatisfied with.	2.39_2	2.30_1	2.39_3	2.46_4	.44(ns)	
Talk friends about products satisfied with.	2.57_4	2.14_1	2.19_2	2.43_3	4.33**	ab, ac
Talk friends about products dissatisfied with.	2.57_3	2.17_1	2.35_2	2.64_4	4.46**	ab, bd

Note. The mean scores represent 1 = almost always to 5 = almost never. The numbers next to adjusted means indicate lowest to highest mean values. Five sociodemographic variables are held constant. Lettering is as follows: a = Anglo, b = African, c = Chinese, and d = Hispanic Americans (ns = not significant).
**Significant at .01.

dissatisfied with," African Americans talked significantly more than both Anglos ($t = 2.71$; $p < .00688$) and Hispanics ($t = 2.71$; $p < .00688$).

The significant findings shown in Table 10.3 suggest the four groups vary in how much they talk about advertising, to whom they talk, and what they talk about. African Americans consistently talk more than the other consumers. They talk more about advertising than products advertised, and they talk to both friends and family about advertising but more to friends about products. To a great extent, these data confirm and expand our understanding of the significant role that media and word of mouth both play in African American consumption decisions (Delener & Neelankavil, 1990; Feick & Price, 1987; Hecht et al., 1993; Hilger & English, 1978; Wilkes & Valencia, 1986). The overall positive attitude African Americans have about the value of advertising, shopping, and buying tells marketers that traditional English-language media may work in tandem with word-of-mouth networks in African American purchasing decisions. Techniques and message strategies in advertisements that simulate and stimulate word of mouth (e.g., "ask a person who owns one") could multiply the impact of media weight with this ethnic group (Robertson, 1971).

In contrast, Chinese Americans talk the least of all groups about either products or advertising, but they are more likely to talk to family members and about products when they do talk. Recognizing the importance of social networks within Chinese American communities (Delener & Neelankavil, 1990; Wiesendanger, 1993), we find it curious that there is so little spontaneous product or advertising talk. A possible implication here for advertisers is to minimize media presence in both English-language and ethnic in-language media and increase the use of Chinese American sales personnel, and to direct marketing efforts to opinion leaders within the community.

Generally, Hispanic Americans talk less about advertising and products than Anglo or African Americans and are even less likely to discuss products with which they are dissatisfied (Hilger & English, 1978; Swan & Oliver, 1989; Webster, 1991). Given that word-of-mouth communication increases the accessibility of product information, efforts should always be made to engage consumers in this behavior. In particular, stimulating advertising and product talk by means of message strategy and a strong media presence in both English and Spanish media may encourage word of mouth among Hispanic Americans. Likewise, marketers should not assume that the lack of complaints from Hispanic Americans signifies high levels of product satisfaction; active efforts must be made to solicit postpurchase feedback from Hispanic Americans.

Anglo Americans, like Chinese Americans, seem to engage in little word of mouth about products or advertisements. However, they are more likely to talk when they are dissatisfied with products than when they are satisfied. Marketers would do well to provide outlets for this word-of-mouth feedback; it is an opportunity to turn dissatisfaction into suggestions for improvement while minimizing negative word of mouth.

Nontraditional Media

The final objective (H_3) of the study was to understand if responses varied among ethnic groups when nontraditional media were incorporated into communication tactics. Ten questions in this section measured amount of coupon use, products ordered from catalogs, desire to receive telephone sales calls, and likelihood of entering contests. A Likert-type scale was used, with response categories ranging from "almost always" to "almost never." The 10 variables were then tested across the four different ethnic groups by use of ANCOVAs. Again, the same sociodemographic characteristics of gender, education level, marital status, household income, and age were held constant. Table 10.4 reports the ANCOVA results and adjusted means, indicating that significant differences between the groups were found for 9 of the 10 statements. No significant difference was found on the question "prefer buying brands that offer a rebate." Support for the third hypothesis was confirmed. Consumers in different ethnic groups do significantly differ in their responses toward nontraditional media in all but one of the cases presented.

The results of a series of pairwise comparisons indicate that ethnic group does make a difference in response to nontraditional media. Table 10.4 shows that African Americans have the highest overall level of involvement with these methods of communication relative to other groups. Chinese Americans were found to use nontraditional media either least or second least often, on 7 of the 10 variables. Anglo and Hispanic Americans' scores demonstrated diverse patterns of response to the integrated marketing communication tools, with no particular preferences overall.

For the question "I like to order products I see in catalogs," the mean scores of all groups ranged from neutral to infrequent use of the medium. Still, African Americans were significantly more in favor of ordering from catalogs than both Anglo ($t = 2.8$; $p < .00525$) and Hispanic Americans ($t = 3.2$; $p < .00140$). Chinese Americans were also significantly more in favor of ordering products from catalogs than both Anglo ($t = 2.8$; $p < .00544$) and Hispanic Americans ($t = 2.7$; $p < .00678$). These findings suggest that African and Chinese Americans may be likely to respond to catalog marketers who are able to reach them with ethnically relevant messages.

With regard to ordering "products via telephone," all groups indicated that they rarely used this medium. However, again African Americans were significantly more favorable to telemarketing than the other groups. The same pattern held for "I try new products when I have a coupon for one," and "I use coupons whenever I can." All four groups indicated neutral to frequent use; African Americans were significantly more favorable. African Americans were also significantly more favorable toward the statement "I like to enter contests or sweepstakes whenever I can" than the other three groups. These findings suggest that a high number of African Americans respond to nontraditional media.

TABLE 10.4
ANCOVA Summary of Purchase Behavior of Nontraditional Media

Dependent Variable	Adjusted Group Means				F Value	Bonferroni ($p < .0083$)
	Anglo American	African American	Chinese American	Hispanic American		
Like to order products seen in catalogs.	3.86_3	3.41_1	3.44_2	3.90_4	5.72^{**}	ab, bd, ac, cd
Order products learned from telephone.	4.83_4	4.26_1	4.73_3	4.59_2	9.41^{**}	ab, bc, bd
Try new products if I have a coupon.	2.84_2	2.36_1	2.87_3	2.92_4	5.91^{**}	ab, bc, bd
Like to enter contests or sweepstakes.	3.45_2	2.75_1	3.95_4	3.59_3	18.52^{**}	ab, bc, bd
Prefer buying brands that offer a rebate.	3.22_4	2.85_2	2.93_3	2.84_1	2.48ns	—
Prefer to buy from companies I've heard good things about.	1.88_4	1.64_2	1.60_1	1.85_3	3.22^{*}	—
Like receiving catalogs or direct mail offers.	3.14_3	2.76_1	3.73_4	2.85_2	11.93^{**}	ac, bc, cd
Like phone calls offering things to buy.	4.63_3	3.87_1	4.79_4	4.19_2	17.91^{**}	bc, cd
Use coupons whenever I can.	2.51_2	2.05_1	2.64_4	2.53_3	5.82^{**}	ab, bc, bd
Like to buy from companies that sponsor my ethnic festivals or sports events.	3.21_4	2.49_2	2.60_3	2.42_1	13.42^{**}	ab, ac, ad

Note. The mean scores represent $1 =$ almost always to $5 =$ almost never. The numbers next to adjusted means indicate lowest to highest mean values. Five sociodemographic variables are held constant. Lettering is as follows: $a =$ Anglo, $b =$ African, $c =$ Chinese, and $d =$ Hispanic Americans ($ns =$ not significant).
*Significant at .05; **Significant at .01.

Chinese Americans were the group least likely to report, "I like to receive catalogs or direct mail from companies offering something to buy" or "I like to receive phone calls from companies offering something to buy." They engaged in these activities significantly less often than all other ethnic groups, with the exception of Anglo Americans, who most disliked telemarketing calls at the same level as Chinese Americans.

The question "I like to buy from companies that sponsor my ethnic festivals or sports events" generated some interesting results. Anglos tended to be neutral but significantly different from the other three ethnic groups: African Americans ($t = 5.11$; $p < .00001$), Chinese Americans ($t - 4.59$; $p < .00001$), and Hispanic Americans ($t = 5.53$; $p < .00001$). No other significant differences were found between the remaining groups. The findings confirm the effectiveness of event sponsorship within ethnic communities.

Finally, although a significant difference was found on the question "I prefer to buy brands from companies I've heard good things about," ($F = 3.22$; $p < .05$), no significant difference was found in the pairwise comparisons between the four ethnic groups at the Bonferroni level of adjustment. This finding conflicts with prior research suggesting significantly more word-of-mouth networks among Hispanic and Chinese Americans (Delener & Neelankavil, 1990; Saegert et al., 1985).

In recent years, integrated marketing communication (IMC) has generated much interest among advertising agencies and academic advertising programs alike. Little prior research has focused on its effectiveness in reaching ethnic consumers. Table 10.4 represents findings that would lead one to promote the use of IMC for African American consumers but to reconsider the use of the nontraditional media in IMC programs in the case of Chinese Americans.

According to the findings, IMC strategies vary in effectiveness both by ethnic group and by specific tactic. In general, African Americans illustrated the greatest use of nontraditional media, and Chinese Americans the least usage. Nevertheless, on specific items the results suggest a need to adapt IMC tactics for different ethnic groups. African Americans tend to favor entering sweepstakes or contests, receiving catalogs or direct mail offers, and using coupons. Chinese Americans are more likely to buy from firms represented at ethnic festivals than to order from catalogs or telemarketers or to enter sweepstakes. Hispanic Americans seem to be best reached through both English-language and ethnic in-language media and sponsorship of ethnic festivals. Anglo Americans indicated that they liked to use coupons, but they appeared negative about other IMC tools. Finally, all four groups reported negative opinions of rebates, perhaps because of delayed gratification—rebates reward purchasers after the fact.

CAVEATS AND FUTURE RESEARCH ISSUES

Before conclusions are drawn, certain caveats of the present study have to be noted. This discussion serves to provide caution against overgeneralization of our results and to offer possible avenues for further research exploration in this area.

Descriptions Versus Explanations

Although the study provided interesting and unique results illustrating that individuals in different ethnic groups attend to communication differently, it was not designed to answer why these differences occur. Future research should examine under what conditions groups are different. Admittedly, explanations other than ethnicity such as situation-specific reasons and availability of media must also contribute to explain the variability in media usage among different ethnic groups.

Individual Versus Group Differences and Felt Ethnicity

Another important issue involves individual versus group differences and the concept of felt ethnicity. Following Stayman and Deshpande (1989), we asked respondents to self-identify to which ethnic group they belonged (self-designated ethnicity). However, once they were categorized, we treated respondents in the same group as similar. A limitation here resides in the fact that although respondents may be similar on this grouping variable, there are surely a great many individual differences between them on other variables that went undetected. As evidence, research by Whittler et al. (1991) illustrated the variation between Black respondents on level of identification with Black culture. Similarly, in a study by Deshpande et al. (1986), differences were found between high and low Hispanic identifiers on dependent measures.

Therefore, even though respondents were grouped as similar on this variable by the operationalization techniques described, individual differences still exist. Furthermore, given that respondents' felt ethnicity was not measured—the strength of identification they had with their self-identified group (Stayman & Deshpande, 1989)—variation within each group may alter future results. It would also be wise to perform follow-up studies (perhaps qualitative) to examine the stability and influence of this variable given that "level of felt ethnicity is seen as more situation specific" (Stayman & Deshpande, 1989, p. 362).

Ethnic In-Language Media

The operationalization of ethnic in-language media may raise some interesting possibilities for future research. Although this variable was defined in the present study on the basis of language, future research might focus on media content that is ethnically targeted regardless of language. The best example would be media that uses the English language but is targeted toward specific groups of people, such as Black Entertainment Television (BET), which directly targets African Americans.

SUMMARY

The study reported in this chapter examined the influence of ethnicity on communication patterns among African, Anglo, Chinese, and Hispanic Americans. Specifically, these four ethnic groups' use of English media, in-language ethnic media, word of mouth, and nontraditional media was researched. Growing ethnic diversity in the United States today demands that marketers come to understand various communication styles of ethnic consumers. Given that culture affects communication patterns, which in turn influence consumer decision-making processes, these questions have to be addressed in a systematic and comprehensive manner. However, until now ethnic groups have been studied either individually or in pairs under differing contexts. Such a patchwork approach does not help provide the whole picture of ethnic consumer communication patterns in the United States. In contrast, the present research set out to establish an initial portrayal of ethnic media behavior by incorporating four ethnic groups from one geographic location, simultaneously, in one study. This necessary first step to studying ethnic communication patterns, therefore, provides a building block for future research in ethnic marketing and communications. Specifically, the results of the present study illustrate how research across several groups and various communication sources is important to understanding and reevaluating current media tactics for reaching specific audiences.

Consumers in different ethnic groups were found to differ significantly in their extent of advertising and product talk, as well as their responses toward most nontraditional media. A closer inspection of the findings reveals that African Americans do tend to engage in media for longer amounts of time than other ethnic groups and are more receptive to a variety of sources, including word of mouth and nontraditional communication tools. In contrast, Chinese and Hispanic Americans spend less time with any one particular medium but obviously have more media choices to which they can allocate their time. Hispanic Americans enjoy a variety of English and Spanish media; radio is favored the most in both languages. In the case of Chinese Americans, it appears that no one particular medium is better at reaching them than another, as all are infrequently used. This suggests that managers must seriously consider how best to effectively and efficiently reach the Chinese American consumer. The results of this study would indicate that although all media avenues are good for targeting African American consumers, Chinese Americans may be better reached by use of community network channels, opinion leaders, and the trickle-down approach (Robertson, 1971).

Technological advances such as the Internet and expanding ethnic in-language media availability suggest that the landscape of ethnic communication will no doubt continue to change in a dynamic way. Therefore, the current investigation of ethnic consumers and their communication patterns should serve as an evolving case study for the American market and as a possible template for countries in

Europe and Southeast Asia that face similar diverse ethnic populations. With an initial ethnic portrayal of communication patterns established, marketers can begin to more effectively target ethnic consumers with the most cost-efficient methods.

ACKNOWLEDGMENTS

We acknowledge the financial support of the American Academy of Advertising, the University of Texas at Austin, College of Communication through a Jamail Research Grant, and the Institute of Latin American Studies' Mellon Fellowship. Their support was essential in collecting the data for the study reported here. We also acknowledge Gigi Taylor and Wen-ling Amber Chen for their help in data collection and entry.

REFERENCES

Arndt, J. (1967). Role of product-related conversations in the diffusion of a new product. *Journal of Marketing Research, 4*, 291–295.

Awhigham-Desir, M. (1997). Cashing in on coupons: Andrew Morrison's Nia Direct Inc. *Black Enterprise, 27*, 171–174.

Bearden, W. O., & Etzel, M. J. (1982). Reference group influence on product and brand purchase decisions. *Journal of Consumer Research, 9*, 183–194.

Bearden, W. O., Netemeyer, R. G., & Teel, J. E. (1989). Measurement of consumer susceptibility to interpersonal influence. *Journal of Consumer Research, 15*, 473–481.

Bejou, D., & Tat, P. K. (1994). Examining black consumer motives for coupon usage. *Journal of Advertising Research, 34* (2), 29–35.

Bone, P. F. (1995). Word-of-mouth effects on short-term and long-term product judgments. *Journal of Business Research, 32*, 213–223.

Brown, J. J., & Reingen, P. H. (1987). Social ties and word-of-mouth referral behavior. *Journal of Consumer Research, 14*, 350–362.

Bureau of the Census (1990). *1990 United States population reports by region: Houston.* Washington, DC: U.S. Department of Commerce, Economics and Statistics Administration.

Burnkrant, R. E., & Cousineau, A. (1975). Informational and normative social influence in buyer behavior. *Journal of Consumer Research, 2*, 206–215.

Childers, T., & Rao, A (1992). The influence of familial and peer-based reference groups on consumer decisions. *Journal of Consumer Research, 19*, 198–211.

Cohen, J. B., & Golden, E. (1972). Informational social influence and product evaluation. *Journal of Applied Psychology, 56*, 54–59.

Dates, J. L. (1993). Advertising. In J. L. Dates & W. Barlow (Eds.), *Split image: African Americans in the mass media* (2nd ed., pp. 461–493). Washington, DC: Howard University Press.

Delener, N., & Neelankavil, J. P. (1990, June/July). Informational sources and media usage: A comparison between Asian and Hispanic subcultures. *Journal of Advertising Research, 30*, 45–52.

de Mooij, M. (1998). *Global marketing and advertising: understanding cultural paradoxes.* Thousand Oaks, CA: Sage.

Deshpande, R., Hoyer, W., & Donthu, N. (1986). The intensity of ethnic affiliation: A study of the sociology of Hispanic consumption. *Journal of Consumer Research, 13*, 214–220.

Deshpande, R., & Stayman, D. M. (1994). A tale of two cities: Distinctiveness theory and advertising effectiveness. *Journal of Marketing Research, 31,* 57–64.

Dichter, E. (1966, November-December). How word of mouth advertising works. *Harvard Business Review, 44,* 147–166.

Faber, R., O'Guinn, T., & McCarty, J. (1987). Ethnicity, acculturation and the importance of product attributes. *Psychology & Marketing, 4,* 121–134.

Feick, L. F., & Price, L. L. (1987). The market maven: A diffuser of marketplace information. *Journal of Marketing, 51,* 83–97.

Ford, J. D., & Ellis, E. (1980). A re-examination of group influence on member band preference. *Journal of Marketing Research, 17,* 125–132.

Frenzen, J., & Nakamoto, K. (1993). Structure, cooperation, and the flow of market information. *Journal of Consumer Research, 20,* 360–375.

Green, C. L. (1995). Media exposure's impact on perceived availability and redemption of coupons by ethnic consumers. *Journal of Advertising Research, 35,* 56–64.

Goldsmith, J. (1996, September 13). Ad sales lag behind boom in Hispanic TV. *The Wall Street Journal,* p. B5.

Hair, J. F., Anderson, R. E., Tatham, R. L., & Black, W. C. (1995). *Multivariate Data Analysis.* Englewood Cliffs, NJ: Prentice-Hall.

Harvard encyclopedia of American ethnic groups. Cambridge, MA: Belknap Press of Harvard University.

Hays, W. L. (1988). *Statistics.* New York: Holt, Rinehart & Winston.

Hayseed, K. M. (1989). Managing word of mouth communications. *The Journal of Services Marketing, 3,* 55–67.

Hecht, M. L., Collier, M. J., & Ribeau, S. A. (1993). *African American communication: Ethnic identity and cultural interpretation.* Newbury Park, CA: Sage.

Herr, P. M., Kardes, F. R., & Kim, J. (1991). Effects of word-of-mouth and product-attribute information on persuasion: An accessibility-diagnosticity perspective. *Journal of Consumer Research, 17,* 454–462.

Higie, R. A., Feick, L. F., & Price, L. L. (1987). Types and amount of word-of-mouth communications about retailers. *Journal of Retailing, 63,* 260–278.

Hilger, M. T., & English W. D. (1978). Consumer alienation from the marketplace. In R. F. Franz, R. M. Hopkins, & A. G. Toma (Eds.), *Proceedings, 1978 Southern Marketing Association Conference* (pp. 78–83). Lafayette, LA: University of Southwestern Louisiana Press.

Hirschman, E. C. (1985). Primitive aspects of consumption in modern American society. *Journal of Consumer Research, 12,* 142–154.

Hofstede, G. (1991). *Cultures and organizations: Software of the mind.* New York: McGraw-Hill.

Jandt, F. E. (1995). *Intercultural communication: An introduction.* Thousand Oaks, CA: Sage.

Koslow, S., Shamdasani, P. N., & Touchstone, E. E. (1994). Exploring language effects in ethnic advertising: A sociolinguistic perspective. *Journal of Consumer Research, 20,* 575–585.

Lee, W. N. (1993). Acculturation and advertising communication strategies: A cross-cultural study of Chinese and Americans. *Psychology & Marketing, 10,* 381–397.

Lee, W. N., & Tse, D. (1994). Changing media consumption in a new home: Acculturation patterns among Hong Kong immigrants to Canada. *Journal of Advertising, 23,* 57–70.

Mehta, R., & Belk, R. W. (1991). Artifacts, identity and transition: Favorite possessions of Indians and Indian immigrants to the United States. *Journal of Consumer Research, 18,* 398–411.

Mick, D. G., & Buhl, C. (1992). A meaning-based model of advertising experiences. *Journal of Consumer Research, 19,* 317–338.

Moschis, G. P. (1976). Social comparison and informal group influence. *Journal of Marketing Research, 13,* 237–244.

O'Guinn, T., & Faber, R. (1985). New perspectives on acculturation: The relationship of general and role specific acculturation with Hispanics' consumer attitudes. In E. C. Hirschman & M. B. Holbrook (Eds.), *Advances in consumer research* (pp. 113–117). Provo, UT: Association for Consumer Research.

O'Guinn, T., & Faber, R. (1986). Advertising and subculture: The role of ethnicity and acculturation in market segmentation. *Current Issues and Research in Advertising, 9*, 133–147.

O'Guinn, T. C., & Meyer, T. P. (1984). Segmenting the Hispanic market: The use of Spanish-language radio. *Journal of Advertising Research, 23*, 9–16.

O'Hare, W. P., Frey, W. H., & Fost, D. (1994, May). Asians in the suburbs. *American Demographics, 16*, 33–38.

Penaloza, L. (1994). *Atravesando fronteras*/border crossings: A critical ethnographic exploration of the consumer acculturation of Mexican immigrants. *Journal of Consumer Research, 21*, 32–54.

Penaloza, L. N., & Gilly, M. C. (1986). The Hispanic family: Consumer research issues. *Psychology & Marketing, 3*, 291–303.

Phillips, C. (1993, February 19). Black entrepreneurship: Data gap. *The Wall Street Journal*, p. R18.

Reingen, P. H., Foster, B. L., Brown, J. J., & Seidman, S. B. (1984). Brand congruence in interpersonal relations: A social network analysis. *Journal of Consumer Research, 11*, 771–783.

Reingen, P. H., & Kernan, J. B. (1986). Analysis of referral networks in marketing: Methods and illustration. *Journal of Marketing Research, 23*, 370–378.

Richins, M. (1991). Social comparison and the idealized images of advertising. *Journal of Consumer Research, 18*, 71–83.

Robertson, T. S. (1971). *Innovative behavior and communication*. New York: Holt, Rinehart & Winston.

Rokeach, M. J. (1968). *Beliefs, attitudes, and values*. San Francisco: Jossey-Bass.

Saegert, J., Hoover, R. J., & Hilger, M. T. (1985). Characteristics of Mexican American consumers. *Journal of Consumer Research, 12*, 104–109.

Schultz, D. E., Tannenbaum, S. I., & Lauterborn, R. F. (1994). *Integrated marketing communications*. Lincolnwood, IL: NTC Business Books.

Sheth, J. D. (1976, June). Word of mouth in low risk innovations. *Journal of Advertising Research, 16*, 15–18.

Singh, J. (1990). Voice, exit, and negative word-of-mouth behaviors: An investigation across three service categories. *Journal of the Academy of Marketing Science, 18*, 1–15.

Solomon, M. R. (1996). *Consumer behavior: Buying, having, and being*. Englewood Cliffs, NJ: Prentice-Hall.

The Sourcebook of demographics Fairfax, VA: CACI, Inc. Federal.

Stafford, J. E. (1966). Effects of group influence on consumer brand preferences. *Journal of Marketing Research, 3*, 68–75.

Stayman, D. M., & Deshpande, R. (1989). Situational ethnicity and consumer behavior. *Journal of Consumer Research, 16*, 361–371.

Stern, B. B. (1994). A revised communication model for advertising: Multiple dimensions of the source, the message, and the recipient. *Journal of Advertising, 23*, 5–16.

Subervi-Vélez, F. A. (1986). The mass media and ethnic assimilation and pluralism: A review and research proposal with special focus on Hispanics. *Communication Research, 13*, 71–96.

Swan, J. E., & Oliver. R. L. (1989). Postpurchase communications by consumers. *Journal of Retailing, 65*, 516–533.

Wallendorf, M., & Reilly, M. D. (1983). Ethnic migration, assimilation, and consumption. *Journal of Consumer Research, 10*, 292–302.

Webster, C. (1991, Winter). Influences upon consumer expectations of services. *Journal of Services Marketing, 5*, 5–17.

Webster, C. (1992, September/October). The effects of Hispanic subcultural identification on information search behavior. *Journal of Advertising Research, 32*, 54–62.

Webster, C. (1994). Effects of Hispanic ethnic identification on marital roles in the purchase decision process. *Journal of Consumer Research, 21*, 319–331.

Whittler, T. E., Calantone, R. J., & Young, M. R. (1991). Strength of ethnic affiliation: Examining black identification with black culture. *The Journal of Social Psychology, 131* (4), 461–467.

Wiesendanger, B. (1993, September). Asian-Americans: The three biggest myths. *Sales & Marketing Management, 145,* 86.

Wilkes, R. E., & Valencia, H. (1986). Shopping-related characteristics of Mexican-Americans and blacks. *Psychology & Marketing, 3,* 247–259.

Williams, J. D., & Qualls, W. J. (1989). Middle-class black consumers and intensity of ethnic identification. *Psychology of Marketing, 6,* 263–286.

Witt, R. E., & Bruce, G. D. (1972). Group influence and brand choice congruence. *Journal of Marketing Research, 9,* 440–443.

CHAPTER ELEVEN

Discovering Brand Equity Through Psycholinguistic Methods

Robert Pennington
National Chung Hsing University

What a brands means to consumers is perhaps the most important component of brand equity. A meaningless brand adds no value to the product to which it is attached. This chapter tells how to apply a psycholinguistic methodology to discover what public affective meanings brands have for consumers. Public affective meaning is the expressive value of the brand; this value may be arbitrarily derived, having no inherent connection with a product, service, or company. Affective brand meanings may be especially important to marketers of parity products, who are competitors with the same essential concrete attributes and functional consequences.

As competition among consumer products diminishes inherent differences, consumers' capacity to differentiate products as objects also diminishes. Brands, however, with a range of arbitrary meanings, augment consumers' capacity to differentiate. Although brands tend to be created by attachment to products, brands are not identical to those products. Brands often do not depend on the physical presence of products for their meanings, which are beyond the meanings of the products themselves. Brands, as abstract entities, can acquire their own meanings to be associated with either abstract objects (products) or social objects (people). Brands, like words, are based on arbitrary, rather than inherent, associations to their referents (Osgood, 1963). Associations with brands are increasingly abstract; they are not determined by the structure of verbal language.

This application can discover consumers' perceived distinctions among publicly consumed brands according to brand personality. The method allows consumers to define brand personality through their own words, rather than through a previously developed list. It then allows the researcher to analyze data for patterns in consumers' responses in order discover those meanings specific to each brand

and those common to a category. In this consumer-based approach, consumers provide all scale items in the research instrument so that the research is not biased by researchers' assumptions about consumers. Because the purpose is to discover what meanings consumers actually associate with brands and products, we do not suggest meanings to them with researcher-selected response choices. Exclusive use of subject-generated responses yields greater validity.

The technique, adapted from previous psycholinguistic research, offers researchers an objective, numerical criterion to retain or reject participants' responses. It utilizes information theory as a tool with several applications related to brand research. For example, we can learn the abstract qualities consumers associate with brands. We can find out which brands consumers think are appropriate within specific contexts. We can identify which brands consumers perceive as belonging together in groupings, or "constellations" (Solomon & Assael, 1987, p. 191). Finally, we can discover which brands consumers consider to have synonymous and antonymous meanings. More broadly, this technique is useful for developing and tracking the morphology of a consumer code that utilizes brands to convey meaning.

RATIONALE

This methodology is useful to advertisers for four reasons. First, an emerging trend in the development of message strategy emphasizes consumers' viewpoints concerning consumption and possession motivations based on values that meaning provides (Richins, 1994a, p. 519). This methodology contributes to a better understanding of consumers' values by examining what meanings consumers associate with brand symbols. Second, this method can establish benchmarks for tracking brand meaning and evaluating meaning transfer from advertisement to consumer (McCracken, 1990, pp. 5–8). Third, when applied to both brands and products, this method can guide decisions concerning brand extensions for congruence in brand and product meanings. Fourth, because this methodology is not culture specific, it is useful for developing and evaluating global creative strategies.

COMPLEMENTING OTHER METHODS

The best use of this methodology is to complement, rather that replace, other methodologies. Previous studies of meaning and advertising, using a range of approaches and methodologies, provide rationale. Researchers often assert, though sometimes implicitly, that consumers actively participate in producing meaning through advertising (Cleveland, 1986; Hirschman & Thompson, 1997; Leiss, Kline, & Jhally, 1986; Levy, 1986; Olson, 1986; Richins, 1994a; Stern, 1988), using advertising meanings to create or reinforce personal identity (Scott, 1994). However, meaning analyses have tended to interpret formal features of advertisements rather than consumer data (Mick & Buhl, 1992).

Investigations of meanings that consumers attach to consumption objects (Johar & Sirgy, 1991; Lunt & Livingstone, 1992; McCracken, 1990, 1988, 1986; Richins, 1994a, 1994b; Williamson, 1978) also suggest applications for the methodology discussed here. Consumers derive meaning from consumption objects, which, in combination, can have syntactical relationships (Englis & Solomon, 1995; Haire, 1950; Holbrook, 1987; Kehret-Ward, 1987; Solomon & Assael, 1987; Solomon & Englis, 1994), which this methodology can discover. Although Solomon and Assael (1987) asserted that products have meaning only in combinations with other products, Richins (1994a, 1994b) demonstrated that single products have meaning. In addition, Haire (1950) found that changing a single product in a list of products resulted in a substantial change in consumer perception. Finding those meanings and perceptual changes is among the uses of this methodology. In fact, Richins explicitly recognized the utility of this methodology (Richins, 1994b, p. 531).

Cultural context often transfers meaning from advertisement to product to consumer (McCracken, 1986, 1988, 1990; Williamson, 1978). A common view is that advertising is primarily about products, although researchers recognize that it reveals much about consumers themselves (Passikoff & Holman, 1987, p. 375). However, in insofar as consumers use the advertising text to create themselves (Scott, 1994, pp. 471–472), advertising is only peripherally about products and is primarily about consumers (Postman, 1985/1987). The text of an advertisement gives cues to its meaning, and readers assemble the cues to derive the actual meaning (Scott, 1994), which then becomes available for transfer to product and consumer.

The meaning derived from an advertisement is a function of each consumer's personal history (Mick & Buhl, 1992), but not all advertising experiences are completely idiosyncratic (Scott, 1994, p. 463). Shared experience allows consumers to use products for artifactual communication (Mick, 1986, pp. 202–203). By early adolescence, consumers use "badge products" to define themselves and their relations with others (Stacey, 1982). We can distinguish the idiosyncratic from the shared meanings by using the methodology discussed here, and we can estimate product potential for artifactual communication.

Research rarely examines the affective meanings that consumers associate with brand symbols, or the process of meaning transfer from advertisement to brand to consumer. Brand equity literature often emphasizes consumer perceptions of product attributes indicated by a brand rather than the affective meaning that brands convey (Aaker, 1991; Kapferer, 1992), although consumer profiles yield some insight into affective meaning (Aaker, 1991, p. 147). Products and brands have been shown to have discursive value and extensional meaning, that is, all objects or phenomena to which the meaning applies; subjects can recognize reference groups that products and brands identify (Englis & Solomon, 1995; Haire, 1950). However, the group qualities or features that the brand signifies have yet to be clearly determined.

Multidimensional scaling techniques often define brands in terms of product or service attributes, leaving brand meaning to be discovered through qualitative research (Aaker, 1991; Ha, 1996). This methodology applies reader-response theory (Scott, 1994) to the study of brand meaning, gathering data from consumers rather than from the formal features of advertisements. The psycholinguistic methods that Richins recognized as useful (Richins, 1994b, p. 531) were developed to study participants' responses to words as stimuli. This study adapts those methods to study participants' responses to brands as stimuli in order to discover affective brand meaning through quantitative techniques.

METHOD DEVELOPMENT

In their exploration of meaning that placed concepts within semantic space, Osgood and others (Osgood, Archer, & Miron, 1962; Osgood, May, & Miron, 1975) utilized information theory in selecting scale items for their research instruments. The manner in which they used information theory tends to find similarities in meaning among concepts rather than differences that distinguish concepts from each other. However, advertisers can modify their use of information theory to reveal distinctions consumers make among brands. The specific technique is the calculation of an H statistic, a criterion for scale-item selection from subjects' responses to a range of stimuli. Researchers rank responses according to the value of H and retain or reject the responses by using rank as a criterion.

The H statistic derives from the definition of conditional uncertainty in discrete noiseless systems, developed by Shannon (Shannon & Weaver, 1963, p. 52), combined with its application by Attneave (1959). The value of H represents the average number of guesses, given an ideal code, that one would have to make in order to guess correctly an occurrence of an attribute of a second variable when the occurrence of an attribute of a first variable is known. It expresses binary digits, or *bits*, of information.

The goal of Osgood et al. (1962, 1975) was to discover the meaning of universal concepts across cultures. However, with their application, if all participants had shown complete agreement through identical responses, that response would have been rejected. Meanwhile, the most intuitively vague response, one given by all participants to all stimuli, would have been retained. Osgood and others' use answers this question: If we know the response, how well can we predict the stimulus?

In the application described here, we do not measure the uncertainty of joint occurrences of stimuli and responses but rather the joint occurrences of individuals and responses. Its use here is a measure of idiosyncrasy, that is, whether a particular response came from a single participant or from multiple participants. A value of $H = 0$ means that, when we know the response, we know the individual. We can calculate a priori a maximum value of H, which would occur if all participants gave the same response to all stimuli. We can also calculate a priori the H value that would occur if all participants gave the same response to one, and only one, stimulus.

The H statistic is calculated by subtracting the uncertainty value of the occurrence of a variable attribute from the uncertainty value of the joint occurrence of the attributes of two variables, or

$$H_{x(y)} = H_{(x, y)} - H_{(x)},$$

where x represents the occurrence of the first variable, y represents the occurrence of the second variable, and $p(ij)$ is "the probability of the joint occurrence of i for the first and j for the second" (Shannon & Weaver, 1963, p. 51). Although x commonly stands for table rows and y commonly stands for table columns, in order to be compatible with Shannon's probability tables (Shannon & Weaver, 1963, p. 41), this discussion presents possible values of x in columns and possible values of y in rows. Across values of y, however, the co-occurrences of specific values of x appear in rows; across values of x, specific values of y appear in columns.

The intention of Osgood and others in their application of this calculation is not clear. They express its utility in combining the criteria of frequency of occurrence—salience—and number of categories for occurrence—diversity (Osgood et al., 1975, p. 87). Diversity is the measure that tends to reveal convergence in meaning. In the proposal appendices that introduced the technique (Osgood et al., 1962), the H statistic is

$$H = \frac{1}{N_i} \left(n_i \log_2 n_i - \sum_i n_{ij} \log_2 \sum n_{ij} \right),$$

where i represents the possible attributes of x and j represents the possible attributes of y. However, in later work that discusses both methodology and results (Osgood et al., 1975), the two terms in parentheses are reversed and presented as

$$H = \frac{1}{N_T} \left[\sum_i \left\langle f_{ij} \log_2 \sum f_{ij} \right\rangle - f_i \log_2 f_i \right].$$

Some confusion results from the use of different symbols. In the first version, n_i and n_{ij} are the equivalent of f_i and f_{ij} in the second version. They represent, respectively, the single occurrence of a response and the joint occurrences of response and concepts. N_i in the first version represents the total number of occurrences of a specific response; N_T in the second version represents the total number of all responses.

The purpose of each is to express, in terms of actual frequencies, Shannon's statement of conditional uncertainty in discrete noiseless systems (Shannon &

Weaver, 1963, p. 52), which he expressed in terms of probability

$$H_{x(y)} = -\sum_{ij} p_{(ij)} \log_2 p_{i(j)},$$

where

$$p_{i(j)} = \frac{p_{(ij)}}{\sum_j p_{ij}}.$$

The probabilities derive from observed or known frequencies of occurrences.

When we use the symbol n to stand for the frequencies of a given occurrence and substitute that symbol for p, Shannon's conditional uncertainty is

$$H_{x(y)} = \frac{\sum_{ij}\left[n_{ij}\log_2\sum_j n_{ij}\right] - \sum_{ij}\left[n_{ij}\log_2 n_{ij}\right]}{\sum_{ij} n_{ij}}.$$

In this expression, the positive term in the numerator represents the uncertainty of a single variable x, and the negative term represents the uncertainty of the joint occurrence of two variables x and y. The original expression of conditional uncertainty,

$$H_{(xy)} = H_{(x,y)} - H_{(x)},$$

subtracted single variable uncertainty from joint variable uncertainty. However, the signs are reversed in the process of expansion because both the joint occurrences and single occurrences, $H_{(x,y)}$, and $H_{(x)}$, respectively, acquire negative values:

$$H_{(x,y)} = \frac{-\sum_{ij}\left[n_{ij}\log_2 n_{ij}\right]}{\sum_{ij} n_{ij}},$$

$$H_{(x)} = \frac{-\sum_{ij}\left[n_{ij}\log_2\sum_j n_{ij}\right]}{\sum_{ij} n_{ij}}.$$

The value of $H_{x(y)}$ expresses the average uncertainty of y for all possible values of x and y (see the matrix). If we express this verbally, to find the uncertainty of y when we know the value of x, we multiply the value of each cell by the base 2 logarithm of its row sum; then we sum the results. From this quantity, we subtract the quantity we obtain from summing the results of multiplying each cell by its own base 2 logarithm. After subtracting the second quantity from the first, we divide by the sum of the values in all cells. The H statistic tells us the average uncertainty of y for all possible values of x: $H_{x(y)} = 0$ whenever $H_{(x,y)} = H_{(x)}$.

	j_1	j_2	j_3	j_4	j_5	j_6	j_7	j_8	j_9	j_{10}	$\sum_j n_{ij}$
i_1	$n_{i_1 j_1}$	$n_{i_1 j_2}$	$n_{i_1 j_3}$	$n_{i_1 j_4}$	$n_{i_1 j_5}$	$n_{i_1 j_6}$	$n_{i_1 j_7}$	$n_{i_1 j_8}$	$n_{i_1 j_9}$	$n_{i_1 j_{10}}$	$\sum_j n_{i_1 j}$
i_2	$n_{i_2 j_1}$	$n_{i_2 j_2}$	$n_{i_2 j_3}$	$n_{i_2 j_4}$	$n_{i_2 j_5}$	$n_{i_2 j_6}$	$n_{i_2 j_7}$	$n_{i_2 j_8}$	$n_{i_2 j_9}$	$n_{i_2 j_{10}}$	$\sum_j n_{i_2 j}$
i_3	$n_{i_3 j_1}$	$n_{i_3 j_2}$	$n_{i_3 j_3}$	$n_{i_3 j_4}$	$n_{i_3 j_5}$	$n_{i_3 j_6}$	$n_{i_3 j_7}$	$n_{i_3 j_8}$	$n_{i_3 j_9}$	$n_{i_3 j_{10}}$	$\sum_j n_{i_3 j}$
i_4	$n_{i_4 j_1}$	$n_{i_4 j_2}$	$n_{i_4 j_3}$	$n_{i_4 j_4}$	$n_{i_4 j_5}$	$n_{i_4 j_6}$	$n_{i_4 j_7}$	$n_{i_4 j_8}$	$n_{i_4 j_9}$	$n_{i_4 j_{10}}$	$\sum_j n_{i_4 j}$
i_5	$n_{i_5 j_1}$	$n_{i_5 j_2}$	$n_{i_5 j_3}$	$n_{i_5 j_4}$	$n_{i_5 j_5}$	$n_{i_5 j_6}$	$n_{i_5 j_7}$	$n_{i_5 j_8}$	$n_{i_5 j_9}$	$n_{i_5 j_{10}}$	$\sum_j n_{i_5 j}$
i_6	$n_{i_6 j_1}$	$n_{i_6 j_2}$	$n_{i_6 j_3}$	$n_{i_6 j_4}$	$n_{i_6 j_5}$	$n_{i_6 j_6}$	$n_{i_6 j_7}$	$n_{i_6 j_8}$	$n_{i_6 j_9}$	$n_{i_6 j_{10}}$	$\sum_j n_{i_6 j}$
i_7	$n_{i_7 j_1}$	$n_{i_7 j_2}$	$n_{i_7 j_3}$	$n_{i_7 j_4}$	$n_{i_7 j_5}$	$n_{i_7 j_6}$	$n_{i_7 j_7}$	$n_{i_7 j_8}$	$n_{i_7 j_9}$	$n_{i_7 j_{10}}$	$\sum_j n_{i_7 j}$
i_8	$n_{i_8 j_1}$	$n_{i_8 j_2}$	$n_{i_8 j_3}$	$n_{i_8 j_4}$	$n_{i_8 j_5}$	$n_{i_8 j_6}$	$n_{i_8 j_7}$	$n_{i_8 j_8}$	$n_{i_8 j_9}$	$n_{i_8 j_{10}}$	$\sum_j n_{i_8 j}$
i_9	$n_{i_9 j_1}$	$n_{i_9 j_2}$	$n_{i_9 j_3}$	$n_{i_9 j_4}$	$n_{i_9 j_5}$	$n_{i_9 j_6}$	$n_{i_9 j_7}$	$n_{i_9 j_8}$	$n_{i_9 j_9}$	$n_{i_9 j_{10}}$	$\sum_j n_{i_9 j}$
i_{10}	$n_{i_{10} j_1}$	$n_{i_{10} j_2}$	$n_{i_{10} j_3}$	$n_{i_{10} j_4}$	$n_{i_{10} j_5}$	$n_{i_{10} j_6}$	$n_{i_{10} j_7}$	$n_{i_{10} j_8}$	$n_{i_{10} j_9}$	$n_{i_{10} j_{10}}$	$\sum_j n_{i_{10} j}$
$\sum_i n_{ij}$	$\sum_i n_{i j_1}$	$\sum_i n_{i j_2}$	$\sum_i n_{i j_3}$	$\sum_i n_{i j_4}$	$\sum_i n_{i j_5}$	$\sum_i n_{i j_6}$	$\sum_i n_{i j_7}$	$\sum_i n_{i j_8}$	$\sum_i n_{i j_9}$	$\sum_i n_{i j_{10}}$	$\sum_{ij} n_{ij}$

In the application described in this chapter, we are not interested in the average uncertainty for all possible values; we are interested in the uncertainty of one variable given specific values of another variable. When we know the specific value of one variable, we want the H statistic to tell us how uncertain we are of the value of the other variable. Specifically, we want to know how well we can guess the subject y when we know the response x in order to distinguish between agreement and idiosyncrasy among subjects. We can use the same calculation of the H statistic for that purpose. When calculating the conditional uncertainty of y given a single known value of x, we ignore the occurrence of all other values of x; thus our matrix has only a single row corresponding to the specific value of the variable for the specific value of x.

What we want to discover determines which variables and which values we will use to calculate the H statistic. When calculating conditional uncertainty given that we know a specific value of a variable, we consider only cells that include occurrences of the specific value. Any cell in which the specific value does not occur contains a frequency of $n_{ij} = 0$. The practical result is that, for any specific value, the matrix has only a single row. The sum of occurrences is equal to the frequency of occurrences of the specific value; that is, $\sum_{ij} n_{ij} = \sum_j n_{ij}$. For example, in the matrix given, the variable x has values i_1 through i_{10}. If we want to know the uncertainty of variable y given that we know the value of x is i_3, we consider only the cells with frequencies of i_3 and any value of y. We then calculate the conditional uncertainty of y as

$$H_{x(y)} = \frac{\sum_j \left[n_{ij} \log_2 \sum_j n_{ij} \right] - \sum_j \left[n_{ij} \log_2 n_{ij} \right]}{\sum_j n_{ij}}.$$

If we choose to consider several values of x, the number of rows in the matrix is equal to the number of values we choose. For example, if we calculate the uncertainty of y given the x values i_3 through i_7, the matrix would have five rows, one for each of the values of x. The sum of occurrences is equal to the sum of the frequencies of the several values of x. We might also want to limit certain alternative values of y in some situations, such as low frequency of one or more values. As we reduce the values of y, we reduce the number of columns in the matrix. However, as we reduce the alternative values of y, we reduce uncertainty until we have $H = 0$, or no uncertainty; with a single value of y, we would be certain given any value of x because we would have no alternative.

As we reduce the number of rows to the point that we know the value of x, one might expect $H_{(x)} = 0$, but that is only the case when $n_i = 1$. Even when all occurrences of a specific x value co-occur with a single, specific value of y, $H_{(x)} \neq 0$. Although we know the specific value of x, we do not know the specific occurrence of that value unless $n_i = 1$. When all occurrences of a specific value of x are contained in a single cell of the matrix, then $H_{(x)} = \log_2 n_i$. Therefore, $H_{(x)} = 0$ if, and only if, $n_i = 1$. For example, assume that subject j_3 is the only subject who gives response i_4 and gives that response to four brands. In the matrix, cell $n_{i_4 j_3}$ will contain a frequency of 4; all other cells will contain a frequency of 0. However, $H_{(x)} \neq 0$ because we do not know the specific brand even when we know the response and subject. In this example, $H_{(x)} = 2$, because that is the number of systematic "guesses" we must make to determine the specific brand.

Rather than calculate the uncertainty of the brand when the response is known, I calculated the uncertainty of the subject when the response is known. In this application, n represented the number of brands to which each subject gave a specific response, and $\sum_{ij} n_{ij}$ represented the total number of that specific response given by all subjects. If a single, and only, subject gave a specific response, $H = 0$ resulted, regardless of the number of brands to which the subject gave the response. If all subjects gave a single, specific response to a single brand, $H = \log_2$ (number of subjects) would have resulted. However, the same would have resulted if all subjects each gave the same, specific response to an equal number of brands.

Using this methodology with several brands in one broad product category, I have obtained useful results. Researchers asked participants to give words that best described the consumers of several brands. The H value of responses was the basis for retention or rejection of the response for further data collection. As described, the selection criteria eliminated idiosyncratic responses, but they retained responses that tended to indicate some agreement on brand meaning and also on category meaning. Several participants, chosen for their sophistication in contemporary verbal language, provided opposites to the retained responses. These became semantic differential scales on which additional participants rated consumers of the original list of brands. Those results were grouped by factor analysis, and the associations among brands and factors were compared by use of an analysis of variance.

The findings showed that participants distinguished among three subcategories within the broad category. Within two subcategories, participants found one brand out of three or four distinguishable from the subcategory. In the third subcategory, participants found no significant distinction among the three brands. That result was not surprising. Each of the three emphasized the same quality in its advertising, a quality central to the target consumers' self-definitions. By emphasizing that quality, none of the brands was able to offer consumers any distinction. Since the completion of this study, however, one of the brands has modified its advertising specifically to distinguish its consumers from those of its competitors.

OTHER APPLICATIONS

This methodology can be useful in continuing the Solomon and Assael study of consumption constellations (Solomon & Assael, 1987). If we take consumer type as variable x and brand as variable y, we can determine the uncertainty of brands when we know the consumer type. Or, if we flip that matrix configuration so that brand is variable x and consumer type is variable y, we can find the uncertainty of consumer types when we know the brand. In either of these situations, the value of H allows us to eliminate idiosyncratic responses.

Brand constellations are not the same as Solomon and Assael's consumption constellations. They identified consumers' brand-level associations with various consumer types. Brand and consumer type are the variables in the matrix. Brands are indirectly related to each other through their direct relationships with consumer types. A study of brand constellations would reveal consumers' direct association of various brands with each other. Brands would be both variables in the matrix. Given a specific brand choice, we would have a measure of uncertainty about other brand choices. The difference between the two constellations is analogous to the difference in another type of test: asking participants to list a typical businessman's vocabulary, and asking subjects to use the phrase "bottom line" in a sentence. The first test may only reveal passive awareness; the second test is more likely to reveal active understanding of meaning and syntax.

In the case of brands, syntax is not the same as the syntax of consumption strings Kehret-Ward discussed (Kehret-Ward, 1987). Consumption strings are likely to have some logical connection or inherent association. For example, shaving cream or gel moistens whiskers so they can be cut easily. A shaver does the cutting, and aftershave lotion soothes skin irritated by shaving. Brand groupings, however, may be completely arbitrary matters of convention, especially among brands of different product categories. Because brand groupings can be arbitrary, we have no basis for guessing which brands belong together. In fact, we may find regional "dialects" of brands groupings. The methodology discussed here is well suited to discovering arbitrary groupings and regional or cultural differences.

Technology now allows delivery of custom media content to individuals through computers and televisions. Instead of turning to special interest channels created for a target audience segment, consumers will be able to create their own personal "brand" channels. This methodology, using information theory, will play a key role in developing those personal channels. Service providers who offer "content constellations" will attract consumers to their media. Based on each consumer's choices, information theory can predict further choices.

CONCLUSIONS

Convergent meanings revealed by greater H values can be useful in developing marketing communication message strategies that surround brands with signs that evoke a specific association. But, when the purpose of marketing communication is to distinguish brands or products, especially in parity situations, marketers must first discover consumers' existing associations and determine whether consumers already distinguish brands and products. For that purpose, the use by Osgood et al. of the H statistic is inappropriate (even using the correct formula). However, using a different combination of variables to calculate the H statistic allows us to retain divergent responses that distinguish brands or products, to reject convergent responses, and to reject idiosyncratic responses.

The use of the H statistic by Osgood et al. discarded highly idiosyncratic responses, but it also discarded responses that showed a high degree of agreement because they did not meet the diversity criterion (Osgood et al., 1975, p. 87). If only one participants had given a specific response one time to a single concept, the result would have been $H = 0$, or no uncertainty of the participant when the response was known, and the response would have been discarded. However, such an interpretation of $H = 0$ in these circumstances would be a conceptual misinterpretation. In these circumstances, $H = 0$ reveals that, when the response is known, the concept is known. In addition, if only one participant had given a specific response to all concepts, the value of H would have been substantially greater than zero and retained for further use when the response was, in fact, completely idiosyncratic.

Further, if all participants had given the same response to one concept, and only one concept, the result would have been an H value of zero, or no uncertainty. That is, when the modifier was known, the concept would have been known. According to criteria from Osgood and others, such a universal response would have been rejected in favor of responses with diverse associations, and greater uncertainty over which concepts occurred jointly with which modifiers. In other words, their research rejected responses that might have indicated divergence of meaning that distinguished concepts from each other, and it retained responses that indicated convergence of meaning and similarities among concepts.

In that early use of conditional uncertainty, which indicated the predictability of a concept when a response was known, $H = 0$ would have revealed a clear distinction between one concept and all others. In the example matrix, i would represent the various responses to the various brands j as stimuli. The cells would contain the number of subjects who gave a specific response to a specific brand. If all subjects give a specific response to a single brand, and only that brand, $H = 0$ would be the result. In the case of marketing communication, we would want to keep such a response because it indicates complete agreement among subjects. If we know the response, we would also know the brand or product.

However, in this configuration of the matrix, $H = 0$ is not an appropriate selection criterion because if one participant gives a response to one, and only one, brand or product, $H = 0$ would also result. In such a case, $H = 0$ indicates the most idiosyncratic responses. If we know the response, we would also know the brand or product, but it would not be of much use, except in personal selling if we knew the participant. We want to select responses that distinguish brands, but we want that distinction to come from as many participants as possible, not just one or a few. We want to eliminate idiosyncratic responses without eliminating agreement among participants.

In this same matrix configuration, using values i and j of response x and brand y, higher values of H represent convergent responses that do not distinguish among brands. If we know the response, we are uncertain of the brand. This can be useful in some situations. If we use brands from a single product category, higher values of H will represent responses that a consumer or consumers associate with the entire category. If we use brands from different product categories, higher values of H will indicate that the brands form a meaningful constellation, or syntactical grouping of brands with an expressive association.

Creating a matrix to calculate the H statistic described herein, that is, the uncertainty of the participants when we know the response, could be cumbersome and tedious were we to use a great number of participants, as Osgood and others did. In their application, the variables were concept and response, verbal modifiers (adjectives) that participants associated with concepts. In our applications, the variables differ, but the matrices can become comparably cumbersome. In the example herein, if we used only 100 participants, each could conceivably give a different response to each of several stimuli. The resulting matrix would have 10,000 cells. Further, when we enter our data, we generally use the participant as a case, or line of data, and responses as the values of the variable stimuli. The responses are nominal measurements, and calculation of uncertainty requires at least ordinal measurement. Therefore, the raw data set is useless for calculating an H statistic.

We must transform the data in some way. Osgood transformed the data so that tables cells contained the number of participants who gave a specific response to a specific stimulus, a ratio measurement. In our application, table cells contain the number of stimuli to which subjects gave a specific response, also a ratio measurement. However, as already illustrated, creating a contingency table and a transformed data set would be a cumbersome and tedious process.

Fortunately, we can compute H statistics without creating matrices and additional data sets. Widely used statistical packages such as SPSS and SAS feature conditional uncertainty calculations, but they do not feature the uncertainty that we want. With a large number of participants, and knowing the response, we want to calculate the uncertainty of the participant without have to create a huge and cumbersome contingency table. Fortunately, SAS can use the original data set with each subject as a case, followed by the responses to brands, to give an H value for each response. Because the most cumbersome part of the process is eliminated by SAS, the process is no longer cumbersome. With the results, building scales for gathering additional data is simple and straightforward.

By using responses from consumers, we are letting consumers build the scales. We are merely using information theory to select their responses. Because our purpose is to discover what meanings consumers really associate with brands and products, we do not suggest meanings to them by injecting our judgments into the selection process. Nor do we create the scales ourselves. Throughout the process, responses come from consumers, who are telling us what our brands mean to them. That is information every marketer should have.

REFERENCES

Attneave, F. (1959). *Applications of information theory to psychology: A summary of basic concepts, methods, and results.* New York: Holt.

Aaker, D. A. (1991). *Managing brand equity: Capitalizing on the value of a brand name.* New York: The Free Press.

Cleveland, C. E. (1986). Semiotics: Determining what the advertising message means to the audience. In J. Olson & K. Sentis (Eds.), *Advertising and consumer psychology* (Vol. 3, pp. 227–241). New York: Praeger.

Englis, B. G., & Solomon, M. R. (1995, Spring). To be and not to be: Lifestyle imagery, references groups, and The clustering of America. *Journal of Advertising, 24,* 13–28.

Ha, L. (1996). Factors countervailing the negative effects of advertising clutter on brand equity. In G. B. Wilcox (Ed.), *Proceedings of the 1996 Conference of the American Academy of Advertising* (pp. 73–74). Austin: University of Texas at Austin.

Haire, M. (1950, April). Projective techniques in marketing research. *Journal of Marketing, 14,* 649–656.

Hirschman, E. C., & Thompson, C. J. (1997, Spring). Why media matter: Toward a richer understanding of consumers' relationships with advertising and mass media. *Journal of Advertising, 26,* 43–60.

Holbrook, M. B. 1987. The study of signs in consumer esthetics: An egocentric review. In J. Umiker-Sebeok (Ed.), *Marketing and semiotics: New directions in the study of signs for sale* (pp. 74–121). New York: deGruyter.

Johar, J. S., & Sirgy, M. J. (1991, September). Value-expressive versus utilitarian appeals: When and why to use which appeal. *Journal of Advertising, 20,* 23–33.

Kapferer, J.-N. (1992). *Strategic brand management.* New York: The Free Press.

Kehret-Ward, T. (1987). Combining products in use: How the syntax of product use affects marketing decisions. In J. Umiker-Sebeok (Ed.), *Marketing and semiotics: New directions in the study of signs for sale* (pp. 219–238). New York: deGruyter.

Leiss, W., Kline, S., & Jhally, S. (1986). *Social communication in advertising: Persons, products, & images of well-being.* Toronto: Methuen.

Levy, S. J. (1986). Meanings in advertising stimuli. In J. Olson & K. Sentis (Eds.), *Advertising and consumer psychology* (Vol. 3, pp. 214–226). New York: Praeger.

Lunt, P., & Livingstone, S. (1992). *Mass consumption and personal identity: Everyday economic experience.* Buckingham, England: Open University Press.

McCracken, G. (1986, June). Culture and consumption: A theoretical account of the structure and movement of the cultural meaning of consumer goods. *Journal of Consumer Research, 13,* 71–84.

McCracken, G. (1988). *Culture and consumption: New approaches to the symbolic character of consumer goods and activities.* Bloomington: Indiana University Press.

McCracken, G. (1990, January). Culture and consumer behavior: An anthropological perspective. *Journal of the Market Research Society, 32,* 3–11.

Mick, D. G. (1986, September). Consumer research and semiotics: Exploring the morphology of signs, symbols, and significance. *Journal of Consumer Research, 13,* 196–213.

Mick, D. G., & Buhl, C. (1992, December). A meaning-based model of advertising experiences. *Journal of Consumer Research, 19,* 317–338.

Olson, J. (1986). Meaning analysis in advertising research. In J. Olson & K. Sentis (Eds)., *Advertising and consumer psychology* (Vol. 3, pp. 275–283). New York: Praeger.

Osgood, C. (1963). On understanding and creating sentences. *American Psychologist, 18,* 735–751.

Osgood, C. E., Archer, W. K., & Miron, H. S. (1962). *The cross-cultural generality of meaning systems: Proposal appendices.* Unpublished manuscript, University of Illinois, Institute for Communications Research, Urbana.

Osgood, C., May, W. H., & Miron, M. S. (1975). *Cross-cultural universals of affective meaning*. Urbana: University of Illinois Press.

Passikoff, R., & Holman, R. H. (1987). The semiotics of possessions and commercial communication. In J. Umiker-Sebeok (Ed.), *Marketing and semiotics: New directions in the study of signs for sale* (pp. 375–390). New York: deGruyter.

Postman, N. (1985, December 23). Interview. *U.S. News and World Report* (pp. 58–59). (Cited by D. G. Mick, 1987. Toward a semiotic of advertising story grammars. In Jean Umiker-Sebeok (Ed.), *Marketing and semiotics: New directions in the study of signs for sale* (pp. 249–278). New York: deGruyter.

Richins, M. L. (1994a, December). Valuing things: The public and private meanings of possessions. *Journal of Consumer Research, 21*, 504–521.

Richins, M. L. (1994b, December). Special possessions and the expression of material values. *Journal of Consumer Research, 21*, 522–533.

Scott, L. M. (1994, December). The bridge from text to mind: Adapting reader-response theory to consumer research. *Journal of Consumer Research, 21*, 461–480.

Shannon, C. E., & Weaver, W. (1963). *The mathematical theory of communication*. Urbana: University of Illinois Press.

Sirgy, M. J. (1985, June). Self-image/product-image congruity and consumer decision making. *Journal of Business Research, 13*, 49–63.

Solomon, M. R., & Assael, H. (1987). The forest or the trees?: A gestalt approach to symbolic consumption. In J. Umiker-Sebeok (Ed.), *Marketing and semiotics: New directions in the study of signs for sale* (pp. 189–217). New York: deGruyter.

Solomon, M. R., & Englis, B. G. (1994, Fall). Reality engineering: Blurring the boundaries between commercial signification and popular culture. *Journal of Current Issues and Research in Advertising, 16*, 1–17.

Stacey, B. G. (1982). Economic socialization in the pre-adult years. *British Journal of Social Psychology, 21*, 159–173.

Stern, B. B. (1988, Summer). How does an ad mean? Language in services advertising. *Journal of Consumer Research, 17*, 3–14.

Williamson, J. (1978). *Decoding advertisements: Ideology and meaning in advertising*. London: Boyars.

IV. THE INFLUENCING ROLE OF SOCIAL AND INFORMATION CONTEXTS IN DIVERSITY IN ADVERTISING

CHAPTER TWELVE

Consumer Distinctiveness and Advertising Persuasion

Sonya A. Grier
Stanford University

Anne M. Brumbaugh
Wake Forest University

The increasing diversity of the global marketplace drives marketing efforts across numerous countries, cultures, and subcultures. The marketer's challenge is to make advertisements relevant to as many people as possible, without offending or alienating others who might "mistakenly" see the ads. In the process of creating targeted advertisements for multicultural marketplaces, marketers look for meaningful characteristics by which to divide a single heterogeneous market into separate homogeneous consumer segments that may be courted more effectively. Almost without exception, these characteristics have been those that are relatively rare within the overall market and that are meaningful to the individual consumer. Distinctiveness theory (e.g., McGuire & Padawer-Singer, 1976; McGuire, McGuire, & Winton, 1979) provides insight into why such numerically rare but meaningful consumer characteristics have been so successful as bases for segmentation as well as into how targeted advertisements work.

Applications of distinctiveness theory (in general, the idea that people define themselves on the basis of traits that are numerically rare in their local environment) to consumer behavior have provided a wealth of insight into how social context and individual characteristics jointly influence consumer responses to advertising. Prior research has shown that members of distinctive groups attend more to targeted advertisements, process and interpret targeted messages differently, and favor targeted ads more strongly relative to nondistinctive consumers (Aaker, Brumbaugh, & Grier, 2000; Deshpandé & Stayman, 1994; Forehand & Deshpandé, 2001; Forehand, Deshpandé, & Reed, 2002; Grier & Brumbaugh, 1999; Grier &

Deshpandé, 2001; cf. Wooten, 1995). Thus, it is important to understand how distinctiveness and cultural group membership together influence which of several possible identities to which one may have access will be made salient by advertising and contextual cues to affect marketing effectiveness.

This chapter discusses the significance of distinctiveness theory for understanding advertising persuasion in multicultural marketplaces. First, we define distinctiveness theory, reviewing the initial empirical tests that formed the distinctiveness postulate and describing its underlying psychological assumptions. We also discuss other research that extends various elements of distinctiveness theory and attests to its robustness. Then, we review consumer applications of distinctiveness theory, and we link this discussion to our understanding of the psychological processes affecting advertising responses. Our goal is to demonstrate how powerful the distinctiveness construct is in understanding advertising persuasion among multicultural audiences. Finally, we suggest directions for future research that capitalize on and extend the distinctiveness construct.

WHAT IS DISTINCTIVENESS?

Prior research on the self-concept has revealed that we can attend to any of our multiple identities at any given time (Markus & Nurius, 1986; Markus & Wurf, 1987). Psychologists have sought to understand the conditions that lead a consumer to feel distinctive on the basis of a particular group characteristic (Smith, Noll, & Bryant, 1999), heightening the salience of that identity over other potential identities. McGuire and colleagues developed distinctiveness theory as a response to a perceived dominance of a "reactive approach" in self-concept research that studied participants' reactions to dimensions of the self-chosen a priori by the researcher. They felt that there was more to learn about an individual's self-concept by exploring the dimensions that one chooses to describe oneself versus those on a given list (McGuire & Padawer-Singer, 1976). Specifically, they hypothesized that the spontaneous salience of a personal characteristic to the self-concept is determined by a process of "perceptual selectivity" (1976, p. 744), whereby the uniqueness of a characteristic in any given context heightens the likelihood that it will become part of one's identity at that moment. Therefore, they proposed that when we are required to consider our identity, those identities that will take precedence over others tend to be those that are rare in our social milieu. This "distinctiveness postulate" suggests, for example, that a Black woman is more likely to be aware of her gender when she is associating with Black men, but more aware of her race when she is associating with White women (p. 744).[1]

Tests of the distinctive postulate have found robust support. The central prediction of distinctiveness theory is that an individual's distinctive traits in relation to other people in the environment will be more salient to the individual than more common traits (McGuire, 1984; McGuire, McGuire, & Winton, 1979, 1980; McGuire, McGuire, Child, & Fujioka, 1978; McGuire & Padawer-Singer, 1976).

Empirically, McGuire and colleagues tested the distinctiveness prediction by using the "spontaneous self-concept" measure. For this measure, participants were asked to describe themselves in response to this open-ended question: "Please tell us about yourself in your own words." The percentage identifying a particular trait represents a measure of trait salience, with higher percentages indicating higher salience. McGuire emphasized that this open-ended approach determines what dimensions are salient to the person versus a structured measure that compels participants to define themselves in only those terms the researcher has selected.

The initial studies conducted by McGuire and Padawer-Singer (1976) asked 1,000 children to "tell us about yourself" and hypothesized that they would reply in terms of their physical characteristics only to the extent that their physical characteristics were different from those of most of their schoolmates. The results confirmed predictions for various traits, including height, weight, hair color, birthplace, and use of eyeglasses. That is, for each of these traits, as the children's characteristic became more distinct from their classmates, the trait became more salient and was more likely to be mentioned as part of their spontaneous self-concepts. McGuire and Padawer-Singer also explored the salience of gender in school classroom groups and found that 26% of the members of the minority gender in these classroom groups spontaneously mentioned their gender, but only 11% of those of the majority gender did so. Another study examined "handedness" and found that left handedness—the more rare of the two—was more salient and mentioned more frequently than right handedness (McGuire & McGuire, 1980).

Empirical support for the distinctiveness prediction has been robust across key multicultural consumer segmentation variables, such as race and ethnicity (McGuire et al., 1978) and gender (Cota & Dion, 1986; McGuire et al., 1979; McGuire & Padawer-Singer, 1976). For example, McGuire et al. (1978) investigated the salience of ethnicity in classes of American grade-school children. They found that 14% of the minority Hispanic and 17% of the minority Black students spontaneously mentioned their ethnicity in describing themselves, whereas only 1% of the majority White students did so. Another study examined the effects of household gender composition on the salience of children's gender (McGuire et al., 1979). This study found that boys spontaneously mentioned being male more often when they came from households in which females were the majority, and girls mentioned being female more often when they came from households with male majorities. Thus, this early research on distinctiveness demonstrates that individuals who belong to a distinctive or numerically rare group tend to be highly aware and mindful of the characteristics shared by that group and are more likely to incorporate that group identity into their self-concept than individuals who do not belong to such a group.

Distinctiveness is Dynamic

The household study just mentioned also introduced McGuire's notion of "chronic distinctiveness" whereby a characteristic can become persistently salient to one's self-concept if the other people in one's reference group are continuously different from oneself on that characteristic (McGuire & McGuire, 1980). People who found themselves consistently in the minority on an important trait experienced chronic accessibility of that trait and felt distinctiveness based on that trait. Along the same lines, in a study of university students on a majority White campus, Black students' ethnicity caused them to experience chronic distinctiveness, whereas White students experienced distinctiveness only when they were minorities in majority Black groups (Pollak & Niemann, 1998). Similarly, female and Black students in an MBA program in which they were in the minority both consistently self-defined on the basis of their minority trait (Mehra, Kilduff, & Brass, 1998).

However, most research has focused on distinctiveness as a dynamic, context-dependent construct, the bases for which may as be varied as people themselves. For example, Cota and Dion (1986) examined distinctiveness and group gender composition, studying ad hoc groups rather than naturally occurring groups. They found that the gender composition of noninteracting groups, put together solely for experimental purposes, affected the salience of gender in the individuals' self-concept. They concluded that one's self-concept is quite fluid and responsive to even transient and leading features of the situational context. Indeed, McGuire argued that context influences identity salience by inducing differential attention to specific features of oneself and that the social context alters the relationship of distinctiveness to the self-concept by providing a reference group. This group is used as the standard against which people compare their characteristics to those of others to know whether they are peculiar or distinctive. Consider again the study by McGuire et al. (1978) that found that numeric minority Hispanic and Black students were significantly more likely to mention their ethnicity in describing themselves than numerically predominant White students. The immediate context, that is, the student's classroom, provided a referent in the form of the other individuals present and their characteristics. Many of the initial studies by McGuire and his colleagues focused on the role of immediate contexts in heightening the spontaneous salience of a demographic or physical characteristic. Alternatively, the study by McGuire et al. (1979), which demonstrated higher gender salience among children who were in the gender minority in their family, assumed a more habitual reference group. Thus, as the context varies, so may the salient trait.

Social Aspects of Distinctiveness

In addition to the aforementioned numeric distinctiveness, which focuses on trait prevalence, research also suggests that the meaning of the trait used to define oneself matters. McGuire noted that "the salience of ethnicity will be affected by many other factors besides distinctiveness such as its social desirability, cultural relevance, and so forth" (1979, p. 518). Similarly, other scholars have argued that the meanings attached to being in the minority, rather than solely its relative (in)frequency, create the increased salience of a category associated with distinctiveness (Abrams,

Thomas, & Hogg, 1990; Oakes, 1987; Smith, 1991; Tajfel, 1981). For example, research has shown that the effects of distinctiveness based on race versus distinctiveness based on gender differ. Racially distinctive individuals in an MBA program tended to socialize together, because of both preference for similar others as well as exclusion by dissimilar others. Thus, the shared experience associated with racial distinctiveness in this setting created both a tendency to socialize with similar others as well as a perceived exclusion by dissimilar others. In contrast, gender distinctive (female) individuals in the same MBA program socialized only because of perceived exclusion by male colleagues (Mehra, Kilduff, & Brass, 1998). For them, being female provided no such shared experience around which they could come together. Thus, the meaning of being female differed from the meaning of being Black, seemingly offering less of a focus for community building. This line of research suggests that the effects of numeric group composition cannot be fully understood if they are considered without reference to corresponding belief systems (Grier & Deshpandé, 2001).

DISTINCTIVENESS AND ADVERTISING

Targeted advertisements are presumed effective because they resonate with a characteristic that is meaningful to the intended audience. Research on persuasion suggests that any factor that leads individuals to make judgments of similarity between themselves and an advertisement source (e.g., cultural orientation, Aaker & Williams, 1998; sexual orientation, Bhat, Leigh, & Wardlow, 1996; social class, William & Qualls, 1989; ethnicity, Wooten, 1995) should enhance positive response to the advertisement. Further, the more personally meaningful the factor, the more likely that similarity with the source will be felt (Tajfel, 1981). As a result, it has been assumed that members of minority groups should have heightened positive feelings toward targeted advertising directed at them on the factor that makes them a numeric minority.

As researchers have explored the impact of source–viewer similarity on advertising responses, they have discovered that mere similarity as they have defined or operationalized it is not sufficient to induce positive responses that target marketing is presumed to cause. Rather, it has become clear that the basis for the similarity underlying the targeting attempt has to be salient to the viewer. That is, the viewer must, on some level (perhaps subconsciously), be aware of the similarity between herself or himself and the ad source. Further, the more meaningful the basis of this similarity, the stronger the favorable target marketing effect. If the basis for similarity is trivial or not self-defining, then favorable target marketing effects are less likely to occur. If the basis is salient and has meaning for one's self-identity (e.g., ethnicity, gender, race, or sexual orientation as implied herein), then the link between the viewer and source is influential in inducing favorable ad responses and creating enduring positive persuasion.

No doubt, there are file cabinets full of experimental studies in which researchers have attempted to manipulate felt similarity on bases they presumed a priori would induce target marketing effects that failed because the bases they chose were either not salient or not meaningful to the viewer. For example, Brumbaugh and Grier (2001) initially expected shared ethnicity to have a favorable impact on identification and ad attitudes among Black and White women viewing one of two identical ads for athletic shoes, one featuring White women and one featuring Black women. In fact, in this study, it was identification based instead on shared role as an athlete, a more salient and meaningful attribute than ethnicity in the case of these ad executions, that caused favorable target marketing effects. Thus, the intended ethnic match between viewer and source fell short of inducing the anticipated favorable effects on advertising. It is likely that such "failures" have motivated a number of researchers to explore when source–viewer similarity will have an impact on ad effectiveness and when it will not. Some of these researchers have found the distinctiveness postulate to be a powerful theory by which to make such predictions. Indeed, a number of insights vital to targeting diverse audiences in a multicultural marketplace have come to light. Results of this body of research have revealed that members of distinctive target markets attend more to targeted advertisements, create more favorable links with themselves, process targeted messages differently, and generally react more favorably relative to nondistinctive consumers (Aaker et al., 2000; Deshpandé & Stayman, 1994; Forehand & Deshpandé, 2001; Forehand et al., 2002; Grier & Brumbaugh, 1999; Grier & Deshpandé, 2001; cf. Wooten, 1995). The contributions of this research to our understanding of advertising effectiveness among culturally diverse audiences merit detailed discussion.

Early Work on Distinctiveness and Persuasion

An important early application of distinctiveness theory to advertising demonstrated that, although being a member of an ethnic minority may be the basis for which one is distinctiveness, being a member of an ethnic minority and being distinctiveness are two different constructs. In this study, Deshpandé and Stayman (1994) applied distinctiveness theory in a study of spokesperson advertising effectiveness. Their guiding premise was that the lower the proportion of ethnic minority group members in the overall population, the more likely that ethnically targeted stimuli, such as the use of an ethnic spokesperson, would be effective. They integrated prior research on strength of ethnic identification, the effect of the race of actors in ads, and distinctiveness theory to derive a model and set of hypotheses concerning how distinctiveness applies to advertising effects. It was hypothesized that consumers who live in a situation where their ethnic group is a numeric minority would have a more salient ethnic identity, and they would be more likely to identify with a spokesperson of their own group. Further, Deshpandé and Stayman proposed that perceptions of similarity should lead to increased credibility of the spokesperson and thus an increase in attitude toward the brand being advertised.

To test this model, Deshpandé and Stayman recruited participants from two similar cities: Austin, Texas, where the majority of residents were Anglo; and San Antonio, Texas, where the majority of residents were Hispanic. Through this manipulation, the authors were able to disentangle the effects of ethnicity (Hispanic vs. Anglo) from their numeric prevalence in the population (minority Hispanics in Austin and Anglos in San Antonio vs. majority Hispanics in San Antonio and Anglos in Austin). In their experiment, participants read a radio commercial script that was described as being spoken by individuals with either Spanish or Anglo surnames. They found that ethnicity was more salient among both Anglo and Hispanic consumers when they were the numeric minorities in the local population than when they were not. Further, for these numerically and ethnically distinctive consumers, similarity between their ethnicity and that of the ad spokesperson resulted in the spokesperson being seen as more trustworthy, which led to more positive brand attitudes. The authors concluded that ethnically targeted stimuli (e.g. an advertisement featuring a spokesperson of the same ethnicity as a targeted viewer) were more effective among numerically distinctive consumers than nondistinctive consumers.

Target and Nontarget Markets

The initial effort to integrate distinctiveness theory into research on ethnicity and target marketing illustrated that target marketing efforts may work differently among distinctive minority consumers as compared to nondistinctive majority consumers. Results suggest that distinctiveness (independent of ethnicity) is a moderator that affects how target marketing works to effect favorable ad reactions. Specifically, favorable target market effects seem to be stronger when the basis for targeting is a distinctive trait for the viewer. Aaker et al. (2000) examined this moderating role of distinctiveness on the effects of targeted advertising among members of an advertiser's intended audience as well as those in the "nontarget market." They built their reasoning on the idea that distinctive viewers who are targeted on the basis of that distinctive trait should perceive heightened similarity and experience stronger persuasion than nondistinctive viewers who are targeted on the basis of a more common trait.

They also reasoned that distinctiveness theory predicts a varying effect of minority versus majority group membership on responses of the nontarget market, based on heightened awareness of dissimilarity (McGuire, 1984). Drawing on this reasoning, the authors proposed that because advertisements targeting numeric minorities are relatively rare in mainstream media, the novelty of such advertisements should be particularly salient to nondistinctive individuals outside the targeted group. This novelty was hypothesized to induce stronger perceptions of dissimilarity between nondistinctive viewers and the distinctive source depicted in the ads, which would lead to less favorable attitudes. In contrast, they argued that advertisements targeting nondistinctive groups should not induce such dissimilarity judgments among distinctive nontarget markets because the prevalence of such advertisements does not make their distinctive trait salient. As a result, they predicted that negative nontarget market effects were not likely to occur for distinctive viewers seeing ads targeting nondistinctive markets.

Results confirmed their predictions and showed that unfavorable nontarget market effects were stronger among members of nondistinctive groups (White consumers and heterosexual consumers in their study), and that favorable target market effects were stronger for members of distinctive groups (African American consumers and homosexual consumers in their study). Further, these asymmetrics resulted directly from different reactions evoked among distinctive versus nondistinctive individuals. Favorable target market effects for distinctive viewers occurred because of heightened levels of felt similarity with a source, as the distinctiveness postulate would predict. However, favorable target market effects for nondistinctive viewers resulted from their felt inclusion in the target market based on some aspects of the entire configuration of advertisement cues rather than from felt similarity to similar sources. Unfavorable nontarget market effects occurred for the opposite reasons. That is, nondistinctive viewers favored nontarget market ads less because of perceived dissimilarity with the depicted sources, and distinctive viewers favored nontarget market ads less because of perceived exclusion from the intended target market. The authors concluded that the mechanism by which targeting works varies drastically for distinctive and nondistinctive viewers. For members of distinctive cultural groups, targeted executions are effective because they make the viewer feel similar to and identify with similar sources, and nontargeted ads fail because of the viewer's perceived exclusion from the target market. Alternatively, for members of nondistinctive groups, targeted executions are effective because they make the viewer feel included in the target market, and nontargeted ads fail because they make the viewer feel dissimilar to the pictured source.

Grier and Brumbaugh (1999) also explored this moderating role of distinctiveness on favorable targeted responses among different subcultural groups by investigating the meanings created by target and nontarget market viewers of advertising created for Black heterosexuals (distinctive based on ethnicity), White heterosexuals (nondistinctive), and White homosexuals (distinctive based on sexual orientation). They proposed that members of distinctive groups would be more likely to read a targeted ad in a self-referential manner than would members of nondistinctive groups. That is, viewers for whom the basis of targeting was salient and self-defining would use this basis to interpret the ad, whereas viewers for whom the basis of targeting was either not salient (viewers were unaware of the basis for similarity) or not self-defining (the basis for similarity did not tap into the viewer's self-identity) would not.

In their study, participants who were members of one of the three subcultures were shown advertisements that had been pretested as being targeted toward each group. Each ad used multiple targeting cues, including sources in the advertisement, advertising copy, and other cultural cues, to indicate their intended target market. After viewing each ad, participants listed the thoughts and feelings they experienced when looking at the ad, and they completed questions to assess the degree to which they believed they were in the target market for the ad. Results of their study showed that both viewer distinctiveness and the cultural meaning of the target market influenced the processes by which people created meaning from the ad stimuli, as well as the specific content of the created meanings. Importantly, their results showed that the relative infrequency with which distinctive groups are targeted and the distinctive viewers' heightened salience of their distinctive characteristics enabled them to create favorable links between themselves and the ad texts more readily than nondistinctive viewers. All viewers drew on their knowledge of the targeted groups to inform their ad responses, but only members of the minority subcultures (Black heterosexuals and White homosexuals) were able to accurately decode cues and meanings in ads targeting their own groups (cf. Brumbaugh, 2002). The two studies established that people use cues in advertisements to determine if they are in the target market for the ad and to assess the meaning the ad has for them (Aaker et al., 2000; Grier & Brumbaugh, 1999). Such ad cues under the control of advertisers appear to have an impact on an individual's felt distinctiveness, depending on the distinctive characteristics of the source as well as the other cues included in the ad stimulus. Forehand and Deshpandé (2001) investigated explicitly how such cues may elicit feelings of distinctiveness that subsequently influence an individual's reaction to the ads.

Elicited Ethnicity

Forehand and Deshpandé (2001) argued that although most previous research has conceptualized distinctiveness as a by-product of the social environment, there is no reason to expect that distinctiveness could not also be elicited by any number of nonsocial contextual factors. Specifically, they proposed that consumers' awareness of their memberships in social groups (and potentially felt distinctiveness based on membership one of those groups) may be elicited by execution factors in a targeted ad as well as by contextual primes that precede exposure to the targeted ad. They built their empirical investigation on a concept they called "ethnic self-awareness," which is defined as a temporary state during which a person is more sensitive to his or her ethnicity. Ethnic self-awareness can be primed by cues in advertising as well as in the consumer's consumption situation, with the latter being the more typical focus of traditional distinctiveness research. It occurs when people are prompted to categorize themselves along ethnic criteria, which happens when people compare themselves to others and assess their relative similarity or dissimilarity. Forehand and Deshpandé hypothesized that ethnic primes in an advertisement would elicit ethnic self-awareness and prompt heightened feelings of targetedness and more favorable attitudes toward same-ethnicity actors featured in ethnically targeted advertisements.

They conducted two experiments, using participants who self-identified as Asian American or White. Their research found that Asians had increased ethnic self-awareness, felt more targeted, and responded more positively to Asian targeted advertising if they were first exposed to an Asian ethnic prime prior to being exposed to the focal advertisement. In contrast, however, ethnic priming had little effect on the responses of White participants, for whom effects were limited to a minor increase in ethnic self-awareness and a decrease in targetedness in response to the Asian targeted advertisements. The authors noted that their results were consistent with the differential numeric distinctiveness of Asians and Whites within the U.S. population. Thus, the ethnic prime for Asian participants successfully raised the salience and meaningfulness of their ethnic identity, which, in turn, affected their responses to advertising in ways consistent with previous research. In contrast, the ethnic prime for White participants failed to have such an effect because their ethnic identity is neither salient nor meaningful for them.

Forehand et al. (2002) followed up on the results of Forehand and Deshpandé (2001) to examine how identity primes delivered prior to a targeted ad and identity cues embedded in an ad work together to influence identity salience and subsequent response to advertising that targets individuals with that identity. In two experiments, they manipulated the numeric distinctiveness of Asian American and White participants (determined by whether participants were chosen from a population in which they were a majority or minority), exposure to either an Asian or White ethnic prime prior to a targeted ad, and exposure to either an Asian or White targeted ad. The results showed that individuals who were exposed to an ethnic prime and an advertisement with cues that directed attention to their ethnic identity and who were numeric minorities in their immediate social environment expressed systematically different attitudes toward the targeted advertising, evaluations of spokespeople in the targeted advertising, and perceptions of being targeted by the advertising. Specifically, Asian (White) participants responded more positively (negatively) to Asian targeted advertising when participants were exposed to identity primes prior to the judgment and were distinctive in their local environment. Surprisingly, they also found that neither identity primes nor numeric distinctiveness independently influenced advertising response.

Social Dimensions of Distinctiveness

The impact that numeric distinctiveness has on making culturally meaningful self-identities salient and its influence on responses to targeted advertising have been well articulated by the previous studies. Grier and Deshpandé (2001) extended work on distinctiveness, culture, and meaning by examining how the meanings associated with a trait in society influence consumers' feelings of distinctiveness and advertising persuasion. They introduced the notion of social distinctiveness: That people's perceptions of the relative meaning and value of an individual characteristic in a social context influences the importance of that characteristic to the person's self-concept. They argued that the meaning of traits such as ethnic group membership acquire significance in relation to other groups within a given context. Therefore, a trait such as ethnicity drives self-attention not only because it may be numerically rare, but also because it implies a set of common group experiences and beliefs. As a consequence, increased ethnic salience should be evoked by factors that create feelings of being socially distinctive independent of being numerically distinctive. They proposed that variations in perceived social status between groups would influence consumer distinctiveness in two ways: through status deficit and status difference. If social status perceptions indicated that one group was more worthy, this group should become the societal referent, and "deviants," that is, members of groups that are perceived as lower in social status (status deficit), should have heightened trait salience caused by chronic distinctiveness. They further reasoned that the relative difference between groups' social status (status difference) also influences the salience and importance of group membership to one's self-identity, and thus social distinctiveness. As a result, individuals who perceived larger relative status differences between groups should have higher salience of their own group membership compared with individuals who perceived less of a difference between groups, regardless of their numeric minority–majority status.

They investigated these hypotheses in an experiment in South Africa, where social status and numeric status are negatively related. There, majority Black individuals are of lower social status than minority White individuals, the opposite of the situation found in the United States, where research on distinctiveness has traditionally been conducted. Results replicated the traditional finding of higher ethnic salience for numeric minorities than for numeric majorities. Further, ethnic salience was also higher among both Blacks and Whites that saw a larger status gap between groups, as well as among those with a status deficit (i.e., chronic salience for Blacks relative to Whites). They concluded that adding consideration of the social dimensions of distinctiveness to the numeric conceptualization increased the explanatory value of distinctiveness theory.

Summary: Distinctiveness Theory and Advertising Response

The cumulative results of the previous studies show that incorporating the distinctiveness construct into research exploring ethnicity, culture, and advertising provides a much-needed theoretic boost to understanding how advertising targeting culturally diverse audiences works, when it is most effective, and why it occasionally fails to have its desired effects. Consistent with a larger body of consumer research on spokesperson ethnicity effects in advertising (Whittler, 1991, 1989; Whittler & DiMeo, 1991; Williams & Qualls, 1989; Williams, Qualls, & Grier, 1995), applications of distinctiveness theory to consumer behavior add insight into how social context and individual characteristics such as ethnicity jointly influence consumer responses to advertising. Thanks to this work, we know that ethnic similarity between the viewer and sources depicted in advertising enhances ad responses among targeted ethnic minorities because similarity judgments are more readily made among these numerically distinctive individuals (Deshpandé & Stayman, 1994) and affect the effectiveness of targeting efforts (Aaker et al., 2000). The salience of the basis of this similarity, whether it be ethnicity, culture, or sexual orientation, is heightened because in the United States such groups are numerically distinctive, and the meaning associated with group membership becomes self-defining (Grier & Brumbaugh, 1999). The meanings associated with ethnic and other cultural group memberships affect ad attitudes favorably among targeted individuals but unfavorably among nontarget majority consumers (Aaker et al., 2000; Forehand & Deshpandé, 2001).

However, it is clear that cultural group membership is not sufficient to induce the target market effects advertisers desire, as cultural group membership and distinctiveness are two different entities that act in concert to induce felt distinctiveness that subsequently affects advertising responses (Forehand & Deshpandé, 2001; Forehand et al., 2002). Importantly, the relationships between groups emerge as important in determining when and which group membership is salient and important in drawing on aspects of one's self-identity to create ad meanings (Grier & Deshpandé, 2001). Though integrating distinctiveness theory into advertising research in a multicultural context has yielded these important insights, much research remains to be done and ample opportunities abound for future research.

DIRECTIONS FOR FUTURE RESEARCH

Because marketers are in the unique position of creating real-life stimuli to attract and persuade market segments, advertising is a natural laboratory in which to study distinctiveness, its antecedents, and its consequences. In the discussion that follows, we outline only some of the opportunities that exist to integrate the distinctiveness postulate into multicultural advertising research. These research avenues include exploration of the following: further cues in ad executions and consumption contexts that lead to felt distinctiveness; the meanings associated with self-defining traits; cues that elicit attention to self-defining traits; intervening processes that affect how distinctiveness influences ad reactions; and the applicability of distinctiveness theory to changing cultural contexts.

Advertising Cues

The most straightforward line of inquiry that derives from the existing research is the exploration of ad cues that lead viewers to make similarity judgments based on a shared distinctive trait with the character(s) depicted in an ad. Aaker et al. (2000) demonstrated that minority group members respond more favorably to an ad when they see someone in it with whom they can identify, but that nonminority individuals will also respond well to the ad if it includes other cues, such as background, consumption occasion, or attire, that they recognize. Combining distinctive sources with other targeting cues that attract nondistinctive viewers may be an effective way of reaching both distinctive and nondistinctive individuals. For example, Brumbaugh (2002) showed that both Black and White participants responded similarly to advertising featuring Black sources combined with mainstream (White) background cues, but that ads featuring both Black sources and Black background cultural cues tapped into subcultural knowledge and self-identity for black viewers. Recent research on identification among gay and lesbian consumers shown targeted ads also supported this notion, with different messages leading to different levels and types of felt identification, distinctiveness, and self-identity (Greenlee & Oakenfull, 2000). This research suggested that an advertiser may be able to reach multiple target segments with one advertising appeal that combines cues viewed favorably by consumers from different cultural backgrounds.

Further, exploring when minority sources depicted in an ad do *not* elicit felt distinctiveness would yield insight into how people decode stimuli that may have multiple meanings for viewers. For example, as Grier and Brumbaugh (1999) noted, it is likely that Michael Jordan, a Black man (a visible, ascribed numeric minority with lower power, lower status, and negative valence), engenders different meanings because of his personal status as a successful professional athlete (an invisible, achieved numeric minority with higher power, higher status, and positive valence; McCracken, 1989). Rather than an indicator of the intended target market, he is likely to serve as an aspirational referent that all people, Black or White, male or female, would like to emulate (Friedman & Friedman, 1979; Mathur, Mathur, & Rangan, 1997). However, his "meaning" may differ subtly depending on if the viewer shares the same cultural affiliation, gender, or interest in sports (Brumbaugh & Grier, 2001). Investigating how viewers interpret complex culture-based sources (such as celebrities from numerically rare social groups) would enhance our understanding of the influence of distinctiveness on how targeting cues are interpreted by different groups.

Contextual Influences

Another line of future research involves studying the situational and contextual antecedents that lead to felt distinctiveness. Thus far, empirical studies of consumer distinctiveness have shown that feelings of distinctiveness are prompted by one's numeric status in the local environment, as well as social status vis-à-vis other groups. Because advertisers are more able to provide ad cues that target consumers based on their distinctive status than to manipulate the local environment in which their ads are seen, it is important to identify the contextual factors that have an impact on how advertisements are processed and interpreted by different audiences. For example, the medium in which an ad is placed may provide the necessary contextual cues to evoke one's distinctiveness. Placing an ad targeting

Black women in *Ebony* may lead to different levels and types of distinctiveness (and thus ad effectiveness) than placing the very same ad in a mainstream medium targeting a broader audience (e.g., *Cosmopolitan*). Similar media effects may occur for targeted radio, television, Web sites, and outdoor advertising whereby the medium provides contextual cues that prime or make salient cultural identities, and the advertisements embedded therein reap the benefits of the observed distinctiveness effects.

Similarly, local demography that affects the cultural composition of consumers patronizing retail establishments might influence felt distinctiveness and the effectiveness of in-store promotions. For example, would consumers be differentially responsive to a targeted supermarket shelf talker depending on whether they are in a supermarket where they are distinctive versus not distinctive? Would their distinctiveness within the supermarket overshadow their nondistinctive status outside the store and vice versa ? Further, prior research highlights that distinctiveness can be both chronic and spontaneous; understanding the relationship between spontaneously evoked identities, and the more chronic importance of identity to one's self-concept, across consumption contexts, and the implications for advertising response, provides an interesting path for continued exploration (cf. Grier & Deshpande, 2001). Consumer research tackling such issues might examine the influence of chronic versus situational distinctiveness in a specific context to identify the unique contributions of each to advertising effectiveness among various segments in a multicultural market.

The Social Meaning of Traits

The research reviewed herein suggests that, in addition to numeric prevalence of a trait, both the meaning of that trait to individuals who use it to self-identify and the broader societal meaning have profound consequences on consumer responses to targeted advertising. For example, Grier and Deshpandé (2001) demonstrated that trait meaning, as reflected by social status perceptions, significantly contributes to a consumer's ethnic salience and response to targeted advertising. Though this research focused predominantly on how distinctiveness enhances favorable ad reactions among targeted consumers, the observations that distinctiveness theory makes about dissimilarity may be fruitfully applied to studies of nontarget markets (Aaker et al., 2000) who may feel excluded from the target of the advertisement and, as a consequence, react unfavorably toward the ad. In such cases, consideration of the meaning of the trait in society may help predict the extent and nature of responses among both target and nontarget market consumers.

For example, Grier and Brumbaugh (1999) drew on research studying "atypicality" (Grier & McGill, 2000), which involves deviation from a norm and encompasses the idea of trait meaning as well as trait prevalence, to argue how consumers' perceptions of social norms, and, importantly, deviations from these norms, affect how people interpret ads targeted toward themselves and others. In their study, White heterosexual viewers, who reflect the norm in American society, were more likely to notice and comment on how ads targeting White homosexual viewers violated their expectations for advertising. White homosexual viewers noted, occasionally with some disdain, how ads targeting White heterosexual viewers reflected and reinforced norms from which they were excluded. Such polarized reactions were not prevalent among either of these groups when viewing ads targeting Black viewers, perhaps reflecting the relative lower status of homosexuals as compared with Blacks in the United States (Grier & Brumbaugh, 1999). Such work highlights the importance of stigma and power to understanding the way group membership influences how consumers create meaning from ads.

Research might also profit from exploring additional social dimensions of distinctiveness. For example, McGuire et al. (1979) argued that one notices a given characteristic to the extent that it is distinctive in the usual environment. The *usual* environment is likely based on the contexts where people spend most of their time—where they live, where they work, and who they associate with. So, although consumers may be part of a numeric minority or majority group, the homogeneity or heterogeneity of their most salient contexts should also influence the meaning associated with their group membership. Thus, for example, exploring the extent and nature of the contact a consumer has with members of other ethnic groups (e.g. the contact hypothesis; Allport, 1954) may also shed insight on how aspects of a person's identity become salient and influence advertising response.

Mechanisms, Mediators, and Moderators

The research reviewed herein also touches on a number of mechanisms by which identity salience and distinctiveness influence ad reactions, including mediators that arise from felt distinctiveness to affect ad responses directly and moderators that change the role that felt distinctiveness plays in persuasion. For example, Aaker et al. (2000) showed that numerically rare consumers targeted on the basis of the trait that makes them distinctive are more likely to infer similarity with a source sharing that trait, enhancing ad attitudes. Such similarity drives one's ability to identify with the similar source (Kelman, 1961), which increases the likelihood that viewers will adopt the favorable disposition the source is implied to have with the product or service being offered, also leading to favorable attitudes toward the ad (Brumbaugh & Grier, 2001). Source similarity effects known to enhance ad reactions are stronger among distinctive ad viewers than nondistinctive ad viewers (Deshpandé & Stayman, 1994). Perceptions of feeling targeted by an ad based on different types of ad cues improve ad attitudes, but less so among distinctive consumers (Aaker et al., 2000). Thus, similarity, identification, source credibility, and targetedness all seem to mediate the impact of distinctiveness induced by an ad or consumption context on advertising reactions. Additional studies that further examine these mediators would help advertisers understand the mechanisms by which target marketing works.

Related research that takes the distinctiveness construct in different directions suggests some of the boundary conditions that limit when felt distinctiveness favorably affects ad reactions. For example, research on tokenism (being one of a kind in a social group) suggests that extreme distinctiveness may be counterproductive to marketers' goals. Results of previous studies show that distinctive individuals react poorly to ads in which their social group was depicted as token (Szybillo & Jacoby, 1974) and that being a token reduces ad effectiveness (Lord & Saenz, 1985). Advertisers who wish to create ads that appeal to many subcultural segments by depicting "one of each" run the risk of making salient a distinctive consumer's identity as "other" to the point where the targeting attempt is seen as exploitative. This notion is consistent with other research that suggests that there is an optimal level of distinctiveness whereby one feels differentiated from others as a unique individual but also part of a larger community in which one shares some common experience (Brewer, 1991). People are motivated to maintain some appropriate balance of individuality and relatedness to others, constantly using cues in their environment to bounce between the two (Brewer, 1991; Snyder & Fromkin, 1977). Advertising may serve as one of these cues, providing information by which individuals negotiate their individual, yet shared, identity.

Applications to A Changing Cultural Landscape

It is important to note that nearly all research on distinctiveness has been done in the United States, where majority White Anglo heterosexuals serve as the nondistinctive group from which others are distinguished (cf. Grier and Deshpande, 2001). Some research shows that people's perceptions of others outside the United States are driven by distinctiveness. For example, a study of Japanese, White Australian, and Hawaiian Japanese found that Japanese described White (but not Japanese) couples in racial terms, White Australians described Japanese (but not White) couples in racial terms, and bicultural Hawaiian Japanese described both in racial terms (Bochner & Ohsako, 1977). However, other research research has argued that distinctiveness may be a uniquely Western phenomenon (Vignoles, Chryssochoou, & Breakwell, 2000), and that the bases for distinctiveness may be very different (Hwang, 1999) in different countries. This raises the issue of whether the effects of distinctiveness are robust cross culturally. Though Grier and Deshpandé (2001) provide some evidence that they are, the question of cross-cultural applicability of distinctiveness theory could use additional empirical support across multicultural contexts worldwide.

Further, as the ethnic, racial, and cultural composition of the U.S. population changes and as boundaries among ethnic, racial, and cultural groups become less distinct through increasing intermarriage, the bases for segmentation that lead to consumer distinctiveness that marketers have previously used to target consumers may no longer be appropriate. Statistics demonstrate that immigration, geographic shifts, birthrates, and other demographic trends are changing the composition of the U.S. population into one quite different from the traditional "White heterosexual mainstream vs. other" notion (Penaloza, 1996). In fact, sociologists conjecture that as White Americans relinquish their majority status, as they currently have in over 48 cities (Visconti, 2001), they may identify with the larger group of European Americans rather than more specific ethnic affiliations such as Irish or Polish American (Alba, 1990). How will demographic changes affect the applicability and validity of consumer behavior theories based on conceptualizations of non-White minorities and white majorities? This is an important area for more research, because there is a pragmatic issue at stake for advertisers in determining expenditures on numeric minority markets. Likewise, there is a need to better understand overlap among multicultural markets. For example, the urban market, which is heavily influenced by rap and hip-hop culture, traditionally thought of as "African American culture," is estimated to be 59.2% White. Understanding how consumer distinctiveness plays out in such "crossover markets" could shed additional insight.

From a more macro perspective, prior research highlights potential negative social consequences of target marketing, including the reinforcement of prejudice and stereotyping, (e.g., Aaker et al., 2000; Grier & Brumbaugh, 1999). For example, Grier and Brumbaugh (1999) noted that the tendency of nontarget market members to use associations of the target segment in assigning meaning to an ad may perpetuate stereotypes and contribute to social fragmentation. Does this vary depending on consumer distinctiveness? Likewise, a body of research has developed describing the influence of idealized advertising imagery on people's self-perceptions (e.g., Gulas & McKeage, 2000; Martin & Gentry, 1997; Richins, 1991). For example, Martin and Gentry (1997) found that young girls compared their physical attractiveness with that of models in advertisements, which sometimes led to a negative effect on self-esteem and self-perceptions. Along the same lines, Gulas and McKeage (2000) found that exposure to idealized images of both physical attractiveness and financial success had a negative effect on the self-evaluations of men. Would such effects be exacerbated or attenuated among distinctive consumers? More generally, understanding the broader social implications of targeted advertising involving distinctive traits in multicultural markets appears necessary.

CONCLUSION

Distinctiveness theory presents a powerful basis for understanding advertising effects in a multicultural market. It is our belief that additional theoretical and practical progress related to multicultural advertising can be made by further exploring advertising cues, consumer contexts, intervening variables, and mechanisms that contribute to the influence of distinctiveness on advertising response. Further, distinctiveness theory highlights the need to consider context in addition to marketer-controlled variables in order to create effective advertising in a multicultural market. Such a focus drives us toward concerns that have traditionally received less attention in investigations of consumer response to advertising, such as the social meanings attached to a particular group, and the dynamics within and between subcultural groups. By broadening the contents of our investigations, we can better anticipate the influence of multicultural marketplaces on how consumers interpret and respond to targeted advertising.

REFERENCES

Aaker, J. L., Brumbaugh, A. M., & Grier, S. (2000). Non-target market effects and viewer distinctiveness: The impact of target marketing on advertising attitudes. *Journal of Consumer Psychology, 9*, 127–140.

Aaker, J. L., & Williams, P. (1998, December). Empathy versus pride: The influence of emotional appeals across cultures. *Journal of Consumer Research, 25*, 241–261.

Abrams, D., Thomas, J., & Hogg, M. A. (1990). Numeric distinctiveness, social identity and gender salience. *British Journal of Social Psychology, 29*, 87–92.

Alba, R. D. (1990). *Ethnic identity: The transformation of White america*. New Haven, CT: Yale University Press.

Allport, G. W. (1954). *The nature of prejudice*. Reading, MA: Addison-Wesley.

Bhat, S., Leigh, T., & Wardlow, D. (1996). The effect of homosexual imagery in advertising on attitude toward the ad. In D. Wardlow (Ed.), *Gays, lesbians, and consumer behavior: Theory, practice, and research issues in marketing* (pp. 161–176). Binghamton, NY: Haworth.

Bochner, S., & Ohsako, T. (1977). Ethnic role salience in racially homogeneous and heterogeneous societies. *Journal of Cross-Cultural Psychology, 8*, 477–492.

Brewer, M. B. (1991). The social self: On being the same and different at the same time. *Personality and Social Psychology Bulletin, 17*, 475–482.

Brumbaugh, A. M. (2002, September). Source and non-source cues in advertising and their effects on the activation of cultural and subcultural knowledge on the route to persuasion. *Journal of Consumer Research, 29*, 258–269.

Brumbaugh, A. M., & Grier, S. A. (2001, October). *Alternative bases for character identification: When culture is not a factor*. Paper presented at the Association for Consumer Research Conference, Austin, TX.

Cota, A. A., & Dion, K. L. (1986, April). Salience of gender and gender composition of ad hoc groups: An experimental test of distinctiveness theory. *Journal of Personality and Social Psychology, 50*, 770–776.

Deshpandé, R., & Stayman, D. (1994, January). A tale of two cities: Distinctiveness theory and advertising effectiveness. *Journal of Marketing Research, 31*, 57–64.

Forehand, M. R., & Deshpandé, R. (2001, August). What we see makes us who we are: Priming ethnic self awareness and advertising response. *Journal of Marketing Research, 28*, 336–348.

Forehand, M. R., Deshpandé, R., & Reed, A., II. (2002). Identity salience and the influence of differential activation of the social self-schema on advertising response. *Journal of Applied Psychology, 87*, 1086–1099.

Friedman, H., & Friedman, L. (1979, October 5). Endorser effectiveness by product type. *Journal of Advertising Research, 19*, 63–71.

Glenberg, A. M., & Swanson, N. G. (1986). A temporal distinctiveness theory of recency and modality effects. *Journal of Experimental Psychology: Learning, Memory, and Cognition, 12*, 3–15.

Greenlee, T., & Oakenfull, G. (2000, February). All the colors of the rainbow: The relationship between gay identity and response to advertising content. Paper presented at the Society for Consumer Psychology, San Antonio, TX.

Grier, S., & Brumbaugh, A. M. (1999, Spring). Noticing cultural differences: Ad meanings created by target and non-target markets. *Journal of Advertising, 18,* 79–93.

Grier, S. A., & Deshpandé, R. (2001). Social dimensions of consumer distinctiveness: The influence of social status on group identity and advertising persuasion. *Journal of Marketing Research, 38,* 216–224.

Grier, S. A., & McGill, A. L. (2000). How we explain depends on who we explain: The impact of social category on the selection of causal comparisons and causal explanations. *Journal Of Experimental Social Psychology, 36,* 545–566.

Gulas,C. S., & McKeage, K. (2000). Extending social comparison: An examination of the unintended consequences of idealized advertising imagery. *Journal of Advertising, 29*(2), 17–28.

Hwang, K.-K. (1999). Filial piety and loyalty: Two types of social identification in confucianism. *Asian Journal of Social Psychology, 2,* 163–183.

Kelman, H. C. (1961). Processes of opinion change. *Public Opinion Quarterly, 25,* 57–78.

Lord, C. G., & Saenz, D. S. (1985). Memory deficits and memory surfeits: Differential cognitive consequences of tokenism for tokens and observers. *Journal of Personality and Social Psychology, 49,* 918–926.

Markus, H., & Nurius, P. (1986). Possible selves. *American Psychologist, 41,* 954–969.

Markus, H., & Wurf, E. (1987). The dynamic self-concept: A social psychological perspective. In A. G. Halberstat & S. L. Ellyson (Eds.)., *Social Psychology Readings* (pp. 79–88). New York: McGraw-Hill.

Martin, M. C., & Gentry, J. W. (1997). Stuck in the model trap; The effects of beautiful models in adds on female preadolescents and adolescents. *Journal of Advertising, 26*(2), 19–33.

Mathur, L. K., Mathur, I., & Rangan, N. (1997, May–June). The wealth effects associated with a celebrity endorser: The Michael Jordan phenomenon. *Journal of Advertising Research, 37,* 67–73.

McCracken, G. (1989, December 3). Who is the celebrity endorser? Cultural foundations of the endorsement process. *Journal Of Consumer Research, 16,* 310–321.

McGuire, W. J. (1984). Search for the self: Going beyond self-esteem and the reactive self. In R. A. Zucker, J. Aronoff, & A. I. Rabin (Eds.), *Personality and the prediction of behavior* (pp. 73–120). New York: Academic Press.

McGuire, W. J., & Padawer-Singer, A. (1976). Trait salience in the spontaneous self-concept. *Journal of Personality and Social Psychology, 33,* 743–754.

McGuire, W. J., & McGuire, C. V. (1980). Salience of handedness in the spontaneous self-concept. *Perceptual and Motor Skills, 50,* 3–7.

McGuire, W. J., McGuire, C. V., Child, P., & Fujioka, T. (1978). Salience of ethnicity in the spontaneous self-concept as a function of one's ethnic distinctiveness in the social environment. *Journal of Personality and Social Psychology, 36,* 511–520.

McGuire, W. J., McGuire, C. V., & Winton, W. (1979). Effects of household gender composition on the salience of one's gender in the spontaneous self-concept. *Journal of Experimental Social Psychology, 15,* 77–90.

Mehra, A., Kilduff, M., & Brass, D. J. (1998, August 4). At the margins: A distinctiveness approach to the social identity and social networks of underrepresented groups. *Academy of Management Journal, 41,* 441–452.

Oakes, P. J. (1987). The salience of social categories. In J. C. Turner, M. A. Hogg, P. J. Oakes, S. D. Reicher, & M. S. Wetherell (Eds.), *Rediscovering the social group: A self-categorization theory* (pp. 117–141). New York: Basil Blackwell.

Penaloza, L. (1996). We're here, we're queer and we're going shopping! A critical perspective on the accommodation of gays and lesbians in the U.S. marketplace. *Journal of Homosexuality, 31*(1–2), 9–41.

Pollak, K. I., & Niemann, Y. F. (1998). Black and White tokens in academia: A difference of chronic versus acute distinctiveness. *Journal of Applied Social Psychology, 28,* 954–972.

Richins, M. L. (1991). Social comparison and the idealized images of advertising. *Journal of Consumer Research, 18*(1), 71–83.

Smith, C. J., Noll, J. A., & Bryant, J. B. (1999, March). The effect of social context on gender self-concept. *Sex Roles, 40*, 499–512.

Smith, E. J. (1991, September/October). Ethnic identity development: Toward the development of a theory within the context of majority/minority status. *Journal of Counseling and Development, 70*, 181–188.

Snyder, C. R., & Fromkin, H. L. (1977, October). Abnormality as a positive characteristic: The development and validation of a scale measuring need for uniqueness. *Journal of Abnormal Psychology, 86*, 518–527.

Szybillo, G. J., & Jacoby, J. (1974). Effects of different levels of integration on advertising preference and intention to purchase. *Journal of Applied Psychology, 59*, 274–280.

Tajfel, H. (1981). *Human groups and social categories.* Cambridge, England: Cambridge University Press.

Vignoles, V. L., Chryssochoou, X., & Breakwell, G. M. (2000). The distinctiveness principle: Identity, meaning, and the bounds of cultural relativity. *Personality and Social Psychology Review, 4*, 337–354.

Visconti, L. (2001). The business case for diversity. Retrieved November 1, 2001, from DiversityInc.com, http://www.diversityinc.com/premium/

Whittler, T. E. (1989). Viewers' processing of actor's race and message claims in advertising stimuli. *Psychology and Marketing, 6*, 287–309.

Whittler, T. E. (1991). The effects of actors' race in commercial advertising: Review and extension. *Journal of Advertising, 20*(1), 54–60.

Whittler, T. E., & DiMeo, J. (1991, December). Viewers' reactions to racial cues in advertising stimuli. *Journal of Advertising Research, 31*(6), 37–46.

Williams, J. D., & Qualls, W. J. (1989). Middle-class Black consumers and intensity of ethnic identification. *Psychology and Marketing, 6*, 263–286.

Williams, J. D., Qualls, W. J., & Grier, S. A. (1995, Fall). Racially exclusive real estate advertising: Public policy implications for fair housing practices. *Journal of Public Policy and Marketing, 14*, 225–244.

Wooten, D. B. (1995). One-of-a-kind in a full house: Some consequences of ethnic and gender distinctiveness. *Journal of Consumer Psychology, 4*, 205–224.

ENDNOTE

1. The term "distinctiveness" has also been used by cognitive scientists to refer to the atypicality of characteristics of any type of memory cues. For example, Glenberg and Swanson (1986) described it as temporal or other novelty of a memory probe. Though related, the term "distinctiveness" in this chapter refers specifically to the construct defined by McGuire and colleagues.

CHAPTER THIRTEEN

Diversity in Advertising: The Influence of Contextual Conditioning Effects on Attitudes

Johan de Heer
Telematica Instituut

Sjaak (J.) G. Bloem
Janssen-Cilag b.v., Unit Business Intelligence

Sofie E. W. M. Paijmans
Valkenbosch Consultancy

Over products, brands, consumer segments and time, advertising messages are characterized by a high degree of variability. Whatever the ads' nature, spatial layout, visual aesthetics, goal, content, target group or medium, the combination of all these aspects provides for a virtually unlimited number of unique and distinct messages. Given ad diversity, this chapter examines whether contextual information influences the attitudes toward the ads. We distinguish between two types of ads: profit ads and nonprofit ads. We also distinguish between two types of contextual information: cognitive laden and affective laden (Yi, 1990a, 1990b). Cognitive laden refers to the "content" of the contextual information (what is it about). Affective laden refers to the affective or emotional feelings from the contextual information (what kind of feeling does it generate). However, we limit our focus to the effect of affective laden contextual information on the attitude toward profit and nonprofit ads. Most studies that have examined the effects of affective contextual information on attitude toward the ad (Aylesworth & MacKenzie, 1998; Kamins, Marks, & Skinner, 1991; Kirmani & Yi, 1991; Lord, Lee, & Sauer, 1994; Stayman, 1994; Yi, 1990a, 1990b) are limited in external validity, because only one advertisement was used as stimulus material. In other words, findings in one study with a particular ad X may be very different from those in a very similar study with a series of ads X, Y, and, Z. Given ad diversity, we examine if the influence of affective laden contextual information will generate its effects on attitude towards multiple ads.

Shimp (1981, 1991) and Shimp, Stuart, and Engle (1991) suggested that the influence of attitude toward the ad on attitudes toward the brand could be explained by a neo-Pavlovian conditioning paradigm. The advertisement functions as the unconditioned stimulus (US) that, by repeated pairings with the brand—the conditioned stimulus (CS)—influences the attitude toward the brand (i.e., CR, or conditioned response). Moreover, these conditioning effects are associated with the peripheral-processing route of the Elaboration Likelihood Model (ELM; Petty & Cacioppo, 1986), in which a consumer's motivation or ability to process the commercial information are medium to low. In particular, under low-involvement processing conditions, affective laden contextual information may show its effect. Note that, in contrast, cognitive contextual information is expected to show its effects on attitudes toward the ad under high-involvement processing conditions—high motivation and ability to process addresses the central processing route of the ELM.

In a forward Neo-Pavlovian conditioning experiment, we paired profit and nonprofit ads (CS) with positive and negative contextual sentences (US). After this learning phase, we serially presented our participants a new set of profit and nonprofit ads and measured viewing time and attitudes toward these ads. We expect that positive contextual information influences a consumer's attitudes positively and negative contextual information influences them negatively, irrespective of ad type.

METHODS

Three pilot studies were conducted. In the first pilot, a subset of 30 ads were selected (15 profit and 15 nonprofit) from 80 Belgium ads (40 profit and 40 nonprofit). Twelve students (4 male and 8 female) from Tilburg University categorized the 80 ads on (a) familiarity of the ad; (b) familiarity of the brand; and (c) profit versus nonprofit ads. Ten profit and 10 nonprofit ads were used for the learning phase of the experiment, and 5 profit and 5 nonprofit ads were used in the measurement phase of the experiment. In the second pilot study, 15 Tilburg University students (6 male and 9 female) rated 160 sentences on the extent of positive or negative affect. In the related third pilot study, 8 Tilburg University students (3 male and 5 female) associated sets of sentences (four sentences per set) with the selected ads from Pilot 1. Pilots 2 and 3 were directed to find the most positive and negative sentence that best belongs to a particular ad. Note that "belonging" is an important criterion for a conditioning experiment.

Learning Phase

In the learning phase of the experiment, each trial consisted of three episodes. In the first episode, participants were exposed to an ad in the center and with a digit in each corner of the computer screen; in the second episode, a contextual sentence was presented in the center and another set of four digits in each corner of the screen; and, finally, in the last episode of each trial, an "equal" button and "unequal" button were presented. To keep participants näive regarding the purpose of our study, we let them perform a simple mathematical task in which they had to sum the four digits (at Episode 1) that had to be compared with the sum of another set of four digits (at Episode 2). If the comparison of the sums of the two sets was equal, then subjects press an "equal" button. The "unequal" button was required to be pressed if the comparison of the sums of the two sets was not equal (at Episode 3). Each episode was exposed for 10 s. So, for each trial, participants at Episode 1 were exposed to four digits; those at Episode 2 were exposed to another set of four digits; and those at Episode 3 were required to press the appropriate button. Our cover story was that previous research had shown that sum comparisons were difficult to make when distracting stimuli were presented, such as pictures and sentences. In addition, we told participants that we were very skeptical about these results, and we briefly argued that adding information should not decrease accuracy at all.

For the learning phase, four conditions were created and 92 Tilburg University students (23 male and 69 female) were randomly assigned to one of the four conditions, resulting in 23 participants per condition. In all the conditions, the respondents were instructed to make 40 sum comparisons (e.g., 40 trials). In half of these trials, no ads or sentences were presented. On 20 trials at Episode 1, an ad was presented; at Episode 2, a sentence was presented. The ads and sentences were presented in the center of the screen so that ad or sentence and digits were clearly visible. Each of 10 profit ads was followed by a positive sentence, and the 10 nonprofit ads were followed by a negative sentence (Condition 1). In Condition 2 the profit ads were followed by a negative sentence, and the nonprofit ads were followed by a positive sentence. In Condition 3 both the profit and nonprofit ads were shown without any sentence. In Condition 4, finally, 5 profit and 5 nonprofit ads were followed by positive sentences and the other 5 profit ads and 5 nonprofit ads were followed by negative sentences. Conditions 3 and 4 served as controls. The ads were presented in random order; however, the order was equal for all conditions.

The aim of the outlined procedure was to condition participants in a biased fashion. In the first condition, we expected that participants would relate a more positive attitude toward the profit ads and a more negative attitude toward the nonprofit ads. In the second condition, the reverse was expected—positive attitudes would be associated with the nonprofit ads and negative attitudes would relate to the profit ads. Thus, we expected differences between attitudes toward profit ads between Conditions 1 and 2 (and the controls, conditions 3 and 4). Similar differences were expected for the nonprofit ads.

Measurement Phase

A second way to test our expectations is related to a transfer conditioning effect with respect to new stimulus material. Therefore, each participant was exposed to 10 "new" ads, that is, 5 profit ads and 5 nonprofit ads, in random order. Participants, in this measurement phase of the experiment, were instructed to look at these ads for as long as they would like to do so. By pressing a button, they selected the next ad. We measured the viewing time of each ad and expected participants in Condition 1 to spend more time viewing the profit ads as compared with the viewing time of profit ads for participants who were assigned to Condition 2. The reverse was expected for the nonprofit ads. In addition, attitudes for each ad were measured. Here we expected to find that participants in Condition 1 had a more positive attitude toward profit ads than did participants in Condition 2. The reverse was expected for the nonprofit ads.

RESULTS

We used five 7-point scales to measure the attitude toward the ad. Cronbach's alpha—a measure for internal consistency—was 0.9 and 0.87 for the profit and nonprofit ads, respectively. It was found that attitudes toward nonprofit ads were more favorable than attitudes towards profit ads. These attitudinal measures were taken before the experiment by means of a general questionnaire in which participants answered 13 questions; 1 question was about attitudes toward profit and nonprofit ads.

The same attitudinal scales were used to rate the ads in the learning and measurement phase. Two one-way analyses of variance (ANOVAs) were performed: one for the profit ads and the other for the nonprofit ads. In contrast to our expectations, none of the expected differences were significant. The F statistic for the profit ads was 1.67 ($p > .05$) and 1.35 ($p > .05$) for the nonprofit ads. The same holds for the attitudes toward the ads in the measurement phase. Again, two one-way ANOVAs were performed. Attitudes toward profit and nonprofit ads did not differ significantly between the conditions ($F = .891$, $p > .05$ for profit; $F = .55$, $p > .05$ for nonprofit). Differences in viewing were expected but, again, not found. The viewing time for profit ads did not differ significantly between the conditions ($F = .407$, $p > .05$) and did not differ between conditions for the nonprofit ads as well ($F = .74$, $p > .05$). Figures 13.1, 13.2, and 13.3 visualize the obtained attitudinal scores for the profit and nonprofit ads in the learning phase (Fig. 13.1) and measurement phase (Fig. 13.2)—Fig. 13.3 shows the viewing time for profit and nonprofit ads in the measurement phase.

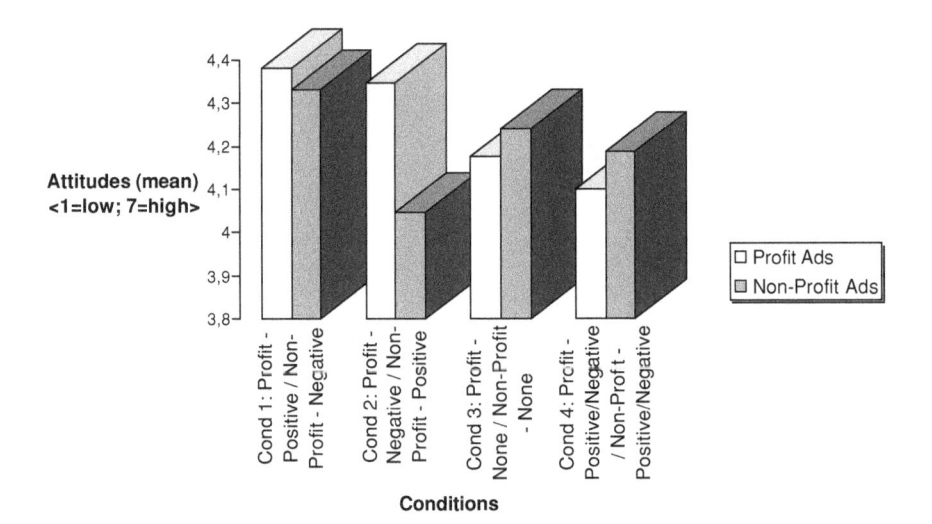

FIG. 13.1.   Learning-phase attitudes toward the ad.

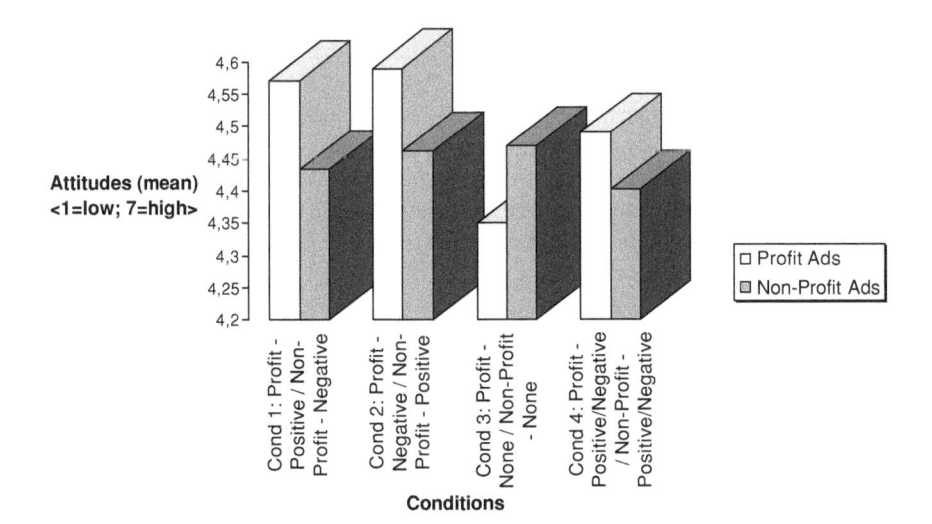

FIG. 13.2.   Measurement-phase attitudes toward the ad.

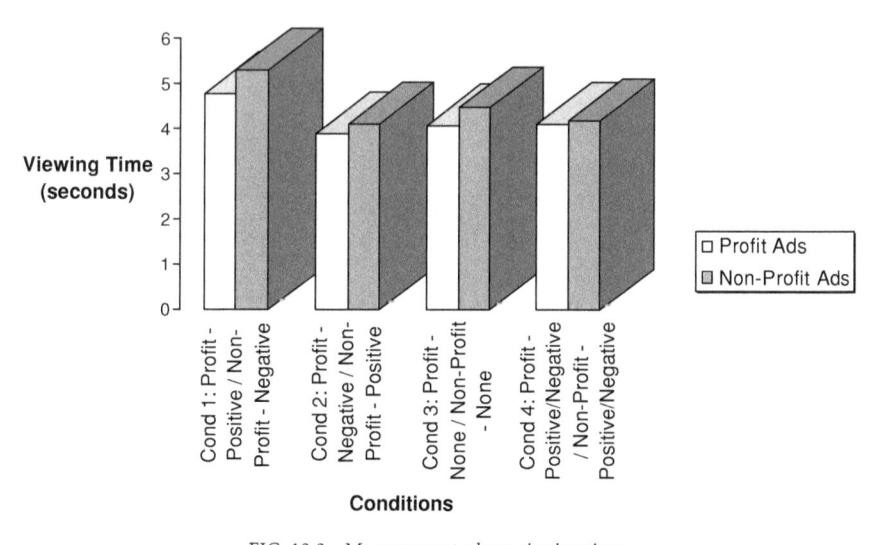

FIG. 13.3. Measurement-phase viewing time.

DISCUSSION AND CONCLUSION

Previous results showed that affective contextual information influences attitude toward the ad (Aylesworth & MacKenzie, 1998; Kamins, Marks, & Skinner, 1991; Kirmani & Yi, 1991; Lord, Lee, & Sauer, 1994; Stayman, 1994; Yi, 1990a, 1990b). As argued, these studies used only one ad as stimulus material, which may cause warrants with respect to external validity. This study examined if affective contextual information is able to show its conditioning effects over stimuli. We distinguished between two types of ads—profit and nonprofit ads. The contextual sentences that were paired with the ads, using a neo-Pavlovian forward conditioning experiment, were either positive or negative affective laden. In one condition, the positive contextual sentences were paired with the profit ad and the negative contextual sentences were paired with the nonprofit ads (for the other condition, this order was reversed). In addition, two control conditions were added. We expected that participants rated their attitudes as more favorable for the profit ads in the first condition in comparison with the second condition, where profit ads were paired with negative sentences (and in comparison with the control conditions). Similar results were expected for the nonprofit ads. In contrast to our expectations, these differences were not significant.

Two lines of argument may be followed to explain these results. One line focuses on the methodological complexities of using the neo-Pavlovian conditioning paradigm. Though all criteria were met to perform such an experiment, there was one important complexity for which we did not control. We assumed that participants could distinguish between the profit and nonprofit ads in the experiment. For example, profit ads were always followed by positive sentences, and nonprofit ads were followed by negative sentences (Condition 1). If participants did not distinguish between the profit and nonprofit ads, then this may have diminished the conditioning effect. To put it differently, we assumed that participants automatically categorized the stimulus material into profit and nonprofit ads. Future studies should check this assumption, because it may bias or diminish results.

The other line of argument is theoretically of interest. If our results are valid, then our advertising communication models may not reflect reality. With the evolution from ad similarity to ad diversity (including Internet advertising and going from singular to integrated advertising), researchers should be cautioned that findings regarding single ad messages are more difficult to generalize today and in the future than in the past. As a consequence, our theoretical models derived from previous experimental findings may be applicable only to a subset of today's ads. Replications of earlier research including multiple diverse ads should be of interest to update our models; this implies that an examination of an ad's effect and effectiveness should incorporate effects of parallel advertising messages. In contrast, ad diversity may influence the sending and receiving of communication efforts; it does not necessarily influence the processing of communication information.

REFERENCES

Aylesworth, A. B. , & MacKenzie, S. B. (1998). Context is key: the effect of program-induced mood on thoughts about the ad. *Journal of Advertising, 27*(2), 17–31.

Brown, S. P., & Stayman, D. M. (1992). Antecedents and consequences of attitude toward the ad: A meta analysis. *Journal of Consumer Research, 19*(1), 34 51.

Burke, M. C., & Edell, J. A. (1989). The impact of feelings on ad-based affect and cognition. *Journal of Marketing Research, 26*(1), 69–83.

Geuens, M., & De Pelsmacker, P. (1998). Feelings evoked by warm, erotic, humorous or nonemotional print advertisements for alcoholic beverages. *Journal of Consumer and Market Research, 1*, http://www.vancouver.wsu.edu/~jcmr/academic/geuens01-98/geuens01-98.html

Homer, P. M. (1990). The mediating role of attitude toward the ad: Some additional evidence. *Journal of Marketing Research,* XXVII, 78–86.

Homer, P. M., & Yoon, S. (1992). Message framing and the interrelationships among ad-based feelings, affect, and cognition. *Journal of Advertising, 21*(1), 19–32.

Kamins, M. A., Marks, L. J., & Skinner, D. (1991). Television commercial evaluation in the context of program induced mood: Congruency versus consistency effects. *Journal of Advertising, 20*(2), 1–15.

Kim, J., Allen, C. T., & Kardes, F. R. (1996). An investigation of the mediational mechanisms underlying attitudinal conditioning. *Journal of Marketing Research, 33*(3), 318–328.

Kirmani, A. , & Yi, Y. (1991). The effects of advertising context on consumer responses. In R. Holman & M. Solomon (Eds.), *Advances in Consumer Research, 18*, 415–416.

Lord, K. R. , Lee, M. , & Sauer, P. L. (1994). Program context antecedents of attitude toward radio commercials. *Journal of the Academy of Marketing Science, 22*(1), 3–15.

MacKenzie, S. B. , Lutz, R. J. , & Belch, G. E. (1986). The role of attitude toward the ad as a mediator of advertising effectiveness: A test of competing explanations. *Journal of Marketing Research,* XXIII, 130–143.

Petty, R. E., & Cacioppo, J. T. (1986). *Communication and persuasion: Central and peripheral routes to attitude change.* New York: Springer 10, 135–146.

Shimp, T. A. (1981). Attitude toward the ad as a mediator of consumer brand choice. *Journal of Advertising, 10*(2), 9–15.

Shimp, T. A. (1991). Neo-Pavlovian conditioning and its implications for consumer theory and research. In H. Kassarjian & T. Robertson (Eds.), *Handbook of consumer behavior* (pp. 162–187). Englewood Cliffs, NJ: Prentice-Hall.

Shimp, T. A., Stuart, E. W., & Engle, R. W. (1991). A program of classical conditioning experiments testing variations in the conditioned stimulus and context. *Journal of Consumer Research, 18*(1), 1–12.

Stayman, D. M. (1994). The influence of affective context on advertising effectiveness. In C. Allen & D. Roedder John (Eds.), *Advances in Consumer Research, 21,* 582.

Yi, Y. (1990a). The effects of contextual priming in print advertisements. *Journal of Consumer Research, 17,* 215–222.

Yi, Y. (1990b). Cognitive and affective priming effects of the context for print advertisements. *Journal of Advertising, 19*(2), 40–48.

V. THE INFLUENCING ROLE OF SOURCE EFFECTS IN DIVERSITY IN ADVERTISING

CHAPTER FOURTEEN

Style or Substance? Viewers' Reactions to Spokesperson's Race in Advertising

Joan Scattone Spira
Consultant

Tommy E. Whittler
DePaul University

In this new millennium, one may find it difficult to imagine marketers showing concern about the race or ethnicity of spokespersons in advertising. However, mainstream mass-targeted magazines and prime-time television still feature predominantly White models (Green, 1991, 1992; Williams, Qualls, & Grier, 1995; Wilkes & Valencia, 1989). Thus, the often-used depiction of America as a "melting pot" may not be accurately portrayed in American advertising. Perhaps some marketers ponder, "If we put minority models in our advertisements, will they turn off our White customers ? If we do not put minority models in our advertisements, will minority consumers go elsewhere to purchase similar products or services ?" These are legitimate concerns given the mounting evidence that various source characteristics may influence an individual's reactions to a persuasive message. For instance, sources that are perceived as more attractive, credible, and similar to the message recipient are more persuasive than their counterparts in delivering the same message (for a review, see Eagly & Chaiken, 1993). A spokesperson's race or ethnicity is often one of his or her most readily apparent physical traits; thus, it may likely influence persuasion. In this chapter we discuss some of the research that has examined individuals' responses to race or ethnicity in persuasive messages. We first discuss what effect a spokesperson's race has on persuasion, and then we consider individual difference, environmental, and contextual variables that may influence who is likely to be influenced by the spokesperson's race and when such influence is likely to occur. Finally, we discuss how these race effects are manifested by considering the psychological processes underlying them.

WHAT EFFECT DOES SPOKESPERSON'S RACE HAVE ON VIEWERS' RESPONSES?

Most of the research examining race effects in advertising has led to the same general conclusion: Viewers respond more favorably to messages presented by a similar-race versus different-race spokesperson (for a review, see Whittler, 1991). For instance, Blacks generate more favorable product and advertisement evaluations when a Black versus White spokesperson is featured in an advertisement (e.g., Schlinger & Plummer, 1972; Szybillo & Jacoby, 1974; Whittler, 1989; Whittler & DiMeo, 1991), whereas Whites respond more favorably to a White versus Black spokesperson (e.g., Whittler, 1989; Whittler & DiMeo, 1991). However, more recent research suggests that responses to spokesperson's race may not be so straightforward. Further study has increased our understanding of the role of race in advertising by shedding some light on who is likely to respond to spokesperson's race, when this response is likely to occur, and how it is manifested.

WHO REACTS TO SPOKESPERSON'S RACE?

An intuitive way to explain the race effect in advertising is that people favor those people who are similar to them over those who are different from them. If this line of thought is extended, then it seems logical that this increased liking could lead to more favorable dispositions toward the product endorsed by a similar (vs. different) spokesperson. These intuitive explanations are aligned with predictions derived from social categorization theory (for a discussion, see Fiske & Taylor, 1991). The basic premise of the theory is that individuals assign individual objects to groups and may apply any affect or beliefs associated with the group to the individual object by virtue of its group membership. The basis for classification may be any important feature that differentiates one group from another. When people assign others to categories, they may use race as a discriminating feature.

An important consequence of social categorization is a phenomenon known as ingroup favoritism (for a discussion, see Fiske & Taylor, 1991). Individuals have a tendency to evaluate people who are members of their own group (the ingroup) more favorably than those who belong to other groups (the outgroup). The advertising studies' results are consistent with this effect: Consumers respond more favorably to a spokesperson who may be classified as a member of their ingroup than one who is classified as a member of an outgroup on the basis of similarities or differences in racial background, respectively.

However, the manifestation of ingroup favoritism relies on the perceiver's classifying others into ingroups and outgroups. With respect to a spokesperson's race, this means that the viewer of the advertisement must use race as a basis for categorizing the spokesperson. A number of variables that influence the salience or importance of race may influence whether and when it is used as a basis for categorization. One individual-difference variable that some marketers have focused on relates to an individual's connection with his or her own ethnic or racial group. The notion is that spokesperson's race may be more meaningful to individuals who feel a strong (vs. weak) affiliation with their own racial group. A few studies have tested this notion.

Ethnic Importance or Identity

In a recent study, we exposed Black consumers to a print ad that featured either a Black or a White spokesperson and contained either strong or weak product claims (Whittler & Spira, 2002). We also assessed Blacks' identification with Black culture by using a measure developed by Whittler, Calantone, and Young (1991). This measure reflects a Black person's sense of belonging to the Black race and his or her concern with issues and causes affecting Blacks. We assigned Blacks to low- and high-identification categories by use of a median split procedure. As in previous research, we found that Blacks responded more favorably to an advertisement given a Black rather than a White spokesperson. Specifically, Blacks' ratings of the spokesperson's likeability, their perceived similarity to her, and their ability to identify with her were greater when she was Black than White. What is important, though, is that these effects were moderated by Blacks' identification with Black culture: High-identification Blacks' product and spokesperson evaluations were more favorable given the Black versus White spokesperson, whereas low-identification Blacks' evaluations did not differ depending on the spokesperson's race. This result indicates that the effect of race is not the same for all ad viewers; the spokesperson's race influenced responses to the advertisement only for those viewers for whom race is particularly important.

Forehand and Deshpande (2001) focused on ethnic self-awareness instead of ethnic identification in their examination of consumer responses to targeted advertising. They defined ethnic self-awareness as "a temporary state during which a person is more sensitive to information related to her or his own ethnicity" (p. 336) that occurs when a person categorizes herself or himself on the basis of her or his own ethnicity. They differentiate ethnic self-awareness from ethnic identification by noting that the former is a relatively temporary state that may be elicited by external factors (i.e., ethnic primes), whereas the latter represents a more enduring association. The distinction is important because elements of advertisements (e.g., cultural symbols) may serve as ethnic primes that influence ethnic self-awareness. Forehand and Deshpande's results indicated that exposure to an ethnic prime increased Asian consumers' ethnic self-awareness and thereby positively influenced their responses to an Asian spokesperson and the advertisement in which she or he was featured.

Racial Prejudice

A related individual-difference variable that may moderate the influence of the spokesperson's race is racial prejudice. In this case, it is the viewer's feelings toward the spokesperson's racial group in general that may influence his or her reactions to both the spokesperson and the advertised product. For instance, we believe that not all Whites will react negatively or less favorably to a Black than White spokesperson. For Whites, who may not feel a similar sense of connection to being "White" as Blacks may to being "Black," the propensity to exhibit such reactions may be linked to feelings of prejudice toward Blacks rather than to feelings of affiliation toward Whites.

We tested this notion by exposing White consumers to an advertisement that featured either a White or a Black spokesperson (Whittler & DiMeo, 1991). We measured Whites' racial prejudice toward Blacks by using 10 items from the Subtle Derogatory Belief Scale of the Multifactor Racial Inventory (Woodmansee & Cook, 1967) embedded in a series of questions assessing participants' opinions regarding various social issues. As we expected, prejudice did moderate Whites' evaluations of the spokesperson. Low-prejudice Whites' perceived similarity to the spokesperson and their ability to identify with her did not differ when she was Black or White, whereas high-prejudice Whites perceived themselves as less similar to the Black than White spokesperson and were less able to identify with her.

WHEN DO VIEWERS REACT TO SPOKESPERSON'S RACE?

Just as individual difference variables (e.g., ethnic identification) may influence the importance that race or ethnicity holds for viewers of advertisements, situational and contextual factors may also affect when the race effect occurs by influencing the felt importance or salience of one's race or ethnicity. Deshpande and his colleagues have examined some of these variables.

The Social Environment

On the basis of McGuire's (1984) distinctiveness theory, Deshpande and Stayman (1994) contended that the racial or ethnic composition of one's social environment may affect the salience of one's race or ethnicity, which may in turn influence one's responses to spokesperson's race. To test this notion, Deshpande and Stayman (1994) exposed Anglo and Hispanic consumers to advertisements that featured either an Anglo or a Hispanic spokesperson. Viewers' ethnic situations were varied by recruiting participants from two cities in Texas, one in which Anglos are in the majority and Hispanics are in the minority (Austin) and the other in which Hispanics are in the majority and Anglos are in the minority (San Antonio). Hispanic participants who lived in Austin (vs. San Antonio) perceived a same-ethnicity spokesperson as more trustworthy and evaluated the product more favorably when an advertisement featured a same-ethnicity spokesperson. The spokesperson's ethnicity influenced Hispanics' responses to the advertisement when the Hispanic viewers were in a social situation in which they were numerically an ethnic minority. Parallel results applied for Anglos.

Grier and Deshpande (2001) extended this research by considering an additional element of the viewers' social environment, that is, their relative social status. They exposed White and Black South African consumers to advertisements that featured either a White or Black spokesperson. Although not necessarily the numeric majority, Whites tend to hold most of the socioeconomic power in South Africa. Participants' ethnic situations were varied by recruiting the participants from Johannesburg (where Blacks are in the majority and Whites are in the minority) and Cape Town (where Whites are in the majority and Blacks are in the minority). The results indicated that both the numeric status and social status of a racial group influenced ethnic salience, and that ethnic salience moderated the influence of spokesperson's ethnicity on brand attitudes.

The Advertising Context

Whereas both Deshpande and Stayman (1994) and Grier and Deshpande (2001) considered factors in consumers' social environments that influence the importance of ethnicity, Forehand and Deshpande (2001) examined contextual or stimulus variables that draw attention to one's ethnicity ("ethnic primes"). They created ethnic primes in their studies by varying both the copy and visual elements of an advertisement that was viewed prior to a focal advertisement. For example, to create an Asian ethnic prime for a nonfocal shampoo advertisement, the copy specified "for Asian hair"; to create an Asian prime for a nonfocal airline advertisement, a photograph of the Great Wall of China was included. The ethnicity of the spokesperson was varied in the subsequently viewed focal ad. The results indicated that exposure to an ethnic prime increased Asian consumers' ethnic self-awareness and led them to respond more favorably to a focal ad that featured a same-ethnicity spokesperson.

HOW DOES SPOKESPERSON'S RACE INFLUENCE VIEWERS' RESPONSES? PSYCHOLOGICAL PROCESSES UNDERLYING RACE EFFECTS

We previously discussed how social categorization theory may account for the influence of a spokesperson's race on consumers' responses to advertising. In this same vein, research in marketing has focused mainly on viewers' evaluations of a spokesperson when it explains why and how spokesperson's race influences product evaluations. Heightened feelings of similarity to, identification with, and trust of a same-ethnicity spokesperson have been associated with more favorable advertisement and product evaluations (e.g., Aaker, Brumbaugh, & Grier, 2000; Forehand & Deshpande, 2001; Grier & Brumbaugh, 1999; Whittler, 1989; Whittler & Spira, 2002).

Although some of our own research has focused on the influence of spokesperson's race on spokesperson and product evaluations, we have also considered other ways that a spokesperson's race might affect product evaluations. Using the Elaboration Likelihood Model (ELM) of persuasion (Petty & Cacioppo, 1986a, 1986b), we examined the role of spokesperson's race in the processing of advertising messages. The ELM posits that there are two routes to persuasion. The *central* route entails careful and thoughtful consideration of the arguments presented in a persuasive message. The *peripheral* route encompasses a variety of other psychological processes in which attitude change may occur without careful consideration of the message's arguments. In particular, a cue in the persuasion setting may activate a simple decision rule that forms the basis for an evaluation. Sometimes these cues relate to characteristics of the message's source. For instance, source attractiveness or likeability has been shown to influence attitudes by functioning as a simple persuasion cue (e.g., Chaiken, 1980, 1987; Petty, Cacioppo, & Schumann, 1983). Greater persuasion occurs with more attractive and more likable sources. We reasoned that, like these other source characteristics, race might also function as a peripheral cue.

Our early research supported this notion of race as a cue in advertising messages; both White and Black consumers responded more favorably to products promoted by a same-race versus a different-race spokesperson, despite identical product information (Whittler, 1989; Whittler & DiMeo, 1991). However, the ELM holds that variables may have multiple roles in persuasion (for a discussion, see Petty & Wegner, 1998), and some research has yielded evidence that race effects do not occur simply through cue processing.

In addition to functioning as peripheral cues, the ELM posits that variables may influence one's motivation to process information. Consistent with this postulate, White and Harkins (1994) concluded that a source's race affects the extent of message elaboration. In a nonadvertising context, they presented White participants with a persuasive message that was attributed to either a White or a Black source. They also varied the strength of the message's arguments (i.e., strong or weak) and manipulated participants' processing motivation (i.e., high or low). Given a White source, participants were more persuaded by strong arguments than weak arguments under the high-involvement condition, but they were equally persuaded by strong and weak arguments under the low-involvement condition. These obtained effects support the predictions of the ELM regarding central and peripheral processing. Central processing, which requires more cognitive effort, tends to occur when message recipients are highly motivated to process the information; peripheral processing is more likely at lower levels of motivation. The strength of the message's arguments influences attitudes only when those arguments have received careful thought, which is likely during central but not peripheral processing.

Interestingly, when White and Harkins' White participants were presented with a message from a Black source, they were more persuaded by strong than weak arguments under both high- and low-motivation conditions. The difference in attitudes depending on argument strength in the low-motivation condition is counter to expectations. Typically, peripheral processing dominates when motivation to process is low with little thought given to the arguments. The researchers contend that the Black source's race motivated Whites to process the message when they would not otherwise have done so in the low-involvement condition (i.e., attitudinal differences appeared between strong and weak arguments). White and Harkins suggested that Whites may have processed the message in the low-involvement condition when presented with the Black (but not the White) source because they did not want to appear prejudicial. They base their explanation on the theory of aversive racism (Gaertner & Dovidio, 1986), which contends that Whites may simultaneously hold negative attitudes toward Blacks while embracing egalitarian beliefs. Their concern about appearing fair to others may lead Whites to act in ways that are seemingly nonprejudicial.

Petty, Fleming, and White (1999) reported findings similar to those of White and Harkins (1994). In a nonadvertising context, they presented White participants with a persuasive message that was attributed to either a White or a Black source and contained either strong or weak arguments. They also measured Whites' racial prejudice toward Blacks. High-prejudice Whites' attitudes were more favorable given the White than the Black source. High-prejudice Whites also appeared to process the message more when the source was White than Black (i.e., the favorability of their attitudes depended more on argument strength given the White than Black source). Interestingly, low-prejudice Whites formed more favorable attitudes given the Black versus White source. Furthermore, low-prejudice Whites appeared to process the message more carefully given the Black than the White source (i.e., the favorability of their attitudes depended more on argument strength given the Black than White source). The authors contend that low-prejudice Whites are sensitive to the fact that stigmatized groups may receive unequal treatment, and so they take on a "watchdog" role. In this case, they gave careful consideration to what the stigmatized (i.e., Black) source had to say.

Although White and Harkins (1994) and Petty et al. (1999) both concluded that source race could motivate processing, their results and corresponding explanations differed in some respects. Petty et al. (1999) found that only low-prejudice Whites engaged in more careful message processing given the Black than the White source, whereas all of White and Harkins' White participants exhibited this effect regardless of their level of racial prejudice. White and Harkins based their explanation of the race effect on the theory of aversive racism (Gaertner & Dovidio, 1986); with the use of this theory, high-prejudice Whites should be expected to process more in the context of a Black source. This prediction is inconsistent with the results obtained by Petty et al. (1999).

Some of our own results may be interpreted as evidence that race may motivate message processing (Whittler & Spira, 2002). However, unlike the studies by Petty et al. (1999) and White and Harkins' (1994), our studies examined Blacks' responses to spokesperson's race and did so in an advertising context. Blacks who viewed an advertisement featuring a Black spokesperson reported equally favorable product evaluations and related thoughts given strong or weak product claims, whereas Blacks who viewed an advertisement featuring a White spokesperson reported more favorable product evaluations and related thoughts when product claims were strong versus weak. One may interpret the fact that argument strength influenced Blacks' attitudes in this latter condition as evidence that Blacks were carefully thinking about the product claims when the spokesperson was White. The lack of any such argument strength effect in the former condition may similarly be interpreted as evidence that Blacks were not carefully considering the product claims when the spokesperson was Black. Because Whites are generally not considered a stigmatized group, the "watchdog" explanation proffered by Petty et al. (1999) is unlikely to explain why Blacks appeared to process the arguments more carefully given the White than Black spokesperson.

We further explored Blacks' cognition by recording their thoughts after they had viewed the advertisement. Thoughts were classified as product, spokesperson, or advertisement related and were also coded as positive, negative, or neutral in valence. The total number of all types of thoughts did not differ depending on the spokesperson's race. However, Blacks did generate more product-related thoughts when the spokesperson was White and more spokesperson- and advertisement-related thoughts when the spokesperson was Black. Thus, the spokesperson's race did have some effect on what Blacks thought about. Interestingly, though, Blacks' message recall was more accurate given the Black versus White spokesperson.

The ELM posits yet another role for variables in the persuasion setting: They may bias processing of the message's arguments (for a discussion, see Petty & Wegner, 1999). A given variable may impart a positive bias on message processing when a perceiver is better able or more motivated to generate positive than negative thoughts about the issue at hand. Subsequent attitudes are more favorable than those formed as a result of objective processing, in which recipients have no ability or motivational predispositions. Likewise, a given variable may negatively bias processing, resulting in attitudes that are less favorable than those formed as a result of objective processing.

Although we did not specifically test this biased-processing notion, some of our results suggest that a spokesperson's race may bias viewers' message processing (Whittler & Spira, 2002). We found that Blacks who identified strongly with Black culture rated an advertisement as stronger and more persuasive when it featured a Black versus a White spokesperson. In contrast, Blacks who had a weak identification with Black culture rated the advertisement as equally strong and persuasive given a Black or White spokesperson. It seems as though the Black spokesperson's race may have positively biased high-identification Blacks' perception of the advertisement. Additional support for biased processing on the part of high-identification Blacks was found in their product evaluations and product-related thinking. When the spokesperson was Black, both their product evaluations and related thoughts were equally favorable given strong or weak product claims. We have argued that high-identification Blacks may have experienced a motivational bias whereby their positive affective reactions to the Black spokesperson may have led them to interpret the product claims favorably, even when these claims were relatively weak, thereby leading to favorable product evaluations. This is consistent with the ELM's contention that a positive bias leads to more favorable rather than unfavorable thoughts and that this bias persists even in the context of weak message arguments (Petty & Cacioppo, 1986b). Although some may interpret these results as evidence of a lack of message processing (see earlier discussion), high-identification Blacks' recall of the product claims suggested that they had indeed thought about the arguments.

Forehand and Deshpande (2001) reported a result that we interpret as suggestive of biased processing. Among their Asian participants, those with high (versus low) levels of ethnic self-awareness produced more positive cognitive responses and fewer negative cognitive responses to an advertisement featuring an Asian spokesperson. This seems to suggest, to us, that the Asian spokesperson's ethnicity may have positively biased the thinking of Asian viewers with high ethnic self-awareness. Clearly, though, additional analyses are necessary to lend more firm support to our interpretation of their results.

CONCLUDING COMMENTS

Although the recent surge of interest in race effects in advertising has shed more light on who, what, when, and how this effect occurs, there are still many unanswered questions. A better understanding of who is influenced by spokesperson's race and when such influence is likely to occur may come from further investigation of individual-difference variables associated with the viewer and contextual factors that characterize the advertisement or situation in which it is viewed. We are personally intrigued by the psychological processes underlying race effects (i.e., how the race effect occurs), which have received little attention in marketing, and we are currently examining the notion that spokesperson's race leads to biased processing of product claims in advertising messages. A preliminary data analysis suggests that this is true, at least in certain situations (Spira & Whittler, working paper).

Limitations in the design of existing research may also open many avenues for additional study. In particular, design aspects of the advertisement itself may influence how viewers respond to race. Much of the current advertising research includes a single spokesperson, but little is known about how viewers respond to advertisements containing multiple individuals of diverse racial or ethnic backgrounds. Further, the apparent relationships between different-race actors in advertisements might also affect viewers' responses. For instance, viewers might have different reactions to a group of Black and White men and women who appear to be friends versus a mixed-race couple who appear to be in a romantic relationship.

In addition, although race may be one of the most obvious physical characteristics of a spokesperson, other personal characteristics might affect how viewers categorize a spokesperson. For instance, White viewers may not react similarly to a Black celebrity versus a Black noncelebrity spokesperson. Whites may not categorize these Black spokespersons similarly because of differences in their celebrity status. Thus, the beliefs and affect accompanying their assigned categories might differ and could lead to differences in responses to the spokesperson, advertisement, and product. The issue of multiple-source cues including race has been virtually ignored in marketing.

These are only a few examples of the many interesting issues that are yet to be examined in this area. Given the continued push to embrace racial and ethnic diversity in American society, the importance of answering these questions is only likely to increase.

REFERENCES

Aaker, J. A., Brumbaugh, A., & Grier, S. A. (2000). Non-target market effects and viewer distinctiveness: The impact of target marketing on attitudes. *Journal of Consumer Psychology, 9,* 127–140.

Chaiken, S. (1980). Heuristic versus systematic information processing and the use of source versus message cues in persuasion. *Journal of Personality and Social Psychology, 39,* 752–766.

Chaiken, S. (1987). The heuristic model of persuasion. In M. P. Zanna, J. M. Olson, & C. P. Herman (Eds.), *Social influence: The Ontario Symposium* (Vol. 5). Hillsdale, NJ: Lawrence Erlbaum Associates.

Deshpande, R., & Stayman, D. M. (1994). A tale of two cities: Distinctiveness theory and advertising effectiveness. *Journal of Marketing Research, 31,* 57–64.

Eagly, A. H., & Chaiken, S. (1993). *The psychology of attitudes.* Fort Worth, TX: Harcourt Brace Jovanovich.

Fiske, S. T., & Taylor, S. E. (1991). *Social cognition* (2nd ed.) New York: McGraw-Hill.

Forehand, M. R., & Deshpande, R. (2001). What we see makes us who we are: Priming ethnic self-awareness and advertising response. *Journal of Marketing Research, 38,* 336–348.

Gaertner, S. L., & Dovidio, J. F. (1986). The aversive form of racism. In J. F. Dovidio & S. L. Gaertner (Eds.), *Prejudice, discrimination, and racism* (pp. 61–89). Orlando, FL: Academic Press.

Green, M. (1991, July). *Invisible people: The depiction of minorities in magazine ads and catalogs.* New York: City of New York Department of Consumer Affairs.

Green, M. (1992, August). *Still invisible: The depiction of minorities in magazine ads one year after the consumer affairs department study.* New York: City of New York Department of Consumer Affairs.

Grier, S. A., & Brumbaugh, A. (1999). Noticing cultural differences: Ad meanings created by target and non-target markets. *Journal of Advertising, 28,* 79–93.

Grier, S. A., & Deshpande, R. (2001). Social dimensions of consumer distinctiveness: The influence of social status on group identity and advertising persuasion. *Journal of Marketing Research, 38*, 216–224.

McGuire, W. (1984). Search for the self: Going beyond self-esteem and the reactive self. In R. A. Zucker, J. Aronoff & A. I. Rabin (Eds.), *Personality and the prediction of behavior* (pp.73–120). New York: Academic Press.

Petty, R. E., & Cacioppo, J. T. (1986a). *Communication and persuasion: Central and peripheral routes to attitude change.* New York: Springer-Verlag.

Petty, R. E., & Cacioppo, J. T. (1986b). Elaboration likelihood model of persuasion. In L. Berkowitz (Ed.), *Advances in experimental social psychology* (Vol. 19, pp. 123–205). New York: Academic Press.

Petty, R. E., Cacioppo, J. T., & Schumann, D. (1983). Central and peripheral routes to advertising effectiveness: The moderating role of involvement. *Journal of Consumer Research, 10*, 135–146.

Petty, R. E., Fleming, M. A., & White, P. H. (1999). Stigmatized sources and persuasion: Prejudice as a determinant of argument scrutiny. *Journal of Personality and Social Psychology, 76*, 19–34.

Petty, R. E., & Wegner, D. T. (1998). Attitude change: Multiple roles for persuasion variables. In D. Gilbert, S. Fiske & G. Lindzey (Eds.), *Handbook of social psychology* (4th ed., Vol. 1, pp. 322–390). New York: McGraw-Hill.

Schlinger, M. J., & Plummer, J. T. (1972). Advertising in black and white. *Journal of Marketing Research, 9*, 149–153.

Spira, J. S., & Whittler, T. E. (2003). *Biased processing and cue effects due to source race in advertising* (working paper).

Szybillo, G. J., & Jacoby, J. (1974). Effects of different levels of integration on advertising preference and intention to purchase. *Journal of Applied Psychology, 59*, 274–280.

White, P. H., & Harkins, S. G. (1994). Race of source effects in the elaboration likelihood model. *Journal of Personality and Social Psychology, 67*, 790–807.

Whittler, T. E. (1989). Viewers' processing of source and message cues in advertising stimuli. *Psychology & Marketing, 6*, 287–309.

Whittler, T. E. (1991). The effects of actors' race in commercial advertising: Review and extension. *Journal of Advertising, 20*, 54–60.

Whittler, T. E., Calantone, R. J., & Young, M. J. (1991). Strength of ethnic affiliation: Examining Black identification with Black culture. *Journal of Social Psychology, 131*, 461–467.

Whittler, T. E., & DiMeo, J. (1991). Viewers' reactions to racial cues in advertising stimuli. *Journal of Advertising Research, 31*, 37–46.

Whittler, T. E., & Spira, J. S. (2002). Model's race: A peripheral cue in advertising messages? *Journal of Consumer Psychology, 12*, 291–301.

Williams, J. D., Qualls, W. J., & Grier, S. A. (1995). Racially exclusive real estate advertising: Public policy implications for fair housing practices. *Journal of Public Policy & Marketing, 14*, 225–244.

Wilkes, R. E., & Valencia, H. (1989). Hispanics and Blacks in television commercial. *Journal of Advertising, 18*, 19–25.

Woodmansee, J. J., & Cook, S. W. (1967). Dimensions of verbal racial attitudes: Their identification and measurement. *Journal of Personality and Social Psychology, 7*, 240–250.

CHAPTER FIFTEEN

Moving Beyond Race: The Role of Ethnic Identity in Evaluating Celebrity Endorsers

Devon DelVecchio
University of Kentucky

Ronald C. Goodstein
Georgetown University

In the late 1960s and throughout the 1970s, the effects associated with the use of ethnic minorities in advertisements were a popular research topic. Between 1965 and 1979, a total of 19 articles on the topic appeared in the *Journal of Marketing,* the *Journal of Marketing Research*, the *Journal of Consumer Research*, the *Journal of Advertising,* and the *Journal of Advertising Research.* That research on ethnic minorities, particularly African Americans, in advertising would be widely published during this time period is certainly not surprising. Among the changes arising from the civil rights movement was a growth in ads targeting Black consumers and an increase in the use of Black models in advertisements. For instance, Kassarjian (1969) reported that the number of ethnic minorities appearing in magazine advertisements doubled between 1965 and 1969. Naturally, researchers reacted to this change in marketing practice by testing the effect that the use of racial minorities had on the advertising audience (12 of the 19 articles specifically tested the effect of the use of Black actors in advertisements).

After the initial flurry of publications on the topic, research on the use of minorities in advertising stagnated. From 1980 through 1998, only five additional articles relating to the appearance of minorities in advertising were published in the previously mentioned journals. This lack of continued research is troublesome for several reasons. First, research in this area continues to be important because of its widespread use as a marketing strategy. During the 1980s, the minority population in the United States grew 9.8%, to reach 24.6% of the total population. This figure is expected to grow to 30.2% by the year 2005. Minorities have also grown in terms of their buying power. In 1990, 45% of White and 42% of Black households earned between $25,000 and $75,000. These figures compare to 28% and 14%, respectively, in 1980. As ethnic minorities have grown in population and buying power, advertising targeting ethnic minorities has risen. For instance, in 1998, advertisers spent $865 million on ads targeting Blacks (Chapelle, 1998). Correspondingly, the use of ethnic minorities in advertising has become more prevalent. In a 1994 study, 45% of ads aired on network television included an African American character (Bristor, Lee, & Hunt, 1995). In contrast, using data from 1986, Wilkes and Valencia (1989) reported finding Black characters in 26% of television advertisements. Given the expectation that the population and buying power of minorities will continue to grow, it is likely that the use of minorities in advertising will also increase.

A second reason for the need for continued research on the use of ethnic minorities in advertising is that reactions to the use of ethnic minorities are likely to be vastly different than they were at the time of the initial research on the topic. Most fundamentally, the growth in the use of ethnic minorities in advertisements should alter the manner in which such ads are perceived. Initial research on this topic was undertaken at a time when the use of minorities in ads was rare. Fundamental differences in the processing of novel versus common social stimuli (see, e.g., Fiske & Taylor, 1991, for a review) may cause past findings to no longer be applicable.

Viewers' reactions to ads that use minorities are likely to have changed not only as the use of minorities has increased but also in response to the change in the manner in which minorities are portrayed in ads. As discussed by Peñaloza (1997), the role of ethnic minorities in advertisements has been shifting from being secondary and often subservient in nature to being more central and more reflective of the wide variety of roles held by minorities in American society.

In addition to changes in advertising practices, viewers' reactions to minority actors in ads will have changed in response to the advancements ethnic minorities have made in terms of the roles they play in American society. As minorities have become more numerous in business management, the arts and entertainment, athletics, and the suburbs, their interactions with, and the way they are perceived by, Anglo Americans have also changed. Thirty years ago, Anglo Americans were less likely to view minorities in a starring role on television (see, e.g., Dates, 1993). Thirty years ago, Anglo Americans were also less likely to work for or patronize a minority-owned business (O'Hare, 1992) or have a neighbor who was a minority (Usdansky, 1992). These social advances have changed the manner in which minorities are viewed by both themselves and the Anglo majority. For instance, opinion polls and surveys show a consistent decline in prejudice toward racial minorities over the past 40 years (Hill, 1993; Wilson, 1999). In turn, changes in the way minorities are viewed in society should alter the way they are interpreted in advertisements, including more acceptance of the presence of minority actors in advertisements (Whittler, 1989).

To this point, the discussion has focused on changes in the societal and advertising environments. A second set of concerns that point to the need for continued research on the effect of minority actors in advertisements stems from the methodological and theoretical shortcomings of earlier research on the subject. Many of the early works in this area conclude that the inclusion of minorities in an ad has little negative effect on Whites exposed to the ad. However, as pointed out by Whittler (1991), many of these studies suffer from demand characteristics, confounds resulting from the use of actual ads, and carryover effects.

In addition to their methodological constraints, the early work in this field suffers, in retrospect, from inadequate theoretical development. The initial research on the use of ethnic minorities focused primarily on the simple main effects arising from the 2 (minority–Anglo) × 2 (minority–Anglo) crossing of viewer and actor's race. The theoretical shortcomings of past research arise primarily as a result of subsequent research on ethnicity. In the past 20 years, research in the areas of social psychology, sociology, and counseling have revolutionized the study of ingroup–outgroup interactivity. Advancements of theories on the manner in which group members are assessed, such as ingroup bias theory (Brewer, 1979) and polarized appraisal theory (Linville & Jones, 1980), have offered new frameworks within which to consider the effect of the presence of minorities in advertisements. Improvements in the techniques used to measure reactions to outgroup members have increased the validity of research investigating phenomena that may suffer from social desirability confounds (e.g., Fazio, Jackson, Dunton, & Williams, 1995). The development of ethnic identity as a construct that is distinct from race has shifted focus from visually observable differences between individuals (race) to ideological differences between people based on shared acculturation (see, e.g., Acre, 1981; Alba & Chamlin, 1983; Gurin & Epps, 1975). Finally, the development of measures of ethnic identity has allowed for application of the construct and the study of its influence on a variety of beliefs and behaviors (e.g., Garcia, 1982; Parham & Helms, 1981; Phinney, 1992).

Our study applies the advancements made in ethnic-identity research to build on existing research on the use of minorities in advertisements. The positive effects of matching endorser and consumer race in advertisements are well documented. Appealing to racial minorities by using same-race spokespeople has been shown to increase liking of and memory for the ad and brand and to elevate purchase intentions (see e.g., Kerin, 1979; Schlinger & Plummer, 1972; Szybillo & Jacoby, 1974; Williams, Qualls, & Grier, 1995). This stream of research highlights the importance of racial diversity in advertising, thereby advancing both marketing theory and, perhaps what is more important, marketing practice.

By ignoring ethnic identity, past advertising research has treated individuals within a given race as being homogenous with respect to the importance they will place on, and manner in which they interpret, ethnic-specific images (Hirschman, 1981). Research on ethnic studies has made important advances in terms of recognizing the limitations of racial classifications that treat members of the same ethnic group as homogeneous. For instance, ethnic identity has been shown to influence behaviors ranging from dating preferences (Mok, 1999) to coupon usage (Donthu & Cherian, 1992). In essence, this research illustrates that ethnic identity is a valuable construct by which to assess intrarace heterogeneity. More specifically, the findings regarding ethnic identity indicate that race is not necessary indicative of a person's behavior or beliefs; rather it is the emphasis that the person places (e.g., Goodstein & Ponterotto, 1997) on her or his racial or ethnic background that is indicative of behavior and beliefs. Given these advancements, it is important that research on advertising using or targeting ethnic minorities incorporates measures of the importance of ethnicity in the formation of one's self-concept. Although prior studies consider the effect of ethnic identity in advertising (e.g., Greene, 1999; Whittler, 1991), additional research is warranted as these studies present conflicting results, do not consider the influence of endorser–actor ethnic identity, and are silent on constructs that are related to ethnic identity such as one's willingness to interact with people from other ethnic groups.

Ethnic identity refers to the value and emotional significance an individual attaches to her or his ethnic group membership (see, e.g., Phinney, 1992; Tajfel, 1981). In contrast to racial identification, which is based on the visible differences between people, ethnic identity is based on one's self-identification and depth of relationship with a cultural group. People who are high in ethnic identity place greater importance on the role of ethnicity in defining their own self-concept and in interpreting social stimuli. In assessing the importance one places on one's ethnicity, ethnic identity captures (a) involvement in ethnic behaviors and practices, (b) affirmation of a sense of belonging to one's ethnic group, and (c) commitment to and sense of comfort with one's ethnic group (Phinney, 1992).

A concept related to ethnic identity is other-group orientation; this is the extent to which an individual places importance on interacting with people from ethnic groups other than his or her own. Although distinct from ethnic identity, other-group orientation is believed to interact with ethnic identity in determining one's social identity (Phinney, 1992). Our research investigates the role of ethnic identity and other-group orientation on the effectiveness of African American and White celebrity endorsers. More specifically, we consider the manner in which a consumer's ethnic identity and other-group orientation interact with his or her perceptions of endorsers' ethnic identity and other-group orientation in affecting liking for the endorser.

We begin by studying liking for the endorser as a dependent variable for two reasons. First, one of the primary means through which advertisements motivate purchase behavior is through the mediating role of attitude toward the ad, that is, A_{ad} (e.g., MacKenzie, Lutz, & Belch, 1986; Mitchell & Olson, 1981; Shimp, 1981). A primary component of A_{ad} is the affective response evoked by an ad (e.g., Hill & Mazis, 1986; Shimp, 1981). Endorser liking plays an important role in the determination of affective responses to an ad and A_{ad} (Petty, Cacioppo, &

Schumann, 1983). Second, our focus on liking stems from the exploratory nature of our research. Ultimately an endorser is employed to generate positive outcomes for a brand by increasing the effectiveness of advertising. Studying the effects of ethnicity on liking for an endorser before placing the endorser in an advertising context allows for better isolation and closer inspection of the process by which ethnicity is expected to influence ad processing, ad liking, and ad-based brand-related outcomes. As discussed in the paragraphs that follow, results of this analysis can then be used to guide the design of future research investigating the link between subject and endorser ethnicity and advertising outcomes.

HYPOTHESES

Research in social psychology indicates that an important variable in the determination of liking for another person is the extent to which the other person is perceived to be similar to one's self (e.g., Stroebe, Insko, Thompson, & Layton, 1971). The positive effect of similarity on liking is quite pervasive. Similarity based on objective traits such as age (Evans, 1963) and clothing (Emswiller, Deaux, & Willits, 1971; Suedfeld, Bochner, & Matas, 1971), as well as ideological traits including political beliefs and religious affiliation (Evans, 1963), has been demonstrated to affect behaviors as trivial as loaning a stranger a dime (Emswiller et al., 1971) and as essential as buying insurance (Evans, 1963). More proximate to the current issue, similarity between the race of an advertising viewer and the race of the actors in the ad has a positive effect on ad and brand evaluations (Kerin, 1979; Schlinger & Plummer, 1972; Szybillo & Jacoby, 1974; Williams et al., 1995). In addition to similarity, another factor in determining liking for a person is the extent to which we feel the other person likes us. In general, there is a predisposition to be attracted to people that are believed to have a positive affinity toward oneself (Berscheid & Walster, 1978).

The first similarity-based hypothesis involves the ethnic group membership of the subject and the endorser. Note that we are studying ethnicity and not race. Although the difference is subtle, by considering ethnicity, researchers allow participants to specify the ethnic group with which they most identify. By focusing on race, the majority of past research implicitly advances the belief that objective classifications (e.g., skin color) are more descriptive of belief structures than self-defined affiliation with a cultural group (ethnicity). As the number of multiethnicity individuals grows and the segregation among individuals of different cultural backgrounds declines, the difference between race and ethnicity and the importance in recognizing this difference increases. In turning to the effect of ethnic group similarity on liking, we expect that the pervasive positive effects of similarity will extend to ethnic group membership. That is, individuals should display greater liking for endorsers who belong to the same ethnic group than they do for endorsers from a different ethnic group.

H1: *Individuals will demonstrate greater liking for endorsers whose ethnic group membership matches their own, relative to their liking for endorsers belonging to other ethnic groups.*

Although ethnic group membership specifies the cultural group with which one most identifies, it does not indicate the importance an individual places on her or his identification with the group. The importance one places on her or his ethnicity plays an important role in the interpretation of social images (Tajfel, 1981). Therefore, we next consider the effect of ethnic identity: the value and emotional significance one places on her or his ethnic group membership (Phinney, 1992). Individuals are capable of making fairly critical judgments on the basis of nominal similarity with a persuasive source (e.g., Brewer, 1979; Sherif, Harvey, White, Hood, & Sherif, 1961). Thus, we expect that ethnic identity will serve as a similarity cue in guiding judgments. Specifically, we expect that matching ethnic identity between the individual and the perceived ethnic identity of the endorser will result in greater liking for the endorser.

H2: *Individuals will demonstrate greater liking for endorsers whose ethnic group membership and level of ethnic identity matches their own, relative to those whose ethnic group membership matches their own but whose level of ethnic identity does not.*

Other-group orientation is defined as the extent to which an individual feels it is important to, and subsequently engages in, activities with members of ethnic groups other than her or his own (e.g., Phinney, 1992). A logical conclusion based on this definition of other-group orientation is that there should be a positive relationship between the other-group orientation of an individual and her or his liking of endorsers from a different ethnic group.

H3: *Individuals with high other-group orientation, relative to those with low other-group orientation, will demonstrate greater liking for endorsers whose ethnic group membership is different from their own.*

The next hypothesis deals with the effects of another's perceived liking of one-self. Perceptions of endorser other-group orientation provide a basis upon which individuals may assess the extent to which an endorser might like them or people ethnically similar to them. Endorsers who are high in perceived other-group orientation have a basis on which individuals may demonstrate reciprocated liking.

H4: *Individuals will demonstrate greater liking for endorsers whose ethnic group membership is different from their own, but whose perceived other group orientation is high, relative to low.*

Finally, similarity effects should extend to other-group orientation as well. Therefore, same-ethnicity endorsers should be more liked when matching the individual in terms of other-group orientation as well.

H5: *Individuals will demonstrate greater liking for endorsers whose ethnic group membership, level of ethnic identity, and other-group orientation matches their own, relative to those endorsers whose ethnic group membership and level of ethnic identity match but whose other-group orientation does not.*

METHODOLOGY

Ethnic identity and other-group orientation are measured by means of the Multigroup Ethnic Identity Measure (MEIM) developed by Phinney (1992). The MEIM scale captures multiple aspects of ethnic identity, including involvement in ethnic activities and practices, affirmation of and a sense of belonging to one's ethnic group, and commitment to one's ethnic group. The MEIM also considers other-group orientation as a construct that is distinct from, yet related to, ethnic identity. The MEIM was selected over competing measures of ethnic identity for several reasons. First, the MEIM is ethnicity neutral, whereas several other measures of ethnic identity are designed to capture affiliation with a specific ethnic group. For instance, Parham and Helms (1981) and Herd and Grube (1996) developed measures specific for Black ethnic identity, Garcia's (1982) scales measured Mexican American identity, and Zak's (1973) scales assessed Jewish ethnic identity. The use of ethnic-specific scales to study differences between divergent ethnic groups introduces measurement confounds. In contrast, the MEIM allows a single measurement tool to be used across ethnic groups. Additionally, the racial neutrality of the MEIM avoids the social desirability bias present in some competing ethnicity measures (e.g., "I often find myself referring to White people as honkies, devils, pigs, etc." in Parham & Helm's Black Racial Identity Attitude Scale from 1981). To adapt the MEIM to our study, we first had to translate the scale from a self-based to an other-based measure of ethnic identity and verify its reliability in this use. These results are reported in the paragraphs that follow.

Our study employed 51 African American and 53 White undergraduate students at a large Midwestern university. In addition to providing measures of her or his own ethnic identity and other-group orientation, each student assessed the ethnic identity and other-group orientation for 6 African American celebrities (of the 12 African American celebrities used in the study) and 3 White celebrities (of the 9 White celebrities used in our study). They also responded to a single item measuring familiarity with the endorser and indicated their liking (using a four item, 7-point scale) for each celebrity.

As a way to minimize potential confounds caused by gender, all endorsers used in the study were male entertainers. Furthermore, the endorsers selected were expected to generally appeal to the undergraduate sample and vary in perceived ethnic identity and other-group orientation. The African American (Black) endorsers included Babyface, Coolio, Cuba Gooding Jr., Ice Cube, Samuel L. Jackson,

Eriq LaSalle, Spike Lee, LL Cool J, Darius Rucker, Will Smith, Wesley Snipes, and Snoop Doggie Dogg. The Caucasian (White) endorsers included Garth Brooks, Jim Carrey, George Clooney, Leonardo DiCaprio, Kenny G., Tommy Lee Jones, Bruce Springsteen, Keanu Reaves, and Bruce Willis. A picture of the endorser accompanied questions pertaining to each endorser in order to facilitate recognition. Responses associated with endorsers for whom an individuals displayed a low level of familiarity (1 or 2 on a 7-point scale) were omitted from further analysis.

Preliminary Analysis

A principle component, confirmatory factor analysis was undertaken to assess the validity of the Phinney scale for our use. This analysis revealed significant cross-loadings for 6 of Phinney's 14 items measuring ethnic identity and 1 of 6 items measuring other-group orientation. These items were subsequently eliminated from our scales. A factor analysis using the remaining items supported the use of the scale for the assessment of one's own ethnic identity and other-group orientation, as well as for the perceived ethnic identity and other-group orientation of others. (Table 15.1 presents the scale items used to measure ethnic identity, other-group orientation, and endorser liking.) Furthermore, this structure was upheld across all relevant subsets of data created by crossing participant ethnicity and endorser ethnicity. This indicates that the scale is ethnicity neutral in terms of participant ethnicity, endorser ethnicity, and participant ethnicity × endorser ethnicity interactions (i.e., it is valid for Black and White participants, as well as for each group's evaluation of own and other ethnic group endorsers' evaluations). Coefficient alphas were .89 for own ethnic identification, .82 for own other-group orientation, .83 for perceived endorser ethnic identification, .80 for perceived other-group orientation, and .90 for liking of the endorser. In addition to the factor analysis results, independence of the constructs is also suggested by the low interconstruct correlations displayed in Table 15.2.

Recall that the hypotheses predicted differences between individuals and endorsers on the basis of their ethnic group membership and their classification as either low or high in terms of their perceived levels of ethnic identity and other-group orientation. (Table 15.3 presents the means and standard deviations for the constructs across participant and endorser ethnicities as well as for each endorser.) For distinctions to be made property between the ethnic identity and other-group orientation of Black and White individuals and endorsers, it is necessary to consider whether ethnic groups differ as a whole in their ethnic identity and other-group orientation and whether celebrities of different races will be perceived differently in terms of their ethnic identity and other-group orientation. To the extent that individuals or endorsers differ on the traits of interest as a function of their ethnicity, categorization of ethnic identity and other-group orientation will have to be ethnicity specific.

TABLE 15.1
Scale Items

Perceived Endorser Ethnic Identity
1. *Endorser name* is likely to have a clear sense of his ethnic background and what it means to him.
2. *Endorser name* is likely to be happy he is a member of the ethnic group he belongs to.
3. *Endorser name* is likely to understand what his ethnic group means to him in terms of how he relates to his own group and to other ethnic groups.
4. *Endorser name* is likely to have spent time trying to find out more about his ethnic group, such as its history, customs, and traditions.
5. In order to find out more about his ethnic group, *endorser name* is likely to often talk to other people about his ethnic group.
6. *Endorser name* is likely to have a lot of pride in his ethnic group and its accomplishments.
7. *Endorser name* is likely to feel a strong attachment towards his ethnic group.
8. *Endorser name* is likely to feel good about his ethnic group.

Perceived Other-Group Orientation
1. *Endorser name* is likely to enjoy meeting people from ethnic groups other than his own.
2. *Endorser name* is likely to feel it would be better if different ethnic groups didn't try to mix together (reverse coded).
3. *Endorser name* is likely to have spent time with people from ethnic group other than his own.
4. *Endorser name* is likely to enjoy being around people from ethnic groups other than his own.
5. *Endorser name* is likely to be involved with people from other ethnic groups.

Endorser Liking
1. I like *endorser name*.
2. I dislike *endorser name* (reverse coded).
3. *Endorser name* is one of my more favorite performers.

Note. Because of the similarity of the items measuring one's own ethnic identity and other-group orientation and those measuring the perceived level of these traits in the endorsers only the modified items (those changed to measure participants' perceptions of endorsers) are included. As an example of how the items have been changed, the original (self-based) version of the first item listed in the endorser ethnic-identity scale herein is "I have a clear sense of my ethnic background and what it means me." See Phinney (1992) for all of the self-based items that correspond to the other-based items presented herein.

TABLE 15.2
Correlations Among the Independent Variables

	Ethnic Identity		Other-Group Orientation	
	Self	*Endorser*	*Self*	*Endorser*
Ethnic identity				
Self	1.00	0.307	0.256	0.194
Endorser		1.00	0.172	0.147
Other-group orientation				
Self			1.00	0.275
Endorser				1.00

Note. All correlations are significant at $p < .01$.

TABLE 15.3
Means and Standard Deviations

	Ethnic Identity			Other-Group Orientation			Liking for the Endorser	
	Self	BE	WE	Self	BE	WE	BE	WE
Subject ethnicity								
Black	6.31 (0.85)	6.09 (0.97)	5.29 (1.09)	5.96 (1.01)	5.38 (1.11)	4.94 (1.06)	5.55 (1.48)	5.07 (1.49)
White	4.86 (0.95)	5.66 (0.77)	4.59 (1.05)	5.28 (0.98)	4.69 (1.21)	4.97 (1.04)	4.63 (1.54)	5.16 (1.53)
All subjects	5.59 (1.15)	5.85 (0.90)	4.90 (1.12)	5.61 (1.05)	5.01 (1.21)	4.96 (1.05)	5.505 (1.58)	5.11 (1.51)

Note. Numbers in parentheses are standard deviations. BE = Black endorsers; WE = White endorsers.

TABLE 15.4
Group Split Points for Ethnic Identity and Other-Group Orientation

	Ethnic Identity		Other-Group Orientation	
	Low	High	Low	High
Subject ethnicity				
Black	<6.14	>6.75	<5.61	>6.60
White	<4.64	>5.13	<4.61	>5.60
Endorser ethnicity				
Black	<5.51	>6.13	<4.41	>5.40
White	<4.26	>5.38	<4.41	>5.40

The results of our preliminary mean comparisons indicated significant differences by ethnic group for both individuals' ethnic identity (Black individuals = 6.31, White individuals = 4.86; $F_{1,94} = 61.77$, $p < .001$) and other-group orientation (Black individuals = 5.96, White individuals = 5.28; $F_{1,99} = 11.73$, $p < .001$). For the endorsers, perceived ethnic identity differs as a function of the ethnicity of the endorser (Black endorsers = 5.85, White endorsers = 4.90; $F_{1,830} = 174.07$, $p < .001$). Perceived other-group orientation does not differ on the basis of the ethnicity of the endorser (Black endorsers = 5.01, White endorsers = 4.96; $F_{1,847} < 0.36$, *ns*). Because of these differences, group splits (low–high) for own ethnic identity, own other-group orientation, and perceived endorser ethnic identity differ across ethnic groups, as displayed in Table 15.4.

Hypotheses Tests

For Hypothesis 1 to be tested, a 2 (subject group membership) × 2 (perceived endorser group membership) analysis of variance was used. The results support the positive effect of matching an individual's ethnic group membership with that of an endorser (see Fig. 15.1). White participants demonstrated a significantly greater liking for White endorsers than they did for Black endorsers (Black endorsers = 4.63, White endorsers = 5.16; $F_{1,464} = 12.13$, $p < .01$). Analogously, African American subjects liked African American endorsers significantly more than they did White endorsers (Black endorsers = 5.55, White endorsers = 5.07; $F_{1,390} = 9.03$, $p < .01$). Thus, Hypothesis 1 was supported for both Black and White participants.

Although Hypothesis 1 demonstrates the importance of matching ethnic group membership in advertising (similar to the earlier findings regarding racial matching), our goal is to highlight the effects of ethnicity that extend beyond group membership. Therefore, Hypothesis 2 investigates the importance of matching individuals and endorsers in terms of their level of ethnic identity. Hypothesis 2 is supported for high-ethnic-identity individuals, as Black individuals who are high

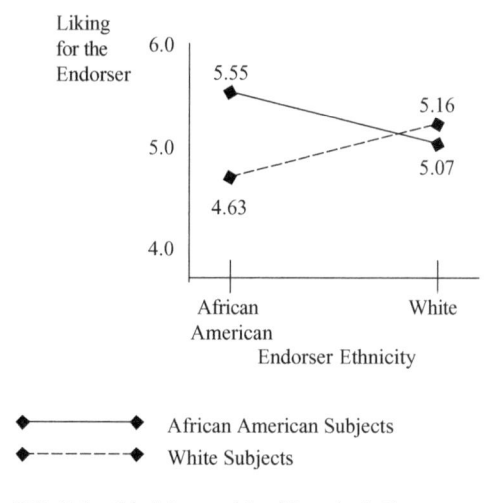

FIG. 15.1.   Ethnicity matching (Hypothesis 1).

in ethnic identity demonstrated significantly greater liking for Black endorsers who are also perceived to be high (HEI) rather than low (LEI) in ethnic identity (LEI Black endorsers = 4.63, HEI Black endorsers = 6.28; $F_{1,64}$ = 20.33, $p < .001$). Similarly, White individuals who are high in ethnic identity demonstrated significantly greater liking for White endorsers who are also perceived to be high rather than low in ethnic identity (LEI White endorsers = 3.13, HEI White endorsers = 5.24; $F_{1,27}$ = 10.59, $p < .01$).

Although the pattern of liking demonstrated by low-ethnic-identity White individuals is directionally consistent with Hypothesis 2, it is not statistically significant (LEI White endorsers = 5.77, HEI White endorsers = 5.13; $F_{1,37}$ = 1.02, $p < .20$). In contrast to expectations, Black individuals with low levels of ethnic identity significantly preferred Black endorsers who are perceived to be high in ethnic identity to Black endorsers who are perceived as low in ethnic identity (LEI Black endorsers = 4.38, HEI Black endorsers = 6.13; $F_{1,59}$ = 21.99, $p < .001$). The results pertaining to Hypothesis 2 are summarized in Fig. 15.2.

Hypothesis 3 examined whether individuals' other-group orientation will be positively related to liking for endorsers from an ethnic group that was different from their own. Consistent with the hypothesis, Black individuals with high other-group orientation (HOGO) liked White endorsers marginally better than did those with low (LOGO) other-group orientation (LOGO Black individuals = 4.83, HOGO Black individuals = 5.31; $F_{1,85}$ = 2.06, $p < .10$). Similarly, White individuals with high other-group orientation liked Black endorsers significantly better than did Whites with low other-group orientation (LOGO White individuals = 4.29, HOGO White individuals = 4.80; $F_{1,212}$ = 5.54, $p < .01$). These results are summarized in Fig. 15.3.

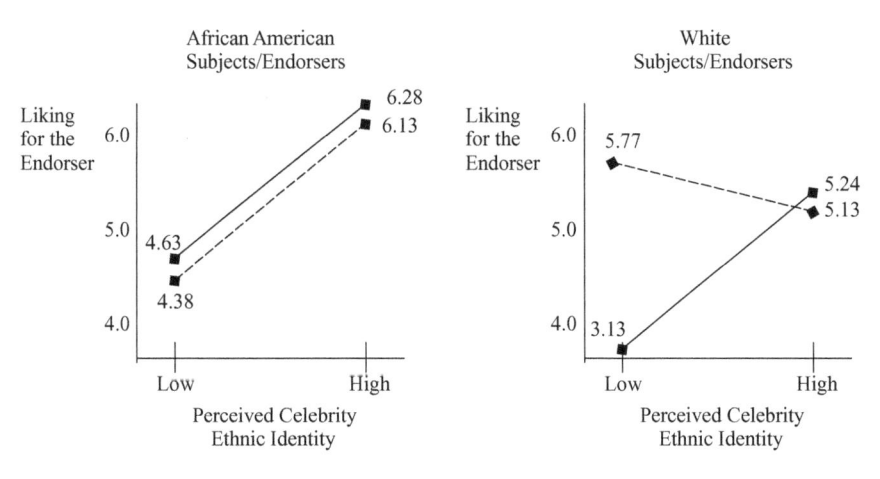

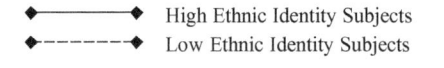

FIG. 15.2. Ethnic identity matching (Hypothesis 2).

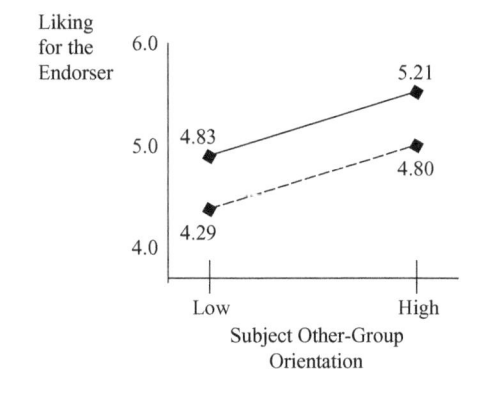

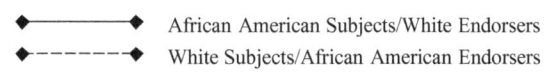

FIG. 15.3. Subject other-group orientation (Hypothesis 3).

Hypothesis 4 proposed that individuals like endorsers from different ethnic groups that are perceived to like them, that is, are high in other-group orientation, relative to endorsers perceived to be low in other-group orientation. The analysis revealed that, for Black individuals, White endorsers with high other-group orientation were significantly better liked than were those with low other-group orientation (LOGO White endorsers = 4.57, HOGO White

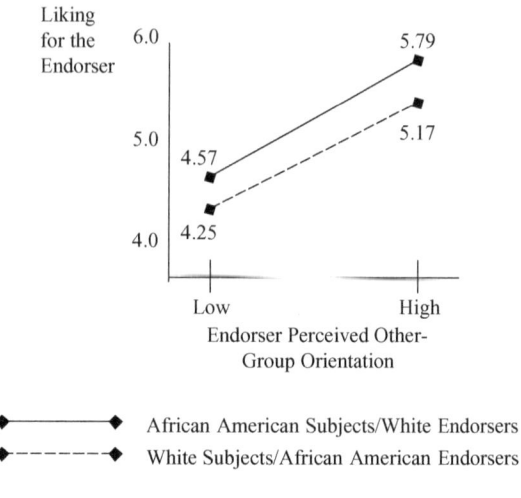

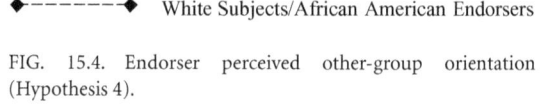

FIG. 15.4. Endorser perceived other-group orientation (Hypothesis 4).

endorsers $= 5.79$; $F_{1,76} = 15.02$, $p < .001$). Analogously for White individuals, Black endorsers with high other-group orientation were significantly preferred to those with low other-group orientation (LOGO Black endorsers $= 4.25$, HOGO Black endorsers $= 5.17$; $F_{1,188} = 18.26$, $p < .001$). Thus Hypothesis 4 was strongly supported and is summarized in Fig. 15.4.

Finally, Hypothesis 5 examined the combined effects of ethnic group membership, level of ethnicity, and other-group orientation on endorser liking. Consistent with the hypothesis, Black individuals with low other-group orientation liked Black endorsers marginally better when they were also perceived to be low in other-group orientation (LOGO Black endorsers $= 5.79$, HOGO Black endorsers $= 5.22$; $F_{1,52} = 2.36$, $p < .10$). However, the pattern diverges from expectations for White individuals with low other-group orientation. Here, these participants showed equal liking for White endorsers regardless of the endorser's level of other-group orientation (LOGO White endorsers $= 4.29$, HOGO White endorsers $= 5.06$; $F_{1,21} = 1.46$, ns).

Individuals with high other-group orientation supported the hypotheses regardless of their ethnic group membership. Black individuals with high other-group orientation liked Black endorsers with high other-group orientation marginally better than they did those low in other-group orientation (LOGO Black endorsers $= 5.23$, HOGO Black endorsers $= 5.99$; $F_{1,59} = 2.10$, $p < .10$). White individuals with high other-group orientation were even stronger in their liking of White endorsers with high versus low other-group orientation (LOGO White endorsers $= 3.20$, HOGO White endorsers $= 5.67$; $F_{1,43} = 26.34$, $p < .001$). Thus,

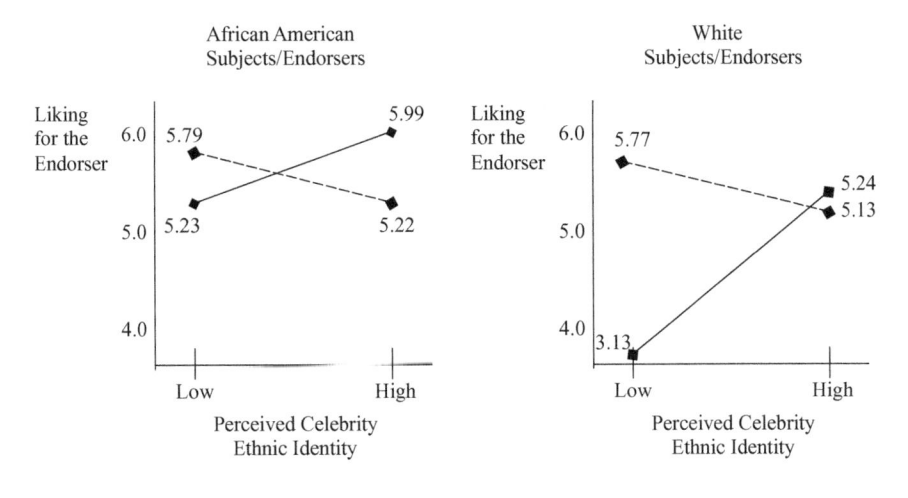

FIG. 15.5. Other-group orientation and ethnicity matching (Hypothesis 5).

Hypothesis 5 is supported in three of the four analyses and is presented in Fig. 15.5.

Additional Analyses

In addition to the formal hypotheses, several differences between groups emerge that may be useful to consider for future research endeavors. These results are presented here, though a discussion of their implications is saved for the following section. For instance, when considering African American endorsers, African Americans participants demonstrate greater liking when the celebrity is high rather than low in terms of his perceived ethnic identity (LEI Black endorsers $= 4.31$, HEI Black endorsers $= 6.06$; $F_{1,188} = 67.64$, $p < .001$). This effect was not found for Whites (LEI White endorsers $= 5.01$, HEI White endorsers $= 5.30$; $F_{1,92} < 1$, ns). Further, Black individuals with high, versus low, levels of ethnic identification liked the Black endorsers significantly better (LEI Black individuals $= 5.50$, HEI Black individuals $= 5.92$; $F_{1,173} = 3.79$, $p < .05$). Surprisingly, the opposite effect was found for White individuals, as those low in ethnic identity liked the White endorsers significantly more than those high in ethnic identity (LEI White individuals $= 5.69$, HEI White individuals $= 4.53$; $F_{1,96} = 14.48$, $p < .001$). The implications of these results, as well as those pertaining to our hypotheses, are discussed in the paragraphs that follow.

DISCUSSION

The effect of endorser and audience ethnicity on advertising effectiveness continues to be an important research topic. The insights provided by research on this topic in the wake of the civil rights movement of the 1960s provided evidence that race is an important factor in determining reactions to advertising images. More recently, however, we have learned of the importance of ethnic identity in influencing relationships. Ethnic identity serves as a manner to recognize the heterogeneity within ethnic groups in terms of the extent to which membership in the ethnic group guides perceptions, attitudes, and behaviors. Although research in advertising has focused predominantly on issues of race, ethnicity holds promising importance in furthering the ways in which to reach growing target audiences.

Our findings take an important step toward furthering our understanding of the role ethnic identity plays in guiding the interpretation of advertising. That the main effect of ethnic group membership matching on liking is significant affirms advertisers' use of racial matching as a tactic to appeal to ethnic minorities. Although Black individuals who are high in ethnic identification demonstrated greater liking for Black endorsers than did Black individuals of low ethnic identity, the opposite effect emerged for White participant–endorser pairings. This result is likely a function of the low level of liking that high-ethnicity White individuals have for White endorsers that are perceived to be of low ethnic identity.

Our results highlight the need to consider the perceived ethnic identity of both endorsers and audiences. Although no main effect for endorser ethnic identity emerges among White endorser–participant pairs, Black endorsers who are perceived to be high in ethnicity were better liked by Black individuals than were endorsers who are perceived to be low in ethnic identity. This finding regarding African American endorsers may explain the inconsistent results of past research efforts. For instance, Greene (1999) found that Blacks with high ethnic identifiers displayed more positive responses to ads featuring Black actors. In contrast, Whittler (1991) found no effect of ethnic identity among his African American participants. This discrepancy in findings may be a result of participants' perceptions of the different actors' ethnic identity, rather than their racial identity.

Another contribution of this research is to introduce the concept of other-group orientation to the marketing literature. Although an endorser may be selected to appeal primarily to target markets of the same ethnicity, marketers can rarely completely ignore the reaction of the nontarget market audience that may view an ad. Our research indicates that one manner in which marketers can appeal to an ethnically diverse audience is through the selection of an endorser who is perceived to have a high other-group orientation. However, the significant interaction between ethnic self-identification and perceived celebrity other-group orientation provides a note of caution. In attempting to appeal to a broad market through the use of an African American celebrity perceived to have high other-group orientation, a marketer appears to run the risk of alienating Black audience members with low other-group orientation. Future research should explore whether media vehicle placement can overcome this potential limitation.

Overall, the results suggest that viewers' ethnic identity and other-group orientation interact with their perceptions of endorsers to affect liking for those endorsers. By considering only liking for an endorser, however, our study is certainly limited to the effects of peripheral route processing if the endorsers' liking is transferred to a brand (cf. Petty et al., 1983). Future research must extend the effects associated with matching ethnicity and other-group orientation directly to ad and brand attitudes, as well as actual purchase behavior. Other advertising effectiveness measures, such as involvement, focus of attention, and memory should be examined for possible influences of ethnic identity and other-group orientation (of both the viewer and spokesperson).

Additional research is also warranted to consider a wider array of ethnic groups. The majority of research in ethnicity focuses on Black consumers. Although African Americans constitute an important segment of the consumer market, virtually every ethnic group in the United States is growing in number (and therefore in importance to marketers) relative to the Anglo majority. For marketers, it is not practicable to simply examine racial identification to meet these demographic changes. To do so would assume that Mexican Americans, for instance, have the same cultural development and background as Puerto Rican Americans. Of course, such assumptions ignore the issue of ethnic identity completely.

The shift in emphasis from race to ethnic identity is a notable advancement in the study of both advertising and ethnicity. For ethnicity researchers in psychology, this application represents a bridge from interpersonal communications to mass communications. For advertisers, the extension of ethnicity to advertising represents the chance to better target consumers with messages that are culturally appropriate for them. Unlike the dearth of research that followed the initial interest in race and advertising, the current advancement in thought will, one would hope, mark the beginning of a stream of research on the role of ethnic identity in an advertising context.

REFERENCES

Acre, C. (1981). A reconsideration of Chicano culture and identity. *Daedalus, 110*, 177–192.

Alba, R., & Chamblin, M. B. (1983). A preliminary examination of ethnic identification among Whites. *American Psychological Review, 48*, 240–242.

Berscheid, E., & Walston, E. (1978). *Interpersonal attraction*. Reading, MA: Addison-Wesley.

Brewer, M. B. (1979). In-group bias in the minimal intergroup situation: A cognitive-motivational analysis. *Psychological Bulletin, 86*, 307–324.

Bristor, J. M., Lee, R. G., & Hunt M. R. (1995). Race and ideology: African-American images in television advertising. *Journal of Public Policy and Marketing, 14*, 48–59.

Chapelle, T. (1998, December–January). Soul for sale. *Emerge Magazine,* 42–48.

Dates, J. L. (1993), Advertising. In J. L. Dates & William Barlow (Eds.), *Split image: African-Americans in the mass media* (pp. 1–21). Washington, DC: Howard University Press.

Donthu, N., & Cherian, J. (1994). Impact of the strength of ethnic identification on Hispanic shopping behavior. *Journal or Retailing, 70,* 383–393.

Emswiller, T., Deaux, K., & Willits, J. E. (1971). Similarity, sex, and requests for small favors. *Journal of Applied Social Psychology, 1,* 284–291.

Evans, F. B. (1963). *American Behavioral Scientists, 6,* 76–79.

Fazio, R. H., Jackson, J. R., Dunton, B. C., & Williams, C. J. (1995). Variability in automatic activation as an unobtrusive measure of racial attitudes: A bona fide pipeline? *Journal of Personality and Social Psychology, 69,* 1013–1027.

Fiske, S. T., & Taylor, S. E. (1991). *Social cognition.* New York: McGraw-Hill.

Garcia, J. (1982), Ethnicity and Chicanos: Measurement of ethnic identification, identity, and consciousness. *Hispanic Journal of Behavioral Sciences, 4,* 295–314.

Goodstein, R., & Ponterotto, J. G. (1997). Racial and ethnic identity and their contribution to self-esteem. *Journal of Black Psychology, 23,* 275–292.

Greene, C. L. (1999). Ethnic evaluations of advertising: Interaction effects of strength of ethnic identification, media placement, and degree of racial composition. *Journal of Advertising, 28,* 49–64.

Gurin, P., & Epps, E. (1975), *Black consciousness, identity, and achievement.* New York: Wiley.

Herd, D., & Grube, J. (1996). Black-identity and drinking in the U.S.—A national study. *Addiction, 91,* 845–857.

Hill, R. B. (1993). *Research on the African-American family.* Westport, CT: Auburn House.

Hill, R. P., & Mazis, M. B. (1986). Measuring emotional responses to advertising. In R. J. Lutz (Ed.), *Advances in consumer research* (Vol. 13, pp 164–168). **CITYCITY:** Association for Consumer Research.

Hirschman, E. C. (1981). American Jewish ethnicity: Its relationship to some selected aspects of behavior. *Journal of Marketing, 45,* 102–110.

Kassarjian, H. H. (1969,). The Negro and American advertising, 1946–1965," *Journal of Marketing Research,* (6), 29–39.

Kerin, R. A. (1979). Black model appearance and product evaluations. *Journal of Communication, 29,* 123–128.

Linville, P. W., & Jones, E. E. (1980). Polarized appraisals of outgroup members. *Journal of Personality and Social Psychology, 38,* 689–703.

O'Hare, W. (1992). Reaching for the dream. *American Demographics, 14*(1), 32–37.

MacKenzie, S. B., Lutz, R. J., & Belch, G. E. (1986). The role of attitude toward the ad as a mediator of advertising effectiveness: A test of competing explanations. *Journal of Marketing Research, 23,* 130–143.

Mitchell, A. A., & Olson, J. C. (1981). Are product attribute beliefs the only mediator of advertising effects on brand attitude? *Journal of Marketing Research, 18,* 318–332.

Mok, T. A. (1999). Asian American dating: Important factors in partner choice. *Cultural Diversity and Ethnic Minority Psychology, 5,* 103–117.

Parham, T., & Helms, J. (1981). The influence of Black students' racial identity attitudes on preferences for counselor's race. *Journal of Counseling Psychology, 32,* 431–440.

Peñaloza, L. (1997). Ya viene Atzlan! Latinos in U.S. advertising. In E. E. Dennis & E. C. Pease, (Eds.), *The media in black and white.* New Brunswick, NJ: Transaction.

Petty, R. E., Cacioppo, J. T., & Schumann, D. (1983). Central and peripheral routes to adverting effectiveness: The moderating role of involvement. *Journal of Consumer Research, 10,* 135–146.

Phinney, J. S. (1992). The multigroup ethnic identity measure: A new scale for use with diverse groups. *Journal of Adolescent Research, 7,* 156–176.

Schlinger, M. J., & Plummer, J. (1972). Advertising in black and white. *Journal of Marketing Research, 9,* 149–153.

Sherif, M., Harvey, O. J., White, B. J., Hood, W. R., & Sherif, C. W. (1961). *Intergroup conflict and cooperation: The Robbers' Cave experiment,* Norman: University of Oklahoma Institute of Intergroup Relations.

Shimp, T. A. (1981). Attitude toward the ad as a mediator of consumer brand choice. *Journal of Advertising, 10,* 9–15.

Stroebe, W., Insko, C. A., Thompson, V. D., & Layton, B. D. (1971). Effects of physical attractiveness, attitude similarity, and sex on various aspects of interpersonal attraction. *Journal of Personality and Social Psychology, 18,* 79–91.

Suedfeld, P., Bochner, S., & Matas, C. (1971). Petitioner's attire and petition signing by peace demonstrators: A field experiment. *Journal of Applied Social Psychology, 1,* 278–283.

Szybillo, G. J., & Jacoby, J. (1974). Effects of different levels of integration on advertising preference and intention to purchase. *Journal of Applied Psychology, 59,* 274–280.

Tajfel, J. (1981). *Human groups and social categories.* Cambridge, England: Cambridge University Press.

Usdansky, M. L. (1992, May 29). USA's decade of change: Diverse nation fits better than "normal." *USA Today,* p. 1A

Whittler, T. E. (1989). Viewers processing of actor's race and message race claims in advertising stimuli. *Psychology and Marketing, 6,* 287–309.

Whittler, T. E. (1991). The effects of actors' race in commercial advertising: Review and extension. *Journal of Advertising, 20,* 54–60.

Wilkes, R. E., & Valencia, H. (1989). Hispanics and Blacks in television commercials. *Journal of Advertising, 18,* 19–25.

Williams, J. D., Qualls, W. J., & Grier, S. A. (1995). Racially exclusive real estate advertising: Public policy implications for fair housing practices. *Journal of Public Policy & Marketing, 14,* 225–244.

Wilson, W. J. (1999). *The bridge over the racial divide.* Berkley: University of California Press.

Zak, I. (1973). Dimensions of Jewish-American identity. *Psychological Reports, 33,* 891–900.

CHAPTER SIXTEEN

Michael Jordan Who? The Impact of Other-Race Contact in Celebrity Endorser Recognition

Geraldine R. Henderson
Howard University/University of Virginia

Jerome D. Williams
The University of Texas at Austin

As the marketplace becomes more ethnically diverse, there will be an increased level of advertising that either features multiethnic celebrity spokespersons, targets multiethnic consumers, or both. With more emphasis placed on courting multicultural consumers, profit-seeking marketers will have to display greater sensitivity to how consumers from different minority racial or ethnic backgrounds perceive they are being portrayed in commercials. Relatedly, they also must assess how responsive consumers from majority racial or ethnic backgrounds are to a greater use of multiethnic celebrity spokespersons and, more fundamentally, how adept they are at even recognizing celebrities from minority racial or ethnic backgrounds. This becomes particularly critical when a multiethnic celebrity spokesperson is used in advertising that targets both majority and minority consumers and the execution of the advertisement does not identify the celebrity spokesperson. This creative strategy perhaps is based on the assumption that the celebrity spokesperson is so recognizable that it is not necessary to identify the celebrity by name. Implicit in this assumption is that the celebrity spokesperson may be equally recognizable among both majority and minority consumers. As an illustration of this point, a perusal of several general interest print magazine advertisements for the first 6 months of 2003 indicates a number of multiethnic celebrity spokespersons for whom only their photo is used and not their name (e.g., Vanessa Williams in *Ebony*, June 2003).

In this chapter, we begin with a discussion of the continued widespread usage of celebrity endorsers in advertising. In particular, we discuss the impact of celebrity endorser race, viewer race, and the amount of experience that the viewer has had with those of the same race as the celebrity endorser. We draw particular attention to a psychological phenomenon that plays a pivotal role in recognition of celebrities by ad viewers, namely the "other-race effect." We then describe a study we previously conducted to explore facial recognition in general and the other-race-effect phenomenon, without necessarily focusing on celebrity facial recognition. In the concluding section, we link the results of our study on general facial recognition with celebrity facial recognition and provide implications for advertisers who use multiethnic celebrity spokespersons to target majority and minority audiences.

LITERATURE REVIEW

Celebrity Endorsers

On July 18, 2003, Kobe Bryant, leading scorer for the Los Angeles Lakers and five-time NBA All-Star, was charged with sexual assault. If convicted, he could face a sentence of anywhere from 4 years to life. Given that a poll conducted the previous fall had rated him the third-best product endorser in sports, behind Tiger Woods and Michael Jordan, most pundits suggested that the charge itself, let alone a conviction, could cost the star millions of dollars in celebrity endorsements (Marshall, 2003):

> Even if he is ultimately cleared, the criminal charge and admission of infidelity will almost certainly change the public perception of Bryant. His squeaky-clean image made him one of the NBA's most recognizable and marketable stars. He recently signed a multimillion-dollar deal with Nike and has endorsement deals with Sprite, McDonald's and Spalding.

However, despite unanticipated issues such as the one raised by the Kobe Bryant charges, the usage of celebrity endorsers is as strong as ever in marketing practice (Till, 1998). Indeed, approximately 20% of all commercials use some type of celebrity endorsement (Bradley, 1996). Recent highly visible examples of both majority and minority celebrity endorsers include Catherine Zeta Jones for T-Mobile, Jason Alexander for KFC, Yao Ming and Emmit Smith for Visa, The Osbournes for Pepsi, Vanessa Williams for Radio Shack, and Tiger Woods for Buick. Although endorsers can be used for a variety of purposes such as getting attention (Kaikati, 1987) and penetrating commercial clutter (Miciak & Shanklin, 1994), the high cost of endorsements suggests that marketers expect to get far more value from the endorsement than simply the use of a clever executional device designed to attract consumer attention. Used appropriately, celebrity endorsers can serve a valuable role in developing brand equity and enhancing a brand's competitive position.

The results of a consumers' views and perceptions study indicate that the consumer has an overall positive attitude toward celebrity endorsement: Such endorsements were perceived to be attention gaining, likable, and impactful, though not generally regarded as overly convincing or believable (O'Mahony & Meenaghan, 1997/1998). According to a survey by Video Storyboard Tests, Inc., more television viewers in 2002 (22%) had very positive feelings about celebrity spokespersons than in 1987 (16%); however, almost twice as many viewers in 2002 as in 1987 indicated that celebrity spokespersons made the advertisement more memorable (Tom et al., 1992). Because celebrity fees and the cost of national advertising are high and the type of spokesperson can affect awareness and recall, the choice of a spokesperson is important to national advertisers. Friedman and Friedman (1979) found that consumers' evaluations of the advertisement would depend on the particular product–endorser combination. The celebrity was found to be the most effective in sustaining brand-name recall and recall of the ad. Just 1 year later, the same authors found that the image of a celebrity may not necessarily spill over onto that of the product, although the celebrity may still be used as an attention getter, source of credibility, aid to recall, or reference group identifier (Friedman & Friedman, 1980). Frieden (1984) found that the type of endorser and the age of the respondent created significant differences in the advertisement's effect, but the gender of the endorser did not.

The primary means that companies use to determine the effectiveness of celebrity spokespersons are Q ratings, also known as Q scores. This "qualitative" score is a measure of both how familiar and likable the public finds a particular actor or celebrity. Q scores measure whether viewers like what they see, unlike the Nielsen numbers, which measure how many people are watching a show. Marketing Evaluations/TVQ, Inc. publishes these scores twice a year, ranking some 1,700 personalities from 21 different categories (MacDonald, 2002). See Table 16.1, which provides Q scores for the top overall performers and sports personalities for Winter 2000[1].

Despite the vast literature on the effects of celebrity endorsements on consumers' brand attitudes and purchase intentions, little is known about the economic value of these endorsements, with the exception of the study by Agrawal and Kamakura (1995). Results indicated that, on average, the impact of these announcements on stock returns is positive, and they suggested the celebrity endorsement contracts are generally viewed as a worthwhile investment in advertising (Agrawal & Kamakura, 1995). For instance, on March 9, 1995, rumors began to circulate on Wall Street concerning Michael Jordan's impending return to the Chicago Bulls. Jordan had previously retired from playing professional basketball in 1993 to play baseball. The results of this study showed that anticipation of Jordan's return to the NBA,

TABLE 16.1
Differences by Race for Top Q-Score Performers and Sports Personalities

Rank	Performer or Sports Personality	Total Sample Q	Non-Black Q	Black Q	Hispanic Q
	Performer				
1	Robin Williams	55	56	50	56
2	Bruce Willis	42	41	48	48
3	The Rock	40	36	61	36
4	Denzel Washington	37	33	65	32
4	Ingo Readmacher	37	39	27	24
5	Noah Wyle	36	36	35	29
5	Will Smith	36	32	60	46
5	Al Pacino	36	35	47	48
9	Della Reese	35	32	49	33
9	Adam Sandler	35	34	41	36
9	Arnold Schwarzenegger	35	34	43	38
9	Julia Roberts	35	37	34	32
9	Colin Mochrie	35	37	23	44
9	Julianna Margulies	35	35	36	40
	Sports Personality				
1	Sammy Sosa	33	31	41	40
2	Joe Montana	32	31	41	32
3	Tiger Woods	30	28	45	35
4	Jerry Rice	28	27	37	27
4	Cal Ripken, JR	28	27	35	22
4	Mark Mcgwire	28	28	26	30
7	Kristi Yamaguchi	27	27	30	31
8	Steve Young	26	25	31	42
8	Kurt Warner	26	26	25	27
10	Randy Moss	25	24	34	31
10	Molan Ryan	25	25	26	30

Note. Marketing Evaluations, Inc. (2000,Winter).

and the related increased visibility for him, resulted in an average increase in the market-adjusted values of his client firms of almost 2%, or more than $1 billion in stock market value (Mathur, Mathur, & Rangan, 1997).

In addition, although a number of scholars have investigated effective celebrity endorser characteristics, with consumer samples using experimental methods, few explored the point of view of practitioners who are responsible for the selection of celebrities (Erdogan, Baker, & Tagg, 2001; Miciak & Shanklin, 1994). Erdogan et al. (2001) investigated British advertising agency managers' consideration of important celebrity characteristics when selecting an endorser, and these factors' importance according to product types. The research findings validated much of the consumer-based research in that managers consider a range of criteria when choosing celebrity endorsers and indicate that the importance of the criteria depends on the product type.

Ethnicity and the Celebrity Endorser

In most of the existing research on celebrity endorsers, it is not clear whether the racial or ethnic background of the endorser, of the viewer, or both are taken into consideration. McCracken (1988) contended that the use of celebrity endorsers in advertisements communicates a number of different messages (i.e., class, gender, age, and lifestyle) to the viewing audience. However, very few studies have addressed the issue of race or ethnicity with respect to celebrity spokespersons (Drugas, 1985). Williams and Qualls (1989) found that the intensity of Black consumers' ethnic identification was positively related to their responses to ads featuring African American celebrities. DelVecchio and Goodstein (2004; see Chapter 15 in this volume) found that matching viewers and endorsers' ethnicity and other-group orientation adds significantly to the explained variance in ratings of endorsers, thus highlighting the need to consider the perceived ethnic identity of both endorsers and audiences in future research. Hsu and Motley (1995) explored the relative effectiveness of a U.S.-based, global celebrity who endorsed a global or local brand in a market outside the United States.

Increasingly so, African Americans are frequently used in advertising as celebrity endorsers. For example, in some years, the semiannual Q scores are dominated by Black sports and entertainment personalities, such as Michael Jackson (Pepsi), Bill Cosby (Jell-O, Kodak), Michael Jordan (Nike, McDonalds), Ray Charles (Pepsi), and Whitney Houston (Coke) ("Black Again," 1989). In recent years, Blacks have frequently been listed among the most popular celebrities. For example, in 2002, there were at least 6 Blacks listed among the 20 most appealing male personalities based on their Q ratings for the year, namely, Denzel Washington, Morgan Freeman, Samuel L. Jackson, Sidney Poitier, James Earl Jones, and Eddie Murphy ("High Q," 2002). Consider the Q scores in Table 16.1 again. First, even though these rankings change over time, typically there are both Blacks and Whites in the top Q-score performers for both entertainers and athletes. However, there can be significant differences in Q scores across ethnic groups, such as the scores for Denzel Washington (65 for Blacks vs. 33 for non-Blacks) and Will Smith (60 for Blacks vs. 32 for non-Blacks). These are just a few examples that illustrate the disparities that can occur in Q scores. The use of these African American celebrities in ads is particularly effective in stimulating attention and recall for an ad among African Americans (Williams & Qualls, 1989). Similarly, *Marketing News* reported that celebrity athletes and celebrity entertainers were the most likely advertising spokespersons that would cause Black consumers to buy a product ("Survey Measures Preferences," 1981). One study indicated that Black consumers were at least twice as likely as Anglos to rate celebrities as being more believable than non-celebrity endorsers (Hume, 1983). It should be noted that the current research focuses on Black–White differences in celebrity recognition. However, given the prevalence of Hispanics in the U.S. population and as celebrity spokespersons, it would be of interest to incorporate Hispanics in future research.

Despite the fact that there are several studies that did at least incorporate race or ethnicity as a variable, few, if any, considered the match up between the celebrity spokesperson and the target market for which the product is being endorsed. One question that was not answered in most existing research is whether it is the similarity between the race of the actor and viewer or the credibility of the celebrity spokesperson that is producing the positive impact.

The importance of fit between the endorser and the endorsed product has been described as the "match-up hypothesis" (Till, 1998; Till & Busler, 2000). The match-up hypothesis deals with the match between a celebrity endorser and the brand that she or he is endorsing; however, we are interested in the match between the celebrity and the viewer, especially in situations in which the celebrity is not identified in the advertisement. In those situations, we recommend that the celebrity be used for ads targeted to individuals of the same race or individuals who have had experience with those of the celebrity's race. In the paragraphs that follow, we discuss celebrity spokesperson recognition in general before we proceed to discussions of cross-race celebrity recognition.

Celebrity Recognition

Arguably, the effectiveness of celebrity spokespersons is dependent on some level of recognition by the viewer. Most researchers have assumed that either the spokesperson has been identified by the advertiser, so that unaided recognition is not an issue, or that the celebrity is so well known that recognition is assumed. Burroughs and Feinberg (1987) found that individuals were able to identify product names much faster when a product identification decision was primed by a correct spokesperson name. Recently, Pashupati, Raman, and Kuhlmeier (2003) found that identifying the celebrity spokesperson in the ad could in fact induce more positive attitude toward the ad than if the celebrity spokesperson was not identified, for consumers who have indicated no previous familiarity with that celebrity. Forehand and Perkins (2003) found a similar effect for celebrity voice. In addition, Pashupati et al. (2003) discussed the variance in whether or not advertisers actually identify the celebrity endorsers. For instance, they mentioned Yogi Berra and the ad that he does for AFLAC. However, in that ad, there is no identification of him at all, as he is sitting in the chair in the barbershop. The advertisers are hoping or assuming that the viewer will recognize him and thus associate whatever positive feelings they have toward him to AFLAC because he is an endorser for the company.

However, existing research on celebrity spokesperson identification or recognition fails to address the issue of multiethnic endorsers or viewers. For instance, Pashupati et al. (2003) used Kirsten Dunst as their celebrity endorser. As Table 16.1 indicates, Q scores may vary for Blacks and Whites, depending on the celebrity endorser. Likewise, recognition of her may be skewed, depending on whether or not the viewer was White or Black.

Other-Race Effect

A psychological phenomenon that plays a pivotal role in the recognition of celebrities by ad viewers is the other-race effect, which is the ability to recognize the faces of those of one race easier than the faces of those from another race. Typically, the race that is easier to recognize is the individual's own race. In this chapter, we suggest a celebrity-recognition framework in which the ability to recognize other-race faces is based on not only the race of the viewer relative to the celebrity but also the amount of exposure or familiarity the viewer has had with other races.

Facial recognition in advertising could become problematic as it becomes increasingly important for ad viewers to recognize a more diverse group of celebrities from different racial or ethnic backgrounds, especially those who are supposedly very popular. Previous research has provided evidence of the other-race effect in the multiracial United States, with its White–Caucasian, African American, Hispanic, and Asian American ethnic or racial groups. Similarly, one would expect to find evidence of the other-race effect in other multiracial societies. To illustrate the impact of the other-race effect in a multicultural society, we report, in the paragraphs that follow, on a previous study we conducted in the multicultural context of Singapore (see Henderson, Williams, Dillon, & Lwin, 1999). In the conclusion, we link it to facial recognition and multiethnic celebrity advertising in the United States.

A STUDY OF FACIAL RECOGNITION AND THE OTHER-RACE-EFFECT PHENOMENON

Background

Researchers have been interested in the phenomenon of differential face recognition for a long time, but, with one exception (Henderson et al. 1999), little attention has been given to the phenomenon in the marketing literature. However, this was done in a services context. Furthermore, most of the nonmarketing research that has been done has been primarily conducted in the context of eyewitness testimony. However, the other-race effect is pertinent for marketing researchers to understand, because it has significant implications for not only multiethnic celebrity facial recognition in advertising but also for other marketing-related issues, including customer service, direct marketing, and personal selling.

In a strict sense, the other-race effect occurs when people display a differential ability to recognize faces of their *own* race compared with those of another race (Bothwell, Brigham, & Malpass 1989; Chance, Goldstein, & McBride, 1975)

Henderson et al. (1999) studied other-race contact by expanding the other-race-effect definition to encompass the differential ability to recognize faces of one race over another, regardless of own versus other race distinction. This expanded definition allows them to replicate the same type of stimuli treatment used in previous other-race-effect studies (i.e., in which individuals are analyzed on their ability to recognize Black and White faces), in a context outside of the United States. Henderson et al. (1999) exposed Asians individuals to Black and White face stimuli, in the same manner in which U.S. White individuals were exposed, thereby allowing a comparison of the results to see if there are differences between Asian individuals and White individuals in the recognition of Black and White faces.

In previous other-race-effect studies, the phenomenon has been observed in several laboratory experiments in which Black and White participants are exposed to Black and White faces. Generally, the results have conformed to a full crossover interaction or an asymmetric interaction. In some studies, Whites were more prone to perform better (higher accuracy) on face-recognition tasks containing White faces over Black faces, and just the opposite was true for Blacks (Bothwell et al., 1989; Lindsay, Jack, & Christian 1991). The sloping line in Fig. 16.1 illustrates the existence of the other-race effect for White individuals. However, the flat line in Fig. 16.1 illustrates the results of other-race-effect studies that have been found by some researchers. In other words, Black individuals performed just as well on White faces as on Black faces (Bothwell et al., 1989). There was an asymmetrical other-race effect, suggesting that the other-race effect may vary by ethnic or racial group.

The closest other-race-effect research to marketing was demonstrated in the context of convenience stores (Brigham, Maass, Snyder, & Spaulding, 1982; Platz & Hosch, 1988). In this environment, if a store clerk does not recognize a repeat customer and therefore fails to establish or maintain some type of ongoing service provider–customer relationship with him or her, it reduces the level of service

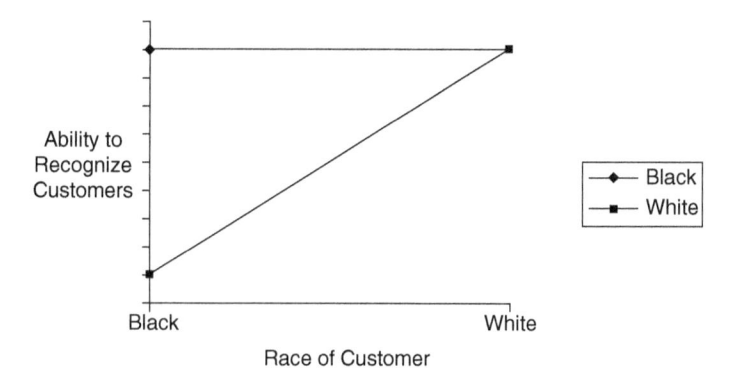

FIG. 16.1. Asymmetric other-race effect.

provided to the customer. As a result, the nature of the overall exchange may be diminished. The repeat customer may spend a great deal of money in the store, but if he or she is treated as if each time is his or her first time in the store, then this may lead to feelings of alienation and an increase in customer dissatisfaction.

There have been some recent attempts to examine how the other-race effect varies across cultures and countries. Henderson, Ostrom, Barnett, Dillon, and Lynch (1997) analyzed differences in the recognition of Black and White faces in the United States and South Africa. They found a main effect for subject race as well as race of face. Interestingly enough, in their study they found that Whites were better at recognizing all faces, regardless of the race of face ($F_{1,103} = 10.17$, $p <$ .0019). This finding was contrary to existing research that found just the opposite: Blacks were generally better at the facial-recognition task. In addition, they also found that all participants were better at recognizing Black faces than White faces ($F_{1,105} = 10.30$, $p < .0018$). Again, this finding was a complete reversal of earlier findings in which White faces were generally better recognized.

In the 1970s, a few studies also attempted to examine the other-race effect as related to Asians, by either including Asians as participants or by using Asian faces as stimuli. For example, Luce (1974) found that Black participants performed poorly on all faces other than Black faces, including Asian faces (both Japanese and Chinese); see Fig. 16.2. In addition, Asians were found to perform well on both Black and Asian faces but poorly on White faces. Whites performed well on both Whites and Asians but poorly on Black faces. Elliott, Wills, and Goldstein (1973) found that both Blacks and Whites were better at identifying own-race faces than Japanese faces. In the study we report on here (Henderson et al., 1999), we analyze the expanded other-race-effect concept by examining the differential ability of the majority racial or ethnic group in two different countries or cultures (Chinese Asians in Singapore and Whites in the United States) to recognize Black and White faces.

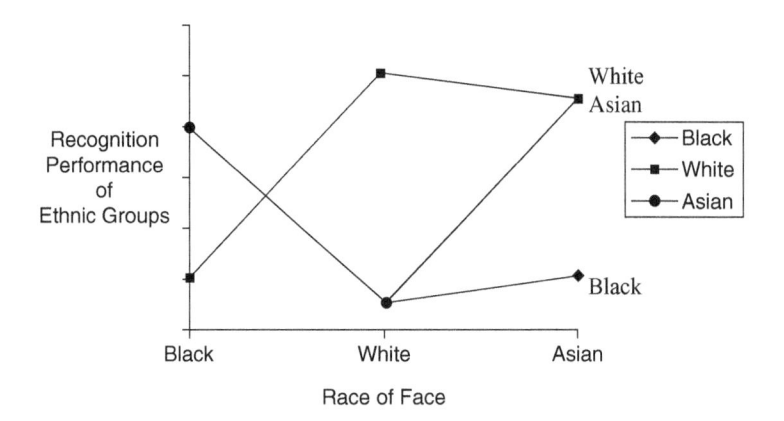

FIG. 16.2. Findings from Luce (1974).

Hypotheses

There are several hypotheses that have been put forth to explain differential facial recognition (Bothwell et al., 1989; Henderson et al., 1997; Lindsay et al., 1991). Each of these hypotheses has some merit; however, many of them have not been rigorously tested, and those that have been tested have not been supported. One such hypothesis is based on the premise that "the more I see people of a different race, the easier it is for me to distinguish between them," and "the more relatedness there is between me and people of another race, the more I can infer about them simply by looking at them than I can infer about someone from another race." Individuals who have more familiarity (exposure or contact) with members of their own race would, therefore, be expected to demonstrate superior performance in the recognition of these faces. This would seem to indicate that as the degree of exposure to, or contact with, members of other races increases, then the other-race effect should decrease.

The results of existing studies based on familiarity and exposure have yielded conflicting findings. For instance, in the two convenience store studies mentioned previously, the field setting was in two different cities, yet both were conducted where there was a moderate degree of intergroup contact. The Brigham et al. (1982) study, which failed to find an own-race bias, was conducted in Tallahassee, Florida, where there was a high degree of intergroup contact (Blacks represented 25% of population.) Surprisingly, the Platz and Hosch (1988) study, which did find an other-race effect among both White and Hispanic participants, was conducted in El Paso, where there was even a higher degree of intergroup contact. Hispanics represented over 63% of the population (Bothwell et al., 1989).

The study reported here (Henderson et al., 1999) examines whether there is a differential ability among Chinese Singaporeans to recognize Black and White faces. Furthermore, it allows us to explore the legitimacy of the familiarity and exposure hypothesis for the other-race effect. If this idea is supported, we should find a crossover interaction effect for familiar–high-exposure faces and less familiar–low-exposure faces for Chinese Singaporeans and U.S. Whites. That is, on one hand, Whites should perform better on facial recognition of Whites (higher familiarity) compared with Blacks (lower familiarity). On the other hand, Chinese Singaporeans should perform better on facial recognition for Blacks (higher familiarity as a result of interaction with people of color, such as Malaysians and Indians) compared with Whites (lower familiarity).[2] More formally, we state the following.

> **H1:** *For Asian (Chinese Singaporean) individuals, face-recognition ability will be greater for Black faces than for White faces.*
>
> **H2:** *For White individuals, face-recognition ability will be greater for White faces than for Black faces.*

Methodology and Procedure

A pretest was conducted to establish eight sets (four White and four Black) of three faces that participants would agree were similar in terms of the physical features of each of the three pictures in each set. In the main study, one of these pictures served as the target face, whereas the other two were distractors (also called foils). Only female faces were used in the study to reduce possible gender effects.

Participants consisted of 203 students enrolled in undergraduate and MBA business courses in one of the national universities in Singapore and a large, Southeastern university in the United States. Although both Blacks and Whites were enrolled in the U.S. classes, only White participants were analyzed in this study. Similarly, although there were a handful of non-Chinese persons enrolled in the Singapore classes, only Chinese Singaporeans were analyzed in the study. This was done to ensure homogeneity within groups representing the majority race in their respective countries. The respondents participated in the study in exchange for monetary compensation or partial course credit. Each participant was told that she or he would be participating in a study concerned with understanding issues in customer service.

For the aforementioned hypotheses to be tested, a pen-and-paper survey was used in conjunction with a timed photoslide presentation. The study used a 2 (race of participant: Asian, (i.e., Chinese Singaporean–White) × 2 (race of customer face: Black–White) mixed-factor design with repeated measures on the latter factor. Participants were not recruited on the basis of race. Instead, race was unobtrusively measured at the end of the experiment along with other demographic data. This step was taken in an effort to reduce demand characteristics that might result from raising the salience of race. Half of the customer or shopper faces were Black and the other half were White, and each participant studied customers of both races. That is, Asians (Chinese Singaporeans) saw Black faces, representing faces that they have more exposure to and are more familiar with as a result of the significant representation of people of color from racial minority groups in Singapore (i.e., Malaysians and Indians). Asians (Chinese Singaporeans) also saw White faces, representing a race to which they have less exposure. This was similar for White participants, except that the reverse was true for familiarity with Black and White faces used in the study. The experiment followed a study–test format. Participants were asked to imagine they were employed in a ladies retail store. They were given approximately 1 min to read a brief scenario in which they were told they would be substituting for a salesperson and would need to recognize that salesperson's regular customers. They were then given 6s to review each of eight face cards, which consisted of a black-and-white photo of each customer.

In the second half of the study (which followed an unrelated distraction task), participants were presented with a second scenario followed by a recognition task in which they were asked whether a pictured shopper was actually one of the salesperson's regular customers. Twenty-four shoppers were shown (eight targets and two pretested foils per target).

A series of relevant questions followed this activity. Among this latter set of questions were those measuring need for cognition, extent of familiarity with and exposure to other races, various other demographic characteristics, and manipulation checks. Participants were then debriefed, compensated, thanked, and dismissed.

The dependent measure analyzed was the recognition ability score, d', calculated by giving participants credit for hits and a penalty for false alarms. Consistent with signal-detection theory, upon which the task involved in our experiment was based, a correct response to a target slide was a hit (Cradit, Tashchian, & Hofacker, 1994; McNicol, 1972). An incorrect response to a target slide was a miss. A correct response to a distractor slide was a correct rejection whereas an incorrect response to a distractor slide was a false alarm.

Results and Discussion

Recognition ability, d', was analyzed in a mixed-models analysis of variance, with customer race as the repeated measure. We found a significant interaction for Asians versus Whites in their ability to recognize Black versus White faces ($F_{1,201} = 4.88$, $p < .0282$); see Fig. 16.3. Asians were better at recognizing Black faces ($\overline{X} = 3.57$) over White faces ($\overline{X} = 2.78$) than Whites were at recognizing White faces over Black faces. There was little difference among Whites in differential recognition between White and Black faces. In fact, White participants did only slightly better in recognizing own-race faces. That is, Whites did slightly better in recognizing White faces ($\overline{X} = 3.89$) than in recognizing Black faces ($\overline{X} = 3.77$), although the difference was not statistically significant. In contrast, Asians were significantly better at recognizing Black faces compared with White faces. Hence, Hypothesis 1 was supported and Hypothesis 2 was not.

FIG. 16.3. Asian (Chinese Singaporean) versus U.S. results.

The results just given suggest that American Whites and Chinese Singaporeans, representing the dominant ethnic or racial group in their respective countries, have similar levels of interaction with their respective ethnic or racial minority groups. Hence both Asians and Whites demonstrate similar ability to recognize faces from people-of-color groups. In other words, Whites in the United States do well in recognizing Black faces as a result of high levels of interaction and exposure between the groups, and Chinese also do well in recognizing Black faces as a result of high levels of interaction and exposure with people of color (e.g., Malays and Indians). However, Chinese perform significantly worse in recognizing White faces, compared with Black faces, as a result of lower levels of exposure and familiarity with that racial group.

In our experimental design, we only explicitly included race of the service provider and race of the shopper in our experimental design. However, additional data we collected from individuals tend to support the suggestion that the dominant racial groups in each country (Whites in the United States and Chinese in Singapore) have similar exposure levels to people of color in each country (Blacks in the United States and Malays and Indians in Singapore, respectively). As already mentioned, participants were asked questions on their extent of familiarity with and exposure to other races. Whites were asked about familiarity and exposure to other Whites, and to other racial or ethnic groups, including Blacks, Hispanics, Asians, and others. Chinese Singaporeans were asked about familiarity and exposure to other Chinese Singaporeans, and to other racial or ethnic groups, including Malays and Indians, Whites, Blacks and so on. As expected, we found that both American Whites and Chinese Singaporeans had significantly higher levels of familiarity and exposure to their own races compared with other races. In addition, we found that the level of familiarity and exposure that American Whites had with Blacks was similar to the level of familiarity and exposure that Chinese Singaporeans had with Malays and Indians, which was significantly greater than the level of familiarity and exposure that they had with Whites. Hence, as already suggested, this may partially account for the similar facial-recognition ability of American Whites for Black faces ($\overline{X} = 3.77$) and Chinese Singaporeans for Malaysian and Indian faces ($\overline{X} = 3.57$).

BLACK AND WHITE INTERACTION: OTHER-RACE-EFFECT IMPLICATIONS FOR U.S. ADVERTISERS AND CONCLUSION

This study found evidence of the other-race effect in the multicultural context of Singapore: Chinese Asians in Singapore, who were more exposed to people of color than to Whites, recognized Black faces better than White faces. This is based on the theoretical premise that people are better at recognizing faces of races for which there is a higher level of interaction, exposure, and familiarity. Blacks are people of color and are more similar in facial features to the major racial minority groups in Singapore, that is, the Malaysians and Indians. On the basis of our hypotheses, because Chinese Singaporeans, the dominant racial group, are more likely to be familiar with and have exposure to people of color, as compared with Whites, they should be better at recognizing Black faces.

However, the study failed to find evidence of the other-race effect among the U.S. sample. As we suggest herein, the ability of the White participants in this study to be as adept at recognizing Black faces as White faces may be accounted for by their extent of familiarity with and exposure to Blacks, based on the additional measures on which we collected data. For advertisers using multicultural celebrity spokespersons, especially without naming them, this raises some interesting implications. Assuming the participants in this study are representative of the U.S. population, then advertisers should feel confident that using Vanessa Williams as a celebrity spokesperson without naming her (the example referred to at the beginning of this chapter) should not have a differential effect among Blacks and Whites in terms of facial recognition. However, we should caution that we conducted a controlled laboratory study using college students in order to maintain high internal validity. In the process, we thereby made a trade-off of sacrificing a certain degree of external validity, thus limiting the generalizability of the results to the entire U.S. population. With that in mind, we find it would be useful to examine the extent of familiarity and interaction between Blacks and Whites in the population in general, as that would provide advertisers with greater insight as to whether to expect, or not expect, evidence of the other-race effect in real-world advertising environments. Our exploratory examination of three environments, namely, residential neighborhoods, schools, and media, suggests Blacks and Whites in the United States may have less interaction and familiarity with each other than is generally assumed and as indicated by our measures among the college students in our study.

Many believe that college campuses tend to be a more diverse and integrated community than many neighborhoods, and therefore Blacks and White students are more likely to have a greater degree of interaction and thus be quite different from the general population. However, one should exercise caution in accepting this assumption. There is mounting evidence that college campuses merely reflect the segregated domains of the population in general. For example, the *Wall Street Journal* ran a front-page story on the two worlds of Black and White students at a major, prestigious university in the United States (Stern & Gaiter, 1994). Furthermore, typically more African American students graduate from historically Black colleges and universities each year than from traditionally White institutions; hence there is that type of segregated environment. However, even on traditionally White university campuses, Black and White students often tend to be in separate fraternities and sororities, separate social organizations, generally separate "housing" (i.e., Blacks tend to have Black roommates), and, in most cases, separate "dining" (i.e., Blacks tend to eat with other Blacks.) Although it may seem that college campuses offer the opportunity for a more diverse community, Blacks and Whites still tend to live in "segregated" campus neighborhoods. The extent of their interaction in many cases, unfortunately, is confined to sitting next to one another in a classroom or playing together on a university athletic team. Even at the precollege level, a recent report from the Civil Rights Project at Harvard University found that the nation's schools are more racially segregated than they were a decade ago (Race Relations Reporter, 2003a). Evidence suggests that the measures of familiarity with and exposure we found among our college MBA student sample may not be typical of school environments in general. We would encourage future experimental research on other-race-effect studies to be expanded to other college campus environments to determine if the results we achieved can be replicated.

In terms of neighborhoods, a number of studies have demonstrated that residential segregation persists in the United States (e.g., Harrison & Weinberg, 1992). Typically, minorities have always had a high degree of concentration, and the recent increase in the size of these populations has accentuated these trends (Frey, 1991); that is, minorities tend to establish residences closer to others of their own race. For example, one recent report on the persistence of racial segregation (Race Relations Reporter, 2002) found that residential segregation has not been reduced over the past several decades, and, for the most part, Blacks and Whites voluntarily choose to live in neighborhoods in which a large percentage of the residents are members of their own race.

Perhaps the media environment is the one most relevant to advertisers in terms of gaining insight about the potential of the other-race effect based on interaction between Blacks and Whites. Although there is some evidence that Blacks and Whites are watching more of the same television shows ("Blacks Again," 2003), a recent study suggests that network television remains largely segregated by race and that Black characters appear most often on predominantly Black shows that are predominantly watched by Blacks (Race Relations Reporter, 2003b). This same study noted that Hispanics received only 3% of the total screen time on network prime-time comedies and dramas, Asians were shown 1% of the time, and American Indians were "invisible." Nielsen Media Research reports routinely indicate that Blacks and Whites essentially are limited in their exposure to each other based on television-viewing preferences (Scott, 2003). For example, during the week of May 12, 2003, "Bernie Mac," one of the highest-rated television shows featuring a minority cast, was No. 1 on Nielsen's list of the most popular African American shows for the week but placed only 17th on the all-inclusive ratings list. Similarly, "My Wife and Kids" ranked 8th with African Americans and 49th on the all-inclusive list, and "Girlfriends," which ranked at No. 87 on the general list, was the 4th-highest-rated show among African American viewers.

The implication of the aforementioned discussion on persistent segregation in American society for advertisers is that the fit between a multicultural celebrity spokesperson and viewer is of paramount importance. This is an extension of the match-up hypothesis (Till, 1998; Till & Busler, 2000) already discussed that suggests a fit between the endorser and the endorsed product. In the case of the current research, that fit must be between celebrity endorser and the viewer. This match becomes even more critical when the celebrity is a multicultural spokesperson and is not identified in the advertisement. In addition, given the degree of persistent segregation between Blacks and Whites in terms of residential housing, educational environments, and media-viewing patterns, the conditions for lessening the other-race effect, that is, familiarity with and exposure to members of the other race, may not be as prevalent as often assumed about a so-called American melting-pot environment. Hence, advertisers need to be more cautious in using crossover celebrity spokesperson appeal without name identification, unless they are extremely confident that the celebrity is equally recognizable between both racial or ethnic segments. In those situations, our recommended strategy is for advertisers to use multicultural celebrity spokespersons in ads targeted to individuals of the same race or individuals who have high levels of familiarity with and exposure to the multicultural celebrity's spokesperson's racial or ethnic group. Otherwise, they may run the risk of encountering a dampening impact on the effectiveness of the celebrity spokesperson that is due to the other-race effect. Recognition of the celebrity spokesperson is somewhat of a surrogate for name identification, which we know from previous research increases effectiveness (Burroughs & Feinberg, 1987, Pashupati et al., 2003).

Future other-race-effect studies should investigate not only the more generally used strict definition of the other-race effect (i.e., whether Blacks and Whites are better at recognizing their *own* race face compared with faces of other races) but also the expanded definition we use in our study based on other-race contact (i.e., the differential ability to recognize faces of one race over another, regardless of own-race vs. other-race distinction, based on level of familiarity with and exposure to that race). Such studies should include other racial or ethnic groups in the United States, such as Hispanics and Asians. This should allow advertisers to gain greater insight into using multicultural celebrity spokespersons targeted to various racial or ethnic segments. For example, for Blacks is there a differential ability to recognize Hispanics versus Asian celebrity spokespersons without names, or, for Hispanics, is there a differential ability to recognize Black versus Asian celebrity spokespersons without names?

Although the focus of this study has been to relate the implications of the other-race effect and other-race contact to advertising, there are a number of other marketing-related contexts to which this research can be applied, such as tourism, retailing, customer service, direct marketing, personal selling—essentially any marketing context in which there is interpersonal interaction or visual communication of race or ethnicity. As researchers continue to explore the phenomenon, they should be able to determine the driving force behind the other-race effect. Therefore, they should be in a better position to identify and recommend strategies to eliminate, or at least reduce, the effect in marketplace exchanges between customers and a marketer's offering involving race or ethnicity in which recognition becomes important, whether that offering be an advertisement, salesperson, or customer service personnel. In advertising, by eliminating, or at least minimizing, the influence of the other-race effect, marketers will be able to deliver more effective advertising to all racial or ethnic segments and capitalize on the growing diversity in the marketplace.

REFERENCES

Agrawal, J., & Kamakura, W. (1995, July). The economic worth of celebrity endorsers: An event study analysis. *Journal of Marketing, 59*(3), 56–62.

Blacks again dominate top marketing Q-ratings. (1989, May 22). *Jet, X,* 50.

Blacks, Whites watching more of same TV shows. (2003, May 19). *Jet, 103,* 6.

Bothwell, R. K., Brigham, J. C., & Malpass, R. S. (1989, March). Cross-racial identification. *Personality and Social Psychology Bulletin, 15,* 19–25.

Bradley, S. (1996, February 26). Marketers are always looking for good pitchers. *Brandweek, 37*(9), 36–37.

Brigham, J. C., Maass, A., Snyder, L. S., & Spaulding, K. (1982). The accuracy of eyewitness identifications in a field setting. *Journal of Personality and Social Psychology, 42,* 673–681.

Burroughs, W. J., & Feinberg, R. A. (1987, September). Using response latency to assess spokesperson effectiveness. *Journal of Consumer Research, 14,* 295–299.

Chance, J. E., Goldstein, A. G. & McBride, L. (1975). Differential experience and recognition memory for faces. *Journal of Social Psychology, 97,* 243–253.

Cradit, J. D., Tashchian, A., & Hofacker, C. F. (1994, February). Signal detection theory and single observation designs: Methods and indices for advertising recognition testing. *Journal of Marketing Research, 31,* 117–127.

DelVecchio, D., & Goodstein, R. C. (2004). Moving beyond race: The role of ethnic identity in evaluating celebrity endorsers. In J. D. Williams, W.-N. Lee, & C. P. Haugtvedt (Eds.), *Diversity in advertising: Broadening the scope of research.* Mahwah, NJ: Lawrence Erlbaum Associates.

Drugas, C. (1985, March). Marketers find celebrity endorsers sell en espano. *Ad Forum, 6*(3), 13–16.

Elliott, E. S., Wills, E. J., & Goldstein, A. G. (1973). The effects of discrimination training on recognition of White and Oriental Faces. *Bulletin of the Psychonomic Society, 2,* 71–73.

Erdogan, B. Z., Baker, M. J., & Tagg, S. (2001, May/June). Selecting celebrity endorsers: The practitioner's perspective. *Journal of Advertising Research, 41,* 39–48.

Forehand, M. R., & Perkins, A. (2003). Unconscious processing of spokesperson information: The influence of implicit cognition. Proceedings of the Society for Consumer Psychology conference, Susan E. Heckler and Stewart Shapiro, (eds). American Psychological Association, 123–126.

Frey, W. H. (1991, October). Are two Americas emerging? *Population Today, 19*(10), 6–8.

Frieden, J. B. (1984, October/November). Advertising spokesperson effects: An examination of endorser type and gender on two audiences. *Journal of Advertising Research, 24,* 33–41.

Friedman, H. H., & Friedman, L. W. (1980, May). Does the celebrity endorser's image spill over to the product? *The Journal of Business, 18*(2), 31.

Friedman, H. H., & Friedman, L. (1979, October). Endorser effectiveness by product type. *Journal of Advertising Research, 19,* 63.

Harrison, R. J., & Weinberg, D. H. (1992, August). *Changes in racial and ethnic residential segregation, 1980–1990.* Paper presented at the 1992 American Statistical Association Meeting, Boston, MA.

Henderson, G. R., Ostrom, A., Barnett, T. D., Dillon, K. D., & Lynch, J. G. (1997). *Confusing consumers: The impact of the other-race-effect on customer service.* (CIBER Working Paper 97–006). Durham, NC: Duke University Fuqua School of Business.

Henderson, G. R., Williams, J. D., Dillon, K. D., & Lwin, M. (1999). The commodification of race in Singapore: The customer service implications of the other-race-effect on tourism and retailing. *Asia Pacific Journal of Management, 16*, 213–227.

High Q. (rating celebrity endorsements). (2002, October 28). Daily News Record, p. 64.

Hsu, C. -K., & Motley, C. M. (1995). A conceptual model of the effects of congruence between the global/local images of the celebrity endorser and the brand on consumer responses. *Cross-Cultural Consumer and Business Studies, 5*, 75–81.

Hume, S. (1983, November 7). Stars are lacking luster as ad presenters. *Advertising Age*, p. 3.

Kaikati, J. G. (1987). Celebrity advertising: A review and synthesis. *International Journal of Advertising, 6*, 93–105.

Lindsay, D. S., Jack, P. C., Jr., & Christian, M. A. (1991, August). Other-race face perception. *Journal of Applied Psychology, 76*, 587–589.

Luce, T. S. (1974). Blacks, Whites and Yellows: They all look alike to me. *Psychology Today, 8*, 105–108.

MacDonald, G. (2002, October 5). The power of Q: A one-letter measurement of the intangible can make or break your career in hollywood. *The Globe and Mail*, Metro Section, p. R17.

Marshall, J. (2003). Bryant fighting for family, image after sexual assault charge. Retrieved July 19, 2003, from Yahoo! Sports, http://sports.yahoo.com/nba/news?slug=ap-lakers-bryantcharged&prov

Mathur, L. K., Mathur, I., & Rangan, N. (1997, May/Jun). The wealth effects associated with a celebrity endorser: The Michael Jordan phenomenon. *Journal of Advertising Research, 37*, 67–73.

McCracken, G. (1988). *Culture and consumption: New approaches to the symbolic character of consumer goods and activities*. Bloomington: Indiana University Press.

McNicol, D. (1972). *A primer of signal detection theory*. London: Allen & Unwin.

Miciak, A. R., & Shanklin, W. L. (1994, Winter). Choosing celebrity endorsers. *Marketing Management, 3*(3), 50–59.

O'Mahony, S., & Meenaghan, T. (1997/1998). The impact of celebrity endorsements on consumers. *Irish Marketing Review, 10*(2), 15–24.

Pashupati, K., Raman, P., & Kuhlmeier, D. (2003). "Do I know that face?" The impact of celebrity identification on attitude toward the ad and brand. In Les Carlson (Ed.), *Proceedings of the 2003 Annual Conference of the American Academy of Advertising.*

Platz, S. J., & Hosch, H. M. (1988). Cross-racial/ethnic identification: A field study. *Journal of Applied Social Psychology, 18*, 972–984.

Race Relations Reporter (2002, December 25). Residential racial segregation persists in New Jersey. E-mail weekly bulletin available from RRR@jbhe.com; retrieved from http://www.jbhe.com/rrr/rrr.html

Race Relations Reporter (2003a, January 25). Racial segregation in schools on the rise. E-mail weekly bulletin available from RRR@jbhe.com; retrieved from http://www.jbhe.com/rrr/rrr.html

Race Relations Reporter (2003b, July 2). Black and White television. E-mail weekly bulletin available from RRR@jbhe.com; retrieved from http://www.jbhe.com/rrr/rrr.html

Scott, T. L. (2003, June 24). Report suggests viewers' choices reflect color line. *The Washington Post*, p. B5.

Stern, G., & Gaiter, D. J. (1994, April 22). Mixed signals: Frustration, not anger, guides race relations on a college campus. *Wall Street Journal*, p. A1.

Survey measures Blacks' media, product, ad preferences, (1981, August 21). *Marketing News*, p. 6.

Till, B. (1998). Using celebrity endorsers effectively: Lessons from associative learning. *The Journal of Product and Brand Management, 7*, 400–409.

Till, B. D., & Busler, M. (2000, Fall). The match-up hypothesis: physical attractiveness, expertise, and the role of fit on brand attitude, purchase intent and brand beliefs. *Journal of Advertising, 29*(3), 1–13.

Tom, G., Clark, R., Elmer, L., Grech, E., Masetti, J., Jr., & Sandhar, H. (1992, Fall). The use of created versus celebrity spokespersons in advertisements. *The Journal of Consumer Marketing, 9*, 45–51.

Williams, J. D., & Qualls, W. J. (1989, Winter). Middle-class Black consumers and intensity of ethnic identification. *Psychology and Marketing, 6,* 263–86.

ENDNOTES

1. It should be noted that the Winter Poll is actually conducted in the late summer to early fall while baseball and football are dominant in the minds of consumers. Thus, there were no NBA players (e.g., Michael Jordan or Kobe Bryant) in the top 10 sports personality Q-score listing.
2. In essence, White faces become the "other" for the Chinese Singaporeans.

VI. BROADENING THE CONCEPT OF DIVERSITY: GOING BEYOND BLACK AND WHITE

CHAPTER SEVENTEEN

Diversity: Population Versus Market

Geraldine Fennell
Consultant

Joel Saegert
The University of Texas at San Antonio

In this chapter, we take a marketing perspective on the topic of advertising in the context of population diversity. In an interdisciplinary context such as we have in this volume, it is useful to reflect on the nature of the *characteristic* contribution from each discipline. What is a reader to assume upon learning that the topic, advertising and population diversity, is to be considered from a marketing perspective? What is the nature of the uniquely *marketing* contribution to the topic of diversity? Addressing that question, we consider how diversity arises in the context of the tasks that are marketing's responsibility. In the first of two major sections in this chapter, we outline essential components of a marketing analysis, that is, the marketer's tasks of strategic development and communication. In the second, we consider such tasks in the context of population diversity. Moreover, in that second section, we make a distinction between population diversity viewed from the perspectives of a marketing analysis (i.e., in light of return on investment) and of social justice. First, however, in the immediately following section, we comment on the nature of diversity itself to clarify the counterpoint between population diversity and market diversity, which is central to the chapter.

DIVERSITY IS DIVERSE

"Diversity" usually evokes characteristics of the general population as, for example, in the words, "the U.S. population becomes more and more diverse" in the Call for

Papers for the present volume. At issue may be the recent perception of increasing numbers and prominence of individuals from non-Caucasian backgrounds and of enhanced readiness, compared with earlier times, of individuals to seek recognition for respects in which they view themselves as different from others. Such "population diversity" is typically at issue in the context of social policy, justice, law, and public relations. However, diversity itself is diverse. Population diversity is usually based on difference as regards one or more relatively enduring characteristics of the person such as age, gender, national origin, race, religious affiliation, or sexual orientation.

In contrast, since the 1950s the diversity that has been central in a marketing context is diversity within product markets, that is, the heterogeneity that underlies market segmentation. That diversity is based, first, on differences in the activities in which people engage: Only people who engage in an activity that corresponds to the focal product category, that is, the focal activity, are included in the market that management addresses. Second, within the market as defined, market segmentation research describes further diversity as found in the context for engaging in the focal activity. It is in conjunction with individual instances of engaging in an activity, such as preparing breakfast, personal grooming, and managing personal finances, that people consider using a good/service, such as a brand of cereal, shampoo, or bank. Using everyday language, people are content to allow a single term, that is, the activity name, such as "preparing breakfast," to embrace the diverse nature of those individual instances in which people engage in preparing breakfast—or any activity. However, such heterogeneity in contexts within activity, interindividually and intraindividually, is the source of the diversity in product markets that is widely recognized under the heading of market segmentation. In contrast to the basis for population diversity, in other words, enduring attributes of the person, an instance of activity arises at a point in time and space, and its form is influenced by enduring and transitory features of intersecting personal and environmental systems (Fennell, 1991, 1997). Accordingly, market diversity and population diversity are distinct phenomena whose counterpoint we explore in this chapter (see Table 17.1).

MARKETING ANALYSIS

Essentially, a marketing analysis is about management's first defining the market in which it plans to compete and going on to identify the nature of diversity *within* that market (Fennell, 1982, 2000, 2001; Fennell & Saegert, 1996). Such analysis is the basis for formulating a strategy for competing in the market to secure a satisfactory return on investment. To provide a realistic background for discussing advertising in a context of diversity, we consider the nature of two important marketing tasks, namely, developing an offering and communicating the offering's existence to its targets.

TABLE 17.1
Two Kinds of Diversity

Population	Market
Diversity as regards relatively enduring characteristics of the person that applies over time and across activities (e.g., age, ethnicity, gender, income, or occupation).	Diversity within the behavioral universe in kind of activity engaged in—relevant for selecting market membership, and the strategic task of market definition.
	Diversity in context within activity—relevant for identifying kinds of demand as found in a market and the strategic tasks of market segmentation analysis and brand positioning.

Strategic Development—What to Offer to Whom

Deciding what to offer is one of the basic tasks that management faces in any venture. The phrase "what to offer" is not sufficiently specific. What management is deciding is *what to offer to whom*: Not everyone in a population is a prospect for any product, and not all prospects want the same thing(s) from a product. "What to offer to whom" in turn implicates two further questions: What/whom to study, that is, which task/interest and the individuals who engage in such activity are relevant to study; What/whom to target with what, that is, which demand-creating conditions within activity, and the individuals who experience them to select as targets, and what kind of good/service management should offer to them (Fennell, 1985).

Identifying Prospects—Whom/What to Study. Developing an offering is about making choices in two universes—the producer's universe and the prospect's universe (Fennell, 1988, 2001). Looking to obtain a satisfactory return from investing resources, the producer chooses the point of entry into these universes. Usually, the producer has in mind a domain of production (e.g., breakfast cereal, shampoo, or banking services) and may eventually formulate a concrete offering that is appropriate to a subset of demand in that domain. Choosing a productive domain for the venture (producer's universe), the producer ineluctably chooses a region of everyday behavior (prospect's universe) corresponding to that productive domain. More specifically, the behavior that corresponds to an individual product category is an activity such as preparing breakfast, washing hair, or managing one's money, that is convenient to refer to as the *focal activity*. Identifying the focal activity,[1] the producer selects as prospects those people in the population who engage in that activity. Reflecting on the initial steps of marketing analysis, then, provides a first view of the kind of diversity that is at issue in marketing, that is, diversity within the behavioral universe: People in a population are distinguished on the basis of the kind of activity that they engage in, namely, the tasks and interests that

TABLE 17.2
Marketing Diversity: Two Steps Within each of Two Universes

Two-Step Diversity	Prospect	Producer
Step 1	Focal activity (e.g., people who prepare breakfast)	Focal Product Category (e.g., breakfast cereal)
Step 2	Concerns/ Interests within Activity	Responsive Brand Attributes/ Benefits

they pursue.[2] For any venture, a first cut through a naturally-occurring population rejects people who do not engage in the focal activity and selects as prospects those who do.[3] Note that there is only a weak-to-moderate association between engaging in particular activities and the usual descriptors referenced by the concept of population diversity (Fennell, Allenby, Yang, & Edwards, 2003). For example, although the incidence of wearing dentures increases with age, it is by no means coextensive with any one age class, such as pensioners. Similarly, although managing tightly curled hair is common among Blacks, it is not confined to that demographic group; although incidence of doing the family laundry is more prevalent among women than men, it is not absent among men; moreover, the incidence of brushing one's teeth shows little association with any of the widely discussed bases for population diversity.[4]

Accordingly, the kind of diversity that is relevant at this first step of marketing analysis is at most moderately associated with the main bases for population diversity. Moreover, once management's first selection from a naturally-occurring population has been made, that is, the step of identifying prospects as individuals who engage in the focal activity,[5] management excludes nonprospects from further consideration and proceeds to study diversity *within* the prospect group as defined; this is the two-step feature of market diversity (see Table 17.2).

Marketing Concept as Rationale. Recent reviews (Fennell & Saegert, 1998, 2003; Fennell, Saegert, & Hoover, 1999, 2002) of their definitions of market, target market, and their treatment of screening and qualifying respondents show that authors of textbooks in principles of marketing[6] and in marketing research,[7] respectively, neglect to discuss systematically identifying prospects as a first step of marketing analysis, and the corresponding operation of using a focal activity to qualify respondents for inclusion in research for strategic development. Moreover, they typically omit any treatment of the strategic task of defining one's market, that is, management's specifying its choice of option for each of the dimensions of a universe relevant to its venture (Fennell & Allenby, 2003). It is, then, appropriate to discuss here management's rationale for restricting its universe to individuals who can be qualified as prospects. With the arrival of the marketing concept in the early 1950s (see, e.g., the annual report of the General Electric Company,[8]) building on action tendencies already in place was articulated as a guiding principle of marketing activity. Embodied in the marketing concept, that is, "respond to wants as found; make what the customer wants to buy," is the notion that management searches for tendencies favorable to the general domain of its venture and, within a universe of favorable action tendencies, investigates how it can put its resources to best use.

Accordingly, for a venture in the domain of cleansing dentures, management defines a universe of individuals who give evidence of being likely to spend resources on denture cleansers. For strategic development, it excludes individuals who are not denture wearers. Although it is undoubtedly true that some individuals, currently nonwearers of dentures, will wear dentures in the future, the principle of putting resources to best use suggests that management give priority to studying the conditions that affect today's denture wearers and denture wearers' views of offerings available to them today. Management's offering, if it develops one or decides to continue supporting an existing offering, is going to have to compete for share of mind and perceived suitability among individuals who qualify as prospective denture-cleanser users currently. Moreover, a further pragmatic consideration argues in favor of management's including only prospects in its research for strategic development: Nonprospects are unable to provide management with information necessary for brand development. As, by definition, they do not engage in the focal activity, nonprospects are not in a position to provide details of the conditions that prompt them to use their resources in this manner. In line with the marketing concept, management wants to imbue its brand with attributes that are responsive to (some of) the conditions that prompt individuals to engage in the focal activity (e.g., Fennell, 1978, 1997). For example, if a prospect for denture cleanser is concerned about removing particular stains from dentures, management wants to know the kinds of stain that she or he finds troubling. Plainly, a nonwearer of dentures will be unable to provide such information. With no concerns or interests that prompt engaging in the activity of cleansing dentures, she or he is not in a position to provide information that could guide management in selecting among its options for brand formulation.

Selecting Targets—Whom/What to Target With What.   The preceding discussion has moved into the second stage of management's deciding what to offer to whom. Once management has decided on the criterion for qualifying individuals as prospects,[9] it has done no more than set an outer limit to the behavioral universe that it considers relevant for the focal venture. Knowing only that an individual engages in the focal activity (e.g., wears dentures), management has no guidance on the conditions that determine the attributes that prospects value in a denture cleanser; it knows nothing that is useful for responding to wants as found. That is true because of heterogeneity *within* activity domain. There is no such thing as "denture cleanser" in any concrete sense; rather the term is an abstraction of all versions of denture cleanser that have been or can be created. The producer must

TABLE 17.3
Strategic Tasks for Each Step of Market Diversity

Strategic Task	Universe	
	Prospect	Producer
Select one from all domains of activity and production	Focal activity (e.g., preparing breakfast, washing hair, or managing one's money)	Focal product category (e.g., cereal, shampoo, or banking services)
Describe kinds of demand within activity and select subset from all kinds (e.g., general classes of DCC):	Concerns/ Interests within Activity (e.g., in context for preparing breakfast):	Responsive brand attributes/ benefits (e.g., for cereal):
Current problem	Feel hungry midmorning	Keeps hunger at bay till lunch time
Potential problem	Concern for image as wise eater	Shows you're a wise eater
Stable state maintenance	Never give breakfast a thought	Breakfast ready when you are
Interest opportunity	Food science is my hobby	Scientifically selected ingredients
Sensory pleasure opportunity	Enjoy taste/texture sensations	Superb taste/texture
Product-related problem	Concerned not to gain weight	Low calorie
Frustration	Can find nothing suitable	Cereal you've been waiting for

decide whether or not to include ingredients for blueberry stains, mouth-odor control, or gum-infection control, or to omit ingredients that may irritate sensitive gums, and so on. To generate such options for brand development, management must explore the varied contexts in which people use denture cleanser. (See Table 17.3 and, for further examples of diverse concerns/interests, within other domains of activity, see the Appendix to Fennell & Saegert, 2002.)

Expanding on the information shown in summary form in Table 17.3, in this second step, management is bent on investigating a number of issues: (a) prospects' varied concerns and interests, i.e., demand-creating conditions (DCCs) arising in the context in which they engage in the focal activity and forming the segments of demand as found in the market; (b) the extent to which prospects view available brands as responsive to their particular DCC; and (c) the likelihood that management, given its own strengths and weaknesses, can obtain a satisfactory return from investing, or continuing to invest, in an offering to compete in this market.

On analyzing such information, management may have identified one or more candidate positionings for a brand, that is, one or more DCC (prospect's universe) where it believes it is able to offer a superior response compared with those currently available (producer's universe). It positions its brand to be responsive to such

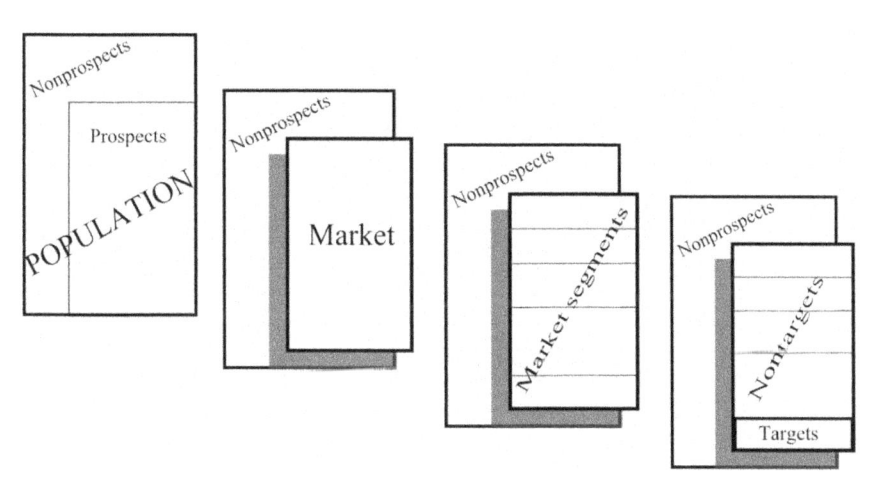

FIG. 17.1. Market diversity: demand segments within prospects.

conditions. Management's targets are the prospects who experience the targeted DCC (see Fig. 17.1).

It should be noted that the usual finding in market segmentation studies conducted in industry is independence between (a) segments as found within product markets and (b) the main bases for population diversity. In other words, the concerns/interests that prompt a prospect to engage in the focal activity are not found exclusively within any demographic group or any class defined in terms of relatively enduring personal descriptors (see Fig. 17.2).

Communicating with Targets

We move on, then, to the second major marketing task, which is letting targets know of the availability of a brand whose attributes are responsive to their concerns/interests—specifically to the concerns/interests that form the context in which they engage in the focal activity[10].

It is relevant to recap what we have said herein about the relationship between the attributes that characterize market segments on the one hand and, on the other, population segments. Recall that market segments are found within a universe of individuals selected because they engage in an activity that qualifies them as prospects. Such market segments are not associated with population segments. Given that the media vehicles that management may use to announce a brand's availability often describe their audiences in terms of demographic characteristics, how does management use such vehicles to reach the targets for their brand (i.e., those prospects who experience the conditions for which the brand has been formulated)?

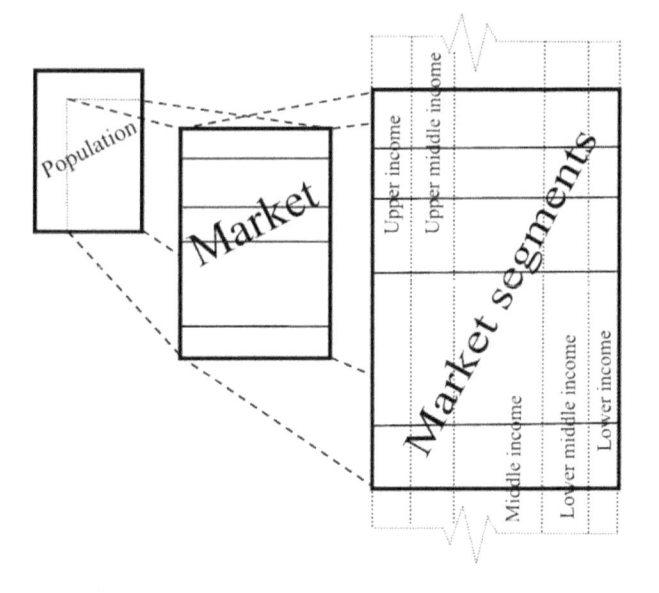

FIG. 17.2. Market segments and population segments (e.g., income).

Reaching Prospects.   Just as in the case of strategic development, the approach here also is two step. The first step is reaching prospects (i.e., the market) and the second is reaching targets. Management selects media vehicles whose audiences contain prospects to a disproportionate degree. Data provided by the media vehicles *may* include information regarding the incidence in their audience of individuals who engage in the focal activity, such as, cat owners or carers. If so, management is able to select a media vehicle based directly on the vehicle's audience containing a disproportionate number of prospects compared with other vehicles. More likely, management must rely on matching the characteristics of prospects with those of media-vehicle audiences. Either directly or indirectly, media vehicles are chosen to provide exposure to prospects for the product category, that is, to individuals who give grounds for believing that they are ready to spend resources to buy/use some brand in the focal product category.

Reaching Targets.   There remains, then, the task of locating targets in the audience of the media vehicle. Facing an audience consisting of prospects and non-prospects and, within prospects, targets and nontargets, how can management ensure that targets (i.e., the prospects for whose conditions a brand was developed) process the brand's message ? Note that, at best, placing an ad in a media vehicle does no more than expose the ad in the environment of a target. Whether or not the target processes the ad depends on the target's selecting the ad in preference to the target's own thoughts or other stimuli present. What can management do to engage the target's attention? Because the message (e.g., the brand's claims) and the underlying brand formulation have been tailored to the targeted conditions, management may rely on elements of the brand's message to elicit an affective response in individuals who experience such conditions, thus compelling their attention. To engage the attention of targets, as distinct from people in general, management has the custom-tailored approach of portraying the targeted conditions (e.g., one or more concerns/interests) or the successful outcome of using the brand in such conditions. Fennell (1979) discussed the implications of various approaches to engaging targets' attention (e.g., presenting the condition that prompts the individual to engage in the focal activity, or presenting the outcome of using the brand in the context of that condition).

As noted earlier, the usual finding of industry market segmentation analysis is independence between segments as found within product markets and the main bases for population diversity. In other words, the specific concerns/interests that prompt an individual to engage in the focal activity are not found exclusively within any demographic group or any class defined in terms of relatively enduring personal descriptors, such as age, ethnicity, or gender. Accordingly, there is no reason to expect that the characteristics of *population segments*, specifically, of any of the main bases for discussing diversity within populations, arise as part of the usual logic of a marketing analysis. For example, if management finds itself selecting a media vehicle that delivers seniors or Blacks disproportionately, it is not because management is interested in senior citizens or Blacks as such but only because analysis has shown that incidence of engaging in the focal activity is somewhat elevated among such demographic categories. As noted, if the media vehicles routinely showed incidence of the activities that correspond to each of the main product categories, management would select media vehicles directly on that basis, rather than via the indirect route of matching demographic characteristics. That media vehicles typically do not show such information is readily explained by considering the expense of showing such a level of detail for audiences of individual vehicles.

On logical grounds, it does not make sense for management to define its prospects, let alone its targets, in terms of membership of population segments. Consider the implications when the management of a venture in cat food defines its prospects as members of a population segment such as seniors or Blacks rather than as individuals who engage in the focal activity, in this case owning or caring for cats. Clearly, a population-segment definition of prospects for cat food implies that all cat owners or carers are senior citizens, or are Black, and that no cat owners or carers are to be found in other population segments, both of which supposed empirical relationships are unrealistic. It would be similarly self-defeating to suggest that seniors or Blacks are targets for a brand of cat food that management would develop. The implication would be that all members of such a population segment (Blacks or seniors) experience identical conditions (concerns or interests) for engaging in the focal activity (i.e., caring for a cat). Aside from having no empirical support, such a notion when subjected to critical reflection is obviously untenable. There is no logical ground for suggesting that Blacks, for example, experience identical conditions, that is, concerns/interests, that would lead them to own or care for a cat. In a similar manner, there is no logical ground for suggesting that seniors or members of other population segments experience identical conditions relevant to owning or caring for a cat. Such a groundless idea risks a charge of stereotyping, whereby all members of such a population segment are viewed as fully described by the class label (here, seniors or Blacks)—in effect, as being clones of each other. Consider how ridiculous it is to suggest that there is a "Black" cat food, or washing machine, tailored to the some specifically "Black" wants. It is as ridiculous as suggesting that there is a "White" cat food or washing machine. There is no reason to suppose that wants within a product market (e.g., cat food or laundry machines) among Blacks are any less heterogeneous than those among Whites. As noted, findings of industry market segmentation research show that, empirically, concerns/interests within an activity are independent of demographic classification.

POPULATION DIVERSITY AND RETURN ON INVESTMENT

Before affirmatively considering the possible relevance for marketing of population diversity, it is important to be clear that, as noted, the logic of a marketing analysis does not have a systematic place for population segments as such. We consider three instances in which management may be required to think in terms of population segments: first, using special-interest rather than general media; second, employing ethnically diverse actors or settings in ads; and third, using language other than English in marketing communications. Note that these three examples arise in connection with the second of the two main marketing tasks that we discussed, that is, marketing communications rather than strategic development. In the following discussion, we assume that strategic development has proceeded as already described. That is, segments within a product market are identified on the basis of the varied conditions that prompt prospects to engage in the focal activity.[11] They are formed from a subset of such heterogeneous conditions, which also specifies the attributes that a brand must have if it is to be responsive to demand as found in the segment. As noted, there is no reason why such segments should be coterminous with, or exclusive to, any population segment[12]; moreover, the empirical relationship is typically one of independence. Accordingly, at issue in the present section are options that management may have to consider as regards communicating a brand's message that has been developed from systematic marketing analysis and research.

Special-Interest Media

For the present purposes, let us distinguish two kinds of special-interest media— vehicles that are designed for (a) devotees of some hobby, sport, or leisure pursuit (i.e., based on activity), and (b) individuals who possess some relatively enduring attribute, including membership in a demographic group defined on the basis of ethnicity, gender orientation, national origin, race, or religion (i.e., based on personal characteristics). We shall have little to say about activity-based special-interest media here, because they are congruent with a systematic marketing analysis as already described. Most likely, the activity domain to which a special-interest media vehicle is dedicated (e.g., sports, or a gardening magazine) comprises the focal activities of a variety of ventures, in which case it offers a direct means of exposing advertising messages in the environment of prospects for those ventures. It is then a matter for the management of such ventures to examine the relative cost of reaching their prospects by means of the special-interest media compared with the general media. A possible drawback of using special-interest media rather than general media is reaching only those prospects who expose themselves to the special-interest media vehicle by buying a subscription (print) or patronizing a broadcast vehicle (radio or TV program). Aside from that drawback, if there is a premium to be paid for locating prospects by means of a special-interest vehicle compared with a general one, then management is in need of guidance as to whether proportionate advantage accrues vis-à-vis competitors who are not using the special-interest vehicle. In contrast, in the event management does not aim to locate prospects by means of such a special-interest vehicle, does it risk putting its brand at a disproportionate disadvantage vis-à-vis competitors who use such a vehicle?

What then about special-interest media of the second kind, that is, those that aim to appeal to individuals who possess a certain personal characteristic, in particular one of the characteristics in the group associated with population diversity as an issue of social concern? As noted, the within-market diversity that a marketing analysis is concerned with is not typically associated with the personal characteristics of population diversity. Such special-interest media, then, are not likely to surface in the normal course of a marketing analysis.

Largely because of the initiative of sales representatives employed by the special-interest media, management is frequently required to decide whether or not to assign some of its advertising budget to buying time or space in such print or broadcast media. Management's response can be considered under three headings: First, does the expenditure make sense, given the usual marketing criteria (e.g., does the vehicle afford a means of efficiently reaching prospects—individuals who engage in the focal activity) ? Second, is the expenditure likely to result in a gain, vis-à-vis competition, among targets who are members of the population segment? The media vehicle's sales representative may present research that claims relevance under the second heading. The relevance and specificity of the questions asked in such research, which are the basis of the findings as presented, should be examined closely. In effect, what is being considered here is, given target indifference between our brand and a competitor's brand, will the sale go to us because we, but not our competitor, advertise in a vehicle that claims special interest for a population segment of which the target is a member? Third, if the decision under the first two headings looks unfavorable to the expenditure, management may consider a further issue: Among targets who are members of the population segment, is our brand likely to lose vis-à-vis competition if we do not make a placement? In effect, what is being considered here is, given target indifference between our offering and a competitor's offering, will we lose the sale because the competitor advertises in a medium that claims special interest for a population segment of which the target is a member?[13]

Ethnically Diverse Actors/Settings

In the strategic development phase, when management chooses a positioning for its brand, it selects from all DCCs[14] a subset for which the brand will be formulated. In this way, prospects who experience such DCCs become the brand's targets. It is now the job of marketing communications to create advertising that implements the brand's strategy. That often means portraying the targeted conditions and the brand's role in helping targets achieve a desired outcome given the DCC. To do so requires management to select actors and settings. It would seem to be an obvious extension of the chosen strategy that the actors or settings should reflect the demographic diversity of the prospects who experience the targeted conditions.[15] If this is not possible within a single ad, then it can be implemented over the set of ads developed for the entire campaign. Simple arithmetic may, however, impose a limit on how far such a strategy can be taken. The number of separate executions that management considers efficient to allocate to a campaign may not be enough to accommodate targets from population segments whose contribution to brand volume is relatively low.

Language or Accent Other Than Mainstream

Considerations similar to those just described for actors or settings should, perhaps, apply to decisions as regards language or accent. However, the pragmatic advantage of acquiring familiarity with a common language or standard accent may lessen the pressure on management to tailor language or accent to those of targets who are also members of nonmainstream population segments. Once again, this is a topic in need of research.

POPULATION DIVERSITY AND SOCIAL JUSTICE

Up to this point, we have focused on strictly marketing considerations. We have considered implications for return on investment of going beyond the logic of a marketing analysis to take specific account of characteristics of population segments in marketing communications. There is another ground on which management may want to take cognizance of characteristics of population segments, namely, considerations of social justice. Aside from drawing attention to such a further perspective, we regard more detailed treatment to be beyond the scope of this chapter. Managerial action based purely on considerations of social justice is outside the scope of a marketing analysis. As regards budgetary allocation, it is more appropriately treated under headings such as community relations, public relations, or social audit.

REPRISE AND CONCLUSIONS

We have drawn a distinction between population diversity, which is based on the presence of a relatively enduring personal characteristic, and market diversity, which is a two-step diversity that first distinguishes prospects (individuals who engage in an activity that corresponds to the product category in focus for a venture) from nonprospects (individuals who do not engage in such activity, i.e., the remainder of the population) and goes on then to describe diversity among prospects (see Tables 17.2 and 17.3, and Fig. 17.1). Such within-activity diversity reflects the varied concerns/interests that lead individuals to engage in a particular focal activity, from which arises the widely recognized fact that demand in product markets is segmented as found. We noted that there is no congruence in logic, or, empirically, between the bases for population diversity and market diversity.

Marketing analysis explores the nature of such market diversity as it is relevant to individual ventures. It guides management bent on putting its resources to best use while choosing a strategic response that takes account of its strengths and weaknesses in a competitive environment. We have followed through the broad outline of a marketing analysis and shown that population segments are not implicated as such at any stage. We then considered instances in which management may be required to consider taking cognizance of population diversity. Prospects and targets for the marketer's brand, defined as a marketing analysis requires, will doubtless include individuals with characteristics that contribute to population diversity. Communicating the availability of its offering to its targets, the actors and settings that management chooses will reflect the population diversity that is found among its targets. As to choosing media vehicles that appeal to population segments, rather than to the population generally, marketing considerations point to assessing such vehicles for their cost worthiness—efficiency and effectiveness—in delivering prospects and targets. Beyond that, a number of other issues require clarification through research. Among members of the relevant population segment, does presence in media dedicated to a particular population segment bring advantage at breakeven cost or above to an advertiser vis-à-vis absent competitors. Does absence in media dedicated to a particular population segment bring disproportionate loss to an absent advertiser vis-à-vis competitors who maintain presence? Similarly in need of clarification through research is whether or not any dividend or liability is incurred by using or not using language, dialect, or accent associated with population segments.

We further clarified that our objective was to carry through an analysis of the counterpoint between population diversity and market diversity from a strictly marketing perspective, such as market share and return on investment. The topics we have considered here may appear in a different light when they are viewed from the perspective of social policy, justice, law, or public relations. Only benefit can accrue from keeping separate distinct bases for assessing such issues, and we leave comment from other perspectives for other occasions.

REFERENCES

Aaker, D. A., Kumar, V., & Day, G. S. (1998). *Marketing research* (6th ed.). New York: Wiley.

Assael, H. (1990). *Marketing: Principles and strategy.* Chicago: The Dryden Press.

Bearden, W. O., Ingram, T. N., & LaForge, R. (1995). *Marketing: Principles and perspectives.* Chicago: Irwin.

Berkowitz, E. N., Kerin, R. A., Hartley, S. W., & Rudelius, W. (1997). *Marketing* (5th ed.) Chicago: Irwin.

Boone, L. E., & Kurz, D. L. (1995). *Contemporary marketing* (8th ed.). Fort Worth, TX: The Dryden Press.

Bovée, C. L., Houston, M. J., & Thill, J. V. (1995). *Marketing* (2nd ed.). New York: McGraw-Hill.

Boyd, H. W., Jr., Westfall, R., & Stasch, S. F. (1989). *Marketing research: Text and Cases* (7th ed.). Homewood, IL: Irwin.

Burns, A. C., & Bush, R. F. (1995). *Marketing research.* Englewood Cliffs, NJ: Prentice-Hall.

Chisnall, P. M. (1992). *Marketing research* (4th ed.). London: McGraw-Hill.

Churchill, G. A., Jr. (1999). *Marketing research: Methodological foundations* (7th ed.). Fort Worth, TX: The Dryden Press.

Churchill, G. A., Jr., & Peter, J. P. (1998). *Marketing: Creating value for customers* (2nd ed.). Burr Ridge, IL: Irwin.

Crask, M., Fox, R. J., & Stout, R. G. (1995). *Marketing research: Principles and applications.* Englewood Cliffs, NJ: Prentice-Hall.

Dillon, W. R., Madden, T. J., & Firtle, N. H. (1993). *Essentials of marketing research.* Homewood, IL: Irwin.

Etzel, M. J., Walker, B. J., & Stanton, W. J. (1997). *Marketing* (11th ed.). New York: McGraw-Hill.

Evans, J. R., & Berman, B. (1997). *Marketing* (7th ed.). Upper Saddle River, NJ: Prentice-Hall.

Fay, C. H., & Wallace, M. J., Jr. (1987). *Research-based decisions.* New York: Random House.

Fennell, G. (1978). Consumers' perceptions of the product-use situation. *Journal of Marketing, 42,* 38–47.

Fennell, G. (1979). Attention engagement. In J. H. Leigh & C. R. Martin, Jr. (Eds.), *Current issues & research in advertising.* (pp. 17–33). Ann Arbor: University of Michigan.

Fennell, G. (1982). Terms v. concepts: Market segmentation, brand positioning, and other aspects of the academic-practitioner gap. In R. Bush and S. Hunt (Eds.), *Marketing theory: Philosophy of science perspectives.* Chicago: American Marketing Association.

Fennell, G. (1985). Persuasion: Marketing as behavioral science in business and nonbusiness contexts. In R. Belk (Ed.), *Advances in Nonprofit Marketing* (pp. 95–160). Greenwich, CT: JAI.

Fennell, G. (1987). A radical agenda for marketing science: Represent the marketing concept! In F. Furat, N. Dholakia, & R. Baggozzi (Eds.), *Philosophical and radical thought in marketing* (pp. 289–306). Lexington, MA: Lexington.

Fennell, G. (1988). Reclaiming form utility for marketing: The human side of the person–technology interface. In S. Shapiro (Ed.), *Marketing: Return to the broader dimensions*. (pp. 380–386). Chicago: American Marketing Association.

Fennell, G. (1991). Context for action = context for brand use = source of valued brand attributes. In K. Haugtvedt (Ed.), *Proceedings of the Society for Consumer Psychology*. (pp. 73–79). Washington, DC: Society for Consumer Psychology (Division 23), American Psychological Association.

Fennell, G. (1995). Globalization and market segmentation: Back to basics. In S. B. MacKenzie and D. M. Stayman (Eds.), *Proceedings of the Society for Consumer Psychology*. (pp. 111–172). Washington, DC: Society for Consumer Psychology (Division 23) American Psychological Association.

Fennell, G. (1996). Representing the Skinner Box: An open letter to behavioral analysts. In P. Herr & J. Kim (Eds.), *Proceedings of the Society for Consumer Psychology* (pp. 120–128). Washington, DC: Society for Consumer Psychology (Division 23) American Psychological Association.

Fennell, G. (1997). Value and values: Relevance to advertising. In L. Kahle and L. Chiagouris (Eds.), *Values, lifestyles, and psychographics* (pp. 83–110). Mahwah, NJ: Lawrence Erlbaum Associates.

Fennell, G. (2000). Coherence in marketing terms. In J. J. Inman, K. Tepper & T. Whittler (Eds.), *Proceedings of the Society for Consumer Psychology* (pp. 137–146). Washington, DC: Society for Consumer Psychology (Division 23) American Psychological Association.

Fennell, G. (2001). Defining the venture-relevant universe: Behavioral implications of a neglected marketing task. In S. Heckler and S. Shapiro (Eds.), *Proceedings of the Society for Consumer Psychology* (pp. 175–181). Washington, DC: Society for Consumer Psychology (Division 23) American Psychological Association.

Fennell, G., & Allenby, G. M. (2003). Market definition: A strategic task. *Marketing Research*. forthcoming.

Fennell, G., Allenby, G. M., Yang, S., & Edwards, Y. (2002). The effectiveness of demographic and psychographic variables for explaining brand and product use. *Quantitative Marketing and Economics*. forthcoming.

Fennell, G., & Saegert, J. (1996). Globalization issues: The myth of prepackaged solutions. In I. McGovern (Ed.), *Marketing: A Southeast Asian perspective* (pp. 1–27). Singapore: Addison-Wesley.

Fennell, G., & Saegert, J. (1998). Implications of the marketing concept: What the textbooks fail to state. In K. Machleit and M. Campbell (Eds.), *Proceedings of the Society for Consumer Psychology* (pp. 65–74). Washington, DC: Society for Consumer Psychology (Division 23) American Psychological Association.

Fennell, G., & Saegert, J. (2002). Psychology and marketing: Scale construction implications of responding to user wants. In J. Edell and R. C. Goodstein (Eds.), *Proceedings of the Society for Consumer Psychology* (pp. 221–231). Washington, DC: Society for Consumer Psychology (Division 23) American Psychological Association.

Fennell, G., & Saegert, J. (2003). Identifying prospects and reaching targets: Neglected distinction within marketing. In I. Skurnik and S. A. Hawkins (Eds.), *Proceedings of the Society for Consumer Psychology*. Washington, DC: Society for Consumer Psychology (Division 23) American Psychological Association, forthcoming.

Fennell, G., Saegert, J. & Hoover, R. (1999). Target market in the textbooks: Oxymoron unexamined. In K. Fatemi and S. Nichols (Eds.), *Proceedings of the International Trade and Finance Association* (pp. 471–492). Calexico, CA: International Trade and Finance Association.

Fennell, G., Saegert, J., & Hoover, R. J. (2002). Marketing's universe: Implicit presence in marketing research texts. In K. R. Evans and L. K. Scheer (Eds.), *Proceedings of the American Marketing Association Winter Educator's Conference* (pp. 188–195). Chicago: American Marketing Association.

General Electric Company. (1952). *Annual Report*.

Green, P. E., Tull, D. S., & Albaum, G. (1988). *Research for marketing decisions* (5th ed.). Englewood Cliffs, NJ: Prentice-Hall.

Hawkins, D. I. & Tull, D. S. (1994). *Essentials of marketing research*. New York: Macmillan.

316 FENNELL AND SAEGERT

Husted, S. W., Varble, D. L., & Lowry, J. R. (1989). *Principles of modern marketing.* Boston: Allyn & Bacon.

Keegan, W. J., Moriarty, S. E., & Duncan, T. R. (1995). *Marketing* (2nd ed.). Englewood Cliffs, NJ: Prentice-Hall.

Kinnear, T. C., Bernhardt, K. L., & Krentler, K. A. (1995). *Principles of marketing* (4th ed.) New York: HarperCollins.

Kinnear, T. C., & Taylor, J. R. (1991). *Marketing research: an applied approach* (4th ed.). New York: McGraw-Hill.

Kotler, P., & Armstrong, G. (1997). *Marketing: An introduction* (4th ed.). Upper Saddle River, NJ: Prentice-Hall.

Kress, G. (1988). *Marketing research* (3rd ed.). Englewood Cliffs, NJ: Prentice Hall.

Lamb, C. W., Jr., Hair, J. F., & McDaniel, C. (1996). *Marketing* (3rd ed.). Cincinnati, OH: South-Western College Publishing.

Lehmann, D. R. (1989). *Market research and analysis* (3rd ed.). Homewood, IL: Irwin.

Luck, D. J., & Rubin, R. S. (1987). *Marketing research* (7th ed.). Englewood Cliffs, NJ: Prentice-Hall.

McDaniel, C., Jr., & Gates, R. (1995). *Marketing research essentials.* Minneapolis/St. Paul: West.

Malhotra, N. K. (1996). *Marketing research* (2nd ed.). Upper Saddle River, NJ: Prentice-Hall.

Nichels, W. G., & Wood, M. B. (1997). *Marketing: Relationships, quality, and value.* New York: Worth.

Parasuraman, A. (1991). *Marketing research* (2nd ed.). Reading, MA: Addison-Wesley.

Perreault, W. D., Jr., & McCarthy, E. J. (1996). *Basic marketing: A global-managerial approach* (12th ed.). Chicago: Irwin.

Peterson, R. A. (1988). *Marketing research* (2nd ed.). Plano, TX: Business Publications.

Pride, W. M., & Ferrell, O. C. (1997). *Marketing: Concepts and strategies* (10th ed.). Boston: Houghton Mifflin.

Semenik, R. J., & Bamossy, G. J. (1995). *Principles of marketing: A global perspective* (2nd ed.). Cincinnati, OH: South-Western College Publishing.

Solomon, M. R., & Stuart, E. (1997). *Marketing: Real people, real choices.* Upper Saddle River, NJ: Prentice-Hall.

Shao, A. T. (1999). *Marketing research: An Aid to Decision Making.* Cincinnati, OH: South-Western College Publishing.

Sudman, S., & Blair, E. (1998). *Marketing research: A problem-solving approach.* Boston: McGraw-Hill.

Tull, D. S., & Hawkins, D. I. (1990). *Marketing research: Measurement and method* (5th ed.). New York: Macmillan.

Weiers, R. M. (1988). *Marketing research* (2nd ed.). Englewood Cliffs, NJ: Prentice-Hall.

Zikmund, W. G. (1997). *Exploring marketing research* (6th ed.). Fort Worth, TX: The Dryden Press.

Zikmund, W. G., & D'Amico, M. (1996). *Marketing* (5th ed.). Minneapolis/St. Paul: West.

ENDNOTES

1. As noted elsewhere (Fennell, 1987), there is both a true relationship between a product and the corresponding region of the behavioral universe and an approximation thereto. In the case of baking soda, the approximation came closer to the true relationship when management included the absorbing of refrigerator smells along with baking as focal activities corresponding to the product category of baking soda. In practice, a producer uses an approximation as a means of identifying prospects.
2. Typically, qualifiers are stated in terms of (a) actual or planned product use or ownership (e.g., persons who use laundry detergent, use headache remedies, own a minivan, or own a calculator), or (b) activities or conditions that do or may involve the use of a marketplace offering (e.g., doing the laundry, having a headache, providing multiperson, short-distance transportation, or doing certain

kinds of mathematical calculation). Probably the most often used type of qualifier is self-reported use or planned use of the focal product category. Acknowledging such activities as using remedies for minor pain, flying for business reasons, having attended live theater in the past 3 years, and planning to apply to graduate school within the next 2 years may qualify a person for inclusion in marketing research for strategic development. In some well-researched product categories in which incidence of product use in the population is high (e.g., mouthwash), the definition may be stated in terms of frequency or heaviness of use (e.g., persons who use mouthwash daily). Other ways in which the prospect universe may be restricted include specifying an objective environment for use (e.g., laundry-detergent prospects residing in hard-water regions) or time of the year (e.g., persons planning to fly to a winter vacation resort or to attend live theater during the summer). This is discussed further in Fennell (1985, p. 106).

3. To avoid possible confusion, we clarify that focal activity refers to individual activities and not to the concept of lifestyle, which refers to style of engaging that comprises multiple activities.

4. Relevant data are in syndicated research services available within industry. Fennell, et al. (2003) used data for 52 product categories from Simmons', The Study of Media and Markets (SMM). This is a survey of the American population that measures media habits, product and brand purchase behavior and beliefs, opinions, and attitudes. Advertising agencies, publishers, advertisers, and media use such data when planning to purchase media vehicles.

5. See findings from a survey of marketing research suppliers concerning aspects of their recruiting practices for respondents in survey research that they conduct for their marketing clients (Fennell, Saegert & Hoover, 2002). With regard to screening for prospects, that is, obtaining evidence of existing interest in the domain of the focal venture, a majority of suppliers reported qualifying respondents for use of the product category, activity, or condition of interest in their qualitative (94% answering always or mostly) and quantitative (86% answering always or mostly) projects.

6. Assael (1990); Bearden, Ingram, and LaForge (1995); Berkowitz, Kerin, Hartley, and Rudelius (1997), Boone and Kurz (1995); Bovée, Houston, and Thill (1995); Churchill and Peter (1998); Etzel, Walker, and Stanton (1997); Evans and Berman (1997); Husted, Varble, and Lowry (1989); Keegan, Moriarty, and Duncan (1995); Kinnear, Bernhardt, and Krentler (1995); Kotler and Armstrong (1997); Lamb, Hair, and McDaniel (1996); Nichels and Wood (1997); Perreault and McCarthy (1996); Pride and Ferrell (1997); Semenik and Bamossy (1995); Solomon and Stuart (1997); Zikmund and D'Amico (1996).

7. Aaker, Kumar, and Day (1998); Boyd Westfall, and Stasch (1989); Burns and Bush (1995); Chisnall (1992); Churchill (1999); Crask, Fox, and Stout (1995); Dillon, Madden and Firtle (1993); Fay and Wallace (1987); Green, Tull, and Albaum (1988); Hawkins and Tull (1994); Kinnear and Taylor (1991); Kress (1988); Lehmann (1989); Luck and Rubin (1987); McDaniel and Gates (1995); Malhotra (1996); Parasuraman (1991); Peterson (1988); Shao (1999); Sudman and Blair (1998); Tull and Hawkins (1990); Weiers (1988); Zikmund (1997).

8. According to General Electric (1952), It (the marketing concept) introduces the marketer at the beginning rather than at the end of the production cycle and integrates marketing into each phase of the business. Thus, marketing, through its studies and research, will establish for the engineer, the design and manufacturing [person], what the customer wants in a given product, what price he [or she] is willing to pay, and where and when it will be wanted. Marketing will have authority in product planning, production scheduling, and inventory control, as well as sales, distribution, and servicing of the product. (p. 9)

9. See endnote 2.

10. Let us connect with the language of market segmentation analysis: What is at issue in our earlier discussion, that is, strategic development, is selecting a segment of demand for which management believes it can position a brand while obtaining a satisfactory return on its investment, given existing competition and its own strengths and weaknesses. Here, under the heading of communicating with targets, we are discussing letting members of the targeted segment of demand know of the availability of the brand that has been positioned for conditions that they experience.

11. How such conditions are to be conceptualized and operationalized is beyond the scope of this chapter, but is discussed elsewhere (e.g., Fennell, 1995, 1996, 1997). One example, in summary form, is included in Table 17.3.

12. The obvious exception is a population segment defined in terms of disability, if the disability is relevant to the focal activity. In such cases, the conditions of disabled individuals who qualify as prospects (i.e., on ground of engaging in the focal activity) will become evident in the normal course of conducting a market segmentation analysis. The problem in which low-incidence disability is neglected as a consequence of adopting a marketing perspective is widely recognized. It is incumbent on society to address such a side effect of enshrining a criterion of return on investment as the gatekeeper of the kinds of good/service that get produced. As noted, such considerations, which go beyond the scope of the present chapter, are properly discussed under the general heading of social justice.

13. The criterion we are suggesting here is advisedly more concrete when compared with the way special-interest media may pose the issue in their promotional material. Their research may claim or suggest that population-segment members who are readers or viewers of their vehicle react "more favorably" (variously operationalized) to ads that appear in special compared with general media. A marketing analysis is essentially concerned to focus management's attention on obtaining the best use of its scarce resources. Accordingly, our criterion is intended to bring to the fore the issue of obtaining a proportionate return for advertising funds allocated.

14. These are concerns/interests in the context for engaging in the focal activity.

15. As noted, it is not expected that targets will be found exclusively in any population segment.

CHAPTER EIGHTEEN

It Must Be the Cues: Racial Differences in Adolescents' Responses to Culturally Embedded Ads

Osei Appiah
Ohio State University

A major goal for product and social marketers is to reach youth with a message they trust and with which they can identify. Teenagers, particularly Black teenagers, may well be the most difficult audience to reach and persuade with product and public service ads, primarily because teens in general doubt messages from mainstream sources and Black teens are particularly skeptical (Fost, 1993).

The critical question, then, is this: How do we get adolescents, particularly Black adolescents, to pay more attention to product and public service ads? One answer may lie in the characters that advertisers choose to use in ads. The most effective way to reach Black adolescents may be through the use of Black characters in ads. The use of Black characters in ads may be an effective way to reach White youth as well.

In addition to the use of Black characters, ads may be made more effective by incorporating cultural cues. Cultural cues refer to the values, symbols, ethics, rituals, traditions, material objects, and services produced or valued by either Black or White members of society that stimulate when, where, and how they respond. Ads rich in cultural cues may be considered *culturally embedded*, which is conceptualized as the degree to which cultural cues are present in each ad. For example, Black character ads that are high in cultural embeddedness are filled with Black cultural cues. Black character ads that are low in cultural embeddedness contain few if any Black cultural cues outside the race of the character. Like ads that simply contain Black characters, culturally embedded ads may be an effective way to reach and persuade Black youth.

Historically, advertisers have been reluctant to use Blacks in advertisements out of fear that Black characters would offend White consumers and adversely affect sales of the advertised product and other products offered by the sponsoring company (Bush, Hair, & Solomon, 1979; Cagley & Cardozo, 1970; Guest, 1970; Qualls & Moore, 1990). Even today, companies are afraid to use Black models in mainstream advertising despite empirical research that has shown that the race of the model has little influence on White consumers (Bush et al., 1979; Pitts, Whalen, O'Keefe, & Murray, 1989; Schlinger & Plummer, 1972; Soley, 1983; Whittler, 1991). Some researchers have argued that using Black characters in ads is a waste of time and money (Wall, 1970) because advertising messages disseminated for White consumers would effectively capture Black consumers as well (Askey, 1995; Gadsden, 1985). This may explain why Blacks remain nearly invisible in national magazines ads (Appiah & Wagner, 2002; Green, 1991) and are infrequently used in television ads (Greenberg & Brand, 1994; Nixon, 1983). For example, in an examination of 962 advertisements in issues of *Cosmopolitan, Glamour,* and *Vogue* from 1986 to 1988, Jackson and Ervin (1991) found that only 2% contained Black women even though 15% of the subscribers to these magazines were Black women. Similarly, a content analysis of more than 2,100 advertisements from 10 prominent national magazines indicated that Blacks appeared in only 3% of those ads although they composed 11% of the readership (Rossman, 1994).

On those occasions when advertisers use Black models to endorse products, the models are primarily used in Black media (Kern-Foxworth, 1994). When Blacks appear in general market ads, they appear primarily for short time periods, in minor and background roles (Greenberg & Brand, 1994), in racially integrated groups, and in nonthreatening or subordinate positions (Wilkes & Valencia, 1989). What is more important is that few Black character ads are culturally embedded. Most Black character ads lack Black cultural cues (e.g., vernacular, dress, images, or symbols) and are often in cultural settings that are so "de-ethnicized" that they are difficult for Black youth to identify with (Fost, 1993). In fact, (Bristor, Lee, & Hunt, 1995) most cultural cues present in ads featuring Black models reflect White cultural values. These Black character ads are, in other words, low in Black cultural embeddedness. This method of advertising to Black audiences could be enhanced by taking into account a broader set of factors, such as marketing to Black audiences' cultural heritage (e.g., jazz, blues, gospel, foods, or history), and using ads that are high in Black cultural embeddedness.

Although there is little if any information on the effects of high culturally embedded ads, there is a solid body of advertising research on the effects of low culturally embedded ads. Previous character race studies have used Black character ads that contained few Black cultural cues. They were, in other words, low in Black cultural embeddedness, although they were not designated as such. Similarly, ads containing White characters have had few White cultural cues, making these ads low in White cultural embeddedness. The evidence from these studies is useful in understanding and highlighting how audiences respond to ads low in cultural embeddedness, and they provide insight into how audiences might react to ads high in cultural embeddedness. However, past advertising research seems to take for granted or completely ignore theoretical explanations of why either the audience or the ad character's race should make a difference in how viewers respond to media messages. For example, what theories provide a better understanding of the psychological mechanisms at work when adolescents are exposed to advertisements with Black and White characters within low or high culturally embedded environments? Identification theory and distinctiveness theory are particularly relevant in addressing this issue; the notion of source similarity provides the conceptual framework necessary to understand and apply these theories.

Source Similarity and Racial Differences in Ad Response

Some researchers argue that ads are most effective when the symbols, characters, and values depicted in the ads are drawn from the intended audience's cultural environment (McGuire, 1984; Pitts et al., 1989), which allows the audience to better identify with the message and the source of the message. Individuals who are more likely to identify with media characters (Huesman, Eron, Klein, Brice, & Fischer, 1983) and perceive themselves to be similar to media characters (Brock, 1965; Burnstein, Scotland, & Zander, 1961) are more influenced by media content in which those characters are portrayed. Studies have shown that high levels of similarity between the viewer of an ad and the characters featured in an ad increase the viewer's belief that he or she is the intended audience for the ad, which in turn leads to more positive attitudes about the ad and the product (Aaker, Brumbaugh, & Grier, 2000).

One significant cue of similarity between a viewer and the character in an ad is race. This may be especially true for racial minorities for whom race is more salient. The race of a model in an ad may be particularly instrumental in inducing racial minorities (e.g., Blacks) to infer similarity or dissimilarity (Whittler, 1989). There is evidence that Black audiences are more likely to identify with, and rate more favorably, ads featuring Black characters than ads featuring White characters (Choudhury & Schmid, 1974; Greenberg & Atkin, 1982; Whittler, 1989, 1991). In contrast, members of a racial majority (e.g., Whites) seem to be less mindful of a model's race and focus on similarities between themselves and the source that are less race specific (e.g., values, dress, lifestyle, or appearance), as evidenced by studies that show that White audiences respond just as favorably to ads with Black models as they do to ads with White models (Bush et al., 1979; Schlinger & Plummer, 1972; Whittler, 1991).

This discussion leads to the following conceptual hypotheses: First, neither the characters' race (i.e., Black or White) nor the ads' cultural embeddedness (i.e., high or low) will affect White viewers' psychological responses (i.e., perceived similarity

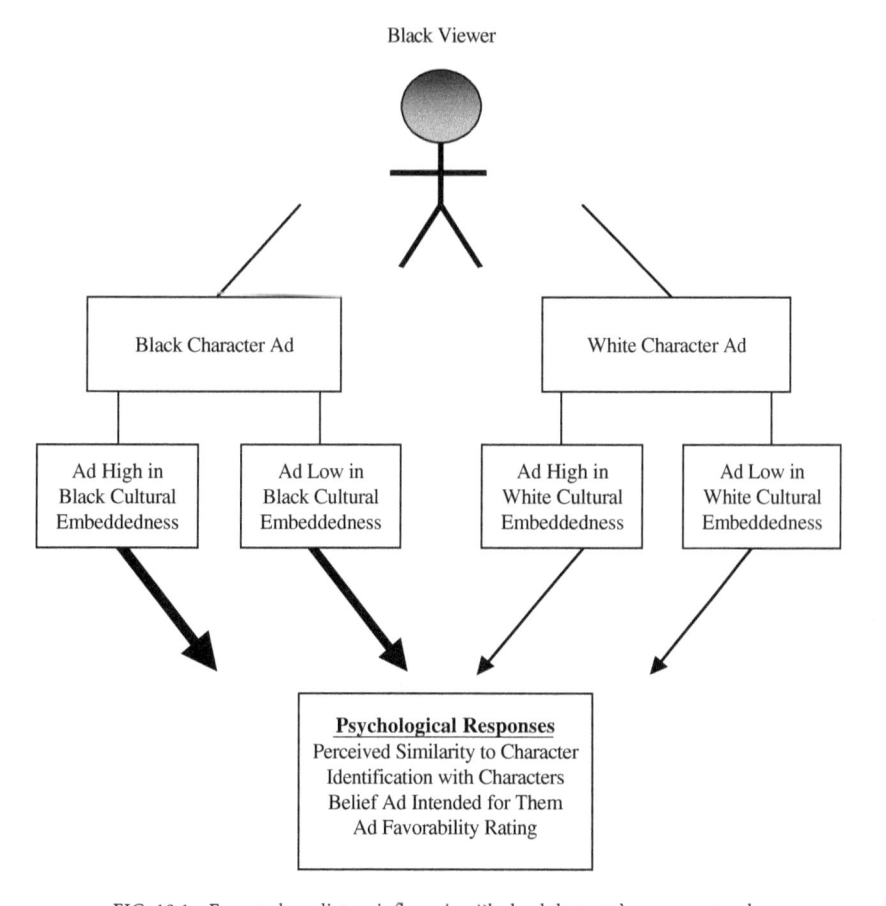

FIG. 18.1. Expected predictors influencing Black adolescents' responses to ads.

to characters, identification with characters, belief that ad is intended for them, and ad-favorability rating). Second, the characters' race and the cultural embeddedness of the ads will affect Black viewers' psychological responses to ads (see Fig. 18.1).

THEORETICAL FRAMEWORK

Identification Theory

Identification theory (Kelman, 1961) maintains that people automatically assess their level of similarity with a source during an interaction and make similarity judgments (Hovland & Weis, 1951; Kelman, 1961). This process drives individuals to choose a model based on perceived similarities between themselves and the model (Basow & Howe, 1980; Kelman, 1961). When viewers perceive that the source possesses characteristics such as race that are similar to their own, they begin to infer that the source will also share other characteristics, all of which lead to greater identification (Brock, 1965; Feick & Higie, 1992). Studies have shown that individuals who are more likely to identify with television characters are more affected by the media content in which those characters are engaged (Huesman et al., 1983).

Among Blacks who maintain strong racial identities, awareness of and preference for Black models is heightened. Racial and ethnic identity is a person's knowledge of membership in a social group and the value and emotional significance attached to that membership (Phinney, 1992). Ethnic and racial identity is an important component of the self-concept and can be particularly salient during adolescence (see Appiah, 2001; Phinney, 1992). This notion was supported by Whittler (1991), who found that Black college students who identified more strongly with Black culture also identified more strongly with Black models in advertising compared with Blacks who were low on cultural identification. Whittler's findings may explain why many Black youth who maintain strong racial identities may develop stronger preferences for Black models in ads.

Among White youth, strength of racial identity may play little if any role in how they respond to advertising. Phinney (1992) showed that minority group members consistently placed higher importance on their racial and ethnic identity than Whites. However, when "whites are the minority, they show traits like ethnic minorities in society" (p. 170). Because majority White viewers are less concerned and less conscious of race, the model's race in an ad does not seem to matter to Whites (Whittler, 1989). What may be more important to White audiences is their ability to understand, relate to, and perceive similarities with Black models in advertising in areas that are not just skin deep.

Viewers who do not identify with television models based on race (i.e., skin color) may identify with other characteristics that the model possesses. Identification often occurs when individuals infer that their tastes and preferences are similar to those of the source (Eagly, Wood, & Chaiken, 1978). For instance, White adolescents may not perceive themselves as racially similar to Black models but may infer that they have other characteristics in common with Black models, and thereby find Black models appealing. For White youth, the simple presence of Blacks in ads may invoke certain race-based stereotypes that characterize Blacks as cool, hip, musical, athletic, and fashionable; many of these traits are highly desirable among White youth. In addition, White youth are likely to identify with and imitate attitudes or behaviors of Black models simply because the models are in a particular social group (e.g., professional athlete, actor, or musician) to which they aspire (see reference group theory, Siegel & Siegel, 1957).

By and large, Black viewers also choose models in the media when they observe some commonalities with these models. For Black viewers, the most striking commonality is often a physical attribute such as skin color. The skin color or race of an actor is a salient communicator characteristic, especially for persons concerned with racial issues or for whom racial identity is central to their concept of self. For these individuals, a model's race could be a positive cue for racially similar viewers, thereby attracting more attention and promoting greater recall (see Appiah, 2002). This phenomenon is addressed by distinctiveness theory.

This leads to the next set of hypotheses. Black viewers will perceive themselves more similar to Black characters than White characters, and more similar to Black characters in high culturally embedded ads than Black characters in low culturally embedded ads. Black viewers will also identify more strongly with Black characters than with White characters, and they will identify more strongly with Black characters in high culturally embedded ads than with Black characters in low culturally embedded ads (see Fig. 18.1). For White viewers, neither the characters' race nor the cultural embeddedness of the ads will influence perceived similarity to characters or identification with characters.

Distinctiveness Theory

Distinctiveness theory maintains that a person's distinctive traits (e.g., being African American or red headed) will be more salient to him or her than more prevalent traits (e.g., being Caucasian or brunette) that are possessed by other people in the environment (McGuire, 1984; McGuire, McGuire, Child, & Fujioka, 1978). This is particularly true for people who belong to a racial group that is part of a numeric minority. Black people, for instance, would be highly aware and mindful of their race in personal and mediated situations as a result of being a numeric minority in the United States. In addition to relatively low numbers of Blacks in the United States, there are also relatively few Blacks in the media, causing Black audiences to be more sensitive to their presence in the media.

Studies using distinctiveness theory demonstrate that targeted media would be most effective in contexts in which the target market is a numeric minority (Aaker et al., 2000; Appiah, 2002; Grier & Deshpande, 2001). Blacks represent a numeric minority group and, compared with whites, have few media messages targeted specifically at them. Grier and Brumbaugh (1999) argued that, unlike Whites, Blacks as ethnic minorities appreciate the acknowledgment associated with being a target market and are more likely to use targeting cues based on their racial distinctive trait in attending and evaluating media than White majority members are to use targeting cues based on their nondistinctive trait. They also mentioned that, because of their increased awareness of the trait that makes them unique, Blacks are more likely to connect with targeted media and make links between the targeted media and themselves. Studies have shown that this leads Blacks to develop more favorable attitudes toward Black-targeted media and its content than toward White-targeted media and content (Aaker et al., 2000; Appiah, 2002).

It appears that racial and ethnic minorities spontaneously evoke their racial and ethnic identities in social and mediated environments where their group is minimally represented. In the United States, racial and ethnic identity or consciousness appears to be of particular importance to Black adolescents (see Appiah, 2001), but its significance for White adolescents is low and not likely to grow until Whites are no longer in the majority in specific settings (Phinney, 1992). These findings lend support to distinctiveness theory, which posits that ads targeting White or Black audiences will be more effective the more the racial group is in a numeric minority (Desphande & Stayman, 1994).

This discussion leads to the next set of hypotheses. Black adolescents—as members of a minority and distinctive group—should be more mindful that they are the intended audience of an ad when the ad features Black characters, particularly those Black characters in high culturally embedded ads, than when the ad features White characters (see Fig. 18.1). White adolescents—as a members of a majority and nondistinctive group—will show no difference in their belief that they are the intended audience for an ad based on the characters' race or the cultural embeddedness of the ad.

In additional, Black viewers will rate Black character ads more favorably than White character ads, and they will rate Black character ads high in black cultural embeddedness more favorably than Black character ads low in black cultural embeddedness (see Fig. 18.1). For Whites, neither characters' race nor cultural embeddedness will affect their ad ratings.

METHOD

Design

The experiment used a 2 (subjects' race: Black or White) × 2 (characters' race: Black or White) × 2 (cultural embeddedness: high or low) between-subjects design to test the hypotheses. The four dependent variables were (a) perceived similarity to characters; (b) identification with characters; (c) ads intended for them; and (d) ad favorability rating.

Subjects

One hundred and seventy-three high school students (ages = 14–19 years, Mdn = 17) participated in the experiment: 81 Black students and 92 White students. Of these students, 62% were male and 38% were female. Participants were drawn from five economically and socially diverse high schools—four in Southern California and one in Northern California.

Each high school principal, in cooperation with teachers, selected three to four classrooms with an average class size of 30 students. Principals at each school issued the students parental consent letters, which described the purpose of the study. Students without parental consent were not allowed to participate in the study.

Stimulus Materials

Stimuli consisted of full-color 8 ½ in. × 11 in. (~ 21.6 cm × 28 cm) photographic ads for three products: Cheerios Cereal, Irish Spring Soap, and Oscar Mayer Wieners. This study examined differences in adolescents' responses to ads filled with and dominated by cultural cues. Ads rich in cultural cues were considered culturally embedded, which is conceptualized as the degree to which cultural cues were contained in an ad. For different levels of cultural embeddedness to be achieved, three product ads that contained either Black or White characters were digitally manipulated to vary the race of the characters and the number of race-specific cultural cues present in each ad while all other visual features were held constant. For example, Black character ads low in Black cultural embeddedness contain few, if any, Black cultural cues outside the race of the character. These Black character ads low in Black cultural embeddedness were then digitally enhanced with the addition of several Black cultural cues such as Black family portraits, Black dolls, and African masks to create Black character ads high in Black cultural embeddedness.

Effort was made to use equivalent Black and White cultural cues in each culturally embedded version of the ad. For example, a picture of a White man hugging his newborn child was one of the White cultural cues added to the White-character Irish Spring ad that was low in White cultural embeddedness to make it high in White cultural embeddedness. Similarly, a picture of a Black man hugging his newborn child was added to the Black-character Irish Spring ad that was low in Black cultural embeddedness when it was transformed into an ad high in Black cultural embeddedness. With the use of this innovative technique, any differences in students' responses to ads with Black characters or ads with White characters must be attributed to the cultural cues present in the ads.

Four ad types were created for each of the three stimulus ads and placed in ½ in. (~1.25 cm) binders. Each binder contained only one of the four ad types. Each student was randomly assigned a binder with one of the four ad types for each product: first, Black-character ads low in Black cultural embeddedness (LBCE); second, Black-character ads high in Black cultural embeddedness (HBCE); third, White-character ads low in White cultural embeddedness (LWCE); and fourth, White-character ads high in White cultural embeddedness (HWCE).

Senior executives at the Burrell Communication Group in Chicago, the largest Black advertising firm in the country, reviewed the low and high culturally embedded ads featuring Black characters, and they confirmed that these ads contained cues specific to Black culture. Similarly, executives at Foote, Cone, and Belding in San Francisco, a leading general-market advertising firm, evaluated the low and high culturally embedded ads featuring White characters, and they confirmed that these ads contained cues specific to White culture. The following is a description of the four versions of each product ad.

Cheerios Cereal Ads. The Cheerios ad shows a father standing in the doorway of the son's bedroom, eating a bowl of Cheerios. The son is sitting in his bed eating a bowl of the cereal. The text reads "Nobody can say no to Honey Nut Cheerios."

With the exception of the race of the characters, the LBCE Cheerios ad and the LWCE Cheerios ad are identical.

Three black cultural cues were digitally added to the LBCE ad to make it an HBCE ad. On the wall is a team photo of the 1931 "Homestead Grays" from the Negro Baseball League. Another picture on the bedroom wall shows a shirtless Black man with his arms raised high in the air. His wrists are handcuffed by the American flag. In large red print the caption says, "BlackLash." The last picture is a poster of a Black face with the text, "Love your self."

Similarly, White cultural cues were added to the LWCE ad to make it an HWCE ad. A Norman Rockwell print entitled "The Rookie" was added to the background wall. The 1957 print shows several all-White Boston Red Sox baseball players in the locker room staring at a young rookie who appears to have just joined the team. The second White cultural cue was another Norman Rockwell print, entitled "Our Heritage." This print shows two White boy scouts holding an American history book while staring in the background at a full-size picture of President George Washington praying on bended knee. An American flag was digitally added to the lower left corner of the print.

Irish Spring Soap Ads.   The Irish Spring ad shows a man posing next to a chair and a large plant. In front of the chair is a large picture of a bar of Irish Spring Sport Deodorant Soap. The text in the center of the ad reads, "Fresh & clean with Irish Spring! The deodorant soap." With the exception of the character's race, both low culturally embedded ads for the White and Black character are identical.

Two Black cultural cues were digitally added to the background wall of the LBCE ad to make it an HBCE ad. A large African mask was placed on the wall to right of the Black character. To the right of the mask a large picture frame was hung on the background wall, which pictured a shirtless 30-something Black man hugging his newborn child. Similarly, two White cultural cues were digitally added to the background wall of the LWCE ad to make it an HWCE ad. A picture of White hands holding a White Greek-like sculpture was added to the wall. To the left of the sculpture was a picture of a shirtless 30-something White man hugging his newborn child.

Oscar Mayer Wieners Ads.   The Oscar Mayer ad shows a man sitting in his home office desk chair with his son standing by his side. The two characters face the camera smiling. To the right of the characters is a small but wide bookshelf. On the top right of the bookshelf is a trophy and a soccer ball. On the floor next to the book shelf is a basketball and a skateboard. Directly below the father and son is the caption, "Being a Dad . . . doesn't come with instructions. It's trusting yourself to make the right choices. Here's one choice that's easy. Oscar Mayer!" Below the text is a picture of a hot dog on a bun with a package of Oscar Mayer Wieners pictured below. The race of the father and son was digitally altered to produce an LBCE ad and an LWCE ad.

Three Black cultural cues were digitally added to produce an HBCE ad. A black family portrait was framed and placed on the bookshelf. A Black female porcelain doll was inserted to the right of the family portrait. In addition, a picture of several runaway Black slaves walking through a forest in search of their freedom was added to the wall. Similarly, three White cultural cues were digitally added to the LWCE ad to produce an HWCE ad. Reminiscent of immigrants arriving to America, a picture of several ships passing the Statue of Liberty during a large fireworks celebration was placed on the wall above the shelf. A White family portrait was framed and placed on the bookshelf, as was a White female porcelain doll.

Procedure

Students were told that they would be participating in an advertising survey designed to determine the types of ads they like best, which would enable researchers to improve the look, style, and content of those ads. After the briefing, students were randomly assigned to one of the four conditions.

Each of the four binders contained five, color, $8\frac{1}{2}$ in. $\times$ 11 in. ($\sim$ 21.6 cm $\times$ 28 cm) photographic ads in clear plastic page protectors. Three products—Cheerios Cereal, Irish Spring Soap, and Oscar Mayer Wieners—made up the experimental ads, while two other ads were used to disguise the purpose of the study. A questionnaire corresponding to each ad (i.e., Cheerios, Irish Spring, or Oscar Mayer) was in the binder next to each ad. Participants completed each questionnaire immediately after they viewed each ad. For example, students opened the binder to the first experimental ad (e.g., Cheerios LBCE), reviewed the ad, and then completed the questionnaire pertaining to that ad. The student would then turn the page to the next ad (e.g., Irish Spring LBCE) and complete the questionnaire pertaining to that ad. The placement of the ads in the binders were as follows: disguise ad, Cheerios cereal ad, Irish Spring soap ad, disguise ad, and Oscar Mayer Wiener ad. Eight percent of the students indicated at least some knowledge of the study purpose and were excluded from the overall analysis. Once the questionnaires were completed, students who did not identify themselves as either Black or White on the questionnaires were excluded from further analysis.

Measures

The measurement instrument collected information for four dependent variables: perceived similarity to characters, identification with characters, ads intended for them, and ad-favorability rating. Scales were developed and alpha coefficients computed to obtain the internal consistency estimates.

Overall Ad-Favorability Rating Scale. For each stimulus ad, an overall ad-favorability rating scale was developed by averaging the mean scores from each of the following three scales: attitude toward the ad scale, attitude toward the characters scale, and attitude toward the product scale. The three scales were each measured by using eleven 7-point semantic differential scales: boring–interesting, bad–good, negative–positive, useless–useful, worthless–valuable, poor–outstanding, not for me–for me, weak–strong, not appealing–appealing, not attractive–attractive, and not likable–likable. The responses to all 11 items were summed to create the three attitude scales. For example, an attitude toward the ad scale was developed by averaging the mean scores from each of the 11 scales. These attitude scales have been used successfully in other character race studies and have shown strong evidence of being highly reliable (see, e.g., Desphande & Stayman, 1994). A reliability analysis was conducted for all scales to assess the degree to which the items measured a single variable or dimension.

For the attitude toward the ad scale, coefficient alphas were computed for each product: Cheerios ($\alpha = .96$), Irish Spring ($\alpha = .96$), and Oscar Mayer ($\alpha = .96$). For the attitude toward the characters scale, coefficient alphas were computed for each product: Cheerios ($\alpha = .96$), Irish Spring ($\alpha = .97$), and Oscar Mayer ($\alpha = .95$). Similarly, the attitude toward the product scale was developed and coefficient alphas were computed: Cheerios ($\alpha = .96$), Irish Spring ($\alpha = .97$), and Oscar Mayer ($\alpha = .97$).

As mentioned earlier, for each product an overall ad-favorability rating scale was developed by averaging the mean scores from the following scales: attitude toward the ad scale, attitude toward the characters scale, and attitude toward the product scale. The coefficient alphas for the Cheerios overall ad-favorability rating scale, Irish Spring overall ad-favorability scale, and the Oscar Mayer overall ad-favorability scale were .85, .79, and .86, respectively.

Perceived Similarity Scale. Students rated their degree of similarity to the characters in each ad in terms of (a) overall lifestyle; (b) cultural background; (c) dress; (d) appearance; and (e) basic values (Whittler, 1989). A similarity scale was created by averaging the mean scores from each of the five scales. For this scale, coefficient alphas were computed for each product: Cheerios ($\alpha = .86$), Irish Spring ($\alpha = .89$), and Oscar Mayer ($\alpha = .91$).

Other Measures. Participants were asked to indicate how strongly they identified with the characters in each ad (Aaker et al., 2000) on a 7-point Likert scale ranging from not at all (1) to very strongly (7). The last dependent measure asked participants to indicate whether they thought each ad was intended for them (Aaker et al., 2000) on a 7-point Likert scale ranging from disagree completely (1) to agree completely (7).

Race and Ethnicity of Participants. Participants were given a list of racial and ethnic groups from which to choose. Participants who identified with more than one racial or ethnic group were not included in the analysis.

RESULTS

An aggregate scale composed of responses from all three ads (i.e., Cheerios cereal, Irish Spring soap, and Oscar Mayer wieners) was created for each dependent variable. For example, the mean scores for the dependent variable "identification with characters" were computed for each of the three ads. The mean scores were then summed and divided by 3 to produce an aggregate scale for the variable "identification with characters." By use of this same procedure, aggregate scales were created for each of the four dependent variables.

Although some researchers have uncovered interesting findings from consumers' responses to ads based on individuals' exposure to only one product ad (e.g., Qualls & Moore, 1990), any generalizations made may be premature because consumers often provide responses that are product specific (Engel, Blackwell, & Miniard, 1995; Muse, 1971). Unlike past research, this study exposed each participant to three product ads. Participants' responses for each of the three ads were aggregated so that more conclusive generalizations could be made. Aggregating the ads helped minimize the skewing effects of any one ad. That is, the aggregate scale summarized the general significance of the set of ads and may provide more conclusive information than a study with just one product ad.

The results of the experiment are presented and discussed according to the hypotheses presented earlier. A series of three-way analyses of variance (ANOVAs) for all hypotheses are given in the paragraphs that follow. These same analyses are conducted for each dependent variable and product ad. The simple means for all independent and dependent variables are presented in Table 18.1, 18.2, and 18.3.

Aggregate Scale Similarity to Characters in Ads

The ANOVA indicated a significant interaction between participants' race and characters' race, that is, $F(1, 158) = 6.50$, $p < .01$. Follow-up analyses were conducted to examine this interaction. As hypothesized, a significant main effect of $F(3, 72) = 32.75$, $p < .001$ for characters' race indicated that Black adolescents perceived themselves more similar to Black characters in ads ($M = 4.50$, $SD = .24$) than they did to White characters in ads ($M = 2.56$, $SD = .24$). Black participants were more influenced by the race of the character than the cultural embeddedness of the ads. This provides only partial support for the hypothesis that characters' race and cultural embeddedness would influence Black participants' perceived similarity to characters in ads.

Surprisingly, White participants' perception of similarity was influenced both by race of the character and by cultural embeddedness of the ads. A significant interaction between character's race and cultural embeddedness, $F(3, 84) = 4.42$,

TABLE 18.1
Black Adolescents' Mean Responses to Culturally Embedded Ads

	White Characters		Black Characters	
	LWCE	*HWCE*	*LBCE*	*HBCE*
Aggregate scale				
Perceived similarity	2.50	2.61	4.46	4.54
Identification	2.60	2.47	4.14	4.09
Ads intended for me	2.92	3.18	4.12	4.21
Ad favorability	3.46	3.45	4.82	4.56
Cheerios Cereal				
Perceived similarity	2.64	2.82	4.58	4.77
Identification	2.60	2.75	4.50	4.19
Ads intended for me	3.20	3.20	4.35	4.05
Ad favorability	3.90	3.94	5.07	5.06
Irish Spring Soap				
Perceived similarity	2.09	2.24	4.07	4.28
Identification	2.40	1.95	3.53	3.95
Ads intended for me	2.25	2.65	4.00	4.45
Ad favorability	2.83	3.36	4.38	4.22
Oscar Meyer Wieners				
Perceived similarity	2.73	2.52	4.77	4.56
Identification	2.80	2.58	4.53	4.05
Ads intended for me	3.30	3.53	4.16	4.30
Ad favorability	3.68	3.47	4.84	4.14

$p < .05$, was found. White participants perceived themselves more similar to White characters in HWCE ads, $M = 3.86$, $SD = 1.13$, than they did to White characters in LWCE, ads, $M = 3.22$, $SD = .95$; $F(1, 40) = 3.93$, $p < .05$.

Aggregate Scale Identification With Characters in Ads

A significant interaction was found between participants' race and characters' race, that is, $F(1, 158) = 6.50$, $p < .01$. A closer examination of these means revealed significant characters' race main effects. Black adolescents identified more strongly with Black characters, $M = 4.11$, $SD = .26$, than they did with White characters, $M = 2.54$, $SD = .26$; $F(3, 73) = 18.00$, $p < .001$. Unexpectedly, White participants were also more likely to identify with Black characters in ads, $M = 2.74$, $SD = .15$, than they were with White characters in ads, $M = 2.23$, $SD = .16$; $F(3, 85) = 5.22$, $p < .05$. The results provide partial support for the hypothesis that Black characters and Black cultural embeddedness would influence Black participants' level of identification with characters in ads.

TABLE 18.2
White Adolescents' Mean Responses to Culturally Embedded Ads

	White Characters		Black Characters	
	LWCE	HWCE	LBCE	HBCE
Aggregate scale				
Perceived similarity	3.22	3.86	3.18	2.88
Identification	2.01	2.45	2.93	2.55
Ads intended for me	2.30	3.00	3.45	2.84
Ad favorability	3.09	3.37	3.89	4.00
Cheerios Cereal				
Perceived similarity	3.56	4.58	3.56	3.17
Identification	2.09	3.00	3.54	3.00
Ads intended for me	3.00	3.38	4.17	2.96
Ad favorability	3.50	3.89	4.16	4.12
Irish Spring Soap				
Perceived similarity	2.55	2.90	2.57	2.46
Identification	1.78	1.86	2.63	2.00
Ads intended for me	2.00	2.86	3.25	2.44
Ad favorability	2.71	3.00	3.62	3.70
Oscar Meyer Wieners				
Perceived similarity	3.56	4.18	3.43	3.02
Identification	2.17	2.60	2.48	2.65
Ads intended for me	1.91	2.85	2.78	3.13
Ad favorability	3.17	3.40	3.40	3.79

Aggregate Scale Ads Intended for Me

The ANOVA indicated a marginally significant interaction between cultural embeddedness and characters' race, that is, $F(1, 158) = 2.84$, $p < .10$. For Black participants, a significant main effect for characters' race, $F(1, 73) = 8.70$, $p < .01$, indicated that Black participants believed Black character ads were more intended for them ($M = 4.17$, $SD = 1.62$) than were White character ads ($M = 3.05$, $SD = 1.68$). The results supported the hypothesis that Black participants would believe ads were more intended for them when the characters were Black than when the characters were White. However, the results failed to support the hypothesis that the cultural embeddedness of the ads would influence Blacks students' belief that ads were intended for them.

White adolescents were significantly more likely to believe ads were intended for them when the characters in the ads were Black, that is, $F(1, 85) = 4.24$, $p < .05$, but this main effect was qualified by a significant interaction between cultural embeddedness and characters' race, $F(1, 85) = 7.43$, $p < .01$. The interaction indicated that White adolescents believed that Black-character LBCE ads were more intended for them, $M = 3.45$, $SD = 1.11$, than White-character LWCE ads,

TABLE 18.3
Mean Responses for Black- and White-Character Ads

	White Participants		Black Participants	
	WC	BC	WC	BC
Aggregate scale				
Perceived similarity	3.53	3.03	3.82	4.21
Identification	2.22	2.74	2.54	4.11
Ads intended for me	2.63	3.14	3.04	4.17
Ad favorability	3.22	3.95	3.45	4.71
Cheerios Cereal				
Perceived similarity	4.05	3.37	2.73	4.68
Identification	2.52	3.28	2.68	4.34
Ads intended for me	3.18	3.57	3.20	4.20
Ad favorability	3.69	4.14	3.92	5.07
Irish Spring Soap				
Perceived similarity	2.72	2.51	2.17	4.18
Identification	1.82	2.32	2.18	3.74
Ads intended for me	2.41	2.85	2.45	4.23
Ad favorability	2.85	3.66	3.08	4.31
Oscar Meyer Wieners				
Perceived similarity	3.86	3.23	2.63	4.67
Identification	2.37	2.57	2.69	4.28
Ads intended for me	2.35	2.96	3.41	4.23
Ad favorability	3.27	3.59	3.58	4.52

Note. WC = White character; BC = Black character.

$M = 2.30$, $SD = .92$; $F(1, 44) = 14.45$, $p < .001$. In additional, White participants believed that White-character HWCE ads were more intended for them, $M = 3.00$, $SD = 1.24$, than White-character LWCE ads, $M = 2.30$, $SD = .92$; $F(1, 41) = 4.42$, $p < .05$. These results failed to support the hypothesis that cultural embeddedness and characters' race would have no influence on White participants' belief of being the intended audience.

Aggregate Scale Ad-Favorability Rating

The hypothesis that characters' race and cultural embeddedness would influence Black participants' rating of ads was partially supported. The cultural embeddedness of Black-character ads did not influence Black adolescents' rating of ads. However, as hypothesized, a significant main effect, $F(3, 53) = 10.77$, $p < .01$, indicated that Black adolescents rated ads featuring Black characters more favorably ($M = 4.69$, $SD = .28$) than ads featuring White characters ($M = 3.45$, $SD = .25$).

Surprisingly, White participants were significantly, that is, $F(3, 74) = 11.92$, $p < .001$, more likely to rate ads featuring Black characters more favorably ($M = 3.95$, $SD = .15$) than ads featuring White characters ($M = 3.23$, $SD = .15$).

DISCUSSION AND CONCLUSION

This study contributed to the field of advertising research by demonstrating the usefulness of an innovative technique that used the latest technology to vary the race of the model and the number of race-specific cultural cues in each experimental ad. Unlike past research that has asked consumers to evaluate Black- and White-character ads that were quite different on dimensions such as body positioning, dress, celebrity, background, and product placement, this study used digital techniques to enable the researcher to control the vast majority of extraneous variables. A computer software program was used to manipulate digitally the race of the model and the cultural cues in each ad while preserving all other visual characteristics of the ad. This procedure ensured that any differences in adolescents' responses to ads with Black characters or ads with White characters must be attributed to the race-related cultural cues.

The results of this study provide much needed information on how White and Black adolescents respond to low and high culturally embedded ads featuring Black or White characters. It was expected that, for Black adolescents, the characters' race and the cultural embeddedness of the ads would play a significant role in mediating their responses to ads. More specifically, it was hypothesized that Black adolescents would be more responsive to Black-character ads than to White-character ads, and more responsive to HBCE Black-character ads than LBCE Black-character ads. In contrast, it was predicted that neither the characters' race nor the cultural embeddedness of the ads would affect White adolescents' responses to ads. These hypotheses were partially supported.

Contrary to predictions, the findings suggest that the level of culturally embeddedness has a stronger influence on White adolescents' responses to product ads than on Black adolescents' responses to ads. White adolescents perceived themselves more similar to White characters than to Black characters, particularly White characters in HWCE ads. Despite this perception, White adolescents identified more strongly with Black characters in ads than with White characters in ads. White adolescents were also more likely to believe they were the target audience of Black-character ads than White-character ads, particularly when those Black-character ads were low in black cultural embeddedness. Moreover, White adolescents rated Black-character ads more favorably than White-character ads. These findings failed to support the hypotheses that White adolescents would display no significant difference in their responses to ads based on the character's race or the cultural embeddedness of the ads.

What appeared to be the most important predictor of adolescents' responses to product ads was the race of the character featured in the ads. For Black adolescents, featuring Black characters in ads significantly influenced their responses to ads. That is, Black individuals were more likely to perceive themselves as more similar to Black characters than to White characters, and they were more likely to believe that ads were more intended for them when they contained Black characters than when they contained White characters. Black teenagers were also more likely to identify with Black characters than with White characters, and they were more likely to rate ads more favorably when the ads contained Black characters. These findings supported the hypothesis that Black individuals would respond more positively to Black-character ads than they would to White-character ads, but they failed to support the hypothesis that Black youths would respond more favorably to HBCE Black-character ads.

The findings support the identification theory, which maintains that people automatically assess their level of similarity with a source during an interaction and make similarity judgments (Hovland & Weis, 1951; Kelman, 1961). Black adolescents perceive themselves to be similar to the models on the basis of race. As a result, they are more likely to identify with Black models, pay more attention to Black models, and recall more information from Black models than they are from White models with whom they are less likely to identify.

Like Black adolescents, White adolescents also seem to identify with Black models. Although White adolescents do not perceive themselves as racially similar to Black models, they may perceive themselves similar to Blacks in other areas such as music, dance, and fashion. As identification theory suggests, identification often occurs when individuals infer that their tastes and preferences are similar to the source (Eagly et al., 1978). For White youth, the simple presence of Black models in ads may invoke particular race-specific stereotypes that characterize Blacks as urban, hip, cool, musical, athletic, and trendsetters, and all of these traits are highly desirable among White youth. In fact, research has shown that Whites stereotype Blacks as possessing innate athletic and musical abilities (Feldman, 1972). These socially desirable traits may drive White adolescents to seek, observe, and emulate Black media characters more than White characters.

Distinctiveness theory provides another explanation as to why White viewers displayed no preference for White-character ads. The theory posits that individuals' distinctive traits will be more salient to them than more prevalent traits possessed by other people in the environment (McGuire, 1984). As members of a racial majority, Whites are less likely to be aware of their racial identity vis-à-vis a member of a racial minority. Because Whites make up a racial majority in society and in the media, they may be less mindful of their race when they view television. In support, the findings show that White adolescents were more likely to believe that an ad was intended for them when it featured Black characters than when it featured White characters. White adolescents do not maintain strong racial identities, and only when White viewers are exposed to HWCE White-character ads do they become mindful of their race and the racial similarities that exist between them and the White characters. However, even after being exposed to HWCE White-character ads, White viewers displayed no preference for HWCE White-character ads over either LBCE or HBCE Black-character ads. The only exception was White adolescents' perceived similarity to White characters.

The results for Black adolescents are also consistent with distinctiveness theory (McGuire, 1984; McGuire et al., 1978). People notice characteristics that are distinctive from other people in their environment. For Black viewers, being part of a racial group that is a numeric minority in America and in the media causes them to be more conscious of Black models in ads. Therefore, it would be expected that Black viewers would spontaneously think about their racial identities while viewing ads and, as a result, display more positive responses to Black characters. Black adolescents, unlike their White counterparts, need few Black cultural cues in ads to summon their racial identities. This was evidenced by the results that show that LBCE ads were just as effective in getting Black adolescents to feel that an ad was intended for them as were HBCE ads.

Some of the more interesting and surprising findings pertain to White adolescents' responses to Black-character ads vis-à-vis White-character ads. For example, why did White teenagers tend to favor Black-character ads over White-character ads? As previously mentioned, the perception that Blacks possess certain socially desirable traits (e.g., they are hip, cool, fashionable, and athletic) may drive White adolescents to seek, observe, and emulate Black media characters. This describes the notion of "cultural voyeurism." In this instance, cultural voyeurism is conceptualized as the process by which a White viewer seeks knowledge about and gratification from Black characters by viewing them by use of a specific medium. White teenagers may seek Black characters in ads, in music, and on television to gain general information about Black dress, Black music, and Black vernacular. Because Blacks often set the trends in many areas such as clothing, language, music, and dance, which not only dominate "U.S. youth culture but the entire global youthmarket" (Rossman, 1994, p. 140), White adolescents may find Black characters in ads particularly appealing. As a result of race-based stereotypes and cultural voyeurism, White adolescents may perceive themselves as more similar to, and identify more with, Black characters than White characters on dimensions such as product use, social activities, sports, fashion, and music. For White adolescents the desire to be cool and hip may override the importance of cultural and racial similarity.

White adolescents' desire to rebel against parental authority and White mainstream culture may provide another explanation for why White adolescents find Black characters appealing. During adolescence, youth may shift from parental values to those that reinforce peer and nontraditional values (Larson, Kubey, & Colletti, 1989). White adolescents may align themselves with more unconventional cultures such as punk culture and Black hip-hop culture because these cultures speak more to their lifestyles and life issues. White adolescents may find certain Black cultural icons and symbols (e.g., rap music or hip-hop fashion) particularly fascinating because they demonstrate strong countercultural messages. This fascination with Black culture by White consumers is evident in their purchase of hard-core rap albums (of which three quarters are sold to White consumers) and Black urban fashion labels such as Mecca, Boss Jeans (Spiegler, 1996), and FUBU. Future research may determine the extent to which the desire to rebel drives White adolescents' responses to Black-character ads.

These findings have practical implications for advertisers for whom a major goal is to reach adolescents with a message they trust and with which they identify. The findings suggest that, when designing campaign messages, planners should make use of Black models in order for Black viewers to best attend and evaluate those messages. A public service or product advertisement with Black characters improves the chances that Black consumers will attend to, recall, comprehend, and be persuaded by the ad (Calvert, Huston, Watkins, & Wright, 1982), and the more affected they will be (Huesman et al., 1983).

Future research in this area should consider using a measure of ethnic identification. The strength of one's ethnic identity may mediate the effects of mass media messages (Appiah, 2001; Williams & Qualls, 1989). For underrepresented racial or ethnic groups—unlike White youth who are less mindful of race—the strength of their racial or ethnic identity may play a role in how they process persuasive communication. Ethnic identity becomes particularly important during adolescence (Phinney, 1992), when youngsters become more aware of people who look and act similar to them. Black youth who maintain strong racial identities may develop stronger preferences for Black models, particularly those models in culturally embedded ads. In contrast, for White youth the strength of their ethnic identity may play little if any role in how they process culturally embedded messages. White adolescents may not think of themselves as distinctly part of a particular racial or ethnic group; as a majority group, they are less conscious of their status in society.

Future research should also look at the effects of culturally embedded ads on Black and White adult audiences. Although research suggests that the values of White adults have changed considerably over time (Bush et al., 1979), it is important to determine whether White adults will respond as positively to Black-character ads that are high or low in black cultural embeddedness as did White adolescents in this study. Findings from adult consumers, as with adolescent consumers, would be invaluable to companies who are interested in using targeted ads to reach Black consumers and who would like to use the same Black-targeted ads to reach the general market.

These findings imply that, irrespective of the cultural embeddedness of ads, the use of targeted advertising to reach Black consumers will continue to appeal to White consumers. Although empirical research shows that White viewers seem just as likely to respond to race-targeted advertising as they would to nontargeted advertising (Fost, 1993; Pitts et al., 1989), race continues to be an important characteristic that guides attention, retention, perception, and behavior for Black viewers.

REFERENCES

Aaker, J., Brumbaugh, A., & Grier, S. (2000). Non-target market effects and viewer distinctiveness: The impact of target marketing on attitudes. *Journal of Consumer Psychology, 9*(3), 127–140.

Appiah, O. (2001). The effects of ethnic identification on Black and White adolescents' evaluation of ads. *Journal of Advertising Research, 41*, 1–16.

Appiah, O. (2002). Black and White viewers' perception and recall of occupational characters on television. *Journal of Communication, 52*(4), 776–793.

Appiah, O., & Wagner, M. (2002). Differences in media buying by online business in Black- and White-targeted magazines: The potential impact of the digital divide on ad placement. *Howard Journal of Communications, 13*(4), 251–266.

Askey, L. (1995, November 13). Is the medium the message? *Adweek, 36,* 57.

Barban, A. M., & Cundiff, E. W. (1964). Negro and White response to advertising stimuli. *Journal of Marketing Research,* 1, 53–56.

Basow, S. A., & Howe, K. G. (1980). Role-model influence: Effects of sex and sex-role attitude in college students. *Psychology of Women Quarterly, 4,* 558–572.

Block, C. E. (1972, Summer). White backlash to negro ads: Fact or fantasy. *Journalism Quarterly, 49,* 258–262.

Bristor, J. M., & Lee, R. G. , Hunt, M. R. (1995). Race and Ideology: African-American images in television advertising. *Journal of Public Policy & Marketing, 14*(1), 48–59.

Brock, T. C. (1965). Communicator-recipient similarity and decision change. *Journal of Personality and Social Psychology, 6,* 650–654.

Bush, R. F., Hair, J. F., & Solomon, P. J. (1979). Consumers' level of prejudice and response to black models in advertisements. *Journal of Marketing Research, 16*(3), 341–345.

Burnstein, E., Scotland, E., & Zander, A. (1961). Similarity to the model and self-evaluation. *Journal of Abnormal and Social Psychology, 62,* 257–264.

Cagley, J. W., & Cardozo, R. N. (1970, April). White response to integrated advertising. *Journal of Advertising Research,* 10, 35–39.

Calvert, S. L., Huston, A. C., Watkins, B. A., & Wright, J. C. (1982). The relation between selective attention to television forms and children's comprehension of content. *Child Development, 53,* 601–610.

Choudhury, P. K., & Schmid, L. S. (1974). Black models in advertising to blacks. *Journal of Advertising Research, 14,* 19–22.

Desphande, R., & Stayman, D. (1994, February). A tale of two cities: Distinctiveness theory and advertising effectiveness. *Journal of Marketing Research, 31,* 57–64.

Eagly, A. H., Wood, W., & Chaiken, S. (1978). Casual inferences about communicators and their effect on opinion change. *Journal of Personality and Social Psychology, 36,* 424–435.

Engel, J. F., Blackwell, R. D., & Miniard, P. W. (1995) *Consumer behavior.* Fort Worth, TX: The Dryden Press.

Feick, L., & Higie, R. A. (1992). The effect of preference heterogeneity and source characteristics on ad processing and judgments about endorsers. *Journal of Advertising, XXI*(2), 9–24.

Feldman, J. (1972). Stimulus characteristics and subject prejudice as determinants of stereotype attribution. *Journal of Personality and Social Psychology, 21,* 333–340.

Fost, D. (1993, May). Reaching the hip-hop generation. *American Demographics,* p. 1.

Gadsden, S. (1985, December). Blowing the whistle on media placement. *Advertising Age, 56,* 26, 28.

Green, M. (1991). *Invisible people: The depiction of minorities in magazines and catalogs.* New York: City of New York Department of Consumer Affairs.

Greenberg, B. S., & Atkin, C. (1982). Learning about minorities from television: A research agenda. In G. Berry & C. Mitchell-Kernan (Eds.), *Television and the socialization of the minority child* (pp. 215–243). New York: Academic Press.

Greenberg, B. S., & Brand, J. E. (1994). Minorities and the mass media: 1970s to 1990s. In J. Bryant & D. Zillmann (Eds.), *Media effects: Advances in theory and research* (pp. 273–314). Hillsdale, NJ: Lawrence Erlbaum Associates.

Grier. S. A., & Brumbaugh, A. M. (1999). Noticing cultural differences: Ad meanings created by target and non-target markets. *Journal of Advertising, 28*(1), 79–93.

Grier, S. A., & Deshpande, R. (2001). Social dimensions of consumer distinctiveness: The influence of social status on group identity and advertising persuasion. *Journal of Marketing Research, 38,* 216–224.

Guest, L. (1970). How negro models affect company image. *Journal of Advertising Research, 10,* 29–33.

Hovland, C., & Weis, W. (1951). The influence of source credibility on communication effectiveness. *Public Opinion Quarterly,* (15), 635–660.

Huesman, L. R., Eron, L. D., Klein, R., Brice, P., & Fischer, P. (1983). Mitigating the imitation of aggressive behaviors by changing children's attitudes about medial violence. *Journal of Personality and Social Psychology, 44,* 899–910.

Jackson, L. A., & Ervin, K. S. (1991). The frequency and portrayal of Black families in fashion advertisements. *Journal of Black Psychology, 18*(1), 67–70.

Kelman, H. C. (1961). Process of opinion change. *Public Opinion Quarterly, 25,* 57–78.

Kern-Foxworth, M. (1994). *Aunt Jemima, Uncle Ben, and Rastus: Blacks in advertising, yesterday, today, and tomorrow.* Westport, CT: Praeger.

Larson, R., Kubey, R., & Colletti, J. (1989). Changing channels: Early adolescent media choices and shifting investments in family and friends. *Journal of Youth and Adolescence, 18,* 583–599.

McGuire, W. (1984). Search for the self: Going beyond self-esteem and the reactive self. In R. A. Zucker, J. Aronoff, & A. I. Rabin (Eds.), *Personality and the prediction of behavior* (pp. 73–120). New York: Academic Press.

McGuire, W., McGuire, V., Child, P., & Fujioka, T. (1978). Salience of ethnicity in the spontaneous self-concept as a function of one's ethnic distinctiveness in the social environment. *Journal of Personality and Social Psychology, 36,* 511–520.

Muse, W. V. (1971). Product-related response to use of Black models in advertising. *Journal of Marketing Research, 7,* 107–109.

Nixon, M. (1983, September 29). Minorities in TV ads a hot topic. *USA Today,* pp. 10–2D.

Phinney, J. S. (1992). The multigroup ethnic identity measure: A new scale for use with diverse groups. *Journal of Adolescent Research, 7,* 156–176.

Pitts, R. E., Whalen, D. J., O'Keefe, R., & Murray, V. (1989). Black and White response to culturally targeted television commercials: A values-based approach. *Psychology & Marketing, 6*(4), 311–328.

Qualls, W. J., & Moore, D. J. (1990). Stereotyping effects on consumers' evaluation of advertising: Impact of racial differences between actors and viewers. *Psychology & Marketing, 7*(2), 135–151.

Rossman, M. L. (1994). *Multicultural marketing: Selling to a diverse America.* New York: American Management Association.

Schlinger, M. J., & Plummer, J. T. (1972). Advertising in black and white. *Journal of Marketing Research, 9,* 149–153.

Siegel, A. E., & Siegel, S. (1957). Reference groups, membership groups, and attitude change. *The Journal of Abnormal Social Psychology, 55,* 361–364.

Soley, L. (1983). The effect of Black models in magazine ad readership. *Journalism Quarterly, 48*(2), 337–339.

Spiegler, M. (1996). Marketing street culture: Bringing hip-hop style to the mainstream. *American Demographics, 18,* 29–34.

Wall, K. (1970). The great waste ignoring blacks. *Marketing Communications, 298,* 42–50.

Whittler, T. E. (1989). Viewers' processing of actor's race and message claims in advertising stimuli. *Psychology of Marketing, 6,* 287–309.

Whittler, T. E. (1991). The effects of actors' race in commercial advertising: Review and extension. *Journal of Advertising, 20*(1), 54–60.

Wilkes, R. E., & Valencia, H. (1989). Hispanics and Blacks in television commercials. *Journal of Advertising, 18*(1), 19–25.

Williams, J. D., & Qualls, W. J. (1989). Middle-class black consumers and intensity of ethnic identification. *Psychology & Marketing, 6*(4), 263–286.

CHAPTER NINETEEN

The Case for Separation of Asian American Ethnic Groups as We Consider Our Target-Market Strategies

David W. Schumann
University of Tennessee

Jinkook Lee
Ohio State University

Kittichai Watchravesringkan
University of Arizona

As we use the term in marketing, "ethnicity" has been typically defined in terms of shared culture and background. Nationality, religion, physical attributes, geographic location, and other factors have been used to segment ethnic groups (Engle, Blackwell, & Minard, 1995). Banks (1981) suggested that an ethnic group could be defined as the sharing of a "common history, tradition, and sense of peoplehood" As it relates to the behavior of consumers, ethnic groups are believed to differ in the types of information sources they use, the types of options they consider, and the types of stores they patronize (Delener & Neelankavil, 1990; Herche & Balasubramanian, 1994).

For many years, marketers, demographers, social psychologists, and other behavioral scientists have used broad categories to capture people of similar ethnic background. For example, in the United States, three broad categories have been used to represent the major ethnic minority populations: African American, Asian, and Hispanic. Both marketing researchers and marketing strategists have focused on these three broad categories as they attempt to segment the population along ethnic lines. Indeed, it is interesting to note that these groups appear to be segmenting themselves on at least one dimension, geographic preference. The largest number of African Americans live in the Southeast and in the larger eastern cities. Most of the Hispanic population in the United States lives in the Southwest, and the largest population of Asians live along the West Coast, Texas, Hawaii, and in the cities of New York and Chicago.

The problem with such broad classification is the fact that it fails to capture significant differences within each category. In the United States, the Asian American category represents a highly significant number of diverse subpopulations. Chinese, Japanese, Korean, Asian Indian, Filipino, and Vietnamese are among the largest of 16 Asian ethnic groups measured by the U.S. Census. Many of these separate ethnic groups vary considerably, and the act of combining them into a single category for purposes of market segmentation is arguably counterproductive. As others have contended in the past (Kang & Kim, 1998; Kim, Laroche, & Joy, 1990), despite the sharing of values and norms of the dominant eastern culture, differential marketing efforts may be warranted given the differences in the groups that comprise the "Asian" category. Diverse languages, religions, and cultural traditions call into question the ability to market to a single segment (Kang & Kim, 1998). This chapter explores this contention: first, it provides an overview of the literature that defines or compares the various ethnic groups within the Asian category; second, it describes the results of a study conducted between three Asian American groups as they respond to ethnic models employed in an advertising strategy.

THE ASIAN SUBCULTURES IN AMERICA

The Superminority

Labeled by the media as the "superminority" (Lee & Um, 1992), the Asian population represents 2.7% of the U.S. population with spending power over $100 billion ("On This Multicultural Front," 1999). The Asian population in the United States, estimated at more than nine million people. By the year 2010, this segment is expected to account for 6% of the total U.S. population (Miller, 1993); by 2050, 11% of the U.S. population is expected to be of Asian heritage. Asian Americans tend to value family, the opinions of male elders (patriarchal family structure), hard work, ambition, education, and knowledge. The U.S. Census reports that, among adults over the age of 25, 42% of "Asian and Pacific Islanders" have earned at least a bachelor's degree, compared with 24% of the general adult population. Likewise, the median income of Asian American households is $45,248, whereas that of all U.S. households is $37,004. The size of the Asian American household is larger than that of the general public, yet Asian Americans are less likely to own their own home (Lach, 1999).

Studies of media usage in the United States reflect mixed results among Asian Americans. Several researchers (Delener & Neelankavil, 1990; Miller, 1993; *World Advertising Expenditures*, 1986) have found that Asian Americans spend the highest proportion of media time watching television. Other studies, however, have discovered that Asian Americans, when compared with Caucasians, read more newspapers (Delener & Neelankavil, 1990) and view less television (Braun, 1991). Regarding the use of products and services, some studies have found that quality is the most important factor in purchase consideration (Braun, 1991; Miller, 1993), whereas others have found that price is the strongest criterion for purchase (Fisher, 1993). Kang and Kim (1998), in considering these varied findings, suggest two possible reasons for these differences: ethnicity and acculturation. This chapter considers both ethnicity and acculturation in its discussion of differences between Asian American ethnic groups.

Asian American Ethnic Groups As Consumers

Several consumer studies have compared Asian ethnic groups with Caucasian populations, revealing distinct differences. For example, Childers and Rao (1992) examined differences in reference-group influence between Caucasians from the United States and citizens of Thailand. The Thai sample reported greater dependence on family for both conspicuous luxuries as well as less conspicuous necessities, whereas the U.S. sample appeared more influenced by their peer group. Lee (1993) examined differences between Taiwanese and American populations on several consumer dimensions. The results revealed that Taiwanese, compared with their American counterparts, felt more positive about advertising, relied less heavily on advice from friends, were more influenced by product trial, and considered product quality more important than price.

Several studies have considered differences between Korean and Caucasian populations. Koreans in general have been found to consider price more important (Choe, 1984). In addition, compared with their Caucasian counterparts, Koreans report being more prone to the influence of national brands, less prone to coupon promotions, are stronger ethical shoppers, are more likely to shop at shopping centers, and are more likely to view shopping as a woman's role (Kim, 1987; Lee & Um, 1992; Shim & Chen, 1996).

There are also studies that have compared the Chinese and Caucasian populations. Yau (1988) found that Chinese citizens are more brand loyal, are more likely to conform to group norms regarding products, and are more likely to purchase the same brand their reference group recommends. Ownbey (1991), in examining Chinese Americans, found them not to be brand loyal, to enjoy shopping at shopping centers, to bargain hunt at less expensive stores, and to be highly store loyal.

Two important studies conducted by Kang and Kim (1997, 1998) examined differences among three cultures in their decision-making processes regarding the purchase of electronic goods and clothing for social occasions. These populations included the Chinese, Japanese, and Koreans. Both studies found ethnicity and acculturation effects. In both studies, Chinese respondents were found to rely on the opinions of family and relatives compared with either the Koreans or Japanese respondents. In the clothing study, the Chinese and Koreans were more likely to rely on their same-ethnic-group friends compared with the Japanese respondents. Likewise, the Chinese and Korean respondent groups were similar when media influence was considered. When they were split into high- and low-acculturation groups, the low-acculturation groups were found to be influenced more by television and radio than the high-acculturation groups. However, for the Japanese groups, the opposite effect occurred. Finally, Chinese and Korean respondents were more likely to consider product-related appeals more important than their Japanese counterparts.

The literature reviewed herein reflects significant differences that lie within the broader Asian category. These Asian ethnic-group differences are likely to produce problems for marketers seeking to segment on ethnicity. Language, religion, culture, and values differ widely among Asian Americans. Both Fost (1990) and Henricks (1992) have suggested that marketers and advertisers need to segment by nationality and not by these broad ethnic groups. However, it appears that we remain confused as to how to handle the fact that the Asian category is composed of many different nationalities. Arguably, we have overlooked the complex differences between Asian subcultures and have been insensitive to cultural practices. Furthermore, we may lack, or may not have thoughtfully considered, the media necessary to reach these varied Asian subcultures.

Acculturation as a Moderating Factor

In today's large metropolitan areas, the mass media offers a significant opportunity for immigrated ethnic groups to learn about other cultures (Lee, 1993). This opportunity to be exposed to the attitudes, values, motives, and behaviors of others has facilitated a high degree of acculturation. In 1954, the Social Science Research Council described the phenomenon of acculturation in the following manner:

> ... the culture exchange that is initiated by the conjunction of two or more autonomous cultural systems. Acculturative change may be the consequences of direct cultural transmission; it may be derived from noncultural causes... it may be delayed, ... or it may be a reactive adaptation of traditional models of life. Its dynamics can be seen as the selective adaptation of value systems, the process of integration and differentiation, the generation of developmental sequences.... (p. 974)

Acculturation can be viewed as the adoption of both subjective and objective aspects of the host culture (Triandis, Kashima, Hui, Lisansky, & Marin, 1982). Subjective culture includes such nonmaterial elements as norms, belief systems, laws, and values; objective culture includes the material aspects of the culture such as tools, foods, and material products. The process of acculturation involves the contact between at least two cultures. The nature and the duration of the contact will undoubtedly determine the amount of impact the contact has on acculturation. It is generally assumed that the longer the duration of the contact, the greater the impact. Regardless of types of contact, either friendly or hostile, some degree of cultural change will occur. It may be confrontation, adaptation, or a mixture of both (Lee, 1993).

To date, there has been no one single variable identified as reflecting acculturation. Instead, it appears necessary to incorporate multiple items that sample and measure relatively orthogonal dimensions of acculturation (Donthu & Cherian, 1994; Kim et al., 1990; Lee & Um, 1992; Mendoza, 1989). Several factors, including generation or length of stay (Lee & Um, 1992; Penaloza, 1994), language (Deshpande, Hoyer, & Donthu, 1986), type of media exposure (Choi, 1984; Choi & Tamborini, 1988; O'Guinn, Faber, & Rice, 1985; O'Guinn, Lee, & Faber, 1986), language use in media (Lee & Tse, 1994), and image associated with products (Lee, 1993), have been suggested as contributing to the identification of acculturation.

Over the past two decades the study of acculturation as it relates to consumer-related activities has gained increased research attention (Lee & Um, 1992). In an important conceptual article in the *Journal of Consumer Research*, Penaloza (1994) presented a framework to explain consumer acculturation. She suggested that individual differences (demographic variables, language, recency of arrival, ethnic identity, and environmental factors) are influenced by two forms of agents, culture of origin and culture of immigration. Included within these agents were a number of influencing factors, such as friends, media, and commercial, educational, and religious institutions. These in turn facilitated the acculturation processes (movement, translation, and adaptation) leading to certain outcomes (assimilation, maintenance, resistance, or segregation). This model demonstrates the complexity of the acculturation process and suggests that, as marketers, we must pay attention to these complexities in order to accurately target ethnic market segments.

A number of consumer researchers have studied different facets of acculturation and have generated a number of important conclusions. For example, several researchers have noted that it seems logical that ethnic consumers enter into the acculturation process in different ways and to different degrees (Jun, Ball, & Gentry, 1993; Lee & Um, 1992). Wallendorf and Reilly (1983) suggested that, diverse levels of acculturation within the same ethnic group would likely result in fundamental differences in consumption behavior, including the use of information surrounding the purchase of products such as food or dress. Solomon (1983) found that, when role dynamics are characterized by uncertainty, there is an increased reliance on the consumption of symbolic products as a guide to behavior. Similarly, Lee (1989) predicted that acculturating individuals who are uncertain about their identities will show accelerated adoption and conspicuous consumption of socially expressive products as a means of asserting self-expression and satisfying role performance.

In sum, the level of acculturation appears to potentially be a key moderating variable as one seeks to explain the consumption behavior of ethnic groups. Further examination is needed to better understand when acculturation level serves as a moderating influence on consumers as they search for information, use media, and select and use products.

A COMPARATIVE STUDY OF ASIAN ETHNIC-GROUP RESPONSES TO ADVERTISING

As a way to continue our study of the contention that marketers need to consider moving away from using large ethnic categories (e.g., African American, Asian, and Hispanic) in their target-market strategies, a study was conducted examining the differential response to advertising stimuli among three Asian ethnic groups: Chinese, Japanese, and Korean.

Over the past two decades, there have been a significant number of studies examining the representation of Asians in commercial messages. However, there have been far fewer studies comparing how ethnic groups respond to advertising stimuli. For example, Cohen (1992), in an analysis of high-tech product advertising, found that when high-tech engineering products were associated with Asian models, they received more favorable attention from Caucasian American respondents than they received from Asian respondents. When Asian models were paired with home and family-oriented products, the Caucasian respondents reported less favorable attitudes than their Asian counterparts.

The larger base of extant literature on Asians and advertising has examined roles within advertising. For example, in a study of 2,000 advertisements in both Korean and U.S. markets, Miracle, Chang, and Taylor (1992) found that advertising in Korea used more indirect and ambiguous messages, more harmony-seeking versus confrontational ads, and more collectivist versus individualistic advertising. In a series of studies, Taylor and his colleagues (Taylor & Lee, 1994; Taylor, Lee, & Stern, 1995; Taylor & Stern, 1997) found that Asian models (a) appeared more frequently in the popular business press and science publications (vs. women's or general-interest magazines), (b) were more likely to be associated with technology-based products (vs. non-technology-based products), (c) appeared in ads more often in business contexts, (d) were depicted more typically as coworkers, and (e) were seldom seen in ads containing family or social settings.

As a way to add to the scant literature examining Asian ethnic response to advertising and to further the case for the separation of Asian ethnic groups (as opposed to the general practice of applying one unifying label), a study was undertaken to compare different Asian ethnic-group responses to advertising stimuli. The purpose of the study was to discover whether different responses to advertising exist between different Asian ethnic groups. More specifically, groups of Chinese, Japanese, and Korean respondents were shown advertisements employing either an ethnically consistent model (a model whose ethnicity is consistent with the respondent's ethnicity) or a Caucasian model. An analysis was conducted on measures of awareness, attitude, and purchase intention. Acculturation was included as a possible moderating variable.

METHODS

Sampling

The populations of interest for this study included the three largest Asian ethnic subgroups: Chinese, Japanese, and Korean. The study was conducted within a moderately large metropolitan area of the southeastern United States. Because there was limited access to these populations in this geographical location (see limitations section), convenience samples were used. Respondents were recruited from ethnic grocery stores, churches, and housing for married students.

The sample consisted of 197 Asian Americans in total (66 Chinese Americans, 65 Japanese Americans, and 66 Korean Americans). Respondents had to be at least 18 years old and either born in their country of origin (i.e., first generation) or born in the United States (i.e., second or third generation). Demographically, because the largest proportion of the respondents was under 30 years of age, the majority of the sample had never been married. Fifty-four percent of the sample was female, and 60% had a bachelor's degree or higher. Sixty-two percent of the sample respondents were graduate students, whereas 26% of the respondents were full-time employees. The majority of the sample earned less than $50,000 annually. Great care was taken to create groups that were similar in demographic construction (e.g., the number of graduate students were nearly equal across groups).

Research Design

Again, the purpose of the study was to examine possible differences between Asian American groups as they respond to an ethnically consistent subgroup model versus a Caucasian model. Acculturation level was also explored as a possible moderating variable. Thus a 3 (respondent ethnicity: Chinese vs. Japanese vs. Korean) × 2 (model ethnicity: ethnically consistent subgroup vs. Caucasian) × 2 (acculturation level: low vs. high) between-subjects design was used.

The respondents were separated into three groups according to ethnicity. The ethnicity of the advertising model was manipulated in the following manner. From a larger set of Chinese, Japanese, Korean, and Caucasian female models drawn from ethnic and general-readership magazines, a pretest was conducted to find two models from each ethnic category, all of whom would be judged as equally attractive. The pretest sample included 60 respondents (20 Chinese, 20 Japanese, and 20 Korean). From the pretest, two models from each subgroup were selected that met the criteria. The acculturation level was manipulated by (a) using an index to measure acculturation, (b) standardizing the items to configure a total score, and (c) using a median split to construct groups low and high on acculturation.

In the actual study, respondents were recruited for the experiment from various locations (ethnic grocery stores, churches, and married-student housing). If they agreed to participate, they were handed a booklet of ads (five in all). The ad appearing third was the target ad, whereas the others were filler ads. The filler ads were for normal products (detergent, automobile, airlines, and a motel chain) and did not contain any people. The target ad was for a popular brand of toothpaste promoting a new feature (baking soda). In the upper left-hand corner was a picture of one of the pretested models. Each ethnic respondent group received either one of two ethnically consistent models (e.g., Japanese respondents received one of two Japanese models) or one of two Caucasian models.

Measurement

As noted earlier, acculturation is not believed to be a unidimensional construct; rather, it has multiple dimensions. In this study, a multiple-item scale was adopted from the work of Donthu and Cherian (1994) and Lee (1993). The factors that were used included (a) strength of ethnic identification (i.e., identification with ethnic group followed by how strongly the individual identifies with his or her ethnic group), (b) assimilation (i.e., importance of assimilating with the dominant culture and importance in maintaining one's own ethnic identity), (c) extent of ethnic-language usage, (d) ethnic composition in one's neighborhood, (e) length of stay in the United States, and (f) media preference. Because different types of scales were used, each scale was standardized, and a total standardized score was determined.

Six dependent variables were included in this study: recall of the product, recall and recognition of the brand, attitude toward the advertisements, attitude toward the brand, and purchase intention. After viewing the last ad (several ads were presented to disguise the purpose of the study and enhance external validity), respondents were asked to list all the products they recalled and the corresponding brands. This was followed by a brand recognition test. These measures of recall and recognition were adopted from a previous study by Petty, Cacioppo, and Schumann (1983).

Attitude toward the advertisement was measured by using five 7-point semantic differential scales anchored by bad–good, unattractive–attractive, unpleasant–pleasant, like very much–dislike very much, and not at all interested–very interested. These scales were used in previous studies by MacKenzie, Lutz, and Belch (1986), and by Mitchell and Olson (1981). As a way to assess attitude toward the brand, three 7-point semantic differential scales were used and anchored by bad–good, unsatisfactory–satisfactory, and unfavorable–favorable. These scales were adopted from previous studies by MacKenzie et al. (1986) and Petty et al. (1983).

The measurement of consumers' intention to purchase the product was measured by four 7-point scales. These scales included the potential for "trying" (anchors: definitely would not try it–definitely would try it), "buying" (anchors: definitely would not buy it–definitely would buy it), "seeking out" (anchors: definitely would not seek it out–definitely would seek it out), and how likely the respondent would want to use this advertised product if it became available in her of his area (anchors: not at all likely–very likely). These scales were drawn from previous studies by Mitchell (1986), Baker and Churchill (1977), and Petty et al. (1983).

RESULTS

Several manipulation checks were conducted. First, as already stated, two models were employed for each ethnic group. The model within an ethnic group was tested as a possible covariate in the initial analyses and was found not to be significant. Thus the model within an ethnic group was dropped as a possible covariate. Second, attractiveness of models was again tested and no significant differences were found.

Analysis of variance (ANOVA) tests were conducted on both product and brand recall. Although no differences were found on product recognition (likely to result from only five ads being used), results of the recall measures revealed some interesting differences between ethnic respondents moderated by acculturation. A simple respondent-ethnicity main effect appeared for product recall, with the Japanese respondents recalling the product more than either the Korean or Chinese respondents, $F(2, 197) = 4.876$, $p < .009$. This main effect must be considered in light of a significant three-way interaction, $F(2, 197) = 3.053$, $p < .05$. As Fig. 19.1 suggests, while the product recall scores for the Chinese and Korean respondents

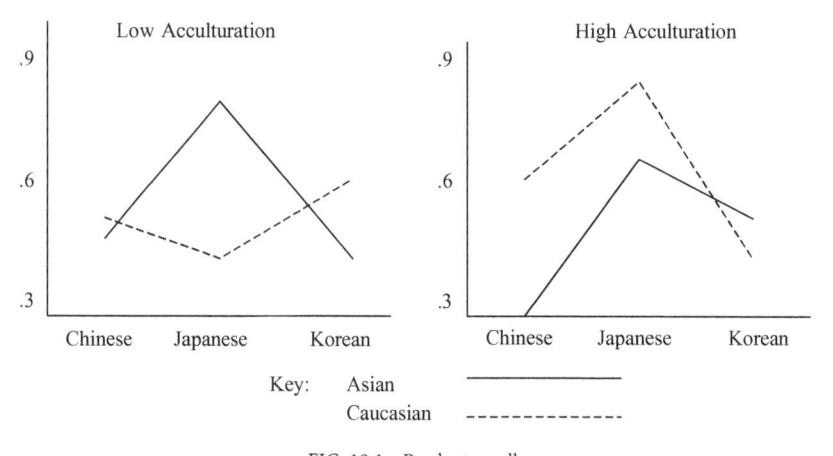

FIG. 19.1. Product recall.

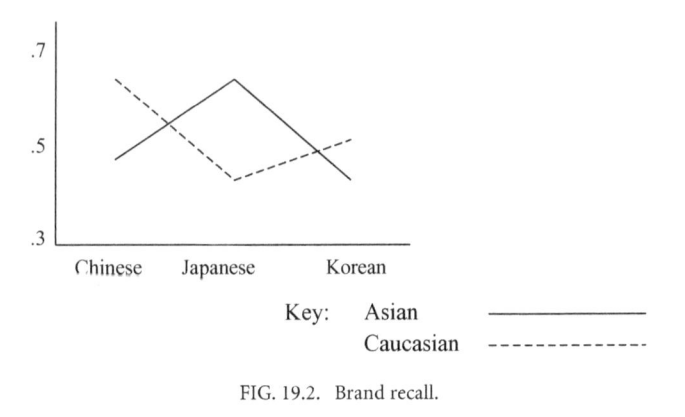

FIG. 19.2. Brand recall.

demonstrated little difference between Asian and Caucasian models across acculturation differences, an acculturation difference did emerge for the Japanese
respondents. When Japanese respondents viewed the Caucasian model, those under the high-acculturation condition recalled the product more often than those
respondents under the low-acculturation condition.

For recall of the brand, a marginal two-way interaction (Model type × Respondent ethnicity interaction) surfaced: $F(2, 197) = 2.492$, $p < .09$. As Fig. 19.2 reflects, for Korean respondents there appears to be no difference between the types
of models. However, for the Chinese and Japanese respondents there appears to
be a crossover effect. For the Chinese respondents, brand recall is slightly higher
when the Caucasian model is employed; for the Japanese respondents, the Japanese
model facilitates more brand recall.

Two indexes of attitude were measured. The results for attitude toward the
advertising revealed respondent-ethnicity differences. A main effect, $F(2, 197) =$
9.01, $p < .001$, reflected that Chinese respondents rated the advertising higher
than the Japanese respondents, who in turn rated the product higher than the
Korean respondents. This respondent-ethnicity main effect also surfaced for the
attitude toward the brand: $F(2, 197) = 7.504$, $p < .001$. However, this latter finding must be viewed in light of both a significant two-way interaction (Model type ×
Respondent ethnicity), $F(2, 197) = 3.480$, $p < .04$, and a three-way interaction,
$F(2, 197) = 3.129$, $p < .05$. As Fig. 19.3 reflects, when respondents were exposed
to an ethnically consistent model (Asian model), the Chinese respondents rated the
brand higher than did the Japanese or the Koreans. It is interesting to note that, for
the Korean sample, acculturation level moderated the influence of the Caucasian
model on brand attitude. Here a somewhat counterintuitive result emerged. When
viewing the Caucasian model, the Koreans who were less acculturated rated the
brand higher than those Koreans who were more acculturated.

Finally, an index of purchase intention was analyzed. Again, a respondent-
ethnicity main effect emerged: $F(2, 197) = 9.629$, $p < .0001$. As experienced in

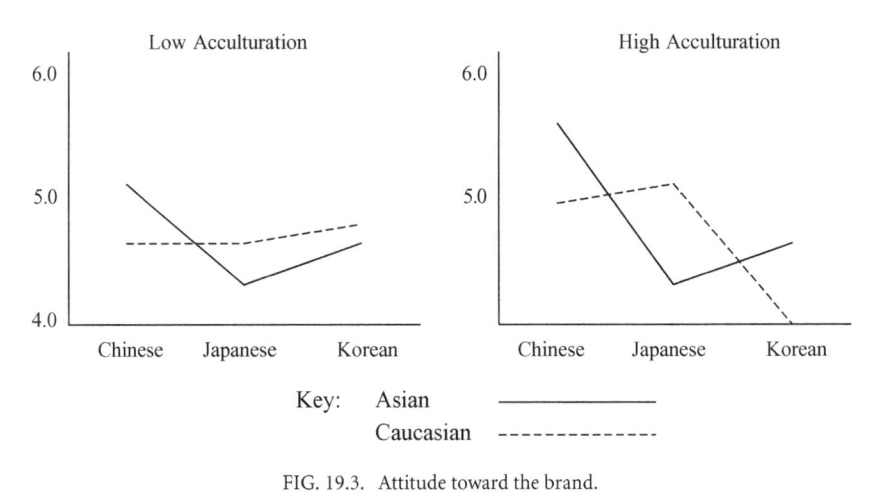

Key: Asian   ——————————
        Caucasian   - - - - - - - - - - - -

FIG. 19.3.   Attitude toward the brand.

both attitude indexes, the Chinese respondents were more likely to want to purchase the product than were the Japanese or the Korean respondents.

DISCUSSION

There were at least two obvious limitations of this exploratory study. First, as mentioned earlier, the respondents were drawn from convenience samples (although placement in conditions was randomly conducted), gathered semisystematically at ethnic grocery stores, churches, and graduate-student housing. An effort was made to ensure an equal proportion of students appeared in each ethnic group. The second limitation addresses potential cultural differences. Toothpaste is considered a common product in the United States. However, no measures were taken to see if these three ethnic respondent groups viewed the product differently in general. If they did, this might have accounted for certain respondent-ethnicity main effects found in the study.

With due notation of the limitations of this study, the results did reflect differences in ethnicity of the respondents in awareness of the product, attitude toward the advertising and brand, and purchase intention. These results potentially reflect the contention of this chapter that important differences exist between ethnic groups within the overall Asian label. In this study, the Chinese respondents consistently rated the advertising and the brand higher than did the Japanese and Korean respondents. Although this might have been a culturally based response, it still is consistent with the notion that there are important differences between Asian ethnic groups and that marketers should take this under consideration when developing target-market strategies.

Acculturation was also found to serve as a moderator of two types of responses. For the Japanese respondents attempting to recall the product when viewing a Caucasian model, those low in acculturation had weaker recall of the product than did respondents higher in acculturation. An acculturation-moderating influence also surfaced with regard to the Korean respondents as they rated their attitude toward the brand. In a counterintuitive finding, for respondents viewing the Caucasian model, those who were lower in acculturation rated the brand higher than did respondents who were higher in acculturation. This seems contradictory to what conventional wisdom would dictate, that stronger acculturation would lead to greater acceptance of products promoted by Caucasian models. Again, the interaction effects involving acculturation found in this study reinforce the fact that significant differences exist between Asian ethnic groups.

CONCLUSIONS

The purpose of this chapter was to reinforce the contention that Asian American ethnic groups should be considered as separate entities when marketers consider their targeting strategies. This chapter reviewed previous literature and reported the results of a recently conducted empirical study. Both the literature and the study presented here support the conclusion that Asian ethnic groups differ in important ways, and, when Asians are targeted as one group, significant potential exists for the creation of ineffective marketing strategies.

In the empirical study, differences were found in responses to advertising stimuli. Such differences in consumption-related activity have been found in previous studies (e.g., Kang & Kim, 1998). The previous literature reflects differences in media choice, store patronage, use of information sources, and so on. The research to date appears to support Kitayama and Markus' Multifactor Interaction Model (presented in Fiske, Kitayama, Markus, & Nisbett, 1998). This model suggests that action results from the interaction of four factors: collective reality, sociopsychological processes, individual reality, and psychological tendencies. The first three factors found in this model support the contention that cultural differences play a critical role in predicting behavior. The collective reality reflects the core cultural ideas, what is good, moral, and the notion of self. Here we find the interplay of ecological, economic, and sociopolitical factors. The sociopsychological processes suggested in Kitayama & Markus's model consider "customs, norms, practices, and institutions reflecting and promoting the core ideas." (p. 918) Finally, the individual reality is based on recurrent episodes in local worlds that personalize the core ideas (e.g., home, school, or workplace). The Multifactor Interaction Model reinforces the importance of considering cultural factors in assessing behavior.

In sum, this chapter presents significant support for the notion that Asian ethnic groups should be considered individually and that marketers should turn away from the tendency to categorize these groups under one umbrella label. This suggestion for greater separation will require marketers to gather group specific information on cultural values, attitudes, acculturation effects, demographic differences, and consumer needs and desires, as ethnically based target-market strategies are considered.

REFERENCES

Baker, M. J., & Churchill, G. A., Jr. (1977, November). The impact of physically attractive models on advertising evaluations. *Journal of Marketing Research, 14*, 538–555.

Banks, J. A. (1981). *Multiethnic education: Theory and practices.* Boston: Allyn & Bacon.

Braun, H. (1991). Marketing to minority consumers. *Discount Merchandiser, 31*, 44–46, 74.

Childers, T., & Rao, A. (1992). The influence of familial and peer-based reference groups on consumer decisions. *Journal of Consumer Research, 19*, 198–211.

Choe, S. T. (1984). *Acculturation and consumption patterns of ethnic consumers: The case of Korean immigrants in Dallas, Texas.* Unpublished doctoral dissertation, Mississippi State University, State College.

Choi, J., & Tamborini, R. (1988). Communication-acculturation and the cultivation hypothesis: A comparative study between two Korean communities in the U.S. *The Harvard Journal of Communications, 1*, 57–74.

Cohen, J. (1992). White consumer response to Asian models in advertising. *Journal of Consumer Marketing, 9*, 17–27.

Delener, R., & Neelankavil, J. (1990). Informational sources and media usage: A comparison between Asian and Hispanic subcultures. *Journal of Advertising Research, 30*, 45–52.

Deshpande, R., Hoyer, W. D., & Donthu, N. (1986). The intensity of ethnic affiliation: A study of the sociology of Hispanic consumption. *Journal of Consumer Research, 13*, 214–220.

Donthu, N., & Cherian, J. (1994). Impact of strength of ethnic identification on Hispanic shopping behavior. *Journal of Retailing, 70*, 383–393.

Engle, J., Blackwell, R., & Minard, P. (1995). *Consumer behavior* (8th ed.). New York: The Dryden Press.

Fisher, C. (1993, February 15). Poll: Hispanics stick to brands. *Advertising Age*, Vol. 64, p. 6.

Fiske, A. P., Kitayama, S., Markus, H. R., and Nisbett, R. E. (1998). The cultural matrix of social psychology. In D. T. Gilbert, S. T. Fiske, and G. Lindzey (Eds.), *Handbook of social psychology* (pp. 915–981). Boston: McGraw-Hill.

Fost, D. (1990, October). California's Asian market. *American Demographics*, Vol. 12, 34–37.

Henricks, M. (1992). Marketing to minorities. *Small Business Report, 17*(3), 47–55.

Herche, J., & Balasubramanian, S. (1994). Ethnicity and shopping behavior. *Journal of Shopping Center Research, 1*, 65–80.

Jun, S., Ball, A., & Gentry, J. (1993). Modes of consumer acculturation. In L. Mcalister and M. Rothschild (Eds.), *Advances in consumer research* (Vol. 20, pp. 76–82). Provo, UT: Association for Consumer Research.

Kang, J. K., and Kim, Y. (1997). Impact of ethnicity and acculturation on Asian-American market segmentation strategies. *Proceedings of the 1997 Summer Marketing Educators' Conference of the American Marketing Association* (pp. 261–270). Chicago: American Medical Association.

Kang, J., & Kim, Y. (1998). Ethnicity and acculturation: Influences on Asian-American consumers' purchase decision making for social clothes. *Family & Consumer Sciences Research Journal, 27*, 91–102.

Kim, S. H. (1987). *A comparative study of shopping orientations between Korean immigrants and whites in Allegheny County.* Unpublished doctoral dissertation, University of Pittsburgh, PA.

Kim, C., Laroche, M., & Joy, A. (1990). An empirical study of the effects of ethnicity on consumption patterns in abi-cultural environment. In T. Kinnear (Ed.), *Advances in Consumer Research* (Vol. 17, pp. 839–846). Provo, UT: Association for Consumer Research.

Lach, J. (1999). Asians at home. *American Demographics, 21*(9), 20.

Lee, W. (1989). The mass-mediated consumption realities of three cultural groups. In T. K. Srull (Ed.), *Advances in Consumer Research* (Vol. 16, pp. 771–778). Provo, UT: Association for Consumer Research.

Lee, W. (1993). Acculturation and advertising communication strategies: A cross-cultural study of Chinese and Americans. *Psychology and Marketing, 10*, 381–397.

Lee, W., & Tse, D. (1994). Changing media consumption in a new home: Acculturation patterns among Hong Kong immigrants to Canada. *Journal of Advertising, 23*, 57–70.

Lee, W., & Um, K. R. (1992). Ethnicity and consumer product evaluation: A cross-cultural comparison of Korean immigrants and Americans. In J. Sherry and B. Sternthal (Eds.), *Advances in Consumer Research* (Vol. 19, pp. 429–436). Provo, UT: Association for Consumer Research.

MacKenzie, S. B., Lutz, R. J., & Belch, G. E. (1986, May). The role of attitude toward the ad as mediator of advertising effectiveness: A test of competing explanations. *Journal of Marketing Research, 23*, 130–143.

Mendoza, R. H. (1989). An empirical scale to measure type and degree of acculturation in Mexican-American adolescents and adults. *Journal of Cross-Cultural Psychology, 20*, 372–385.

Miller, C. (1993, May). Researcher says U.S. is more than a pot. *Marketing News, 27*, 6.

Miracle, G. E., Chang, K., & Taylor, C. R. (1982). Culture and advertising executions: A comparison of selected characteristics of Korean and U.S. television commercials. *International Marketing Review, 9* (4), 5–17.

Mitchell, A. A. (1986). The effects of verbal and visual components of advertisements on brand attitudes and attitude toward the ad. *Journal of Consumer Research, 13*, 12–24.

Mitchell, A. A., & Olson, J. C. (1981). Are product attribute beliefs the only mediator of advertising effects on brand attitude? *Journal of Marketing Research, 18*, 318–332.

O'Guinn, T. C., Faber, R. J., & Rice, M. D. (1985). Popular film and television and consumer acculturation agents: America 1900 to present. In J. Sheth & C. T. Tan (Eds.), *Historical perspectives in consumer research: National and international perspectives* (pp. 297–301). Singapore: National University of Singapore.

O'Guinn, T. C., Lee, W., & Faber, R. J. (1986). Acculturation: The impact of divergent path on buyer behavior. In R. J. Lutz (Ed.), *Advances in Consumer Research* (Vol. 13, pp. 579–583). Provo, UT: Association for Consumer Research.

On this multicultural front, mystique holds back marketers (1999, May 3). *Advertising Age, 70*, 19, p. 36.

Ownbey, S. (1991). *Chinese Americans: Cultural values and shopping orientations*. Unpublished doctoral dissertation, Texas Tech University, Lubbock.

Penaloza, L. (1994). Atravensando fronteras/border crossings: A critical ethnographic explanation of the consumer acculturation of Mexican immigrants. *Journal of Consumer Research, 21*, 32–54.

Petty, R. E., Cacioppo, J. T., & Schumann, D. W. (1983). Central and peripheral routes to advertising effectiveness: The moderating role of involvement. *Journal of Consumer Research, 10*, 135–146.

Shim, S., & Chen, Y. Q. (1996). Acculturation characteristics and apparel shopping orientations: Chinese students and spouses from the People's Republic of China residing in the southwest. *Clothing and Textile Research Journal, 14*, 204–215.

Social Science Research Council. (1954). Acculturation: An exploratory formation. *American Anthropologist, 56*, 973–1002.

Solomon, M. (1983). The role of products as social stimuli: A symbolic interactionism perspective. *Journal of Consumer Research, 10*, 319–329.

Taylor, C. R., & Lee, J. Y. (1994). Not in vogue: Portrayals of Asian-Americans in U.S. Advertising. *Journal of Public Policy and Marketing, 13*, 239–245.

Taylor, C. R., Lee, J. Y., & Stern, B. B. (1995). Portrayals of African, Hispanic, and Asian Americans in Magazine Advertising. *American Behavioral Scientist, 38*, 608–621.

Taylor, C. R., & Stern, B. B. (1997). Asian-Americans: Television advertising and the "model minority" stereotype. *Journal of Advertising, 14*, 47–61.

Triandis, H. C., Kashima, Y., Hui, C. H., Lisansky, J., and Marin, G. (1982). Acculturation and bi-culturalism indices among relatively acculturated Hispanic young adults. *Interamerican Journal of Psychology, 16*, 140–149.

Wallendorf, M., & Reilly, M. (1983). Ethnic migration, assimilation and consumption. *Journal of Consumer Research, 10*, 292–302.

World Advertising Expenditures (20th ed.). (1986). Mamaroneck, NY: Starch INRA Hooper.

Yau, O. (1988). Chinese cultural values: Their dimensions and marketing implications. *European Journal of Marketing, 22*, 44–57.

CHAPTER TWENTY

Mainstream Marketers Advertise To Gays and Lesbians: Strategic Issues and Research Agenda

Timothy B. Greenlee
Miami University

The past 10 years have been witness to an increasing number of mainstream marketers who direct various elements of their promotional efforts at the gay and lesbian consumer market, often referred to as the "dream market" (Lukenbill, 1995). Because it is characterized as an over $500 billion market comprising approximately 18 million consumers (Johnson & Levin, 1993), mainstream marketers have found it increasingly difficult to ignore such a consumer group. The lucrative nature of this market segment has fueled significant growth in the advertising revenue generated by gay and lesbian print media, making it the fastest growing category in the advertising print market industry. Advertising revenue in the gay and lesbian press increased from $74 million in 1996 to $100 million in 1997 to $110 million in 1998. In addition, there are now over 152 gay and lesbian magazines and newspapers across the country reaching over 5 million consumers (Nicholson, 1999). Such growth rates underscore the movement of mainstream marketers to attract and retain a portion of the gay and lesbian consumer dollar.

As the number of mainstream marketers appealing to the gay and lesbian consumer segment increases, firms must continue to increase their level of commitment to the gay and lesbian community. In doing so, mainstream marketers must understand the effectiveness of various communication strategies for targeting gay and lesbian consumers in gay media. Increasing levels of commitment and corporate involvement can be achieved via internal and external paths. Internally, mainstream marketers may consider a wide range of corporate policies toward gay- and lesbian-specific issues. Externally, mainstream marketers may consider advertising strategies that specifically target the gay and lesbian community. Ideally,

358

GREENLEE

corporations will have enacted internal corporate policy that reflects positively on its gay and lesbian employees prior to targeting external promotional efforts toward gay and lesbian consumers.

This chapter focuses on the strategies available to mainstream marketers as they attempt to secure a portion of the gay and lesbian consumer dollar. As a backdrop, a brief historical perspective of gay- and lesbian-oriented advertising is offered. In addition, evidence is presented to substantiate exactly what the dream market entails. Next, a discussion of the role of corporate policy in targeting the gay and lesbian community is presented along with a hierarchical promotional strategy model. The chapter concludes with a research agenda designed to provide insight for mainstream marketers attempting to target gay and lesbian consumers.

HISTORICAL PERSPECTIVE

Consider the following "firsts" that have propelled numerous mainstream marketers into the gay and lesbian consumer market debate. As one of the earliest mainstream advertisers to target the gay and lesbian market, Carillon Importers placed an ad for Absolut vodka in the first edition of the *Advocate* in 1979. With continued advertising support, this brand enjoys enormous loyalty within the gay and lesbian community. Featuring its Benson & Hedges brand in *Genre*, Philip Morris became the first tobacco-related company to advertise in a gay publication. In 1994, using a depiction of two men selecting a dining table, Ikea, a Swedish furniture company, was the first to use gay characters in an advertisement for mainstream television. Today, numerous mainstream marketers, including AT&T, MCI, Banana Republic, The Gap, IBM, and Apple, direct elements of their promotional mix toward the gay and lesbian consumer market.

With such efforts becoming more commonplace, critics may be hard pressed to question the practitioners' acceptance of the existence of the gay and lesbian market segment. Two major factors have contributed to the growth of gay- and lesbian-targeted advertising and promotional efforts, especially by mainstream advertisers. First, there has been a softening in mainstream America's views toward homosexuality. Although perhaps not fully condoned, homosexuality is arguably less taboo than once viewed by the general public. A recent Gallop study reported 84% of Americans favor employment discrimination protection for gays and lesbians. As a result, a new generation of marketing decision-makers has been educated with less bias toward gay- and lesbian-oriented issues and is more apt to consider targeted appeals toward these groups. Furthermore, several gay- and lesbian-oriented media have modified their editorial policies to eliminate explicit sexual material from their pages. Such editorial decisions have made these gay- and lesbian-oriented media outlets less risky for mainstream marketers.

Not surprisingly, the growth in the gay and lesbian consumer movement has been paralleled by the rise of the gay and lesbian social movement. As noted by

Penaloza (1996), members of a social movement tend to have a heavily sensitized concern for the impact of marketing communications on group interests. Traditionally, marketing studies prescribing how to target specific groups have paralleled respective social movements. During the 1970s, numerous marketing studies focused on targeting women and African Americans, whereas studies during the 1980s focused on the Latino market. Although the gay and lesbian consumer movement has experienced significant growth during the 1990s, academic marketing research focusing on this movement lags behind.

DEFINING THE DREAM MARKET

As previously noted, the gay and lesbian consumer segment is estimated to consist of approximately 18 million consumers with expenditures in excess of $500 billion (Johnson & Levin, 1993), a lucrative market segment by most standards. However, evidence substantiating the existence of such a dream market is often called into question, as much of the data were gathered from biased sampling frames. For example, a 1990 study by Overlooked Opinions (Lukenbill, 1995) drew a sample from readers of gay and lesbian publications and from sign-up sheets gathered at gay and lesbian events, such as Gay Pride celebrations. The study concluded that 34% of gay and lesbian households had incomes greater than $50,000 versus 25% in the general population and that 26% of gays and lesbians held graduate degrees versus 5% in the general population; it also estimated the gay and lesbian community's total income to be approximately $518 billion.

Critics note that sampling frames based on readers of gay and lesbian media and attendance at gay and lesbian events are highly unrepresentative of the entire gay and lesbian community. Thus, it should not be surprising that people who read more magazines and newspapers and attend special gay and lesbian events are likely to have higher levels of income and are unlikely to be representative of the gay and lesbian population at large.

Although studies using biased sampling frames may lead to inaccurate projections concerning the entire gay and lesbian community, these studies do offer valuable insight into a specific segment of the gay and lesbian community, namely the readership of gay and lesbian print media. Estimated to account for approximately 5 million consumers, this segment of the gay and lesbian community represents an identifiable, accessible, and sizable target audience. In addition to the previously noted demographics provided by the Overlooked Opinions study, consider the income and education demographics pertaining to the readership of gay and lesbian print media generated from various studies.

In 1988 (Lukenbill, 1995), Simmons Market Research Bureau estimated readers of gay and lesbian print media to have an average personal income of $36,900 and an average household income of $55,430. In addition, Simmons estimated that 49% of the readers of gay and lesbian print media held college degrees whereas only

18% of the general population held college degrees. In 1992 (Lukenbill, 1995), the National Gay Newspaper Guild estimated readers of gay and lesbian print media to have an average personal income of $41,300 and an average household income of $63,700. (Lukenbill, 1995), Simmons Market Research Bureau estimated that 28% of readers of gay and lesbian print media had personal incomes over $50,000 and 21% had household incomes over $100,000.

With a readership composed of above-average wealth and education, gay and lesbian print media offer mainstream marketers a lucrative outlet for advertisements designed to appeal to the gay and lesbian community. Mainstream marketers of goods and services designed for such a demographic segment would be well advised to utilize gay and lesbian print media when appealing to this market segment. As an example, in 1996, 90% of gays and lesbians took a domestic trip compared with 65% of the general population (Wilke, 1997). Marketers in product categories such as travel, medicine, finance, law, and entertainment should take advantage of the natural linkages between their products and this specific market segment. In doing so, mainstream marketers should be able to target more effectively their promotional expenditures and eliminate wasted coverage. In addition, by targeting the readership of gay and lesbian media, mainstream marketers may avoid the majority of heterosexual backlash that may accompany marketing efforts outside of the targeted covers of gay- and lesbian-oriented print media.

COMMUNICATION STRATEGIES

Although various communication strategies exist to appeal to the previously identified gay and lesbian consumer segment that possesses above-average personal or household incomes and education levels, most strategies can be classified as being "more" or "less" in the public eye. Corporations may choose to take a "less public" approach to appealing to the gay and lesbian community through a strategy that is less in the general public's eye. Corporate sponsorship of gay- and lesbian-specific events and direct marketing appeals targeted to gay and lesbian consumers are examples of such tactics.

Conversely, corporations may choose to take a "more public" approach to appealing to the gay and lesbian community through a strategy that would be more in the general public's eye. Although they still target the gay and lesbian consumer segment, these tools may be more open to the scrutiny of the general public. Corporate policy toward gay and lesbian issues and advertisements in gay- and lesbian-oriented print media are examples of such efforts. Although these efforts are arguably not more public in the sense that the advertisements are not placed in mainstream media outlets, the placement of advertisements by mainstream marketers in gay- and lesbian-oriented print media more overtly identifies a marketer's efforts than does a direct mail promotional effort targeted at gay and lesbian consumers.

Event Sponsorship and Direct Marketing

For years, corporations including Tanquerey, Absolut, and Anheuser-Busch have maintained a sponsorship status at numerous gay- and lesbian-oriented events such as gay rodeos, marathons, bicycle races, and pride celebrations. Logic dictates that companies attempting to capture a presence in the gay and lesbian market would benefit from such sponsorships. In addition, corporations have utilized these events as a means of developing targeted mailing lists for use with their direct marketing initiatives. Both AT&T and MCI have utilized direct marketing campaigns as an attempt to gain a foothold in the gay and lesbian community. With both of these tactics, corporations are more able to focus their efforts on the targeted segment and are less likely to encounter a negative "spillover" effect on nontargeted segments.

Corporate Policy

In the purchase decision-making process, gay and lesbian consumers may be persuaded by evidence of a firm's corporate policy toward related issues. Thus, marketers interested in capturing a share of the gay and lesbian market may be well served to consider the corporation's position toward gay- and lesbian-related issues. Various gay- and lesbian-related organizations, including the Human Rights Campaign and The Wall Street Project, stand ready to provide firms with direction in developing appropriate policy.

For a firm to communicate a position of equality to gay and lesbian consumers, The Human Rights Campaign recommends that a firm establish corporate policies that address three specific issues. First, the firm should include the phrase "sexual orientation" in its nondiscrimination policies. Although numerous companies advocate a position of nondiscrimination on the basis of race, sex, color, religion, national origin, or disability, federal civil rights law already covers these categories. Inclusion of sexual orientation, a category not included in federal civil rights law, would communicate a higher level of commitment to gay- and lesbian-related issues. As of March 2003, 2,249 employers, including 313 Fortune 500 companies, have adopted nondiscrimination policies that include sexual orientation (Human Rights Campaign, 2003).

Second, the firm should provide its employees with domestic partner benefits. In 1982, the *Village Voice*, a New York City weekly, became the first employer to offer domestic partner benefits to its gay and lesbian employees. In 1992, Lotus Development Corporation became the first publicly traded company to do so. Domestic partner benefits should include the same benefits that are made available to the spouses of heterosexual married employees. Given that benefits comprise nearly 40% of overall compensation, firms that offer domestic partner benefits demonstrate evidence of providing equal pay for equal work. As of March 2003, 5,760 employers, including 186 Fortune 500 companies, offer domestic partner health benefits (Human Rights Campaign, 2003).

Third, the firm should support the formation of gay and lesbian employee groups. Such groups serve as channels of information and can assist the firm in developing its gay- and lesbian-related policies.

In addition, The Wall Street Project, an organization of gay and lesbian shareholder activists, designed a list of equity principles on sexual orientation as a voluntary code of conduct aimed at achieving equality in the workplace. Similar initiatives, including the Sullivan Principles on South Africa, the MacBride Principles on Fair Employment in Northern Ireland, and the Ceres Principles on the Environment, established shareholder activism as a practicable tool in creating social change (Lukenbill, 1995). The Wall Street Project Initiatives address the following issues:

1. Discrimination based on sexual orientation is prohibited.
2. Discrimination against HIV-positive employees or those with AIDS is prohibited.
3. The formation of employee groups based on sexual orientation is promoted.
4. Information concerning sexual orientation is incorporated in diversity training.
5. Domestic partner benefits are provided.
6. Company advertising avoids negative sexual stereotypes and does not discriminate in media advertising on the basis of sexual orientation.
7. Company does not discriminate in the sell and purchase of goods and services on the basis of sexual orientation.
8. Throughout the company, written nondiscrimination policies on sexual orientation are disseminated and corporate compliance is monitored.

Specific corporate policy issues to be considered could vary but would likely address the following issues. At a minimum, a company should provide recognition of the benefits of a diverse workplace. Such a statement should be a part of written corporate policy and could be highlighted in corporate advertising. Proceeding one step further, a company should adopt a stated policy of nondiscrimination based on sexual orientation in both its hiring and promoting practices. Such policy would strengthen a company's commitment from a general diversity position to one of more specific action.

Following the development of nondiscriminatory policies based on sexual orientation, a company should focus efforts on developing programs that benefit all its employees. Possible programs may include a sensitivity training program and a corporate-sponsored gay and lesbian employee group. In addition, domestic partner benefits would signal a high level of commitment to gay and lesbian consumers.

Externally, the company should consider providing support for gay and lesbian philanthropic organizations and should avoid sending contradictory messages to the gay and lesbian community by supporting political action committees known to have low levels of tolerance for gay and lesbian issues. A firm's efforts to offer domestic partner benefits may be overshadowed if the firm also makes financial contributions to political action committees known not to support gay and lesbian initiatives. Finally, the company may want to consider incorporating an appropriate level of advertising directed to the gay and lesbian consumer. The basis for such an advertising strategy is developed in the following section.

Hierarchical Advertising Strategy Model

In addition to gay- and lesbian-friendly corporate policy, the placement of advertisements in gay- and lesbian-oriented print media is suggested as another more public approach to appealing to the gay and lesbian community. As previously discussed, advertising revenue in the over 150 gay and lesbian newspapers and magazines increased from $74 million in 1996 to $110 million in 1998. Although many of the gay- and lesbian-oriented print media are local or regional in scope, several outlets cater to a national audience, including *The Advocate, Curve, Genre, Men's Style, Next, Out, 50/50, 10 Percent, POZ, Victor,* and *Wilde.*

When corporate decisions have been made to follow such a strategy, what type of advertising tactics should be used? Should the firm take a more cost-effective approach and simply run promotional tools designed for traditional markets and outlets? Or should the firm develop promotional tools specific for gay and lesbian media outlets? Furthermore, if specific tools are developed, what level of "gayness" is most effective? In a study conducted by Wilke (1996), 54% of gay and lesbian consumers wanted advertisements that addressed gay and lesbian themes, 33% stated that support for such advertisements would depend on how the gay content was handled in the advertisements, and 13% stated that the advertisements should concentrate on the product, not the consumer. As is evident from the survey results, differing views exist among members of the gay and lesbian consumer segment.

As a means of addressing this issue, this chapter proposes a five-stage hierarchical advertising strategy model for targeting the gay and lesbian market through gay- and lesbian-oriented print media. These strategies communicate varying degrees of marketer commitment and openness toward gay and lesbian issues. Refer to Fig. 20.1 for a diagram of the advertising hierarchy.

The model's initial stage begins with marketers' utilizing traditional, mainstream advertisements in gay- and lesbian-oriented media outlets. Marketers adopting such a technique simply place the advertisements designed to run in a more mainstream medium into a gay- and lesbian-specific medium. In doing so, marketers opt for a more cost-effective approach to reaching the gay and lesbian community because advertising and production costs are kept to a minimum. In addition, potential backlash from the heterosexual audience may be less severe as the

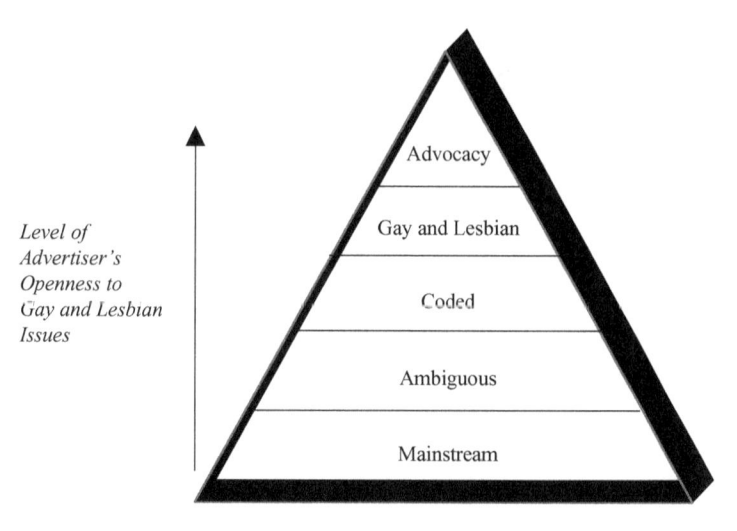

*Level of
Advertiser's
Openness to
Gay and Lesbian
Issues*

FIG. 20.1.   Advertising strategy hierarchy to target gays and lesbians.

advertisements were not explicitly gay or lesbian in orientation. However, such a strategy must be balanced against the potential that gays and lesbians may perceive it as a low level of commitment to the gay and lesbian community. Companies including Movado watches, Saab automobiles, Propecia (the hair loss prevention drug), and Gardenburger have used this tactic.

The second stage uses more tailored efforts to target the gay and lesbian consumer with promotions that include ambiguous copy or layout. Through such efforts, marketers intentionally attempt to present a vague message that may be interpreted multiple ways by multiple markets. Marketers intend for a specific target market, such as the gay and lesbian community, to "see" in the advertisement a message that is pertinent to their market while with the same advertisement another target market, such as a heterosexual market, will see a message that targets their market. Examples of this tactic include (the kitchen and dining superstore) Kitchen and Company's use of the slogan "23,000 gifts that won't stay in the closet" (ambiguous: gifts vs. people staying in the closet) and Meridian Settlement Company's use of the slogan "we help people diagnosed with a terminal illness achieve a higher quality of life (ambiguous: terminal illness such as HIV or AIDS vs. cancer). In addition, an advertisement for Parliament Cigarettes provides the ambiguous situation of two shirtless men and one clothed woman as the backdrop for individual interpretation.

The third stage builds on the second stage by making the ambiguousness of the advertisement more gay- and lesbian-targeted with the use of gay- and lesbian-specific code. Possible codes that could be used include specific words or slogans that have special meaning within the gay and lesbian community. Examples of such words include "pride, family, and coming out." In addition, specific symbols such as the inverted triangle, the rainbow flag and freedom rings could be incorporated into the layout of an advertisement. In both instances, the marketer is attempting to communicate with words or symbols that have specific meaning to the targeted group and may be meaningless to nontargeted groups. Gay and lesbian consumers may find this type of advertising especially appealing, as it acknowledges the existence of a specific subculture rich with its own language and meaning. Sea-Doo Watercraft has utilized gay code in an advertisement that includes the word "family" in quotes and a set of freedom rings and a rainbow flag sticker. Budweiser has also utilized code by dressing a bottle of Bud Light with a rainbow-colored top hat, a string of rainbow-colored beads and rainbow-colored balloons.

The fourth level of the hierarchy taps a higher level of involvement as marketers take their efforts one step further by directly appealing to gay and lesbian consumers with the use of gay- and lesbian-specific advertisements. Such a tactic demonstrates to the gay and lesbian community a marketer's direct interest, because the marketer has developed advertisements that openly target the community. The message from the marketer is one of equality. The marketer has identified and acknowledged the existence of the gay and lesbian target market as a meaningful market segment that will be directly targeted. Examples include an IBM advertisement featuring two men stating "we're not your typical mom and pop operation" and American Express Financial Advisors' use of a photograph of two women embracing and an accompanying caption stating "how do you plan your future together." In addition, the Hartford Insurance Agency utilized combinations of pink and blue cars to represent services to gay, lesbian, and heterosexual couples. For gay couples, two blue cars are shown with the tagline "The Hartford offers auto insurance discounts to gay couples." For lesbian couples, two pink cars are shown with the tagline "We also offer discounts to lesbian couples." Lastly, for heterosexual couples, one blue and one pink car are shown with the tagline "Heck, we even offer discounts to heterosexual couples."

Marketers may make the ultimate pitch by means of corporate advertising designed to portray a specific image or highlight a certain advocacy or cause. With these tactics, marketers are not necessarily promoting specific brands; instead, marketers are stressing the corporation's overall culture with respect to gay and lesbian issues. With corporate advertising, mainstream marketers are afforded the opportunity of communicating to the target market the firm's corporate policy as it relates to gay and lesbian issues. In doing so, a firm is able to demonstrate that its overall corporate commitment to the gay and lesbian community goes beyond merely advertising goods ands services and extends into the company's overall policies. Coors provides an example of an advocacy advertisement with its tag line "perception isn't always reality" and an ensuing discussion of the company's progressive employee practices. EDS also offers an example of this hierarchical level with its "sea of diversity" advertisement. Clos Du Bois winery also utilizes this strategy by announcing its support of the NAMES Project and the AIDS Memorial

Quilt. In addition, The Dun and Bradstreet Corporation asks the question "Does it matter whether he's straight or gay?" as a means of promoting its diverse workforce.

RESEARCH AGENDA

Despite the growing interest in the gay and lesbian consumer market from mainstream marketers, the field has received scarce attention from academic researchers. Two of the previously discussed areas are prime for empirical research and would provide practitioners with insight on how best to secure a portion of the gay and lesbian consumer dollar.

Specifically, research investigating the effects of various levels of corporate involvement with respect to gay and lesbian issues would offer marketers initial insight into structuring their internal policies. Descriptive research assessing the overall awareness of and importance to gay and lesbian consumers to related corporate policy issues would provide insight and offer a benchmark for future comparison. This could be followed by experimental research designed to assess the impact of corporate policy awareness and importance on traditional measures such as attitudes toward the advertisement, attitudes toward the brand, and purchase intentions. Following a determination of the effects of various levels of corporate involvement with gay- and lesbian-oriented issues, companies could target the desired level of corporate involvement appropriate for the organization's desired outcomes.

Further direction could be provided by empirically studying the hierarchical promotional strategy model. Is one level of the hierarchy consistently more effective, or is the effectiveness of the various levels dependent on other issues? What conditions render various levels of the hierarchy more effective at generating positive attitudes and behaviors for sponsoring organizations? Again, initial descriptive research should assess the overall awareness and importance of the hierarchical model. Subsequently, experimental research should assess the impact of the hierarchy on the traditional measures of attitudes toward the advertisement, attitudes toward the brand, and purchase intentions.

CONCLUSION

As is often the situation, recent history serves as a conservative estimate of the near future; thus, more corporations will be drawn into the competition for a portion of the gay and lesbian community's purchasing dollar. The pullover effect begins to take place as a firm's initiative toward the gay and lesbian community is countered by a competitor's marketing movement. Whether the initiative involves corporate policy or advertising strategy, a move by a major competitor will likely generate a competitive reaction.

A continuing softening of society's stance toward gay and lesbian issues will likely fuel increased marketing activities directed to the gay and lesbian community as well. As issues such as corporate policy and advertising strategies utilized in gay- and lesbian-oriented media are resolved, marketers' attention may begin to focus on strategies to achieve crossover advertising, gay-oriented advertising in mainstream media. Throughout this process, academic and practitioner research will be needed to assess the effectiveness of initiatives designed to attract the gay and lesbian consumer segment through mainstream channels.

In addition, as advertising strategy evolves to include more than just gay- and lesbian-oriented print media, organizations will have to develop appropriate assessment tools for measuring the number of people watching, listening, or reading who are gay or lesbian. Currently, no organization provides this level of service; thus, data that are used to inform networks and advertisers are not broken down by sexual orientation. Therefore, no one in mainstream media knows which programs and publications have sizeable gay and lesbian audiences. Thus, guesswork and stereotypes will likely govern media buying decisions, techniques that are without question unacceptable for other market segments. As is evident from this review, there is yet much to know about the dream market.

REFERENCES

Human Rights Campaign. (2003). *The state of the workplace for lesbian, gay, bisexual and transgendered americans.* Retrieved from the Human Rights Campaign Web site, www.hrc.org

Johnson, B., & Levin, G. (1993). The gay quandary: Advertising's most elusive, Yet lucrative target market proves difficult to measure. *Advertising Age, 64*(3), 29.

Lukenbill, G. (1995). *Untold millions.* New York: Harper Business.

Nicholson, J. (1999). Big national advertisers are eyeing gay press. *Editor & Publisher, 132,* 30–31.

Penaloza, L. (1996). We're here, we're Queer, and we're going shopping! A critical perspective on the accommodation of gays and lesbians in the U.S. marketplace. *Journal of Homosexuality, 3*(2), 9–41.

Wilke, M. (1996). Ad survey shows appeal of gay themes. *Advertising Age, 67*(19), 19.

Wilke, M. (1997). United is first major airline to target gays. *Advertising Age, 68*(22), 6.

CHAPTER TWENTY ONE

Targeting Consumer Segments Based on Sexual Orientation: Can Advertisers Swing Both Ways?

Gillian K. Oakenfull
Miami University

Many marketers have begun to refer to the gay and lesbian consumer market as a "dream market," attracted by promises of above-average disposable income and a willingness to spend. A study by Overlooked Opinions, a gay-focused market-research firm, estimates that the gay market consists of 18.5 million people with total annual income of $514 billion (Johnson, 1993). More conservative estimates, such as those of Nile Merton, publisher of *The Advocate*, put the number of gay and lesbian consumers in the United States at 5 million (Johnson, 1993), and gays' and lesbians' annual spending estimated at $450 billion (Garden, 2001).

Firms interested in targeting the gay and lesbian market can choose from a growing number and variety of print media. Most metropolitan areas have both free and paid newspapers and magazines with gay-related content specific to the area. Additionally, a number of nationally distributed gay and lesbian magazines have joined traditional, and more politically inclined, outlets such as *The Advocate*, *On Our Backs*, and *Outweek* to offer marketers more stylish and consumer-oriented vehicles through which to reach a gay and lesbian audience. In 1997, marketers flooded the more than 140 gay magazines and newspapers in the United States with ads totaling over $100 million last year.

Although marketers have little trouble in targeting gay and lesbian consumers in gay-oriented media, a short survey of advertising history will chart a similar path in targeting racial and ethnic groups that led to a crossover to mainstream media. Several firms such as IKEA, Calvin Klein, Banana Republic, and Benetton have used gay imagery in ads that have appeared in mainstream media. However, with this crossover comes an exposure of gay-targeted ads to nongay consumers. Although the gay and lesbian market may seem appealing to marketers, its size is far less significant than the heterosexual audience, many of whom are far from ready to welcome gays and lesbians into mainstream society. In a recent Gallop Poll, a majority of those surveyed believed that being gay is not an "acceptable alternative lifestyle" (Goldstein, 2003). Thus, given the significant negative attitude toward homosexuality in mainstream America, marketers may risk the nightmare of alienating a far greater percentage of the market in pursuit of the "dream market." It is important, therefore, that marketers fully understand the nature of their market before they can determine whether the attractive gay market is worth pursuing.

Marketers must also consider whether the most effective method of reaching gay and lesbian consumers is to treat them as one segment based solely on sexual orientation without considering other bases of segmentation. It may be naïve of marketers to assume that all gay consumers are eager to "go mainstream." Many gay consumers are concerned with the erosion of the gay subculture that may be a direct result of marketplace acceptance of gay consumers. Such a situation may result in marketers' antagonizing the very consumers that they seek to court.

This study puts forth the idea that gays and lesbians should be treated as a distinct subculture rather than a consumer segment in traditional marketing terms. Such a consideration would allow for differences within the group based on the degree and stage of subcultural identity (Cass, 1984; Penaloza, 1994; Troiden, 1989), and it would guide advertisers toward advertising strategies that may more effectively target gay consumers. Additionally, segmentation based solely on sexual orientation may overlook economies that may be gained by targeting gay-friendly heterosexuals with the same ads as gay consumers.

Hence, we need to examine the advertising strategies available to marketers carefully before we chase the pot of gold at the end of the rainbow. This chapter presents a discussion of how marketers should treat gays and lesbians as a consumer group, drawing from the subculture literature to examine how issues of subcultural identity and meaning may provide marketers with a meaningful differentiation strategy for gay and lesbians consumers. This argument provides the basis for an examination of the advertising strategies that are available to advertisers in pursuit of the gay market, and it reflects on the issues that advertisers must consider to carefully balance gay goodwill with the potential stigma attached to courting the gay market. In this way, a framework is offered based on sexual orientation, gay identity, and attitude toward homosexuality within which advertisers may identify the appropriate message and medium for their target market. Drawing from subculture research, the chapter considers advertising strategies that may allow marketers to target gay and gay-friendly consumers without risk of alienating heterosexual consumers who may disapprove of such a strategy.

THE REALITY OF THE DREAM MARKET

Much of the argument for a distinct gay and lesbian consumer segment has stemmed from scientifically questionable studies that have led to the dream market label (Lukenbill, 1995). Compared with heterosexual consumers, gays and lesbians were found to have higher average incomes, more education, and fewer kids. In short, gays and lesbians were seen as a group of DINKs (dual income, no kids), which had marketers rubbing their hands together in anticipation of enormous amounts of disposable income just waiting to be courted (Miller, 1990). However, none of these studies used a representative sample of the gay and lesbian population; they were, in fact, based on readers of gay media publications, a group that is estimated to represent less than half of all gays and lesbians in the United States. The Simmons Market Research Bureau conducted a survey of readers of free gay newspapers circulated in large metropolitan areas throughout the United States that form the National Gay Newspaper Guild (NGNG) (Lukenbill, 1995). When we compare this information with data collected by the 1994 Yankelovich Moniotor (Lukenbill, 1995) on a representative sample of all gays and lesbians, we see some dramatic differences between readers of gay media and the overall gay and lesbian population. Given that the NGNG comprises free publications, these numbers may provide a conservative estimate of the differences between readers of gay media and the overall gay and lesbian population. However, these publications are circulated in large metropolitan areas in the United States, which usually account for above-average incomes for gays and lesbians compared with those living in rural areas. As Table 21.1 shows, readers of gay media are demographically very different from the overall gay and lesbian population in terms of income, both personal and household; gender; occupation; and education.

In additional, it is believed that there are attitudinal differences between readers of gay media and the overall population of gay and lesbian consumers (Lukenbill, 1995). Readers of gay media are more likely to live within gay communities and react differently to marketing actions than nonreaders of gay media (Kates, 1998; Rudd, 1996). Thus, although the 5 million gay and lesbians that read gay media represent a large and accessible group, marketers know very little about the remaining 5 to 9 million gays and lesbians that are estimated to reside in the United States who do not read gay media (Poux, 1998). As we see in Table 21.1, all gays and lesbians cannot be treated similarly by marketers. For a start, a placement of an ad in a gay magazine will only reach 50% of the gay and lesbian population, at most. There are also fundamental demographic and attitudinal differences between gays and lesbians who do not read gay media and those who do. In this research, it is contended that the attitudinal differences may be attributed to the degree and manner in which individuals identify with being gay.

TABLE 21.1
Demographic Differences Between Readers of Gay Media and Overall Population
of Gays and Lesbians

Characteristic	Gays and Lesbians	Readers of Gay Media
Age distribution (%)		
16–34 years[a]	43	46.1
35–44 years	21	32.6
45–44 years	13	14.6
Gender%		
Male	44	89.9
Female	56	10.1
Occupation%[b]	38	62.9
Income $[c]		
Personal	16,908	41,300
Household	36,508	63,700
Education(%)[d]	26	59.6

Note. Source was Simmons Market Research Bureau (1996) and the Yankelovich Monitor (as cited in Lukenbill,1995).

[a] This age range was 18–34 for readers of gay media.

[b] Percentages given indicate white-collar occupations.

[c] Personal incomes were less than $ 25,000, 81% of gays and lesbians; less than $ 30,000, 46.1% of readers of gay media.

[d] Four-year college or more.

Thus, to truly segment gay and lesbian consumers into meaningful segments with homogeneous preferences and behaviors, it would seem that marketers would benefit from considering the extent to which these consumers identify with the gay subculture and the direction that they feel the gay social movement in relation to mainstream society.

THE IMPORTANCE OF GAY SUBCULTURE IN TARGETING GAY AND LESBIAN CONSUMERS

The issue of whether the gay market can indeed be considered a target market segment is one that has been disputed in academic research. Bhat (1996) argued that sexual orientation can serve only as a "descriptor" of a segment rather than as a "base" of segmentation. He added that using a descriptor as a base for segmentation results in "stereotyping," that is, the assumption that everyone who fits the segment behaves in the same way. Thus, by designating gays and lesbians as a market segment, we are assuming that every member of the segment possesses a common set of preferences and behaviors. Fugate (1993) contended that gay consumers do not meet the segmentation criteria of being identifiable, accessible, and of sufficient size (Cravens, Hills, & Woodruff, 1987). Penaloza (1996) criticized Fugate's (1993) characterization of gays and lesbians as a "lifestyle" and drew on the literature on social movements and subcultures to define a gay and lesbian market segment. This chapter builds on the idea of a gay subculture and social movement and investigates the role that these concepts may play in identifying effective advertising strategies to target gay and lesbian consumers.

A subculture may be defined as a minority group with distinct social practices, community formation, and identity. This identity may be communicated by using "code." This code may include clothing styles, mannerisms, language, and symbols that hold meaning for members of the subculture but have little meaning to non-members. Past research has shown that people vary in the degree to which they identify as members of a subculture. Gay studies have identified four distinct stages of gay identity: sensitization, identity confusion, identity assumption, and commitment. Furthermore, gay identity is just one of several identities incorporated into an individual's self-concept (Troiden, 1989), and it may be expressed to others in varying degrees.

Thus, gay and lesbians will vary in the degree to which they identify with the gay subculture. At one extreme, gays and lesbians that are at the "committed" stage of gay identity fear that, as society becomes increasingly accepting of homosexuality, the separateness between heterosexuals and homosexuals dissolves and the gay identity goes with it. The formation, and thus maintenance, of a subculture requires the formation of a community that is distinct from the mainstream society. However, other gays and lesbians are increasingly reluctant to define themselves as "all gay, all the time" (Wilke, 1998). These consumers feel that gay media fail to deliver a picture of how many gays and lesbians see themselves.

As a result, not all gays and lesbians will be equally receptive to the same advertising targeting the group. Gay and lesbian consumers who feel that the course of the gay social movement is acceptance into mainstream society would require a separate advertising strategy from more identified gay and lesbian consumers. They would be less likely than more identified members of the gay subculture to read gay media and they would interpret marketers' placement of gay-friendly ads in mainstream media as supportive of the gay social movement. However, more radical gay consumers may interpret the same strategy as an effort to dilute the gay identity, and they would be best targeted with ads containing more overtly gay images placed in exclusively gay media.

A COMPARISON OF GAYS AND LESBIANS TO HETEROSEXUAL CONSUMERS

Whereas proponents of the dream market have promoted demographic differences between gay and lesbian consumers and heterosexual consumers, a recent study by Yankelovich and Associates (as cited by Lukenbill, 1995), which was the first to

TABLE 21.2
Demographic Differences Between Gays and Lesbians and Heterosexuals

	Gay and Lesbians	Heterosexuals
Age Distribution	Same	Same
Gender(%)		
Male	44	48
Female	56	52
Occupation(%)		
White Collor	38	39
Blue Collor	27	26
Income ^{a}		
Male		
Personal	21,500	22,500
Househeld	37,400	39,300
Female		
Personal	13,300	13,200
Househeld	34,800	34,400
Political Affiliation(%)		
Democrat	45	44
Republican	27	26
Parenthood(%)^{b}		
Male	27	60
Female	67	72

Note: Source was Yankelovich and Associates Survey (as cited in Lukenbill, 1995).
[a] Personal incomes were under $25,000 as follows. For gays and lesbians: male, 81%; female, 87%.
For heterosexuals: male, 65%; female, 88%.
[b] For parenthood, 50% of gays and lesbians and 66% of heterosexuals were parents.

use a representative sample of gays and lesbians, found little difference between the two groups demographically, as can be seen in Table 21.2.

Unlike less scientifically representative surveys, the Yankelovich survey painted a very different picture of the gay and lesbian group. Considering the fact that men's incomes are generally 70% higher than women's, one would expect a gay household comprising two men to have a higher household income than a heterosexual household with a relatively lower income woman. However, the study found that, on average, both the personal and household incomes of gays and lesbians were lower than those of heterosexuals. In addition, the percentage of gay men who earn less than $25,0000 was significantly lower than that for heterosexual men.

The concept of DINKs is reliant on the presence of two childless individuals sharing a household. However, the study showed that 67% of lesbians and 27% of gay men are parents. Furthermore, gays and lesbians show no difference in their pattern of political affiliation than heterosexuals. However, they did tend to be more liberal in their beliefs.

From these statistics, it would appear that gays and lesbians are demographically more similar to heterosexuals that previously suggested, although the study did find that gay and lesbians tended to be more educated, more likely to be self-employed, and more likely to live in a large metropolitan area than heterosexuals. The key areas of difference between gays and lesbians and heterosexuals, and those that substantiate the need for distinct targeting by marketers, are in the importance placed on certain dimensions of the life. Gays and lesbians tended to place more importance on individuality and self-understanding, social interaction, experiencing life's diversity, maintaining independence, and self-protection (Lukenbill, 1995). These attitudinal differences can be traced to feelings of marginalization and "living outside of the mainstream" that are common in subcultural groups (Penaloza, 1996). These differences may account for the disproportionate amount of "gay dollars" that are spent on leisure activities and vacations, entertainment, and home décor, among other products and services.

Thus, it would appear that the difference between gays and lesbians and heterosexuals is more attitudinal and emotional than demographic, which would explain the difficulties in targeting the group as a meaningful consumer segment on the basis of demographic variables. In fact, to communicate effectively with gays and lesbians, advertisers must have a keen understanding of the gay subculture. From here, marketers can understand which products and brands take on a specific meaning within the gay and lesbian subculture, and how subcultural code can be effectively used in reaching these consumers with advertising.

REACHING THE GAY MARKET

A number of strategies have been developed to target gay and lesbian consumers. Figure 21.1 shows a framework that can aid advertisers in identifying the most effective strategy in terms of ad content and media placement for reaching gay and lesbian consumers. The top row of the framework focuses on the content of ads placed in gay media. Each box identifies the effect of the interaction between the ad content and the media placement on various audiences based on sexual orientation and gay identity.

In the top left-hand corner of Fig. 21.1, we see that the most cost-effective process and the least risky in terms of alienating heterosexual consumers is to redirect an advertising campaign that had been designed for a heterosexual audience, simply by placing the ad in a gay media vehicle. Firms such as Calvin Klein, Levi's, and Evian have used this strategy to communicate their desire to do business with gays and lesbians (Penaloza, 1996).

However, many gays and lesbians who are skeptical of companies who seek the gay dollar without taking a stance on the issue will require a more direct appeal by advertisers. Thus, separate advertising campaigns for gays and lesbians with readily identifiable appeals may be more effective in targeting gays and lesbians.

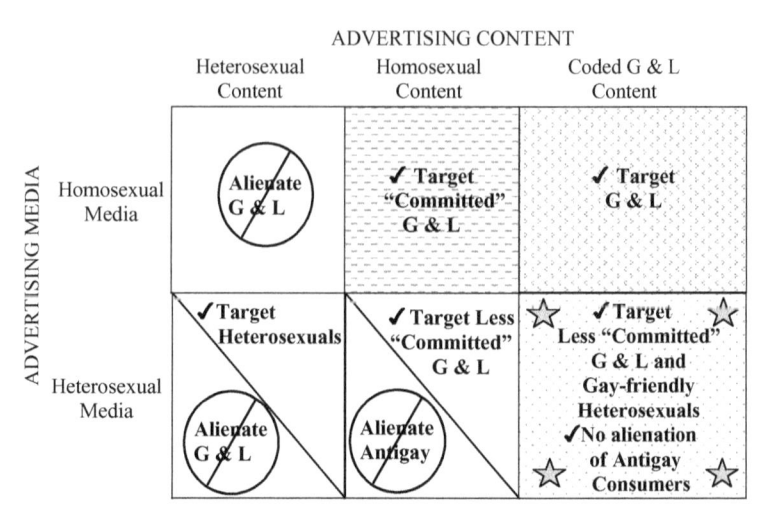

FIG. 21.1.   Ad content and media selection for targeting segments on the basis of sexual orientation and identity with gay subculture (G & L = gay and lesbian).

The downside for advertisers is the increased cost of developing distinct advertising campaigns for mainstream and gay media placements. If the ads are placed in gay media, we can assume that heterosexuals, especially those who tend to hold negative attitudes toward homosexuality, would not be exposed to these ads. Thus, this strategy, which is represented in the top right-hand corner of Fig. 21.1, is unlikely to result in a great risk of antagonizing or alienating heterosexual consumers. However, although it is likely that the readership of gay magazines will be receptive to gay imagery, the mere placing of advertisements in gay media or within gay-oriented programming has resulted in negative publicity for some firms.

Carillon Inc., distributors of Absolut Vodka and the first major company to advertise in the *Advocate* in 1979, has regularly received criticism from antigay consumers who refuse to purchase the product because they feel that the company is promoting homosexuality by advertising in a gay magazine (Levin, 1993). Although Absolut vodka advertisements have remained a constant in gay magazines, other advertisers such as Phillip Morris have relented to pressure from religious groups and pulled their ads from gay magazines (Levin, 1993). Thus, marketers cannot assume that by placing ads in gay magazines they run no risk of alienating heterosexual consumers, as the publicity generated by such a strategy may affect the attitudes of consumers who hold negative attitudes toward homosexuality.

Despite the stigma that may be attached to a brand advertised in gay audiences, many firms recognize the potential of the gay market. As a result, the number of advertisers who place ads in gay media continues to grow. However, advertisers have remained far more reluctant to target gay readers through mainstream media. As shown in the bottom right-hand corner of Fig. 21.1, in addition to the risk of alienating a far larger heterosexual consumer audience with content specifically oriented to gay consumers, it would simply be bad economics to use a mainstream media outlet to target a relatively small consumer group. However, the placement of gay-oriented advertising in mainstream media may provide advertisers with access to a larger number of gay consumers than a similar placement in gay media.

Targeting Gays and Lesbians in Mainstream Media

IKEA, the Swedish furniture company, created much controversy when it included a gay male couple in its "lifestyles" ad campaign, which was broadcast on network television in the United States. It is reasonable to assume that IKEA considered its target audience to consist of both gay consumers and heterosexual consumers who hold a positive attitude toward homosexuality. Images suggesting homosexuality have also been used in mainstream advertising for fashion labels such as Calvin Klein, Banana Republic, and Benetton. Similarly, the fashion industry has consistently been a gay-friendly industry where such imagery is accepted without resistance.

Why should marketers risk alienating heterosexual consumers by placing ads with gay content in mainstream media? First, the cost of developing and implementing a standardized ad campaign is considerably less than that involved with testing, developing, and implementing separate ad campaigns to reach distinct audiences. Second, by bringing gay issues into the mainstream, marketers may stand to gain from the goodwill of gay and lesbian consumers who, unlike those who are deeply grounded in the gay subculture, strive for the acceptance of gays and lesbians into mainstream society. Penaloza (1996) contended that many gay and lesbian consumers consider their inclusion in marketplace activities as recognition of the progress of the gay social movement, with less concern for the preservation of a distinct gay subculture.

Thus, it is feasible that some gay and lesbian consumers may feel that a firm's decision to place a gay ad in a mainstream media vehicle is a greater endorsement of support for the gay social movement than a similar placement in a gay medium. Hence, we may expect these consumers to hold a more positive attitude toward ads with gay content placed in mainstream media vehicles than those placed in gay media.

Despite this, most advertisers remain reluctant to target gays ands lesbians in mainstream media, and they confine themselves to the proportion of gays and lesbians who read gay media. Given that a sizeable amount of gay and lesbians do not read gay media, advertisers who seek to penetrate the gay and lesbian market should be prepared to place ads in mainstream media to target these consumers. Compared with readers of gay media, these gays and lesbians will tend to be less identified with the gay subculture and have a more positive attitude toward blending with mainstream society (Kates, 1998).

For gays and lesbians to be targeted effectively in mainstream media, a few precautions must be taken. First, all products do not necessitate a separate campaign for gays and lesbians. Advertisers of toothpaste will not benefit from a gay-oriented campaign, as gays and lesbians are unlikely to have specific needs for the product or be made to feel marginalized during the purchase process. In contrast, American Express has successfully targeted gays and lesbians who in the past would find difficulty in making financial arrangements that were oriented toward the mainstream concept of "married with children." Although gays and lesbians have a need for financial planning, their needs and concerns are different than those of mainstream consumers. Second, advertising for products and brands that hold subcultural meaning will be most effectively placed in gay media so as to target gays and lesbians who identify strongly with the subculture. Third, advertisers must use different messages from many of those used in gay media as a result of both demographic and attitudinal differences between the two gay and lesbian audiences. Whereas many of the ads that appear in gay media tend to rely on sexual innuendo or overtly physical imagery, ads placed in mainstream media will require more subtle content.

How, then, may marketers balance the costs and risks involved in targeting a gay and lesbian audience with advertising in mainstream media? One strategy that has been used by advertisers such as Calvin Klein, Parliament cigarettes, and U.S. West is the idea that "gayness is in the eye of the beholder." Thus, a U.S. West ad with imagery depicting two women in a business setting, smiling and making eye contact, accompanied by the caption "Keep all your connections strong," may be perceived by an antigay heterosexual as a scene of two friends chatting, while gay and lesbian consumers would see a picture of a lesbian couple. However, gay and lesbian consumers may see this as a lack of conviction by advertisers and require a more direct appeal.

Although gays and lesbians who cannot be reached with gay media will be less likely than readers of gay media to be in the "committed" stage of gay identity, they will still be familiar with the gay iconography and symbolism that are linked with the gay subculture. Examples of such gay iconography include the rainbow, freedom rings, the pink triangle, and references to "family" and "pride." Subaru has placed a coded ad in gay media to take advantage of its popularity with lesbian consumers. This ad cleverly incorporates gay symbolism and code on the license plate and bumper sticker of each car so as to appeal to different types of gay and lesbian consumers with little risk of offending antigay customers. The car on the left has the license plate "XENA LVR," referring to the television show "Xena: The Warrior Princess," which has a heavy lesbian following. The middle car has the license plate "P-TOWNIE," which implies that the car owner is a resident of Provincetown, a predominantly gay town in New England. The car also has a subtle Human Rights Campaign sticker on the bumper. The car on the right has "CAMP OUT" on its license plate, which may be a double-entendre reference to the gay practice of "camp," which incorporates elements of dressing in drag. Finally, this car has a rainbow sticker, the most universal symbol of the gay subculture, on its bumper. However, a reader who was unfamiliar with the gay subculture would simply perceive the ad message to be focused on using Subaru cars for a variety of uses. Thus, Subaru may reach gay and lesbians consumers in mainstream media with a well-targeted message that has little risk of alienating or offending other consumers.

Thus, advertisers may reach gays and lesbians in mainstream media with minimal risk of alienating heterosexuals by combining the use of gay iconography with the reading strategies for gay or lesbian consumers (Grier & Brumbaugh, 1999). Such a strategy would allow gay consumers to identify with the advertising and have a more positive attitude toward the advertisement than an ad with purely heterosexual content. In fact, such a strategy has the characteristics of an inside joke, allowing gay consumers to feel bonded with the advertiser against less-informed heterosexual adversaries (Penaloza, 1996).

Advertisers Can Swing Both Ways

The use of more subtle content will also be required for marketers to lessen the risk of offending the larger heterosexual population while pursuing a niche market. However, although the statistics cited earlier from the Gallop poll serve to illustrate the negative attitudes toward homosexuality that exist in mainstream America, these numbers also indicate that almost half of the population is in fact gay friendly. Thus, it would be naïve to assume that all heterosexual consumers would react negatively to gay content in ads. Whereas heterosexual images in advertising are the norm and should continue to be used to target antigay consumers, a consumer's attitude toward an ad with gay content would be influenced by the consumer's attitude toward homosexuality (Bhat, Leigh, & Wardlow, 1996). Thus, a heterosexual consumer who holds a positive attitude toward homosexuality is unlikely to be offended by gay content in an ad and may hold a positive attitude toward the ad as it reflects the consumer's societal beliefs.

Thus, as shown by the shaded box in the extreme right-hand corner of Fig. 21.1, it may be possible for advertisers to target heterosexuals and gays and lesbians who are less "committed" to the gay subculture with the same ad in mainstream media. As previously mentioned, heterosexual consumers who hold a positive attitude toward homosexuality are also likely to "get the joke" and appreciate the inclusion of subtle inclusion gay-oriented material in advertising. Additionally, gay-friendly heterosexual consumers are unlikely to hold a more negative attitude toward an advertisement with overtly gay imagery than one with heterosexual imagery as a result of an aversion to the content. However, advertisers are keenly aware of the need to provide consumers with images with which they may identify. Thus, while condoning the content, these consumers are unlikely to identify with the imagery of the gay-oriented ad, and they are likely to hold a more favorable attitude toward ads with a subtler gay reference than those with overtly gay imagery.

Gay-friendly heterosexuals may be familiar enough with the gay subculture to recognize the gay symbols, whereas individuals who hold a negative attitude toward homosexuality would be unaware of the gay imagery. Hence, those consumers who would be positively affected by its inclusion, both gay and gay friendly, would recognize its meaningfulness, with a reduced risk of alienating antigay heterosexual consumers.

CONCLUSIONS

The growth in the number of media and marketing firms serving gays and lesbians, coupled with the promise of a dream market, has enticed many mainstream firms to attempt to target the gay and lesbian segment. Many mainstream marketers have used the shield afforded by gay media to target the gay and lesbian market while minimizing their risk of offending antigay consumers. However, few have offered gays and lesbians a readily identifiable appeal with gay content even within gay media. Furthermore, less than 50% of all gays and lesbians read gay media. Thus, marketers must take steps to understand the entire gay and lesbian population and not just those that can be conveniently reached with a survey of those who subscribe to gay magazines.

This paper contends that there are both demographic and attitudinal differences between readers and nonreaders of gay media that will influence the efficacy of various advertising strategies in targeting gay and lesbian consumers. A study of gay subculture will allow marketers to understand what gays and lesbians expect from them. Gays and lesbians vary in the degree to which they identify with the gay subculture and will respond differently to gay content in ads as a result. Advertisers may use messages and symbols in ads that have subcultural meaning to gay or lesbian consumers and gay-friendly heterosexuals but that would be meaningless to heterosexual consumers who are unfamiliar with the gay subculture. As a result, marketers may run ads in mainstream media that provide a crossover appeal to both heterosexual and homosexual audiences.

REFERENCES

Bhat, S. (1996). Some comments on "marketing to the homosexual (gay) market: A profile and strategy implications." In D. Wardlow (Ed.), *Gays, lesbians, and consumer behavior: Theory, practice, and research issues in marketing* (pp. 213–217). Binghamton, NY: Haworth.

Bhat, S., Leigh, T., & Wardlow, D. (1996). The effect of homosexual imagery in advertising on attitude toward the ad. In D. Wardlow (Ed.), *Gays, lesbians, and consumer behavior: Theory, practice, and research issues in marketing* (pp. 161–176). Binghamton, NY: Haworth.

Cass, V. (1984). Homosexual identity: A concept in need of definition. *Journal of Homosexuality, 9,* 105–126.

Cravens, D., Hills, G., & Woodruff, R. (1987). *Marketing management.* Homewood, IL: Irwin.

Fugate, D. L. (1993). Evaluating the U.S. male homosexual and lesbian population as a viable target market segment: A review with implications. *Journal of Consumer Marketing, 10*(4), 46–57.

Gardyn, R. (2001, November). "A market kept in the closet," American Demographics, 23(11) p. 36.

Goldstein, R. (2003, September 9). Get Back! The gathering storm over gay rights. The Village voice online newsletter.

Grier, S., & Brumbaugh, A. (1999). Noticing cultural differences: Ad meanings created by target and non-target markets. *Journal of Advertising, 28*(4) 79–93.

Johnson, B. (1993, January 18). The gay quandary: Advertising's most elusive, yet lucrative target market proves difficult to measure. *Advertising Age, 64*(18), 34.

Kates, S. M. (1998), *Twenty million new customers—Understanding gay men's consumer behavior.* Binghamton, NY: Haworth.

Levin, G. (1993, January 18). Mainstream's domino effect: Liquor, fragrance, clothing advertisers ease into gay magazines. *Advertising Age, 30.*

Lukenbill, G. (1995). *Untold millions.* New York: Harper Business.

Now for a queer question about gay culture. (1997, July 12). The Economist, pp. 75–76.

Penaloza, L. (1994). *Atravesando fronteras/border crossings: A critical ethnographic exploration of the consumer acculturation of Mexican immigrants. Journal of Consumer Research, 21*(1), 32–54.

Penaloza, L. (1996). We're here, we're queer, and we're going shopping. In D. Wardlow (Ed.), *Gays, lesbians, and consumer behavior: Theory, practice, and research issues in marketing* (pp. 9–42). Binghamton, NY: Haworth.

Poux, P. D. (1998). Gay consumers MIA from media surveys. *Advertising Age, 69*(16), 26.

Rudd, N. (1996). Appearance and self-presentation research in gay consumer cultures: Issues and impact. In D. Wardlow (Ed.), *Gays, lesbians, and consumer behavior: Theory, practice, and research issues in marketing* (pp. 109–134). Binghamton, NY: Haworth.

Simmons market research bureau (1996). Survey of gay and lesbian consumers.

Troiden, R. (1989). The formation of homosexual identities. *Journal of Homosexuality, 5*(3), 43–73.

Wilke, M. (1998, June 22). Ads targeting gays rely on real results, not intuition. *Advertising Age, 69*(25), p. 3.

Yankelovich, X. (1994). *Gay/lesbian/bisexual monitor survey.* New York: Yankelovich and Associates.

CHAPTER TWENTY TWO

Health Promotion and Interactive Technology: Do Gender Differences Matter in Message Design?

Patricia A. Stout
The University of Texas at Austin

Jorge Villegas
University of Florida

Issues surrounding women's health demand our attention. The notion of differences in communicating health messages to men and women has received scant attention (Gabbard-Alley, 1995), although a significant body of literature addresses gender differences in persuasion and communication (Meyers-Levy, 1989; Meyers-Levy & Sternthal, 1991; Darley & Smith, 1995). Meanwhile, the Internet is one of the major sources of health information. More specifically, researchers from the Pew Internet & American Life Project found that respondents of a national survey are as likely to look for information on the Internet as they are to contact a health professional (Horrigan & Rainie, 2002). Although there is the belief that this new technology can help to transform both personal and public health, how interactive technology can best be used to address health-related issues facing individuals is little understood.

Both policymakers and communication researchers are increasingly concerned that a "digital divide" may result from the evolution of Web-based delivery of communication (Peterson Bishop, 2000). However, perhaps a more pressing concern centers on the impact of the addition of "interactivity" into the equation of information processing on message effectiveness. How does interactivity influence individuals' processing and their subsequent behavior? Furthermore, although the role of individual differences, such as gender, in message processing has received some attention in studies using traditional media (Darley & Smith, 1995), how these differences might influence message design for delivery using interactive technology has yet to be seriously addressed. Should Web sites be designed differently for men and women to facilitate knowledge, attitudes, and behavior? And, if this is so, what are the key design elements for an effective Web site targeted to women versus men?

The selectivity hypothesis (Meyers-Levy, 1989) provides an explanatory framework for understanding gender differences in communication design. This model proposes that the main source of differences between cognitive abilities of male and female individuals is the different configuration and use of the brain's cortical hemispheres. This difference might explain why women take a holistic approach to processing whereas men focus on one aspect of the message (Meyers-Levy, 1994). Using the selectivity hypothesis, researchers such as Darley and Smith (1995) have found that, in general, women grasp the information of a stimulus in a comprehensive fashion by using objective and subjective information. In contrast, men select information through heuristic processes, thereby increasing the possibility of missing not clearly stated informational cues.

Our inquiry is driven by two questions. First, how can Web-based media best be used for health promotion? Second, how are gender differences in message processing relevant in the study of Web-based media? In this chapter we propose that interactive technology can be a feasible and effective medium for a theory-based approach to health promotion by specifically addressing key variables in theories of health-protective behavior. Street and Rimal (1997) argued that, when interactive technology is compared with other health-promotion media, several features such as interactivity, networkability, sensory vividness, modifiability, availability, cost, and ease of use can enhance effectiveness. In this chapter, we assess these structural features of interactive technology as they may interface with gender differences of Web users. On the basis of the selectivity hypothesis (Meyers-Levy, 1989), we outline a set of propositions that address expected differences in health-message effectiveness between men and women.

UNIQUE CAPABILITIES OF THE WEB

Most scholars agree that *interactivity* is the main characteristic and driver of change of the new media (Ha & James, 1998). The Web is unique as a means of communication in its ability to combine text, video, and sound while allowing for interactivity between users and messages, between the individual and the machine, and between senders and receivers (Cho, 1999). According to Biocca (1992), interactivity refers to "(a) the number and forms of input and output, (b) the level of responsiveness to ... user actions and states, and (c) the range of interactive experiences (including applications) offered by the system" (p. 64). Although there is a lack of consensus in the literature on a precise definition of interactivity (Liu & Shrum, 2002), most researchers would agree that interactivity allows for user control and responsiveness (Street & Rimal, 1997). User control is the "extent to which users can participate in modifying the form and content of a mediated environment in real time" (Steuer, 1992, p. 84). Responsiveness is the extent that the form, content, and nature of a previous action are taken into account following a specific action by the user (Rafaeli, 1988; Street & Rimal, 1997). Although we agree that interactivity might be used as an umbrella term to encompass all the components relevant to the technology and content that might allow a message to be more or less responsive to the users' actions, we note that, for many researchers, reference to interactivity pertains specifically to the speed of response of the machine (Novak, Hoffman, & Yung, 2000; Street & Rimal, 1997) and the relative control of the user as the machine responds to the person (Liu & Shrum, 2002; McMillan & Hwang 2002). In this chapter, we consider interactivity to mean the speed of the response of the machine to the person using it.

Bagui (1998) claimed that characteristics such as a multimedia environment, modularity, and the user's control of the direction and pace of the medium, all of which are important features of our definition of interactivity, boost learning by using more senses, parallel the way people learn, and motivate learners. Researchers have viewed interactivity in different ways, including the result of elements that are present in the site (Frazer & McMillan, 1999; Ghose & Dou, 1998; Ha & James, 1998); the speed of response of the system (Street & Rimal, 1997); the possibility of the user to look for information in different patterns (Ariely, 2000; Bezjian-Avery, Calder, & Iacobucci, 1998); and the use of hyperlinks in a site (Sundar, Brown, & Kalyanaraman, 1999).

Street and Rimal (1997) considered that interactive technology fared well compared with other health-promotion media, such as videotapes, brochures, telephone systems, and professional consultations, on several structural features that enhance effectiveness, including networkability, sensory vividness, modifiability, availability, cost, and ease of use.

Networkability is the ability of a medium to connect users with the sender of the information, databases, and other users. This ability of computer-mediated communication has been proven to be an effective provider of social support (Braithwaite, Waldron, & Finn, 1999; Shaw, McTavish, Hawkins, Gustafson, & Pingree, 2000) and medical expertise essential to health-related decision making. *Sensory vividness*, although currently restricted by technological limitations of the WWW, allows the multimedia capacity of the Web that makes possible the realization of compelling messages using text, audio, and video to create a memorable and persuasive sensorial experience. Information might be delivered by means of multiple modalities (e.g., text, streaming video, narration, music, and graphics), resulting in a more vivid presentation experienced through more sensory stimulation (e.g., sound, sight, color, and movement). The use of multiple channels can enhance information processing (Biocca, 1992; Steuer, 1992).

Modifiability allows developers and even users to change the computer-mediated environment (i.e., background color or use of or nonuse of frames) or the content of the medium (i.e., personally tailored messages or search engines). This capability of interactive technology starkly contrasts with more traditional media, such as videotape, brochures, and so forth, which cannot be easily adapted to different needs of different target audiences. Other traits, such as availability, cost, and ease of use, although not exclusive to the Web, can enhance the effectiveness of health-related messages. Because these first four components of Web-based media—interactivity, networkability, sensory vividness, and modifiability—are most unique to the Web, we focus more on them in this chapter.

The effects of interactive media in users have been documented with mixed results by researchers. On one hand, media perceived as more interactive create a more positive attitude than less interactive interfaces (Ariely, 2000; Cho, 1999; Liu & Shrum, 2002; Villegas & Stout, 2001). Similarly, interactive functions have been found to be a good indicator of the perceived quality of a commercial Web site (Ghose & Dou, 1998).

The finding of positive affect toward more interactive messages might be due to higher levels of engagement with the medium that lead to immersion (Vorderer, 2000) or the feeling of "being there," a state called telepresence (Lombard & Ditton, 1997).

Besides the positive affect created by interactivity, there is evidence that this trait of media can have a positive impact on learning. Ariely (2000), who defined interactivity as control of the information flow, found that more control led people to a better understanding of the attributes of models of a product. However, there is a considerable body of research that addresses the uncertain link between communication or educational objectives and the use of interactive technologies (Unz & Hesse, 1999).

The use of interactive media might also have a price for users by requiring a greater amount of individuals' cognitive resources (Ariely, 2000; Eveland & Dunwoody, 2001). Distraction created by the interactive nature of the medium can be a possible negative outcome, particularly for novices (Wiedenbeck & Zila, 1997). Other researchers have found that people using interactive media can feel lost in the medium (Eveland & Dunwoody, 2001). Surprisingly, Bezjian-Avery et al. (1998) found that the persuasiveness of an interactive message was lower than that of a static message.

ADDRESSING GENDER DIFFERENCES

Although many feel that messages communicated to women about women's health issues are in serious need of examination by communication scholars (Parrott & Condit, 1996), a paucity of research has addressed differences in communicating health messages to men and women. Although a body of research has investigated differences in men's and women's processing of information and formation of judgment (Meyers-Levy, 1989), a great deal of uncertainty remains (Meyers-Levy & Maheswaran, 1991). For example, Eagly (1978) found that women are more prone to accede to a persuasive message. Research on emotions has shown that women are better nonverbal encoders and decoders (Hall, 1984), have greater empathy for others (Hall, 1984), and experience more intensity in both positive and negative emotions (Larsen & Diener, 1987). Because emotion is considered to influence attitudes and subsequent behavior (Batra & Ray, 1986), these differences can be important in considering message processing by men and women.

However, some scholars consider research that looks at gender differences in cognitive processing to be inconclusive and flawed. Eagly (1978) believes that the research is not conclusive enough to consider women as easier targets for persuasive messages. Others (Caplan, 1979; Caplan, MacPherson, & Tobin, 1985; Eagly & Carli, 1981) consider the research of gender differences suspect because of methodological or context confounding elements. Researchers' belief that differences are independent of the context of the situation and the nature of the message poses a significant problem for this research stream (Meyers-Levy, 1989). For example, past research regards men as more analytical and logical and women as more subjective and intuitive (Broverman, Klaiber, Kobayashi, & Vogel, 1968). Now we know that this interpretation of data might be explained by using the selectivity hypothesis (Meyers-Levy, 1989), which we detail in the paragraphs that follow.

In the specific area of computer use, some researchers have consistently found gender differences. In a recent study, Pearson, Bahmanziari, Crosby, and Conrad (2002–2003) found that gender and age are more important factors of computer efficacy than corporate culture. More specifically, the authors found that female employees of a sample of large multinational companies perceived themselves as less effective at using computers than male employees. In addition, female college students showed a significantly higher level of computer anxiety than male college students (Gilroy & Desai, 1986). Shashaani (1997) similarly found that women displayed less interest in computers, were less confident, and had less experience than men. However, other researchers such as Scott and Rockwell (1997) and Pope-Davis and Vispoel (1993) did not find significant gender differences in the use of and attitudes toward computers.

Whitley (1996) presented one possible explanation for the lack of consistent results. He suggested that gender differences in computer attitudes are not a unidimensional phenomenon. He believed that the differences have three dimensions: An affective factor (i.e., anxiety) and two cognitive factors (positive and negative beliefs concerning the social impact of computers). Applying this model, he found a moderate difference for anxiety, a small contrast for negative beliefs, and no significant difference for positive beliefs.

Using the Technology Acceptance Model, Gefen and Straub (1997) found that e-mail systems are used similarly by women and men; however, they have different perceptions of usefulness and ease. It seems that women are less comfortable with e-mail than men, but they believe that this means of communication has a higher utility value. The researchers also found that more women than men believed that e-mail had a higher social presence.

Use of the Internet is another of the new technologies where gender issues surface. In the beginning of the Internet boom, men were the main users of the Internet. However, by 2000 the gap between male and female Internet usage was practically erased (Clark & Gorski, 2002). This surge of women's use of the Internet does not necessarily mean that gender differences are disappearing on the Web. For instance, women have a more positive attitude than men toward catalog and retail shopping, but this gender difference disappears in the case of online shopping (Alreck & Settle, 2002). Another researcher (Zhang, 2002) found that female college students had a more positive attitude toward the Internet than male students; however, the trend reversed in a sample of industrial employees. The use of Internet tools was also found to differ across gender.

Gender differences go beyond how the Web is perceived. Women and men also differ on how they use the Internet. College female students use more e-mail and use the Web to do research, whereas male students perform more online leisure activities such as reading news, playing games, and listening to music (Odell, Korgen, Schumacher, & Delucchi, 2000). Using a teen sample, LaFerle, Edwards, and Lee (2000) obtained similar results.

In the WWW as well as in other media such as CD-ROMS, video games can be used as a way to create an interactive learning environment (Lieberman, 1997). Research indicates, however, that video games are less popular among women than among men and provides a number of possible explanations for this (Brown, Hall, Holtzen, Brown, & Brown, 1997). One explanation considers that women are not attracted to video games because in general they focus on competitiveness, violence, and aggression, traits that are noncharacteristic to female players (Perry, Perry, & Boldizar, 1990). In contrast, this lack of popularity among women has been attributed to women's higher levels of anxiety and discomfort while using computers (Shashaani, 1997). Finally, from a cognitive perspective, researchers have found gender differences that might affect video game performance (Brown et al., 1997). For example, tasks that involve moving visual stimuli are more challenging for women than for men (Schiff & Oldak, 1990).

Research on gender and computer use, use of the Internet, and other interactive media point to differences as highlighted herein. Although some of these differences may be accounted for by means of socialization, it is likely that differences in information processing also play a role.

THE SELECTIVITY HYPOTHESIS AS
AN EXPLANATORY FRAMEWORK

The selectivity hypothesis presented by Meyers-Levy (1989) is a commonly used framework to explain the differences in information processing between men and women. Meyers-Levy found that, for messages that do not elicit any particular process strategy (i.e., recall vs. recognition), women's processing style tends to be comprehensive. As comprehensive information processors, women try to grasp all of the relevant points of the message and to assimilate all available cues (Meyers-Levy & Maheswaran, 1991). Their objective is an effortful and comprehensive analysis of information. Women have a psychological orientation toward a communal outlook characterized by emphasis on interpersonal relationships, affiliation, and attachment to the self and other (Carlson, 1971, 1972). This is manifested in their orientation to information that is both self-related and other related.

In contrast, the selectivity hypothesis suggests that men use a more selective information processing style. Their strategy is to use heuristic devices that involve single cues or cues that convergently imply a single inference (Meyers-Levy, 1989). Their objective is to strive for efficiency in processing by reliance on cues that are highly available and particularly salient. Men's psychological orientation tends more toward agency that is characterized by instrumental, self-assertive and self-purposive concerns. This orientation is reflected in men's tendency to focus more on self-related (vs. other-related) information (Meyers-Levy, 1989). Thus it seems that men choose a single idea or inference from the message in congruence with a personal perspective, whereas women process the information by trying to understand all of the elements of the message.

Meyers-Levy proposed that the main source of differences between cognitive abilities of men and women is the different configuration of and use of the brain's cortical hemispheres. The right hemisphere shows the capability of understanding comprehensive stimuli such as images, making it the main driver of visual spatial tasks. Meanwhile, the left hemisphere's ability to differentiate elements and analyze them is appropriate to performing verbal functions.

Cognitive research suggests that men perform better at right-hemisphere-driven tasks, whereas women have an advantage over men when doing activities that are processed in the left hemisphere. Men have also been found to have more specialized hemispheres than women. That is, it seems that women have better communication between the left and right hemispheres. This difference might explain why women take a holistic approach to processing whereas men focus on one aspect of the message (Meyers-Levy, 1994). Table 22.1 presents a synthesis of how the

TABLE 22.1
How the Selectivity Hypothesis Accounts for Differences in Information Processing

Women	Men
Comprehensive information processors	Selective information processors
Assimilate all available cues	Use heuristic cues
Comprehension	Efficiency
Focus is equally divided on self and others	Focus is on self-related information

Note. Adapted from Meyers-Levy (1989).

selectivity hypothesis accounts for differences in information processing between men and women.

APPLYING THE SELECTIVITY HYPOTHESIS TO WEB SITE USE: PROPOSITIONS

The use of interactive media is a promising new area for health promotion. The Internet, CD-ROMS, and other multimedia are changing the way mass marketers and public health organizations communicate with their audiences. However, in this rapidly evolving field, gender is as important an issue as in all traditional media. The implications of the selectivity hypothesis in interactive media that present health information are multiple.

One interesting research question driving this line of inquiry concerns message design: Do men and women need different messages delivered by different sites, or do they process the same site differently but ultimately experience similar outcomes regarding degrees of knowledge, attitudes, and behavior?

The selectivity hypothesis makes predictions about how gender differences might affect information processing of Web-based messages. The selectivity hypothesis has been used to account for a variety of gender differences in selectivity in numerous facets of men's and women's behavior, including the performance of spatial and linguistic skills, conversational style, interpretation of information, influenceability, and determination of self-evaluations. In the paragraphs that follow, we consider how gender differences in information processing might matter in Web-based message design by considering the four main traits that distinguish interactive technology from more traditional modes of communication (Street & Rimal, 1997). We outline a series of propositions that consider as outcomes the impacts on information processing, attitudes toward the site, and online behavior (e.g., time spent on a site or number of pages visited). These three dependent variables are important to assessing the effectiveness of interactive messages (i.e., Ariely, 2000; Chen & Wells, 1999; Lohse, Bellman, & Johnson, 2000).

It is important to acknowledge that in developing these propositions we are considering objective tools essential to Web-site design as well as information that is useful on a site. Therefore, the issue is not so much the number of tools present in any particular Web site but whether the tools assist in message processing. The propositions must be interpreted with consideration that the appropriateness of the tools is important relative to the nature of the site as well as the balance of how much any set of tools may "tax" (or perhaps more appropriately "overtax") the mechanical system of the machine (i.e., hardware and software).

We would expect that this relationship can be represented by an inverted U-shaped curve. Thus, for example, the selectivity hypothesis suggests that women might stay in a site longer if the tools are appropriate and the site is "assisting" them (both by the objective tools and the capability of the machine). In contrast, men will move around the site more and look at pieces of the message and not assimilate the characteristics of the site. With this caveat in mind, we summarize a series of propositions in Table 22.2.

Interactivity

For most researchers of the Web, interactivity is conceptualized as the speed of response of the machine (Novak et al., 2000; Street & Rimal, 1997). Whether a site is more or less interactive, then, is dependent on tasks or processes that slow down the speed of response. Examples of such processes include the registration process to gain access to a site or to access some part of the site for further interaction; the use of numerous or complex graphics that require a lengthy loading time; and the use of these graphics that limit the accessibility of the site, such as the need for additional software to access part of a site (e.g., Acrobat) or the use of pull-down menus or links to other software (that will speed up access).

Interactivity is a property of the machine over which the individual has no control (similar to sensory vividness but unlike the characteristics of networkability and modifiability, in which the individual controls the interaction with the machine). We assume that speed facilitates processing by creating positive affect and by providing immediate feedback that validates processing. With the qualification that the speed of the sites is equal (i.e., men and women use comparable equipment), we propose the following:

P1a: *Highly interactive sites will facilitate processing for both men and women. Both men and women will have positive attitudes when the machine responds.*
Therefore:
P1b: *For highly interactive sites, there will be no differences in attitudes toward the site for men and women.*

Because men tend to strive for efficiency in processing and want to "cut to the chase," we expect men to have less favorable attitudes toward the site if the machine does not respond quickly. Because women's processing style tends to be comprehensive, we would expect women to search more and spend more time when the machine responds quickly. Therefore:

P1c: *For highly interactive sites, women will visit more pages and spend more time on the site than men.*

Networkability

Networkability is the ability of a medium to connect users with the sender of the information, databases, and other users. Networkability enables the creation of relationships between and among users as evidenced by a number of different interactive tools. For example, users may be required to register prior to gaining

TABLE 22.2
Propositions for Gender Differences in Processing Interactive Messages

	Interactivity	Networkability	Sensory Vividness	Modifiability
Information processing	P1a: Highly interactive sites will facilitate processing for both men and women.	P2a: When networking tools are available on a site, women will use the tools more frequently than men.	P3a: For sites with more multimedia tools, information processing will be enhanced for women.	P4a: When sites provide options to personalize sites and to filter information, women will use these options less frequently than men.
Attitude	P1b: For highly interactive sites, there will be no differences in attitudes toward the site for men and women.	P2b: For sites with more networking tools, women will have more favorable attitudes toward the site than men.	P3b: For sites with more multimedia tools, women will have more favorable attitudes toward the site than men.	P4b: For highly modifiable sites, women will have less positive attitudes toward the site than men.
Behavior	P1c: For highly interactive sites, women will visit more pages and spend more time on the site than men.	P2c: For sites with more networking tools, women will spend more time on the site than men.	P3c: For sites with more multimedia tools, women will visit more pages and spend more time on the site than men.	P4c: For highly modifiable sites, women will spend less time modifying the site than men.

access to a site or some part of a site; various tools that allow contact, such as e-mail and chat rooms, allow users to contact the Web master, other users, professional experts, or moderators of a site; and the site might provide other modes of connection, by means of newsletters or classes online. When these tools are available, access to the opportunities that they afford are within the control of the user.

One key notion of the selectivity hypothesis centers on differences in psychological orientation between men and women. Women are more oriented toward a communal outlook and emphasize interpersonal relationships, affiliation, and emphasis on the self and other. In conversation, women are more likely to invite others to express their feelings and thoughts. Men, in contrast, tend to be more self-related and take a personal perspective. These selective tendencies are evident in research on conversation or style of interaction, which suggests that men interact with others to suit their own agenda and are less sensitive to others whereas women manifest comprehensiveness by drawing out and sharing in others' views (Meyers-Levy, 1989). Women express more active and attentive listening, acknowledging and encouraging others' utterances, and sharing emotions (Thorne, Kramarae, & Henley, 1983). Evidence also suggests that partner visibility enhances conversation and fluency for women whereas men are more fluent when their partners are concealed (Siegman & Reynolds, 1983). Presumably, partner visibility allows women more cues for comprehensive processing whereas lack of visual contact allows men to focus selectively on the topic at hand (Meyers-Levy, 1989). These differences have important implications for Web-based messages.

Women may be more likely to use the possibility to connect to other people (e.g., chatrooms or e-mail) and sources of information (e.g., databases) to obtain a thorough understanding of the problem at hand. Men will use networking tools only when they bring an easy access to the understanding of the issue at hand and enable heuristic processing. Therefore we propose the following.

P2a: *When networking tools are available, women will use the tools more frequently than men.*

P2b: *For sites with more networking tools, women will have more favorable attitudes toward the site than men.*

P2c: *For sites with more networking tools, women will spend more time on the site than men.*

Sensory Vividness

By incorporating use of text, audio, and video, sensory vividness allows the multimedia capacity of the Web to create a memorable and persuasive sensorial experience. Sensory vividness is important to creating effective messages given the complexity of health-related information, because the use of multiple channels can enhance information processing (Biocca, 1992; Steuer, 1992) and subsequent learning (Bagui, 1998).

Sensory vividness of a Web site can be enhanced by use of such interactive tools as video, audio, virtual reality, and text only, among others. The sensory vividness of a site could be greater or lesser depending on the number of such tools used and the degree to which they are used in the site.

Research has noted differences in men's and women's visual spatial skills, in their style of interaction, and in how they interpret information. The selectivity model suggests that men may have more difficulty integrating information in a highly interactive medium. Men's tendency to "cut corners" while processing information might lead to judgments of Web sites based on tools and not on content. That is, the bells and whistles of a site might be used as a proxy of quality. Similarly, more accessible or easy to use Web sites would be considered better because of their availability. Therefore, we propose the following.

P3a: *For sites with more multimedia tools, information processing will be enhanced for women.*

We assume that there will be some ceiling to the number of multimedia tools that can be mentally processed. With the use of too many multimedia tools, any positive effect for women will be eliminated (as a result of sensory overload). The ceiling may differ for various reasons, depending on an individual's technical skill, category expertise, or motivation, among others.

Because women tend toward comprehensive information processing and assimilation of all available cues, they are likely to have more favorable attitudes toward sites with greater levels of multimodal presentation. Similarly, because men desire to learn as efficiently as possible with the least number of distracters, they are likely to have less favorable attitudes toward more complex multimodal sites. Therefore, we state the following.

P3b: *For sites with more multimedia tools, women will have a more favorable attitude toward the site than men.*

P3c: *For sites with more multimedia tools, women will visit more pages and spend more time on the site than men.*

Modifiability

Modifiability allows users and content developers to change both the computer-mediated environment (e.g., background color, or selection of a graphic-enhanced or simpler text-based interface) and the content of the medium (e.g., personally tailored messages or search engines).

For women, the goal to obtain a comprehensive amount of information will counter their desire to reduce the information into a more manageable format. For men, the goal to be more efficient in message processing to make efficient use of their time will encourage their attempt to reduce the information into a more manageable format to facilitate decision making. Therefore, we propose the following.

P4a: *When sites provide options to personalize the site and to filter information, women will use these options less frequently than men.*

Given their need to assimilate all new cues, women are likely to have less positive attitudes toward sites that afford tools that allow rapidly changing the site or having highly personalized Web sites. Women may also feel "lost" in a site given their need to thoroughly comprehend a site in combination with their lower navigational abilities. Therefore, we state the following.

P4b: *For highly modifiable sites, women will have less positive attitudes toward the site.*

P4c: *For highly modifiable sites, women will spend less time modifying the site than men.*

For women, the time they spend in the site is more likely to be spent on processing existing information rather than filtering or modifying the site (which men are more likely to do).

FUTURE RESEARCH

A better understanding of how men and women use Web-based messages in decision making is important to developing effective Web sites that enhance learning, attitudes, and behaviors related to health. However, is it preferable to deliver different messages to men and women by different Web sites to enhance message effectiveness? Or will men and women process the same message on a site in a different manner but with outcomes that render the message effective? In this chapter, we have used the selectivity hypothesis to develop a series of propositions that relate some specific characteristics of interactive messages to differences in message processing. Systematic empirical research is still needed to begin to answer the questions posed here.

Several other psychological constructs should be examined in conjunction with the selectivity hypothesis and interactivity, as they are likely to be important in explaining gender differences in processing. These include level of technical skill of the user, previous experience with the topic category, level of involvement with the topic, degree of risk, motivation, and direction of the message (i.e., for the self or for another). Other message factors, such as the type of information (e.g., subjective or objective; see Darley & Smith, 1995), credibility of the information source, and amount of information may also be important to processing differences. Affective cues, such as emotion, may also affect message processing. Future research should consider these variables as they relate to gender differences in processing interactive messages.

For many of these constructs, useful and validated measures are available. However, future research should examine the transferability of existing measures to an interactive environment. Qualitative methods can also illuminate our understanding of the underlying processes. Personal interviews with participants in experimental studies, when used in tandem with software that tracks the surfing behavior of individuals, can do much to illuminate why respondents behave the way they do online.

It is important that future research strike a balance in assessing how the presence of objective tools of interactivity used in a Web site assists message processing. To understand how the appropriateness of the tools, relative to the nature of the site, and the capability of the equipment work together requires a research approach providing a blend of simple quantitative counting of tools in combination with a broader approach that enables an understanding of the gestalt of how elements of Web message design influence how men and women process interactive messages. The degree to which gender differences matter in how we communicate health-related messages on the Web to enhance learning, attitudes, and behaviors deserves serious attention.

REFERENCES

Alreck, P., & Settle, R. B. (2002). Gender effects on Internet, catalogue, and store shopping. *Journal of Database Marketing, 9*, 150–163.

Ariely, D. (2000). Controlling the information flow: Effects on consumers' decision making and preferences. *Journal of Consumer Research, 27*, 233–248.

Bagui, S. (1998). Reasons for increased learning using multimedia. *Journal of Educational Multimedia and Hypermedia, 7*, 3–18.

Batra, R., & Ray, M. L. (1986). Affective responses mediating acceptance of advertising. *Journal of Consumer Research, 13*, 234–249.

Bezjian-Avery, A., Calder, B., & Iacobucci, D. (1998). New media interactive advertising vs. traditional advertising. *Journal of Advertising Research, 38*, 43–54.

Biocca, F. (1992). Virtual reality technology: A tutorial. *Journal of Communication, 42*, 23–72.

Braithwaite, D. O., Waldron, V. R., & Finn, J. (1999). Communication of social support in computer-mediated groups for people with disabilities. *Health Communication, 11*, 123–151.

Broverman, D. M., Klaiber, E. L., Kobayashi, Y., & Vogel, W. (1968). Roles of activation and inhibition in sex differences in cognitive abilities. *Psychological Review, 75*, 23–50.

Brown, R. M., Hall, L. R., Holtzer, R., Brown, S. L., & Brown, N. L. (1997). Gender and video game performance. *Sex Roles, 36*, 793–812.

Caplan, P. J. (1979). Beyond the box score: A boundary condition for sex differences in aggression and achievement striving. In B. Maher (Ed.), *Progress in experimental personality research* (pp. 41–87). New York: Academic Press.

Caplan, P. J., MacPherson, G. M., & Tobin, P. (1985). Do sex-related differences in spatial abilities exist? A multilevel critique with new data. *American Psychologist, 40*, 786–799.

Carlson, R. (1971). Sex differences in ego functioning: Exploratory studies of agency and communion. *Journal of Consulting and Clinical Psychology, 37*, 267–277.

Carlson, R. (1972). Understanding women: Implications for personality theory and research. *Journal of Social Issues, 28*, 17–32.

Chen, Q., & Wells, W. D. (1999). Attitude toward the site. *Journal of Advertising Research, 39*, 27—37.

Cho, C. H. (1999). How advertising works on the WWW: Modified elaboration likelihood model. *Journal of Current Issues and Research in Advertising, 21*, 33–50.

Clark, C., & Gorski, P. (2002). Multicultural education and the digital divide: Focus on gender. *Multicultural Perspectives, 4*, 30–40.

Darley, W. K., & Smith, R. E. (1995). Gender differences in information processing strategies: An empirical test of the selectivity model in advertising response. *Journal of Advertising, 24* (1), 41–56.

Eagly, A. H. (1978). Sex differences in influenciability. *Psychological Bulletin, 85*, 86–116.

Eagly, A. H., & Carli, L. L. (1981). Sex of researchers and sex-typed communications as determinants of sex differences in influenciability: A meta-analysis of social influence studies. *Psychological Bulletin, 90*, 1–20.

Eveland, J. R., & Dunwoody, S. (2001). User control and structural isomorphism or disorientation and cognitive load? Learning from the Web versus print. *Communication Research, 28*, 48–78.

Frazer, C., & McMillan, S. (1999). Sophistication on the World Wide Web: Evaluating structure, function and commercial goals of Web sites. In D. W. Schumann & E. Thorson (Eds.), *Advertising and the World Wide Web* (pp. 119–134). Mahwah, NJ: Lawrence Erlbaum Associates.

Gabbard-Alley, A. S. (1995). Health communication and gender: A review and critique. *Health Communication, 7*, 35–54.

Gefen, D., & Straub, D.W. (1997). Gender differences in perception and use of e-mail: An extension to the technology acceptance model. *MIS Quarterly, 21*, 389–400.

Ghose, S., & Dou, W. (1998). Interactive functions and their impacts on the appeal of Internet presence sites. *Journal of Advertising Research, 38*, 29–43.

Gilroy, D. F., & Desai, H. B. (1986). Computer anxiety: Sex, race and age. *International Journal of Man-Machine Studies, 25*, 711–719.

Ha, L., & James, E. L. (1998). Interactivity reexamined: A baseline analysis of early business Web sites. *Journal of Broadcasting and Electronic Media, 42*, 457–474.

Hall, J. A. (1984). *Nonverbal sex differences: Communication accuracy and expressive style.* Baltimore: Johns Hopkins University Press.

Horrigan, J., & Rainie, L. (2002). *Counting on the Internet.* Washington, DC: The Pew Internet & American Life Project.

LaFerle, C., Edwards, S., & Lee, W. (2000). Teens' use of traditional media and the Internet. *Journal of Advertising Research, 40*, 55–66.

Larsen, R. J., & Diener, E. (1987). Affect intensity as an individual difference characteristic: A review. *Journal of Research in Personality, 21*, 1–39.

Liu, Y., & Shrum, L. J. (2002). What is interactivity and is it always a good thing? Implications of definition, person and situation for the influence of interactivity on advertising effectiveness. *Journal of Advertising, 31*, (4), 53–65.

Lieberman, D. A. (1997). Interactive video games for health promotion: Effects on knowledge, self-efficacy, social support and health. In R. L. Street, Jr., W. R. Gold, & T. Manning (Eds.), *Health promotion and interactive technology* (pp. 103–120). Mahwah, NJ: Lawrence Erlbaum Associates.

Lohse, G. L., Bellman, S., & Johnson, E. J. (2000). Consumer buying behavior on the Internet: Findings from panel data. *Journal of Interactive Marketing, 14* (1), 15–29.

Lombard, M., & Ditton, T. (1997). At the heart of it all: The concept of presence. *Computer Mediated Communication, 3* (2), 1–43.

McMillan, S. J., & Hwang, J. S. (2002). Measures of perceived interactivity: An exploration of the role of direct communication, user control, and time in shaping perceptions of interactivity. *Journal of Advertising, 31*, (3), 29–42.

Meyers-Levy, J. (1989). Gender differences in information processing: A selectivity interpretation. In P. Cafferata & A. M. Tybout (Eds.), *Cognitive and affective responses to advertising* (pp. 219–260). Lexington, MA: Lexington.

Meyers-Levy, J. (1994). Gender differences in cortical organization: Social and biochemical antecedents and advertising consequences. In E. Clark, T. Brock, & D. Stewart (Eds.), *Attention, attitude and affect in response to advertising* (pp. 107–122). Hillsdale, NJ: Lawrence Erlbaum Associates.

Meyers-Levy, J., & Maheswaran, D. (1991). Exploring males' and females' processing strategies: When and why do differences occur in consumers' processing of ad claims? *Journal of Consumer Research, 18*, 63–70.

Meyers-Levy, J, & Sternthal, B. (1991). Gender differences in the use of message cues and judgements. *Journal of Marketing Research, 28*, 84–96.

Novak, T. P., Hoffman, D. L., & Yung, Y. F. (2000). Measuring the customer experience in online environments: A structural modeling approach. *Marketing Science, 19*, 22–42.

Odell, P. M., Korgen, K. O., Schumacher, P., & Delucchi, M. (2000). Internet use among female and male college students. *CyberPsychology & Behavior, 3*, 855–863.

Parrott, R. L., & Condit, M. C. (Eds.) (1996). *Evaluating women's health messages: A resource book.* Thousand Oaks, CA: Sage.

Pearson, J. M., Bahmanziari, T., Crosby, L., & Conrad, E. (2002–2003). An empirical investigation into the relationship between organizational culture and computer efficacy as moderated by age and gender. *Journal of Computer Information Systems, 43* (2), 58–71.

Perry, D. G., Perry, L., & Boldizar, J. P. (1990). Learning of aggression. In M. Lewis & S. M. Miller (Eds.), *Handbook of developmental psychopathology* (pp. 135–146). New York: Plenum.

Peterson Bishop, A. (2000). Technology literacy in low-income communities. *Journal of Adolescent & Adult Literacy, 43* (5), 473–476.

Pope-Davis, D. B., & Vispoel, W. P. (1993). How instruction influences attitudes of college men and women towards computers. *Computers in Human Behavior, 9*, 83–93.

Rafaeli, S. (1988). Interactivity: From new media to communication. In R. P. Hawkins, J. M. Weimann, & S. Pingree (Eds.), *Advancing communication science: Merging mass and interpersonal processes* (pp. 110–134). Beverly Hills, CA: Sage.

Schiff, W., & Oldak, R. (1990). Accuracy of judging time to arrival: Effects of modality, trajectory, and gender. *Journal of Experimental Psychology, 16*, 303–316.

Scott, C. R., & Rockwell, S. C. (1997). The effect of communication, writing, and technology apprehension on likelihood to use new communication technologies. *Communication Education, 46* (1), 44–62.

Shashaani, L. (1997). Gender differences in computer attitudes and use among college students. *Journal of Educational Computing Research, 16*, 37–51.

Shaw, B. R., McTavish, F., Hawkins, R., Gustafson, D. H., & Pingree, S. (2000). Experiences of women with breast cancer: Exchanging social support over the CHESS computer network. *Journal of Health Communication, 5*, 135–159.

Siegman, A. W., & Reynolds, M. A. (1983). Effects of mutual invisibility and topical intimacy on verbal fluency in dyadic communication. *Journal of Psycholinguistics Research, 12*, 443–455.

Steuer, J. (1992). Defining virtual reality: Dimensions determining telepresence. *Journal of Communication, 42*, 73–93.

Street, R. L., Jr., & Rimal, R. N. (1997). Health promotion and interactive technology: A conceptual foundation. In R. L. Street, W. R. Gold, & T. Manning (Eds.), *Health promotion and interactive technology* (pp. 19–38). Mahwah, NJ: Lawrence Erlbaum Associates.

Sundar, S. S., Brown, J., & Kalyanaraman, S. (1999, May). *Reactivity vs. interactivity: Impression formation effects of message contingency in political Web sites.* Paper presented at the meeting of the International Communication Association Conference, San Francisco, CA.

Thorne, B., Kramarae, C., & Henley, N. (1983). Language, gender, and society: Opening a second decade of research. In B. Thorne, C. Kramarae, & N. Henley (Eds.), *Language, gender and society* (pp. 7–24). Rowley, MA: Newbury House.

Unz, D. C., & Hesse, F. W. (1999). The use of hypertext for learning. *Journal of Educational Computing Research, 20*, 279–295.

Villegas, J., & Stout, P. A. (2001, March). *Measurement and the role of emotions while browsing on the Web.* Paper presented at the meeting of the Advertising and Consumer Psychology Conference, Seattle, WA.

Vorderer, P. (2000). Interactive entertainment and beyond. In D. Zillmann & P. Vorderer (Eds.), *Media entertainment: The psychology of its appeal* (pp. 21–36). Mahwah, NJ: Lawrence Erlbaum Associates.

Whitley, B. E. (1996). Gender differences in computer-related attitudes: It depends on what you ask. *Computers in Human Behavior, 12,* 275–289.

Wiedenbeck, S., & Zila, P. L. (1997). Hands-on practice in learning to use software: A comparison of exercise, exploration, and combined formats. *ACM Transactions on Computer-Human Interaction, 4*, 169–196.

Zhang, Y. (2002). Comparison of Internet attitudes between industrial employees and college students. *CyberPsychology & Behavior, 5,* 143–150.

CHAPTER TWENTY THREE

The Presence of Religious Symbols and Values in Advertising

David Fairfield
Madeline Johnson
University of Houston-Downtown

Reports of investigations into the frequency of religious thought and symbols in advertising are nonexistent. Therefore, little is known about religious diversity in advertising, even though religions significantly influence culture in many countries. The primary purpose of this research is to investigate whether advertising content reflects religious symbols and values in print publications from a country with a strong religious presence. India was chosen as the country from which to gather print advertisements because Hinduism is an integral part of Indian society.

BACKGROUND

Although the relationship between religion and advertising has not been studied, the relationship between advertising and other components of culture has been investigated. The cultural context of an ad may capture lifestyles, demographic characteristics, or values. It is argued that "to create the economic impact of selling goods, advertising operates psychologically, changing attitudes, images, cognitions, feelings and values" (Pollay & Gallagher, 1990, p. 359). Creating culturally congruent advertising can result in more positive attitudes toward the ad and toward the brand advertised (Zhang & Gelb, 1996).

Cultural diversity is reflected in advertising content to some extent. Gender roles portrayed in advertising have been the subject of a number of studies. The relationship between gender roles portrayed in advertising and cultural context was the focus of two recent studies. A comparison by Browne (1998) of advertising during children's television in the United States and Australia revealed substantial similarity in gender stereotyping. Advertisements from both countries portrayed men and boys engaging in domination and action behaviors whereas women and girls were portrayed as engaging in deference and touching behaviors. Although Browne did not directly address the question of culture-based differences between the United States and Australia, the lack of differences in gender stereotyping may reflect strong cultural similarities between these two countries.

A direct attempt to look at cultural differences and sex role portrayals was made by Milner and Collins (2000). Using Hofstede's masculinity index rankings, they classified Sweden and Russia as feminine countries and the United States and Japan as masculine countries. They expected that sex-role differences would be more defined in masculine countries than in feminine countries. Their findings revealed that, on some characteristics such as marriage, spokesperson, and credibility, the sex roles were more defined in the United States and Japan than in Sweden and Russia. However, there were no differences in sex-role definition among the four countries with respect to such traits as helpfulness and advising.

Another component of culture that has been studied extensively is the use of sexual content or messages in advertising. Soley and Kurzbard (1986) expected that cultural changes in the United States resulting from the "sexual revolution" would be reflected in more sexual content in 1984 ads than in 1964 ads. They found that there was an increase in sexually oriented ads in general-interest magazines and that sexual illustrations had become more overt. In a cross-cultural comparison of sexual content in French and American print ads, Biswas, Olsen, and Carlet (1992) found that sexual appeals were more frequently used in French ads than in American ads. The more frequent use of sexual appeals was expected in French ads because France is more sexually liberated than the United States.

The finding of culture-based differences in advertising is mixed. The frequency of use of a subset of advertising appeals that capture the cultural value of uncertainty avoidance was found to relate to cultural differences. However, the frequency of other advertising appeals that also capture uncertainty avoidance did not differ by culture (Albers-Miller & Gelb, 1996). Some characteristics of gender role in advertising do appear to be culturally determined, whereas others do not (Milner & Collins, 2000).

The explanations for the mixed findings on the extent to which advertising is a reflection of a country's culture are varied. There is evidence that cultural congruency as a predictor of advertising effectiveness may be moderated by the product use conditions (Zhang & Gelb, 1996). The globalization of marketing, particularly international advertising campaigns, may explain the lack of cultural differences reflected in advertising. For example, despite cultural differences between the United States and Korea with respect to individualism–collectivism, these differences were not found in a comparison of U.S. and Korean ads (Cho, Kwon, Gentry, Jun, & Kropp, 1999).

Another explanation is that advertising reflects only some aspects of a culture. Advertisements are distortions of a society's attitudes, behaviors, and values rather than a complete reflection of them (Pollay, 1986). Advertising content will include some lifestyles, demographic characteristics, and values but not others. In a longitudinal study involving the content analysis of advertisements from 2,000 magazines from 1900 to 1980, Pollay and Gallagher (1990) found that the variation in values portrayed was modest. The frequency of ads containing values relating to leisure, productivity, being modern, and traditional did change. However, the use of the remaining 21 values was constant over time. The three most common values in advertisements included pleasure, wisdom, and family security. The study concluded that advertising has a more constant cultural character than it may appear on casual inspection. According to Pollay and Gallagher, "commercial communication has been relatively consistent in its cultural character" (p. 370).

Religion and Advertising

If advertising content reflects only some cultural characteristics and values, then religious thoughts and symbols may not be reflected in advertising content. Religion operates within a society in a number of ways, such as personal values, beliefs, icons, symbols, rituals, and social gatherings. Its most pervasive social affects are through its influence on the personal values and beliefs of its followers. Religious organizations have led very successful boycotts of products as well as promoted the use of other products. The Pontifical Council for Social Communication for the Vatican issued its standards for ethics in advertising in 1997 in an attempt to influence the behavior of advertisers around the world. These activities by religious organizations and their followers influence marketers by establishing standards of acceptability in advertising. An advertiser who wants to garner the endorsement of a religious group may incorporate religious symbols and values in an advertisement. Choosing the religious symbol or value to incorporate into an ad campaign, however, could be difficult. In a culture that supports a wide variety of religious beliefs, there is the potential to offend one set of believers while supporting another. This would be less of a problem in a culture in which only one or two religions thrive.

Throughout its history, India has had strong relationships between its economic development and religious thought (Dehejia & Dehejia, 1993). Hinduism, a major religion in India, has evolved over the past 5,000 years to form one of the most complex religions in the world. For many in India, it defines a way of life, including daily rituals as well as rituals that mark significant passages, such as the birth of a child. In addition to the significant number of rituals, Hinduism is also characterized by a large number of gods, and goddesses representing different characteristics and values intimately tied to day-to-day living. For example, Rama, one of the more popular gods, is known as the ideal man and is often depicted in a family setting. Lakshmi is the goddess that embodies loveliness, grace, and charm.

It is expected that if religious symbols and thought are reflected in advertising content, this would most likely occur in print advertisements from a country such as India. The social affect of religion is high in the Indian culture. In addition, the dominating effect of Hinduism in the country would make the choice of religious symbols and values less risky for the advertiser. For these reasons, India was considered to be a good prospect for finding religious symbols in advertising. Therefore, the research questions were as follows. First, to what extent are religious symbols found in print advertisements distributed in India? Second, which values are most often reflected in print advertisements distributed in India?

METHOD

The magazines for this sample were collected from a number of rural and urban outlets in southern India over a 3-week period. Publications came from Chennai, Madurai, and Kanniyakumari. Local temples, shrines, places of worship, and bookstores were the primary sources of materials. Magazine publications included everything from expensive, high-end glossy publications to free black-and-white publications. Of the 80 magazines that were collected, 50 were selected randomly for inclusion in this study. The magazines were dated 1997 or 1998 and included both English and Tamil languages. Five advertisements from each magazine were selected randomly for analysis. Of the ads chosen for this study, 72% of the advertisements were written in Tamil and 28% were written in English.

The three coders are natives of India and permanent residents of the United States. The coders are fluent in English, Tamil, and Hindi. All of the coders are also Hindus who are very familiar with the religious practices, values, and symbols of the Hindu religion. The coders frequently return to India for religious festivals and holidays. Although each coder was assigned the review of the same set of advertisements, only 177 of the 250 ads were actually reviewed by all three coders.

Each coder was provided an instruction booklet that contained instructions, a copy of the coding instrument, and a reference guide to Hindu gods, goddesses, and symbols. The coding instrument consisted of two parts: the Rokeach Value Scale and a religious appeals questionnaire created by the authors. The religious appeals questionnaire consisted of five topic areas: religious icons, colors, the setting, words or phrases, and religious theme. The coders were asked to identify the number of religious icons or symbols used in the advertisement. To facilitate the identification of religious symbols, the coders used the reference guide. The coders were also asked to identify the colors found in the advertisement. The options included orange–burnt yellow and blue–green—colors associated with Hinduism. The listing of settings or activities in the advertisement included temple or shrine, prayer or meditation, family gathering, and private or communal religious ritual. The coders also identified the presence of key words or phrases relating to love, duty, and courtship. Finally, the coders were asked the extent to which they agreed with this statement: "This ad contains a religious theme."

The Rokeach Value Scale included 18 terminal values and 18 instrumental values. The terminal values were a comfortable life, an exciting life, a sense of

TABLE 23.1
Magazine Titles and Number of Ads

Magazine Title	No. of Ads
Woman's Era	4
Femina	3
Taj	2
Outlook	4
Business India	3
Business Today	3
Liebas	5
Cosmopolitan	6
India Today	2
Various Titles in Tamil	102
Total (all titles)	134

accomplishment, a world at peace, a world of beauty, equality, family security, freedom, happiness, inner harmony, mature love, national security, pleasure, salvation, self-respect, social recognition, true friendship, and wisdom. The instrumental values were being ambitious, broadminded, capable, cheerful, clean, courageous, forgiving, helpful, honest, imaginative, independent, intellectual, logical, loving, obedient, polite, responsible, and self-controlled. A brief definition accompanied each of these values. The coders were asked to identify which of these values were evident in the ad.

For purposes of classification, the coders identified the size of the ad (full page or half-page) and the orientation of the publication as Western, Hindu, or other. Each coder was given a detailed briefing on the study, including a review of the coding instrument. Following the completion of a "practice set," the researchers met with the coders to review the results and answer questions about coding.

Following completion of the coding, the data were analyzed to determine the degree of intercoder reliability. The degree of agreement for each pair of coders was calculated and then an average degree of agreement was calculated for each of the 177 advertisements. Only those advertisements for which the average degree of agreement exceeded .67 were chosen for further analysis. This resulted in 134 useable advertisements. The number of advertisements by magazine title included in the final sample is shown in Table 23.1.

RESULTS

Of the 134 advertisements, 16% (21) were considered by the coders to be in publications having a Hindu theme and 17% (23) were considered to be in publications having a Western theme. The remaining advertisements were in publications

TABLE 23.2
Religious Symbols and Percentage of Total

Religious Symbol in Ad	Hindu	Western	Other	All
Yes (%)	7 (9)	0	1 (2)	8 (11)
No(%)	9 (12)	17 (23)	66(88)	92 (123)
Total	16 (21)	17 (23)	67 (90)	100 (134)

Note. Frequencies are given parenthetically.

lacking either a clearly Hindu or Western theme. The analysis was divided into two areas: use of religious symbols in the advertisements and the values reflected in the advertisements. Religious or spiritual symbols were found in only 8% (11) of the advertisements. The religious settings found in the ads included a temple, community religion, and social religious gathering. Only 2% (3) of the advertisements were considered to have a religious theme. Most of the advertisements (59%) were in black and white. There was no evidence that colors, such as oranges and blues, associated with Hinduism were used.

When the classification of the publication is taken into account, 9 of the 11 ads containing religious or spiritual symbols were from publications having a Hindu theme. The remaining two ads were from magazines that fell into the "other" category. None of the ads were in publications having a Western cultural theme. Table 23.2 contains more information on the breakdown by religious or cultural theme.

The second area of inquiry focused on the values found in the advertisements. The coders were asked to identify which of the 36 values listed in the Rokeach Value Scale were reflected in the advertisement. Table 23.3 contains the results of this analysis. The most frequently occurring value reflected in the ads was a comfortable life (75%). Other values occurring often in the ads included an exciting life (57%), pleasure (48%), a sense of accomplishment (40%), and family security (37%). The value of salvation was found in nine ads (7%). A review of the ads by religious or cultural theme revealed a similar value pattern. A comfortable life appeared the most frequently in all categories. However, it should be noted that the values of happiness and salvation were reflected in a disproportionately higher percentage of Hindu-theme publications: 43% (9) of the Hindu ads contained the value of happiness compared with 4% (1) of the Western-theme ads. Salvation as a value was reflected in 29% (6) of the Hindu-theme ads and did not appear in any of the Western-theme ads.

DISCUSSION

Although Hinduism is considered to be an integral part of Indian culture, particularly in southern India, it does not appear to have a significant influence on advertising content. To the extent that religious symbols are used in print advertisements,

TABLE 23.3
Values Appearing in Ads and Percentage of Total Ads

Value	All	Hindu	Western	Other
A comfortable life %	75 (101)	86 (18)	87 (20)	70 (63)
An exciting life %	57 (76)	81 (17)	61 (14)	50 (45)
Pleasure %	48 (64)	52 (11)	78 (18)	39 (35)
A sense of accomplishment %	40 (53)	57 (12)	39 (9)	36 (32)
Family security %	37 (49)	48 (10)	26 (6)	37 (33)
A world of beauty %	31 (41)	19 (4)	57 (13)	27 (24)
A world at peace %	24 (32)	24 (5)	48 (11)	18 (16)
Happiness %	21 (28)	43 (9)	4 (1)	20 (18)
Freedom %	11 (15)	14 (3)	4 (1)	12 (11)
Salvation %	11 (15)	29 (6)	0	10 (9)
Ambitious %	9 (12)	9 (2)	9 (2)	9 (8)
Other Values (< 10/value)	42 (56)	71 (15)	22 (5)	40 (36)

Note. Percentages will not total to 100% because some ads contain multiple values. Frequencies are given parenthetically.

they appear to be limited to those publications that have a definite Hindu theme. All of these ads were found in magazines that are written in Tamil and are distributed free at religious shrines throughout southern India. Therefore, the use of religious symbols in these magazines may be a function of the target market for the publication rather than the centrality of Hinduism in Indian culture.

The values reflected in the print ads may be more consistent with Western values than Indian values. In a recent study on the personal values of undergraduate students in India, the top values among male students were equality, a world of peace, a world of beauty, national security, and self-respect; and among female students, the top values were wisdom, equality, true friendship, freedom, and family security (Rustogi, Hensel, & Burgers, 1993). In contrast, the top five values in the print advertisements reviewed for this study were a comfortable life, an exciting life, pleasure, a sense of accomplishment, and family security. This comparison would suggest that advertisers are not choosing advertising content that captures the dominant values of the culture.

The low incidence of religious symbols and icons in advertising may be explained in a number of ways. First, because this was designed as an exploratory study, the sample size was intentionally small. The number of different publications included in the survey may not adequately represent the variety of publications in India. However, in planning this exploratory study we did focus our collection efforts on local publications that we thought would be less influenced by global marketing campaigns. If religious symbols were being reflected in advertising content, it would most likely be present in these very localized publications distributed at religious shrines and temples in southern India. The low incidence here would suggest some other explanation.

One explanation worthy of further investigation would be to explore the attitudes of advertisers and advertising agencies toward the use of religious symbols and themes in advertising. To what extent do advertising professionals or the companies they represent consider the use of religious symbols appropriate in advertising? The separation of the secular from the spiritual in many cultures would support the separation of religious symbol themes from advertising content. Advertisers may also believe that the use of religious themes and symbols in advertising is too risky. Specifically, the public may find such a use to be offensive and even sacrilegious. Finally, advertisers may find that religious themes are inconsistent with the universal themes of advertising that promote consumption as the path to the good life.

Our research findings are consistent with the theory that the value content of advertisements reflects only some of the values of a society. In our case, the values chosen by the advertiser are not necessarily considered to be most important to the population of that country. Despite the importance of Hinduism in the lives of people living in southern India, advertisers are not choosing to include religious settings, colors, or symbols in their advertising content. Research from other countries in which a religion plays an integral role would help in further understanding the role of religion in advertising.

REFERENCES

Albers-Miller, N. D., & Gelb, B. D. (1996). Business advertising appeals as a mirror of cultural dimensions: A study of eleven countries. *The Journal of Advertising, 25* (4), 57–70.

Biswas, A., Olsen, J. E., & Carlet, V. (1992). A comparison of print advertisements from the United States and France. *The Journal of Advertising, 21* (4), 73–81.

Browne, B. A. (1998). Gender stereotypes in advertising on children's television in the 1990s: A cross-national analysis. *The Journal of Advertising, 27* (1), 83–96.

Cho, B., Kwon, K., Gentry, J. W., Jun, S., & Kropp, F. (1999). Cultural values reflected in theme and execution: A comparative study of U.S. and Korean television Commercials. *The Journal of Advertising, 28* (4), 59–73.

Dehejia, R. H., & Dehejia, V. H. (1993). Religion and economic activity in India: An historical perspective. *American Journal of Economics and Sociology, 52,* 145–153.

Milner, L. M., & Collins, J. M. (2000). Sex-role portrayals and the gender of nations. *The Journal of Advertising, 29* (1), 67–79.

Pollay, R. W. (1986). The distorted mirror: Reflections on the unintended consequences of advertising. *Journal of Marketing, 49,* 24–37.

Pollay, R. W., & Gallagher, K. (1990). Advertising and cultural values: Reflections in the distorted mirror. *International Journal of Advertising, 9,* 359–372.

Rustogi, H., Hensel, P. J., & Burgers, W. P. (1996). The link between personal values and advertising appeals: Cross-cultural barriers to standardized global advertising, *Journal of Euromarketing, 5* (4), 57–79.

Soley, L., & Kurzbard, G. (1986). Sex in advertising: A comparison of 1964 and 1984 magazine advertisements. *The Journal of Advertising, 15*(3), 46–54, 64.

Zhang, Y., & Gelb, B. D. (1996). Matching advertising appeals to culture: The influence of products' use conditions. *The Journal of Advertising, 25* (3), 29–46.

CHAPTER TWENTY FOUR

Ethics, Machiavellianism, and Social Values: Implications for Advertising

Swee Hoon Ang
National University of Singapore

Jerome D. Williams
The University of Texas at Austin

There have been several discussions on the benefits and challenges of having a standardized ad campaign versus one that is customized to selected markets (cf. de Mooij & Keegan, 1991). Besides cost efficiency, a uniform ad campaign is espoused particularly for international brands as the values of such brands are consistently communicated throughout the world. In contrast, researchers acknowledge that not all consumers are similar in their values and preferences. Even when the same ad is used, consumers from various cultural backgrounds may interpret the ad differently. Hence, there is a need to develop customized ads to suit the preferences of the target audience, especially when such a market is a significant one. Mueller (1987) showed that, in general, advertising tends to reflect the prevalent values of the culture in which it exists.

One of the emerging markets that companies are interested in is the youth market. Called Generation Y, teenagers aged 12 to 19 form a huge market that is expected to grow at some 5% annually ("Understanding Generation Y," 1998). Another market of interest is the Asian market, with a population of over 5.3 billion people or almost 56% of the world's population. Although the economic crisis has slowed the growth in this region somewhat, its youth market remains a thriving one. In fact, as the crisis has hit the middle-income highly leveraged Asians, the youth market has become an alternative viable segment. Asian youths are not leveraged and generally live with their parents. Therefore, although their disposable income is low, they are somewhat insulated from the economic crisis. Survey findings indicate that Hong Kong and Singapore teenagers have weekly allowances of $14.50 and $13.50, respectively, the highest in the Asia Pacific (" Rich Pickings," 1998). These compare favorably with the weekly income of U.S. youths, which is estimated at less than $8 (" More Than Play Dough," 1997). Indeed, Pepsi noted that, despite the Asian economic crisis, its turnover has registered double-digit growth in 1997 and 1998, attesting to the resilience of the Asian youth market (Business Asia, 1998).

There is also anecdotal evidence of the interest among international brands toward customizing their ad campaigns for the Asian youth market because of differing values. Nike found that Asian youths were more interested in their studies and in making money than in sports ("Nike Chases American Dream," 1997). Their international ad campaigns of showing various sports celebrities were thus not as well received in Asia as in the United States. Therefore, a customized ad campaign was commissioned to encourage Asian youths to dare to dream and challenge their parents by excelling in sports. Levi's, known for its standardized campaigns, also created one especially for Asia. Playing on the theme of social acceptance, the ad showed the popularity of a high-school kid, even with his female teacher.

The objective of this study is therefore to examine selected value differences among youths from different countries, and their implications for advertising. Specifically, youths from two major Asian cities—Hong Kong and Singapore—were studied. Their counterparts, youths of East Asian descent living in Hawaii, were also studied for comparison, along with Caucasian youths from North America. The difference in geography (East vs. West) as well as ethnicity (East Asian vs. White) offers an interesting investigation in whether youths differ in their values, and whether acculturation—the learning of another culture—is likely to evolve among youths. The findings will have implications on whether advertising appeals should be tailored accordingly and, if so, the extent to which customization should take place.

Four sets of values were investigated, two that have generally been studied in Western research and two others that are usually associated with the East. The belief in business ethics and social responsibility is an issue that has much interest in Western literature. Potentially, it is of interest in East Asia as well. The prevalence of corruption (de George, 1997) and counterfeiting (Tan, Lim, & Lee, 1997) in Asia suggests that studying this value would indicate the extent to which corporate ethics and responsibility would be acceptable as an advertising issue in Asia. Another value concerns self-interest. Although Machiavellianism is touted as a Western concept, it is not limited in its application to Western management. Hence, studying this construct will offer implications on the extent to which self-interest should be portrayed in Asian advertisements.

Several Eastern values pertaining to social values are studied. Asians have been described as being more collectivistic than Westerners (Hofstede, 1980).

Collectivism refers to the need for social acceptance and maintaining group harmony. Included in this value is the need to avoid public confrontation. Also of interest are the need for outward recognition of one's success and respect for elders or superiors. Studying such social values offers implications on the use of testimonials and endorsements in advertising as well as the extent to which comparative advertising will be favorably received.

The next section provides the literature on the values studied. This is followed by the research methodology. The results are then discussed and advertising implications furnished together with directions for future research.

LITERATURE REVIEW

Business Ethics and Social Responsibility

Much research on ethics and social responsibility is conducted among Americans and Europeans. In general, the findings indicate a high level of corporate ethics. Robertson & Schlegelmich (1993) described American businesses as having a high degree of institutionalized ethics, whereas Dunfee and Werhane (1997) observed that there has been major developments in the observance of business ethics in the United States.

However, research in this area in Asia is scarce. Among Singaporeans, it has been observed that they are less ethical compared with Americans. Mehta and Kau (1984) found that, in 9 of 10 situations, Singaporeans demonstrated that they were less ethical than Americans. For instance, padding expense accounts was not considered as unethical by Singaporeans. Some 64% of Singaporeans were also found to approve of the philosophy that the ends justify the means, including tolerating unethical practices (Kau & Yang, 1992). Similar findings were observed for Hong Kong. McDonald and Kan (1997) found that Hong Kong managers were significantly less ethical than expatriate managers from the United States and Britain. They were more agreeable to practicing deceptive advertising and labeling, among others. In comparing Hong Kongers and Canadians, Nyaw and Ng (1994) showed that Hong Kongers were more tolerant of unethical behavior toward customers and suppliers than their Canadian counterparts. On a personal level, the China Association for Promoting Democracy (CAPD, 1997), found that 43% of Chinese youths would rather betray others than let others betray them, and 52% indicated that with stiff market competition, one need not pay heed to the conscience and to morality.

As a summary test of ethics and social responsibility in these economies, the *World Competitiveness Yearbook* (1998) rated Hong Kong lowest at 5.42, whereas Canada and the United States scored highly at 6.63 and 6.06, respectively. Therefore, we expect Hong Kongers to value ethics and social responsibility least, whereas Canadians will most harbor this value.

Machiavellianism

Named after Niccolo Machiavelli, Machiavellianism is defined as a "negative epithet, indicating at least an amoral (if not immoral) way of manipulating others to accomplish one's objectives" (Hunt & Chonko, 1984, p. 30). Machiavellian individuals are therefore less emotionally involved with others. They are less concerned with the others' feelings and pursue self-interest instead by engaging in behaviors that would protect or enhance themselves.

Empirical evidence suggests that Hong Kongers are somewhat Machiavellian. McDonald and Pak (1996) observed that managers in Hong Kong and Malaysia employed self-interest as one of the frameworks when they were deciding on an ethical problem. The CAPD study showed that Chinese youths displayed Machiavellian characteristics. Some 63% believed that telling lies is necessary or else nothing great can be accomplished, and 57% believed interpersonal relations were all about mutual exploitation. A comparative study showed that Hong Kong professionals more so than Americans would engage in Machiavellian tactics for power (Ralston, Giacolone, & Terpstra, 1994; Ralston, Gustafson, Cheung, & Terpstra, 1993). Therefore, we hypothesize that Hong Kongers will possess more Machiavellian values than Singaporeans and their Western counterparts.

Social Values

Collectivism. Triandis, Bontempo, Villareal, Asai, and Lucca (1988) described collectivism as the state in which members of a group seek stable relationships and harmony. Conformity is endorsed and deviant behaviors not tolerated. Hence, confrontation is highly undesirable. East Asians have been observed to have higher collectivism than Westerners (Hofstede, 1980; Triandis et al., 1986). Leung (1987) reported that, as a way to avoid confrontation, East Asians engaged in more subtle forms of conflict-resolution procedures. As a further indication, there are fewer lawyers per capita in East Asian countries than Western countries. On the basis of this information, Hong Kongers and Singaporeans are therefore expected to value group harmony and avoid public confrontation more than Canadians or Hawaiians.

External Recognition of Success. Researchers have observed East Asians to be self-effacing with a high level of humility. As part of the Confucian ethic, Chinese, in particular, tend to attribute success to hard work or luck rather than innate skill (cf. Crittenden, 1994). In studies on Chinese students, the general findings indicated that, when they do well, they attributed it to luck or effort rather than to personal skills. These findings suggest that when success is encountered, Chinese would rather not "boast" of their success and would rather attribute it to luck. In contrast, when failure is encountered, they tend to blame it on themselves as being because of their low ability or laziness.

However, Chinese are also known for their concern with saving or enhancing face or *mianzi*. In some instances, when successful, they like others to know so that they gain respect in return and elevate their standing in the society. For instance, East Asians' penchant for high-end labels is in part for others to know that they have arrived and, hence, enhance their face. Lau and Kuan (1988) found that Hong Kongers often use material possessions as a primary base for normative judgments. As they noted, "a finely graded stratification structure, based on the criterion of wealth, was generally held" (p. 65) in Hong Kong. Thus, East Asians rely on brand names to reinforce their social identity. Name brands, especially for visible products, are used as social tools to increase distance from other social groups and to identify with peers of similar social status. The "Orange Tribe" youth group in Korea, for instance, has a strict membership code in which youths must drive a top-end foreign car; have visited the United States at least once, and preferably as a student; and have tycoon parents. Youths who do not fulfill any of these criteria are considered as the outgroup. Such contradictory evidence regarding East Asians' external attribution for success while at the same time being motivated for external recognition, does not provide a clear indication regarding how they will be different from Westerners.

Respect for Elders or Superiors.   Hofstede's (1980) study showed that, in general, Asians have a strict hierarchical structure in which power distance is observed. Individuals know their place in the society and those who are above and below them in social standing. Such marked differentiation suggests that Asians are respectful of elders and superiors. Further, with their strong sense of collectivism, respect for those higher in the hierarchy is necessary to maintain group harmony. Therefore, we expect Hong Kongers and Singaporeans to value respect for elders or superiors more strongly than their Western counterparts.

METHOD

Subjects and Procedure

Self-administered survey questionnaires were distributed to 393 business undergraduates—80 from Hong Kong, 113 from Singapore, 101 from Hawaii, and 99 from Canada. The Hong Kong and Singapore participants were East Asian, generally Chinese. The Hawaiian sample consisted of American citizens of East Asian descent. These included Chinese, Filipinos, Japanese, and Koreans. The Canadian sample consisted of Caucasian individuals. Thus, comparisons between Hong Kong and Singapore versus Hawaii would indicate differences within the same ethnicity (East Asian) in different geographic environments (East vs. West). Comparisons between Hawaii and Canada would indicate differences in ethnicity (East Asian vs. Caucasian) in similar geographic locations.

Participants were told that the survey was to find out about their opinions on various business practices. They were also informed that there were no right or wrong answers. Participation in the survey was voluntary. The average time taken to complete the questionnaire was 8 min. All items were on 9-point scales from "disagree" (1) to "agree" (9).

Business Ethics and Social Responsibility

This variable was measured by using the scale developed by Singhapakdi, Vitell, Rallapalli, and Kraft (1996). It consisted of 13 items. The higher the score, the more an individual believed in business ethics and social responsibility. Five of the items were reverse scored. A reliability test conducted showed that the scale was reliable with Cronbach alphas ranging from .64 (for Canada) to .83 (Hawaii). Thus an average score across the 13 items was used in the analyses.

Machiavellianism

The 20-item Mach IV Scale developed by Christie and Geis (1970) was used in this study. Cronbach alphas obtained exceeded .66 for each country sample. Thus an average score across the items was used to compute Machiavellianism. The more Machiavellian an individual, the higher the score.

Social Values

Collectivism. Four items measured the level of collectivism. On the aspect of being part of a group, participants were asked how much they disagreed or agreed that being in the "inside" circle helps in obtaining preferential treatment, and that maintaining good relationships is important. The higher the score, the more collective with regard to belonging to a group an individual is.

On the aspect of avoiding conflict, the two items asked were whether one should avoid embarrassing others in social interactions and whether public confrontations should be avoided if possible. The higher the score, the more an individual wants to avoid conflict to maintain group harmony.

External Recognition for Success. Participants indicated how much they disagreed or agreed that it is important to be recognized as successful by others, and that one should be seen with ostentatious possessions for social enhancement. Higher scores reflect greater importance placed on external recognition.

Respect for Elders or Superiors. A single item was used to measure this variable. The higher the score, the more participants agree that one should respect elders or superiors.

RESULTS

The business ethics and social responsibility and Machiavellian items were analyzed on the basis of their composite average scores as these scales are well established. For the social values, each item was analyzed separately to provide more insights into specific differences.

Table 24.1 furnishes the descriptive statistics for each sample. Post hoc comparison tests (Tukey B) were run to test for differences across the four samples. The results are summarized in Table 24.1.

Consistent with the hypothesis, Canadians were the most ethical and socially responsible ($x = 7.11$), followed by Hawaiians ($x = 6.75$), Singaporeans ($x = 6.39$), and finally, Hong Kongers ($x = 5.51$). Significant differences were observed across all pairs ($F = 35.68$, $p < .01$).

In terms of Machiavellianism, the hypothesis was also supported ($F = 22.81$, $p < .01$). Hong Kongers were the most Machiavellian ($x = 5.04$), followed by Singaporeans ($x = 4.80$). Hawaiians and Canadians were the least Machiavellian, with insignificant differences between their scores ($x = 4.30$ and 4.45, respectively).

Collectivism was measured on two aspects—ingroup membership and conflict avoidance. The hypothesis concerning the ingroup aspect of collectivism was not supported. Canadians believed more in the virtues of being in the "ingroup" than did Hong Kongers ($x = 7.68$ vs. 6.96; $F = 4.43$, $p < .05$). Moreover, the item on

TABLE 24.1
Descriptive Statistics

Descriptor	Hong Kong	Singapore	Hawaii	Canada
Business ethics and social responsibility	5.51[a]	6.39[b]	6.75[c]	7.11[d]
Machiavellianism	5.04[a]	4.80[b]	4.30[c]	4.45[c]
Being in the inside circle helps in obtaining preferential treatment	6.96[a]	7.27[a,b]	7.40[a,b]	7.68[b]
Maintaining a good relationship is the best way to enhance business	7.68[a]	7.86[a]	7.67[a]	8.03[a]
One must avoid embarrassing others in social interactions	7.06[a]	7.64[b]	7.51[a,b]	7.57[a,b]
Public confrontation should be avoided if possible	6.09[a]	6.86[b]	6.51[a,b]	6.40[a,b]
It is important to be recognized as successful by others	6.64[a]	6.76[a]	6.56[a]	6.49[a]
One way to enhance one's station in life is to be seen with ostentatious possessions	6.34[a]	4.38[b]	3.97[b]	4.34[b]
One should respect one's elders or superiors	7.54[a,b]	7.77[b,c]	7.21[a]	8.03[c]

Note. In terms of rows, pairs of mean values with different letters indicate a significant difference ($p < .05$).

maintaining good relationships drew no significant differences across samples. Therefore, the ingroup hypothesis for collectivism was not supported.

The conflict avoidance aspect of collectivism drew interesting findings. Consistent findings were observed for both items, although they partially supported the hypothesis. Singaporeans scored highest in terms of avoiding social embarrassment ($x = 7.64$) and public confrontation ($x = 6.86$), thus supporting the hypothesis that Chinese are collectivistic. However, Hong Kongers scored the least and significantly less than Singaporeans on these two items ($x = 7.06$ and 6.09, respectively), thus contradicting the hypothesis. Canadians and Hawaiians scored between these two Chinese samples.

External recognition for success was measured by two items. On the item that it is important to be recognized as successful by others, no difference was observed across the samples ($F = .46$, $p > .10$). However, on the item that ostentatious possessions can enhance one's social standing, Hong Kongers scored the highest, as expected ($x = 6.34$), followed by Singaporeans ($x = 4.38$). Hawaiians and Canadians scored lower ($F = 16.88$, $p < .01$). Therefore, support was provided for this hypothesis on this aspect of external recognition.

Finally, in terms of respect for elders or superiors, Canadians gave the highest score at 8.03, whereas Hawaiians the lowest at 7.21. Hong Kongers and Singaporeans scored between these Western samples ($F = 6.63$, $p < .01$).

These tests concerned comparisons across samples. Post hoc tests were also conducted to determine, for each sample, whether these values differed significantly from each other. This is of interest as it indicates those values that are more central to each sample. Bonferonni tests were conducted to control for Type I error. In general, the values can be prioritized into two or three clusters. Cluster 1 consisted of the more strongly held beliefs. Good relations was the most strongly held value across the four samples. This was followed by respect for elders or superiors in all samples except Hawaiians, for whom avoiding embarrassing others was the second most important value. The other values in Cluster 1 for all samples were importance of being on the "inside circle" and avoiding embarrassing others. Cluster 2 consisted of a second set of values that were less strongly held. For Singapore, Hawaii, and Canada, this consisted of recognition by others of one's success and avoiding public confrontation. Cluster 3 for these samples was ostentatious possessions for enhancing one's station in life. This value was the least important to them. In contrast, Hong Kongers believed in this value as strongly as social recognition and avoiding public confrontation.

DISCUSSION

In general, the findings indicate that the youth market is not homogeneous in terms of the strengths of values held. This suggests that developing a global ad campaign for the youth market has to be carefully carried out to take into account cultural nuances.

The results partially supported the hypotheses concerning how values differ among youths across different countries in the East and the West. Consistent with the hypothesis, Canadian youths were observed to believe more in business ethics and social responsibility, followed by Hawaiians, Singaporeans, and, finally, Hong Kongers. This has implications for advertising and promotions. It may pay well for businesses in Canada to engage in promotions that demonstrate their corporate responsibility more than businesses in Singapore or Hong Kong. For instance, affinity credit cards, where a percentage of dollar expenditure is donated to a chosen charity, may appeal to Canadians and Hawaiians, but less so to Singaporeans or Hong Kongers. Similarly, corporate sponsorships that are social work in nature are more likely to enhance corporate image in Canada and Hawaii rather than in the East Asian countries. In terms of advertising, corporate advertising espousing the good works that a company has engaged in would see more mileage in the West than in the East.

The results in this study also showed that Hong Kongers were the most Machiavellian, followed by Singaporeans, and then youths from the Western countries. This suggests that advertising appeals that focus on a somewhat Machiavellian nature will attract such East Asian youths. For instance, advertising that discusses or demonstrates how a product brings career success in a competitive world will appeal to the Machiavellian streak in Hong Kongers and Singaporeans. To avoid negative publicity for encouraging such selfish advancements, these ads should be subtly couched in terms of helping consumers become more successful in a competitive environment.

The two findings just given are interesting because, although they are consistent with past research, specifically in the fields of ethics and Machiavellianism, they contradict those concerning cultural masculinity or femininity observed by Hofstede (1980). Hofstede (1980) found that Asian cultures tended to be more feministic in their outlook. This means that such cultures are more socially responsible and place greater emphasis on environmental concern and welfare. In contrast, Western cultures are more masculine, in which aggressiveness and competition prevailed. The aforementioned marketing implications derived from the ethics and Machiavellian findings would contradict those suggested by Hofstede's (1980) masculinity–femininity observations. Instead of appealing to femininity needs of Asian cultures, the present findings suggest that a masculine appeal is needed to fulfill the Machiavellian needs of Hong Kongers and Singaporeans. In contrast, the masculinity appeal, thought to be appropriate there for individuals from Western cultures, would not be appropriate as it does not address their ethical and social responsibility concerns. Rather, a feministic appeal is recommended. Such contradictions suggest that future research is needed to integrate these various cross-cultural constructs and differentiate how they are similar or different. In particular, future research may study the masculinity–femininity dimension together with Machiavellianism and social responsibility to tease out the differences.

Several social values were also investigated in the present study. Collectivism was studied both in terms of ingroup membership and conflict avoidance for harmony. The findings did not support the contention that East Asians are more ingroup minded than Westerners. Instead, Canadians were found to value ingroup membership more so than Hong kongers on one of the two items measured. A possible explanation is the strong level of Machiavellianism observed among Hong Kongers. Being selfish and competitive at the expense of others may have reduced Hong Kongers' value for ingroup membership. Managerially, this finding suggests that ads demonstrating social or group activities may appeal more to Canadians than Hong Kongers. For Hong Kongers, ads that show individual success are likely to be more appealing.

In terms of avoiding public confrontation to preserve harmony, the present study found that the two East Asian cultures split on this count. Singaporeans consistently believed in avoiding social embarrassments, but Hong Kongers consistently scored the lowest on this belief. Although the literature suggests the importance of group harmony in East Asian cultures, anecdotal evidence of Hong Kongers' being rude abounds, thus suggesting that they may have no qualms about publicly embarrassing others.

Managerially, this finding has implications on the use of fear appeal in advertising. Fear appeal on avoiding social embarrassment may find more favorable reception among Singaporeans than Hong Kongers. Ads demonstrating how a product can minimize social embarrassment or be used as a reconciliatory tool between two opposing parties may be more effective in Singapore than in Hong Kong. For instance, in an ad by a Singapore bank, it promoted its corporate credit card by emphasizing its unique selling proposition—a higher credit limit than a personal credit card. The ad suggested that this higher limit would avoid embarrassments such as inability to pay for banquet bills, especially when one was entertaining very important clients. This ad thus hinges on the fear appeal associated with public embarrassment. As another example, a contact lens ad in China showed a bespectacled girl suffering embarrassingly from misty glasses during a dinner date. Her date then went on to advise her on the benefits of contact lens, which invariably included avoiding such social embarrassments in addition to enhancing her looks. This ad demonstrated the important role of social influence in avoiding embarrassments as well as enhancing belongingness.

The need to avoid public confrontation also has implications on product positioning as a reconciliatory tool. The brand can be positioned as one that preserves family harmony. For example, a washing detergent can be positioned as the brand of family choice for both the mother and daughter-in-law. Among youths, a product can be positioned as reconciliatory present between a boy and his girlfriend to patch up after a disagreement. Among siblings, a product can be positioned as one that reduces sibling rivalry.

The findings on conflict avoidance also suggest that the effectiveness of comparative advertising will vary between Singapore and Hong Kong. Comparative advertising is more likely to find better reception in Hong Kong than Singapore. The very nature of comparative ads in promoting confrontation between two or more brands is consistent with Hong Kongers' smaller concern for public embarrassment. In contrast, Singaporeans may perceive such ads as unnecessary as they ridicule the referenced brand and provoke aggression.

East Asian youths were also found to place more importance on social recognition of success than their Western counterparts. In particular, Hong Kongers believed the most in ostentatious possessions to elevate one's social standing. This was followed by Singaporeans, Canadians, and, finally, Hawaiians. Managerially, this implies that ads espousing social recognition will be more effective in Asia, especially in Hong Kong. For brand name goods, their ads should suggest recognition from others and appeal to the audience's external ego or esteem needs. For regular brands, their positioning can be enhanced by adopting an ostentatious image. The ads should show social approval of and admiration toward the person possessing the product. The ads can also capitalize on classical conditioning. Knowing that Hong Kongers believe ostentatious possessions elicit a perception of high standing, marketers can ensure that brands associate their name with other existing ostentatious possessions to elicit a similar perception of high status. Therefore, Tag Heuer in Hong Kong associates itself with prestigious sporting events such as the Four Peaks Boat Race to elicit association with elitism.

The more strongly held values placed on conflict avoidance and social recognition among East Asians in general suggest that the use of such creative ad strategies as drama style, psychological appeal, and symbolic association should be more effective than a lecture style in conveying brand benefit claims. The values of conflict avoidance and social recognition involve interpersonal interactions that are consistent with drama and psychological appeals. Symbolic associations involving celebrity endorsements in which the brand is associated with the celebrity allow for social recognition and enhancement. In contrast, a lecture style is less appropriate because this style is more suited for a discussion of the functional merits of a product.

The present study did not find East Asians to respect elders or superiors more so than Westerners. Instead, Canadians demonstrated the highest level of hierarchical respect. This suggests that the use of a lecture-style format in advertising may not be as appealing to East Asians as it would be to Canadians. A lecture format where someone of authority (e.g., an expert) tells another what to do may not go over as well, especially in Hong Kong, as it would in Canada. Instead, in line with the external recognition finding already discussed, celebrity advertising with an image appeal may work more effectively among Hong Kongers than expert endorsements with a lecture format.

Comparisons between East Asian Hawaiians and Caucasian Canadians, and the former versus Hong Kongers and Singaporeans, suggest acculturation at work. Hawaiians tended to provide responses that are more akin to those given by Canadians compared with those given by their East Asian counterparts. This is consistent with Webber's (1969) thesis that convergence in values will result as individuals adapt to the values of their adopted culture. That acculturation occurred among

Hawaiian youths is also consistent with Kelley, Whatley, and Worthley's (1987) finding. They observed that Japanese (Chinese) Hawaiians were more similar to Caucasian Hawaiians than Japanese (Chinese) on work attitude. Thus, although the present findings showed differences in values that call for adaptation in advertising strategies, the extent of such adaptation may vary depending on the degree of acculturation.

Despite these cultural differences across the four samples, the post hoc tests showed similarities in terms of how centrally held these values were within each sample. Maintaining good relations and respect for elders were the highest in terms of how much the youths believed in these values. Possession of ostentatious brands to enhance social standing was the least important for all, except Hong Kongers. Collectively, the findings therefore imply that, for advertising, focusing on good relations (especially those that are intergenerational in nature) will be the most favorably received among the values studied. Therefore, ads for products such as soft drinks, fast food, and clothes should focus on how these products can enhance social harmony, especially between members of a hierarchy such as parent and child, teacher and student, and boss and subordinates.

The present study examined youths' responses to these values. Future research may extend this to other groups such as the older and younger generation to see whether a convergence or divergence in values is occurring over time within and across cultures. Other values can also be investigated. Besides the masculinity–femininity value cited earlier, others such as uncertainty avoidance and paternalism may also be of interest.

REFERENCES

Business Asia (1998). *Managing Asia's dwindling consumer markets.* Hong Kong: Economist Intelligence Unit.

China Association for Promoting Democracy. (1997, March 20). Self-interest comes first for Guangzhou youths. *The Straits Times (Singapore)*, p. 20.

Christie, R., & Geis, F. L. (1970). *Studies in Machiavellianism.* New York: Academic Press.

Crittenden, K. (1994). Causal attribution processes among the Chinese. In M. H. Bond (Ed.), *The handbook of Chinese psychology.* Hong Kong: Oxford University Press.

de George, R. T. (1997). Ethics, corruption, and doing business in Asia. *Asia Pacific Journal of Economics & Business, 1*(1), 39–52.

de Mooij, M. K., & Keegan, W. (1991). *Advertising worldwide: Concepts, theories, and practice of international, multinational, and global advertising.* London: Prentice-Hall.

Dunfee, T. W., & Werhane, P. (1997). Report on business ethics in North America. *Journal of Business Ethics, 16*, 1589–1595.

Hofstede, G. (1980). *Cultural consequences: International differences in work-related values.* Beverly Hills, CA: Sage.

Hunt, S. D., & Chonko, L. B. (1984, Summer). Marketing and Machiavellianism. *Journal of Marketing, 48*, 30–42.

Kau, A. K., & Yang, C. (1991). *Values and lifestyles of Singaporeans: A marketing perspective.* Singapore: Singapore University Press.

Kelley, L., Whatley, A., & Worthley, R. (1987). Assessing the effects of culture on managerial attitudes: A three-culture test. *Journal of International Business Studies, 18*(2), 17–31.

Lau, S. K., & Kuan, H. C. (1988). *The ethos of the Hong Kong Chinese.* Hong Kong: Chinese University Press.

Leung, K. (1987). Some determinants of reactions to procedural models for conflict resolution: A cross-national study. *Journal of Personality and Social Psychology, 53*, 898–908.

McDonald, G. M., & Kan, P. C. (1997). Ethical perceptions of expatriate and local managers in Hong Kong. *Journal of Business Ethics, 16*, 1605–1623.

McDonald, G. M., & Pak, P. C. (1996). It's all fair in love, war, and business: Cognitive philosophies in ethical decision making. *Journal of Business Ethics, 15*, 973–996.

Mehta, S. C., & Kau, A. K. (1984). Marketing executives' perceptions of unethical practices: An empirical investigation of Singapore managers. *Singapore Management Review, 6*(2), 25–35.

More than play dough. (1997, November 24). Brandweek, *XXXVIII* (44), 18.

Mueller, B. (1987, June–July). Reflections of culture: An analysis of Japanese and American advertising appeals. *Journal of Advertising Research, 27*, 51–60.

Nike chases Asian dream. (1997, June 27). *Asian Advertising & Marketing*, p. 9.

Nyaw, M.-K., & Ng, I. (1994). A comparative analysis of ethical beliefs: A four country study. *Journal of Business Ethics, 13*, 543–555.

Ralston, D. A., Giacolone, R. A., & Terpstra, R. H. (1994). Ethical perceptions of organizational politics: A comparative evaluation of American and Hong Kong managers. *Journal of Business Ethics, 13*, 989–999.

Ralston, D. A., Gustafson, D. J., Cheung, F. M., & Terpstra, R. H. (1993). Differences in managerial values: A study of U.S., Hong Kong, and PRC managers. *Journal of International Business Studies, 24*, 249–275.

Rich pickings for kids. (1998, August). *Market Asia Pacific, 7*(8), p. 3.

Robertson, D. C., & Schlegelmich, B. B. (1993). Corporate institutionalization of ethics in the United States and Great Britain. *Journal of Business Ethics, 12*, 301–312.

Singhapakdi, A., Vitell, S. J., Rallapalli, K. C., & Kraft, K. L. (1996). The perceived role of ethics and social responsibility: A scale development. *Journal of Business Ethics, 15*, 1131–1140.

Tan, S. J., Lim, G. H., & Lee, K. S. (1997). Strategic responses to parallel importing. *Journal of Global Marketing, 10*(4), 45–66.

Triandis, H. C., Botempo, R., Betancourt, H., Bond, M., Leung, K., Brenes, A., Georgas, J., Hui, C. H., Marin, G., Setiadi, B., Sinha, J. B. P., Verma, J., Spangenberg, J., Touzard, H., & de Montmollin, G. (1986). The measurement of the ethic aspects of individualism and collectivism across cultures. *Australian Journal of Psychology, 38*(3), 257–267.

Triandis, H. C., Bontempo, R., Villareal, M. J., Asai, M., & Lucca, N. (1988). Individualism and collectivism: Cross-cultural perspectives on self-ingroup relationships. *Journal of Personality and Social Psychology, 54*(2), 323–338.

Understanding generation Y: A look at the next wave of US consumers. (1998, December). *Drug & Cosmetic Industry, 163*(6), 90.

Webber, R. A. (1969). Convergence or divergence? *Columbia Journal of World Business, 4*(3), 75–83.

World Competitiveness Yearbook. (1998). Lausanne, Switzerland: Institute for Management Development.

Author Index

423

Subject Index

CPSIA information can be obtained
at www.ICGtesting.com
Printed in the USA
BVHW042348191218
531601 9BV00013B/60/P